WebSphere Certification Study Guide

Developing J2EE Applications with IBM WebSphere Studio

IBM Certified Enterprise Developer

WebSphere Certification Study Guide

Developing J2EE Applications with IBM WebSphere Studio

IBM Certified Enterprise Developer

Edited by Howard Kushner,
with Michael Brown, Kameron Cole, Ken Greenlee,
Gene Van Sant, Doug Weatherbee, and Colin Yu

Developing J2EE Applications with IBM WebSphere Studio
IBM Certified Enterprise Developer

Edited by Howard Kushner, with Michael Brown, Kameron Cole, Ken Greenlee, Gene Van Sant, Doug Weatherbee, and Colin Yu

Published under IBM Press by MC Press Online, LP
IBM Associate Publisher: Tara B. Woodman, IBM Corporation
IBM Press Alliance Publisher: David M. Uptmor, MC Press

For information on translations and book distribution outside the United States or to arrange bulk-purchase discounts for sales promotions or premiums please contact:

MC Press Online, LP
Corporate Offices:
125 N. Woodland Trail
Lewisville, TX 75077

Sales and Customer Service:
P.O. Box 4300
Big Sandy, TX 75755-4300

First edition
First Printing: August 2003
Second Printing: February 2004

ISBN: 1-931182-10-8

Dedication

In loving memory of my mother, Ida W. Kushner, who believed in me and believed in this book but was not able to receive the copy that I so wanted her to have. Also in honor of my father, Meyer Kushner, who encouraged and inspired me to capitalize on my intellect.

Acknowledgments

My deepest thanks go to my wife, Jennifer, without whom this book would not have been possible and who, with unbounded patience, shares with me her love, encouragement, and three most treasured gifts—our children: Matthew, Samuel, and Natalie.

I would like to thank CrossLogic Corporation. I was given with the opportunity to write this book for IBM Press, because IBM recognizes the technical excellence and leadership that CrossLogic provides.

I would like to give special thanks to Tara Woodman of the WebSphere Retail Publishing Program for providing CrossLogic and myself with the opportunity to develop this certification study guide and also for facilitating the entire process.

I would like to thank our technical reviewers who did such a great job, giving unselfishly of their time to provide thoughtful feedback on chapters: Neil Canham of Know Sense Limited, Gary Craig of Superlative Software Solutions, Fabio Ferraz of e-voilà, Neville Harrison of Cirrus Technologies, Ken Kousen of Golden Consulting Group, Krista Meyer of IBM, Jeff Mitchell of IBM, Jan Rysz of TPartners, Stephanie Trunzo of IBM, and Neil Weightman of IBM.

Thanks also to Al White of IBM, who helped me find real answers to some really tough questions, and Merrikay Lee of MC Press, who guided me through the creation of a manuscript and its ultimate transformation into a book.

Howard Kushner
Raleigh, North Carolina
July 2003

About the authors

Howard Kushner, editor: Howard Kushner is a Senior Consultant with CrossLogic Corporation. In this role he specializes in the development and delivery of Java and WebSphere-related training as well as consulting and mentoring services. He has been working in Information Technology since the 1970s, and has been a Sun-certified Java Programmer since 1999. He currently specializes in distributed J2EE architectures, Web Services, and XML.

Howard's most recent IBM certifications include Enterprise Application Development using WebSphere Studio Application Developer Version 5, and WebSphere Application Server Version 5 Multiplatform Administration. Prior certifications from IBM include Certified Solution Developer using VisualAge for Java, and Object Oriented Analysis and Design with UML.

Contributors

Michael Brown: Mike is currently the WebSphere Team Lead within IBM Learning Services and is involved in the development and delivery of many courses in IBM's WebSphere curriculum, beginning with Version 3.02, and continuing with Version 3.5, Version 4.0, and now Version 5.0. Previously, Mike has been involved in a number of enterprise applications written in Java, Python, C/C++, and Eiffel, with over 10 years of experience in Web and application development.

Mike received his degree in Mechanical Engineering from Auburn University and holds a number of professional and technical certifications, including IBM Certified Enterprise Developer.

Kameron Cole: Kameron is an Advanced Education Specialist/Systems Programmer with IBM. He teaches the entire core WebSphere Curriculum. Kameron is an IBM Certified Systems Expert for WebSphere Administration and a Sun Certified J2EE Developer.

Kameron holds a B.Mus. in Cello Performance, an M.A. in Theoretical Linguistics (focus on Logic and Artificial Languages), and a B.A. in Computer Science, all from the University of Iowa. He is experienced primarily in Unix/Linux operating systems, and he programs in CORBA (Orbix), Java, Prolog, C, C++, Miranda, ML, LIFE, and SmallTalk.

Ken Greenlee: Ken is the Chief Technology Officer of Kenetiks, Inc., a Java-WebSphere training and consulting company he founded in 1997. He has written many courses covering J2SE, J2EE, WebSphere Studio Application Developer, WebSphere Application Server, and WebSphere Portal Server.

Prior to founding Kenetiks, he worked for IBM in North Carolina, where he worked on development teams responsible for such products as VisualAge Smalltalk and OS/2. He holds a B.S. degree in Computer Science from Indiana University along with numerous professional certifications in Java and WebSphere.

Gene Van Sant: Gene works as an Integration Solutions Architect / Implementor with loofa. He teaches IBM's entire WebSphere and e-business solution design curricula. In addition to teaching IBM products and technologies for the past decade, Gene works on contracts with IBM extensively as both an architect and implementor.

Gene has an M.S. in Computer Science / Artificial Intelligence and a B.S. in Space Sciences / Physics from Florida Institute of Technology.

Doug Weatherbee: Doug is an IBM Certified WebSphere Instructor who has been working with J2EE, WebSphere, and VisualAge for Java technologies since 1999. Doug has consulted with many companies representing a wide range of industry sectors on WebSphere development, administration, deployment and performance optimization. He has presented at the 2001 IBM Wireless University Conference in Atlanta and the 2002 IBM WebSphere Technical Exchange Conference in Las Vegas.

Prior to his WebSphere consulting, Doug was employed as a Program Analyst, Business Analyst, and Software Project Manager by the Ontario Government. In addition to his IBM Certifications, he holds an M.A. degree from the University of Toronto and a Diploma in Applied Information Technology. When not on client WebSphere engagements, Doug enjoys spending time with his spouse, Kate, at their cottage in a small lobster fishing village on an island off the south coast of Nova Scotia.

Colin Yu: Colin is currently working as a technical designer of WebSphere Business Scenario Development team at IBM Software Solutions Toronto Lab. Prior to his current job, he has participated in high-level system analysis and design with customers, worked on customer critical situations, and provided solutions and consulting to IBM customers with a variety of WebSphere Platform products. He has also worked for a national bank as a senior developer for four years before he joined IBM.

Colin received a Bachelor of Engineering degree in 1995 and a Master of Applied Science degree from the University of Waterloo, Ontario, in 2000. He is an IBM Certified Enterprise Developer and Systems Expert on WebSphere Application Server and an IBM Certified Solution Developer on WebSphere Studio Application Developer and VisualAge for Java. He has contributed many articles on WebSphere platform products for *WebSphere Technical Journal*, WebSphere Developer Domain, and DB2 Developer Domain.

Contents

Preface

When we "certify" something, we attest to that something being true or genuine, and we tend to think in terms of meeting a certain predefined standard. When we search for excellence, we give recognition to those who have attained higher levels of certification. We believe that certifications can prove something to us . . . something that might not be too easy for us to prove for ourselves.

And now, more than ever before, the industry of e-business is developing standards for the knowledge and practical skills that we as programmers are expected to possess in order to perform highly specialized jobs for which qualified candidates are in short supply.

Today's marketplace has a critical need for technical professionals who can fulfill these newly emerging roles that are defined in terms of specific objectives along with standardized sets of skills.

So, if . . .

- You want to keep pace with the complex technologies and products in today's constantly changing world . . .
- You want to gain proficiency in the latest IBM technology and solutions . . .
- You want to differentiate yourself, as being capable of delivering higher levels of service and technical expertise . . .

- You want to truly excel at your job, providing your employer confidence that your skills have been tested . . .

. . . then you are ready to move your career to a higher level. Start charting your course today!

IBM Certified Enterprise Developer - WebSphere Studio, Version 5.0

The book you now hold in your hands, *Developing J2EE Applications with IBM WebSphere Studio,* was written to fit into the Professional Certification Program from IBM. In particular, it has been designed to help you prepare for the role of IBM Certified Enterprise Developer - WebSphere Studio, Version 5.0. That credential speaks volumes about the person who holds it. It speaks of competency at performing certain required tasks, and it speaks of productivity gained by effectively leveraging the IBM WebSphere platform for e-business.

For WebSphere Studio Version 5.0, IBM defines three roles, increasing in sophistication from the entry-level Associate Developer, who is new to WebSphere and the use of IBM products for Web development, through the intermediate level Solution Developer, and progressing finally to the Enterprise Developer. The role this book addresses is the highest and most challenging of three roles: the Enterprise Developer, who designs, develops, and deploys distributed enterprise-level applications. The following table shows the three different roles and their associated IBM test numbers.

WebSphere Certification Roles and Associated Tests

Role	Head
IBM Certified Associate Developer - WebSphere Studio, Version 5.0	Developing with IBM WebSphere Studio, Version 5.0 (Test 285)
IBM Certified Solution Developer - WebSphere Studio, Version 5.0	Application Development with IBM WebSphere Studio, Version 5.0 (Test 286)
IBM Certified Enterprise Developer - WebSphere Studio, Version 5.0	Enterprise Application Development with IBM WebSphere Studio, Version 5.0 (Test 287)

Focusing now on the role of IBM Certified Enterprise Developer - WebSphere Studio Version 5.0, let's see how this book helps you prepare to demonstrate to the world that you have mastered the skills and knowledge necessary to accomplish the tasks required in the fulfillment of this role.

How does one qualify and prepare?

In order to qualify for the role of IBM Certified Enterprise Developer, you must pass four tests:

- Sun Certified Programmer for the Java 2 Platform 1.2 (Test 155)
- Object Oriented Analysis and Design with UML (Test 486)
- Enterprise Connectivity with J2EE V1.3 (Test 484)
- Enterprise Application Development with IBM WebSphere Studio, Version 5.0 (Test 287)

In preparing to take Test 287, IBM recommends you follow either the self-study or the tutor approach. This book is written primarily for those candidates who have chosen the self-study approach. If that is the path you have chosen to follow, then we strongly encourage you to test your skills and identify those areas where you may need improvement. IBM provides free of charge, over the Internet, a pre-assessment sample test for Test 287. Take advantage of the IBM Certification Exam (ICE) Tool, where sample questions are available. For more information, and to register to take the pre-test, go to the ICE home page at *http://certify.torolab.ibm.com*.

The best way to use this book will depend largely on your own individual needs and preferences. You may wish to read it sequentially starting with Chapter 1, or you may wish to review the chapter descriptions included here in the Preface and then focus on those chapters in which you are most interested. Another possible approach is to begin by looking at the certification objectives in order to select the chapters in which you are most interested. Yet another approach would be to look at the end-of-chapter materials, and decide from there which chapters you want to take on first.

Prerequisites

IBM recommends the prerequisites (i.e., knowledge and skills one needs to possess before beginning to prepare for this job role certification) listed in this section. Chances are, you already have some familiarity with the items on the list. But if you feel you lack sufficient knowledge regarding these items, you'll find the additional coverage in this book helpful. If you need more background than what is included, we recommend that you review the original specifications, which are generally available on the Web.

- Knowledge of the following Java APIs:
  - Servlet API 2.3
  - JSP 1.2
  - Java 2 SDK 1.3.X
  - JMS 1.0.2
  - JCA 1.0

- JTA 1.0
- JDBC 2.1
- EJB 2.0

- Plus knowledge of Web Services technologies:
  - SOAP
  - WSDL
  - UDDI
- Knowledge of object-oriented analysis and design:
  - UML
  - Design Patterns
- Experience working on actual object-oriented projects:
  - Participation in the analysis and design phases
  - Participation in building, deploying, and tuning J2EE-compliant enterprise applications that include EJBs and Web modules

---

Note: There is no substitute for actual project development experience. A candidate who lacks practical experience using Java on an object-oriented project, preferably a J2EE enterprise application, will be at a disadvantage as compared to the candidate who has learned certain valuable lessons from having applied this knowledge to work in the real world.

What is covered in this book?

The 15 chapters in this book have been specifically designed to address the objectives for Test 287. Here, at a high level, is what they cover.

Chapter 1, *Introduction to IBM WebSphere,* introduces the WebSphere platform as an enabling technology for enterprise computing (also known as e-business). It does so within the context of the Java 2 Enterprise Edition (J2EE) architecture, and it introduces several key members of the WebSphere product family.

Chapter 2, *Developing Enterprise Applications with WebSphere Studio,* introduces the reader to WebSphere Studio Application Developer, Version 5, and the role it plays in component-based development of J2EE enterprise applications. As we highlight the development of a simple J2EE application, we look at the most commonly used perspectives, and introduce the reader to the WebSphere Test Environment (WTE) and the Universal Test Client (UTC).

Chapter 3, *Servlets,* covers the design, development, and testing of servlets, filters, and listeners. It addresses issues regarding session management and options for maintaining conversational state with the user. It also introduces Model-View-Controller (MVC) and shows the part that servlets play. The latest additions to the Servlet Version 2.3 API, including filters and Web application lifecycle events and listeners, are included in this chapter as well.

Chapter 4, *JavaServer Pages (JSP),* covers JSP syntax and then goes on to show how to design, develop, and test JSP pages using WebSphere Studio as well as the role of JSP pages in MVC. The design, development, and use of custom tag libraries are also covered.

Chapter 5, *Developing EJBs: Session Beans and the EJB Architecture,* introduces the EJB architecture and the role of Session beans as a façade. We show how Session beans are developed in WebSphere, and we explain their deployment descriptors. The proper use of EJBs in enterprise applications distinguishes the Enterprise Developer from the other development roles.

Chapter 6, *Developing Entity EJBs with WebSphere Studio,* explores both container-managed persistence (CMP) and bean-managed persistence (BMP) for Entity beans. We discuss WebSphere specifics for Entity beans and the use of EJB Query Language for finding CMP Entity beans. We will also cover relationships between Entity beans.

Chapter 7, *Message-Driven Beans,* presents a Java Message Service (JMS) primer, and then shows how Message-Driven beans are developed in WebSphere Studio.

Chapter 8, *Transactions,* covers the proper use of transactions, which is one of the most important and complex topics in J2EE. The chapter introduces basic concepts and then goes on to discuss the transactional support required by J2EE and EJBs in particular. The topics of concurrency and transactional isolation available in WebSphere are covered, followed by a section on best practices.

Chapter 9, *Security,* begins with a review of the basic concepts regarding security, followed by the J2EE requirements to support declarative and programmatic access to security services. In particular we will explore role-based security, which reduces the application developer's burden with regard to implementing security policies. We will then continue our discussion to show how to configure security for J2EE applications using WebSphere Studio.

Chapter 10, *JCA Tools and Supports,* provides a high-level overview of J2EE Connector Architecture and the characteristics of connection management, transaction management, security management, and the Common Client Interface.

Chapter 11, *Profiling Analysis Tools in WebSphere Studio,* shows you how to measure performance so that you can manage it. The profiling tools in WebSphere enable the Enterprise Developer to gather and analyze data regarding the runtime behavior of code inside a Java Virtual Machine. The profiling perspective assists the developer in visualizing program execution. This chapter presents the goals of profiling and the profiling architecture upon which WebSphere relies.

Chapter 12, *Implementing Clients,* discusses how to implement clients in a distributed system. Behaving as J2EE components themselves, clients take advantage of a contract with their container that allows J2EE to offer a rich set of services, vastly simplifying the complexity of the client.

Chapter 13, *Packaging and Deployment,* covers areas of critical importance to the Enterprise Developer, who must first assemble a set of Web components, EJB components, and client components into a complete enterprise application, which is represented by an enterprise archive (EAR) file. Then the Enterprise Developer must deploy (i.e., install and configure) that enterprise application into an operational environment.

Chapter 14, *WebSphere Administration,* focuses on the aspects of the WebSphere Version 5 J2EE Server that influence the design of an enterprise application and its performance, particularly those aspects that are under the control of the developer. It is incumbent upon Enterprise Developers to understand the nature of the WebSphere Application Server Version 5, since that is the platform that will ultimately host their applications.

Chapter 15, *Remote Debugger and Java Component Test Tools in WebSphere Studio,* covers two very useful tools in WebSphere Studio Application Developer: (1) remote debugging and (2) the Component Testing Framework. The chapter first provides some background on the Remote Debugger and then outlines the steps required for remotely debugging applications that have already been deployed. The chapter then goes on to cover the Component Testing Framework and its associated perspective and concludes by outlining the procedures for creating, executing, and reviewing the results of Java Testcases.

Certification objectives

The following table lists, section by section, the individual certification objectives of Test 287, along with the chapter in this study guide in which they are addressed.

Test 287, Enterprise Application Development using WebSphere Studio Version 5.0

Section 1: Design, build and test reusable enterprise components (25%)	
1A: Design and develop Session EJBs	Chapter 5
1B: Design and develop Message-Driven EJBs	Chapter 7
1C: Design and develop Entity EJBs	Chapter 6
1D: Access container and server services from enterprise components	Chapters 5, 6, 7, 9, and 10
1E; Implement mechanisms for efficient inter-component calls	Chapters 5 and 6
1F: Test and debug enterprise components	Chapters 2 and 15
Section 2: Design, build and test Web components (19%)	
2A: Design, develop and test Java servlets, filters, and listeners	Chapter 3
2B: Design, develop, and test JSP pages	Chapter 4
2C: Manage end-user state and understand performance tradeoffs of using HTTP sessions	Chapters 3 and 14
2D: Design and develop custom tags	Chapter 4
Section 3: Develop clients that access the enterprise components (8%)	
3A: Implement Java clients calling EJBs	Chapter 12
3B: Implement Java clients calling Web Services	Chapter 12
3C: Implement mechanisms that support loose coupling between clients and components	Chapter 12
Section 4: Demonstrate understanding of database connectivity and messaging within IBM WebSphere Application Server (8%)	
4A: Create, configure, and tune connection pools	Chapter 14
4B: Interact with connection pools to obtain and release connections	Chapter 14
4C: Configure JMS connection factories and destinations	Chapter 7
Section 5: EJB transactions (10%)	
5A: Build EJBs that satisfy transactional requirements	Chapter 8
5B: Use JTA to control transaction demarcation	Chapter 8
5C: Manipulate transactional behavior of EJBs using deployment descriptors	Chapter 8

Test 287, Enterprise Application Development using WebSphere Studio Version 5.0 (Continued)

Section 6: Assemble enterprise applications and deploy them in IBM WebSphere Application Server (15%)	
6A: Assemble Web components, EJB components, and client application components into enterprise applications	Chapter 13
6B: Deploy enterprise applications into servers	Chapters 9 and 13
6C: Configure resource and security-role references	Chapter 9 and 13
6D: Create and configure WebSphere test environment servers	Chapter 2
Section 7: Validate, tune, and troubleshoot an application within an IBM WebSphere Application Server environment (15%)	
7A: Use tracing and profiling tools to analyze and tune applications	Chapters 11 and 14
7B: Explain implications of resource management on application design and implementation	Chapters 11 and 14
7C: Identify misbehaving application components	Chapter 11, 14, and 15
7D: Describe the effects of a server failure on the application	Chapter 14
7E: Validate operational parameters of application server to support the enterprise application	Chapter 14

Contributors

You may have noticed that this book is written by multiple contributors. This was not by chance. We wanted to make sure that the book was written by a team of subject matter experts, each selected and assigned individual chapters according to their particular areas of expertise. For this reason we chose people from within IBM as well as consultants and IBM business partners. The resulting team combines the best mix of real-world project development, consulting experience, and classroom teaching experience. We include authors who have previously published articles, developers of Java and J2EE course materials, and presenters at technical conferences such as the WebSphere Technical Exchange.

Whether you are using this book to help you prepare for your certification or simply to gain knowledge of enterprise application development using WebSphere, we hope this book will be a valuable tool and a welcome addition to your bookshelf.

CHAPTER 1

Introduction to IBM WebSphere

Kameron Cole

Chapter topics

- *What is WebSphere?*
- *A brief history of J2EE*
- *J2EE architecture*
- *Introducing WebSphere*

Certification objectives

- *This chapter does not address any specific certification objectives*

As companies the world over struggle to remain competitive, e-business is emerging as a way to reach a potential global marketplace while drastically reducing costs. But the complexities of developing distributed, industrial-strength applications have been growing at a frightening pace ever since client/server computing caught on. Web-based business applications, once a rarity, are now the norm as companies invest in customer self-service applications as well as in systems intended for internal use behind the corporate firewall, supporting their day-to-day operations.

When a company's network is down, even for a short while, business can virtually come to a standstill. Without access to corporate information, which is the lifeblood of the company, workers wander out of their cubicles and chat, waiting for the announcement that the network is back up. The network has become synonymous with the business. When the network is down, we may as well turn off the lights and go home.

The systems we design and build are limited only by our imagination. The companies that thrive will be the ones that can effectively and intelligently harness the technology of the Internet to set themselves apart from their competition. We need an enabling technology in order to make these dreams a reality. The IBM Certified Enterprise Developer plays a key role in helping invent that future.

An Enterprise Developer develops and deploys distributed enterprise-level applications that model an organization's processes, practices, and concepts. He accomplishes these tasks by designing, creating, and maintaining Java 2 Platform, Enterprise Edition (J2EE) 1.3 components, deploying and configuring these components, and supporting the development of application clients that access them.

The Enterprise Developer works with business analysts, application architects, application assemblers, and administrators. He is expected to apply sound object-oriented analysis and design techniques during development. This Developer understands application assembly within the business domain across a multi-tier architecture. This individual has the system administration skills required to tune the application to meet performance requirements.

The IBM Certified Enterprise Developer has the enabling technology available today. That technology is WebSphere.

What is WebSphere?

WebSphere is a software platform for e-business. Understanding WebSphere is key to becoming an IBM Certified Enterprise Developer. In this book we will focus on the latest versions of two products within the WebSphere family. IBM WebSphere Application Server provides the infrastructure for e-business enterprise applications. IBM WebSphere Studio, and in particular IBM WebSphere Studio Application Developer, supports enterprise application development. Because this book addresses the role of Enterprise Developer, most of the focus will be on WebSphere Studio Application Developer (hereafter referred to as Application Developer).

Beginning with version 4 and continuing with version 5, WebSphere Application Server and Application Developer are fully compliant with the Java 2 Enterprise Edition (J2EE) specification. This is important, because it delivers open-standard interoperability, just as Java delivers platform independence. Furthermore, J2EE allows developers to focus on the business. A brief history of J2EE can help us understand how WebSphere supports modern enterprise computing.

A brief history of J2EE

Work on J2EE began with Sun, IBM, and others in the late 1990s in an effort to enhance enterprise computing by simplifying the tasks of development and deployment. At the heart of the roadmap to enterprise computing, J2EE promised to separate the business from the plumbing. Developers could focus on the business aspects of computing as they developed Java components, and the infrastructure would provide the necessary services in an open, platform-independent way. J2EE represents the evolution of client/server computing to a fully distributed model. As businesses became more dependent on their networks, the architecture needed to develop distributed business solutions evolved.

Major challenges of e-business include security, dynamic processing, and growth. These are real business requirements, rather than computing concepts.

First, to conduct e-business, information has to be made usable, available, and secure. In a traditional storefront business, security is achieved in physical ways, such as with locks and keys. In order to do e-business, our computing model must emulate those physical security mechanisms.

Second, data that just sits there is not business: The data needs to be manipulated—manipulated in such a way as to resemble actual, intuitively satisfying business processes, e.g., transactions. A transaction models the concept of an indivisible unit of work that supports the business.

Once we have secure transactions involving business data, there is still one ingredient left to complete an e-business application: growth. Businesses that do not grow do not survive. To support growth, a business often must acquire new physical property and hire new employees, because growth implies that each new customer receives the same, if not improved, quality of service. In computing terms, this means that throughput must be scalable in order to accommodate increased demand.

The Common Object Request Broker Architecture (CORBA) led the way to vendor-independent distributed computing. Many of the good ideas of J2EE, such as services, which we will be discussing shortly, actually appeared in CORBA first.

The Java solution for the incorporation of CORBA functionality was EJB (Enterprise JavaBeans), a way to incorporate the robustness of the CORBA Object Request Broker (ORB)'s transactional and secure services into a standard architecture. Existing CORBA implementations, although based on the same, robust CORBA standards, were not "standard" (i.e., portable and interoperable). But EJB went beyond CORBA: The designer of Java wanted their remote procedure-calling architecture to be more intuitive than the complicated and nongenial CORBA code. Incorporating the intuitiveness and ease of use of JavaBean technology into CORBA-compliant components was the deciding factor in the acceptance of EJB over CORBA as the e-business solution of choice.

With EJB, Java provided a technological basis for implementing robust e-business solutions, addressing and going beyond the technologies provided by CORBA. However, the picture was not complete. As programmers began to incorporate the new Java technologies into their solutions, it became apparent that there was no true *architectural* standard to which a programmers could apply the new technologies. In other words, Java needed to evolve from a set of technologies into a *framework* that would standardize not only the technologies used but also the way in which they were used in architecture. This would become the J2EE Specification, which is the basis for this entire book.

J2EE architecture

When the J2EE Specification (henceforth, although not always stated explicitly, this discussion is limited to the J2EE 1.3 Framework Specification) mentions architecture, it clearly refers to runtime architecture. Every discussion of this architecture must begin with this picture from the specification itself:

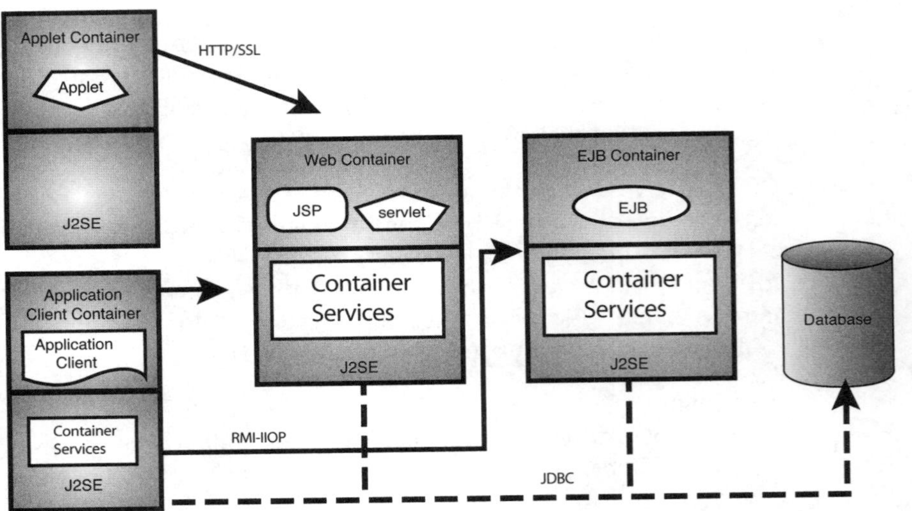

Figure 1.1: J2EE architecture.

While Figure 1.1 may imply a programming architecture, at some level, its main purpose is to outline two things:

1. That there are specific components such as servlets, JSPs, and EJBs, and
2. That those components need specific runtime support, which is provided by containers such as the Web container and the EJB container.

Also implied in the figure is a connectivity specification (those arrows that connect the containers/components to one another). Although obviously blank in this diagram—really absent from any diagram in the actual spec—the transports are "filled in" in the text of the J2EE Specification. This discussion of these three "architectural elements" (components, containers, and transport mechanisms) will begin with the components, because their definition really implies, and was ultimately responsible for, the services provided by the containers, as well as the transport protocols.

J2EE architecture: components

This might be a good time to bring out a salient point in the definition of J2EE components: The J2EE specification (J2EE Platform Specification: J2EE.2.2.1) says, "Application components can be divided into three categories according to their dependence on a J2EE server:

- "Components that are deployed, managed, and executed on a J2EE server. These components include web components and Enterprise JavaBeans components.
- "Components that are deployed and managed on a J2EE server, but are loaded to and executed on a client machine. These components include HTML pages and applets embedded in HTML pages.
- "Components whose deployment and management is not completely defined by this specification. Application Clients fall into this category."

The Application Client

I won't start in the upper left-hand corner of the diagram, as is typical in these reviews. Instead, I'll begin with the component called Application Client. Historically, this is what we've always known, simply, as a computer program. Before J2EE was released, the name for this component in Java terms was just "application": a set of related methods, linked together by a runnable method, namely, the main() method. At other times, this component is referred to as "stand-alone," which implied that it required only the Java Virtual Machine (JVM)—no container—to execute: The JVM was given the name of the class, as an argument, which contained the main() method, and the JVM executed that method. At some point, the J2EE architecture designers realized that the fact that the application was "stand-alone" was inconsistent with the component model, which had been already applied to servlets and EJBs. In other words, everything, including the application, should be a component, which by definition, was a software element that required a container. Thus was born the Client container, which was to run application client components.

In the J2EE 1.3 architecture, the Application Client is a largely graphical program, which gets its data from EJBs, running in an Application Server, via access to the JNDI namespace. So, put another way, the application that formerly could stand alone will now be a Client to a J2EE Server, with the Client Container providing access to both the JNDI namespace of that server and the necessary libraries (e.g., javax.Naming).

Application clients also require a JVM to execute in—not the JVM of the application server variety, but a basic JVM that resides on the client side. We will try to flesh out the nature of these components in both the container section to follow and in the packaging/development discussion of another chapter. (If, on the whole, you find the treatment of application clients "vague," it is. The J2EE Spec says, "Future versions of this specification may more fully define deployment and management of Application Clients.")

The applet

The applet (the name implies "little application") is often compared to the application (the application client, which we have just discussed above) in early literature. In fact, many texts contained exercises that asked the developer to convert an application into an applet and vice versa.

The servlet

Servlets are among the "web components" in the first category of components mentioned at the beginning of this section. Servlets will be covered in detail in Chapter 3. The strength of servlets lies in their ability to generate and deliver dynamic content in response to requests.

The JSP

JavaServer Pages (JSP) were a response to the problems inherent in embedding HTML in servlet code that was ultimately to be compiled by an ordinary Java compiler. Escape characters need to be included to differentiate between similar notions recognized by the compiler. Also, the compiler, or the Java editor in WebSphere Studio, cannot check the validity of the HTML. JSP technology, on the other hand, enables an Enterprise Developer to write the functionality of a servlet in purely HTML form, whose syntax is protected by her HTML editor, such as the Page Designer in WebSphere Studio.

Moreover, a "best-practice" idea has been developing that recognizes a design pattern from SmallTalk called Model-View-Controller (MVC). Simply put, MVC requires that the code in each element of an application restrict itself solely to the role of that element in the overall architecture of the application. In other words, code that processes business data (fulfilling the role of model) should remain separate from code that displays the results of that processing (fulfilling the role of view). Code that which delegates and coordinates between functions in the view and model, i.e., code that controls the flow between other functions, falls into the role of controller. The JSP fulfills the role of view. When used as part of MVC, the JSP page is commonly referred to as a display page. A more complete discussion of MVC is included in Chapter 4.

The EJB

In the earliest stages of development of the EJB specification, one could say that an EJB was an inherently remote, network aware, distributed transactional component. Certainly, the EJB was conceived as Java's response to the remote procedure call, of which CORBA and, now, Web Services are also attempts at a solution. The notion of "bean" in the name Enterprise JavaBeans stems from the design intent of making EJBs reusable components similar to JavaBeans, which are intended to be self-describing Java software components. Also, EJBs advertise their properties via getters and setters, and they use Java Reflection in a comparable way to JavaBeans. But it is important to make a clear distinction between JavaBeans and Enterprise JavaBeans.

With the advent of EJB 2.0, one can no longer define an EJB as being *inherently* remote, since local EJBs are inherently not remote but are still EJBs. Insofar as local EJBs are not remote, they are also not network aware and, likewise, not truly distributed.

Whereas the J2EE 1.3 Specification directly states that the EJBs "typically contain the business logic of a J2EE application," the Entity EJB is probably used more for persistence than for execution of business logic. The Session EJB is used to execute business logic, but there are contending design patterns, most notably the EJB Command pattern, that would place the business logic in JavaBeans and use the Stateless Session EJBs as "transactional listeners."

This concludes our list of components as listed in the J2EE architecture segment of the Specification. We now move on to the component managers, the containers.

J2EE architecture: Containers

A container's basic function is to manage and provide the runtime support for the components it contains. This support can be broken down into four separate functions:

1. To provide access to all the necessary J2EE and J2SE APIs (essentially, class libraries) that the components will call;
2. To isolate the contained components from the other components in the J2EE Server, and consequently
3. To take care of the communication between components running in different containers;
4. To manage the life cycles of objects, creating them so that they are available when requested and destroying them when they are no longer needed. The final function includes providing a way for the objects to persist themselves.

The necessity of the first function is clear: Precompiled class libraries have long been used as a means of deferring many of the mechanical complexities of the runtime from the programmer. This makes programming more intuitive, closer to resembling human thought. The second function, that of isolation, provides the essence of this programming model: It allows the runtime to be uniquely configured and managed through the use of *deployment descriptors*, which are read and implemented at deployment time by the containers. As stated, the third function is really a logical follow-on of the first two: The complexities of intercomponent communication are deferred to the containers, thus freeing the programmer from the "details," while at the same time allowing for isolation or grouping of varied processes.

With regard to the first function of providing necessary APIs, it can be seen from Figure 1.1 that all containers must provide the Java 2 Standard Platform Edition (J2SE) APIs (whose package names all begin with the topmost directory of *java*, e.g. java.sql).[1] Also shown in the diagram is that containers must provide access to additional APIs from the Java 2 Enterprise Extensions (J2EE), although not uniformly but on a per-container basis. (These packages all have *javax* [x for extension] as the topmost directory, indicating they are standard extensions to Java.) These APIs often work in conjunction with the J2SE packages to support the services the containers provide, which are discussed in the following section.

Since containers must perform the functionality outlined in the deployment descriptors, it goes without saying that the containers must understand the packaging conventions and instructions contained in the deployment descriptors.

J2EE architecture: J2EE server

While JVMs are all based on the standard J2SE technology, they can be highly specialized to provide a server-side functionality. Such a JVM is referred to as a J2EE server or, variously, an application server (the "server" being simply a set of threads running through instances of classes running on a standard JVM). The J2EE server is minimally a JVM that is capable of managing the containers described above, with some additional standard transaction-processing infrastructure. Also, there must be some mechanism for interaction with application clients. The J2EE server must, ultimately, fully implement the J2EE Specification.

J2EE architecture: drivers

The functionality of J2EE servers will be extended through their coupling (network connectivity) with external resource managers, by implementing J2EE Service Provider Interfaces (SPIs). The SPI guarantees that the implementation classes will work with any and all J2EE products. These implementation classes are packaged software collections, referred to as resources manager drivers, or, most commonly, just drivers. Many external resource applications have corresponding Java APIs, such as JDBC. Other external applications using non-Java APIs can be connected to Java drivers through connectors.

J2EE architecture: database

As stated in J2EE Specification 1.3 (J2EE.2.5, Database), the J2EE Platform *requires* a database that is accessible by all components, with the optional exception of applets, through the JDBC API. It follows then that all such database vendors and/or third-party vendors would have to provide JDBC drivers.

---

[1]The Applet container, uniquely, can provide the J2SE through the Java Plugin product; most of us have seen the dialog concerning this plugin after installing a new browser.

J2EE architecture: services

In its effort to standardize the computing environment, the J2EE Platform requires a set of services. The term *services* is rather all encompassing and so might benefit from a bit of delineation at this point. The following paragraphs outline elements of the Specification that are considered "services."

J2EE services: naming and directory

The Java Naming and Directory Interface (JNDI) delivers a critical piece of the puzzle with regard to distributed enterprise computing, by providing the ability to organize and locate components. Seen from the outside, this is simply the ability to bind a name to an object so that that same object can later be located by only its name. A "name" object is simply a string identifier bound to a specific location in memory or on a network. A "directory" is a more robust "name" object that has attributes. For example, a Microsoft Windows shortcut is example of an icon that is bound, somehow internally within the operating system (OS), to the location of the executable that is launched when the icon is clicked. Likewise, the directory C:\WINNT is the string identifier "C:\WINNT" bound to the location in storage at which "files" (another type of "directory") for the OS are located. This WINNT directory has attributes, such as size and access permissions.

Services: resource processing and compilers

Extensible Markup Language (XML) has become an integral format for structured data transfer. Its powerful structured-data processing is reliant on a strict parsing mechanism that can load highly configurable parsing grammars. Two such parsing engines are referred to as Document Object Model (DOM) and SAX. DOM parses documents by creating a tree structure from the grammar and storing that tree along with the parsed data, so that it can be reconstructed. The SAX parser parses without the tree structure, i.e. in a linear, event style, thus saving on memory space. The Java API for XML Parsing (JAXP), described in J2EE Specification 1.3: J2EE.2.6.11, has APIs for both these parsing paradigms as well as APIs for XML Stylesheet Language for Transformations (XSLT) transform engines. Thus, J2EE components are guaranteed interoperability with XML-centric applications.

Services: EIS interoperability enablement

The J2EE Connector Architecture (JCA) is perhaps the most powerful service added with the 1.3 release of the J2EE Specification. The goal was to enable existing information systems (EIS) that had over the years proven their robustness, but were not necessarily object-oriented nor CORBA-enabled, to be incorporated into the J2EE architecture. Examples of such systems include the industry-tested Customer Information Control System (CICS), from IBM; "in-house" applications, such as those employed by J.D. Edwards; and third-party workflow systems, such as PeopleSoft. It was clear that such systems could, on an individual basis, connect to Java objects in much the same way the messaging and database connectivity had been achieved—through a type of "adapter." JCA is discussed in detail in Chapter 10.

Services: security

Clearly, the most difficult standardization effort would be security. Security mechanisms, even physical ones, can be characterized as "nonstandard"—that is, we wouldn't want just one key that would allow entry to any car! In the J2EE 1.2 Specification, inroads to such a standardization were attempted with a broad set of application requirements, including authentication, application-internal (thus, portable) authorization, and a delegation mechanism for EJB, referred to as "run-as" mode. At the 1.3 level, rather than relying on generalities (which would, of necessity, be implemented in a wide variety of proprietary ways), the Specification brought to the fore a set of Java APIs referred to collectively as Java Authentication and Authorization Service(s) (JAAS). JAAS is actually an extension of the Pluggable Authentication Module (PAM) Framework. Security is discussed in Chapter 9.

Services: asynchronous messaging

Often in an e-business application, processes must be "synchronous"—in this sense, we mean that the pieces of a transaction must be executed serially, waiting for completion before continuing on. For example, the output of one action must be the input of another action. The subsequent action cannot proceed before the prior action has completed successfully.

While this is desirable for transactions whose flow must be serial, it has serious performance implications. The locking behavior in databases, connections, EJBs, etc. can slow the processing of many such transactions to an unacceptable level—even to the point of halting the processing of the entire set of transactions inexorably (deadlock). Yet, given the critical nature of transactional integrity of today's e-business applications, this is a necessary evil.

The J2EE architecture requires that its components have access to such systems in a standardized way. The Java Message Service (JMS) offers to J2EE components both point-to-point and publish-subscribe asynchronous messaging, and it requires an external service that can offer these options. Point-to-point messaging is characterized by the notion that there must be a unique receiver for a given message and that that receiver must be connected at the time of delivery. The message delivery is considered successful when the specific receiver acknowledges receipt of the message. Publish-subscribe implies that messages are sent to many interested receivers, but the messages are retained in a queue and delivered when a subscriber connects. Message delivery is said to be successful when all subscribers have received a given message.

The message provider is configured administratively, and the service is offered through a JNDI lookup. JMS is covered within the context of Message-Driven beans in Chapter 7

Services: transactions

The backbone of any enterprise application is the ability to provide transactional integrity for all the components and services mentioned in the J2EE Architecture. This is made possible through two sets of Java interfaces: the Java Transaction API (JTA) and the Java Transaction Service (JTS). Chapter 8 provides a thorough discussion of transactions.

J2EE architecture: roles

At this point most of our discussion is complete. We have defined a programming model, the "component" style, delineating thoroughly the types of software components that are required. In turn, the component design model implies a highly stylized runtime environment, and we have delineated all of the services required of this runtime, even breaking the runtime down into tiers of runtime support. Thus, the "mechanics" are in place and ready to go. Due to the complexities of full J2EE implementations, certain responsibilities must be assigned to persons and firms having specific *roles* so that all the tasks necessary for the development and deployment of enterprise applications are accomplished.

Roles: J2EE Product Provider

IBM WebSphere Application Server is a J2EE product. It provides the containers and services as well as other related features. The products generally refer to servers in the architecture. They provide the runtime infrastructure. They do not refer to development tools, which have their own role distinction. Thus, vendors such as IBM provide J2EE-compliant application servers, database servers, and Web servers. Since many of the services required of these servers are at the system level, operating system vendors such as IBM are well suited as Product Providers. The Product Provider must provide the system level integration with all the services required by the containers and server, but not necessarily the services themselves, and vendors of messaging services, transaction services, email services, and the like are not necessarily J2EE Product Providers.

It is important to note that J2EE describes the minimum requirements for Product Providers, specifically outlining the places where proprietary value-adds and enhancements may be offered and where they may not.

The Product Provider is also responsible for the mapping to services tools, deployment tools, and systems administration tools.

Roles: Tool Provider

Tool Providers make tools for packaging and development of components, for deployment into J2EE-compliant containers. IBM is such a provider. IBM WebSphere Studio Application Developer Version 5 and the Application Assembly Tool included with the IBM WebSphere Application Server are prime examples of IBM's contributions as a J2EE Tool Provider.

The Specification draws a distinction at the point of deployment. Up to deployment, these tools can be platform independent. Deployment and post-deployment tools may be platform dependent; that is, tools for deployment, monitoring, and management of applications do not have to be interoperable.

Roles: Application Component Provider

Component Providers are developers of J2EE Components. The Specification implies subroles, such as HTML designers and EJB programmers, but ultimately leaves the sub-list open. An IBM Certified Enterprise Developer using WebSphere Studio Version 5.0 is a prime example of an Application Component Provider.

Interestingly, Application Component Providers do not assemble their components into complete enterprise applications. Also, they do not necessarily implement security in their EJB/Web methods. These functions are deferred to the Application Assembler and the System Administrator, respectively, per the strict definition in the J2EE specification.

Roles: Application Assembler

The Application Assembler puts it all together. He optionally assembles components and modules into enterprise applications. Because of the advanced tool-to-tool integration between WebSphere Studio Application Developer and WebSphere Application Server, an Application Assembler is not always required. The complete enterprise application is ultimately packaged into an enterprise archive, known as an EAR file. In Chapter 13 we will explore packaging, as well as deployment and installation.

Roles: Deployer

The Deployer is responsible for installation and configuration of an enterprise application, which can include customization for the operating environment. In J2EE, deployment can entail generation and compilation of the Java source in order to generate the stubs, ties, and implementation classes specific to the operating environment. During the installation of the application, the Deployer maps the logical security roles onto real principals (users and groups) defined in the authentication server. Thus, he may need to understand the application, as well as the security infrastructure of the enterprise, in order to assign the roles to users correctly. The Deployer does not establish security policy but does, in a sense, implement security policy. Also, it is at this point that JNDI names are configured and placed in the Java namespace. Finally, the Deployer runs the application.

Roles: System Administrator

The System Administrator's role doesn't really begin until the application is installed. Of course, it will probably fall to the Administrator to install WebSphere Application Server in the first place, create additional clones of that application server, and federate nodes on a multiserver environment. Clearly, the Administrator is solely responsible for the configuration of networking and the general computing environment. Finally, it is the Administrator's job to keep the application running, and running as quickly as possible. To this end, the Administrator must collect performance data, using the Performance Monitoring Infrastructure (PMI) and Java Virtual Machine Profiler interface (JVMPI)—special interfaces implemented by the JVM to produce performance data, which will be discussed in detail in the chapter on WebSphere administration (Chapter 14)—and understand the application's baseline performance. Eventually, the Administrator will tune the J2EE server.

Introducing WebSphere

As stated at the beginning of this chapter, WebSphere is a software platform for e-business. Let us now introduce in further detail the two products we will be concerned with for the remainder of this book.

WebSphere Application Server

WebSphere Application Server Version 5 drives most of the discussion, because it is IBM's latest implementation of the J2EE Application Server. While compliant with the J2EE 1.3 Specification we have examined, WebSphere Application Server Version 5 includes a great deal of added functionality (as allowed in the J2EE Specification), including a state-of-the-art Web services runtime and delivery system. (Since Web services are not part of J2EE, a discussion of this technology is beyond the scope of this book.)

Let's take a more detailed look at WebSphere Application Server Version 5. Here we have a fully J2EE 1.3-compliant Application Server. It can be thought of as the "single-server" packaging, comparable to WebSphere Application Server Advanced Single Server Edition Version 4.0. The administrative model of this edition is almost identical to that of the Version 4 single-server edition: The server configuration is maintained entirely in XML, not a relational database; also, the administrative console is Web browser-based. This product includes all the features of the entry level WebSphere Application Server Express Version 5 but adds EJB, thus rounding out the J2EE component set.

As for J2EE services, this edition provides both JMS and JAAS, in addition to all the services in Express Version 5, once again rounding out to the complete set of J2EE service APIs.

The Remote Agent Controller is provided with this edition, allowing for remote-debugging integration with the WebSphere Studio set of development products.

Finally, WebSphere Application Server Version 5 comes with IBM HTTP Server, Version 2.0—the latest build of IBM's adaptation of the Apache open source Web server.

WebSphere Studio

As a J2EE Tool Provider, IBM offers a wide selection of development tools to fit a wide variety of developer needs. It is important to note here that WebSphere Studio is based on the open-source Eclipse platform (*www.eclipse.org*). Varying degrees and types of functionality are added to the Eclipse platform to suit individual development needs. IBM has sought to provide a broad set of configurations of WebSphere, which support varying degrees of functionality, built on the Eclipse platform. Because it is based on Eclipse, WebSphere Studio makes it easy to plug in and integrate third party offerings.

WebSphere Studio Application Developer sets a new standard for J2EE development. This advanced Integrated Development Environment (IDE) has support for the development of all J2EE components, as well as multiple options for application server testing, using either one of the built in test environment servers, including WebSphere Application Server Version 4, Version 5, and Tomcat, or remote installations of WebSphere Application Server Version 4 or Version 5. The major portion of this book will be specific to WebSphere Studio Application Developer Version 5.

WebSphere Studio Application Developer Integration Edition is a special build of WebSphere Studio Application Developer, which adds on to the functionality of that IDE by providing rapid application development aids for creating custom JCA adapters as described in Chapter 10. Additionally, there are wizards to help deploy those adapters as web services. Finally, this IDE has support for all the "bonus" features of WebSphere Application Server Enterprise Edition.

Summary

We have now introduced WebSphere within the context of enterprise computing, also known as e-business. We added the context of J2EE, which was a major influence on the evolution of WebSphere. And finally we introduced the products that are of most importance to the IBM Certified Enterprise Developer: WebSphere Studio, Version 5.0.

In the next chapter we will introduce the component-based development of enterprise applications using WebSphere Studio Application Developer Version 5.

Test yourself

Key terms

Java
servlet
J2EE
component
container
Enterprise JavaBeans
service
framework
e-business
JavaServer Pages
CORBA
JavaBeans
applet
J2EE server

Review questions

1. List the services provided by a J2EE server.
2. What is the relationship between containers and components?
3. List the various roles defined by the J2EE architecture.
4. What is the difference between WebSphere Application Server and WebSphere Studio Application Developer?

CHAPTER 2

Developing enterprise applications with WebSphere Studio

Kameron Cole

Chapter topics

- *Introducing perspectives, views, and editors*
- *Commonly used perspectives*
- *WebSphere Studio testing scenarios*

Certification objectives

- *Create and configure WebSphere test environment servers*
- *Test and debug enterprise components*

The purpose of this chapter is to introduce the reader to the use of WebSphere Studio Application Developer for developing enterprise applications. We will introduce the workbench and introduce the notions of perspectives, views, and editors. We will demonstrate navigation around the workbench and walk though several of the perspectives most commonly used by enterprise developers. We will introduce the perspectives one by one, as we present a few highlights from the creation and testing of a simple, yet architecturally complete enterprise application. The complete application is available on the accompanying CD for those who wish to load it into the workbench, explore, and work with it.

Introducing perspectives, views, and editors

WebSphere Studio Application Developer Version 5 is based on the Eclipse workbench and supports a role-based development model. These roles are supported by task-oriented perspectives, which are designed to present the developer with functions most relevant to the task at hand. For example, the Web perspective is generally better suited to the development of servlets and JavaServer Pages (JSPs). Any perspective can be customized, and those custom perspectives can be saved and reused. Perspectives are aptly named, since they provide alternative ways of looking at, organizing, and interacting with the workspace.

A perspective consists of a synchronized collection of views and editors. Views provide alternate presentations of resources and a means of navigation. Editors provide a means of viewing or modifying the details of resources. Different types of resources will be associated with different editors based on the type of file for that particular resource. For example, Java source files having the (.java) extension will be associated with the Java editor, while files having the (.html) extension will be associated with Page Designer.

We will show a running example throughout this chapter as we develop an enterprise application. The first perspective is the J2EE Perspective, one of the more commonly used perspectives.

Starting up the workbench

If you're running Windows, you can start WebSphere Studio Application Developer by using **Start → Programs → IBM WebSphere Studio → Application Develop 5.0.** This will bring up the pop-up window shown below in Figure 2.1. You are starting the workbench using a workspace that is the default.

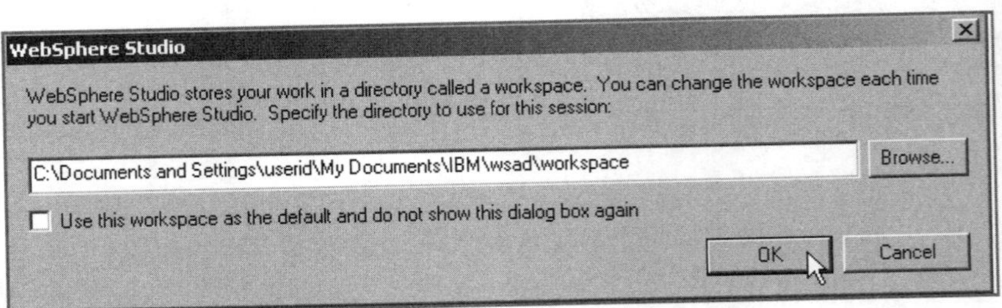

Figure 2.1: Default workspace pop-up.

Instead of using the default, it is generally preferable to create a new workspace. In this example, we will call it "MyAudio." Type the path to the desired directory for this work space in the box in the dialog, as shown in Figure 2.2. WebSphere Studio Application Developer will create this directory for you if it doesn't exist.

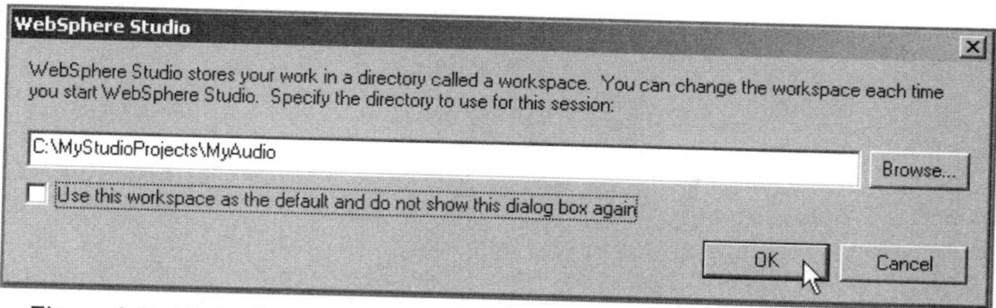

Figure 2.2: MyAudio workspace.

By being able to define the workspace directory, you can make use of multiple workspaces to manage separate projects.

Command line options

The developer has other ways to start the workbench. From the command line one can use the -data option to specify the workspace as shown in the following code.

```
"C:\Program Files\IBM\WebSphere Studio\wsappdev" -data
"C:\MyStudioProjects\MyAudio"
```

Note that this command would be entered all on a single line with a space after **-data.**

Another very useful command line option is -showlocation, which will result in the workspace location being shown in the title bar of the workbench.

```
"C:\Program Files\IBM\WebSphere Studio\wsappdev" -data
"C:\MyStudioProjects\MyAudio" -showlocation
```

These strategies can be incorporated into the target for a Windows desktop shortcut, by dragging the wsappdev.exe file onto the Windows desktop (which creates a shortcut rather than moving the file) and then modifying the shortcut target property.

One last useful command line option can help the developer who has checked the option as shown in Figure 2.3.

WebSphere Studio
WebSphere Studio stores your work in a directory called a workspace. You can change the workspace each time you start WebSphere Studio. Specify the directory to use for this session:
C:\Documents and Settings\userid\My Documents\IBM\wsad\workspace
Browse...
Use this workspace as the default and do not show this dialog box again
OK
Cancel

Figure 2.3: Getting rid of the workspace dialog box.

The dialog will not be shown again if this option is checked. But there is a way to reset this option from the command line:

```
"C:\Program Files\IBM\WebSphere Studio\wsappdev" -setworkspace
```

This little trick can come in quite handy.

Commonly used perspectives

We will use a running example to introduce six commonly used perspectives. We will create and test a simple but architecturally complete enterprise application. The application will consist of two Enterprise JavaBeans (EJBs), a servlet, and an HTML form.

We will create and configure two servers for testing, and we will demonstrate the debugging facilities of the workbench.

The J2EE perspective

The focus of the Enterprise Developer using WebSphere Studio Application Developer is the development of J2EE applications. Everything that pertains to the configuration and packaging of a J2EE enterprise application can be found in the J2EE perspective. This comprises the deployment descriptors and the ability to package the various modules that make up an enterprise application. For example, double-clicking the icon for an Enterprise Application project opens the editor for the application.xml file, which is the deployment descriptor for the entire J2EE enterprise application. As we build an enterprise application, the deployment descriptor is automatically modified. When it comes time to export the enterprise application, J2EE gives us the ability to package the application in the form of an .ear file. Let's work through an example.

Enterprise Application project

Select **File → New → Enterprise Application Project** from the menu at the top of the workbench, to begin creating an enterprise application. The Enterprise Application Project Creation wizard provides the opportunity to name the projects and modules associated with that Enterprise Application project, as shown in Figure 2.4. Notice that the project names follow a pattern. By default, they are all based on the name of the Enterprise Application project. The developer is free to change any of the individual names, and optionally select the module projects that are to be created as part of the enterprise application.

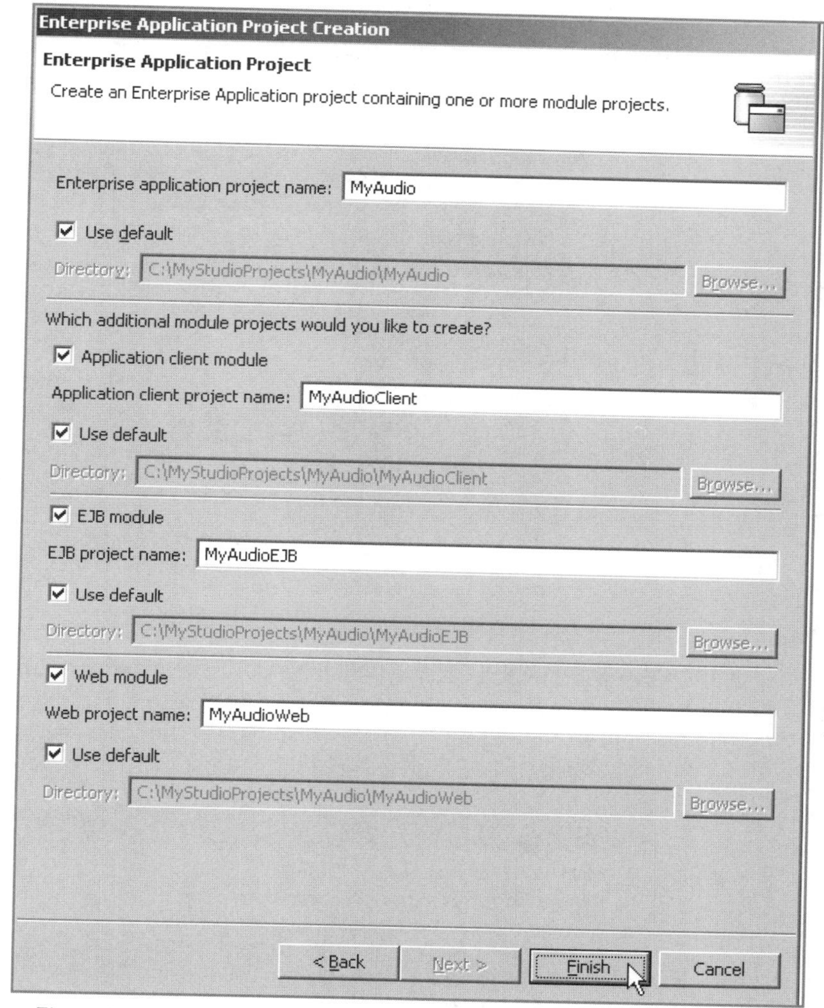

Figure 2.4: Picking names for the Enterprise Application and modules.

At this point, we have an Enterprise Application project that contains three modules: a Web module, an EJB module, and an ApplicationClient module. Let's continue by adding EJBs to the EJB module.

Enterprise JavaBean project

Since there are three chapters devoted to EJB development, the example here will be just to familiarize you with the basics of the user interface for working with EJB modules.

We can add an EJB to the MyAudioEJB module. This can be done in the J2EE Hierarchy view of the J2EE perspecive as shown in Figure 2.5, by right-clicking the **MyAudio** module, which brings up a pop-up menu, from which we can select **New → Enterprise Bean.**

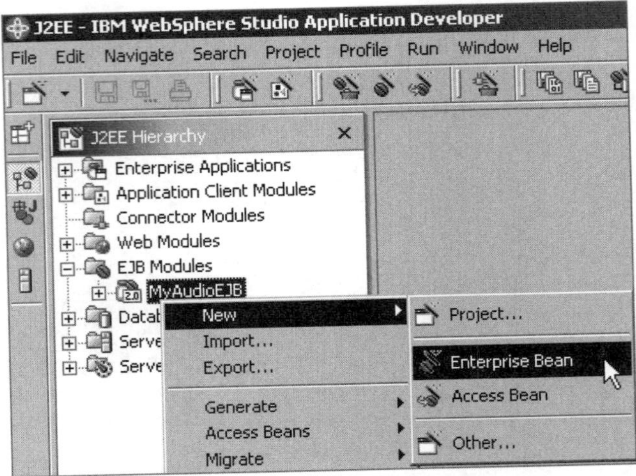

Figure 2.5: Creating a new Enterprise bean.

After verifying the project name, click **Next.** On the next panel, name the bean and place it in a package as shown in Figure 2.6. You must also select the type of bean. In this example, we will create an Entity bean with container-managed persistence (CMP) 2.0; the remaining details in the creation of a CMP EJB will be covered in Chapter 6.

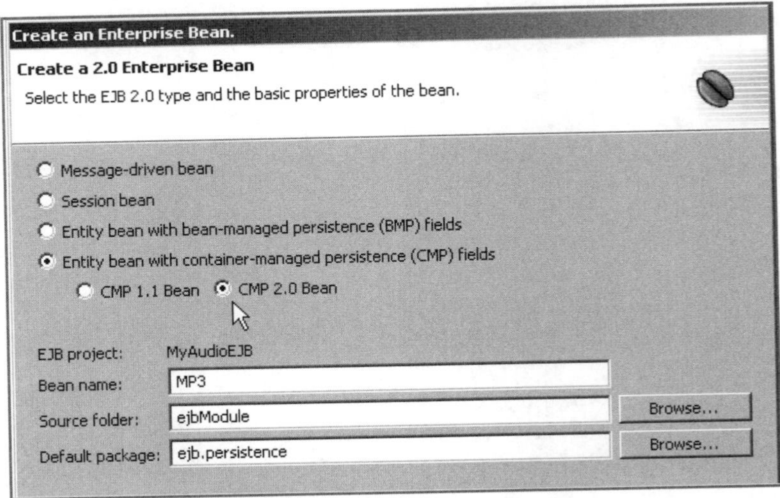

Figure 2.6: Basic bean properties panel.

Figure 2.7 shows the net result after creating a CMP EJB and a Session bean.

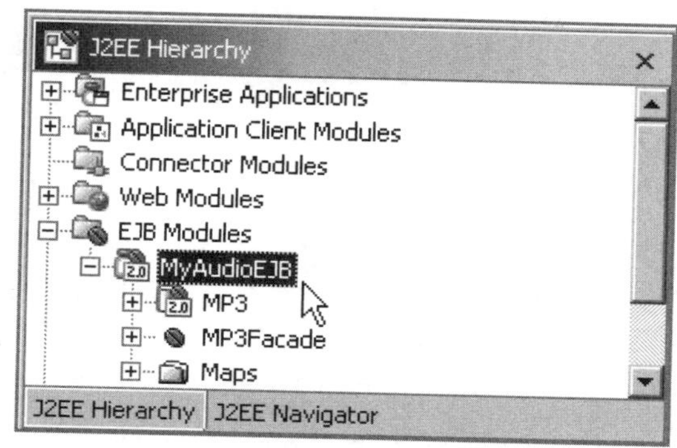

Figure 2.7: The completed EJB module.

The Java perspective

We move now to the Java perspective. Although it is an oversimplification, for the sake of some conceptual grounding we could characterize the Java perspective as a basic integrated development environment (IDE) for Java development, much like VisualAge for Java. Let's open the Java perspective using the shortcut bar. This is the vertical bar at the leftmost edge of the Application Developer window. Look in the upper left-hand corner of Figure 2.8 for an icon that resembles a multi-paneled IDE window, with a plus sign in the corner.

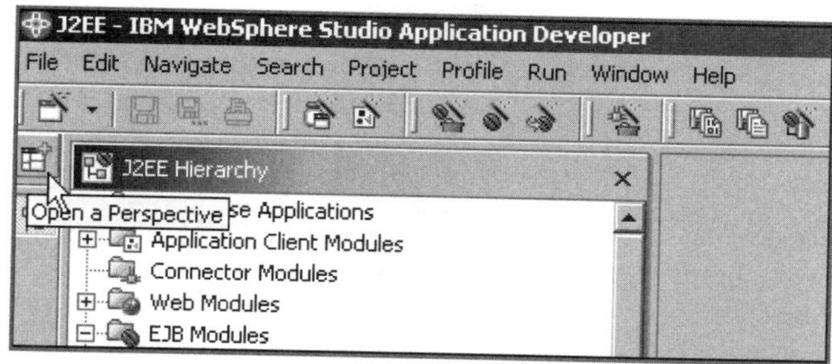

Figure 2.8: Using the shortcut navigation bar to open a new perspective.

Click the icon and select **Java**; the Java perspective will open as shown in Figure 2.9.

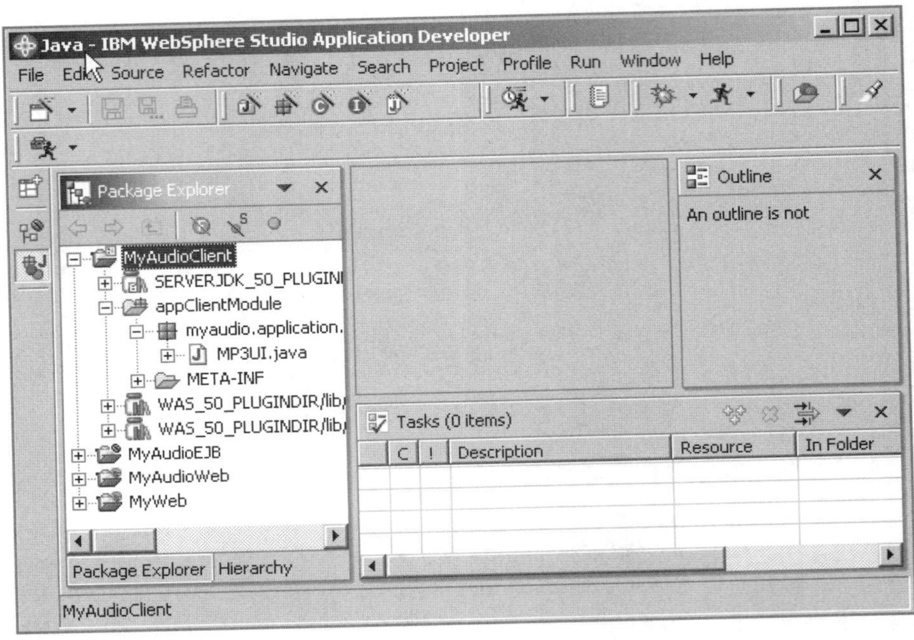

Figure 2.9: The Java perspective.

The Java perspective consists of multiple views: the Hierarchy view, which shares a tabbed space with the Package Explorer view and is open by default; the Tasks view, which is most like the All Problems page of VisualAge for Java; the Outline view, which, as the name suggests, is an outline of all the source code in a given Project. In the Package Explorer view, we have purposefully opened the application client created at the beginning of this chapter to point out that every Java project has its classpath set to the J2SE runtime (rt.jar). Since this is a J2EE module, the J2EE class libraries are also on the classpath as is an additional runtime set of libraries for interacting with EJBs, called ivjejb.jar. While the J2SE runtime is common to all Java projects, the other two jars provide Client container functionality, since this Project was created as a J2EE Application Client project.

Let's walk through the creation of a simple application client. Begin by creating a Java package, using the wizard icons in the top toolbar. Click the icon that resembles a package, as shown in Figure 2.10.

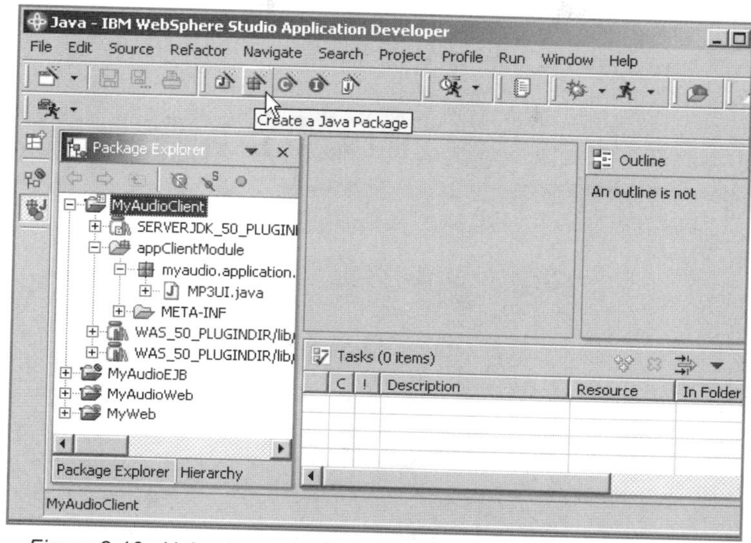

Figure 2.10: Using the wizard icons to create a new package.

The wizard enables us to name the package. The default location for the source files is set to a directory called appClientModule. Fill in a package name and click **Finish**.

We can create a new Java class inside this package by selecting the new package in the Package Explorer view and then clicking the New Class wizard icon, also on the top toolbar, as in Figure 2.11.

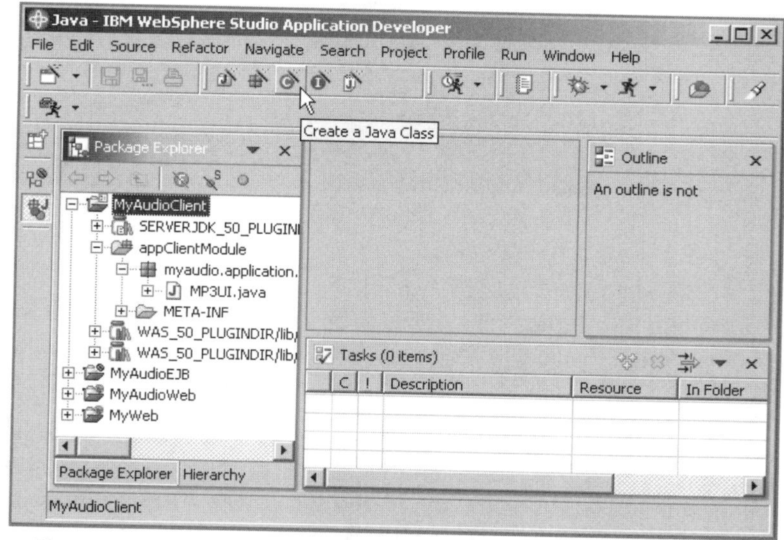

Figure 2.11: Invoking the New Class wizard from the top toolbar.

Although we could have used the icon without having first selected the package, doing it this way sets the containing package to the one we want automatically. The first panel of the resulting wizard, displayed in Figure 2.12, enables us to give the class a name and select whether to create various stubs. In this example we are creating an application client rather than an applet, so turn on the check box for creating a stub for the **public static void main(String[] args)** method and deselect the check boxes for the creation of superclass constructors and inherited abstract method stubs.

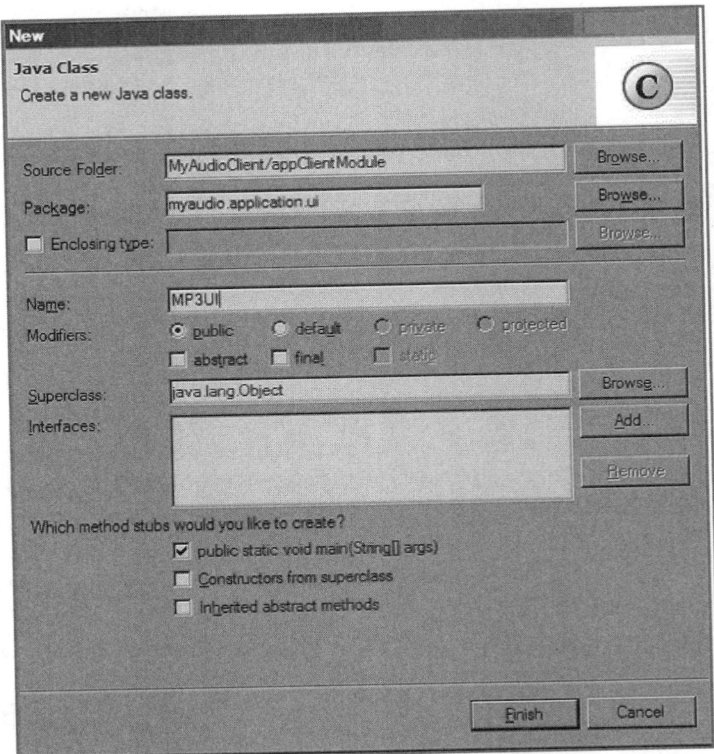

Figure 2.12: The New Java Class wizard.

Clicking Finish causes the class to be created with the appropriate package declaration and the Java Editor view opens. Now, we can enter fields and methods. (For those coming from a VisualAge for Java background, note that WebSphere Studio Application Developer has neither a New Method wizard nor a New Field wizard.)

If we enter a field declaration for a new JFrame, we see a special feature of Application Developer: the Solutions utility. It is the small light bulb icon that immediately appears next to our field declaration. Clicking it reveals a suggestion as to how to fix our code. In the Figure 2.13 example, it suggests that we add an import statement.

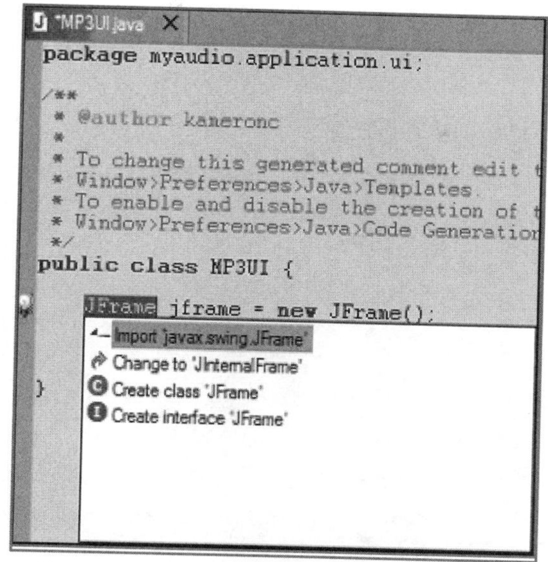

Figure 2.13: The Solutions utility makes a suggestion to correct potential coding errors.

Double-click the solution (**import javax.swing.JFrame**), and the import statement is added. At this point, we can compile our class simply by saving the source file. Type **Ctrl+S**.

Another very useful utility in Application Developer is Code Assist. Typing Ctrl+space while on an incomplete line of code pops up a suggestion box listing possible completions to the line, as shown in Figure 2.14.

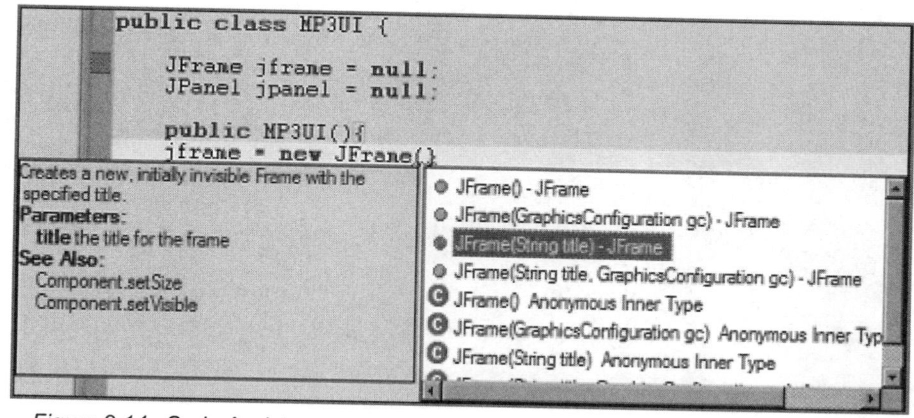

Figure 2.14: Code Assist.

Suppose you type a very long line of code, so long that it goes beyond the visible area in the Java Editor view, as in Figure 2.15.

Figure 2.15: A poorly formatted source file.

If you right-click anywhere in the Editor and select **Format** from the pop-up context menu, the default formatting settings will be applied as in Figure 2.16.

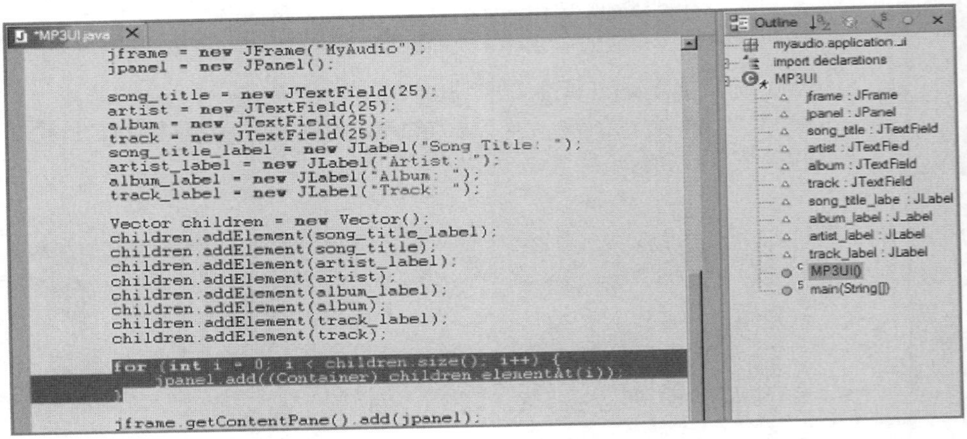

Figure 2.16: Formatting applied.

To review or change these settings, select **Window → Preferences** from the main menu. In the resulting panel, select **Java → Code Formatter** as shown in Figure 2.17.

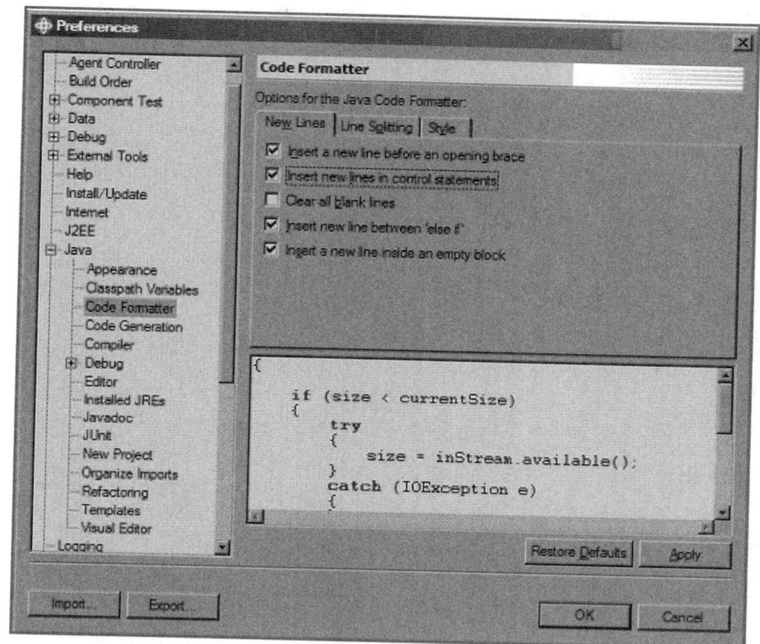

Figure 2.17: Code formatting options.

Once your code is complete, you have many options for testing it. See the section at the end of this chapter for testing using the standard JVM launcher and the Application Client launcher.

The Web perspective

As with the other perspectives we have examined thus far, the Web perspective provides a set of Views designed to meet the generalized needs of a front end Web component developer. Designing, building, and testing Web components is one of the key roles of the IBM Certified Enterprise Developer. Let's open the Web perspective using the shortcut bar on the left of your Application Developer GUI, as we previously did with the Java perspective. Figure 2.18 displays this default Web perspective.

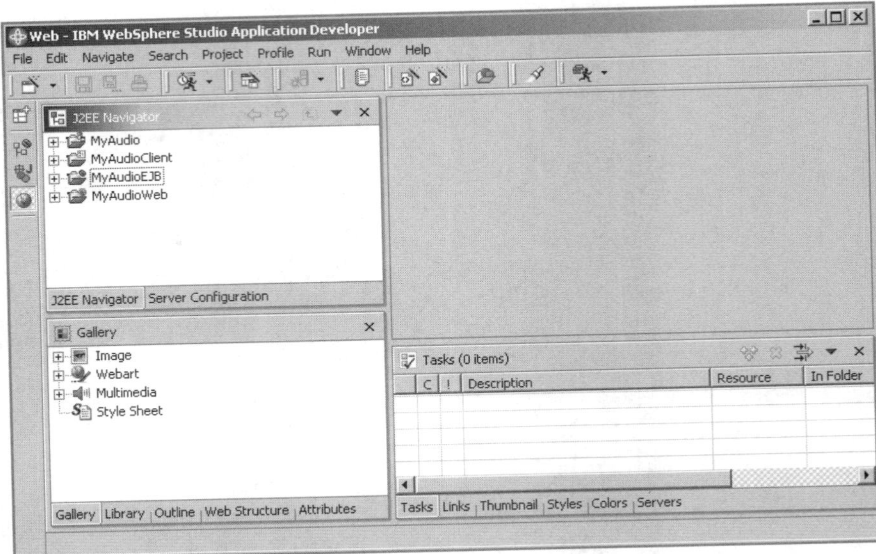

Figure 2.18: The (default) Web perspective.

Numerous Views are displayed. We will defer a more detailed discussion to Chapters 3 and 4, which focus on Web component development. We will explore several of the Views by way of continuing our example: We will add an HTML file and a servlet front end to our EJB back end.

Begin by expanding out the Web project and right-clicking the **Java Source** folder. Select **New → Servlet** from the pop-up context menu, as in Figure 2.19 (we could also have used the New Servlet wizard in the Java perspective).

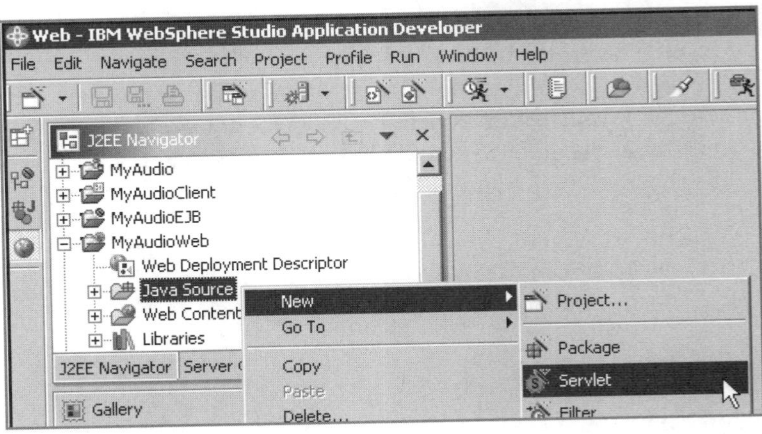

Figure 2.19: Adding a new servlet.

On the first panel of the resulting wizard, we add the name of a package (Application Developer will create the package for us; of course, we could have used the New Package wizard in the Java perspective) and the name of our servlet class, and click **Next**.

On the subsequent panel we accept the defaults for stub creation. This panel also takes care of adding our servlet definition to the Web deployment descriptor, web.xml.

Clicking **Finish** on the wizard opens the Java Editor View in the Web perspective. Figure 2.20 displays the results of using this New Servlet wizard.

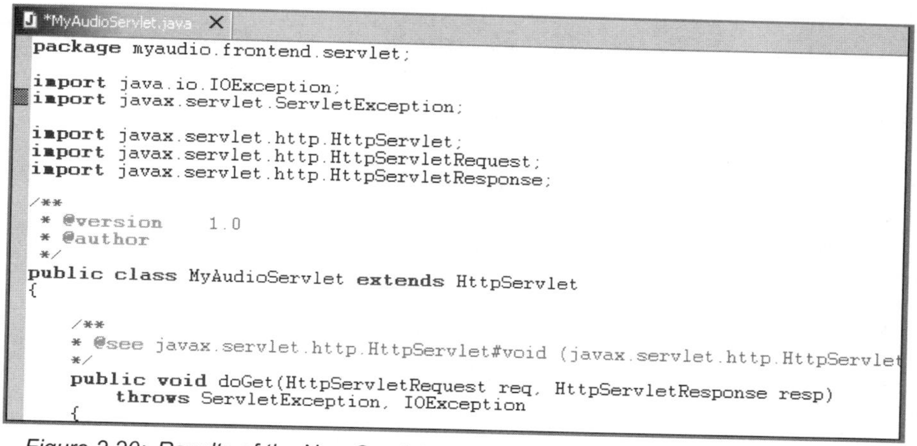

```
*MyAudioServlet.java
package myaudio.frontend.servlet;

import java.io.IOException;
import javax.servlet.ServletException;

import javax.servlet.http.HttpServlet;
import javax.servlet.http.HttpServletRequest;
import javax.servlet.http.HttpServletResponse;

/**
 * @version     1.0
 * @author
 */
public class MyAudioServlet extends HttpServlet
{

    /**
    * @see javax.servlet.http.HttpServlet#void (javax.servlet.http.HttpServlet
    */
    public void doGet(HttpServletRequest req, HttpServletResponse resp)
        throws ServletException, IOException
    {
```

Figure 2.20: Results of the New Servlet wizard.

In our servlet we can use similar code to that used in the application client to call a Session Façade EJB, effectively delegating the work required to perform the database entry. Since we are calling an EJB, we need to place the EJB JAR on the Java Build Path and add a reference to the EJB JAR to the Project References page of the Web project, as well as adding the appropriate import statements to our servlet class for the EJB Home and Remote stubs. Additionally, we add a JAR dependency on the Java JAR Dependencies page. We begin by right-clicking on the Web project and selecting properties from the pop-up context menu. The following Figure 2.21 shows the Java JAR dependencies in the project properties dialog.

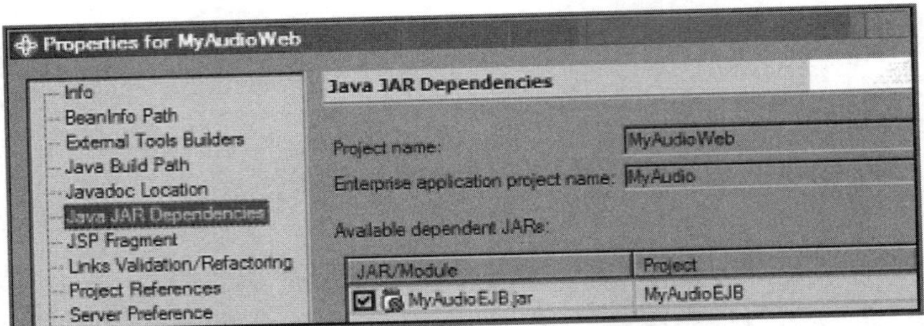

Figure 2.21: Adding an EJB JAR dependency to the Web project.

We also need to add an ejb-ref to the web.xml. This procedure is essentially the same as adding an ejb-ref to the application-client.xml: simply double-click the Web Deployment Descriptor in the J2EE Navigator View, go to the References page, and add the reference as shown in Figure 2.22.

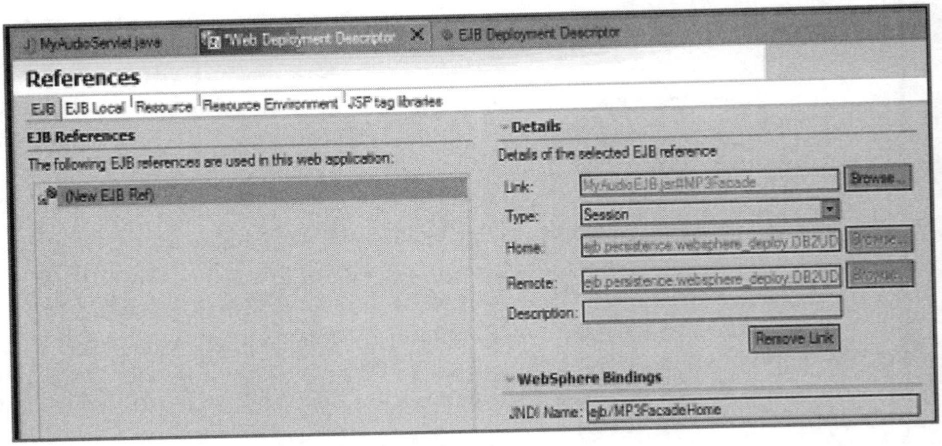

Figure 2.22: Adding an ejb-ref to the web.xml.

We continue by adding an HTML page to access our servlet. This task will give us the opportunity to explore some of the HTML editing features of the Web perspective. To insert an HTML page into your Web application in the J2EE Navigator view, drill down in the Web project until your find the folder called Web Content. Right-click, and from the pop-up context menu, select **New → HTML/XHTML file**, as shown in Figure 2.23.

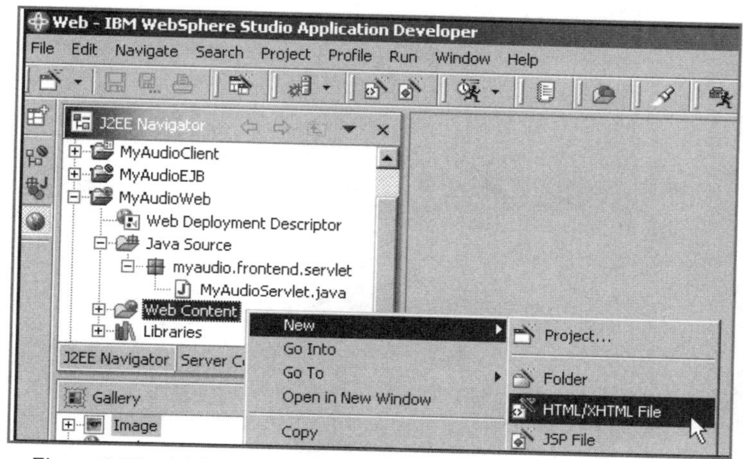

Figure 2.23: Adding an HTML page.

The wizard is straightforward. We simply name the file **addmp3.html** and click **Finish**. Doing so results in opening the new file in the HTML editor, also known as Page Designer. This editor provides three tabbed views: Design, which is the drag-and-drop visual editor; Source, which reveals the HTML code; and Preview, which essentially renders the page in a browser.

It's possible to just type into the Design view, but we'll familiarize ourselves with the Insert file menu. Select **Insert → Paragraph → Heading 1**. This will present you with a flashing box, where you can type your text. To manipulate the attributes of any tag, simply right-click the element (in this case, the text you just entered). Select **Attributes** from the context menu. Doing so will bring us to the screen shown in Figure 2.24 and enable us to modify attributes of a selected object.

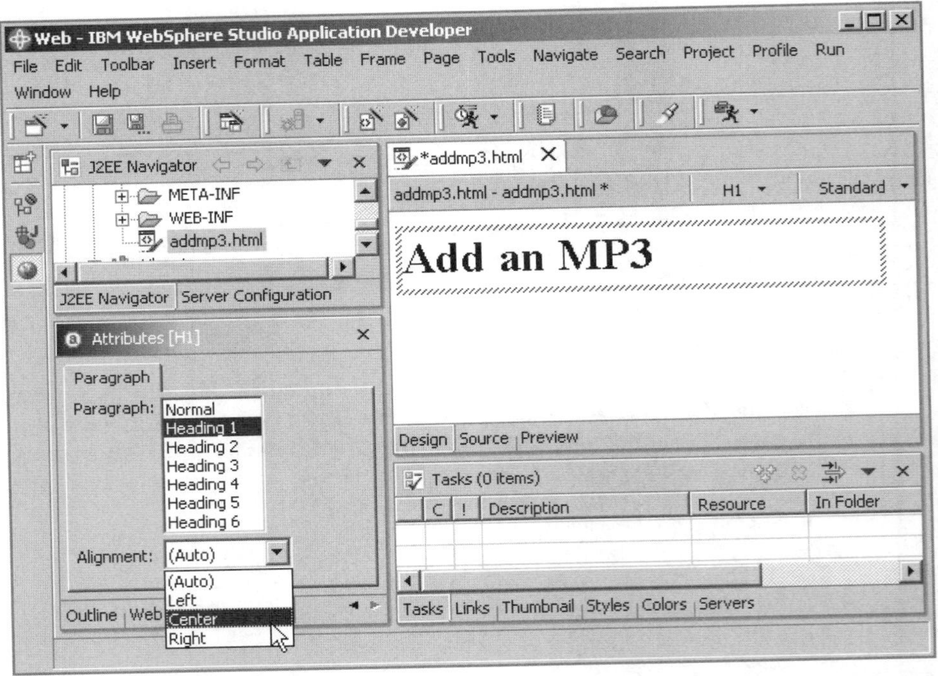

Figure 2.24: Modifying attributes.

The Attributes view, in the lower left-hand corner of the Web perspective, gains focus. Here the developer can manipulate the Attributes of the selected object, such as by switching the alignment to Center, as shown.

We will skip over the details of creating a form and go straight to setting the form's action to reference our servlet. In the Outline view we can select the form, and then switch to the Attributes view.

The Attributes view now shows the configuration of the form. If we click the dropdown list next to Action, the (only) choice is Servlet. Selecting that option brings up a dialog with our servlet listed. Select the servlet, and click OK, as shown in Figure 2.25.

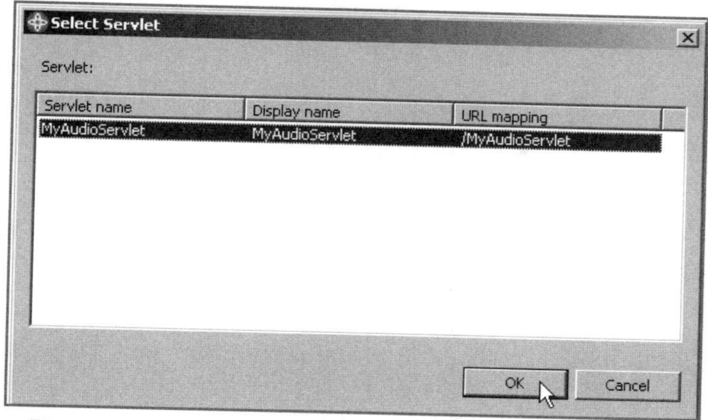

Figure 2.25: Setting the form's Action to invoke MyAudioServlet.

This completes our example of developing a simple Web application in the Web perspective. We will test the servlet using the Remote Server Attach. The testing is described in the next section.

WebSphere Studio testing scenarios

In this section we will introduce the WebSphere Test Environment of WebSphere Studio Application Developer. This facility allows the developer to perform unit testing of J2EE components using an actual WebSphere Application Server included with the workbench.

Testing EJBs using the Universal Test Client and the WebSphere Test Environment

In this section we will show how the enterprise developer can perform unit testing of EJBs by taking advantage of the simplified approach made possible by the Universal Test Client (UTC) in WebSphere Studio Application Developer Version 5. The UTC is a Web application that provides a prebuilt user interface for testing EJBs without requiring the developer to write any client code.

Before we can test an EJB, we must generate deployment code. This code provides the logic that connects the server-independent deployable bean to the server-dependent implementation of the standard J2EE services. In the J2EE Hierarchy view of the J2EE perspective (the same is possible, using identical menu options, in the J2EE Navigator view), we right-click on the EJB module and select **Generate → Deploy** and **RMIC Code . . .** (it is also possible to right-click only the bean and then select **Generate Deploy Code**). This topic of generated code will be discussed in further detail in the EJB chapters.

The next step would be to right-click the bean (you could alternatively right-click the module or, in the J2EE Navigator view, the source file for the bean, e.g., **mp3.java**) and, from the pop-up context menu, select **Run On Server**. However, we have a CMP bean, and so that step would be premature if we tried it prior to configuring the appropriate data source on an application server.

We need to configure a DataSource for the EJB container to use to connect to the database. In order to have a DataSource, we need to make sure that we have a JDBC Provider, also known as a driver, available to the server. But we don't even have a server yet, so that is the next task.

We can now create our first test server. In fact, we will create several test servers before we are done with this chapter in order to illustrate the unit testing capabilities of Application Developer. The first test environment we will use will utilize the internal WebSphere 5.0 Test Environment. This comprises an internal instance of WebSphere Application Server Version 5 and its attendant XML configuration file. We begin the process by creating a Server Project.

Begin by opening the Server perspective. The Server perspective provides the developer with five views by default: the Navigator view, which is exactly the same as the J2EE Navigator, except that this navigator shows the folder for our Server project; the Server Configuration view; the Editor view; and the Servers and Console views, tabbed together at the bottom.

Now, from the workbench menus in the Server perspective, we can select **File → New → Server Project**. The Create a New Server Project wizard appears as shown in Figure 2.26.

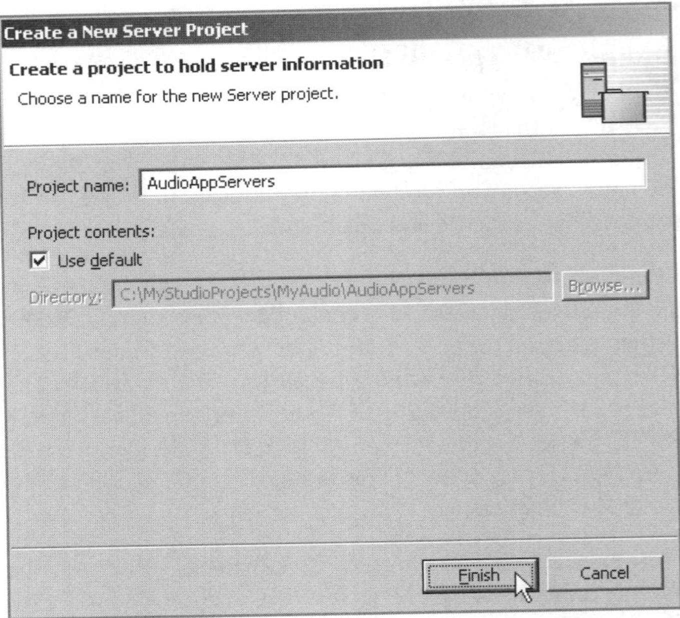

Figure 2.26: Start your new server project by giving it a name.

We will use this project to hold all of our test server configurations. Clicking **Finish** provides us with an empty folder to hold Server Instances and Server Configurations.

Setting up the WebSphere Test Environment

We have two equivalent ways to begin creating a server instance and configuration: Either right-click the Server Project folder in the Navigator View, or right-click the Servers icon in the Server Configuration View. Either way, we select **New → Server and Server Configuration** from the pop-up context menu as shown in Figure 2.27.

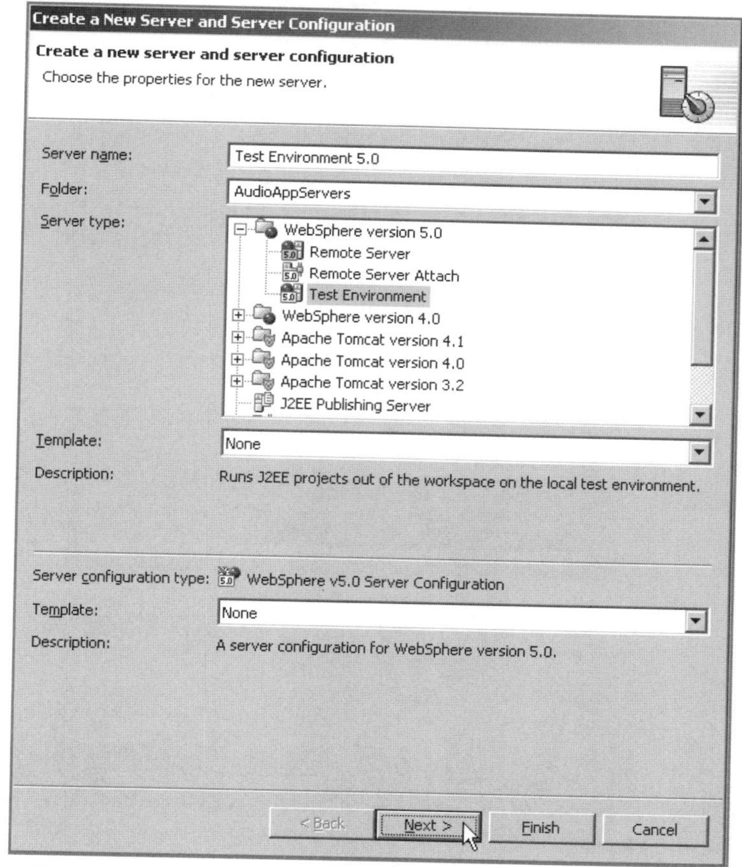

Figure 2.27: New Server and Server Configuration wizard.

This time, we are using the internal WebSphere Version 5.0 Test Environment as our server type. We can give the server instance a meaningful name. The subsequent panel allows us to specify a port number or accept the default. As Figure 2.28 demonstrates, we have to make sure that we avoid port conflicts. Then click **Finish**.

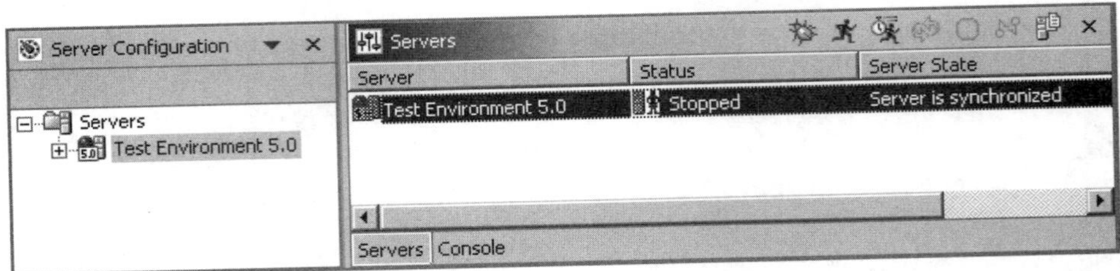

Figure 2.28: New server and server instance.

The Server view displays the server instance, and the Server Configuration view displays the name of the configuration just created. We can double-click on the Configuration, which opens the Server Configuration editor. As in Figure 2.29, we then select the **Data sources** tab.

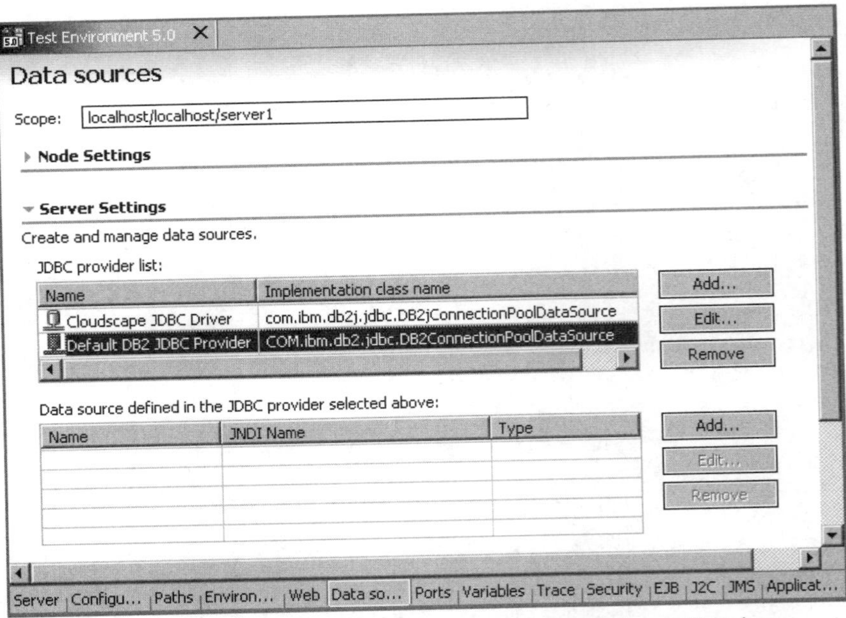

Figure 2.29: The Data sources tab of the Server Configuration Editor view.

We will use the JDBC provider listed as Default DB2 JDBC provider, but, before we can use it, we need to set the environment variable to the path to the driver archive. On the Variables tab, we scroll down in Node settings to select **DB2_JDBC_DRIVER_PATH**, click **Edit**, and enter the full path to the directory containing db2java.zip. Figure 2.30 displays how the driver path is set as a Node variable.

Figure 2.30: Setting the DB2 JDBC driver path as a Node variable.

Back on the Data source tab, we select the **Default DB2 JDBC Provider** from the JDBC provider list, and click the **Add** button located to the right of the list of data sources directly below the list of providers, as shown in Figure 2.31.

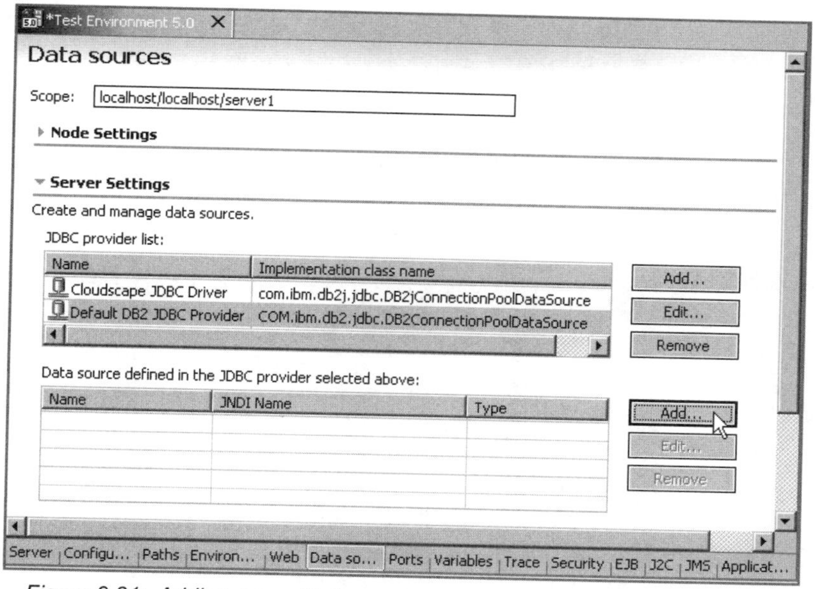

Figure 2.31: Adding a new Data source.

In the resulting wizard we select the **DB2 JDBC Provider** and specify the creation of a **Version 5.0 data source** as shown in Figure 2.32.

After clicking **Next**, we can specify the remaining details of the data source and click **Finish**, as shown in Figure 2.33.

Data sources are covered in more detail in Chapter 14.

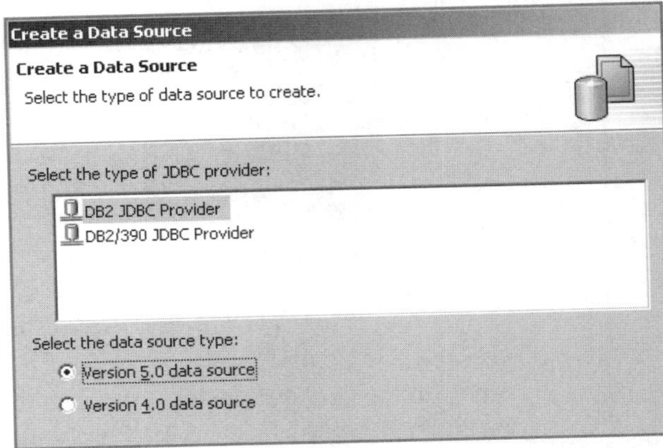

Figure 2.32: Creating a Data source.

Modify Data Source

Modify Data Source

Edit the settings of the data source.

Name:	MyAudioDataSource
JNDI name:	jdbc/AudioDS
Description:	
Category:	
Statement cache size:	10
Data source helper class name:	com.ibm.websphere.rsadapter.DB2DataStoreHelper
Connection timeout:	1800
Maximum connections:	10
Minimum connections:	1
Reap time:	180
Unused timeout:	1800
Aged timeout:	0
Purge policy:	EntirePool
Component-managed authentication alias:	
Container-managed authentication alias:	

☑ Use this data source in container managed persistence (CMP)

< Back | Next > | Finish | Cancel

Figure 2.33: Defining a Data source.

The Universal Test Client application

Now that we have a WTE server and server instance set up, we are ready to unit-test our EJBs. In the J2EE Hierarchy view, we simply right-click on the EJB we wish to test and select **Run on Server** as shown in Figure 2.34.

Once the server starts, the UTC is presented in its own view. Click on the triangular icons to expand down to the create method, as shown in Figure 2.35.

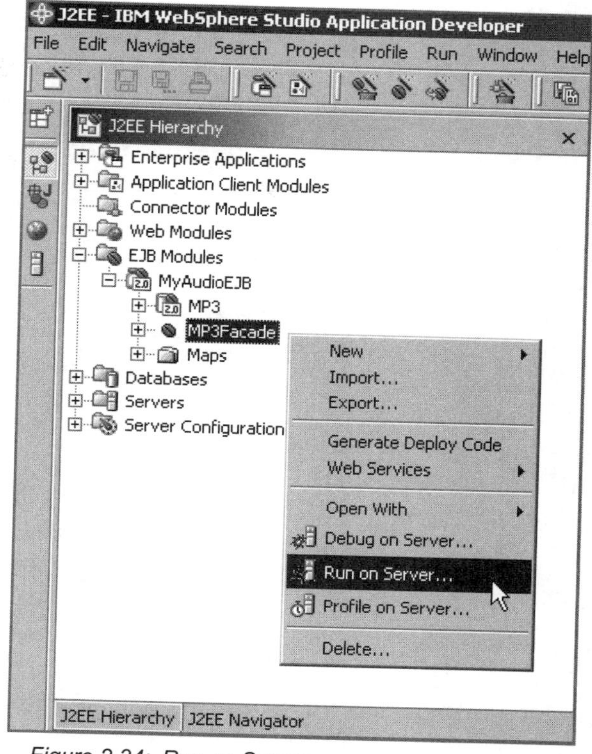

Figure 2.34: Run on Server.

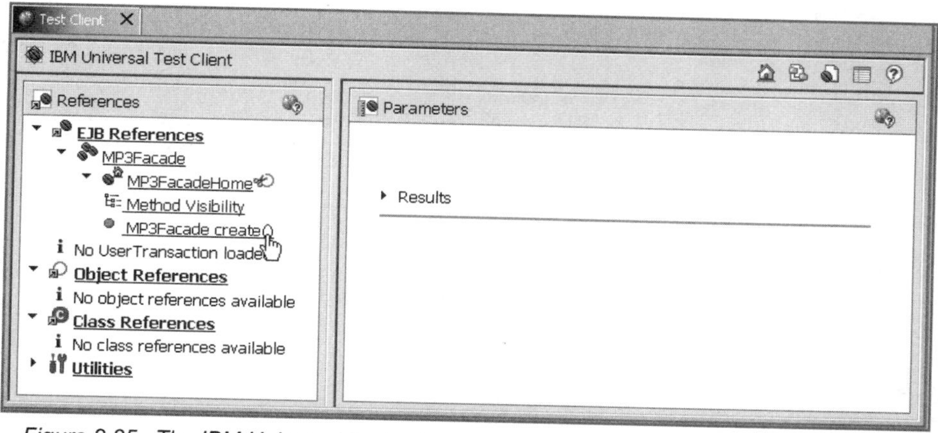

Figure 2.35: The IBM Universal Test Client.

Next, click on the **Create** method and then click the **Invoke** button as shown in Figure 2.36.

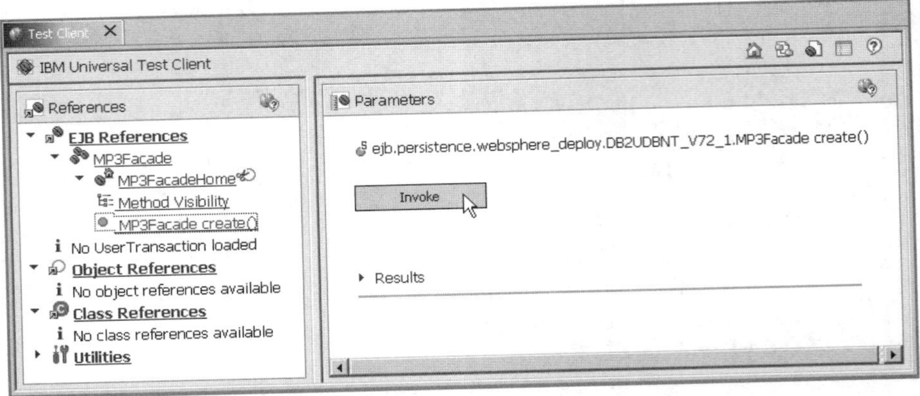

Figure 2.36: Invoking the create method in the UTC.

The create method returns a reference to an MP3Facade object instance. In order to work with this reference, click on the button labeled **Work with Object** as shown in Figure 2.37.

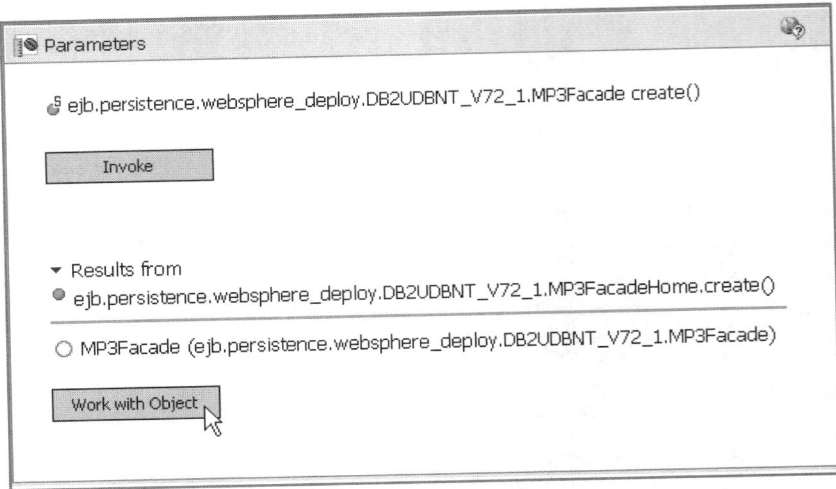

Figure 2.37: Obtaining a reference.

Having obtained an object that implements the MP3Facade interface, we are almost ready to invoke business methods using it. In our example we will demonstrate the addition of an MP3 to the database using the addMP3 method of the MP3Facade. In the references pane, expand the remote reference, whose name is MP3Facade 1, to expose the addMP3 method and then click on that method, as shown in Figure 2.38.

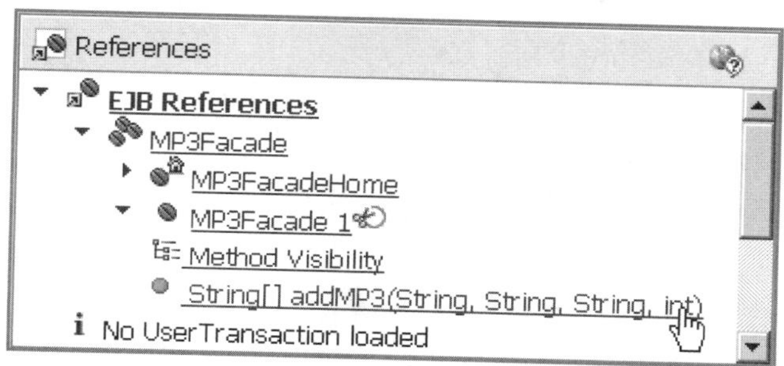

Figure 2.38: Selecting a business method on the remote reference.

Now we are ready to invoke the method. First we fill in values for the four input parameters. The three strings and the integer are the title, artist, album, and track for the song that we are adding to the MP3 table in the MYAUDIO database. See the example in Figure 2.39.

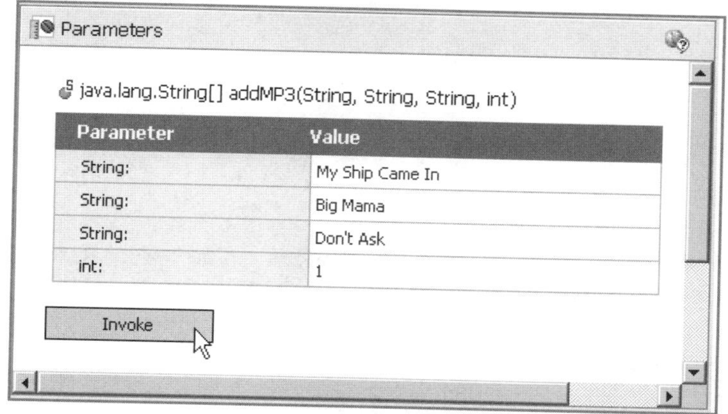

Figure 2.39: Invoking a business method on a session EJB.

At this point we can verify that a new row was actually created in the database. In our example we will use the DB2 Control Center to do this, as shown in Figure 2.40.

Figure 2.40: Using the DB2 Control Center to sample contents.

Unit testing: the application client launcher

Now we can test our application client in a Client container, provided by the Web-Sphere Test Environment. The Client container will attach to the JNDI Namespace of our J2EE server, so we need to ensure that that server is up and running before proceeding. This can be done in the Servers view at the bottom of the Server perspective, as shown in Figure 2.41.

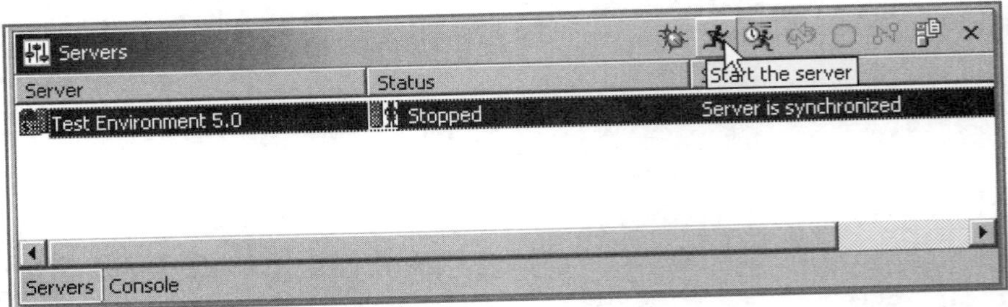

Figure 2.41: Starting the server.

The Console view is displayed, and we see the server starting up. Finally the message "Server server1 open for e-business" appears in the console. Having started the server, we are now ready to start the client. Switch back to the J2EE perspective and select **Run → Run . . .** from the workbench menu. In the Launch Configurations dialog shown in Figure 2.42, select **WebSphere Version 5 Application Client** and press the button labeled **New.** Name the new configuration **MP3UI** and select **MyAudio** as the enterprise application.

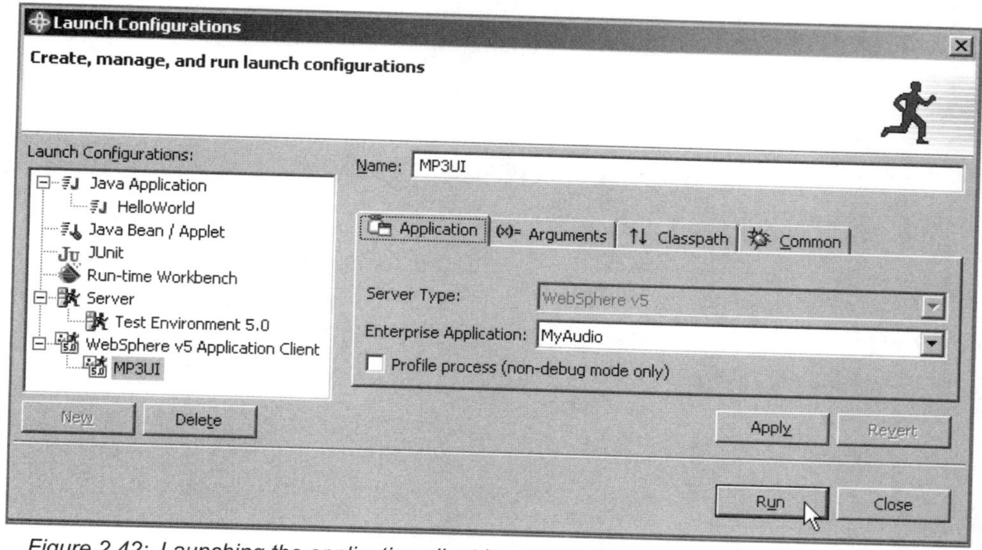

Figure 2.42: Launching the application client in a WTE client container.

After we click **Run,** the Client container is initialized, the application client class is invoked, and the MyAudio user interface is displayed. Figure 2.43 shows the user interface.

Figure 2.43: The user interface of the MyAudio application client.

Every time we enter values for title, artist, album, and track and click the Add button, another row is inserted into the database. Figure 2.44 shows the database after several songs have been added using the J2EE Application Client.

ALBUM	SONG_TITLE	ARTIST	TRACK
Don't Ask	My Ship Came In	Big Mama	1
Bubba Sings the Blues	Same Old Song	Bubba	1
Bubba Sings the Blues	A Brand New Song	Bubba	2
Bubba Sings the Blues	Sing Me A Song	Bubba	3

Figure 2.44: The MP3 table with additional songs added from the application client.

Testing Web components using the Remote Server Test Environment

We will test the Web application we developed using a local instance of WebSphere Application Server Version 5 installed on our local machine, although it could be remote as well. We will use the AudioAppServers server project previously created to show that an existing server project can hold a variety of servers and server configurations, since the server project is essentially a container. The instance and configuration constitute a test environment.

We begin by switching to the Server perspective. In the Navigator view in the Server perspective, you can right-click on the AudioAppServers folder and select **New → Server and Server Configuration** from the pop up context menu as shown in Figure 2.45.

Figure 2.45: New Server and Server Configuration.

We saw the next panel before when we created our WebSphere Test Environment server and server configuration. This time, we select **Remote Server** and give it a name that will differentiate it from the internal WTE server as shown in Figure 2.46.

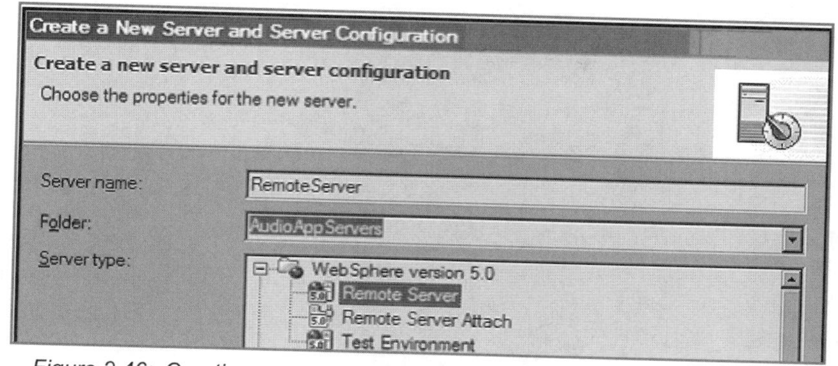

Figure 2.46: Creating a remote server instance and configuration.

On the next panel, shown in Figure 2.47, enter the IP address or machine name where the remote server is located. The default value, 127.0.0.1, is called the *loopback address,* which is a computer's alias for itself. If we leave the default, we will invoke a server on our local machine.

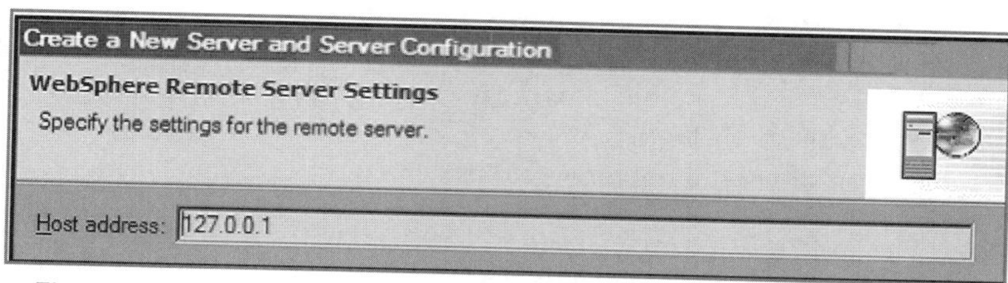

Figure 2.47: A remote server on the local machine.

With the Agent controller installed and configured correctly, we next see the following panel, in which the wizard has discovered the necessary settings as shown in Figure 2.48.

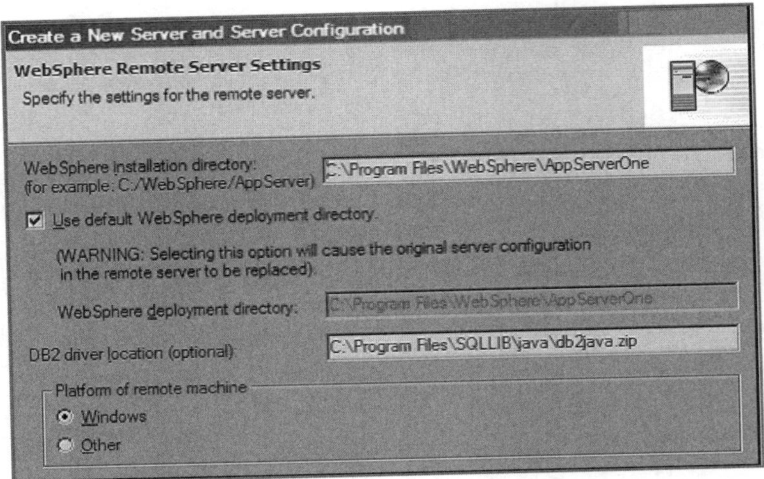

Figure 2.48: Setting paths.

One thing to note in Figure 2.48 is that we have chosen the option to "Use default WebSphere deployment directory." This means that the server-cfg.xml will be overwritten by the configuration from within Application Developer. We could have unchecked that option, which would then leave the original server-cfg.xml file intact, and specified a different WebSphere deployment directory in which to store the server-cfg.xml associated with our WTE remote server. This would clearly be necessary in situations when the remote server did not belong to us.

The subsequent panel determines how we will copy the necessary application files to the default deployment directory.

Since we choose to create a new file copy mechanism, we get the subsequent panel in the wizard. It should be clear from this panel what the file copy mechanism is supposed to do: copy the application files from within our Application Developer Server project to a similar place on the remote server installation, as Figures 2.49 and 2.50 detail.

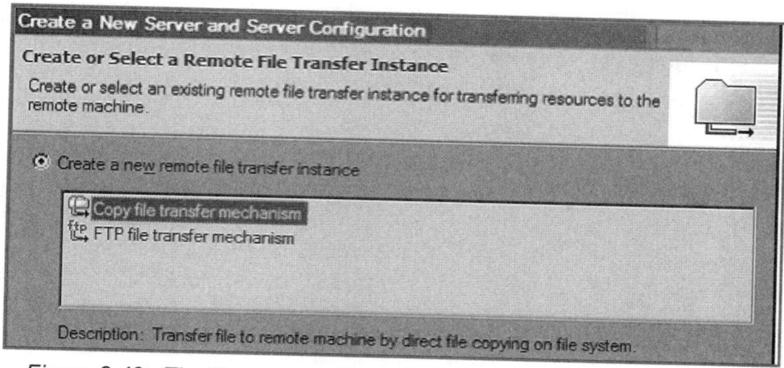

Figure 2.49: The file copy mechanism.

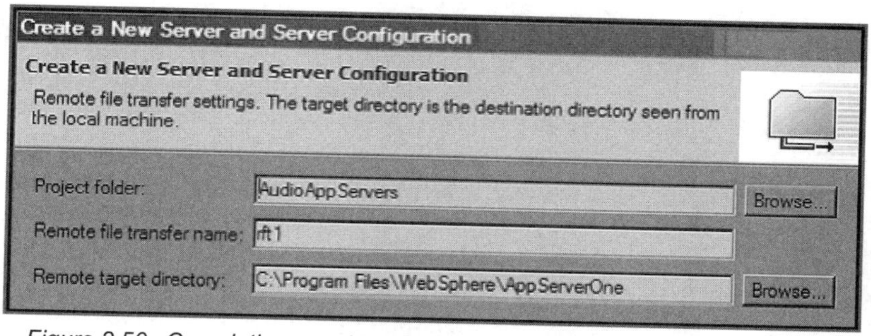

Create a New Server and Server Configuration
Create a New Server and Server Configuration
Remote file transfer settings. The target directory is the destination directory seen from the local machine.
Project folder: AudioAppServers Browse...
Remote file transfer name: rft1
Remote target directory: C:\Program Files\WebSphere\AppServerOne Browse...

Figure 2.50: Completing creation of a new file transfer mechanism.

We finish by clicking **Finish**.

The final panel we omit here, since it is the port assignment for the remote server and can be any value, as long as a port conflict is avoided. Clicking **Finish** at this point will yield in our Server perspective the results shown in Figure 2.51.

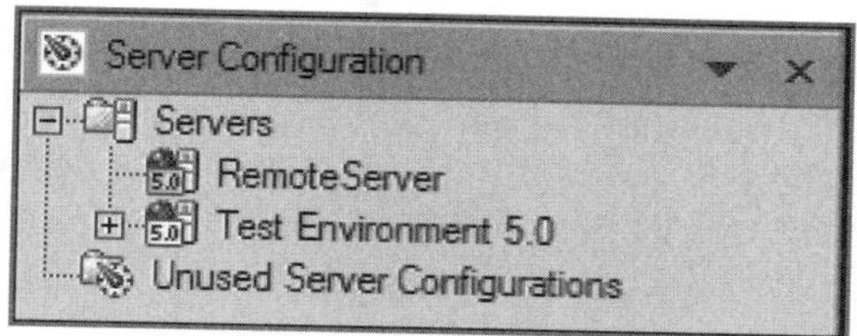

Figure 2.51: New server instance and server configuration, Server perspective.

We need to add our enterprise application project to the configuration. Right-click the configuration, select **Add** from the context menu, and choose the **MyAudio** project as shown in Figure 2.52.

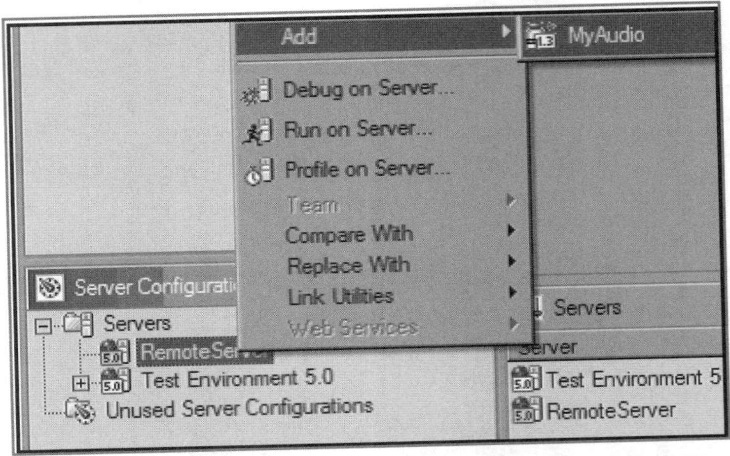

Figure 2.52: Installing our enterprise application on the new server.

We're almost ready to start the remote server, but first we must add the data source to the server configuration. The process is exactly the same as in the WTE section. We open the **Server Configuration** by double-clicking it in the Server Configuration view, go to the Data source tab, select the appropriate driver, and click **Add** in the Data source section.

With the exception of being slower, starting the remote server is not visibly different from starting the local WTE, so we won't try to start it now, at least not in its normal mode. Instead, we will take this opportunity to explore the last of the main perspectives in Application Developer: the Debug perspective.

Before we get to the Debug perspective, however, we will do a bit of setup first. If we were to right-click the addmp3.html file and select Run on Server, WebSphere Studio would attempt to start the WTE server instead of running the application on the Remote server. We can remedy this by setting the server preferences for the Web application, using the file-base approach. Our Web project contains a file called .serverPreference, which can be seen in the Navigator view of the Server perspective. Double-clicking this file will open it in an Editor. We simply need to substitute the .wsi file path for the .rwsi file path to our remote server, as in Figure 2.53.

```
.serverPreference
<?xml version="1.0" encoding="UTF-8"?>
<server-preference>
    <deployable factoryId="com.ibm.etools.webtools.server"
        memento="MyAudioWeb" server="/AudioAppServers/RemoteServer.rwsi"/>
</server-preference>
```

Figure 2.53: Setting the server preference using the serverPreference configuration file.

Now the remote server will automatically start up if we right-click any runnable file in this Web project.

The Debug Perspective

At this point, we will open the Debug perspective, set a breakpoint in our servlet, and step through the code. The Debug perspective (Figure 2.54), just like any other perspective we have examined so far, can be opened either through the shortcut bar on the left-hand side of the workbench or from the menu item **Window → Open Perspective → Debug**.

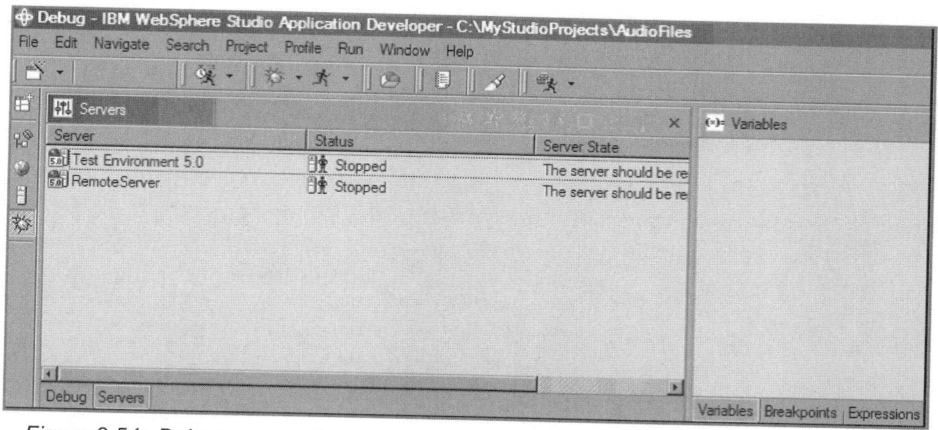

Figure 2.54: Debug perspective.

To set a breakpoint, we can open the MyAudioServlet .java source file using the Navigator view in the Web perspective. In the Java Editor, which opens on the file, the leftmost margin is referred to as the prefix area. Double-clicking on any line of code in this area will cause a breakpoint, signified by a blue dot, to appear. (Be sure to double-click on a line of executable code, not on a method declaration.) In MyAudioServlet we will set a breakpoint on the line of code just before the while loop assigns to the local variables the values it retrieves from the HttpServletRequest, as shown in Figure 2.55.

```
MyAudioServlet.java
    processRequest(req, resp);
    }

    /**
    * @see javax.servlet.http.HttpServlet#void (javax.servle
    */
    public void doPost(HttpServletRequest req, HttpServletR
        throws ServletException, IOException
    {
        processRequest(req, resp);

    }
    public void processRequest(HttpServletRequest req, Http
        String song_title = "";
        String artist = "";
        String album = "";
        String track = "";

        Enumeration names = req.getParameterNames();

        String value = "";
        String name = "";

        while (names.hasMoreElements()){
            name = (String) names.nextElement();
            value = req.getParameter(name);
            if (name =="song_title") song_title = value;
            if (value =="artist") artist = value;
            if (value =="album") album = value;
            if (value =="track") track = value;

        }
```

Figure 2.55: Setting a breakpoint.

We will now debug the code using the remote server, which is visible in the Servers view, in the upper left-hand corner of the Debug perspective. To enable our breakpoint, we must start this server in Debug mode. As Figure 2.56 shows, this is accomplished by right clicking the remote server and selecting **Debug** from the pop-up context menu.

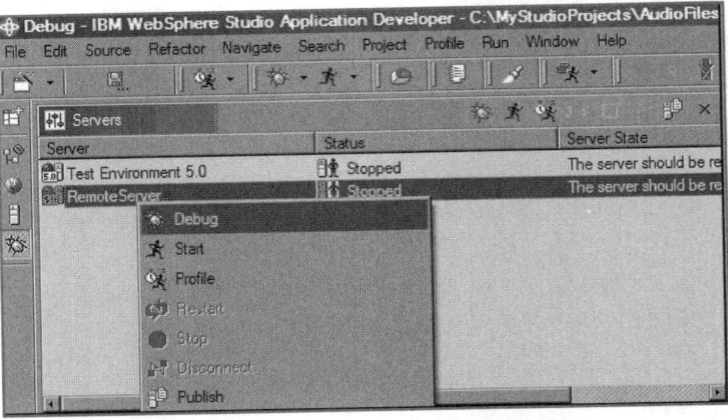

Figure 2.56: Starting the remote server in Debug mode.

Once the server has started, we can return to the Web perspective, right-click on the **addmp3.html** file, and select **Run on Server**. Note in Figure 2.57 that the URL reflects the fact that the server is remote.

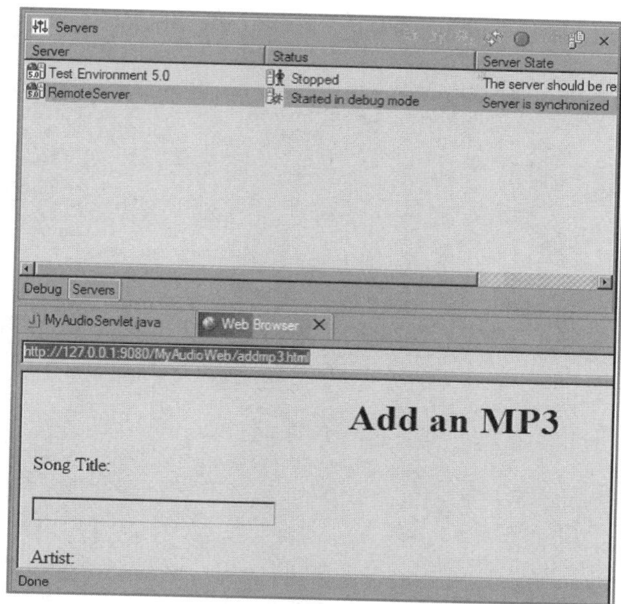

Figure 2.57: Beginning the remote server debugging session.

We won't hit our breakpoint until we have filled in some values and clicked the **Add** button on the Web page. Having done this, we are presented with a dialog asking whether we wish to "step into" the doPost method. Before clicking **Yes**, check the box at the bottom of the dialog labeled **Disable step-by-step debugging**. The view in the left center pane switches to the Java Editor, stopping on the first (and only) line of the doPost method (see Figure 2.58).

```
MyAudioServlet.java   Web Browser
    }

    /**
    * @see javax.servlet.http.HttpServlet#void (javax.se
    */
    public void doPost(HttpServletRequest req, HttpServ
        throws ServletException, IOException
    {
        processRequest(req, resp);

    }
    public void processRequest(HttpServletRequest req,
        String song_title = "";
        String artist = "";
        String album = "";
        String track = "";
```

Figure 2.58: Entering the doPost method.

In the upper right-hand pane, switch from the Server view to the Debug view. Notice that the top instruction in the stack in the currently suspended thread is highlighted. Notice also that the navigation icons at the top of the Debug view are enabled. We now click the middle of the three arrow buttons. Step Over appears if the mouse pointer hovers over the button for a few moments, as shown in Figure 2.59.

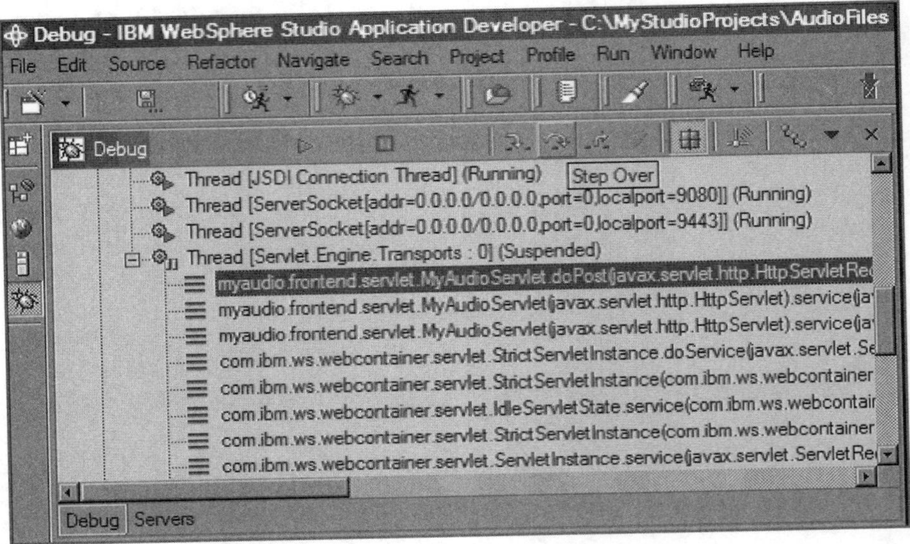

Figure 2.59: Stepping over an instruction in the stack.

This brings us to the breakpoint. If we continue stepping over the lines of code in the for-loop, with the Variables view visible in the upper right-hand pane, we can watch the variables as they get values assigned, as shown in Figure 2.60.

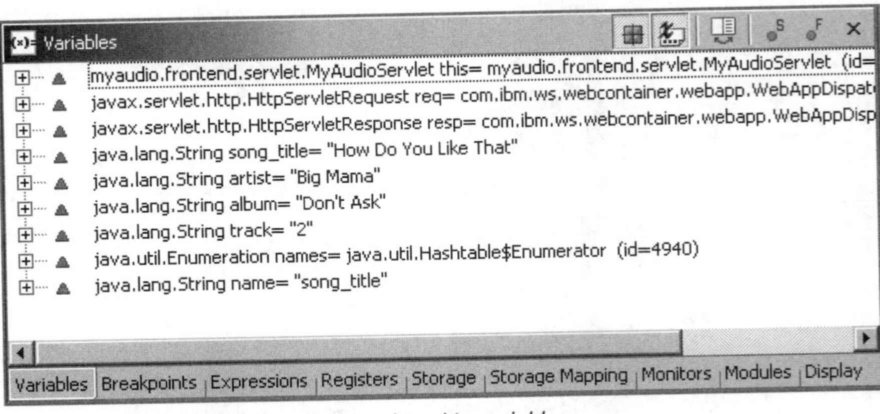

Figure 2.60: Viewing the values assigned to variables.

Once the while loop is complete, we can right-click any of the initialized variables in the Variables view and, from the pop-up context menu, select **Change Variable Value,** as Figure 2.61 shows.

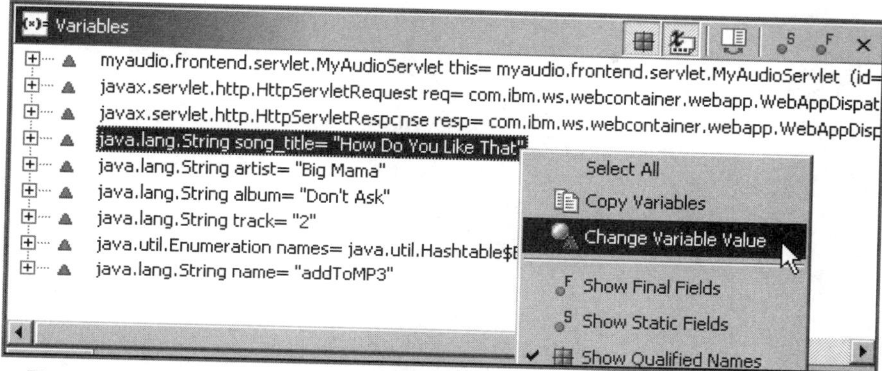

Figure 2.61: Changing the value of a variable during execution.

When finished, we can click the resume icon, which is the leftmost icon in the Debug view, displayed as a green triangle. This will allow the program to run until it either encounters another breakpoint or terminates, as shown in Figure 2.62.

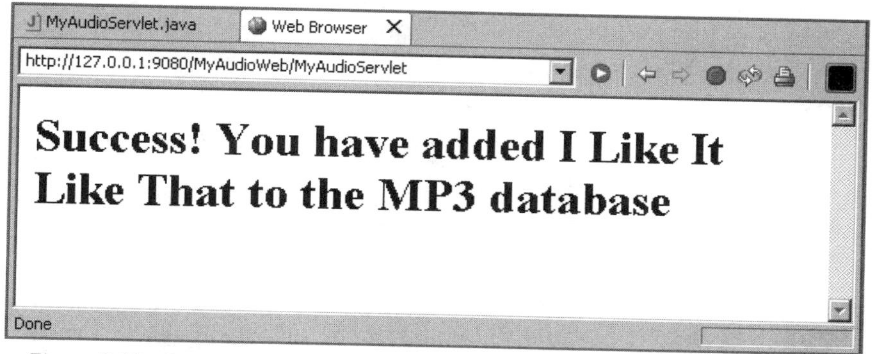

Figure 2.62: Completed debugging session.

Summary

There is much to cover regarding WebSphere Studio Application Developer. Much more will be covered in the following chapters. In this chapter our goal was to introduce the reader with the terminology regarding perspectives and views. The second goal was to strengthen the understanding of the reader by providing examples. We introduced six commonly used perspectives and their default views: the J2EE perspective, the EJB perspective, the Java perspective, the Server perspective, the Web perspective, and the

Debug perspective. Subsequent chapters will go into more detail appropriate to the enterprise developer. The third goal of this chapter was to introduce you to the unit-testing facilities and options available in Application Developer: the WebSphere Test Environment, the UTC, the Remote Server environment, the Agent Controller, the Application Client runtime environment, and the standard JVM test environment.

Test yourself

Key terms

perspective	*ear*
view	*war*
IDE	*deployment descriptor*
workbench	*modules*
workspace	*project*

Review questions

1. Looking at the MyAudio enterprise application, which parts of it (if any) are not portable?
2. The so-called application client module also requires a container for execution. Why is this?
3. What is the shortcut to bring up Code Assist?
4. How do you access a view that is not available in the current perspective?

CHAPTER 3

Servlets

Ken Greenlee

Chapter topics

- *Introducing servlets*
- *Servlet architecture*
- *Creating and testing servlets*
- *Maintaining conversational state*
- *Model-View-Controller*
- *Application lifecycle events*
- *Filters*

Certification objectives

- *Design, develop, and test Java servlets, filters, and listeners*
- *Manage end-user state and understand performance trade-offs of using HTTP sessions*

In this chapter we will begin a detailed discussion addressing the design, construction, and testing of Web components. Our discussion will be primarily within the context of WebSphere Studio Application Developer, Version 5, which is fully compliant with the Java Servlet Specification Version 2.3. We will also include best practices, which are important to the IBM Certified Enterprise Developer.

Introducing servlets

A servlet is a Web component written in Java, whose purpose is the generation of dynamic content. Its execution and life cycle are managed by a Web container within an application server, which for our discussion is the WebSphere Application Server.

Servlets can interact with Web clients indirectly via the container, using the HTTP request-response protocol. A client, typically using a Web browser, can invoke a servlet by entering a URL in the Web browser, clicking a hypertext link, or submitting an HTML form.

Companies choose servlets for many reasons. Foremost is that servlets are platform-independent Java classes. Because the WebSphere Application Server, version 5, is J2EE version 1.3 compliant, enterprise developers have only to develop servlets in accordance with the specification, and they can be confident that their servlets will run correctly. After developing a few servlets, many developers realize that most servlets look similar; that is, the servlets all share the same structure and basic method calls. Experienced developers thus create new servlets with ease. Also, since a servlet is written in Java, developers may integrate almost any existing Java code. Training expenses are reduced because skilled Java developers learn to write servlets with little training.

A traditional Web server can serve static HTML pages, and an application server, such as WebSphere, greatly extends that functionality by its ability to run Java code within its Java Virtual Machine. We can think of servlets as extending the function of a traditional Web server, which is limited to serving out only static content. Since servlets are capable of generating dynamic content at execution time, the developer can create new servlets to add new functions.

Using servlets

Servlets extend the function of a server to include server-side programming as a Java class. The servlet may do anything the Web server cannot inherently do, such as query a database or calculate the tax on a purchase. Since servlets are portable and the runtime environment is standardized, the application servers' handling of requests is also standardized.

Server-side programming

Server-side programming has been available for many years. Before Java came into use on the server side, developers used languages such as C, C++, or Perl to implement server-side dynamics. Most traditional Web servers support a technology known as Common Gateway Interface (CGI). CGI is a standard way to add server-side function to a Web server. Using CGI, the Web server has a consistent mechanism for calling the server-side function. Developers may think of a servlet as really just a CGI program written in Java, but CGI is not used to communicate with the servlet.

Process flow

Remember that a client such as a Web browser initiates the call to the servlet. Figure 3.1 illustrates the process.

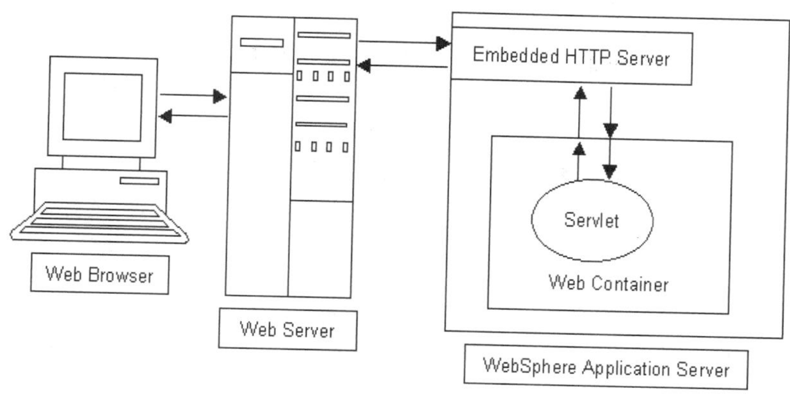

Figure 3.1: Servlet process flow.

The Web browser sends an HTTP request to the Web server. The Web server determines that the request is not for static content, such as a standard HTML Web page file, image file, or sound file, but for dynamic content—in this example, a servlet. So the Web server forwards the request to the application server, again using HTTP, to an embedded HTTP server. The Web container within the application server handles communication with the servlet, passing the request and response in as objects. Since the servlet is Java code written using standard Java interfaces, the servlet may collaborate with other classes and objects to accomplish additional work, such as accessing a database to perform a query. The servlet now has the answer for the client. Since the answer is ultimately meant for a Web browser, the servlet formats the answer in a language understood by the Web browser: HTML. So the servlet, either directly or indirectly, dynamically generates the HTML response that ultimately goes back to the Web browser.

This example illustrates a common use of servlets: to generate HTML to be sent using HTTP. However, servlets may generate any output required by the requesting program. For example, a servlet may generate Wireless Markup Language (WML) for a wireless device.

Servlet architecture

The servlet architecture is geared toward one goal: performance. Servlets easily handle multiple, concurrent requests.

Concurrent requests

Unlike traditional CGI programs, the servlet architecture can be more efficient when multiple users call the same servlet. In a traditional Perl CGI architecture, the Web server handles multiple requests for the same CGI program by launching each request in its own process. Process creation is a resource-intensive activity for a server. So the more requests handled means more time spent creating processes, which can ultimately degrade the server's performance, resulting in slower responses and unhappy users. Creating many processes may also fragment the server's memory, which could also impair performance.

In the servlet architecture, the Web server passes the request to the application server. The application server uses a JVM to execute the servlet, as with any other Java program. The difference is that the JVM allows a servlet to handle multiple requests simultaneously on separate, lightweight threads of execution. The overhead of loading and starting a servlet is significantly reduced to only one occurrence. Additionally, when a request is completed, the application server keeps the servlet in memory waiting for another request.

Life cycle

The JVM executes a servlet in a predefined manner. Figure 3.2 illustrates the life cycle of a servlet.

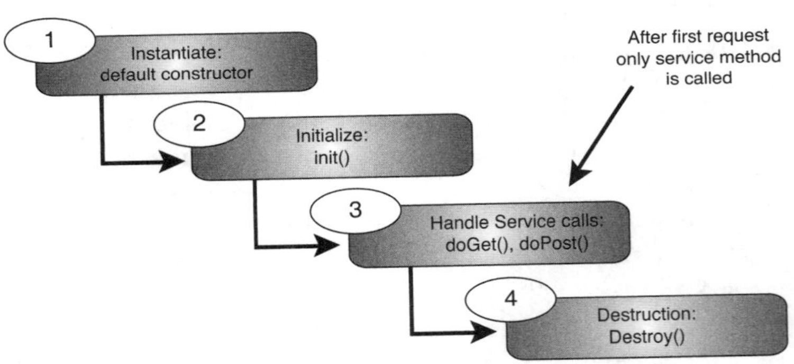

Figure 3.2: Servlet life cycle.

When an application server receives a request for a servlet, the application server first determines whether the servlet is already loaded into memory and available. The developer can optionally specify in the web.xml deployment descriptor that a servlet is to be loaded on startup. If the servlet is not yet loaded, the application server loads the servlet class and creates an instance of the servlet, calling the servlet's default constructor. Next, the application server calls the servlet's init() method. Developers use the init method to accomplish any onetime housekeeping tasks for the servlet, such as loading any resources the servlet will need. After the init method completes, the servlet is ready to handle requests. The application server calls the servlet's service() method repeatedly to handle individual requests. For HTTP servlets, the service method calls another method, typically either doGet() or doPost(), depending on which type of request is received. When the service method completes, the handling of the request is complete. The application server keeps the servlet instance in memory to handle future requests.

When another request is received, the application server need not start the life cycle process at the beginning. Instead, since the servlet is still in memory, the application server simply calls the service method again. In fact, if multiple concurrent requests are sent, the application server calls the service method once for each request, possibly simultaneously.

This leads to an interesting problem: What happens when multiple requests need to be serviced simultaneously? Technically, the application server uses multi-threading to handle the requests, with each request in its own thread. Threads are much less resource intensive than processes. Requests for the same servlet use the same servlet instance kept in the application server's memory, which means that all requests share the fields defined in the servlet. Consider this example: Bank customers use a servlet to query and display their checking account balance. If the balance is kept in a field, a customer may see some other customer's balance.

To resolve the incorrect balance issue, the developer of the servlet cannot use a field to store the balance but should use a variable within a method. A field has the scope of the servlet class, whereas a variable has the scope of an individual servlet method. For example, in the Web container's multi-threaded implementation, threads share fields, which are stored on the heap, but not variables, which are stored on the stack. By using variables rather than fields we ensure that our servlet remains stateless.

There is one notable exception to the stateless rule: the init method. The application server calls the init method only once, regardless of the number of requests on the servlet. The init method is really the only safe place to store values in a field for later retrieval in the service methods.

The application server does not keep the servlet instance in memory indefinitely. Application server administrators may set a timeout value. The timeout value indicates how long the application server waits to destroy the servlet instance. The timeout value resets with each new request. So the application server keeps the servlet in memory as long as new requests arrive. The application server calls the servlet's destroy() method and removes the instance from memory once the timeout expires. If a new request arrives after the servlet has been destroyed, the entire life cycle process starts over from the beginning.

Servlet request and response

The Web browser interacts with the Web server using HTTP, which involves HTTP headers going back and forth. The application server is responsible for converting these headers into Java objects that can be processed by the servlet. The two objects are the servlet request and the servlet response.

In a Web-based servlet, the servlet request is an instance implementing the javax.servlet.http.HttpServletRequest interface. The servlet request provides all input values to the servlet. For example, HTML form data, cookies, and information about the requested URL are all available in the servlet request. Additionally, the servlet request contains environmental information, such as the current session and security settings.

In a Web-based servlet, the servlet response is an instance implementing the javax.servlet.http.HttpServletResponse interface. The servlet response provides methods to output data from the servlet. For example, the servlet response contains methods to create various I/O streams to send data to the client. The servlet response also contains methods to store information either on the client (as a cookie) or to cause the Web browser to display another URL (known as a redirection).

One thing to remember about servlets is that the application server in both the servlet request and the servlet response supplies all information needed by a servlet.

Encoded data

There are a few rules about Web-based URLs that affect how the Web browser sends the request to the Web server. For example, a URL must be a single string that does not contain spaces or certain punctuation characters. The servlet client must encode (or change) the request to conform to these rules.

The Web browser encodes the request; for example, data from an HTML form is encoded when sent to the Web server. If the client of the servlet is not the Web browser but some other program, such as a Java applet, that program must encode the request before initiating the servlet. It would use the java.net.URLEncoder.encode(String) method to encode data.

Encoded data consists of a set of key/value pairs separated by ampersand (&) characters. The key is the name of the data value, and the value is the encoded value.

On the receiving end, the servlet decodes the request to retrieve the original data. Use the servlet request's getParameter(String) method to retrieve the decoded value of the incoming data.

GET requests and POST requests

There are two main methods for sending data to the servlet: GET and POST. Table 3.1 compares GET requests and POST requests.

Table 3.1: GET and POST request comparison

GET Request	Post Request
Initiated from a URL	Initiated from an HTML form
Data passed as part of the URL	Data passed as form fields
May send only a limited amount of data	May send an unlimited amount of data
May be “bookmarked”	May “bookmark” only the URL containing the HTML form

The result of a GET or POST request is always the same: Data values are made available to the servlet. The difference between a GET and POST request is the manner in which the data values are sent, which leads to a few side effects.

A GET request is sent to the servlet when the user selects a URL, either by entering the URL in the Web browser's address field or by clicking a hypertext link. Clicking an HTML form's submit button, on the other hand, sends a POST request to the servlet, as defined by the form's method and action attributes.

In a GET request, data values are passed to the servlet as encoded values as part of the servlet's URL. In a POST request, data values are passed as HTML form fields.

Since a GET request sends encoded data values as part of the servlet's URL, the Web browser can send only a limited amount of data (depending on the browser's implementation). The opposite is true in a POST request. A POST request sending data values through HTML form fields may send an unlimited amount of data.

Technically, in a GET request, the Web server makes the data values available to the servlet in environment variables. In a POST request, the Web server sends the data values to the servlet through an input stream.

Finally, in a GET request the URL to the servlet may be "bookmarked" (some browsers call this a "favorites list") for later retrieval. Loading the bookmark reinitiates the GET request, including the data values, since the GET request is initiated through a URL. Since a POST request requires an HTML form, however, the bookmark is for the HTML form and not for the POST request itself. Returning to this bookmark simply reloads the HTML form, not the form data.

As a general rule, use a POST method in an HTML form's action; never use a GET method. An HTML form does allow the use of a GET method, but the amount of data is limited in that case. By always using a POST method in an HTML form, you avoid the need to worry about the amount of the data as the number of fields in the form grows.

Handling GET requests

Handling a GET request in a servlet is very simple. As mentioned earlier, use the servlet request's getParameter method, as in the following example.

```
String value = request.getParameter("data");
```

The getParameter method takes one parameter: the name of an incoming data value. The result of the getParameter method is the decoded data value. For example, if the incoming data contains the encoded string "data=Learn+servlets," the request.getParameter("data") call returns the decoded value "Learn servlets."

The string name of the data value is case sensitive. Giving the wrong case of the data name to the getParameter method returns a null.

The code in Figure 3.3 illustrates a servlet that displays two encoded parameters: *chaptername* and *goal.*

```
import java.io.*;
import javax.servlet.*;
import javax.servlet.http.*;

public class GETRequest extends HttpServlet {
   public void doGet(HttpServletRequest request,
   HttpServletResponse response)
   throws ServletException, IOException {
      // tell client we're sending back html
      // send a valid mime type
      response.setContentType("text/html");

      // get the output stream
      PrintWriter out = response.getWriter();

      // send back html
      out.println("<html><head>");
      out.println("<title>GETRequest Servlet</title>");
      out.println("</head><body>");
      out.println("<p>chaptername=" +
         request.getParameter("chaptername") + "</p>");
      out.println("<p>goal=" + request.getParameter("goal") + "</p>");
      out.println("</body></html>");
   }
}
```

Figure 3.3: Extracting parameters from the request.

Handling POST requests

Handling a POST request is as simple as handling a GET request. Use the request's get-Parameter(String) method. In other words, handling a POST request is identical to handling a GET request. Take the HTML form shown in Figure 3.4 as an example.

```
<form method= "POST" "action="/myweb/POSTRequest">
<table><tbody>
<tr><td>Name</td><td><input type="text" name="NAME" size="40"></td></tr>
<tr><td>Street</td><td><input type="text" name="STREET" size="40"></td></tr>
<tr><td>City</td><td><input type="text" name="CITY" size="40"></td></tr>
<tr><td>State</td><td><input type="text" name="STATE" size="40"></td></tr>
<tr><td>ZIP</td><td><input type="text" name="ZIP" size="40"></td></tr>
<tr><td></td><td><input type="submit" value="Submit" name="SUBMIT">
<input type="reset" value="Reset" name="RESET"></td></tr>
</tbody></table>
</form>
```

Figure 3.4: An HTML form for collecting input data.

Figure 3.5 illustrates this HTML form as displayed in a Web browser.

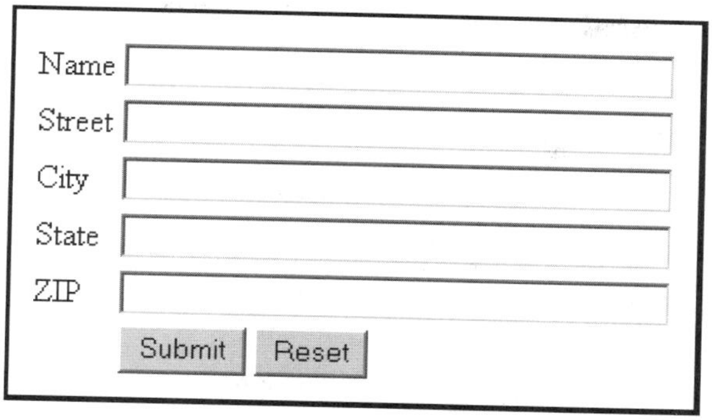

Name
Street
City
State
ZIP
Submit Reset

Figure 3.5: HTML form as displayed in the Web browser.

In the HTML each input field has a name. The servlet uses the name of the field in the getParameter method to retrieve the data entered for that field. The HTML form also defines the method, which in this case is set to POST, and the action, which in this case is set to /myweb/POSTRequest.

An HTML form may contain elements other than single-line text entry fields. An HTML form may include a text area, which contains multiple lines of text. The syntax for a text area is the following.

```
<textarea rows="4" name="ADDRESS" cols="40">
</textarea>
```

Calling request.getParameter("ADDRESS") for the text area returns all text entered. In this example the text area is four rows tall and 40 columns wide.

An HTML form may contain two types of list: drop-down lists and traditional scrolling lists. In HTML syntax a list is known as a *select*, as in the following example.

```
<select size="3" name="ITEMS">
<option value="1">Root beer</option>
<option>Ice cream</option>
</select>
```

The size of the select determines the type of list displayed in the Web browser. A size of one yields a drop-down list; a size greater than one yields a standard, scrolling list. In this example the size is three, which means the list displays at most three items. If the list contains more than three items, only three are displayed, but a vertical scroll bar appears from which to navigate the items.

The items in the list are called options. This example illustrates the two ways of declaring an option. The option for "Root beer" contains a value; the option for "Ice cream" does not contain a value. The value, if present, is not displayed in the Web browser; only the option text is displayed.

To query the selected option, use the same getParameter call. In this example, request.getParameter("ITEMS") returns the selected option. If "Root beer" is selected, getParameter returns 1, since the "Root beer" option has that value. If "Ice cream" is selected, getParameter returns "Ice cream" since the "Ice cream" option does not have a value.

A checkbox indicates a selection: on/off, yes/no, or true/false. HTML form checkboxes are created as in the following example.

```
<input type="checkbox" name="C1" value="ON">
```

Using the ever faithful getParameter method, request.getParameter("C1") returns the string "ON" if the checkbox is selected. If the checkbox is not selected, getParameter returns null.

Finally, HTML forms may contain radio buttons, which are a simple way of allowing a selection of at most one item. The following example defines a set of radio buttons.

```
<input type="radio" name="R1" value="V1">
<input type="radio" name="R1" value="V2">
```

The call request.getParameter("R1") returns the string "V1" if the first radio button is selected and returns the string "V2" if the second radio button is selected. If neither radio button is selected, getParameter returns null.

In all cases the getParameter method returns the value of the form field. If multiple fields have the same name or if a single field allows multiple selections, in either case the getParameter method returns the first value. For this scenario, use the getParameterValues(String) method instead to return all values for the given fields.

The code in Figure 3.6 illustrates a complete servlet that displays the contents of the earlier HTML form.

```
import java.io.*;
import javax.servlet.*;
import javax.servlet.http.*;
public class POSTRequest extends HttpServlet {
    public void doPost(HttpServletRequest request,
    HttpServletResponse response)
    throws ServletException, IOException {
        // tell client we're sending back html
        // send a valid mime type
        response.setContentType("text/html");

        // get the output stream
        PrintWriter out = response.getWriter();

        // send back html
        out.println("<html><head>");
        out.println("<title>Form Data</title>");
        out.println("</head><body>");
        out.println("<p>name=" + request.getParameter("NAME") + "</p>");
        out.println("<p>street=" + request.getParameter("STREET") + "</p>");
        out.println("<p>city=" + request.getParameter("CITY") + "</p>");
        out.println("<p>state=" + request.getParameter("STATE") + "</p>");
        out.println("<p>zip=" + request.getParameter("ZIP") + "</p>");
        out.println("</body></html>");
    }
}
```

Figure 3.6: A servlet that echoes form data.

Creating and testing servlets

Before the introduction of WebSphere Studio Application Developer, creating and testing servlets was a tedious process. Not only was the developer required to compile the servlet code; the developer also had to package the servlet class file in a form recognized by the application server. Application Developer makes creating and testing servlets simple.

J2EE packaging

Figure 3.7 shows many things about the J2EE packaging structure.

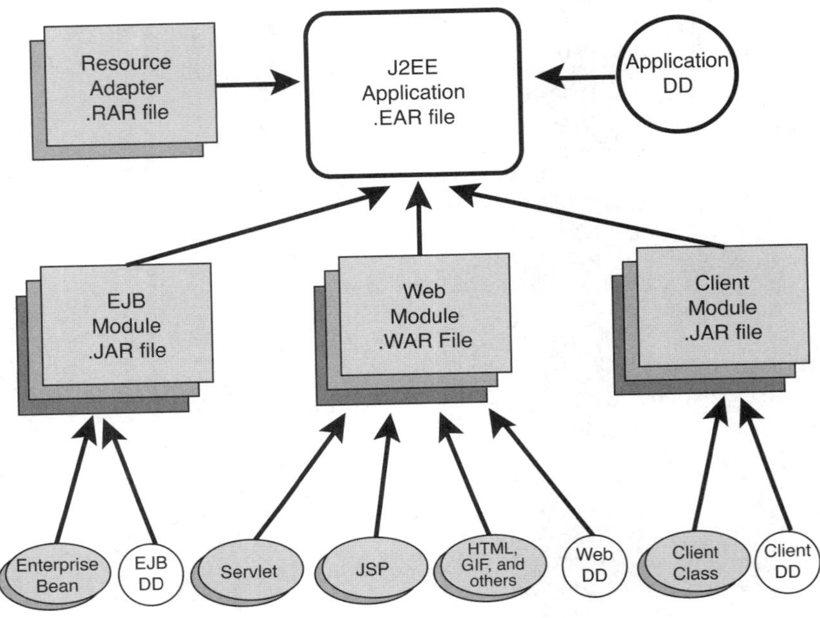

Figure 3.7: J2EE packaging.

The boxes represent the J2EE application packaging structure. Since this chapter focuses on servlets, the nonservlet pieces will be ignored. Web modules, which correspond to Web projects in Application Developer, contain servlets, JSPs, and other Web resources, along with a deployment descriptor (web.xml). A deployment descriptor (DD) is an XML file containing information about a J2EE application or component. An enterprise application, which corresponds to an Enterprise Application project in Application Developer, contains zero or more Web modules and a deployment descriptor (application.xml).

The Application Developer project structure is identical to the J2EE packaging structure in that an enterprise application project contains zero or more Web projects. The deployment descriptors are manipulated in Application Developer with specialized editors that hide the intricate XML syntax from the developer.

Therefore, Application Developer's project structure matches exactly the J2EE packaging structure. Since the two structures match, the effort to move from development to test to production is minimized.

Creating Web projects

As stated previously, creating Web projects and their components is done in the Web perspective. To create a Web project, we select **File → New → Web Project**. The Create a Web Project window (Figure 3.8) begins the wizard to create a Web project.

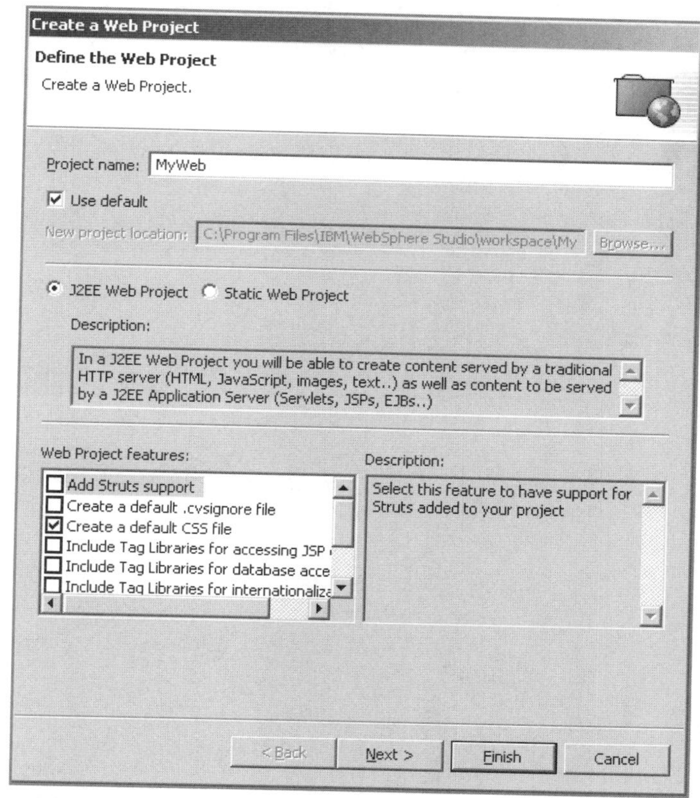

Figure 3.8: Create a Web project (page 1).

In the Project name field, we enter a project name. Developers may wish to alter the other options on the window (prior to proceeding to the next page of the wizard, Figure 3.9), such as the following:

- The New project location specifies where to save the Web project's files; unselect the **Use default** option to change the project location.
- The J2EE Web project radio button is selected if one is creating a Web project that contains servlets or JavaServer Pages (JSPs) as well as files found in a static Web project. The Static Web Project button is selected if the a Web project contains only traditional Web site files, such as HTML files, images, sounds, or JavaScript libraries.

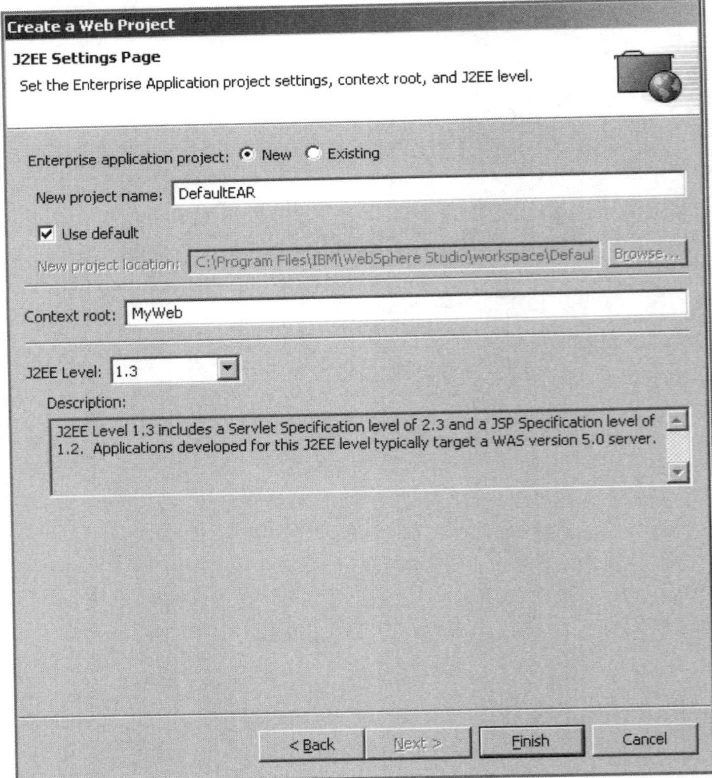

Figure 3.9: Create a Web project (page 2).

To complete the wizard and create the Web project using the default values, simply click **Finish**. The options on the second page of the Create a Web Project wizard are:

- Enterprise application project: Select **New** to create a new Enterprise Application project; select **Existing** to use an existing Enterprise Application project. J2EE and compliant implementations such as WebSphere require that Web projects be packaged as part of an Enterprise Application project even if no Enterprise JavaBeans are used.

- New project name: When the radio button for a new Enterprise Application project is selected, this field is the name to give the new Enterprise Application project; when the button for Existing Enterprise Application project is selected, this field contains the name of an existing Enterprise Application project.

- New project location: This field specifies where to save the Enterprise Application project's files; unselect the **Use default** option to change the project location.

- Context root: The context root defines the Web application. The context root becomes part of the URL to access the servlet. For example, to invoke the ABCServlet with a mapping of *abc* and using a context root *myweb*, associated to the MyWeb Web module in the application.xml, we can use the URL *http://server/myweb/abc*. The context root is case sensitive, which makes the URL case sensitive. Developers generally change the context root to all lower case to make entering URLs easier. The context root must be unique among all Web projects within the same Enterprise Application project. Additionally, the context root must be unique among all Enterprise Application projects loaded by the application server.

- J2EE level: J2EE level 1.2 includes a servlet specification level of 2.2 and a JSP specification level of 1.1; features such as servlet filters and lifecycle event listeners cannot be used if this level is chosen. J2EE level 1.3 includes a servlet specification level of 2.3 and a JSP specification level of 1.2. Applications developed in accordance with J2EE Version 1.2 are appropriate for WebSphere Application Server Version 4. Applications developed in accordance with J2EE level 1.3 typically target a WebSphere Application Server Version 5.

Web project folder structure

Creating the Web project creates the folder structure as shown in Figure 3.10:

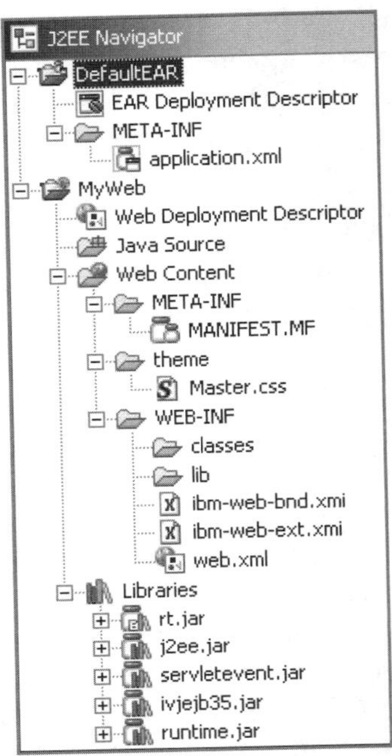

Figure 3.10: Web project folder structure.

The DefaultEAR folder is the enterprise application project. Opening the EAR Deployment Descriptor opens the META-INF\application.xml file. Use the EAR Deployment Descriptor as a shortcut to access the application.xml file.

The MyWeb folder is the Web project. All Java source code (servlets, JavaBeans, etc.) goes in the Java Source folder. All Web files (HTML, JSPs, images, etc.) go in the Web Content folder. The Libraries folder contains all J2SE/J2EE JAR files referenced by the Web project. Opening the Web Deployment Descriptor opens the WEB-INF\web.xml file. Use the Web Deployment Descriptor as a shortcut to access the web.xml file.

Other notable folders in the MyWeb folder are those within the WEB-INF folder. The WEB-INF\classes folder contains the class files compiled from the files in the Java Source folder. The WEB-INF\lib folder contains any Web application-specific JAR files, such as helper classes needed by servlets. The developer can add JARs to the WEB-INF\lib folder using Windows Explorer to drag and drop the JAR files into the WEB-INF\lib folder.

Creating servlets

After creating a Web project, we can add servlets to it. To create a servlet, select **File → New → Servlet** and complete the first page of the wizard (Figure 3.11).

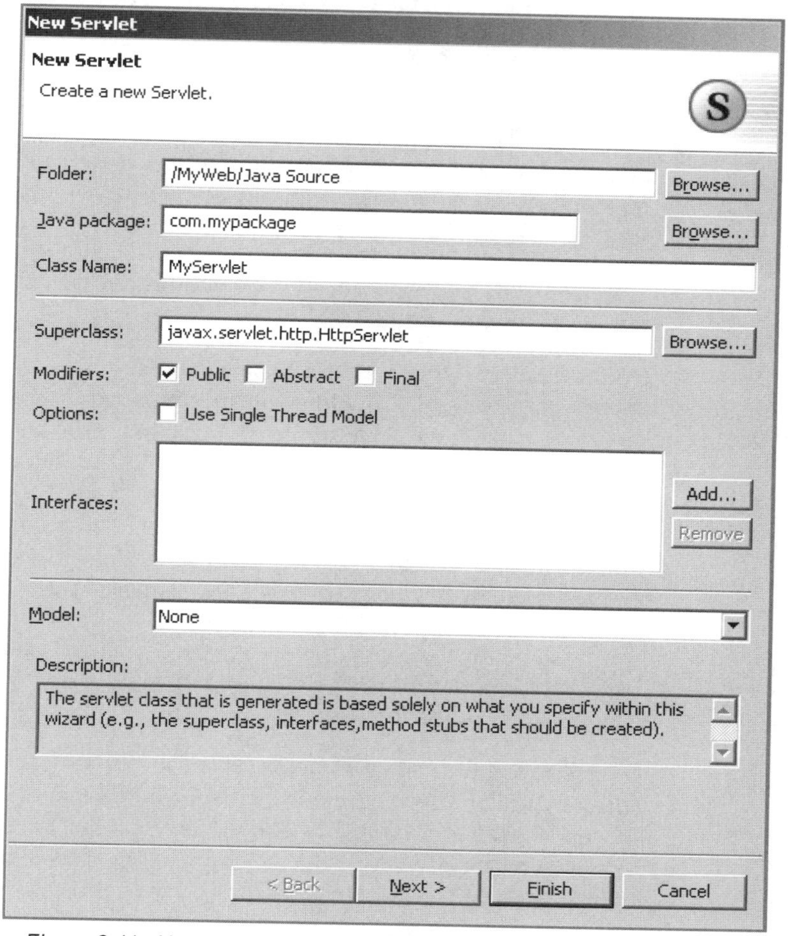

Figure 3.11: New servlet wizard (page 1).

The options are as follows:

- Folder: The folder specifies the location of the new servlet. This folder should be the Java Source folder of the Web project. If not, click the **Browse** button on the right to select the correct folder.

- Java package: The Java package specifies the package to contain the new servlet. This field may be empty, signifying that the servlet is to go in the default package, which does not have a name, but this is not good practice. Always supply a package name and do not use the default package. If the package name is incorrect, either type the correct name or select an existing package name using the Browse button.
- Class name: The class name defines the servlet's Java class name.
- Superclass: The superclass defines the superclass of the servlet's Java class. Usually, the superclass should be set to **javax.servlet.http.HttpServlet**. If the superclass name is incorrect, either type the correct name or select an existing class name using the Browse button.
- Modifiers: The modifiers section sets options for the servlet class. Usually only the public option is selected.
- Options: Select the **Use Single Thread Model** option to disable concurrent threads in the servlet. Disabling concurrent threads prevents the application server from using the same servlet instance to handle concurrent requests. Application servers may use a pool of single-thread-model servlet instances. Each single-thread instance handles only one request; when the request finishes, the instance returns to the pool to be reused by another request. Developers should generally avoid selecting the single-thread model option, because it will decrease throughput of the application server. Instead, use synchronized code to manage concurrent access to critical code sections.
- Interfaces: Use the Add and Remove buttons to change the set of Java interfaces that the servlet class implements.
- Model: Select the code generation model for the servlet class. This is not currently used for servlets but is there for future support. As the description below the model selection explains, "The servlet class that is generated is based solely on what you specify within this wizard (e.g., the superclass, interfaces, method stubs that should be created)."

Click **Next** to go to the second page of the wizard (Figure 3.12).

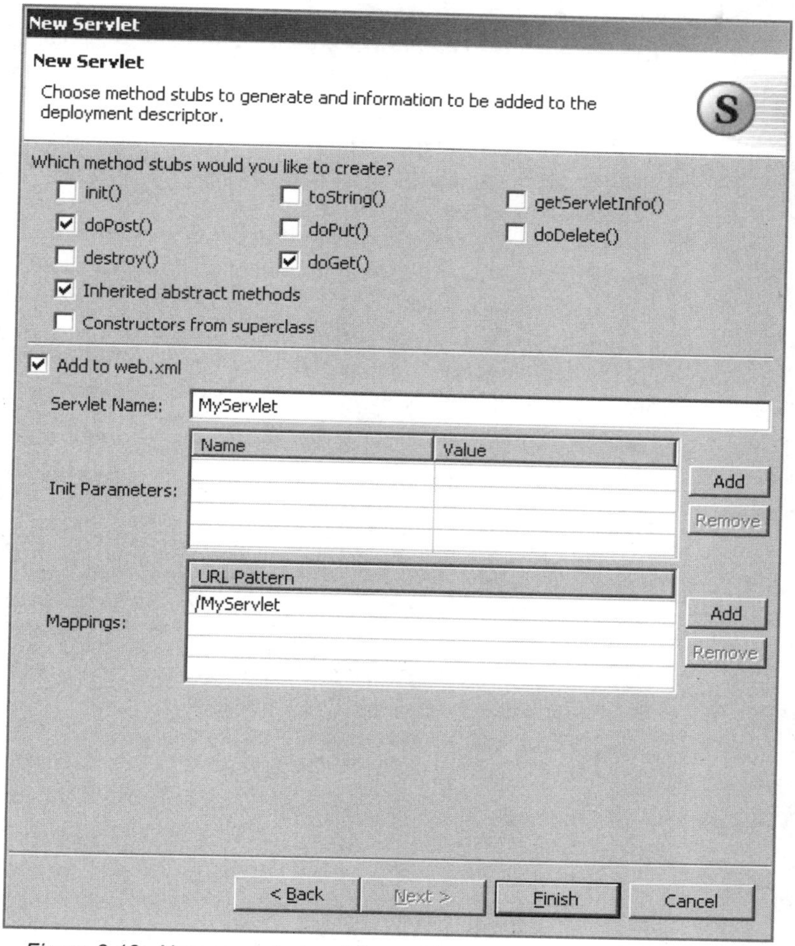

Figure 3.12: New servlet wizard (page 2).

The options on the second page are the following:

- Which method stubs would you like to create?: Select which methods to create in the servlet. These stubs apply only to creating a new servlet. These methods may be manually added later.

- Add to web.xml?: Select this option to add a servlet entry in the web.xml deployment descriptor.

- Servlet name: Servlet name defines the servlet name in the web.xml file. The name may be anything as long as all servlets in the web.xml have unique names.

- Init Parameters: The init parameters section defines the servlet initialization parameters section in the web.xml file. The initialization parameters are available to the servlet using the getInitParameter(String) method. The getInitParameter method is a convenience method that gets the value of the named parameter from the ServletConfig associated with the servlet when it is initialized. The actual values are included in the web.xml deployment descriptor for the Web module. as shown in Figure 3.13. In this figure, using getInitParameter("param1") would return "value1" as a String. Note that these initialization parameters are unique for each individual servlet (there is a different way, presented later in the chapter, to share initialization parameters among all of the servlets in a Web module using the ServletContext). Use the **Add** and **Remove** buttons to change the initialization parameters.

```
<servlet>
    <servlet-name>MyServlet</servlet-name>
    <display-name>MyServlet</display-name>
    <servlet-class>com.mypackage.MyServlet</servlet-class>
    <init-param>
        <param-name>param1</param-name>
        <param-value>value1</param-value>
    </init-param>
    <init-param>
        <param-name>param2</param-name>
        <param-value>value2</param-value>
    </init-param>
</servlet>
```

Figure 3.13: Initialization parameters for an individual servlet.

- Mappings: The mappings section defines the servlet mapping section in the web.xml file. The mappings define the URL pattern or patterns used to invoke a servlet. This feature is important because it can be used to effectively hide the names of servlets. By default the servlet mapping is the same as the servlet name. Use the **Add** and **Remove** buttons to change the mappings at the time that the servlet is being created. Later it is still possible to change the mappings by editing the deployment descriptor. Even if no mappings are associated with the servlet, it may still be possible to invoke the servlet anonymously, using the servlet's package and class name, in this example com.mypackage.MyServlet. It is good practice to disable this feature by editing the deployment descriptor, as shown in Figure 3.14. This setting will apply to the entire Web module.

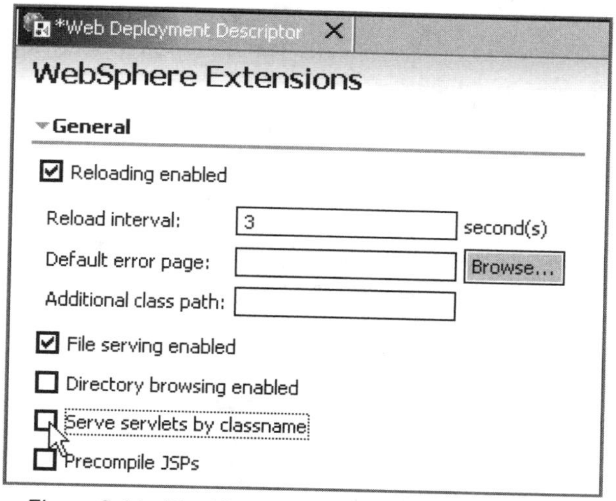

Figure 3.14: Disabling anonymous servlets.

Click **Finish** to complete the wizard. Application Developer creates the servlet class file and opens the class file in a Java editor.

Servlet deployment descriptors

Creating a servlet using the wizard adds the entries shown in Figure 3.15 to the web.xml deployment descriptor file.

```
<servlet>
   <servlet-name>MyServlet</servlet-name>
   <display-name>MyServlet</display-name>
   <servlet-class>com.mypackage.MyServlet</servlet-class>
   <init-param>
      <param-name>param1</param-name>
      <param-value>value1</param-value>
   </init-param>
   <init-param>
      <param-name>param2</param-name>
      <param-value>value2</param-value>
   </init-param>
</servlet>
<servlet-mapping>
   <servlet-name>MyServlet</servlet-name>
   <url-pattern>/doit</url-pattern>
</servlet-mapping>
```

Figure 3.15: Servlet element in the Web module deployment descriptor.

The <servlet> section defines the servlet's name, display name, and class file and any initialization parameters. There is one <servlet> section per servlet in the module. The <servlet-mapping> section defines the URL mapping to call the servlet. Provide multiple

<servlet-mapping> sections to define multiple URL mappings. In our example, with anonymous servlets disabled, we invoke MyServlet using *http://servername/myweb/doit*, where *myweb* is the context root associated to the Web module and *servername* is the name of the server.

Running the servlet

To perform unit testing of a servlet, select the servlet source file in the J2EE Navigator list. From the source file's pop-up menu, select **Run on Server**. If the Web module has not yet been deployed to a server, as is the case here, the Server Selection window appears (Figure 3.16).

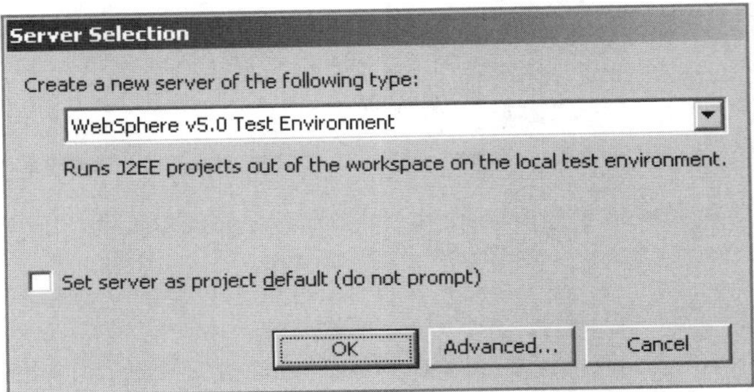

Figure 3.16: Server selection.

There are two ways to use this window.

1. Simply select **WebSphere v5.0 Test Environment** from the drop-down list and click **OK**. Application Developer creates a new server instance and uses the server instance to run the servlet. Recall that a server instance represents a distinct and configurable application server.

2. To avoid creating a new server instance, click the **Advanced** button, and use the Server Selection dialog to select an existing server and optionally set it as the project default.

After a few moments, the server instance starts and runs the servlet. A Web browser opens inside the workbench, and the output from the servlet is displayed.

Using the debugger

Debugging a servlet is very similar to debugging any method in an ordinary Java class. We set a breakpoint and invoke the servlet, with the difference that, instead of selecting Run on Server as before, we select **Debug on Server**.

Setting breakpoints

As was stated in Chapter 2 for application clients, to set a breakpoint, open the source and double-click the vertical gray bar on the left side of the Java source editor. A blue dot appears where a breakpoint is set, as shown in Figure 3.17.

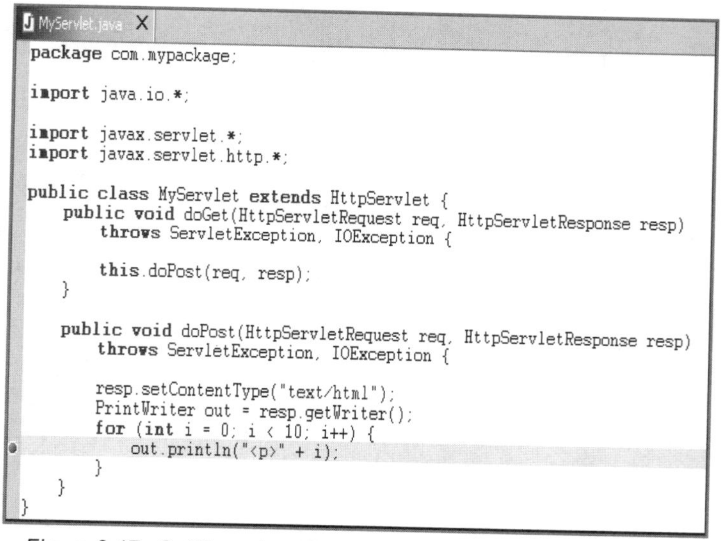

```
MySerlet.java X
package com.mypackage;

import java.io.*;

import javax.servlet.*;
import javax.servlet.http.*;

public class MyServlet extends HttpServlet {
    public void doGet(HttpServletRequest req, HttpServletResponse resp)
        throws ServletException, IOException {

        this.doPost(req, resp);
    }

    public void doPost(HttpServletRequest req, HttpServletResponse resp)
        throws ServletException, IOException {

        resp.setContentType("text/html");
        PrintWriter out = resp.getWriter();
        for (int i = 0; i < 10; i++) {
            out.println("<p>" + i);
        }
    }
}
```

Figure 3.17: Settting a breakpoint.

To remove a breakpoint, double-click again on the blue dot. The breakpoint and blue dot are removed. The blue dot turns green once the breakpoint is successfully registered with a debug-enabled JVM.

Debug on Server

To debug the servlet, select the servlet source file in the J2EE Navigator list. From the source file's pop-up menu, select **Debug on Server**. From the Select Server window, select an existing server or create a new one. The Select Server window does not appear when a default server has been selected. Click **Finish** to start debugging. As stated previously, the Step-by-Step Debug window appears.

The Step-by-Step Debug window shows which servlet method the server will execute. Choose whether to step into the method or skip it. This window appears when selecting the Debug on Server option and is not related to the existence of any breakpoints in the source.

Select **Disable step-by-step mode** to skip this dialog. Once the server is stopped, this option is automatically reset. Use the standard Debug view with its step over, step into, and run to return button to navigate through the source.

Managing conversational state

HTTP, the protocol on which HttpServlets are based, is a stateless protocol. This means that each request elicits a response that is in no way connected to previous or subsequent requests. However, to build enterprise applications the developer generally needs to keep track of conversational state, so that the user's experience appears to be a logical flow from one Web page to the next. Since servlets themselves are stateless, we find ourselves looking for a simple mechanism for maintaining separately the conversational state of each individual user of our enterprise applications. Hidden fields in forms as well as cookies can be appropriate options, depending on the nature of the information that must be retained. However, each has limitations with regard to size and security.

Cookies

A cookie is a relatively small quantity of textual data that is kept on the client. Many Web sites use cookies to save user-specific information such as Web site preferences. In addition to holding the actual data values, cookies can be used to hold references or keys to data kept securely on the server. With the HTTP request-response protocol, the Web server may optionally send cookies back to the client's Web browser along with other response headers based on the processing of individual HTTP requests. As you will see, some cookies are short lived, while others are kept for a longer time on the client.

Architecture

The user's Web browser manages the cookie files and automatically sends the cookies with each request to the Web server. The Web browser sends only those cookies specific to the Web server visited. That is, when visiting server *abc.com*, the Web browser sends only abc.com's cookies.

One limitation on the use of cookies is that most Web browsers allow users to disable cookies. With cookies disabled, the Web browser no longer sends any cookies to the Web server. Servlets that expect to receive cookies and do not receive them may display a message requesting the user to enable cookies.

Using cookies in a servlet is quite simple. Basically, there is one constructor to create a cookie with the usual accessor methods. Saving a cookie on the client is equally simple, since there is only one method to use within the servlet.

Creating cookies

Use the javax.servlet.http.Cookie class to create and manage cookies. Each cookie contains a name and a value; both the cookie name and cookie value are strings. From the servlet, save the cookie onto the Web browser using the response object's addCookie(Cookie) method.

For example, to create a cookie named "scheme" with a value of "default," use the following code in the servlet's service method.

```
javax.servlet.http.Cookie cookie = new javax.servlet.http.Cookie(
   "scheme", "default");
response.addCookie(cookie);
```

Each cookie may have an optional expiration date. The expiration date represents the number of seconds the Web browser continues to send the cookie to the Web server. When the number of seconds elapses, the cookie expires and is no longer sent. By default, the expiration date is minus one (–1), which means the cookie expires when the user closes the Web browser. An expiration date of zero (0) means the Web browser should immediately delete the cookie. All other positive numbers represent the expiration in seconds until the Web browser deletes the cookie.

The following example illustrates setting a cookie's expiration date to ten minutes (600 seconds) using the setMaxAge(int) method.

```
javax.servlet.http.Cookie cookie = new javax.servlet.http.Cookie(
   "scheme", "default");
cookie.setMaxAge(600);
response.addCookie(cookie);
```

Retrieving cookies

To retrieve a cookie, first use the request's getCookies() method, which returns an array of all cookies sent to the servlet. Then loop through the array searching by name to find the desired cookie. Figure 3.18 illustrates a search for a cookie called "scheme". When the cookie is found, a boolean variable, cookieFound, is set to true.

```
// retrieve the cookies
Cookie cookies[] = request.getCookies();

Cookie cookie = null;
boolean cookieFound = false;

for (int i = 0; i < cookies.length; i++) {
   // find the cookie
   cookie = cookies[i];
   if (cookie.getName().equals("scheme")) {
      cookieFound = true;
      break;
   }
}
```

Figure 3.18: Retrieving a particular cookie.

Updating cookies

To update the value of a cookie, call the cookie's setValue(String) method before adding the cookie to the servlet's response.

```
cookie.setValue("newValue");
response.addCookie(cookie);
```

Deleting cookies

To delete a cookie, set the expiration to zero (0).

```
cookie.setMaxAge(0);
response.addCookie(cookie);
```

Session management

In this section we will focus on the HttpSession mechanism, which allows us to maintain the conversational state of individual users securely on the server. A session allows the developer to associate an HttpServletRequest with the conversational state unique to a particular client. When needed, the servlet obtains a new instance representing an HttpSession. This new instance is associated, by a unique session ID, with the user from whom the request originated. The application server creates and maintains the session in memory. Servlets use sessions to save objects that will be needed later by other servlets. This enables the developer to maintain the flow of information from one servlet to the next. One of the more obvious results of session management is the ability to maintain unique online shopping carts for individual users on the World Wide Web. Another use of sessions might be to store an object for reposting form data, instead of requiring the user to re-enter all the data on a form that could not be processed due to validation errors.

Architecture

When the servlet requests creation of a session, the Web container generates a unique session ID and allocates the necessary storage for the session data. The application server maintains the session in memory for performance and can optionally replicate the session to a database table for improved fault tolerance.

The Web container typically tracks the session ID in a transient HTTP cookie that is discarded when the Web browser exits. A session-tracking cookie is just like an ordinary cookie. The Web browser stores the session-tracking cookie and sends it to the server along with each request. When the servlet requests creation of a session, the Web container creates the session-tracking cookie with a name and value. The Servlet Specification Version 2.3 requires the name of the session-tracking cookie to be JSESSIONID, and the value is the session ID, which is simply a unique identifier generated by the container. The maximum age of a session-tracking cookie is always minus one (–1), which means that the session-tracking cookies are not persistent and expire when the user closes the Web browser. Since the Web container completely manages all session-tracking cookies, a servlet never needs to access the session tracking cookie directly.

Creating a session

To create a session, the servlet invokes the method getSession(boolean) on the HttpServletRequest. If the input boolean parameter is true, the existing session for that client is returned or a new one is created. When using true, we can determine whether the client has "joined" the session, by invoking the method isNew on the session. If the Web container uses only cookie-based sessions and the client has disabled the use of cookies then a session would be new on each request.

If the input boolean parameter is false, the application server returns the existing session for that client or returns null if the request has no valid session. The developer must be careful when using false, in order to avoid potential null pointer exceptions.

The code example in Figure 3.19 illustrates creating a new session.

```
javax.servlet.http.HttpSession session = request.getSession(true);
if session.isNew() {
    // a new session was just created for this request
}
else {
    // a session was already associated with this request
}
```

Figure 3.19: Creating a new session.

Destroying a session

To invalidate, or destroy, a session programmatically and unbind any objects bound to it (the session data), use the session's invalidate() method as in the following code example. A session can also be destroyed after a period of inactivity based on a specific timeout value. There is a default value for the Web container, which defaults to 30 minutes. The developer can programmatically set the timeout value on an individual session by invoking the setMaxInactiveInterval method on the session, specifying the number of seconds.

```
session.invalidate();
```

The garbage collector's rules for destroying instances of HttpSessions still apply after the invalidate method is called. As long as any other object maintains a reference to that session, it will not be garbage collected.

Storing and removing data

An HttpSession behaves much like a keyed collection, such as a Hashtable. Each item added to the session has a name, which acts as the key, and an associated value, which can be any object. There are three basic methods for manipulating the session data.

- public void setAttribute(String name, Object value) binds an object to the session using the name specified. The name cannot be null. If an object of the same name is already bound to the session, it is replaced. If the value is null, the result is the same as invoking removeAttribute.
- public Object getAttribute(String name) returns the object bound with the specified name in this session, or returns null if no object is bound under that name.
- public void removeAttribute(String name) removes the object bound with the specified name from this session. If the session does not have an object bound with the specified name, this method does nothing.

These methods are not thread safe. Concurrent-access session data should be managed using synchronized code, as shown in the shopping cart example that follows.

Objects can optionally be notified when they are bound to, or unbound from, a session. The object in question must implement the HttpSessionBindingListener interface, and classes that implement this interface must have the methods valueBound and valueUnbound defined. The valueBound method will be invoked on the object, after the setAttribute is invoked on a session for that object. The valueUnbound method will be invoked on the object after (1) the removeAttribute is invoked on a session using the name associated to that object; (2) the session to which the object is bound is invalidated programmatically; or (3) or the session to which the object is bound times out. An HttpSessionBindingEvent is passed as a parameter to the valueBound and valueUnbound methods.

Developers should be wary of storing complex object types into the session. When the object instance is stored, the complete object graph is stored, which means that all contained object instances and any object types in the hierarchy are also stored. So using large object types with a complex hierarchy may mean that many kilobytes, even megabytes, of data are ultimately stored into the session. Always use the smallest and simplest object definition possible to minimize the amount of required memory. When it is not possible to store all necessary data in the session due to size limitations, the developer can consider storing the data in a database and keeping just the keys in the session. When persistent sessions are being used, all objects being stored in the session must implement the Serializable interface.

Classic shopping cart example

Online shopping carts regularly use sessions to store the shopping cart items. The following code example queries the session and retrieves the shopping cart (a java.util.Vector in this example) from the session. If the shopping cart vector doses not exist, the code creates a new vector and saves the vector in the session data. The code queries the item to store by calling getParameter(String). Finally, the code adds the item to the shopping cart (Figure 3.20).

```
javax.servlet.http.HttpSession session = request.getSession(true);
java.util.Vector cart = (java.util.Vector)
session.getAttribute("cart");
// we definitely have a session, but may not have a cart
if (cart == null) {
     cart = new java.util.Vector();
     // setAttribute is not thread safe
     synchronized (session) {
          session.setAttribute("cart", cart);
     }
}
// we definitely have a cart in the session now
String item = request.getParameter("item");
if (item != null) {
     cart.add(item);  // add method is synchronized
}
```

Figure 3.20: Adding an item to an online shopping cart.

URL encoding

One issue with sessions remains. When cookies are disabled in the Web browser, how does the application server retrieve the session ID? With cookies disabled, the session ID is not sent with each request and is not available.

Limitations

Servlets may use the response's encodeURL(String) method to allow for the case when cookies are disabled in the Web browser. The encodeURL takes one parameter: a URL.

```
String url = response.encodeURL("/myweb/MyServlet");
```

The encodeURL method is very smart. If cookies are available in the Web browser, the encodeURL method does nothing and simply returns the given URL. If cookies are not available in the Web browser, the encodeURL method alters the URL to include the session ID. An encoded URL might look like "/myweb/MyServlet;JSESSIONID=123". Notice how the session ID is included with the original URL.

Enabling URL encoding within Application Developer

To enable URL encoding within Application Developer, switch from the Web perspective to the Server Configuration view. Expand the Servers folder as shown in Figure 3.21.

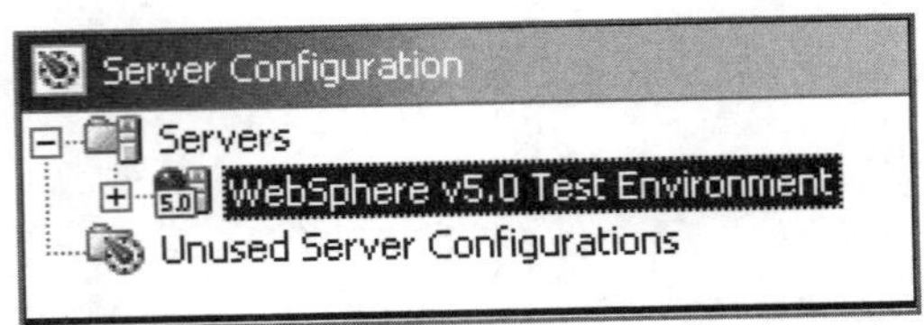

Figure 3.21: Server configuration.

Double-click the server in the Server folder. In this example, double-click **WebSphere v5.0 Test Environment**. The server's editor window opens. Select the Web tab. On the Web Options page, select the **Enable URL rewriting** option as shown in Figure 3.22.

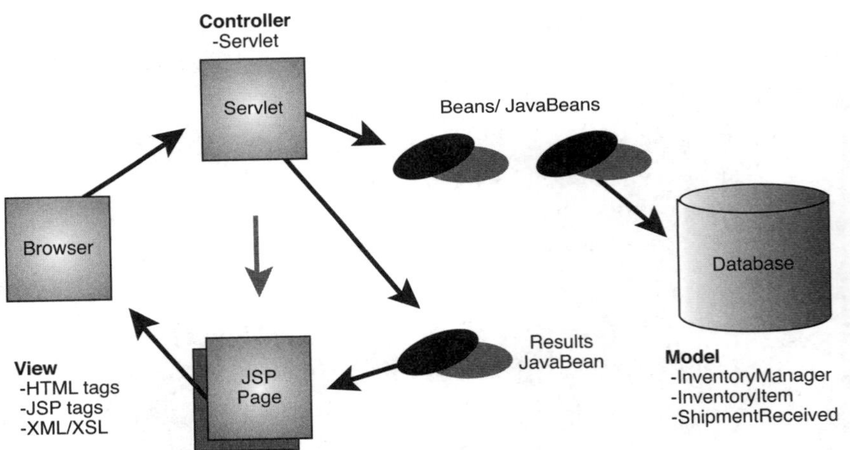

Figure 3.22: Server Web options.

Close the editor window, saving changes. If the server is running, stop the server before testing any code.

If URL encoding is not enabled within Application Developer or the application server, the encodeURL method does nothing and returns the given URL string.

Model-View-Controller

Model-View-Controller (MVC), considered by some to be a design pattern, provides a clean separation of concerns and distributes responsibilities in a time-proven manner to the three roles that represent information, presentation, and interaction. JavaBeans or Enterprise JavaBeans represent the business model. A page in JavaServerPages, which will be covered in detail in Chapter 4, acts as a display page. Finally, servlets act as interaction controllers, meaning that they control the way that a user interacts with the application.

Importance of MVC

J2EE applications should take advantage of MVC when possible. By separating the view from the model, the presentation can be made pluggable and interchangeable, so that users of Web browsers, personal digital assistants (PDAs), cell phones, or other networked (or wireless) devices could all be looking at different views of the same business objects.

Also, when developers create separate model classes, they may reuse the same model class in other enterprise applications. Reuse is a tremendous benefit of using an object oriented programming language, such as Java, and developing components, such as JavaBeans and Enterprise JavaBeans, to gain developer productivity and to reduce development costs. MVC helps to realize this promise.

Finally, when the command and control logic are separated, the responsibilities of the controller are limited to coordination between user, model, and view. By limiting the responsibilities of the servlet, we enable the developer to create a component that can "do one thing and do it well." The developer creating the controller need not worry about how to display the result—merely how to arrive at the result.

Servlets within MVC

Figure 3.23 illustrates the relationship among the MVC components.

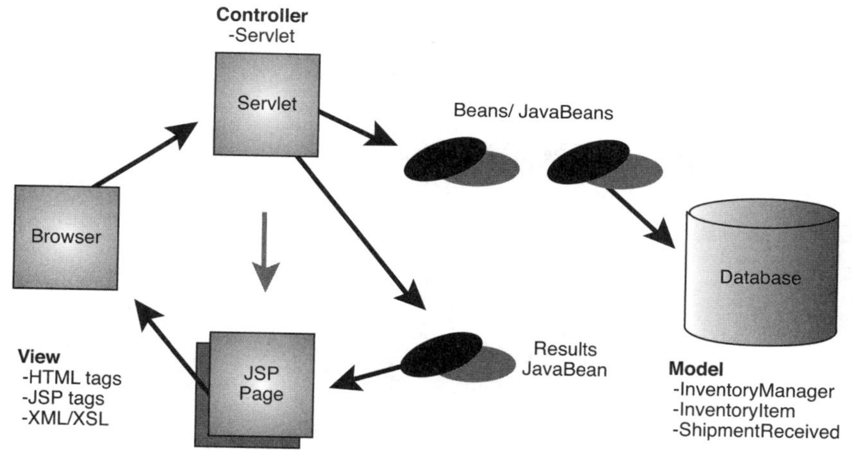

Figure 3.23: MVC components.

When the user interacts with the content by clicking a hypertext link or submitting a form in their browser, the servlet takes control. The servlet coordinates the use of JavaBeans, Enterprise JavaBeans, or both to perform business tasks and access information. The servlet encapsulates the results in one or more JavaBeans, which it stores in some context (typically the request) that is accessible to the JSP, before transferring control to that JSP. The JSP retrieves the JavaBean(s) containing the result and formats the result for display in the browser.

One potential weakness of this approach is that servlets can proliferate, since typically a separate servlet is developed for each type of action that can be requested by a user of the application. However, the developer can mitigate that problem by using the command design pattern. The command design pattern allows the developer to replace many servlets with a single servlet, which collaborates with command objects that encapsulate and perform the individual operations.

Servlet redirection

One way the servlet passes control to any URL (JSP, servlet, or HTML file) is with the response's sendRedirect(String) method, which accomplishes the redirection using the client. The given string is the URL. The container is responsible for converting relative URLs to absolute URLs that can be used by the client. The following code example shows a servlet redirecting to a JSP whose location is specified relative to the current requests location.

```
response.sendRedirect("OutputJSP.jsp");
```

Since the redirection is happening through the browser, any JavaBeans containing results must be stored in the session when using sendRedirect, since a new request will be issued by the client as a result of this type of redirection.

Saving data into the request

As an alternative to storing the result JavaBean instance in the session, a developer can use the request to store the result JavaBean instance. The following code example illustrates storing a string as the JavaBean instance in the request.

```
String result = "Result goes here.";
request.setAttribute("result", result);
```

The request uses the same methods of getAttribute, setAttribute, and removeAttribute as the session does.

This is the narrowest scope and should be used when data does not need to be kept around beyond the duration of a single request. A developer should favor the narrowest scope possible when considering possible alternatives.

Request forwarding

To transfer control directly from the servlet to a JSP without involving the client, the developer uses a RequestDispatcher, which is available from either the ServletRequest or the ServletContext. Because the transfer is direct from the servlet to the JSP and does not involve the client, the request context can be used to pass data. To do so, use the request's getRequestDispatcher(String) method to create a RequestDispatcher for the given path. The path can be expressed as relative to the context root if it begins with a slash or relative to the current request if it does not. The following example illustrates creating a RequestDispatcher for the path *OutputJSP.jsp* relative to the current request and then invoking the forward method on that RequestDispatcher.

The forward method should be called before the response has been committed to the client (before response body output has been flushed). If the response already has been committed, this method throws an IllegalStateException. The developer should beware of conditional logic that is intended to forward the request and response to one of several possible JSPs. If a servlet should attempt to invoke forward more than once, an exception will likely result. The best practice is to explicitly code a return statement immediately following the invocation of forward.

```
javax.servlet.RequestDispatcher rd =
    request.getRequestDispatcher("OutputJSP.jsp");
rd.forward(request, response);
return;
```

Saving data into the ServletContext

Yet another way to share data is with the javax.servlet.ServletContext class. Servlets use the ServletContext object to communicate with the Web container. There is one context per Web application per Java Virtual Machine. Recall that a Web application corresponds to a Web module. The ServletContext provides many methods to retrieve runtime application server information. In addition, the ServletContext can provide initialization parameters that are shared by all servlets in the entire Web module. The getInitParameter method is invoked on the ServletContext, which the servlet can obtain using the getServletContext convenience method. The ServletContext may also be used to save data that is global to the Web application. Therefore, the ServletContext implements the by-now-familiar methods setAttribute, getAttribute, and removeAttribute.

Like HttpSessions, data access within the servlet context is not thread safe. Use synchronized code to manage concurrent access.

Best practices for saving servlet data

Why use the request instead of the session? Why not use the servlet context? A servlet context persists as long as the Web application is available in the application server. A session persists across servlets and JSPs as long as the user's Web browser remains open, unless it times out. A request persists as long as the application flow is servicing the request; the request ends when the output JSP (in MVC) completes. As a rule, use the session when sharing data across multiple servlets or JSPs. Use the request when data is not shared but merely passed from a servlet to a JSP for output. In other words, best practices dictate to put data into the narrowest scope possible.

Alternative ways to pass data between servlets and JSPs include imbedding hidden HTML tags with an HTML form or using cookies. Using hidden HTML tags requires that every page be generated within the application in order to embed the correct value. Using cookies would violate the best practice to limit the scope of the data, since any servlet on the Web site may access the same cookie. In other words, continue using the request or session to save servlet data.

Application lifecycle events

Application-level events are new in Version 2.3 of the Servlet specification. These events provide the enterprise developer greater control over interactions with ServletContext and HttpSession objects. Application event listeners are provided by the developer and are packaged in the Web module. They are instantiated and registered by the Web container.

ServletContext events either are lifecycle events or are triggered by changes to attributes. The lifecycle events indicate that either the servlet context has just been created and is available to service requests or that the servlet context is about to be shut down. This provides the developer an opportunity to accomplish certain housekeeping chores, which might have been done in the past in the init method of a servlet loaded on startup as part of a bootstrap mechanism. Attribute events are triggered when attributes are added, removed, or replaced in the servlet context for a Web module.

HttpSession events are also related either to lifecycle events or to changes to attributes. The lifecycle events are triggered whenever an HttpSession is created, invalidated, or timed out. An attribute-related event is triggered when attributes have been added, removed, or replaced in an HttpSession.

Event types

There are four new interfaces defined to support these events.

javax.servlet.ServletContextListener

A ServletContextListener receives notification about the ServletContext of the Web application. Specifically, the application server notifies the listener when the application server initializes and destroys the Web application.

Listeners of this event must implement the following methods:

- public void contextDestroyed(javax.servlet.ServletContextEvent): Notification that the ServletContext is about to be destroyed. This method could be used to accomplish any cleanup operations, which might be related to initialization tasks performed at startup, when the context was initialized.
- public void contextInitialized(javax.servlet.ServletContextEvent)–: Notification that the Web application is initialized and ready to process requests. This method could be used to perform initialization of resources that are shared throughout a Web application.

In all methods the ServletContextEvent provides a getServletContext method to retrieve the related ServletContext.

javax.servlet.ServletContextAttributeListener

A ServletContextAttributeListener receives notification when attributes in the ServletContext change.

Listeners of this event must implement the following methods:

- public void attributeAdded(javax.servlet.ServletContextAttributeEvent): Notification that a new attribute was added to the servlet context. This method is called after the attribute is added.
- public void attributeRemoved(javax.servlet.ServletContextAttributeEvent): Notification that an existing attribute has been removed from the servlet context. This method is called after the attribute is removed.
- public void attributeReplaced(javax.servlet.ServletContextAttributeEvent): Notification that an attribute on the servlet context has been replaced. This method is called after the attribute is replaced.

In all methods the ServletContextAttributeEvent provides a getName and getValue methods to inspect the related attribute.

javax.servlet.http.HttpSessionListener

An HttpSessionListener receives notification when changes occur to a session of the Web application.

Listeners of this event must implement the following methods:

- public void sessionCreated(javax.servlet.http.HttpSessionEvent): Notification that a session was created.
- public void sessionDestroyed(javax.servlet.http.HttpSessionEvent): Notification that a session was invalidated.

In all methods the HttpSessionEvent provides a getSession method to retrieve the related session.

javax.servlet.http.HttpSessionAttributeListener

An HttpSessionAttributeListener receives notification when changes occur to the attributes stored in a session. We can compare this interface to the HttpSession BindingListener discussed previously. Although both listeners receive an HttpSession BindingEvent during notification, an HttpSessionAttributeListener is notified for all attributes added, removed, or replaced in session within the entire Web application. The HttpSessionBindingListener is notified only when the object itself is bound or unbound from a session.

Listeners of this event must implement the following methods:

- public void attributeAdded(javax.servlet.http.HttpSessionBindingEvent): Notification that an attribute has been added to a session. This method is called after the attribute is added.
- public void attributeRemoved(javax.servlet.http.HttpSessionBindingEvent): Notification that an attribute has been removed from a session. This method is called after the attribute is removed.
- public void attributeReplaced(javax.servlet.http.HttpSessionBindingEvent): Notification that an attribute has been replaced in a session. This method is called after the attribute is replaced.

In all methods the HttpSessionBindingEvent provides a getSession method to retrieve the related session and getName and getValue methods to retrieve the related attribute.

Creating Web application lifecycle event listeners

One way to create a new lifecycle listener is to double-click the Web Deployment Descriptor in the Web project folder, which opens the web.xml deployment descriptor. When you select the **Listeners** tab and click the **New** button, the New Life-cycle Listener wizard opens (Figure 3.24).

The wizard is similar to those we have seen earlier. The folder, Java package, and model are identical to the New Servlet wizard. The listener name is the listener's Java class name. In the listener types section we can select the desired listeners. Note that a single class can implement all four interfaces if so desired. On the second page of the wizard, the developer can choose to have method stubs created for inherited abstract methods (Figure 3.25). This is a good idea in implementing multiple interfaces. The developer can simply add code to the empty method bodies that are generated.

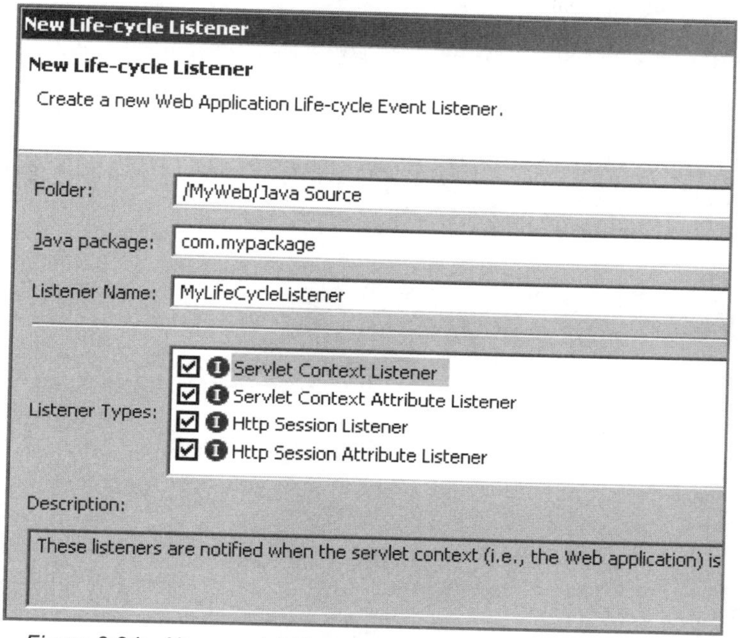

Figure 3.24: New servlet lifecycle listener.

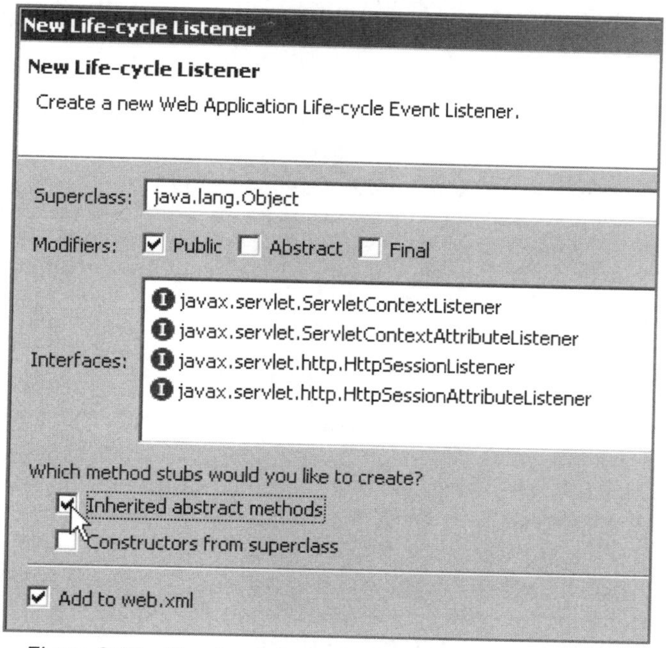

Figure 3.25: Creating inherited abstract methods.

Application Developer creates the listener class and opens the source in a Java editor. The developer can finish coding the methods that were stubbed in and compile, as with any other Java class.

Lifecycle listener deployment descriptors

Creating a Web application lifecycle listener using the wizard adds the following elements to the web.xml deployment descriptor.

```
<listener>
    <listener-class>com.mypackage.MyLifeCycleListener</listener-class>
</listener>
```

The <listener> element defines the listener class file. The Web container registers the listeners according to the interfaces they implement and the order in which they appear in the deployment descriptor. At runtime the listeners are notified in the order in which they were registered. On application shutdown, listeners are notified in the reverse order of their declarations. Session listeners get notified before context listeners. Session listeners also get notified of session invalidations before context listeners are notified of application shutdown.

Debugging application event listeners

Debugging an application event listener follows the same process as debugging a servlet. Set a breakpoint in the source and test the listener.

To debug a servlet context listener, select the **Web project**; from the Web project's pop-up menu, select **Debug on Server**. To complete the test, stop the server to debug all methods in the servlet context listener.

To debug a servlet context attribute listener, session listener, or session attribute listener, select a servlet that manipulates the servlet context attributes or session and debug the servlet on the server.

Filters

A filter is typically used to provide additional processing before or after the invocation of a servlet. Filters can be used for logging and auditing, image conversion, data compression, encryption, tokenizing, and even XSL transformation. Filters typically manipulate the request and response objects. The application server invokes all associated filters both prior to and after invoking the servlet, using a mechanism called a *filter chain*. The ordering of the filters is defined in the filter-mapping entries in the web.xml deployment descriptor, and the developer can change the order by editing the deployment descriptor. Filters may be associated with any URL, which means that filters may be applied to HTML files and JSPs in addition to servlets.

Filters must implement three methods: init, doFilter, and destroy. The init method, called once by the application server, initializes the filter, enabling it to acquire any needed resources. The doFilter is where the main processing of the filter takes place. The application server calls the doFilter method once for each request of the associated servlet. Finally, the destroy method, called once by the application server, allows the filter to release any resources acquired in the init method.

The application server passes the doFilter method three parameters: a ServletRequest, a ServletResponse, and a FilterChain. Within the doFilter method, filters may access the servlet request and response before passing control to the next servlet. To pass control to the next filter, the developer invokes the doFilter method on the FilterChain passing along the request and response objects. Developers can even use filters to wrap the original request and response objects in order to customize (decorate) using their own specialized subclasses of HttpServletRequestWrapper and HttpServletResponseWrapper, respectively. Methods default to calling through but can be overridden.

Figures 3.26a and 3.26b illustrates a simple filter that saves a counter into the servlet context. The counter is incremented on each call to the filter. The System.out.println invocations are included only for demonstration purposes.

```
import java.io.*;
import javax.servlet.*;

public class MyFilter1 implements Filter {
    private FilterConfig fc;

    public void destroy() {
        System.out.println(">>> In MyFilter1 destroy");
    }

    public void doFilter(ServletRequest req, ServletResponse resp,
    FilterChain chain) throws ServletException, IOException {
        Integer counter = null;

// retrieve the counter from the servlet context
        ServletContext sc = this.fc.getServletContext();

        synchronized (sc) {
            counter = (Integer) sc.getAttribute("counter");
        }

        if (counter == null) {
            counter = new Integer(0);
        }

        System.out.println(">>> In MyFilter1 doFilter");
        System.out.print(">>>   Before calling the chain:");
        System.out.println("counter=" + counter);
```

Figure 3.26a: A filter for counting invocations.

```
        // increment the counter
        int newValue = counter.intValue() + 1;
        counter = new Integer(newValue);
        synchronized (sc) {
            sc.setAttribute("counter", counter);
        }

        // continue processing the chain
        chain.doFilter(req, resp);
        // control returns here after all downstream processing
        synchronized (sc) {

            counter = (Integer) sc.getAttribute("counter");
        }

        System.out.println(">>> In MyFilter1 doFilter");
        System.out.print(">>>   After returning from chain:");
        System.out.println("counter=" + counter);
    }

    public void init(FilterConfig config) throws ServletException {
        System.out.println(">>> In MyFilter1 init");
        this.fc = config;
    }
}
```

Figure 3.27b: A filter for counting invocations.

Creating servlet filters

To create a servlet filter, double-click the **Web Deployment Descriptor** in the Web project's folder to open the web.xml deployment descriptor file. Select the **Filters tab** and click the **New** button. The New Filter wizard opens (Figure 3.27).

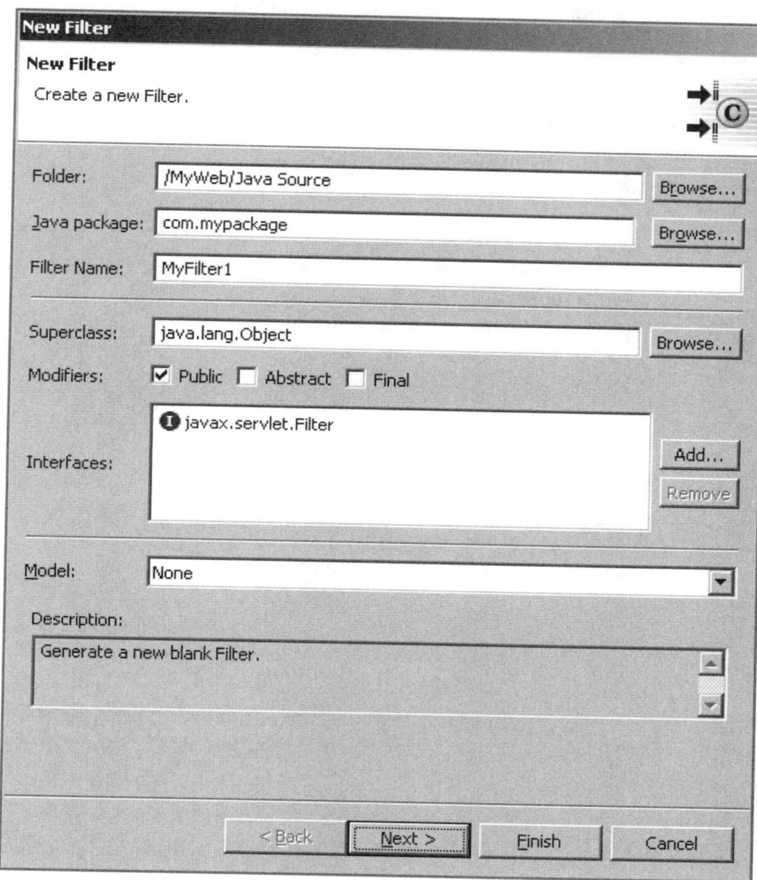

Figure 3.28: New servlet filter wizard (page 1).

The wizard contains many elements from wizards we've described previously. The folder, Java package, and model fields are identical to those in the New Servlet wizard. The filter name is the filter's Java class name. The superclass, modifiers, and interfaces define the filter's superclass (usually java.lang.Object), class modifiers, and interfaces. The filter must implement the Filter interface and may implement additional interfaces as necessary. Click **Next** to go to the second page of the wizard (Figure 3.28).

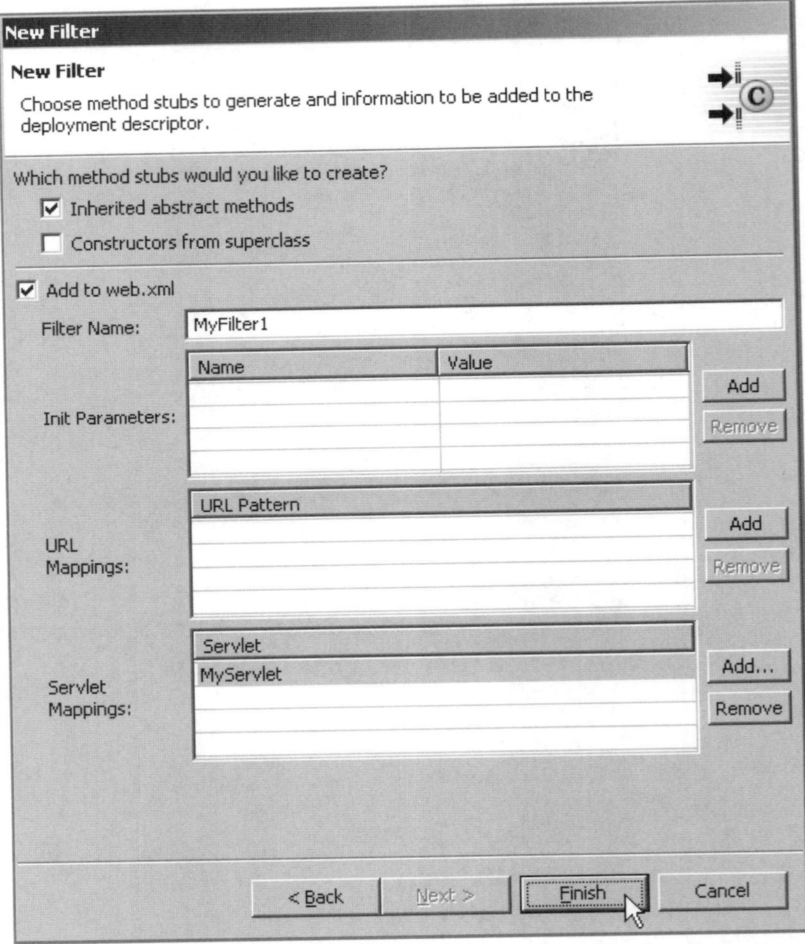

Figure 3.29: New servlet filter wizard (page 2).

The second page of the wizard defines the filter in the web.xml deployment descriptor file. In the init parameters section, the developer can use the Add and Remove buttons to define initialization parameters to the filter if necessary. In the URL Mappings section, the default URL mapping is shown. Even though the filter can have a URL, the developer should remove it to prevent the filter from being invoked directly. It is better to use a servlet mapping to invoke the filter as part of a chain. In the Servlet Mappings section, use the **Add** and **Remove** buttons to define the servlets associated with this filter. Before the developer can add a servlet to the Servlet Mappings list, the servlet must already have been created with a URL mapping in the web.xml deployment descriptor file.

Application Developer creates the filter class and opens the source in a Java Editor. Make changes to the source and compile as with any other Java class.

Servlet filter deployment descriptors

Creating servlet filters using the wizard adds the following entries to the web.xml deployment descriptor file. In this example two filters have been created, but the order of the mappings has been changed to put MyFilter2 ahead of MyFilter1 in the chain mapped to MyServlet. So that is the order in which they are invoked by the container, as shown in the sample output in Figure 3.29.

```
<filter>
    <filter-name>MyFilter1</filter-name>
    <display-name>MyFilter1</display-name>
    <filter-class>com.mypackage.MyFilter1</filter-class>
</filter>
<filter>
    <filter-name>MyFilter2</filter-name>
    <display-name>MyFilter2</display-name>
    <filter-class>com.mypackage.MyFilter2</filter-class>
</filter>
<filter-mapping>
    <filter-name>MyFilter2</filter-name>
    <servlet-name>MyServlet</servlet-name>
</filter-mapping>
<filter-mapping>
    <filter-name>MyFilter1</filter-name>
    <servlet-name>MyServlet</servlet-name>
</filter-mapping>
```

Figure 3.30: Filter ordering defined in the deployment descriptor.

Each <filter> element defines the filter's name, display name, and class. Each <filter-mapping> element defines a mapping. The first <filter-mapping> associates MyFilter2 with MyServlet. The second <filter-mapping> associates MyFilter1 with MyServlet also. Although MyFilter1 is defined first, the mappings establish the order in which the filter will participate in the chain. All servlets specified in the <servlet-name> element of a <filter-mapping> element must already have a <servlet> element in the web.xml deployment descriptor. Sample output is shown in Figure 3.30.

```
>>> In MyFilter2 init
>>> In MyFilter1 init
>>> In MyFilter2 doFilter
>>>   Before calling the chain: counter=0
>>> In MyFilter1 doFilter
>>>   Before calling the chain: counter=1
>>> In MyServlet doGet
>>> In MyFilter1 doFilter
>>>   After returning from chain: counter=2
>>> In MyFilter2 doFilter
>>>   After returning from chain: counter=2
```

Figure 3.31: Demonstration of filter ordering in the chain.

Debugging servlet filters

Debugging a servlet filter follows the same process as debugging a servlet. Set a breakpoint in the source and test by calling the servlet associated with the filter.

Summary

Servlets provide a powerful and portable way of extending the function of the Web server. As developers learn the servlet API, they will see that their prior Java knowledge and experience is very valuable. Servlets produce the dynamic results seen in many of today's popular commercial Web sites. In fact, the servlet API is usually the first J2EE technology learned by developers.

New to WebSphere Application Server Version 5 is J2EE Version 1.3, which provides support for servlet listeners and filters. These two new technologies will become important tools to manage content changes within the Web application.

Test yourself

Key terms

servlet
request and response
cookies
session
servlet listeners
servlet filters

Review questions

1. What are the types of requests that can be handled by servlets?
2. HttpServlet extends the abstract class GenericServlet, which contains the abstract method abstract void service(ServletRequest req, ServletResponse res). Whereas the HttpServlet class is also abstract, it contains no abstract methods. How is the service method implemented in HttpServlet? In other words, what happens when a GET request is received by an HttpServlet subclass?
3. When a URL is typed into a browser, what kind of HTTP request is generated?
4. How would you initialize attributes in a servlet? What method would you override? What method would you use to access values provided in the deployment descriptor?
5. Describe the differences between the HttpSessionListener, HttpSessionBindingListener, and HttpSessionAttributeListener interfaces.
6. Google (*http://www.google.com*) search queries use an HTTP Get request. Why? Most forms use an HTTP Post request. Why is that?
7. What is the difference between using the sendRedirect(String) method in the HttpServletResponse interface and calling forward(request, response) from a RequestDispatcher?
8. The HttpServletRequest class has both a getParameter(String) method and a getAttribute(String) method. What is the difference?
9. There is an addCookie(Cookie) method in the HttpServletResponse interface but no corresponding removeCookie(Cookie) method. How can you remove a cookie?
10. Application Developer provides a nice graphical front end on the XML-based Web deployment descriptor, which means a developer doesn't need to remember the various tags and rules for using them. The rules can be found, however, in a Document Type Definition (DTD) file. Its location appears at the top of the file, as part of the <!DOCTYPE> tag. What is the URL for the deployment descriptor DTD?

CHAPTER 4

JavaServer Pages (JSP)

Ken Greenlee

Chapter topics

- *Introducing JavaServer Pages*
- *JSP syntax*
- *Creating and testing JSP Pages*
- *Custom tags*

Certification objectives

- *Design, develop, and test JSPs*
- *Design and develop custom tags*

The name "JavaServer Pages" (JSP) refers to a technology for J2EE components that can be used in enterprise applications, very much like servlets, for generating dynamic output. Typically the generated output is HTML, but DHTML, XHTML, and XML can be generated as well. As we mentioned in the previous chapter, JSP pages (or, more familiarly, JSPs) can be used very effectively as the display page technology in Model-View-Controller collaborations with servlets and JavaBeans. WebSphere Studio Application Developer makes it easier than ever for the enterprise developer to design, develop, test, and debug JSPs.

Introducing JavaServer Pages

Anything that might be done by a JSP page could also be done by a servlet. The problem with using a servlet is that a servlet must generate the markup, and with the current generation of tools it is difficult to verify that the markup is correct in a Java program, since the compiler knows the markup only as strings. This makes it difficult if not impossible to determine whether the markup is well formed or whether it is valid. As the markup becomes increasingly complex, its generation by a servlet also becomes more difficult.

JSP technology has been designed to simplify integrating static and dynamic Web content. The static content remains as markup, while a scripting language, usually Java, generates the dynamic content. The markup generally does a good job of formatting the embedded dynamic results from executing the script. A prime example is any Web page showing the latest news headlines. A separate information source provides the text of the headline, or content. The scripting portion of the JSP page queries the source to obtain the content, and the markup portion of the JSP page, which is typically HTML, formats the content for output.

By separating the content from the formatting, we are once again separating model from view. A JSP page enables Web site developers to specialize in writing the Java code, in writing the HTML, or even in both, but with tools such as WebSphere Studio that are highly specialized to each of these now separate tasks. The HTML developer will use an editor such as Page Designer in WebSphere Studio and incorporate various scripting elements into the markup. Java developers provide reusable JavaBeans, either previously written or newly developed. Page Designer makes it much easier to create valid markup along with the necessary scripting elements and JavaBeans.

The compilation process

JSP pages typically consist of a mixture of HTML, which is the static content, and Java code, which generates the dynamic content. In order to merge the static and dynamic content, Java code must be generated, compiled, and executed. When the application server receives a request for a JSP page, or when a servlet forwards a request to a JSP page, the application server first compiles the JSP file to a Java source file and then compiles the Java source file into a class file, which is executed to output both the static and dynamic content. The result of the running class file is the result of the JSP page displayed in the web browser. For efficiency, WebSphere provides an option to precompile JSP pages.

If the content of a JSP file ever changes, the application server repeats the conversion and compilation process. Otherwise, the application server reuses the existing compiled class file.

Comparison of JSP pages with servlets

Because of the way that the Java interfaces have been designed, a JSP page is a servlet (and performs like one at runtime), but a servlet is not a JSP page. When the application server compiles the JSP page to a Java source file, that source code defines a Java class that implements the HttpJspPage interface. The HttpJspPage interface extends JspPage; the difference between HttpJspPage and JspPage is that HttpJspPage is a JSP page capable of responding to HTTP requests, whereas JspPage provides generic JSP support and is not limited to HTTP requests. One further important piece of information links JSP with servlets: The JspPage interface extends the Servlet interface. Therefore, a JSP page is a servlet.

The generated Java source compiled from the JSP page contains a _jspService method, similar to the service method of a servlet. For each portion of HTML, the _jspService method invokes a method on a JspWriter, which outputs a portion of the results. This is very similar to the way a servlet might use a PrintWriter. All Java code embedded within the JSP page also ends up interleaved in the _jspService method, So, between the invocations to output portions of static content, Java code is executed to produce dynamic content, which then gets merged into the output stream.

Since a JSP page is a servlet, the application server treats the compiled JSP class file as it would any other servlet. Once loaded, the application server keeps the class file in memory to respond to future requests. In other words, the application server typically creates one instance of the generated servlet and uses that instance to handle multiple requests. When the original JSP source is changed, the application server takes note of that fact and recompiles the JSP page. The application server unloads the old class file and loads the new one.

JSP syntax

Developers familiar with HTML generally have little difficulty learning the JSP syntax. The best way to learn the JSP syntax is with practice: Create simple JSP pages with various tags to see the result. Then try adding more complex features to experiment.

Comments

Two types of comments are may be used in JSP pages: (1) regular HTML and XML comments and (2) JSP comments. The following example shows both types of comments.

```
<!-- This is an HTML/XML comment. It will wind up in the output -->
<%-- This is a JSP comment. It does not get into the output. --%>
```

Elements

For the purpose of this discussion, we will consider JSP pages as consisting of elements and text (technically speaking, they are called *elements* and *template data*). There are three types of elements: directives, scripting elements, and actions. *Directives* provide global information for translation. There are three directives: page, taglib, and include. *Scripting elements* enable the developer to manipulate objects, and they perform computations supporting the generation of dynamic content. There are three types of scripting elements: declarations, scriptlets, and expressions. *Actions* are used for request processing by the JSP page. Actions are either *standard* or *custom*. Standard actions are those that are defined in the JSP specification. Custom actions are additional actions that are made available from tag libraries. All actions follow standard XML syntax. They can have a start tag including the element's name and attributes, an optional body, and an end tag, or they can be empty, with only the element's name and attributes. The following example demonstrates what we mean by "empty" as opposed to non-empty elements.

```
<jsp:useBean id="user" class="com.mypackage.User">
    <jsp:setProperty name="first" value="John" />
    <jsp:setProperty name="last" value="Doe" />
</jsp:useBean>
```

The jsp:useBean action has a start tag, <jsp:useBean . . . >, a body (consisting of two jsp:setProperty elements), and a separate end tag, </jsp:useBean>. Therefore, it is considered to be non-empty.

Both of the jsp:setProperty actions are considered to be empty, since they are self-ending. Each of them has two attributes, yet technically speaking each of them is empty, since they have no bodies and each consists of only one tag, which ends with a slash and a greater- than sign (/>).

The page directive

The page directive tag defines attributes that apply to the entire JSP page. The syntax of the page directive is <%@ page . . . %>, which is not XML compatible. The page directive provides the developer various options, which are expressed as attributes. Each of these attributes has a default value, so the page directive is optional. The developer need only specify the parameters for which the default values are not acceptable. A list of valid attributes follows.

- autoFlush: The autoFlush option defines whether the output buffer is automatically flushed when full. A value of *true* automatically flushes the buffer when full; a value of *false* causes an exception to be raised when the buffer is full. The default is *true*.
- buffer: The buffer option defines the buffer size used by the default output writer. To specify a buffer, supply the buffer size in kilobytes followed by the letters *kb*; for example, to specify a buffer size of one megabyte (1024 kilobytes), the value of the buffer option would be 1024kb. If not specified, the default used is 8kb.
- contentType: The contentType option defines the MIME type or format of data used within the JSP page. Most JSP pages will have a contentType of *text/html*, which instructs the Web browser to interpret the content returned by the JSP page as HTML.

- errorPage: The errorPage option defines the error JSP page that is displayed when any uncaught exception occurs. The location of the error page depends upon the errorPage value. If the value begins with /, the error page is found relative to the Web project's context root. Without a beginning /, the error page is found relative to the current JSP file. If not specified, the default is */error.jsp*.

- extends: The extends option defines the fully qualified name (package name and class name) of the superclass of the Java class to which this JSP page will be compiled. This option is rarely used. If not specified, the default is the standard superclass defined for the JSP class on this application server.

- import: The import option defines any Java classes or packages to be imported within the JSP page. To specify multiple classes or packages, the developer can use either multiple page directive tags (generally easier to read) or a comma-delimited list. By default, the java.lang.*, javax.servlet.*, javax.servlet.http.*, and javax.servlet.jsp.* packages are already imported within the JSP page. The default is that no additional classes or packages are imported.

- info: The info option defines a text string that is incorporated into the compiled JSP class. Use the getServletInfo() method within the JSP page to retrieve this value.

- isErrorPage: The isErrorPage option defines whether this JSP page is an error page; that is, whether the page has access to the exception implicit object instance, which is a reference to the Throwable object originating in the JSP page where an exception occurred. A value of *true* identifies this JSP page as an error page; a value of *false* indicates that this JSP page is not an error page. The default is *false*.

- isThreadSafe: The isTheadSafe option determines whether the application server may send multiple requests to this JSP page simultaneously. A value of *true* indicates that the JSP page is thread safe and can be accessed by multiple threads concurrently. A value of *false* indicates that the JSP page is not thread safe; this value causes the compiled servlet to implement the Single Thread Model discussed in Chapter 3. The default is *true*.

- language: The language option defines the scripting language used in scriptlets, declarations, and expressions in the JSP page and any included files. In the JSP 1.2 specification, the only defined and required value for this attribute is *java*. WebSphere, however, allows JavaScript to be used as the scripting language for JSP pages. It is important to remember that JSP pages are executed in the Web Container in the application server. Therefore, if *javascript* is specified as the scripting language for a JSP page, then any JavaScript within the JSP scripting elements (declarations, scriptlets, and expressions) will be run on the server. However, JavaScript within standard HTML <SCRIPT language="javascript"> . . . </SCRIPT> elements will still execute in the client browser. The example in Figure 4.1 illustrates both client-side and server-side use of JavaScript in the same JSP page. The default for the language attribute is *java*.

```
<!DOCTYPE HTML PUBLIC "-//W3C//DTD HTML 4.01 Transitional//EN">
<HTML>
<HEAD>
<%@ page language="javascript" %>
<TITLE>TestJavaScript.jsp</TITLE>
</HEAD>
<BODY>
<H2>Countdown...</H2>

<%-- This runs in the browser --%>
<SCRIPT language="javascript">
<!--
var ns = (navigator.appName.indexOf("Netscape")  >= 0);
var ie = (navigator.appName.indexOf("Microsoft") >= 0);
if (ns) {
window.status = "Netscape";
}
if (ie) {
window.status = "Internet Explorer";
}
//-->
</SCRIPT>

<%-- This runs in the web container --%>
<%
var i = 0;
for (i = 10; i >= 0; i--) {
out.println(Math.round(i) + "<BR />");
}
%>

<H2>Done!</H2>
</BODY>
</HTML>
```

Figure 4.1: Example of JavaScript used as scripting language for a JSP page.

- pageEncoding: The pageEncoding option defines the character encoding that the JSP page uses for the response. The default is ISO-8859-1.
- session: The session option defines whether an HttpSession needs to be created for the JSP page. A value of *true* indicates that a session is required, and either the current session will be obtained or a new session will be created. A value of *false* indicates that a session is neither to be retrieved nor created. The default is *true*.

The following example page directive defines imports for packages java.util.* and java.text.*, instructs the application server not to create a session, and defines myerror.jsp as the error page for this JSP.

```
<%@ page
    import="java.util.*,java.text.*"
    session="false"
    errorPage="myerror.jsp"
%>
```

The taglib directive

The taglib directive is used to extend the set of tags, by identifying a tag library and associating it with a prefix. In the following example, the prefix *c* is associated with the Java Standard Tag Library (JSTL) core set of tags, and the prefix *fmt* is associated with the JSTL formatting tags. Recall that the prefix *jsp* is associated with the standard actions; for example, <jsp:setProperty . . . />. Tag libraries will be discussed later in this chapter in the “Custom Tags” section.

```
<%@ taglib uri="http://java.sun.com/jstl/core" prefix="c" %>
<%@ taglib uri="http://java.sun.com/jstl/fmt" prefix="fmt" %>
```

The include directive

The include directive is used to include a JSP fragment into a JSP page statically, before it is translated and compiled. Later we will see another way to include another JSP file dynamically, at execution time. The following is an example of the include directive.

```
<%@ include file="copyright.html" %>
```

Declarations

Declaration tags declare fields and methods in the JSP class. The syntax <%! . . . %> defines the declaration. The following example declares a field. Any Java field may be declared using a declaration tag.

```
<%! private String pattern = "MM/dd/yyyy"; %>
```

The following example declares a method. Any Java method may be declared using the declaration tag.

```
<%!
public String format(java.util.Date d, String pattern) {
   java.text.SimpleDateFormat sdf =
      new java.text.SimpleDateFormat(pattern);
   String result = sdf.format(d);
   return result;
}
%>
```

The declared field or method has the scope of the JSP page and can be referenced anywhere within the page.

Scriptlets

The scriptlet tag embeds code, typically Java, within the JSP page. Scriptlets are not required to produce any output. The <% . . . %> syntax is use to define a scriptlet. Variables defined within a scriptlet have the scope of the body of the JSP. The following example of a scriptlet uses a Java *for* loop to change the font size of the string "Hello" that is displayed using the *out* implicit object.

```
<%
for (int i=1; i<=5; i++) {
   out.println("<P><FONT SIZE=" + i + ">Hello</FONT></P>");
}
%>
```

Implicit objects

Developers writing JSP pages may use any of the implicit object instances within scriptlets and expressions. Using these instances makes writing a JSP page easier, since these instances are created and initialized in the generated JSP Java code. The JSP writer need not do anything other than use these instances.

The instances listed in Tables 4.1 and 4.2 function similarly, in most cases, to their servlet counterparts. The Table 4.1 lists implicit object available in all JSP pages. Table 4.2 lists the implicit object available only in error pages.

Table 4.1: Implicit objects available in all JSP pages.

request	The HttpServletRequest
response	The HttpServletResponse
pageContext	Provides access to implicit objects, also supports forwarding, inclusion, and error handling
session	The HttpSession, available if the session option is set to *true* (the default) in the page directive
application	The ServletContext
out	JspWriter for the output stream
config	The ServletConfig
page	Equivalent to *this* when the scripting language is Java

Table 4.2: Implicit objects available only in error pages.

exception	The uncaught Throwable object that comes from the page where the exception occurred

The following example illustrates using these instances within a scriptlet to retrieve a string from the request and then display the string as a paragraph in HTML.

```
<%
String message = request.getAttribute("message");
if (message != null) {
   out.println("<P>" + message + "</P>");
}
%>
```

Expressions

The express tag inserts the result of an expression into the JSP result. The syntax <%= . . . %> defines the expression. The following example uses an expression tag to display the result of calling the previously defined format method.

```
<%= this.format(new java.util.Date(), this.pattern) %>
```

An expression tag is ultimately converted to an out.print(expression); statement in the generated servlet, so be careful not to include a semicolon at the end of the expression.

Standard action: forwarding a request

The <jsp:forward> tag forwards the client request to a given HTML page, JSP page, or servlet within the same Web application context. The following examples forward the request to an HTML page, a JSP page, and a servlet.

The developer must be careful when forwarding, because an IllegalStateException can result, if page output was buffered, and the buffer was flushed.

```
<jsp:forward page="file.html" />
<jsp:forward page="main/file.jsp" />
<jsp:forward page="LoginServlet" />
```

The page attribute specifies a relative URL of the component to forward to. Additionally, the page attribute value may be the result of an expression tag, as in the following example. In this example, "expression" represents any valid expression.

```
<jsp:forward page="<%= expression %>" />
```

Any JSP text following the <jsp:forward> tag is not processed.

If the page forwarded to is a JSP page or servlet and requires input, use the <jsp:param> tag to supply input values on the request, as in the following example.

```
<jsp:forward page="LoginServlet">
    <jsp:param name="user" value="john_doe" />
    <jsp:param name="password" value="<%= pwd %>" />
</jsp:forward>
```

Notice that the value attribute of the <jsp:param> tag may be an expression.

Standard action: dynamic include

The <jsp:include> tag embeds an HTML file or the result of a servlet or JSP page within the current JSP page. This happens dynamically, at request time, as compared to the include directive discussed previously, which takes place at translation. The following examples include an HTML file, a JSP page, and a servlet.

```
<jsp:include page="header.html" />
<jsp:include page="body.jsp" />
<jsp:include page="FormatServlet" />
```

The page attribute specifies a relative URL of the component to include. If the page attribute specifies a static component such as an HTML file, the HTML file is embedded within the JSP page. If the page attribute specifies a dynamic component such as another JSP page or a servlet, the application server passes the request to the dynamic component; the result of the dynamic component is then embedded within the JSP. Additionally, the page attribute value may be the result of an expression tag, as in the following example.

```
<jsp:include page="<%= expression %>" />
```

Once the application server includes the given component, the remaining JSP text lines are processed.

If the included page is a JSP page or servlet and requires input, use the <jsp:param> tag to supply input values on the request as in the following example.

```
<jsp:include page="DateFormatServlet">
<jsp:param name="pattern" value="MM/dd/yyyy" />
<jsp:param name="date" value="<%= new java.util.Date() %>" />
</jsp:include>
```

Notice that the value of the <jsp:param> tag may be an expression.

Standard action: integrating JavaBeans

The term "JavaBeans" refers to a particular software component architecture, and JavaBeans are also the software components themselves. JavaBeans are self-describing software components written in Java. Technically speaking, JavaBeans must be serializable and have a public default constructor, also known as a zero-argument constructor. JavaBeans are always Java classes. JavaBeans are self-describing in that they support introspection, both implicitly, and explicitly. The explicit support is via BeanInfo classes. The implicit support is through the use of certain naming conventions. JavaBeans are self-describing, by exposing properties, methods, and events. For the purpose of the following discussion, we will consider JavaBeans primarily as data holders that allow the developer to manipulate their encapsulated state through accessor and mutator methods (also known as getters and setters).

As outlined in Chapter 3, the Model-View-Controller (MVC) design pattern is very important to J2EE developers. The MVC pattern divides an application into the model (JavaBeans or Enterprise JavaBean Entity beans), the view (HTML files or JSP pages), and the controller (servlets or Enterprise JavaBean Session beans). JSP pages function as the view, which means that JSP pages can actually gather input, display results, or both. Gathering input usually employs an HTML form. Displaying a result requires at least minimal code to retrieve and display a value out of the model. To minimize the amount of Java code within a JSP, the developer uses the <jsp:useBean> tag to retrieve or create a JavaBean. Create the <jsp:useBean> tag by selecting the option in the JSP menu, by entering the tag in the JSP editor's source view, or by dragging a Java class into the JSP editor's design view.

The <jsp:useBean> tag has the following attributes.

- id: The id attribute names the variable used by the developer to identify the JavaBean instance. Unfortunately, "id" is somewhat misleading, but we must live with it because that is the way the specification is written. The net result is that we use the id attribute in the jsp:useBean element, and that corresponds with the name attribute in the getProperty and serProperty elements. It is important for the developer to understand this connection.
- scope: The scope attribute defines the scope in which the JavaBean exists. Think of the scope of defining how a JavaBean instance is shared among a set of JSP pages. Allowable values are *page*, *request*, *session*, and *application*. The default value is *page*.
  - page: A value of *page* indicates that the JavaBean instance exists only on the current JSP page and on any included JSP pages.
  - request: A value of *request* means that the JavaBean instance is shared among all pages and servlets fulfilling the current request; the request object may also be used to store and retrieve the JavaBean instance.
  - session: A value of *session* is very similar to *request* except that the JavaBean instance exists in the current session. Any JSP page using a session scope must have a page directive with session="true".
  - application: A value of *application* means that the JavaBean instance may be used from any JSP pages or servlets within the same application.
- class: The class attribute specifies the JavaBean class to instantiate. The class must not be abstract and must have a public default constructor. If the bean is not found in the specified scope, and the class is specified, the bean is instantiated using the default constructor. Processing continues by execution of the body of the jsp:useBean tag if the element is non-empty.
- type: If the JavaBean already exists in the scope, the type attribute allows the developer to specify a type for the reference that is different from that of the class from which the bean was instantiated. One can think of the type attribute as casting the bean instance to a compatible type. Therefore, the type must be either a superclass of the bean's class or an interface implemented by the bean's class. Using the type option without providing either a class attribute or a beanName attribute prevents instantiation of the bean, and the consequences of this are

important. If the bean is found in the specified scope, then processing continues as expected. If however, the bean is not found in the specified scope and only the type is specified, an InstantiationException is thrown. This may be the desired behavior, if it is truly an error when the bean is not found in the specified scope. An error page should be registered to handle this situation gracefully.

- beanName: The beanName attribute specifies the name of a bean to instantiate via static invocation of the instantiate() method on the class java.beans.Beans. It can be either the name of a class or the name of a serialized resource.

The following example creates a JavaBean instance called formatter, using the default constructor of the class com.mypackage.DateFormatter. Since no scope is specified, it defaults to page.

```
<jsp:useBean id="formatter" class="com.mypackage.DateFormatter" />
```

The following example attempts to retrieve a bean instance called message from the session. If the instance does not exist in the session, then it is instantiated using the default constructor.

```
<jsp:useBean id="message" class="com.mypackage.Message" scope="session" />
```

The following example attempts to retrieve from the request a bean instance called formatter of type com.mypackage.DateFormatter (a subclass of com.mypackage.Formatter). The bean instance is cast to com.mypackage.Formatter. If not found in the request, the bean is instantiated using the default constructor of DateFormatter.

```
<jsp:useBean id="formatter" class="com.mypackage.DateFormatter"
type="com.mypackage.Formatter" scope="request" />
```

Standard action: displaying JavaBean properties

Use the <jsp:getProperty> tag to retrieve the value of a JavaBean property. The JavaBean must already be defined using a <jsp:useBean> tag. The <jsp:getProperty> tag has the following attributes.

- name: The name attribute identifies the JavaBean to use, as declared in the id attribute of a <jsp:useBean> tag.
- property: The property attribute specifies the JavaBean property to display in the JSP result. The property must have a corresponding getter method in the JavaBean class.

The following example accesses a JavaBean from the session using a <jsp:useBean> tag followed by a <jsp:getProperty> tag to display the JavaBean's text property.

```
<jsp:useBean id="message" class="com.mypackage.Message" scope="session"/>
<jsp:getProperty name="message" property="text" />
```

Standard action: setting JavaBean properties

Use the <jsp:setProperty> tag to set a property's value within a JavaBean. The JavaBean must already be defined using a <jsp:useBean> tag. No output is included in the JSP result from the <jsp:setProperty> tag. The <jsp:setProperty> tag has the following options.

- name: The name attribute identifies the JavaBean to use as declared in the id attribute of a <jsp:useBean> tag.
- property: The property attribute specifies the JavaBean property to set. The property must have a corresponding setter method in the JavaBean class.
- param: The param attribute specifies the name of an incoming request parameter. The request parameter's value is used as the value to which the property is set. When using the param attribute, do not use the value attribute.
- value: The value attribute specifies the value to which the property is set. An expression tag may be used to specify the value.

The following example creates a JavaBean using a <jsp:useBean> tag followed by a <jsp:setProperty> tag to set the JavaBean's text property to a value of "Action complete."

```
<jsp:useBean id="message" class="com.mypackage.Message" />
<jsp:setProperty name="message" property="text" value="Action complete."/>
```

The following example is a variation of the first example. In this example the value of the "text" property of the Message bean is taken from the incoming request's parameter named "text". When both the value option and the param option are omitted, the name of the bean's property is assumed to be the same as the name of the parameter in the incoming request. Therefore, the value is simply copied from the incoming parameter to the correspondingly named property.

```
<jsp:useBean id="message" class="com.mypackage.Message" scope="request" />
<jsp:setProperty name="message" property="text" />
```

The following example is another variation, demonstrating how the developer can set all properties from their corresponding parameters in the incoming request.

```
<jsp:useBean id="message" class="com.mypackage.Message" scope="request" />
<jsp:setProperty name="message" property="*" />
```

If the incoming request's parameter and the property to be set do not have the same name, specify both the property and param options, as in the following example.

```
<jsp:useBean id="message" class="com.mypackage.Message" />
<jsp:setProperty name="message" property="text" param="status" />
```

Finally, a common use of the <jsp:setProperty> tag is to initialize a bean instance created with a <jsp:useBean> tag. If the bean has been successfully retrieved from the specified scope, then setting properties would not be required. On the other hand, if the bean is not found in the specified scope and the class attribute is provided, the default constructor is used to instantiate the bean, and the <jsp:setProperty> element must be used to set the properties. To get this conditional behavior, use a variation of the <jsp:useBean> element with a body, in which the <jsp:setProperty> element is nested, and a separate ending tag, as follows.

```
<jsp:useBean id="message" class="com.mypackage.Message" scope="session">
    <jsp:setProperty name="message" property="text" value="Complete." />
</jsp:useBean>
```

Error handling and error pages

As mentioned in the page directive tag section, JSP pages may specify an error page. The designated error page is automatically invoked whenever any uncaught exception occurs. To illustrate, consider the JSP page in Figure 4.2:

```
<HTML>
<HEAD><TITLE>Today.jsp</TITLE></HEAD>
<BODY>
<%@ page import = "java.util.*,java.text.*" %>
<%@ page errorPage = "TodayErrorPage.jsp" %>
<%!
   public String format(String pattern) {
      SimpleDateFormat sdf = new SimpleDateFormat(pattern);
      return sdf.format(new Date());
   }
%>
<% String pattern = request.getParameter("pattern"); %>
<P>Today is <%= this.format(pattern) %></P>
</BODY>
</HTML>
```

Figure 4.2: Today.jsp, an example of a JSP that defines an error page.

This JSP code incorporates a format method to format today's date according to a given pattern string. Notice that this JSP page defines an error page. This error page is shown in Figure 4.3:

```
<HTML>
<HEAD><TITLE>TodayErrorPage.jsp</TITLE></HEAD>
<BODY>
<%@ page isErrorPage = "true" %>
<H1>Error</H1>
<P>Exception: <%= exception %></P>
</BODY>
</HTML>
```

Figure 4.3: TodayErrorPage.jsp, the error page defined for Today.jsp in Figure 4.1.

If any uncaught exception occurs in the page Today.jsp, the page TodayErrorPage.jsp is invoked. Since the required pattern string is supplied in the request, any unacceptable pattern character causes an exception. So a URL of *http://server/MyWeb/Today.jsp?MM%2Fdd%2f%yyyy* indicates to format today's date using the *MM/dd/yyyy* pattern, which does not raise any exception. A URL of *http://server/MyWeb/Today.jsp?abc* does raise an exception because the java.text.SimpleDateFormat class does not allow *b* as a pattern character. When the exception occurs, the application server invokes the error page, TodayErrorPage.jsp.

Creating and testing JSP pages

Creating and testing a JSP page begin with a process very similar to that of creating and testing servlets. We will skip the discussion with regard to creating a Web project, and go directly to the creation of JSP pages usng WebSphere Studio Application Developer.

Creating JSP pages

After having created a Web project, the developer can create JSP pages in it. To create a JSP page, select **File → New → JSP File** and complete the first page of the wizard (Figure 4.4).

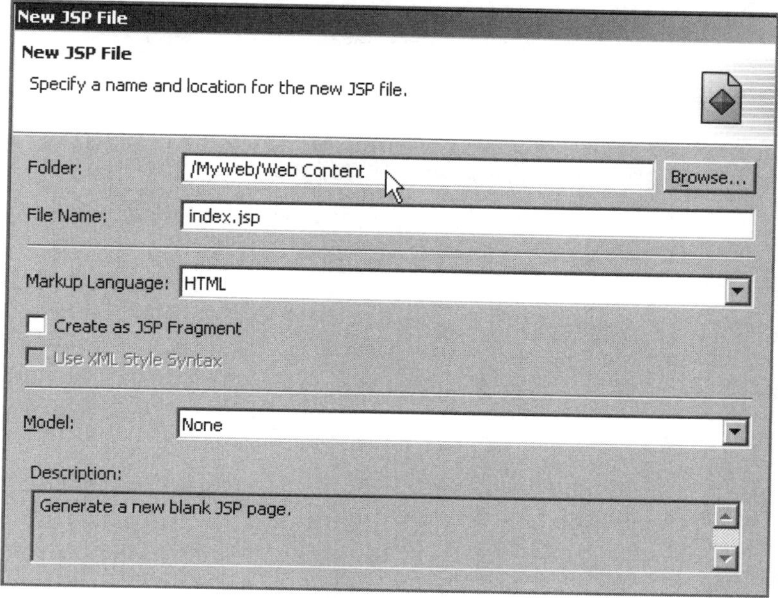

Figure 4.4: New JSP File wizard (page 1).

The options are

- Folder: The folder specifies the location of the new JSP file. This folder should be the Web Content folder of the web project. If not, click the **Browse . . .** button on the right to select the correct folder.
- File name: The file name defines the JSP page's file name.
- Markup language: The markup language option defines the language used to create the JSP file. Choose **HTML** or **XHTML**.

- Create as JSP Fragment: Select this option to create a JSP file that is to be included within another JSP file.
- Use XML Style Syntax: This option is available only when the XHTML markup language is selected. Selecting this option enforces XML tag style when creating the JSP file. This option affects code assist.
- Model: Select the code generation model for the JSP class. Currently the only options available are “None” and “Struts JSP”.

Click **Next** to go to the second page of the wizard (Figure 4.5).

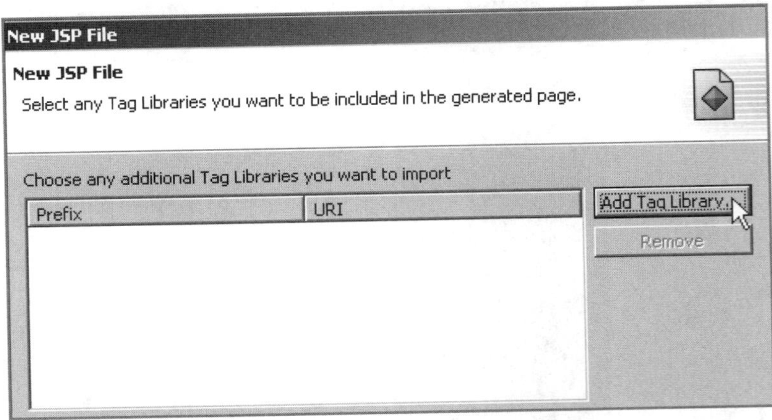

Figure 4.5: New JSP File wizard (page 2).

The second page of the wizard allows the developer to specify any tag libraries to be used within the JSP page. Use the **Add Tag Library . . .** button to add tag libraries to the JSP definition. The appropriate taglib directives will be generated (see example below). After you click the Add Tag Library button, the Select a Tag Library dialog is presented. The developer can select a tag library from the list, and the available tags in the library are displayed (Figure 4.6).

```
<%@ taglib uri="http://java.sun.com/jstl/core" prefix="c" %>
```

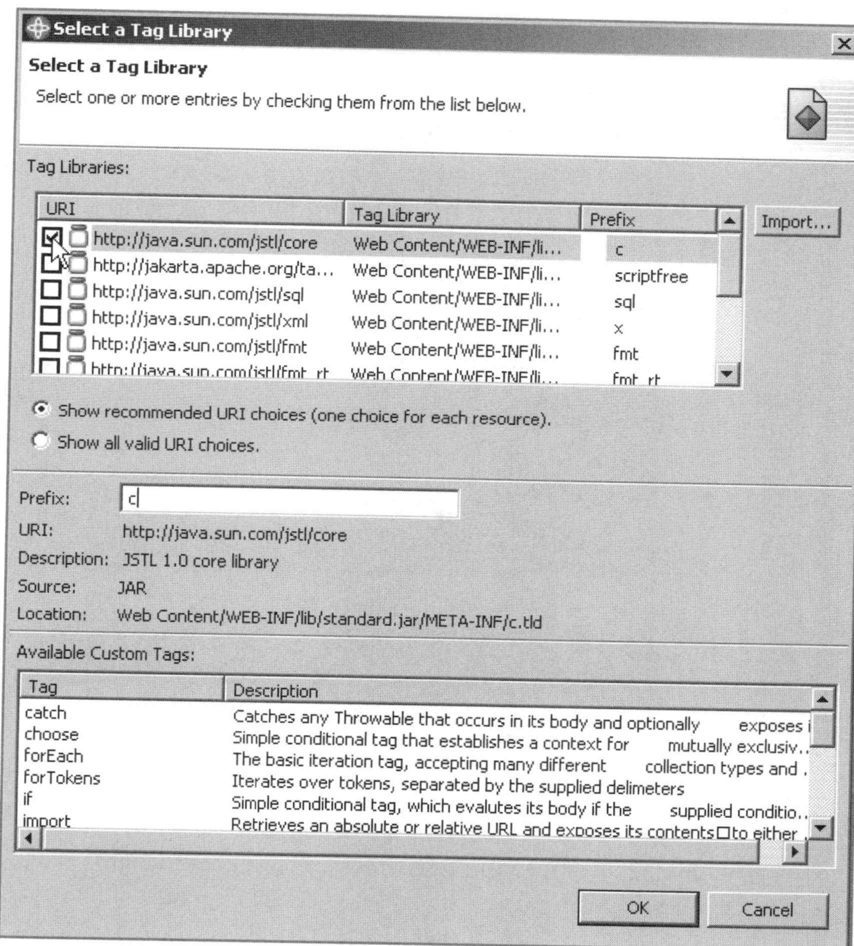

Figure 4.6: Select a Tag Library dialog.

Click **Next** to go to the third page of the wizard (Figure 4.7).

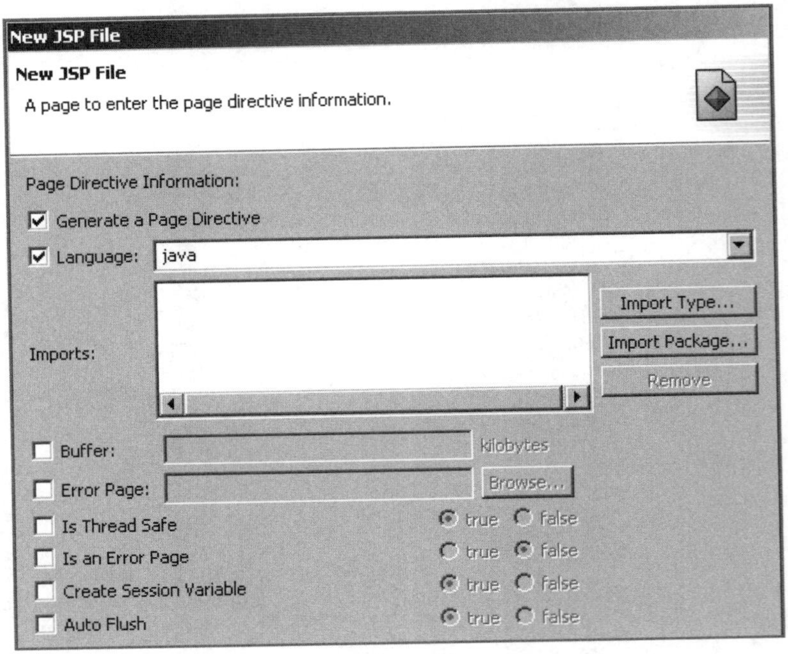

Figure 4.7: New JSP File wizard (page 3).

The third page of the wizard defines any page directive information. These details were discussed in detail previously in this chapter. This part of the wizard is for generating a page directive for the JSP page. The main options on this panel are

- Generate a Page Directive: Checking this option instructs the wizard to generate a page directive tag in the JSP page. The tag definition depends upon the settings of the other options on this page. Deselecting this option disables all other options on this page.
- Language: This option specifies the language used within the JSP page. The default is *java*.
- Imports: This list defines any Java classes or packages to be imported within the JSP page. The default is that no additional classes or packages are explicitly imported via the page directive.

Click **Next** to go to the fourth page of the wizard (Figure 4.8).

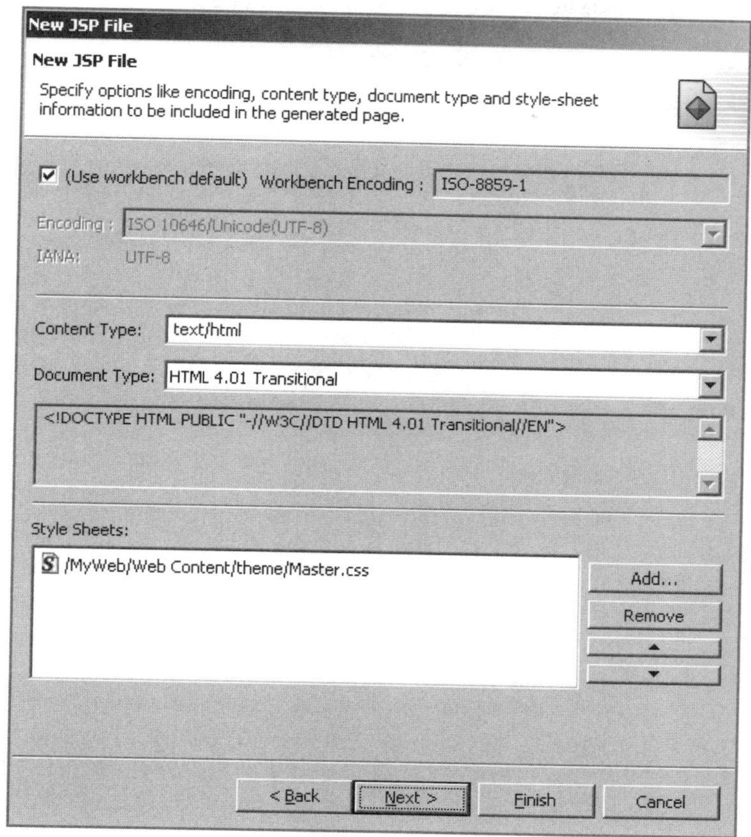

Figure 4.8: New JSP File wizard (page 4).

The fourth page of the wizard defines more JSP options:

- Workbench Encoding: When this option is checked, the JSP page is generated using the workbench's default encoding. The encoding instructs the Web browser how to interpret the characters in the JSP file. Most developers select this option.
- Encoding: When the "(Use workbench default)" encoding option is not checked, use the encoding list to select an available encoding.
- Content Type: Defines the content type or format of data used within the JSP page. Most JSP pages will be *text/html*, which instructs the Web browser to interpret the content of the JSP file as HTML.
- Document Type: Selecting a document type changes the allowed set of HTML and XHTML tags available in the JSP file. Most developers select the HTML 4.01 Transitional option, because it allows the most flexibility.

- Style Sheets: Use the **Add** and **Remove** buttons to change the set of HTML style sheets used by the JSP page.

Click **Next** to go to the fifth page of the wizard (Figure 4.9).

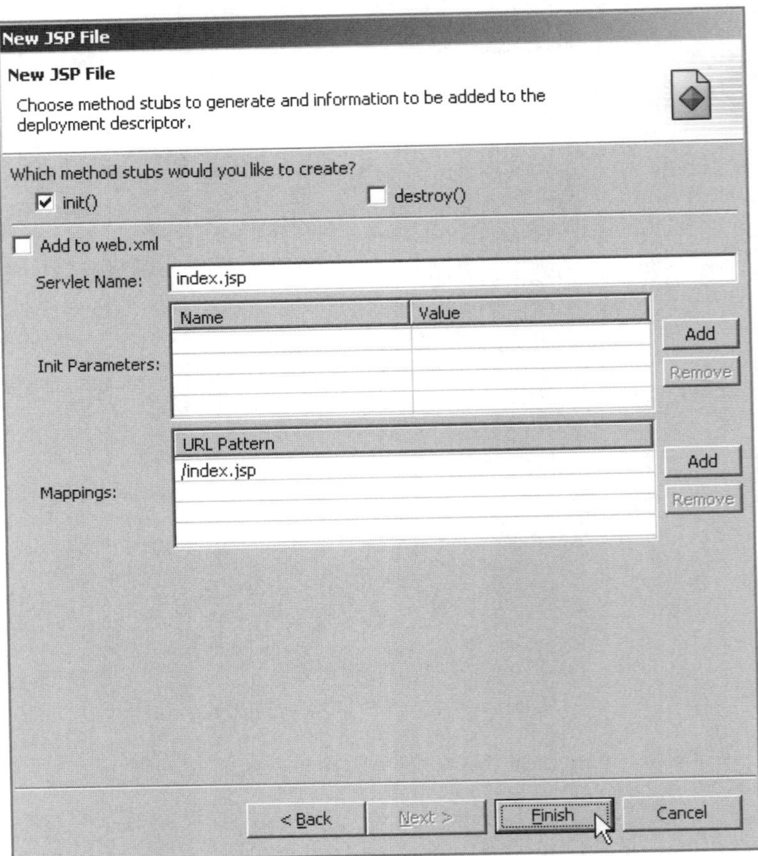

Figure 4.9: New JSP File wizard (page 5).

The fifth page of the wizard defines values added to the web.xml deployment descriptor file for the JSP page. The options are

- Which method stubs would you like to create? Select the **init()** option to generate a jspInit() method within the JSP page; select the destroy() option to generate a jspDestroy() method within the JSP page.
- Add to web.xml: Select this option to add an entry for the JSP page in the web.xml deployment descriptor file. As with servlets (Chapter 3), adding an entry allows the JSP page to have initialization parameters and URL mappings.

- Servlet Name: This field defines the name of the JSP page within the web.xml deployment descriptor file.
- Init Parameters: Use the **Add** and **Remove** buttons to alter the set of initialization parameters defined for the JSP page. These initialization parameters function identically to those defined for servlets.
- Mappings: Use the **Add** and **Remove** buttons to define the URL mappings associated with the JSP page. These URL mappings function identically to those defined for servlets.

Click **Finish** to create the JSP page.

Editing JSP files

After creating the JSP file, Application Developer opens it in the Page Designer editor in the Web perspective. The Page Designer editor is an HTML/JSP editor with three views: design, source, and preview (the preview option may not be available on Application Developer support platforms). The design view is a WYSIWYG editor; the source view shows the actual JSP and HTML tags; and the preview shows a static representation of the JSP content.

The Library view in the Web perspective (Figure 4.10) contains shortcuts for inserting JSP tags. Double-click on a tag in the Library view to insert the tag into the JSP page. The tag now exists with the default settings. To change the settings, select the tag in the Page Designer editor and switch to the Attributes view. The Attributes view is tabbed along with the Library view. Use the Attributes view to change the settings for the selected tag.

When you have finished editing, save and close the file. Double-click on the JSP file again to reopen the Page Designer editor.

Unit-testing JSP files

To run the JSP page, select the JSP source file in the J2EE Navigator list. From the source file's popup menu, select **Run on Server**, if server is already configured, as discussed previously. After a few moments, the server starts and runs the JSP page. A Web browser displays the result of the JSP page.

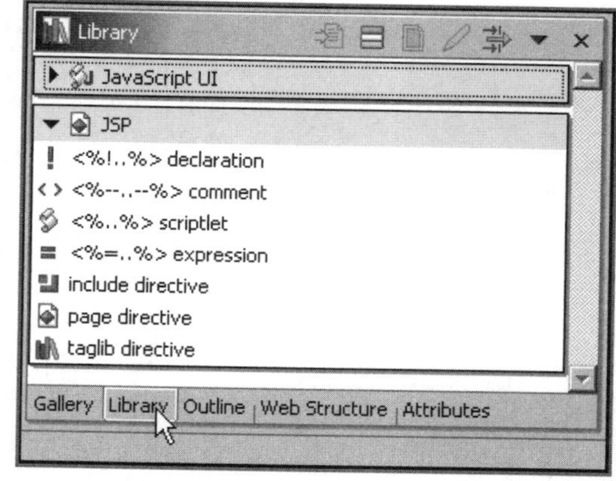

Figure 4.10: Library view.

Debugging JSP files

Traditionally, debugging JSP pages has been difficult, but it is made much easier in WebSphere Studio

Application Developer. With less sophisticated tools, a developer might see a stack trace in the browser, which is usually of limited value in diagnosing and correcting the problem. Developers need to step through the code in a debugger to troubleshoot effectively, but with JSP pages the generated Java source is not available for debugging. However, Application Developer allows developers to set breakpoints in the JSP source and then step through the JSP code. The values of variables can be viewed and modified as needed.

Setting breakpoints

To set a breakpoint, open the JSP source, switch to the Source view in the Page Designer editor, and double-click on the vertical gray bar on the left side of the Java source editor. A blue dot appears where a breakpoint is set, as shown in Figure 4.11.

```
<BODY>
<%
for (int i = 0; i < 10; i++) {
    out.println(i + "<BR />");
}
%>
<P>Place index.jsp's content here.</P>
</BODY>
```

Figure 4.11: Breakpoint in JSP.5

To remove a breakpoint, double-click again on the blue dot. The breakpoint and blue dot are removed.

Debug on Server

To debug the JSP, select the JSP source file in the J2EE Navigator list. From the source file's pop-up menu, select **Debug on Server**. From the Select Server window, select an existing server or create a new one. The Select Server window does not appear when a default server has been selected. Click **Finish** to start debug. The Step-by-Step Debug window appears (Figure 4.12).

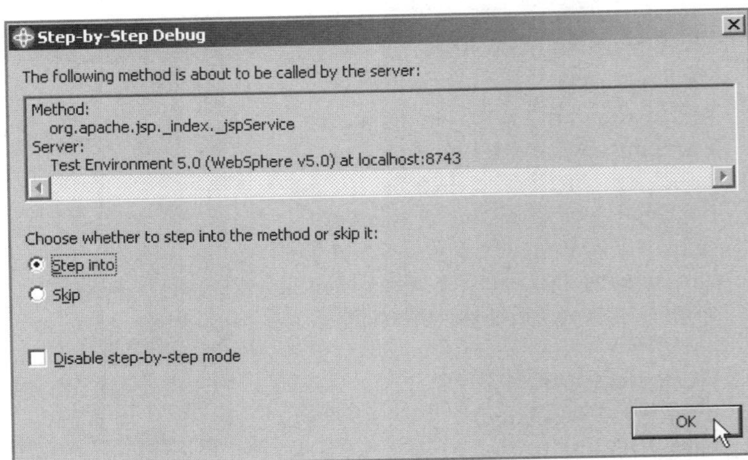

Figure 4.12: Step-by-Step Debug.

The Step-by-Step Debug window shows which JSP method the server will execute. Choose whether to step into the method or skip it. This window appears when you select the Debug on Server option. This window is not related to the existence of any breakpoints in the source.

Use the various views within the Debug perspective as to step through the code and view and modify variables as needed (see Figure 4.13).

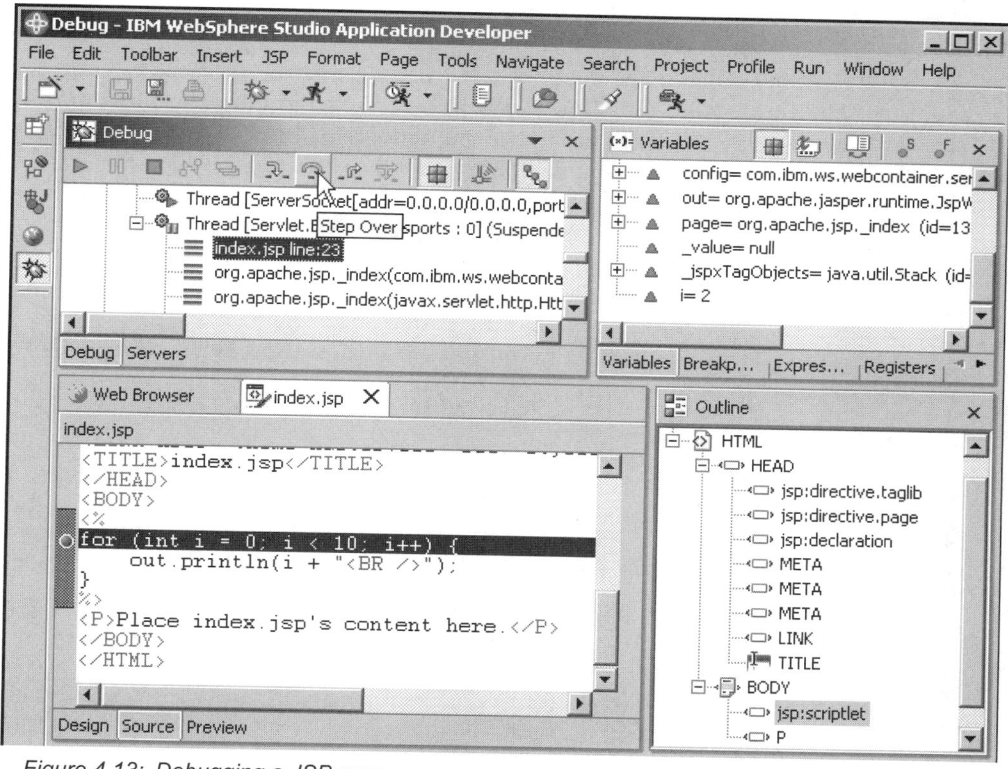

Figure 4.13: Debugging a JSP page.

Custom tags

A custom tag is a user-defined JSP tag. Each custom tag has its own, developer-written function. When the application server encounters a custom tag, the application server invokes the tag's function, inserting the function's result into the JSP's result.

Custom tags follow the syntax of other JSP tags such as <jsp:useBean>. Custom tags may have default attributes or, if supported, may be customized using attributes; for a comparison, the scope attribute customizes the <jsp:useBean> tag.

Custom tags allow developers to create tags specific to their projects. Think of a custom tag as extending the JSP language. For example, developers creating an employee database application may create an employee tag to display employee related data instead of using the standard JSP tags. An employee custom tag vastly simplifies the syntax for retrieving and formatting an employee. The syntax becomes much more like markup and much less like Java programming. Also, any changes to the formatting of the displayed employee are now centralized in the custom tag implementation.

Creating custom tags

Creating a custom tag requires two files: a tag library descriptor (TLD) file and tag handler class. The TLD file is an XML file defining information about the tag library as a whole and about each individual tag within the library. The tag handler class is a Java class containing the function defined for the custom tag.

Creating tag library descriptor files

To create a TLD, switch to an existing Web project. The TLD file must be in the Web project's WEB-INF folder. Follow these steps to create an empty TLD file:

1. From Application Developer's menus, select **File → New → Other**.
2. In the New wizard, select **Simple → File** and click **Next**.
3. Select the Web project's **WEB-INF** folder in the folder list
4. Enter a file name ending with the **.tld** extension.
5. Click **Finish** to create the file.

In the TLD's editor, switch to the Source view and enter the following lines:

```
<?xml version="1.0" encoding="ISO-8859-1" ?>
<!DOCTYPE taglib
    PUBLIC "-//Sun Microsystems, Inc.//DTD JSP Tag Library 1.2//EN"
    "http://java.sun.com/j2ee/dtds/web-jsptaglibrary_1_2.dtd">
```

The first line defines the XML version and character encoding of the file. The second line defines the file as a tag library with the associated XML DTD file. Every TLD file begins with these two lines.

Use the <taglib> tag to define a new tag library. Each TLD may have only one <taglib> tag. The syntax of the <taglib> tag is as follows:

```
<taglib>
        <tlib-version></tlib-version>
        <jsp-version></jsp-version>
        <short-name></short-name>
        <uri></uri>
        <description></description>
</taglib>
```

The attributes in the <taglib> element are

- tlib-version: This attribute defines the tag library's version.
- jsp-version: This attribute defines the minimum required JSP version to use this tag library.
- short-name: This attribute defines a name, which may be used by a JSP authoring tool, for the tag library. This attribute is optional.
- uri: This attribute defines a Universal Resource Identifier (URI) to identify the tag library uniquely.
- description: This attribute contains text to describe the tag library.

The <taglib> element includes one or more <tag> tags. The <tag> tag defines each tag within the tag library. The syntax of the <tag> tag is as follows:

```
<tag>
       <name></name>
       <tag-class></tag-class>
       <body-content></body-content>
       <description></description>
</tag>
```

The attributes in the <tag> tag are

- name: This attribute defines the name that will be used within a JSP page to invoke the tag.
- tag-class: This attribute defines the Java class containing the code to handle the custom tag.
- tei-class: This tag extra info class attribute defines a Java class containing the code to validate the custom tag's attributes; it is required if one or more of the tag's attributes must be one of a set of allowable values.
- body-content: This attribute defines whether the custom tag has a body. A tag with a body is written as a begin tag, followed by other JSP content, followed by an end tag.
- description: This attribute defines text to describe the tag.

Additionally, if a tag allows attributes, the <tag> tag may contain one or more <attribute> tags. The syntax of the <attribute> tag is as follows:

```
<attribute>
        <name></name>
        <required></required>
</attribute>
```

The attributes of the <attribute> tag are

- name: This element defines the name of the attribute.
- required: This element defines whether the attribute is required

As an example, consider the TLD file shown in Figures 4.14a and 4.14b. This TLD file defines a set of tags to format and return the current date. There are two tags defined in the library: <simpletoday> and <attrtoday>. The <simpletoday> tag simply returns the current date as a result of calling the java.util.Date class's toString method. The <attrtoday> tag also returns the current date, but this tag allows an optional pattern attribute to format the date. For an added twist, the <attrtoday> tag also allows an optional color attribute, which may have a value only of "red", "green", or "blue".

```
<?xml version="1.0" encoding="ISO-8859-1" ?>
<!DOCTYPE taglib
    PUBLIC "-//Sun Microsystems, Inc.//DTD JSP Tag Library 1.2//EN"
   "http://java.sun.com/j2ee/dtds/web-jsptaglibrary_1_2.dtd">

<taglib>
   <tlib-version>1.0</tlib-version>
   <jsp-version>1.2</jsp-version>
   <short-name>today</short-name>
   <uri>MyTLD</uri>
   <description>Today custom tags</description>

   <tag>
      <name>simpletoday</name>
      <tag-class>com.mypackage.SimpleTodayTagHandler</tag-class>
      <body-content>empty</body-content>
      <description>Prints the current date</description>
   </tag>

   <tag>
      <name>attrtoday</name>
      <tag-class>com.mypackage.AttributeTodayTagHandler</tag-class>
      <tei-class>com.mypackage.TodayChecker</tei-class>
      <body-content>empty</body-content>
      <description>Prints the current date</description>
```

Figure 4.14a: Tag library descriptor file example.

```
<attribute>
         <name>pattern</name>
         <required>false</required>
      </attribute>

      <attribute>
         <name>color</name>
         <required>false</required>
      </attribute>
   </tag>
</taglib>
```

Figure 4.14b: Tag library descriptor file example.

Creating tag handler classes

To create a tag handler class, create a Java class in the web project's Java Source folder. The tag handler class must extend the javax.servlet.jsp.tagext.TagSupport class.

The tag handler class to support the <simpletoday> tag is shown in Figure 4.15.

```
import java.util.*;
import javax.servlet.jsp.*;
import javax.servlet.jsp.tagext.*;

public class SimpleTodayTagHandler extends TagSupport {
   public SimpleTodayTagHandler() {
   }

   public int doStartTag() throws JspException {
      try {
         JspWriter out = this.pageContext.getOut();

         Date today = new Date();

         // Write the date into the generated page
         out.print(today);
      } catch (Exception e) {
         System.err.println(e);
         throw new JspException(e.getMessage());
      }
      return SKIP_BODY;
   }

   public int doEndTag() {
      return EVAL_PAGE;
   }
}
```

Figure 4.15: Tag handler class for the <simpletoday> tag.

The tag handler classes include two methods: doStartTag and doEndTag. The application server invokes the doStartTag method when the tag's start tag is encountered and invokes the doEndTag method when the tag's end tag is encountered.

In this example the doStartTag retrieves the JspWriter for the current request, creates and instance of java.util.Date, and writes the date instance into the generated result. The output is the result of the date's toString method. The doStartTag returns SKIP_BODY because the <simpletoday> tag does not have a body. Tags with a body return EVAL_BODY_INCLUDE.

The doEndTag tag returns EVAL_PAGE to indicate to the application server to continue processing any JSP tags within the JSP file. To stop processing any remaining tags, return SKIP_PAGE.

The tag handler class to support the <attrtoday> tag is shown in Figures 4.16a and 4.16b.

```
import java.text.*;
import java.util.*;
import javax.servlet.jsp.*;
import javax.servlet.jsp.tagext.*;

public class AttributeTodayTagHandler extends TagSupport {
   private String pattern;
   private String color;

   public AttributeTodayTagHandler() {
      this.pattern = "MM/dd/yyyy";
   }

   public int doStartTag() throws JspException {
      try {
         JspWriter out = this.pageContext.getOut();

         Date today = new Date();
         SimpleDateFormat sdf = new SimpleDateFormat(this.pattern);
         String result = sdf.format(today);

         String hexColor = null;
         if (this.color != null) {
            if (this.color.equals("red")) {
               hexColor = "#FF0000";
            } else if (this.color.equals("green")) {
               hexColor = "#00FF00";
            } else if (this.color.equals("blue")) {
               hexColor = "#0000FF";
            }
```

Figure 4.16a: Tag handler class for the <attrtoday> tag.

```
                result = "<font color=\"" + hexColor + "\">" + result +
                "</font>";
            }

            out.print(result);

          } catch (Exception e) {
            System.err.println(e);
            throw new JspException(e.getMessage());
        }
        return SKIP_BODY;

    }

    public int doEndTag() {
        return EVAL_PAGE;
    }

    public String getPattern() {
        return pattern;
    }

    public void setPattern(String pattern) {
        this.pattern = pattern;
    }

    public String getColor() {
        return color;
    }

    public void setColor(String color) {
        this.color = color.toLowerCase();
    }
}
```

Figure 4.16b: Tag handler class for the <attrtoday> tag.

In this example the tag handler class includes fields for pattern and color, which match the names of the allowed tag attributes. Each tag attribute is saved within a field; during process of the tag, the application server calls the tag's (the field's) setter method to save the given attribute value. Optional tags must have a default value. In the <attrtoday> tag the pattern attribute defines a java.text.SimpleDateFormat pattern string to format the current date. If no pattern attribute is found, the default is "MM/dd/yyyy". Also, the color attribute defines the color to output the formatted date.

The doStartTag method begins like most other doStartTag methods: by retrieving the JspWriter for the current request. Then, an instance of SimpleDateFormat formats the current date according to any given pattern attribute. Next, the color of the formatted date is set based upon any given color attribute. Finally, doStartTag method writes the formatted and colored date into the generated result.

One additional class is required to support the <attrtoday> tag. Since the color attribute may have only a value of "red", "green", or "blue", code must be written to ensure that the value is one of the three allowed values. The class listed in Figure 4.17 validates the color attribute.

```
import javax.servlet.jsp.tagext.*;

public class TodayChecker extends TagExtraInfo {
   public boolean isValid(TagData data) {
      Object obj = data.getAttribute("color");

      if ((obj != null) && (obj != TagData.REQUEST_TIME_VALUE)) {
         String color = (String) obj;
         if (color.toLowerCase().equals("red") ||
             color.toLowerCase().equals("green") ||
             color.toLowerCase().equals("blue")) {
            return true;
         } else {
            return false;
         }
      } else {
         return true;
      }
   }
}
```

Figure 4.17: Tag extra info class for the <attrtoday> tag.

The TLD defines a <tei-class> attribute for the <attrtoday> tag, which means that at least one of the attributes of <attrtoday> must be validated against a set of allowable values. The application server automatically calls the tag extra info class's isValid method for each tag attribute. The isValue method returns *true* when the attribute value is valid and returns *false* when the attribute value is not valid.

In this example, the color attribute must be validated, but the pattern attribute needs no validation. The isValid method uses the getAttribute method to retrieve the given value of the color attribute. If no color value is given, isValid returns *true*. since color is an optional attribute. (If the color attribute value were required, we would change the return value for a null color value to *false*.) The main part of isValid method compares the given color attribute value against the allowed set of values and returns *true* only when one of the given values is present.

The isValid method ensures that the result of getAttribute is not TagData.REQUEST_TIME_VALUE. REQUEST_TIME_VALUE is currently not supported by J2EE.

Using custom tags

JSP files using custom tags must include a <%@taglib> tag, as in Figure 4.18.

```
<!DOCTYPE HTML PUBLIC "-//W3C//DTD HTML 4.01 Transitional//EN">
<HTML>
<HEAD>
<TITLE>Today Custom Tags</TITLE>
</HEAD>

<%@ taglib uri="/WEB-INF/MyTLD.tld" prefix="dates" %>

<BODY>
<H1>Today is <dates:simpletoday />.</H1>
<H1>Today is <dates:attrtoday pattern="MMMM d, yyyy" />.</H1>
<H1>Today is <dates:attrtoday pattern="d MMM yyyy" color="blue" />.</H1>
</BODY>
</HTML>
```

Figure 4.18: Example illustrating the use of custom tags.

Include one <%@taglib> tag for each needed TLD. In this example, the taglib's URI attribute references the TLD file in our Web project. The prefix attribute defines the tag prefix that is used within the JSP page for all custom tags defined within that tag library. The prefix allows the JSP page to distinguish among identically named custom tags, and prevents collisions and ambiguities.

There are three custom tags in this example. The first example uses <dates:simpletoday> and calls the <simpletoday> tag to display the current date. The second example uses <dates:attrtoday pattern="MMMM d, yyyy"> and calls the <attrtoday> tag to display the current date in "MMMM d, yyyy" format. The third example also uses the <attrtoday> tag. In the third example, the current date appears in "d MMM yyyy" format in the color blue. Figure 4.19 shows the output of this JSP page.

Today is Sun Feb 02 13:36:45 EST 2003.

Today is February 2, 2003.

Today is 2 Feb 2003.

Figure 4.19: Custom tag output.

Summary

JavaServer Pages make today's Web site come alive with dynamic content. JSP pages (or JSPs) play a critical role within MVC, supporting the development of complex J2EE enterprise applications. With custom tags, the enterprise developer has the ability to extend the JSP syntax to suit the needs of the business better.

Test yourself

Key terms

JavaServer Pages
comments
JSP directives
JSP page directive
JSP include directive
JSP taglib directive
JSP declarations
JSP expressions
JSP scriptlets
implicit objects
JSP actions
standard actions
tag library
JSTL
tag library descriptor
tag handler
JavaBeans

Review questions

1. Describe the phases in the lifecycle of a JSP page.
2. What method in the translated servlet is executed during every request?
3. If a JSP page is altered, is it necessary to restart the server?
4. What is the difference between the include directive and the include action?
5. Must variables appearing in a JSP page be declared in JSP declarations or JSP scriptlets before their first use?
6. Does the order of scriptlets in a JSP page matter?
7. Must scriptlet variables be initialized before their first use? What about variables in declarations?
8. What packages are automatically included in every JSP page?
9. To which classes or interfaces do the implicit objects correspond?
   a. application
   b. session
   c. request
   d. response
   e. out
   f. page
   g. pagecontext
   h. config
   i. exception
10. When are the implicit objects instantiated?
11. The <jsp:setProperty> tag has attributes called “name”, “property”, and “param”. When are each used?

CHAPTER 5

Developing EJBs—Session beans and the EJB architecture

Michael Brown

Chapter topics

- *Session beans and the EJB architecture*
- *The role of Session beans in the J2EE architecture*
- *Developing a Session bean in WebSphere*
- *The deployment descriptor*

Certification objectives

- *Design and develop Session EJBs*
- *Access container and server services from enterprise components*

In many J2EE architectures, Session Enterprise JavaBeans represent the gateway into the business model. Therefore, it is fitting that this chapter begins with a discussion of the Session EJB. This chapter will also cover the basic architecture of Enterprise JavaBeans and the development of Session beans.

Session beans and the EJB architecture

It is easy to think of J2EE components as single Java class files. In most object-oriented environments, developers are conditioned to model an application and its nouns as types, and in Java that would usually mean a new class. It is only natural, therefore, to think of J2EE components as single types, and in most cases that assumption would be correct.

As you have already learned, the content for a servlet or for a JSP is contained in a single file. In this chapter, though, you will learn about another type of component that is made up of many different new types, requires a file to configure it properly, and is managed strictly by the application server.

The Enterprise JavaBean is a J2EE component written to leverage a number of services provided by the application server. This text addresses the J2EE 1.3 specification, which includes a number of related components and services. The EJB 2.0 specification, part of this J2EE specification, defines the architecture of an EJB and the way it interacts with the rest of the application server. This new EJB specification introduces many new features to the EJB architecture and gives component developers many options for producing scalable, reusable, and robust components for Web applications.

The EJB 2.0 specification defines the architecture and behaviors for three different types of EJBs. In doing so, it establishes the behavior of an environment for the management and support of these components. Developing an Enterprise JavaBean involves producing the behavior of the bean with new code as much as understanding the operation of the environment and how that logic will be managed by an application server. Enterprise JavaBeans are not difficult to learn, but they can, like most things, take quite a bit of time to understand fully.

Of the three types of EJBs, Session beans are usually considered to be the most basic. A Session bean has very similar behavior to the single-class type with which most developers are familiar, with the addition of a list of common services. This chapter will cover Session beans, with a discussion of Entity beans and Message-Driven beans in later chapters.

To understand the types of EJBs and their uses better, it is probably a good idea to review the EJB Architecture and come up with a basic summary of EJB management and operation.

EJB architecture

To produce a J2EE component that could support the services required of an enterprise-capable application server, it was easy to utilize some of the features of existing technologies. The producers of the original EJB specification built on technologies such as component transaction managers, distribution services, and persistence mechanisms, yielding a number of components that capitalize on the strengths of those technologies and try to overcome some of their weaknesses.

For most people, it is enough to know that the EJB architecture borrows heavily from Object Management Group's (OMG) Common Object Request Broker Architecture (CORBA) and Java's Remote Method Invocation (RMI). Many of the services available to EJBs have a direct ancestor in the list of CORBA services. CORBA's naming, lifecycle management, security, persistence, and distribution structures have all made their way into the existing EJB architecture. One of the major strengths (and, in some cases, biggest headaches) offered by CORBA was its language neutrality. Two components developed in two different languages could work together.

CORBA was also a distributed architecture; two (or more) run-time environments could cooperate to produce the full application. This type of cooperation required some degree of networking and data marshaling. Fortunately, Object Request Brokers (ORBs) handled most of the work, but, unfortunately, the developer still had to produce interface definitions. To produce these interface definitions, the developer needed another language for describing interfaces, which was labeled, interestingly enough, the Interface Definition Language (IDL). Using the IDL one could define a component's relationship with its ORB (which establishes the interface it shares with its clients). Dealing with all the possibilities of data marshaling between different languages makes it easy to see why some people would prefer an architecture that is language-specific.

Java's RMI has some strengths of its own. It is very easy to work with, is Java-centric, and supports communication between JVMs. Unfortunately, though, it doesn't offer many of the services that one would expect to have in an enterprise-services environment.

Imagine, though, an architecture that supports the best features of RMI and CORBA and tries to eliminate any weaknesses that they may have. Combining the services of CORBA and the Java focus of RMI would remove the language independence (and the need for IDL) but maintain the services. This combination would eliminate the data-marshaling headache and enable a much more powerful structure. It would run inside a JVM and would allow communication between instances that are remote (or co-located). It also has the additional benefit of being able to work with prior technologies, just in case. This combination is the basic idea behind Enterprise JavaBeans (EJBs), a service-rich, Java-centric component for the enterprise.

So, EJBs are distributed, and they capitalize on services present in the application server. But how do they work? What does one have to develop to produce an EJB?

To begin to answer those questions, it is important to understand the EJB architecture. How is it that a method call from a client can produce the correct synchronous behavior on an object in a separate runtime environment? What if that operation is transactional? What about security implications?

The EJB architecture, at it most basic, is much like the remote control of a television set. Television control technology has made some tremendous advances since the earliest days of broadcasting. There was a point, many years ago, when one would actually have to move to the television and tune it manually. The television provided the function, receiving the information present in a given area of the broadcast spectrum, but it was the television operator's job to tune to the correct frequency in the spectrum-stated in terms of cycles per second. The logic for adjustment and good function was present in the user's head. By bumping, tapping, or twisting the knob, the user was responsible for managing the state of the television. Hopefully, the user's modifications would leave it in a functional state.

Soon afterwards, the TV was given more capability to control its state. The unfortunate TV user still had to approach the unit physically, and the electronics (the actual mechanics of the reception) didn't change much, but now the TV set had some small measure of logic that enabled a viewer to select a particular channel, and the set would then translate that selection into the corresponding frequency setting. Imagine this use of logic as a new layer of functioning around the old TV set. A request from the user was handled, but logic in the set modified or controlled the real result. For example, suppose the TV was tuned to channel 13 and the user issued the command to increment the channel number (by turning the channel selector knob one more step). The TV set, "aware" that channel 13 was the highest possible channel number at that time, would translate the channel number to 2 (the lowest possible) and thence to the corresponding frequency (55.25 MHz).The television set's state was closely managed. Unfortunately, one still had to approach the television set to manipulate it.

More time passed, and the television saw yet another feature added. The remote control was invented. This wonderful device allowed a user to modify the television set's state without actually touching it! With this device, the user could choose from a list of functions present on an interface (a keypad), and then see his commands passed to the television. Usually, this operation resulted in the modification of the state of the unit. The user did not need to be aware of the way the signal was passed from remote to set, or how the message was structured, only that the desired result was achieved. The user had to trust that the television would handle the request correctly or that the interface he possessed would be enough to produce the desired result.

Explanation of architecture

The EJB Architecture is very similar to this television example. As developers, we must provide a way for our clients to make requests to an object in a remote, managed environment. Our task is a bit more complex than this example in some ways, and much simpler in others. The EJBs that we develop will be written to a strict specification. This specification defines the structure that we must cooperate with in order to receive the benefits of all of the available services.

First, remember that all J2EE components, including EJBs, will run in some sort of container. This container will handle requests, lifecycle, security, and (if capable) transactions for this EJB. It is easy to see, therefore, that any component must have a well-defined relationship with its container. EJBs will be managed by an EJB container. By developing components around the capabilities of the EJB container, developers can produce types that can be assembled to form an EJB component.

The anchor for this functionality in the EJB container is the bean class. Every EJB will have a bean class, which will implement a certain interface (depending on bean type) and will also implement any business logic required of the EJB. From our previous example, this bean class represents the television's electronics. It is the real reason the television exists: to display a picture. The container, therefore, is the layer of logic around this functionality, ensuring that any request is executed in the correct context and produces a reliable state. Our clients will never touch this bean class directly; instead, they will always act through the container. The two interface types are shown in Figure 5.1.

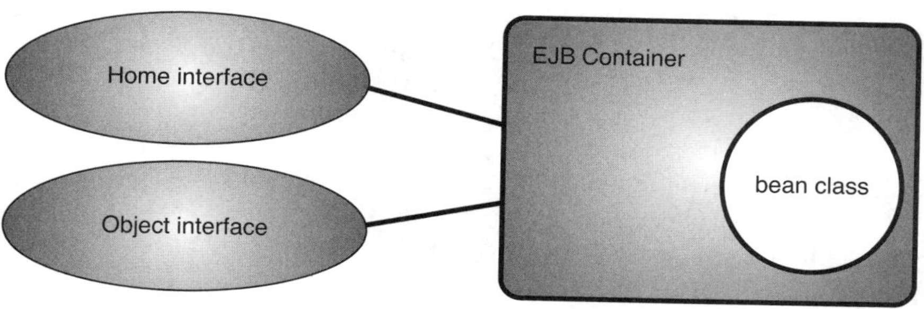

Figure 5.1: The EJB interfaces.

While the container and the bean class define most of the EJB's behavior, it is critical that the bean's clients be able to make contact and request the execution of certain behavior. This is the job of the *object interface*. A client's call on an object interface method should result in the execution of business logic on the "real" component in the container (an instance of the bean class). This object interface is specific to an EJB in the container: To work with the logic or state of a particular EJB, you must have its object interface.

Under some circumstances, an EJB can be a client to itself. In such situations, an EJB must access itself through the container in order to preserve transaction semantics. Therefore, an EJB should not invoke business methods from its own public interface, referring to itself with the Java keyword "this". Rather, it should use the EJBObject (or EJBLocalObject) interface. Furthermore, an EJB should use the EJBContext (of which SessionContext is a subtype) to obtain a reference to itself, either for use as a parameter or as a return value, rather than using "this". We will discuss these interfaces in further detail later in the chapter. The key concept to grasp at this point is that the developer must ensure that the container is involved when accessing the business methods of an EJB.

There is another interface, called the *home interface*, that allows a different level of control over the EJBs in the container. While it is unlikely that someone would have multiple TVs (of the same or different types) in any single room, and even more doubtful that they could cause TVs to be created and destroyed as the situation demands, this is exactly the case with beans in the EJB container. Because EJBs can be created and destroyed, just like their interfaces, the EJB architecture must provide a means of manipulating some of a bean's lifecycle.

To enable this management behavior, the EJB specification defines the home interface. Using this type of interface, the client can create or remove a bean or even find a bean whose state matches a certain set of criteria.

The EJB 2.0 specification defines these two interface types, home and object, as *client views* of an EJB. The home interface will see most of its use in managing some of the lifecycle issues of a type of EJB (think of it as housekeeping), and the object interface will expose the logic of a single EJB object.

Because there are two subtypes of each of these interfaces, an EJB can have as many as four different interfaces. These two subtypes are *remote* and *local*. A remote interface is used by a client accessing an EJB from outside the JVM that is managing the bean class. This type of access imposes a certain set of restrictions on the use of remote interfaces. They will pass by value, and they can accept only parameters that are serializable.

EJB 2.0 also defines local interfaces. Local interfaces are used by clients that share a JVM with an EJB, and are similar in practice to using the controls on the front of a television set rather than the remote control. Because of their proximity, there are some benefits to local interfaces: They do not involve network traffic, they pass by reference, and they allow the association of EJBs.

This basic structure required for an EJB doesn't seem like much, considering the features they promise. There are many benefits to the structured environment defined for EJBs, one of which is its simplicity. The environment allows the developer to focus on business logic, leveraging many services present in the application server. Small sections of code in an EJB can have big results because of the services available in the application server.

What about the remote interfaces? With the interfaces present in one container and the bean class present in another, how can a method call on the client side be passed to the bean class? How are results passed back?

The Proxy pattern and its relation to the architecture

If two Java classes implement the same interface, they will certainly share a common list of methods. Those methods may be implemented differently in each class, but the two classes will share a certain set (or subset) of methods. The fact that different types can appear to be similar is one of the most useful features of object-oriented programming.

If a developer were to define an interface with a single method, such as doSomething(), and then implement that interface in two different classes, where the doSomething() of one class didn't do anything more than call the doSomething() of the other class, this would be a simple implementation of the Proxy pattern.

The Proxy pattern is nothing new. It has been used in many architectures. It is a very useful pattern if, for whatever reason, a developer would like to allow a client to perform some task or modify some object but is unable to provide the client with a direct link to do so.

In Figure 5.2, a client could acquire the Proxy object and, by making a method call, actually call a method on the Subject object. The Proxy code does not contain the logic to perform the real operation, but it does contain the logic necessary to make a method call on an object that *does* implement the true logic (the Subject).

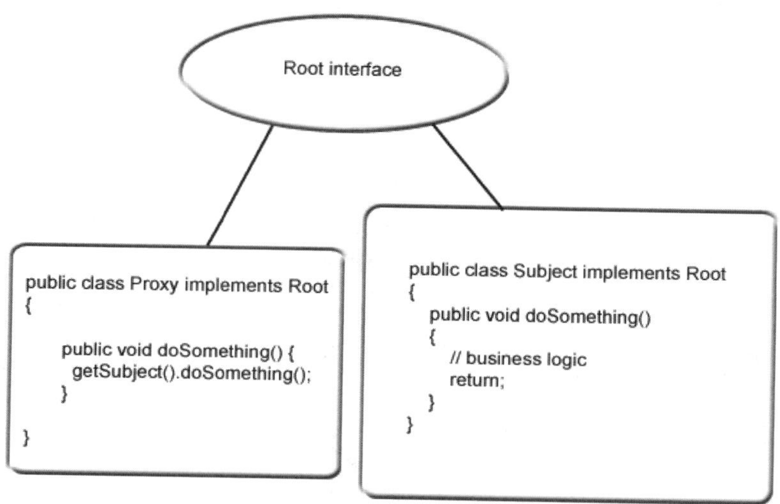

Figure 5.2: The Proxy pattern.

You can be sure that each object, the Proxy and the Subject, have similar interfaces, because they implement the same methods (i.e., they implement the same interface type). The important point to remember, though, is that the behavior of a method call on each type is very different, even though the interface is shared.

The basic behavior present in the EJB architecture is that the interfaces that developers define are used as the root types for a Proxy/Subject pair that allows a client to exercise logic present in the container. These Proxy/Subject pairs are generated by the container, because they contain the networking code (among other things) required for a method call by an EJB client to be properly propagated to the corresponding method on the bean class.

Both interface types (local and remote) implement this Proxy pattern. The remote interfaces are similar in concept to the stub/tie paradigm from other architectures (RMI and CORBA, for example). Even though it isn't immediately clear, the local interfaces also implement this pattern. To support transactions and workload management, a client will never be able to work with a bean class directly.

To go much further with EJB development, it is important to begin talking about the specifics of EJBs. Therefore, it is time to learn about one of the three types of Enterprise Beans and how to assemble one.

Session beans and their types

Session beans are components written to provide a transactional, distributed, and managed resource that does not support any persistence. These properties do not mean that Session beans will not have state, only that the state of the Session bean will not be persisted by the container. Moreover, the Session bean's lifecycle does not address the possibility of its changing state. For this reason, Session beans see quite a bit of use as task processors or flow controllers. Other EJB types are much more suited to representing or managing the state of an object.

Most simple discussions of EJBs label Session beans as "verbs" or "processors". With the basic EJB knowledge covered to this point in the chapter, the definition can go a bit further. Session beans will have a bean class and the interfaces necessary for clients to make calls on some of the methods found there. The EJB container will handle all lifecycle management, security, distribution, and operational details ofthe EJB.

A good way to think of a Session bean is that it represents the capability to perform a task. The actual state of objects before or after the task will be managed elsewhere, and the Session bean will modify these objects to reflect the results of this task, or session.

A drive-up bank teller is a good analogy of a Session object. The bank teller really only represents the capability to perform banking functions. The fact that he may have children, pets, blue hair, even a name, doesn't really matter. You pass the parameters of your request with all necessary information into the magic pneumatic tube machine, receive your results, and go on your way.

There are two types of Session beans, stateless and stateful, the difference being how the container manages the bean's state with respect to a client. In both cases, the Session bean can have instance state, or state that any client of that bean would have access to. The big difference is actually in the management provided by the container.

Stateless Session beans

Stateless Session beans are the most common (and most simple) of the beans, which is probably the reason why most texts begin with this type of EJB. Stateless Session beans are managed by the container as if they have no state. Their bean class can still declare variables, but the container assumes that any instance of a bean of this type is the same as any other. Because of this, it is very easy to share stateless Session beans, and the container is free to pass any method call on a bean of this type to any instance of the bean class (unless that instance is involved in a transaction). Consequently, any modification of this instance's state by any client may be seen by any other client.

This behavior is called *instance pooling* and allows the EJB container to serve multiple requests, and multiple clients, with a small pool of bean instances, in an effort to make more efficient use of resources.

Thus, a drive-up bank teller can be likened to a stateless Session bean. For the purpose of handling a request, any individual bank teller is probably as capable as any other. Additionally, even though each operator has some degree of state, the state really isn't important in the context of the task. As a client, I will supply all necessary information for my request when I actually make the request.

Stateful Session beans

The behavior for a stateful Session bean is fundamentally different from that of a stateless one. A stateful Session bean is managed in such a way that its state, even though it is not persisted, is assumed to be client-specific. From the point of view of a client to a stateful Session bean, the bean appears to "remember" information from previous interactions, similar to a conversation. For this reason, clients do not usually share stateful Session beans. Each client will appear to have its own instance.

Instead of a drive-up bank teller, imagine a phone-based teller. The capability to handle bank transactions is still the same,. You would probably have a conversation with this teller that allowed him to gather the information required for a particular operation. For the purpose (and extent) of this operation, that teller is your teller. No one else can use him at that moment.

The course of the conversation would establish some unique state that only you and the teller share, which is analogous to a stateful Session bean.

Of course, because this one stateful Session bean is unique (its state is for this client's use alone), there is an issue with management. This unique instance cannot be used by any other client. Therefore, it cannot be pooled. In effect, your personal bank teller will sit idly waiting for your next request. Without proper management, this would be remarkably inefficient. WebSphere will handle this management, with a process that allows it to switch the state of these stateful objects in and out, by managing the bean's lifecycle. You will learn more about this later.

The role of Session beans in the J2EE architecture

Session beans occupy a special role in the development of Web applications. In any application with EJBs, a Session bean usually serves as a gateway, or process handler, for the logic of the application (the model). In this way, Session beans can encapsulate actions with the business logic, serve as transaction boundaries, and even group operations for certain client types.

The fact that there are two types of Session beans gives developers additional flexibility in designing Web applications that capitalize on the strengths of the EJB architecture. There are cases in which one type of Session bean is more suited to the current application than another.

To better understand the role that Session beans play in the architecture, it is important to understand how the application server will manage their behavior and how the different pieces of a Session bean come together to form the entire component.

Enterprise JavaBeans have a lifecycle that differs considerably from the lifecycle of a simple Java class. The EJB container will be responsible for establishing the required class instances that represent the structure of the EJB. In the case of Session beans, the container has some flexibility in the way that it will manage client requests.

Figure 5.3 shows that there are two basic states in the lifecycle of a stateless Session bean: Does Not Exist and Pooled. The EJB container will choose to add bean instances to the pool if the current number of instances in the pool is not sufficient for the current workload.

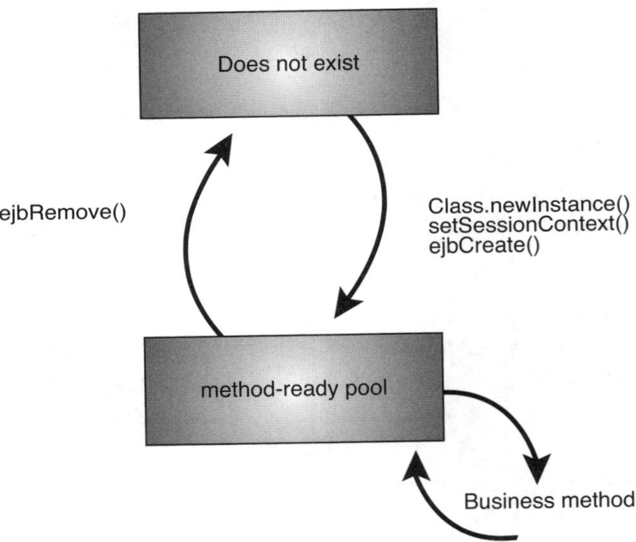

Figure 5.3: The stateless Session bean lifecycle.

The stateful Session bean state diagram (Figure 5.4) differs from the stateless Session bean in one key detail: The stateful Session bean can be *passivated*. In cases where the bean is not being used (no current client request), the EJB container can passivate the current state of the EJB to some temporary store. This capability is not the same as real persistence, because this state record is temporary and will be lost if the application server is restarted. The temporary store is simply an area for the application server to serialize state information, freeing resources for active components. In WebSphere, this temporary store is a directory, set up as part of the administration of the application server.

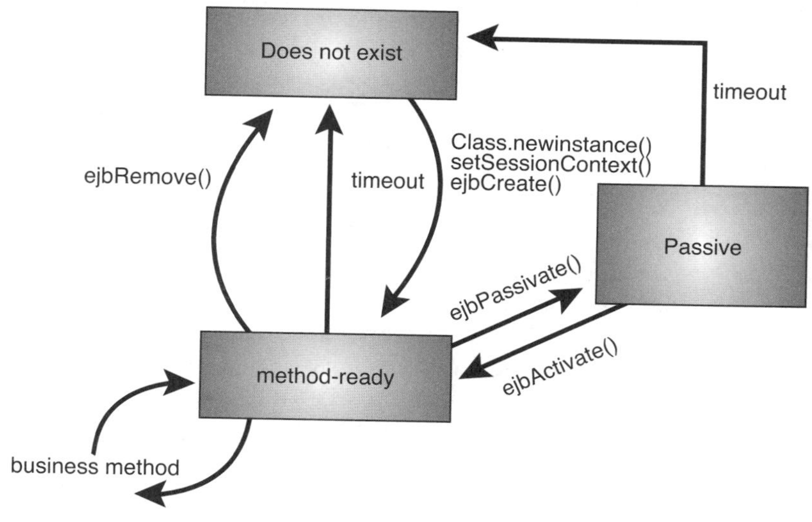

Figure 5.4: Stateful Session bean lifecycle.

Of the three possible states (two for stateless Session beans), Does Not Exist is the simplest. In this state, the Session bean is not available for service because the bean does not exist. The application server can move an EJB from this state with operations to create a new bean class instance, tie it with the container (establish its context), and finally, initialize it for operation (call the ejbCreate() method).

At this point, the instance is pooled and is available for service. As clients make method calls to stateless Session beans, those calls will be "matched" to an available instance. Thus, it is possible for a single bean to serve the requests of many clients. For stateful Session beans, remember that the client will have an interface to a particular instance, and the container is responsible for making it available.

The operation of stateless Session beans can lead to a bit of confusion. One of the methods on the home interface is called create(). You might expect that a call to the create method would, indeed, create a new instance of a Session bean for any client and return an object reference for it. The truth is that if the container can find an instance of the stateless Session bean that already exists, it may not perform the create process but will return an object reference to the existing bean instead. WebSphere goes one step further and may not actually create an instance until the first call on the object interface.

This pooling behavior is an example of the lifecycle services offered by the EJB container. As developers, we will produce the pieces necessary for the component to function, knowing that the EJB container is responsible for managing the instances and contexts as it sees fit. For some developers, learning to give up this control is a difficult process. To learn to rely on the EJB container for these management issues, though, is a big step toward using EJBs to their full capability.

This pooling behavior is different for stateful Session beans. Because each instance is unique (or at least treated as unique), these instances are not pooled in the same fashion. WebSphere will manage a pool of stateful instances, passivating and then activating them as necessary to serve client requests, in effect, "switching" the client's state in and out of instances as required by requests. This passivation (and activation) involves serialization of the object to a directory location defined on the application server. To some, this would seem to be a means of persistence (some people actually call this "lightweight persistence"), but because this information is not available after a server restart, this does not qualify as a means of durable storage, and it should not be relied on for data that should be permanently stored.

In addition, because of the way that these beans are managed, the object references to stateful Session beans are unique and represent the only channel available to a particular stateful instance. It is important that clients to a stateful Session bean store the object reference to their bean instance in some location that is available in the future.

Why passivate? Passivation allows WebSphere to manage a small pool of available instances. It can switch the state for many clients in and out of just a few real stateful instances. This is a much more efficient use of resources than maintaining an instance for every previous client.

Developing a Session bean in WebSphere

At this point, it may be difficult to see how to develop a Session bean. There are many items that must come together to produce a functional EJB component. Of these, the bean class is the center point; it will represent the logic of the bean and give the container the interface necessary to manage any instance's state.

The interfaces will provide the means for clients to access the functionality present in that bean class. For that reason, many of the methods present in the bean class will also be present in an interface.

To produce an Enterprise JavaBean in the WebSphere Studio family of products, one must first create an enterprise application project and an Enterprise JavaBean project. With this step completed, Enterprise JavaBean development usually begins with the Enterprise Bean Creation wizard, shown in Figure 5.5.

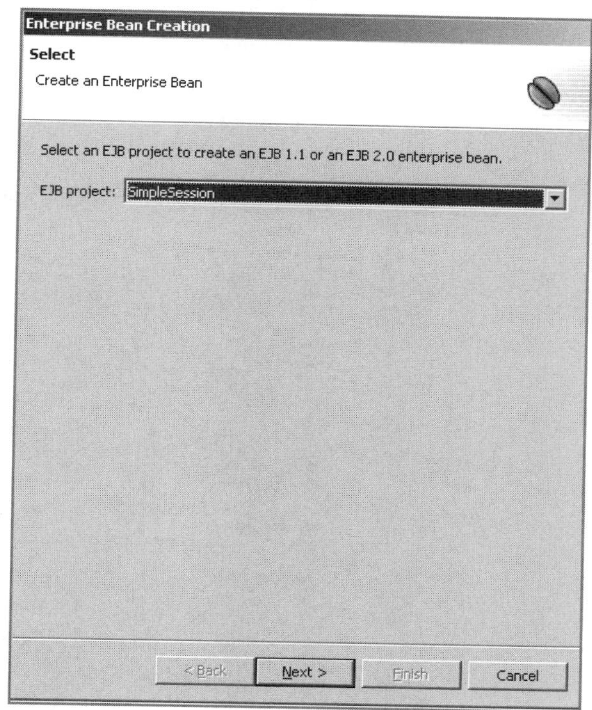

Figure 5.5: The first page of the Enterprise Bean Creation wizard.

The first step of Enterprise Bean creation is the selection of an EJB Project. In this case, the new EJB will be added to the **SimpleSession** EJB Project.

The next screenshot, Figure 5.6, shows the options for the types of Enterprise JavaBeans, with **Session bean** selected. There is also a text box to indicate the name of the finished component, which, in this case, is **CounterEJB**. The Source folder box allows a developer to specify the location of this bean's code in the project folder; **ejbModule** is the default. You can enter a new folder name, which WebSphere Studio will create if it does not exist, or use the Browse . . . button to navigate to an existing folder. Finally, notice that this EJB will be added to a new Java package, **simple.book**. Again, there is a Browse . . . button, allowing you to browse to an existing package; otherwise, you can enter a package name, and if that package does not exist, it will be created.

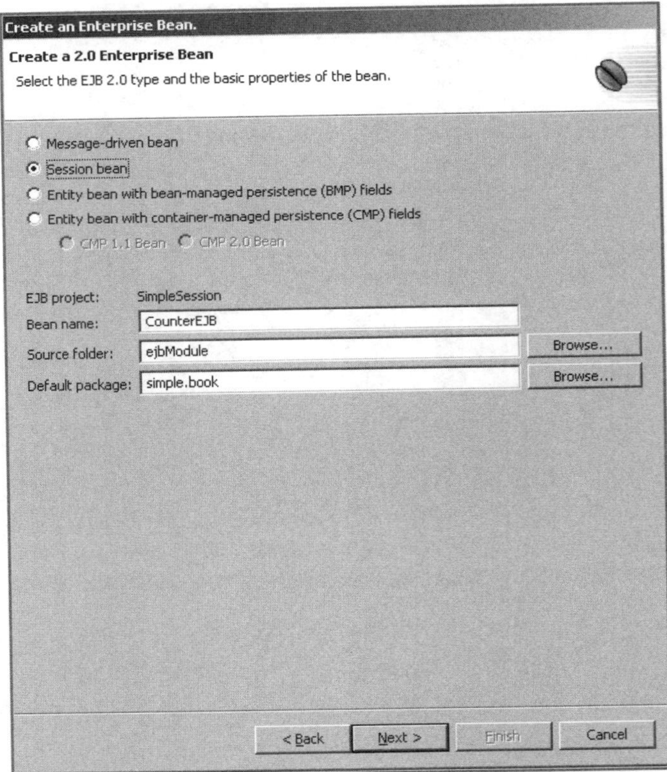

Figure 5.6: The second page of the Enterprise Bean Creation wizard.

Click the **Next** button to proceed to the section of the wizard that deals with this component's interfaces, as shown in Figure 5.7. The session type and transaction type are selected using radio buttons; in this case, **Stateless** for a stateless Session bean and **Container** for container-managed transactions. (Transactions will be discussed in a later chapter.) The entries included for the bean class name and JNDI binding name are automatically generated based on the EJB name and package name given on the previous page of the wizard.

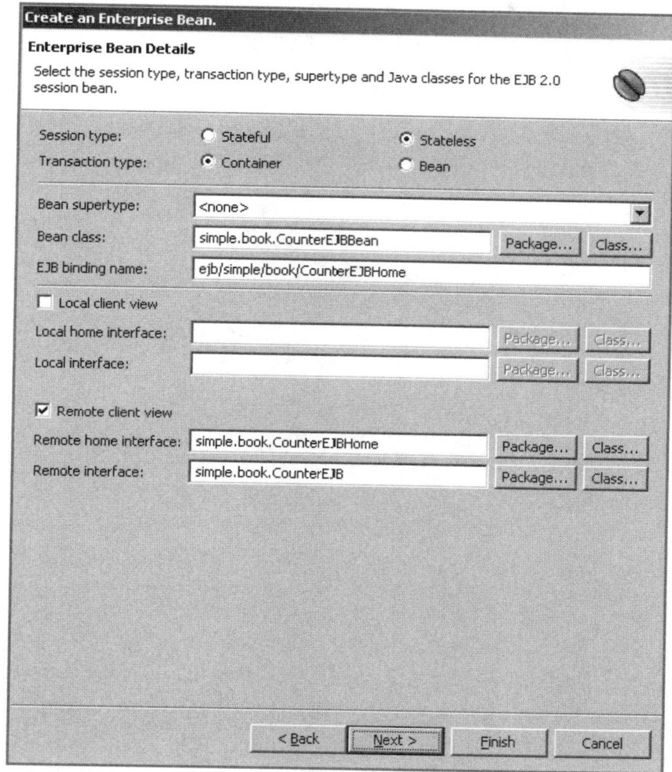

Figure 5.7: The third page of the Enterprise Bean Creation wizard, creating an EJB.

The next set of options determines which of the interfaces (client views) will be produced. Either or both of the checkboxes can be selected. It is rare for an EJB to be produced with both interfaces. Usually, one is sufficient. In the case of Session beans, the Remote interface is the most common. Usually employed as a façade, the Session bean represents the gateway to the model, so most method calls will have to come from remote clients.

The final page of the wizard allows a developer to add interfaces to the remote or local object interfaces. Doing this forces the creation and promotion of methods to these interfaces, which can be a useful tool in structured environments.

When the **Finish** button is clicked, the tool will create the bean class and any selected interfaces. At this point, one can edit this code to produce the desired results. The new components are shown in Figure 5.8. These files can be opened for editing by double-clicking on them in the J2EE Hierarchy view.

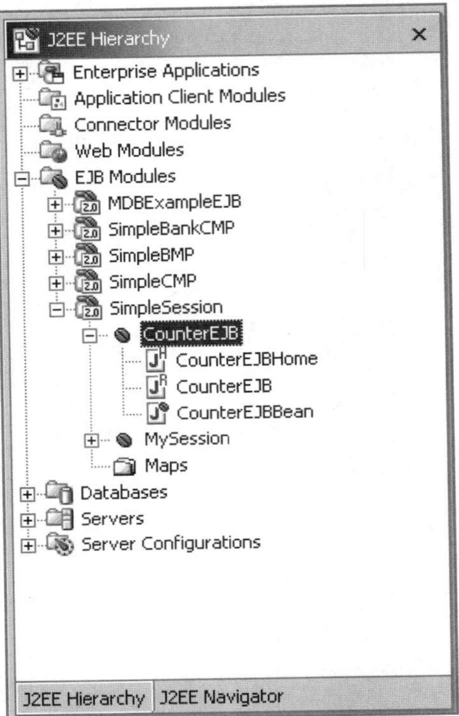

Figure 5.8: The generated components, CounterEJB.

Session bean: A bean class

The bean class is a type that represents the encapsulation of the functionality for all of the component-specific behavior of the bean. Because this bean class will be closely managed by a container, it must be written to support the container's operations. To ensure this behavior, there is a Java interface that this bean class must implement: javax.ejb.SessionBean. The methods that this Session bean interface declares are all methods that this bean class must support. The methods and their signatures are listed in the code in Figure 5.9.

```
abstract public interface javax.ejb.SessionBean implements
        javax.ejb.EnterpriseBean
{

        abstract public void setSessionContext(SessionContext ctx)
            throws javax.ejb.EJBException, java.rmi.RemoteException;

        abstract public void ejbRemove()
            throws javax.ejb.EJBException, java.rmi.RemoteException;

        abstract public void ejbActivate()
            throws javax.ejb.EJBException, java.rmi.RemoteException;

        abstract public void ejbPassivate()
            throws javax.ejb.EJBException, java.rmi.RemoteException;

}
```

Figure 5.9: javax.ejbSessionBean interface.

This interface defines most of the methods necessary for a Session bean to function. If you consider the lifecycle of a Session bean, it should be clear which state transition each of these methods is responsible for supporting. The methods, commonly called the lifecycle methods, represent notifications from the container that a certain lifecycle event is about to occur. Clients will not call these methods, and the methods are present to allow the bean developer to supply logic to be performed *in addition to* the state management performed by the container.

An example of such a need would be the process of passivation. The container is expected to manage the process of serializing all non-transient data and storing it in the proper location. If a bean were to have an instance variable that was not serializable, the passsivation process could not store the full state of the instance. If, though, a developer wrote a method that took that instance field and modified it so that it was serializable, or at least had the information necessary to reproduce it, this bean could be safely passivated. To do this, one could write an ejbPassivate method that takes the state of some unserializable instance variable, such as an array, and encodes it (tokenizes it) so that its state is represented in a String variable. Naturally, this would mean that the ejbActivate method would be written to take the tokenized String and reproduce the array.

Remember, though, that the lifecycles of the stateful and stateless Session beans differ. The fact that some lifecycle methods are available in the SessionBean interface, but may not be used, should not be confusing; if a particular Session bean is marked as stateless, the container will never passivate (or activate) this bean, so these methods will never be called.

It would seem as if there were a kind of method missing in this interface. It would certainly seem that creation is a lifecycle event. Why isn't there a method on this interface for creation?

Because of the differences in lifecycle and management, stateful and stateless Session beans have different patterns for creation methods.

Any instance of a stateless Session bean is, in the eyes of the container, identical to any other instance of that type. It would be counter to that logic, therefore, if there were methods presented to the client (and written in the bean class) that would allow the creation of a stateless Session bean with anything other than some standard state. For this reason, stateless Session beans will have one, and only one, create method, and that method will not have any arguments. Lifecycle methods for EJBs will appear in the bean class with a prefix of "ejb". If we stick to this idea, the create method signature will look like this:

```
public void ejbCreate() throws javax.ejb.CreateException
```

The body of this method could then be added with the code necessary to initialize an instance of this bean.

We will expose this method to clients by placing it in either home interface as create, with the same list of parameters (none).

Create methods for stateful Session beans are different. Stateful sessions are required to have at least one method to support creation, but this create method can accept any number of arguments. It is also possible for a stateful Session bean to have many create methods, each with its own set of arguments. These additional create methods will follow a similar pattern but can be named to express their true function more closely. The name must begin with ejbCreate but can continue with text to indicate its use, similar to the following code:

```
public void ejbCreateAtValue(int init) throws javax.ejb.CreateException;
```

The existence of create methods must be enforced as a development rule, but it cannot be enforced with the features of inheritance. It would not be possible to add the full list of possible create methods to the SessionBean interface, an infinite set of possibilities. Neither would it be efficient to define two different interfaces for each type of Session bean.

We can now develop a bean class. The first example will be a very simple example of a stateless Session bean.

The Session bean listed in Figure 5.10 is implemented to serve as a counter. Beyond the basics of lifecycle, it will support operations to increment, query, or reset its value. The bean will always begin with a count of 0, and will add 1 to that count whenever its increment() method is called. The reset and query methods will also work as expected, resetting the count to 0 or returning the present value of the counter.

```
public class CounterEJBBean implements javax.ejb.SessionBean
{
    private javax.ejb.SessionContext ctx;
    private int counter;

    public javax.ejb.SessionContext getSessionContext(){
        return ctx; }

    public void setSessionContext(SessionContext thisCtx){
        ctx = thisCtx; }

    public void ejbActivate() {}
    public void ejbPassivate() {}
    public void ejbRemove() {}

    public void ejbCreate() throws javax.ejb.CreateException {
        counter = 0;
    }

    public int getCount(){
        return counter;
    }

    public void reset(){
        counter = 0;
    }

    public int increment(){
        return (counter++);
    }

}
```

Figure 5.10: The Counter Bean class.

At this point, there is no code difference between this bean as a stateless component and as a stateful one. The bean class for either case would be the same. It is useful to note, though, that a stateful Session bean could introduce another create method, allowing the client to initialize an instance with a different counter value, as seen in Figure 5.11.

```
public void ejbCreate(int initValue) throws javax.ejb.CreateException {
    counter = initValue;
}
public void ejbCreateAtValue(int init) throws javax.ejb.CreateException{
    counter = init;
}
```

Figure 5.11: Sample create methods for a stateful counter.

Since stateful Session beans have a different lifecycle than stateless Session beans do, how would the behavior of this bean differ if it were set up as a stateful bean instead of a stateless one? Where does one go to make the change, if the same bean class can be used for a stateful and a stateless Session bean?

To answer the first question, remember that stateless Session beans are pooled and shared between clients. Each client works with an instance that is moved from the pool to service the request and returned to the pool upon completion. The container assumes that any instance in the pool is identical to any other, and method calls will be passed to any bean class instance in the pool.

With a stateful Session bean, the container is required to match a client's method call to an instance that matches the state at the completion of the last call from that object interface. Therefore, 10 increment() calls from 10 clients on a container managing a stateful example of this EJB will result in up to 10 instances of this bean, any of which will respond to getCount() with the value of 1.

If this container is managing this bean as a stateless component, however, 10 calls will results in a pool of instances whose sum (of their counter values) will equal 10. In this example, there could be three instances with values of any combination that reflect the 10 calls.

To answer the second question, you'll have to learn more about interfaces and deployment descriptors.

Interfaces

This chapter has mentioned interfaces many times up to this point. The number of different interfaces can be confusing: interfaces to define type behavior, interfaces to expose functionality, interfaces to allow bean management, and interfaces to allow client contact. We will now look in detail at the interfaces clients will have available to work with Session beans.

Remember, there are two types of interfaces: home and object. Each of those interfaces will have local and remote subtypes. We will deal with these interfaces now.

Home interfaces

The home interface is the first EJB interface most clients will access. It allows the client some control over the lifecycle of an EJB. For Session beans, these interfaces will be fairly lightweight, with only a few methods. These methods will usually be whatever create methods are available for this bean type.

There will be some type dependence, because the application server is going to create and manage these home interfaces. For this reason, the home interface must extend javax.ejb.EJBHome. With this information, it should be fairly easy to write a home interface.

```
public interface CounterEJBHome extends javax.ejb.EJBHome
{
    public CounterEJB create()
        throws javax.ejb.CreateException, java.rmi.RemoteException;

/* optional, stateful session bean only */
    public CounterEJB create(int initValue)
        throws javax.ejb.CreateException, java.rmi.RemoteException;

    public CounterEJB createAtValue(int init)
        throws javax.ejb.CreateException, java.rmi.RemoteException;
}
```

Figure 5.12: The CounterEJB home interface.

The code found in Figure 5.12 is an example of a remote home interface. A client to the EJB container can use this remote interface to work with or manipulate the state of an EJB. This remote home interface will have one or two methods matched to the ejbCreate(. . .) methods present on the bean class to allow a client to contact the EJB container and create a relationship with a CounterEJB Session bean. A call to the create() method on a home interface will be passed to the ejbCreate method with a matching set of arguments.

Remember, the names of the stateful create methods, present to establish the bean at some initial state, must begin with *create* but can contain a suffix that more accurately represents their specific purposes.

Because this is an interface, the developer will not be able to implement any of these methods here. The container (or development toolset) will use this interface as the root interface for a Proxy/Subject relationship similar to the one described earlier in this chapter.

Notice the exceptions present in the method declarations. Our bean class defined the true behavior of these create methods but did not declare the same list of exceptions, because the container-generated code (the Proxy and Subject) will be handling network traffic and must be able to notify the client of network problems (among other things), using the RemoteException.

A client can use a remote interface from almost any location. The types generated from this interface will have the logic necessary to invoke methods across the network, passing any information required.

Local interfaces behave differently. They will function only if the client is located in the same JVM as the desired instance. For this reason, they can be much more efficient than remote interfaces. A local interface does not involve any network traffic, will pass by reference instead of passing by value, and does not have some of the data-marshaling limitations of remote interfaces.

The code for local interfaces will have a few key differences from the code for remote interfaces. The code for a local interface might look like this:

```
public interface CounterEJBLocalHome extends javax.ejb.EJBLocalHome
{
    public CounterEJBLocal create() throws javax.ejb.CreateException;
}
```

This interface is much simpler. There is no need for the RemoteException, because this interface does not support network traffic. Additionally, instead of a reference to a remote object interface, a call to create will return a local object interface.

Object interfaces

The object interface is the client's gateway to the logic of a Session bean. In the CounterEJB example, the real function of the component is in its function as a counter: the methods that allow one to increment, reset, and query the counter. These methods will be placed on the object interfaces (remote, local, or both).

During development, it is left to the developer to determine which of the bean's business methods should be added to the object interface. It is usually a simple procedure. In WebSphere Studio Application Developer one *promotes* a method to a desired interface. Promotion is equivalent to adding the correct method signature to the desired interface. The increment method of the CounterEJB cannot be added to the home interface. In fact, only a subset of methods with the "ejb" prefix can be promoted to the home interface. Remember, the client cannot control lifecycle, so ejbPassivate is not meant to be exposed.

To promote a method, it is selected in the outline view. A context menu, available by right-clicking on the method signature, will supply the options necessary to promote a method to the EJB's interfaces. This is shown in Figure 5.13.

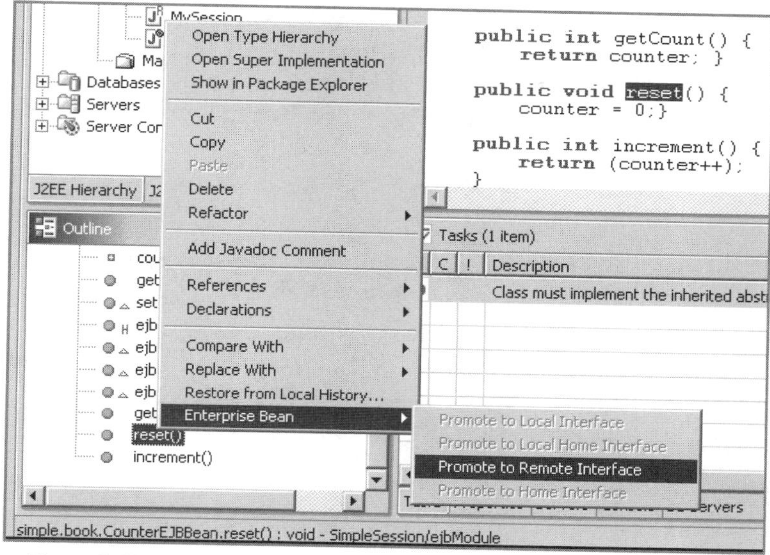

Figure 5.13: Promotion, using the Outline View.

With the business methods promoted, the remote object interface would look something like the code in Figure 5.14.

```
public interface CounterEJB extends javax.ejb.EJBObject{
    public int getCounter() throws javax.rmi.RemoteException;
    public int increment() throws javax.rmi.RemoteException;
    public void reset() throws javax.rmi.RemoteException;
}
```

Figure 5.14: The CounterEJB remote object interface.

The corresponding local interface is shown in Figure 5.15.

```
public interface CounterEJBLocal extends javax.ejb.EJBLocalObject{
    public int getCounter();
    public int increment();
    public void reset();
}
```

Figure 5.15: CounterEJB's local object interface.

Using either of these interfaces, a client would have the ability to work with the logic of the CounterEJB.

In summary, a Session EJB begins as a few pieces of developer-written code: two (or four) interfaces and a bean class. This code is then augmented with the addition of tool-generated structure, Proxies and Subjects (called stubs and ties) for each interface, and a collection of other types to enable the Session bean to cooperate with the EJB Container and any required services. The final structure is similar to that represented in Figure 5.16. This figure should not indicate that one must produce both local and remote interfaces. Developers will usually produce one or the other, and with Session beans it is most common to produce a remote interface.

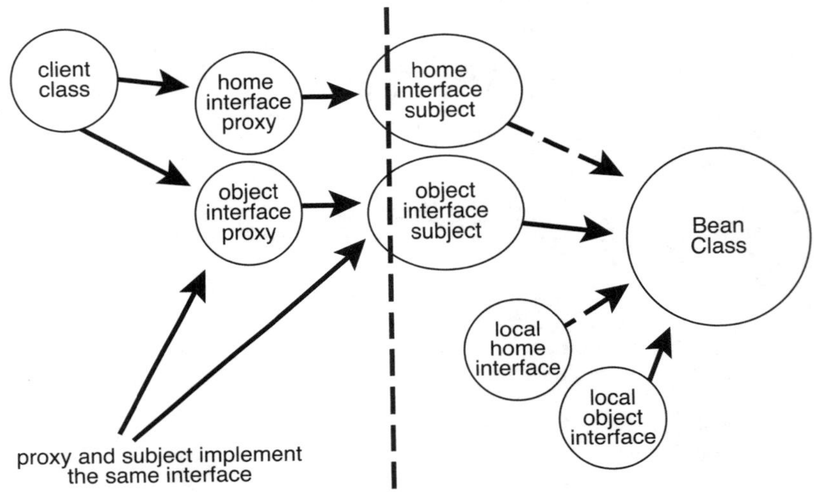

Figure 5.16: The full EJB interface architecture.

At this point, this code does not represent everything necessary for the component to function. Indeed, the container can't really hope to generate the balance of its code without some additional information.

The deployment descriptor

A deployment descriptor is a file, organized into the J2EE file hierarchy, that is present in every Web module, EJB module, and Enterprise Application. Each module will have its own descriptor, and the sum of the settings in all of the descriptors for an enterprise application will define the application's ultimate behavior. The deployment descriptor for an EJB module will contain all of the information necessary for an EJB (or group of EJBs) to be generated and loaded.

A very simple descriptor follows, with the settings required for the CounterEJB. Most of this information is self-explanatory. For example, it will define the type names of the interfaces and bean class. There may be more here than meets the eye, or some things that have not yet been addressed, so don't be shocked to see something new.

Deployment descriptors are written in XML, which is tag-based, and are written to a certain tag structure, defined in a DTD (Document Type Definition). Figure 5.17 contains an example of an EJB module's deployment descriptor.

```
<?xml version="1.0" encoding="UTF-8"?>
<!DOCTYPE ejb-jar PUBLIC "-//Sun Microsystems, Inc.//DTD Enterprise
     JavaBeans 2.0//EN" http://java.sun.com/dtd/ejb-jar_2_0.dtd>
<ejb-jar id="ejb-jar_ID">
    <display-name>BookExamplesEJB</display-name>
    <enterprise-beans>
        <session id="CounterEJB">
            <ejb-name>CounterEJB</ejb-name>
            <home>ejb.CounterEJBHome</home>
            <remote>ejb.CounterEJB</remote>
            <local-home>ejb.CounterEJBLocalHome</local-home>
            <local>ejb.CounterEJBLocal</local>
            <ejb-class>ejb.CounterEJBBean</ejb-class>
            <session-type>Stateless</session-type>
            <transaction-type>Container</transaction-type>
        </session>
    </enterprise-beans>
</ejb-jar>
```

Figure 5.17: A simple deployment descriptor.

This deployment descriptor defines a single Session EJB, called CounterEJB. The CounterEJB is included in an EJB module named BookExamplesEJB. Most of the information included in a Session bean's deployment descriptor is involved with naming the interfaces and types required to construct the component. At the end of the list of attributes for this bean, there is an entry for session-type. This entry will be stateless or stateful, depending on the behavior desired.

The final entry is transaction-type. The possible values here are container and bean, based on the desired transactional behavior. Transactions will be covered in a later chapter, but it is important to be aware that the changes made to the deployment descriptor will allow the modification of bean behavior.

WebSphere Studio has an editor for deployment descriptors. To open it, select an EJB Module, and then, using the Open With option, select the Deployment Descriptor editor. The Deployment Descriptor editor is shown in Figure 5.18. There are six tabs included in the editor, with the Source tab selected, showing the source of the deployment descriptor.

EJB Deployment Descriptor

```
<?xml version="1.0" encoding="UTF-8"?>
<!DOCTYPE ejb-jar PUBLIC "-//Sun Microsystems, Inc.//DTD Enterprise
<ejb-jar id="ejb-jar_ID">
    <display-name>SimpleSession</display-name>
    <enterprise-beans>
        <session id="MySession">
            <ejb-name>MySession</ejb-name>
            <home>simple.session.MySessionHome</home>
            <remote>simple.session.MySession</remote>
            <ejb-class>simple.session.MySessionBean</ejb-class>
            <session-type>Stateful</session-type>
            <transaction-type>Container</transaction-type>
        </session>
        <session id="CounterEJB">
            <ejb-name>CounterEJB</ejb-name>
            <home>simple.book.CounterEJBHome</home>
            <remote>simple.book.CounterEJB</remote>
            <ejb-class>simple.book.CounterEJBBean</ejb-class>
            <session-type>Stateless</session-type>
            <transaction-type>Container</transaction-type>
        </session>
    </enterprise-beans>
</ejb-jar>
```

Overview | Beans | Assembly Descriptor | References | Access | Source

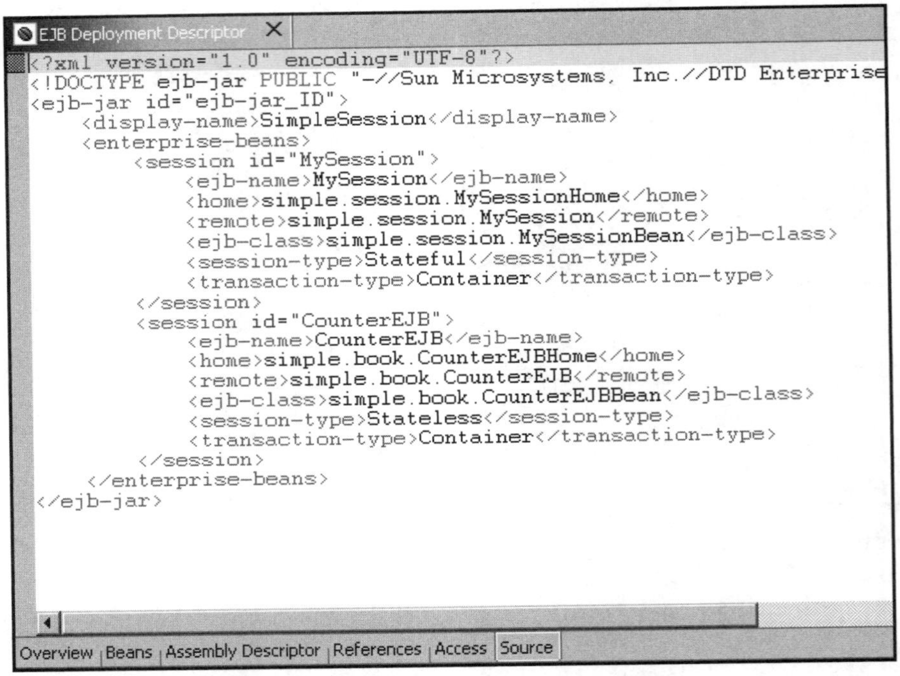

Figure 5.18: The Deployment Descriptor editor.

Using this editor, one can change the many settings contained in a deployment descriptor. Of these, the most common are security settings and transactions. The Deployment Descriptor editor will be covered in more detail in a later chapter.

Summary

In addition to providing a gateway to the model, as a façade, the Session bean also represents an excellent boundary for transaction processing, or a distributed interface for application logic.

Development of a Session bean requires the development of a bean class, at least one set of interfaces (local or remote), and a deployment descriptor. The bean class will contain the logic required for the bean to perform its responsibilities, and the bean's clients will access that logic through the use of the bean's interfaces.

Session beans can be either stateless or stateful. This setting is defined in the deployment descriptor and will determine the behavior of a given bean with respect to its clients. If a bean is marked as stateful, the rules for development change, and the Session bean can have multiple create methods, used to establish a working state for a particular client.

The WebSphere Studio suite of tools will assist in the development of these components. Using some of the wizards and editors present in WebSphere Studio Application Developer, component developers can accelerate the development process, allowing them to focus on business logic, instead of the basic architecture.

Test yourself

Key terms

Enterprise JavaBeans
stateless Session beans
stateful Session beans
home interface
remote interface
local interface
object interface
EJB container
EJB component
CORBA
resource pooling
lifecycle management

Review questions

1. Can stateless Session EJBs have attributes?
2. An application contains four EJB classes. Which one should be a stateless Session bean?
   a. TravelAgent
   b. CreditCardValidator
   c. Cruise
   d. Cabin
3. Which of these should be a stateful Session bean?
   a. TravelAgent
   b. CreditCardValidator
   c. Cruise
   d. Cabin
4. Why are stateless Session beans more efficient than stateful Session beans?
5. What happens when Session beans are passivated and then activated?

6. A Session bean requires a home interface, a remote interface, and a bean class. What interface must the bean class implement? What methods are in that interface?
7. As a related question, if the Session bean class implements all the methods listed above, it will compile but not work. What additional method must be implemented, but does not appear in the interface?
8. Most Session beans (even stateless ones) keep an attribute of type SessionContext. Why? What is the SessionContext used for?
9. Assume you already have a stateless Session bean implemented, and the bean class has attributes. You decide to change the type of bean from stateless to stateful. What changes need to be made?
10. Notice that though the bean class has methods that correspond to those in the home and remote (or local) interfaces, the bean class does not actually implement those interfaces. Where are they implemented?

CHAPTER 6

Developing entity EJBs with WebSphere Studio

Mike Brown

Chapter topics

- *Entity beans*
- *Bean-Managed Persistence*
- *Container-Managed Persistence*
- *WebSphere specifics for Entity beans*
- *Finding CMP beans using EJB Query Language*
- *Relationships between Entity beans*

Certification objectives

- *Design and develop entity EJBs*
- *Access container and server services from enterprise components*
- *Implement mechanisms for efficient intercomponent calls*

Entity EJBs represent a persistent layer in J2EE applications. This chapter will cover the basics of creating and configuring the different types of Entity beans in the WebSphere suite of tools.

Entity beans

Entity EJBs represent a persistent layer in J2EE applications. Like the Session beans discussed in Chapter 5, Entity beans have a bean class and at least one of the sets of interfaces (local and or remote), consisting of home and component views. Entity beans add a feature, called the Primary Key Class, which will be discussed later in this chapter. Their role in J2EE applications is significantly different from that of the Session beans, though.

Role of Entity beans in J2EE applications

Entity beans are meant to represent the persistent features of J2EE applications. They allow a developer to produce an object-oriented view of some persistence structure. Usually, this persistence will be managed by a relational database.

Entity beans will be added to provide a layer that abstracts the use of persistence and presents a more logical interface to the application. Other components in the application will be able to rely on this layer for persistence services. The EJB container in the Application Server will manage when the EJB should be stored and when its state should be loaded, among other things. Once again, as developers, we will provide the business logic, leveraging off of available services, and the container will determine when to exercise that logic, based on the specification.

Because the overwhelming majority of all persistent stores are relational databases, the examples and terminology in this chapter will assume that data is being stored in one of these relational databases. It is also assumed that the reader has a basic understanding of the fundamentals of database function: records, keys, tables, columns, and so forth.

Lifecycle of Entity beans

The lifecycle of an Entity bean is governed by the responsibility it holds in J2EE applications. This object type is required to be robust and to support concurrent access. For that reason the Entity bean's state cycle is focused on allowing the container to manage its instances as efficiently and effectively as possible.

Entity beans will be closely associated with common database operations. Using method calls present on the interfaces, clients will be able to create, remove, and update records in the database. One of the most common operations, though, is finding a record present in the database and associating that state with an EJB. This is called a *query,* and it is as fundamental as creation in the use of Entity beans. The creation of an Entity bean will require the development of logic to support each of these operations.

States of Entity beans (lifecycle states)

Entity beans have three states: Does Not Exist, Pooled, and Ready. A diagram of these states can be seen in Figure 6.1.

At the point before an instance exists, it has no state (Does Not Exist). The container creates an instance by instantiating a bean class and assigning it an entity context. Because entity beans can be pooled, the container will manage when instances are created and destroyed.

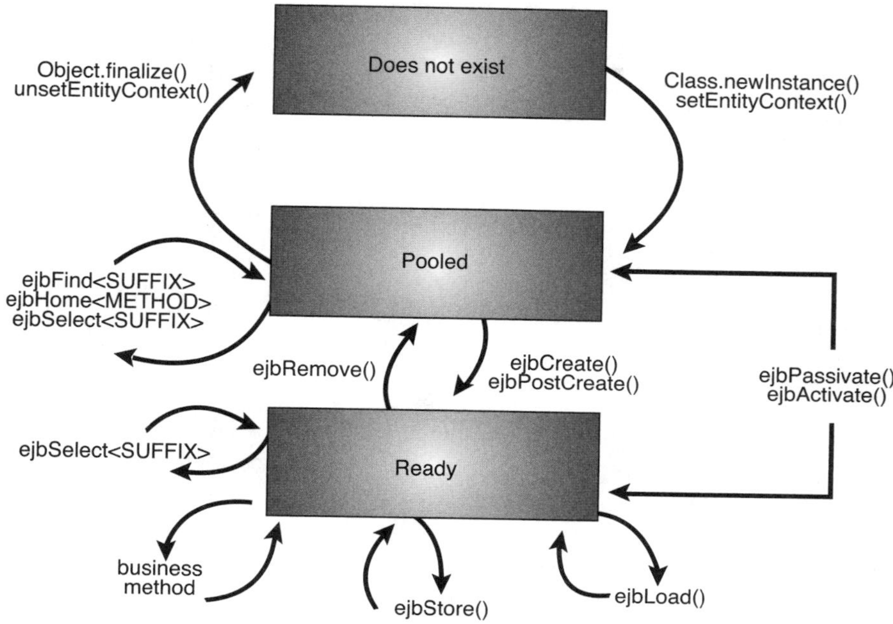

Figure 6.1: Life cycle of an Entity bean.

Newly created instances are Pooled. They are not yet associated with any particular state (no information has been loaded from the database). A Pooled instance is a "plain" instance and a candidate for use by a client. As clients make requests that would require a bean instance, such as the creation of a record, instances are moved from this Pooled state. Instances in the pool can also be used to service requests that do not require any state. Because query operations do not require a bean to have state (data), but are actually a search for a bean (or beans) with a certain state, these Pooled instances are often used to provide an instance necessary for a query to be performed.

The third state is the Ready state. In this state, the bean can accept client requests for business methods. A Ready instance is associated with an EJB object and represents a particular state.

An Entity bean can make the transition from the Pooled state to the Ready state as a result of one of three operations. As a result of a create call, the container chooses an available instance out of the pool, creates an EJB Object interface, then calls the create lifecycle methods present in the bean instance. This instance is associated with a primary key object and, as a result, is available for service.

The second means of transition is based on queries. If a successful query is performed, an instance is pulled from the pool for every record that matches the search. As in a create, it is bound to an EJB Object interface and is activated when a client makes a method call.

The third process that moves beans from the pool and to the Ready state is activation. The container can passivate ready beans to the pool and then activate a pooled bean when it is next requested. Activation and passivation are complementary processes used by the EJB container for managing its working set of bean instances.

Management of Entity bean state and pooling

This state management behavior allows the container to appear to be managing many more instances than is actually the case. In the current Web environment, the duration of a request or operation is usually short compared to the "travel" time or the time required for a response to leave the container, return to the client (the real client, i.e., a browser), and have the next request issued. To have all of these specific object instances sitting idly, waiting for the next request from a particular client, would be very inefficient.

To combat this inefficiency, the EJB container is allowed the freedom to manage its working set of instances. By switching instances between the Pooled and Ready states, a container can appear to have many more instances under control than it actually possesses. When requests are received for a particular entity, the container can switch an instance to the Ready state that represents the current state of the object of interest. In this way, a small pool of instances can serve a large number of clients. Although it would seem that a client's object reference is bound to a particular instance, the truth is that by using instance switching, the object reference is really just bound to a particular state, or even a particular record (a particular object identity). The instance is just an object-oriented layer for viewing or manipulating that state.

Types of Entity beans

There are two types of Entity beans in the EJB 2.0 specification: the Container-Managed Persistence (CMP) Entity bean and the Bean-Managed Persistence (BMP) Entity bean. Each has a role in the architecture; the two types enable the developer to make the trade between deploy-time flexibility and ease of use (CMPs) and the design-time flexibility that only a hand-coded persistence object can offer (BMP).

CMP

CMPs are named such because of the involvement of the container in this object's persistence. The EJB container generates the code necessary to persist this object's state. In When creating a version 2.0 Enterprise Bean using WebSphere, you designate the fields that should be persisted by the container; at deploy time (when the code is generated), the container produces code that persists those features to the correct datastore. The CMP feature allows more flexibility once the bean is generated, and it certainly reduces the amount of work required to produce the bean, but CMPs will only support databases for which a JDBC 2.0 driver is available.

There are some advantages that make CMPs very popular, and there are some features that are supported only with CMPs. Because the EJB Container is involved in the generation of this object's persistence code, CMPs can participate in associations with other CMPs and have quite a bit of support available for database queries and finders.

BMP

The BMP is the entity bean for the do-it-yourself type. Although the container will still manage lifecycle, the production of all persistence code is left to the developer. In the lifecycle management methods of a BMP's bean class, developers will have to add the code necessary to access the desired datastore and manage this object's state correctly.

It can become quite a bit of work, but for flexibility of design at development time it is hard to beat a BMP. Often, in complicated situations, BMPs are the only solution.

Even though BMPs are often the more complex of the entity beans, it is helpful to see the structure necessary for a BMP to function before seeing the development of a CMP. Doing so can make it much easier to understand the container's responsibility when it comes time to develop a CMP.

Bean-Managed Persistence

The BMP is the most flexible of the two entity bean types, because the developer must produce all of the code necessary for persistence. This allows quite a bit of variation (at design time) in the persistence features of a BMP. On the other hand, a CMP can be much more flexible once development is finished, as we will learn later in this chapter. The persistence operations of any entity bean go beyond the basic requirements of loading or storing an instance's state, they are also involved in the way that the container will manage multiple instances of a type and find records that represent instances.

Entity beans (BMP or CMP) are much more than objects that represent state. These objects are used to *manage* state. They carry the state of an object through the operations to modify it, and they ensure that it maintains its integrity along the way. Entity beans, fundamentally, represent an object-oriented view of the database, with a nearly one-to-one relationship between an entity bean instance and a record (or set of records) in a database. The beans that we develop, then, will be required to support the expected operations—storing and loading the fields present in the columns of databases—but they will also be required to support the operations required by the container in managing that data when it is present in the EJB Container.

Diagram of Entity bean structure

Remember from Chapter 5 the basic layout of the EJB architecture, shown in Figure 6.2.

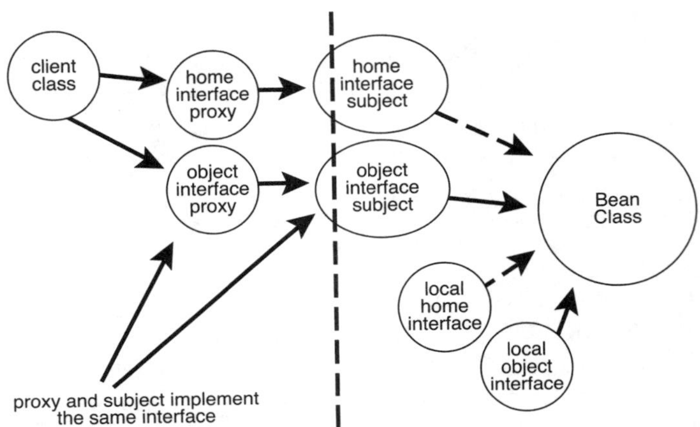

Figure 6.2: EJB runtime execution model.

Entity beans can be developed to support both local and remote interfaces. In most cases, though, Entity beans are developed with only local interfaces because of the advantages offered by that interface type. We will produce interfaces to allow our clients to access the logic present in the bean class.

The bean class

The bean class for a BMP represents the lifecycle defined for an entity bean. The lifecycle methods are present to support the operations required by the container as it manages an object of this type. The bean class will implement the javax.ejb.EntityBean interface, which declares the methods shown in Figure 6.3.

The context methods are similar to the methods present in a Session bean. They enable a container to bind or unbind a specific instance to the container during the course of execution. You will also see the ejbPassivate and ejbActivate methods. Although Entity beans are not passivated or activated as stateful Session beans are (there is no reason to, because the container can use the database), the ejbActivate and ejbPassivate methods are present to allow the container to notify an instance that it is being moved into or out of the instance pool. This may be useful if this bean has a connection to some transient

```
public interface javax.ejb.EntityBean implements javax.ejb.EnterpriseBean {

    void setEntityContext(EntityContext ctx);

    void unsetEntityContext();

    void ejbRemove() throws javax.ejb.RemoveException;

    void ejbActivate();
    void ejbPassivate();

    void ejbLoad();

    void ejbStore();
}
```

Figure 6.3: The EntityBean contract.

resource. When the bean is moved out of the Ready state and back to the pool, its ejb-Passivate method is called, notifying the bean that it should close that connection. Then, as it is moved from the pool and back into the Ready state, the ejbActivate callback enables it to re-establish that connection.

While it is often acceptable not to populate some callback methods, some methods are critical to a BMP's function. The three other methods in this interface (ejbLoad, ejb-Store, and ejbRemove) are present to address some of the persistence requirements of the bean. They are implemented on the bean class to allow the container to load a record, update the state of a record, and remove a record, respectively.

The code placed in these methods will contain the logic necessary to acquire a connection to the datastore and send the proper commands. In SQL terms, the ejbLoad method will implement a SELECT, the ejbStore method will implement an UPDATE, and the ejbRemove method will implement a DELETE.

All that remains for basic persistence is the insertion of a new record. We will use the create methods for this purpose. Create methods will be defined on the bean class and promoted to the home interface. Because this is a stateful object, it is expected that create methods will exist that initialize some of the state of any new instance. Again, as with stateful Session beans, these create methods can be named to represent their function better.

With Entity beans, though, another method must be defined: the ejbPostCreate() method. This method makes up the third of the set of methods required by the EJB specification for the creation of EJBs. It has to do with the lifecycle of Entity beans. Some operations may be necessary in the creation of a bean that are not possible until the bean is fully loaded and set up. For this reason, the ejbPostCreate is called as the final step in creation and allows the developer to access these methods. An example is the use of the EJB context to acquire a bean's object interface. Until the bean is fully established (when the ejbPostCreate method is called), there is no way for a bean to acquire its own reference.

Each of these three methods (the create method on the home interface and the two methods defined in the bean class: ejbCreate and ejbPostCreate) is matched using its parameter list and the suffix following its corresponding name. The code in Figure 6.4 represents the different methods more clearly.

```
public class PersonBMP implements javax.ejb.EntityBean
{
…
// On the bean class:
    public PersonBMPKey ejbCreate() throws javax.ejb.CreateException {…}
    public void ejbPostCreate() throws javax.ejb.CreateException{…}
// a more complex example, still on the bean class
    public PersonBMPKey ejbCreateWithName(String name) throws
        javax.ejb.CreateException {…}
    public void ejbPostCreateWithName(String name) throws
        javax.ejb.CreateException {…}

}
```

Figure 6.4: Examples of creation methods defined for the BMP.

This bean is created through the corresponding local home interface as shown in Figure 6.5.

```
public interface PersonBMPLocalHome extends javax.ejb.EJBLocalHome{
…
    public PersonBMPLocal create() throws javax.ejb.CreateException;
    public PersonBMPLocal createWithName(String name) throws
        javax.ejb.CreateException;
}
```

Figure 6.5: Corresponding creation methods declared in the BMP local home interface.

Using our knowledge at this point, we can begin to write a full BMP bean class. The code in Figures 6.6a and 6.6b is an example of part of a BMP bean that manages the state of a person.

```
public class PersonBMP implements javax.ejb.EntityBean
{
    public int id;
    public String name;
    public int bday;

    public EntityContext ctx;

    public PersonBMPKey ejbCreateWithName(String name)
        throws CreateException
    {
        this.id = getNewID();
        this.name = name;
        Connection conn = null;

        PreparedStatement ps = null;
        try{
            conn = this.getConnection();
            ps = conn.prepareStatement(
                "insert into PERSON (id, name, bday) values (?,?,?)");
            ps.setInt(1,this.id);
            ps.setString(2,this.name);
            ps.setInt(3,0);
            if (ps.executeUpdate() != 1) {
                throw new CreateException("Failed to create new Person");
            }
            return new PersonEJBKey(id);
        }
        catch (SQLException sqle) {
            throw new EJBException(sqle);
        }

        finally {
            try {
                if (ps != null) ps.close();
                if (conn != null) conn.close();
            }
            catch (SQLException sqle) {
                sqle.printStackTrace();
            }
        }
    }
```

Figure 6.6a: Managing the state of a BMP bean.

```
public void ejbPostCreateWithName(String name){
}

public void ejbLoad() {
    PersonBMPKey primaryKey = (PersonBMPKey)(ctx.getPrimaryKey());
    Connection conn = null;
    PreparedStatement ps = null;
    ResultSet rs = null;

    try{
        conn = this.getConnection();
        ps = conn.prepareStatement(
            "select id, name, bday from person where id=?");
        ps.setInt(1,primaryKey.getId());

        rs = ps.executeQuery();
        if (rs.next()){
            id = primaryKey.getId();
            name = rs.getString("name");
            bday = rs.getInt("bday");
        } else {
            throw new EJBException();
        }
    }
    catch (SQLException sqle) {
        throw new EJBException (sqle);
    }
    finally {
        try {
            if (rs != null) rs.close();
            if (ps != null) ps.close();
            if (conn != null) conn.close();
        } catch (SQLException sqle) {
            sqle.printStackTrace();
        }
    }
}

...

public String getName(){
    return this.name;
}

public int ejbHomeCalculateSalary() {
    // add code to support the operation of finding
    // the total salary expense of the company.
}
```

Figure 6.6b: Managing the state of a BMP bean.

This is a basic example of a BMP bean. Most of the code should be familiar if you've ever worked with JDBC™. Each of the persistence-related methods contains the code required for that stage of the bean's lifecycle. Many methods have been left out of this example for the sake of simplicity.

You should notice that business methods are added to the bean class, as are queries and, new to EJB 2.0, home methods, which will be discussed shortly.

Business methods will be added to the bean class and then promoted to the Object interface. These methods are usually associated with operations that are specific to a certain record or a certain state. Common examples are accessors and mutators for acquiring or modifying the state of a particular instance (also called getters and setters).

There is another set of methods that we will add to the bean class of a BMP. The finder query methods are used to find the EJBs (records) that match a certain criteria. One method that is required is ejbFindByPrimaryKey(). This method, present in the bean class and also on the home interface (as findByPrimaryKey), provides the logic necessary to find an EJB that has a given primary key. The container uses this method to search for a record with the given primary key and pulls an instance from the pool to contain the record's state. It is possible, and often desirable, to declare other finders. In a BMP, the developer is left to write these methods. The method must begin with ejbFind, and the method body contains the Java and SQL code necessary for the query to execute.

Finders can return a single object reference or a collection of object references that match the given query. Figure 6.7 shows an example of a finder method for the PersonBMP.

```
public Collection ejbFindByName (String name) throws FinderException {
    Connection conn = null;
    PreparedStatement ps = null;
    ResultSet rs = null;

    try{
        conn = this.getConnection();
        ps = conn.prepareStatement("select id from person where name = ?");
        ps.setString(1,name);
        rs = ps.executeQuery();

        Vector keys = new Vector();
        while (rs.next()) {
            keys.addElement(rs.getObject("id"));
        }
        return keys;
    }
    catch (SQLException sqle) {
        throw new EJBException (sqle);
    }
    finally {
        // close connection, prepared statement and resultset
    }
}
```

Figure 6.7: A custom finder method defined for a BMP.

This finder has a matching method on the home interface, it will look like this:

```
public Collection findByName(String name) throws FinderException;
```

The final set of methods consists of the home methods, which are new to EJB 2.0. They declare methods that will be added to the home interface. These methods can be used for logic that does not involve a specific instance of a bean but, instead, focuses on the entire set of this type. They must begin with ejbHome and have a matching home method in the home interface. A very simple example would be a method that finds the sum of the salaries of a group of employees. Home methods are declared with the prefix of ejbHome and are then promoted to the home interface. Home methods can be very useful for working with the information present across an entire Entity bean type.

This is the signature for a home method in the bean class:

```
public int ejbHomeGetPersonCount() {}
```

It has a matching method in the home interface:

```
public int getPersonCount()
```

The primary key class

The primary key class is a Java representation of a record's primary key. The EJB container uses the information present in this object as a means of comparing and managing EJB instances and their various states. In this sense, the primary key class will be used as an object identifier.

Figure 6.8 is an example of a primary key class:

```
public class PersonBMPKey implements java.io.Serializable {
    int id;

    public PersonBMPKey(int id){this.id = id};

    public int getId() {return id};

    public boolean equals(java.lang.Object otherKey) {
        // used by container to compare 2 keys
        if (otherKey instanceof PersonBMPKey) {
            PersonBMPKey o= (PersonBMPKey) otherKey;
            return (this.id.equals(o.id));
    }

    public int hashCode() {
        // used to calculate a hash for this key
       return (super.hashcode());
    }
}
```

Figure 6.8: Example of a primary key class for a BMP.

The container uses this primary key class to track the identity of the instances it is managing. Using this class, the container can manage each of the instances in its pool and associate them with records as needed.

For the Entity bean this primary key class is usually written, but that is not required. The primary key class can be an existing class that contains the information necessary for this object's primary key. Good examples are some of the "wrapper" classes present in Java.

If your Entity bean has a primary key that is an int, you can use the Integer class as a primary key class.

Entity bean interfaces

Entity beans, like Session beans, have client interfaces. Those interfaces represent the "view" that any client has of the bean's lifecycle and logic. Home interfaces for Entity beans are usually much more feature-rich than home interfaces for Session beans, because most processes that involve Entity beans are concerned with creating or finding a particular entity, and many options must be supported. In most architectures, the component interface will contain a set of getters and setters and not much else, but Entity beans can be written with very rich sets of methods here, as well.

The home interface

To work with an Entity bean (remember, think of it as working with an object-oriented view of the database), it is important to support many stateful operations. A client may desire to create a new record, find an existing record, or remove an existing record. To perform these tasks, we will need different methods available on the home interface of any Entity bean.

As with Session beans, Entity bean home interfaces will implement the javax.ejb.EJBHome or javax.ejb.EJBLocalHome interface.

It is possible to have many create methods in any home interface. Each create method's signature must match the ejbCreate and ejbPostCreate set present in the bean class. To match, all three must have the same parameter list. An example of the code required, and its location, is given in Figure 6.9.

```
// On the bean class
public PersonEJBKey ejbCreate (int SSN) throws CreateException {…}
public void ejbPostCreate (int SSN){…}

// On the home interface
public PersonEJBKey create (int SSN) throws CreateException;
```

Figure 6.9: Corresponding creation methods in the bean and the home interface.

This requirement could make it difficult to support operations that require similar arguments, for example, to create a record using an SSN and phone number. If this phone number were also an int, it could be confusing (which comes first?) and this signature, create (int, int) would be "taken". No other set of create methods (for example, a create method that uses a phone number and employee number) could use that signature.

For this reason, EJB 2.0 supports create methods that can be written with suffixes. It is possible to supply an optional suffix to the create signature to make the operation's purpose more clear. In the example shown in Figure 6.10, a suffix has been added to make it clear that the argument will create a new bean using the supplied SSN.

```
// On the bean class
public PersonBMPKey ejbCreateWithSSN (int SSN) throws CreateException {…}
public void ejbPostCreateWithSSN (int SSN) {…}

// On the home interface
public PersonBMPKey createWithSSN (int SSN) throws CreateException;
```

Figure 6.10: Improved names for creation methods in the bean and the home interface.

This suffix can be nearly anything (subject to the requirements Java places on method names); the only requirement is that it matches across the "triad" represented by the ejbCreate() and ejbPostCreate() on the bean class and the create() on the home interface.

Clearly, this capability allows the development of create methods that are much more understandable, but it can also eliminate method naming collisions and make it possible to support many options that may not have been possible before—for example, createWithSSNAndPhone(int, int) and createWithPhoneAndEmpID(int,int).

Finders

A very useful feature, also present in the home interface, is the ability to support finders. In some applications it is common to create new records, but in others it is much more common to retrieve an existing record. The purpose of a finder is to support queries that return an EJB or Collection of EJBs that match a certain criteria.

In BMPs, the developer adds the logic for the finder to the bean class and adds a corresponding signature to the home interface.

One finder method is required; it is present on the bean class as ejbFindByPrimaryKey() and present on the home interface as findByPrimaryKey(). Finders, like other home-interface methods, are associated based on parameter list and suffix. In the case of finders, this will mean that all finders will begin with find or ejbFind, depending on their location.

The ejbFindByPrimaryKey method is required on the bean class, because the container uses it to support many of its operations. It is not required that the findByPrimaryKey method be present on the home interface. It may not be desirable that our clients be able to find using primary keys.

Other finder methods can be added to the bean class. In a BMP, this method will contain all of the logic necessary for this finder to function. It can return either a single EJB Object reference or a collection of the EJB Object references that meet the criteria present in the method. It is also acceptable that these finders accept multiple arguments. Basically, anything is allowed, as long as it results in a valid return.

The code in Figure 6.11 is an example of a finder method written on the bean class. This finder will return the key of the customer who has the supplied phone number.

```
public PersonEJBKey ejbFindByPhone (int phone) throws FinderException
{
    int keyValue;
    Connection conn = this.getConnection();
    String stmtText = "SELECT ID FROM PERSON WHERE PHONE="+phone;
    try {
        PreparedStatement pStmt = conn.prepareStatement (stmtText);
        ResultSet rs = pStmt.executeQuery();

        if (rs.next()){
            keyValue = rs.getString("ID");
            return new PersonEJBKey(keyValue);
        }
        else {
            throw new ObjectNotFoundException();
        }
    }
    catch (SQLException sqlE)
    {
        throw new EJBException(sqlE);
    }
    finally
    {
        // place code here for cleanup
        // close the connection, statements, etc.
    }
}
```

Figure 6.11: Custom finder method.

The corresponding method on the home interface will look like this.

```
public PersonEJBKey findByPhone (int phone) throws FinderException;
```

Home methods

Home methods, new to EJB 2.0, allow the development of "general" methods for use in gathering or returning information for a type of entity bean. The example given previously, returning the sum of salaries for all employees, is a fairly simple one. To implement it, one would write an ejbHomeCalculateSalary() method on the bean class and promote it to the home interface.

The remove method

Remember that the lifecycle methods present on the home interface are for finding, creating, or removing the records associated with this type of entity bean, and they really don't have much to do with the instances of the actual bean. The remove method is a perfect example. Remove is used to remove the record associated with the bean instance from the database. The bean class has a method, ejbRemove(), that can be promoted to the home interface, where it allows the client to remove a record from the database.

The object interface

The object interface allows a client to access the stateful logic of an Entity bean. After finding or creating a specific Entity bean, the client can use the object interface to access the state this bean represents. This logic may be as simple as accessors or mutators, but it could also perform complex business tasks.

Local and remote interfaces

Each of the interface types, home and component, can be developed as a local or remote interface. The local interfaces have the advantage that they are specific to the container and must be used by a client that is co-located with the bean. These calls can be much more efficient, because they do not involve network overhead. In addition, local interfaces pass parameters by reference, which eliminates the need to create copies of object parameters.

The remote interface allows application-wide access to Entity beans. A client can be in any container associated with the J2EE application that contains the EJBs, or it can be any CORBA client with network access to the Application Server. This remote access is a big advantage of the EJB architecture. Usually, EJB interfaces will be developed to combine the best features of remote interfaces (distribution) with the advantages of local interfaces (efficiency).

At this point in time, most applications are being written to use remote interfaces on Session beans. Those Session beans will act as façades, to manage the model. Entity beans, then, are usually written with local interfaces. In this way, Session beans present an almost API-like interface to the model, while the Entity beans will encapsulate the state of the model.

The deployment descriptor

The deployment descriptor is used to describe the EJB module to the Application Server's EJB container. It provides the information that the container requires for establishing and supporting the Entity bean. The deployment descriptor for an Entity bean will be very similar to the descriptor for a Session bean but will naturally contain some additional information.

A BMP's deployment descriptor will have only the information necessary to manage the components of the BMP. We will learn, shortly, that as the container's role increases, the deployment descriptor will require quite a bit more information.

The descriptor for the PersonBMP is listed in Figure 6.12.

```
<enterprise-beans>
    <entity id="PersonBMP">
        <ejb-name>PersonBMP</ejb-name>
        <local-home>book.ejb.PersonBMPLocalHome</local-home>
        <local>book.ejb.PersonBMPLocal</local>
        <ejb-class>book.ejb.PersonBMPBean</ejb-class>
        <persistence-type>Bean</persistence-type>
        <prim-key-class>book.ejb.PersonBMPKey</prim-key-class>
        <reentrant>False</reentrant>
    </entity>
</enterprise-beans>
```

Figure 6.12: Deployment descriptor for a BMP entity bean.

This descriptor section defines the BMP. It names the interfaces and bean class the container must use when running this bean type. There is also an entry for the primary key class. There is a new entry here, for persistence type. With a BMP, this is marked as Bean. This declares to the container that the bean contains the code necessary for persistence. As we have mentioned, there is another option.

Container-Managed Persistence

If a BMP is a do-it-yourself Entity bean, a Container-Managed Persistence (CMP) Entity bean is the do-it-yourself kit. The considerable logic required to develop a BMP can, in the case of a CMP, be categorized into things that the developer *must* do and things that the container *can* do if the developer is willing to declare the details. While the container will always manage transactions, security, and distribution for either of the Entity bean types, a CMP's persistence will be managed by the container as well.

CMP bean class (the primary difference)

The primary difference between a BMP and a CMP is in the bean class. As we have learned, the bean class for a BMP contains code for all of the lifecycle events of the entity bean. For the BMP to support persistence, there must be code in the ejbLoad and ejbStore methods to provide that support. The development of that code is basically a matter of writing SQL code that records (or retrieves) data values from a particular schema.

Wouldn't it be useful to enable the container, if given a schema and a "map" of bean class fields to schema columns, to produce the required SQL?

That is exactly what a CMP is meant to do. The developer of a CMP bean produces an abstract bean class, which defines the code that goes beyond the basics of persistence management. Then, when the bean is generated, the container (or development tool) generates classes to handle the persistence.

The information that the container uses to generate this code will be stored, primarily, in the deployment descriptor. Most of this information will be generated by wizards and tools within the development environment. It is probably best to work through those tools and wizards as we cover the details of CMP development.

Using the Enterprise Bean Creation wizard, one can work through the process of creating a CMP. The first step is to choose which EJB project this bean will be added to, as shown in Figure 6.13.

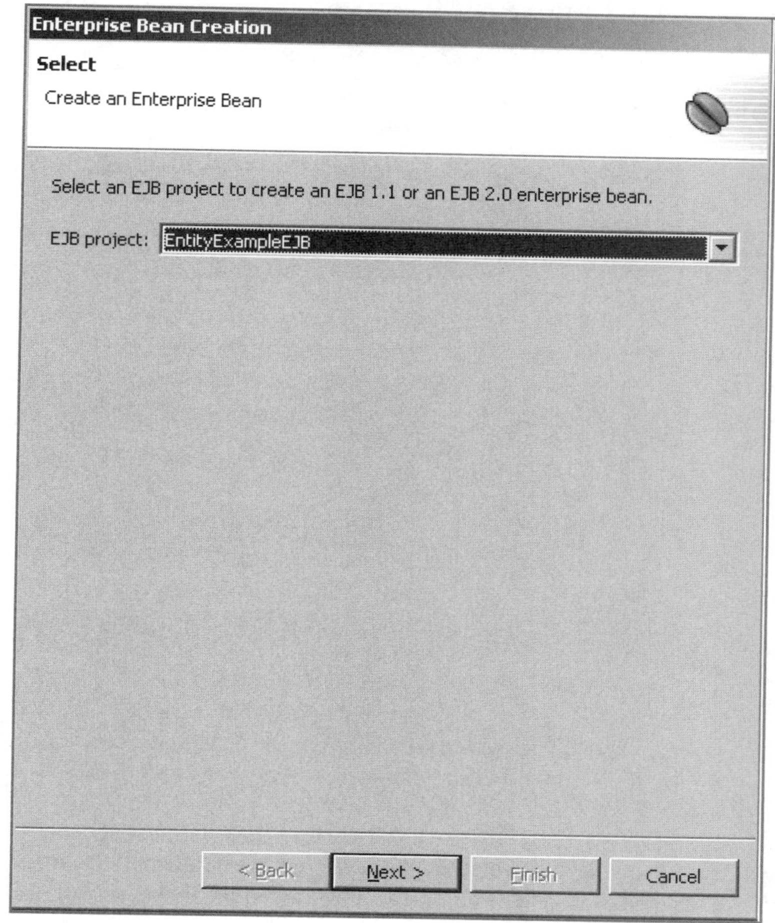

Figure 6.13: EJB Creation wizard.

On the next page, there are options to select a bean type and give the basic information required for creation. This is shown in Figure 6.14.

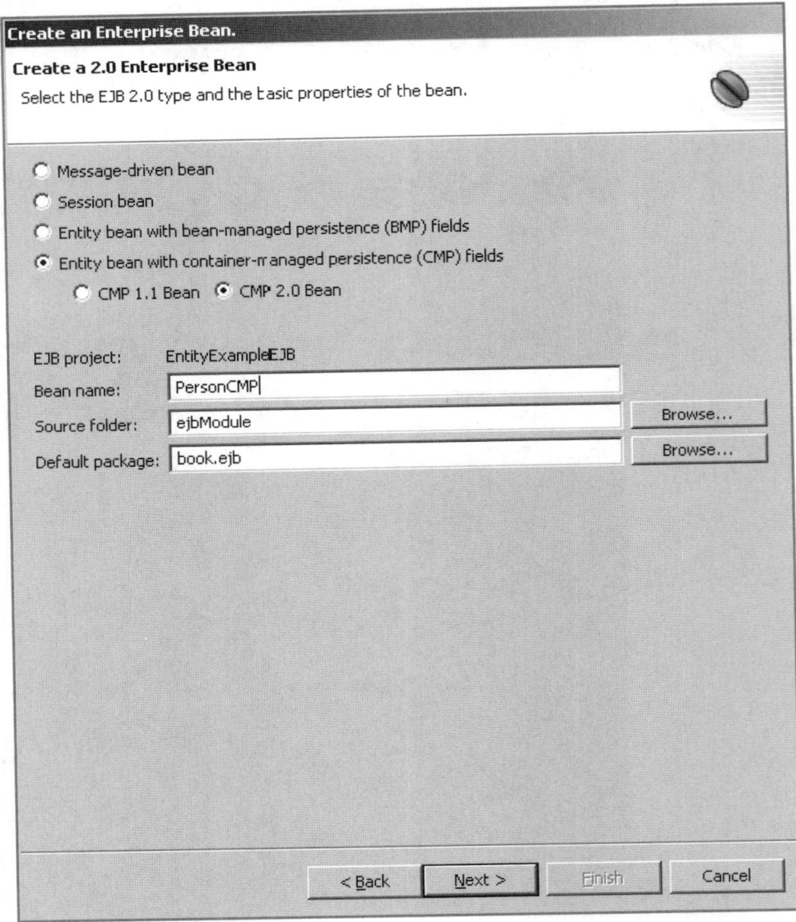

Figure 6.14: EJB Creation wizard (continued).

To create a CMP, select the radio button labeled **Entity bean with container-managed persistence (CMP) fields**. Beneath this button, there is another radio button to determine persistence type. Using this button, a developer can choose to use the "old" EJB 1.1 persistence model or the current EJB 2.0 model. This text will address the current model, so select **CMP 2.0 Bean**. There are also options here for the bean's name, the location where the code will be stored in the project, and the default package name for all resources dealing with the creation of this bean.

Examining Figure 6.15, you can see that the tool has determined the names of the bean class, primary key class, interfaces, and even the JNDI name using the EJB name and default package name provided. It is possible to change them here, but the defaults are usually sufficient.

There are two check boxes here to indicate interface type. Although it is acceptable to have both interfaces, Entity beans are usually created with only local interfaces. Many architectures use the idea of Session bean façades for working with Entity beans, so remote interfaces are not necessary.

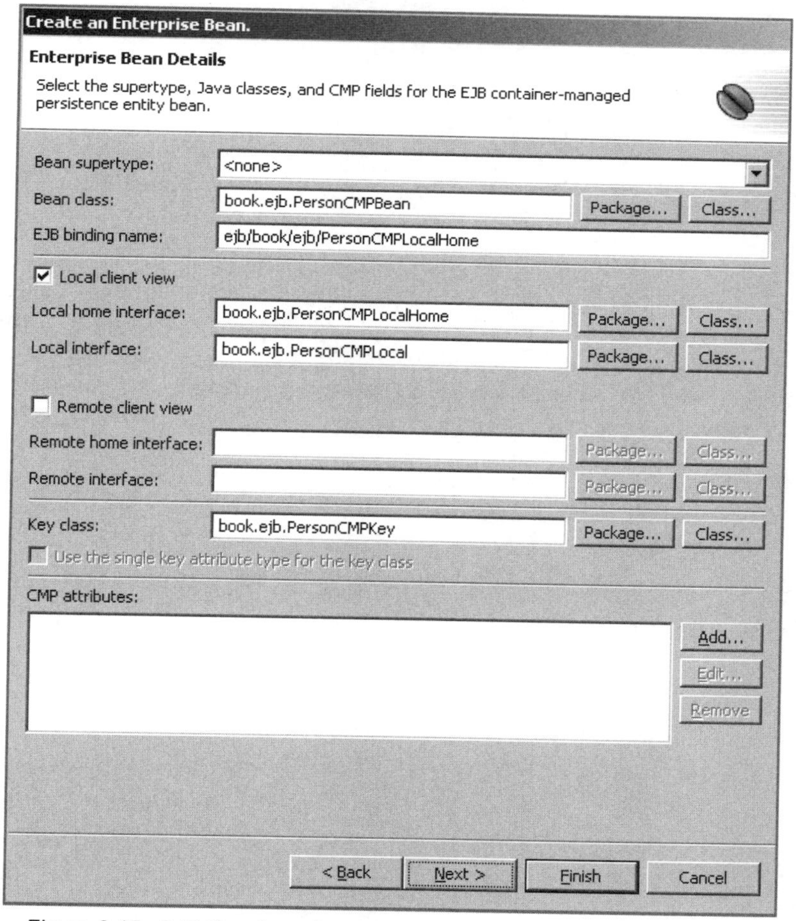

Figure 6.15: EJB Creation wizard (continued).

Because the container is going to play such a large role in the management and creation of CMPs, the wizards are very capable. The bottom portion of this section of the wizard shown in Figure 6.15 represents the capability to add persistent fields to the CMP. By clicking the **Add…** button, you can add the fields that should be persisted by this bean. The Add button will bring up another window to allow the addition of persistent fields. This window is shown in Figure 6.16.

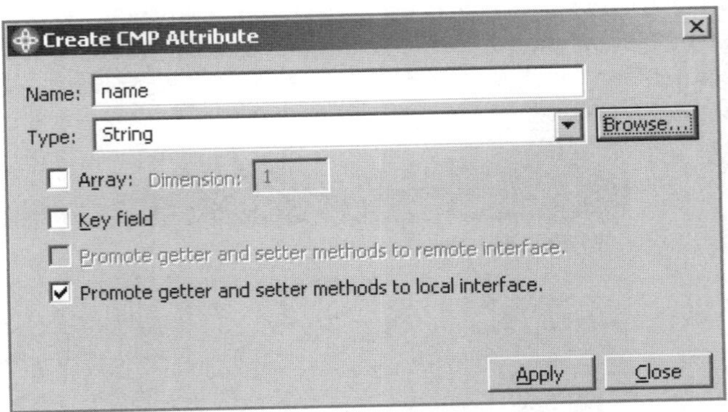

Figure 6.16: CMP Attribute definition dialog.

There are options on this dialog to cover the requirements of adding a field to the CMP. In effect, this dialog will allow us to declare a new field for the resulting CMP. When you click **Apply**, the current entries will be added to the bean, but the dialog will remain open to add other fields. When all of the required fields have been added, click **Close** to return the focus back to the wizard.

If this step was completed correctly, there should be entries present in the bottom window of the wizard. They will probably be similar to Figure 6.17.

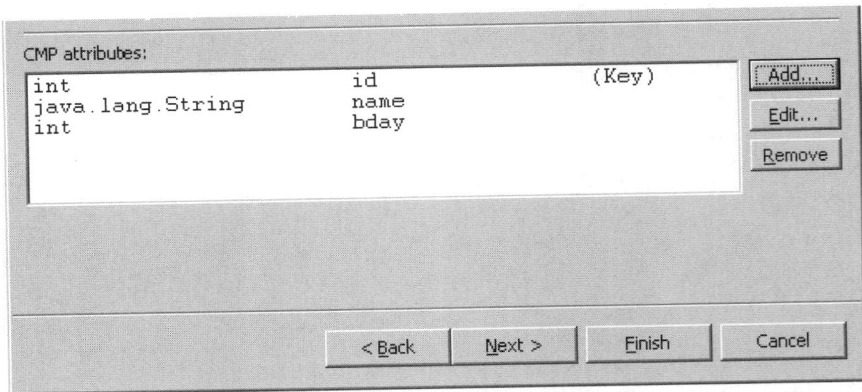

Figure 6.17: CMP Attributes list in EJB Creation wizard.

Click **Finish** to complete the creation of this CMP bean. Quite a bit of the basics are completed by the tool. The new CMP should show up in the J2EE Hierarchy view so that work can begin. Figure 6.18 is an example.

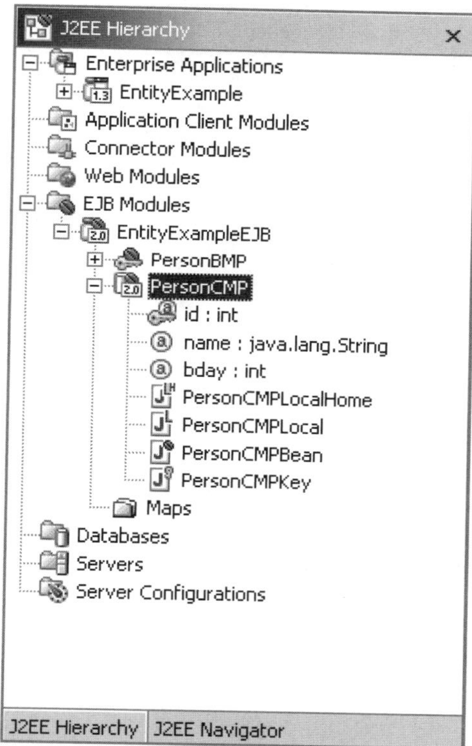

Figure 6.18: J2EE Hierarchy view of EJB artifacts.

The bean class that is created will be an abstract class, similar to the code shown in Figure 6.19. You can open the bean class, **PersonCMPBean**, by double-clicking it in the J2EE Hierarchy view.

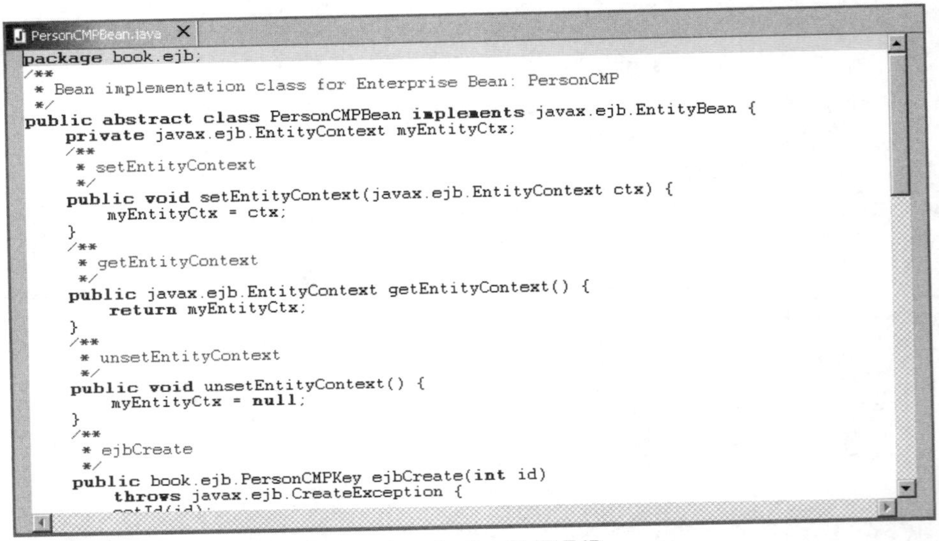

```
package book.ejb;
/**
 * Bean implementation class for Enterprise Bean: PersonCMP
 */
public abstract class PersonCMPBean implements javax.ejb.EntityBean {
    private javax.ejb.EntityContext myEntityCtx;
    /**
     * setEntityContext
     */
    public void setEntityContext(javax.ejb.EntityContext ctx) {
        myEntityCtx = ctx;
    }
    /**
     * getEntityContext
     */
    public javax.ejb.EntityContext getEntityContext() {
        return myEntityCtx;
    }
    /**
     * unsetEntityContext
     */
    public void unsetEntityContext() {
        myEntityCtx = null;
    }
    /**
     * ejbCreate
     */
    public book.ejb.PersonCMPKey ejbCreate(int id)
        throws javax.ejb.CreateException {
```

Figure 6.19: The implementation class for the CMP EJB.

This abstract class represents the "working area" for a CMP developer. The container uses this class to implement fully the features required for persistence. This class will contain all of the lifecycle methods and business methods required for operation. To add logic to the bean, a developer will make changes to this class.

CMPs support all of the behavior covered in BMPs, but because the container will play such an important role in management, many things will be declared in wizards rather than defined in code.

To write a finder in a CMP, you use the deployment descriptor editor and define a query for this CMP. On the Beans tab of the deployment descriptor editor, select the EJB to be modified, and scroll down to find the Queries section, as shown in Figure 6.20.

Click **Add . . .** to open the Add Finder Descriptor wizard and allow the definition or modification of finder descriptors. Finder descriptors are used by the container to generate the code necessary for finder function. This dialog is shown in Figure 6.21.

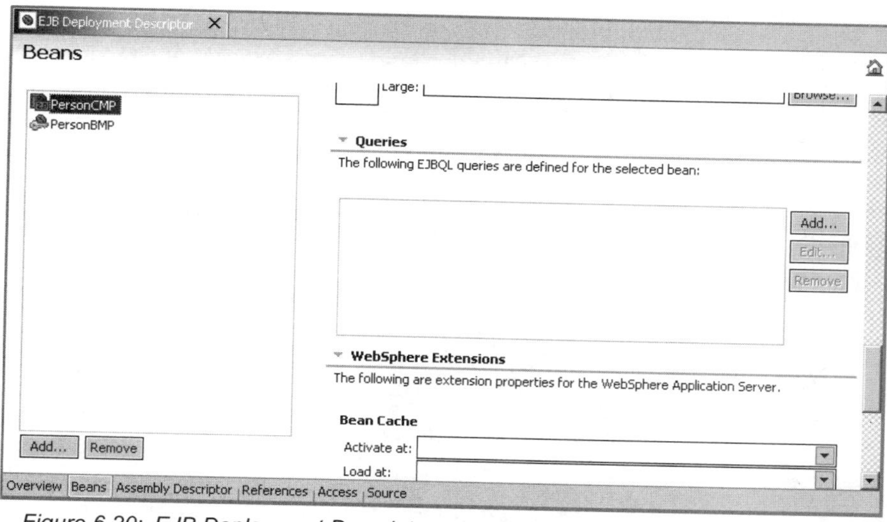

Figure 6.20: EJB Deployment Descriptor editor.

Add Finder Descriptor

Enterprise Java Bean 2.0 Query

Add an enterprise bean finder method.

Method: New Existing

Method Type: find method ejbSelect method

Type: Local Remote

Return remote entities:

Name: findByName

Parameters: java.lang.String name

Add...

Edit

Delete

Return type: java.util.Collection

< Back Next > Finish Cancel

Figure 6.21: Finder Descriptor wizard (page 1).

The Finder Descriptor wizard has a second page, for allowing the definition of a query. This is basically a "hint" to the container on how to write a SQL query. We will cover some of the basics of the EJB query language later in this chapter. It is a simple language, much like SQL. An example is included in Figure 6.22.

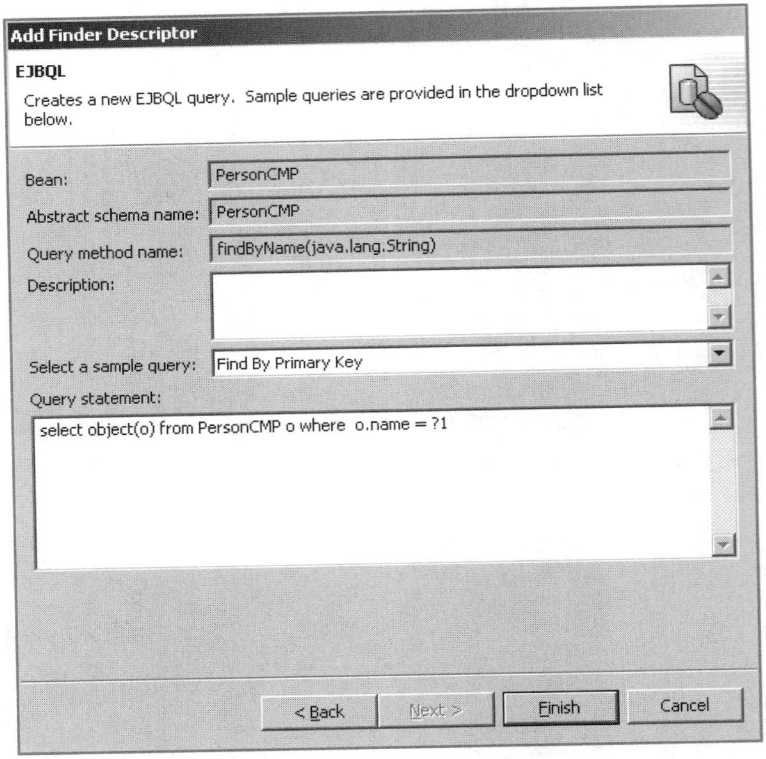

Figure 6.22: Finder Descriptor wizard (page 2).

Selects are an additional feature for CMPs, similar to finders. Whereas a finder returns an object interface (or collection of interfaces) that meet certain criteria, a select function allows one to query the fields present in a set of EJBs. A good example is a method such as selectLastNames(), which return the set of all last name values present in *all* records of the type this EJB represents. The same tool used for adding finders will allow the creation of selects. However, whereas finders are exposed to clients, select methods are private and are available for use only by business methods in the bean class.

Selects are developed much like finders, with a select clause on the home interface and a "hint" supplied in the entity bean's deployment descriptor. This query specification will be used to generate the real query used to access the database.

Another feature that CMPs support, beyond the basics of persistence, is relationships. Relationships (or associations) are a CMP feature that allows the relation of one CMP to another. For example, a CustomerCMP could have a relationship with a ShippingAddressCMP. This is very similar to the relation of database tables to one another through the use of foreign keys, to allow the management of fairly complex object graphs. Relationships are a very powerful feature and will be discussed later in this chapter.

The deployment descriptor, dealing with CMPs

Because of the special role the EJB container plays in the management of CMPs, quite a bit of information is stored in the deployment descriptor of any module with CMPs. Let's take a look at some of those new elements now, illustrated in Figure 6.23.

```
<entity id="PersonCMP">
    <ejb-name>PersonCMP</ejb-name>
    <local-home>book.ejb.PersonCMPLocalHome</local-home>
    <local>book.ejb.PersonCMPLocal</local>
    <ejb-class>book.ejb.PersonCMPBean</ejb-class>
    <persistence-type>Container</persistence-type>
    <prim-key-class>book.ejb.PersonCMPKey</prim-key-class>
    <reentrant>False</reentrant>

    <cmp-version>2.x</cmp-version>
    <abstract-schema-name>PersonCMP</abstract-schema-name>
    <cmp-field>
        <field-name>id</field-name>
    </cmp-field>
    <cmp-field>
        <field-name>name</field-name>
    </cmp-field>
    <cmp-field>
        <field-name>bday</field-name>
    </cmp-field>
</entity>
```

Figure 6.23: Deployment descriptor for a CMP entity bean.

There is quite a bit more information in the CMP's deployment descriptor than in the BMP's descriptor (Figure 6.12). Remember that in the WebSphere Studio tooling these deployment descriptors are written based on the information supplied in wizards or dialogs. This descriptor represents the sum of all of the entries to this point. The biggest difference from BMP to CMP is the addition of the CMP fields. These fields are declarations to the container that it will manage the persistence of the state represented by that field in every instance of this type.

There is a final detail required in the development of a CMP. CMPs must be mapped to a database schema. In a BMP, the developer writes SQL that is specific to a database schema. One of the strengths of CMP is its portability—that is, the code is not bound to a particular schema. To support this portability, CMPs must be mapped to multiple database schemas. This mapping function is a capability of the WebSphere Studio tooling. An example of mapping is shown in Figure 6.24. In this case, we are mapping the PersonCMP to a database created specifically for this example.

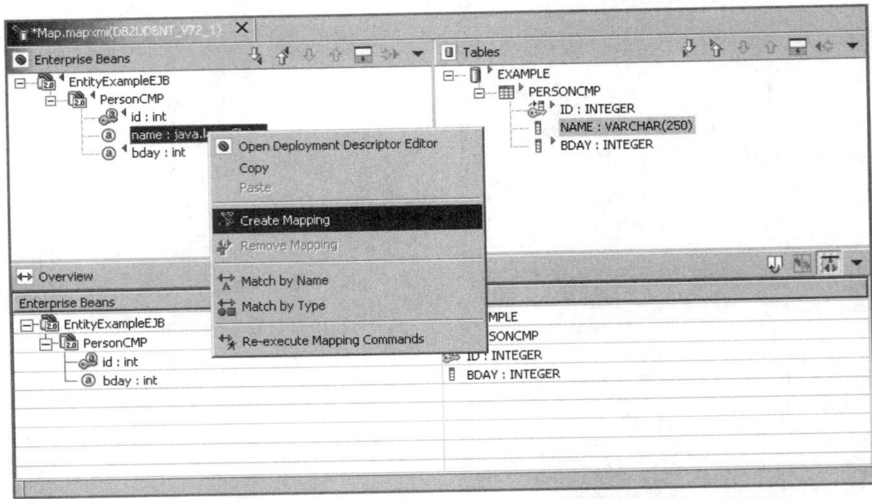

Figure 6.24: Mapping an attribute in a bean to a column in a database table.

WebSphere specifics for Entity beans

There are many cases in the specification where a responsibility is established, but not the implementation (behavior is specified, but not logic). Many of these responsibilities must be included in the deployment descriptors, but because the implementation of these behaviors could differ significantly from application server to application server and thus negatively affect portability, IBM has chosen to list this information in files that are very similar to deployment descriptors but contain information specific to the WebSphere Application Server.

Binding

There are two additional deployment files present in many EJB modules bound for a WebSphere Application Server and the EJB Container. One of those files covers the details of binding. It will contain JNDI naming information for EJBs and the datasources that a CMP will use for its persistence. This file will be modified using the EJB deployment descriptor editor, and the tool will manage the construction of the bindings file necessary for the WebSphere Application Server.

Extensions

WebSphere also allows the declaration of certain “extra” J2EE features. These are usually operations that J2EE does not specify but that are supported in the WebSphere Application Server. Again, extensions will be modified using the deployment descriptor editor, but the tool will create the necessary files for the Application Server.

Finding CMP beans using EJB query language

BMPs are useful, because they allow the developer (nearly) complete control over the function of an Entity bean. As we have learned, CMPs share the same lifecycle, without the need for the developer to produce the code necessary for persistence.

There are some other differences between the two types. Because the container will generate the code necessary for the function of the CMP, it is possible to declare certain behaviors or provide a specification for certain behaviors. This can significantly ease the burden on developers and allow much more than basic behaviors.

One of the drawbacks of a BMP is the fact that the SQL may not be portable. The query structure is often specific to a database schema and database vendor and would have to be modified to work with each change. CMPs have the advantage that any persistence code is produced in concert with a map. For a CMP to move from one schema to another would require only a new map.

When working with BMP finders, a developer writes the query directly into the bean class. So, just like the persistence methods, the query methods are specific to a schema. It would be foolish, then, if CMPs did not have a process that would allow a developer to specify queries that would not be portable if given a new map.

The EJB Query Language (EJBQL) was developed to allow this to happen. EJBQL is very similar to SQL but uses "EJB-side" names as its references instead of "schema-side" names.

EJBQL syntax

The EJBQL syntax is primarily a subset of SQL. There are a few features added to the EJBQL syntax that are not supported in SQL, and there are many features in SQL that do not need to be supported in the operation of EJBs. So, many of the common operators are present, such as WHERE and SELECT. Because EJBQL will be almost completely focused on queries for EJBs or EJB fields that meet certain criteria, some of the EJBQL's operations will take on nearly critical importance, such as DISTINCT.

In the section "CMP Bean Class (The Primary Difference)," there was an example of adding a query method to a CMP. This query statement (see Figure 6.22) contained the following text:

```
SELECT object(o) FROM PersonCMP o WHERE  o.name = ?1
```

SELECT, FROM, and WHERE will work as expected, considering the similarity between SQL and EJBQL. They define a scope (FROM) of where to look, a set (SELECT) of what to retrieve, and a list of conditions (WHERE) to be met in the results.

Because these queries are interpreted in object-space, instead of data-space, it will be important to use names from the objects and fields present as they are defined in the container instead of the tables and rows present in the database schema. When the EJB is generated, this information will be used to produce queries specific to a given schema.

The OBJECT keyword is required when the query will be returning one or more EJBs. In this case, the query will return the EJBs that contain a given name, and the client will receive object references for all EJBs that match, so the OBJECT operator must be used.

When you are writing SELECT queries, the OBJECT keyword may not be required, as the query may return a specific field. An example of this is the following:

```
SELECT o.bday FROM PersonCMP o WHERE o.name = ?1
```

This statement would return the birthday (an int) of all people whose names match the argument supplied in the method call.

WHERE conditionals can use literals or method arguments for their criteria, as follows:

```
SELECT object (o) FROM personCMP WHERE bday<01011900
SELECT object (o) FROM personCMP WHERE id < ?1
```

The first example uses a literal and would probably be matched to a method such as find-TriCenturians (to find people born before Jan 1, 1900). The second example would return the list of PersonCMPs that had an id less than some value, supplied as an argument to the method. These argument numbers will extend sequentially, so the second argument could be used as ?2, the third as ?3, and so on.

The WHERE operator has many options, such as BETWEEN for supplying a condition that a value rests between to boundaries or IN for requiring that a value be in a set of values supplied as a part of the query. Examples of these follow.

```
SELECT object(o) FROM personCMP WHERE o.id BETWEEN 10 AND 100
SELECT object(o) FROM personCMP WHERE o.bday IN ('01011901', '01011902')
```

The WHERE operator also supports NULL, NOT NULL, IS EMPTY, MEMBER OF, and LIKE expressions.

There are some modifiers that can be very useful, such as DISTINCT. We might, for example, desire a list of all the last names present in our list of people. Assuming that we have a lastName field (a modification on the basic PersonCMP), the obvious way to write this query is something like this:

```
SELECT o.lastName FROM PersonCMP WHERE o.lastName IS NOT NULL
```

This statement may have a somewhat different behavior than expected, however, because it would return the list of every last name found in every record with a last name. If there are two people with the last name of Jones, we would see that name in the results twice.

To eliminate this behavior, we can use the DISTINCT operator. If the query statement were rewritten to include DISTINCT, it would return the set of last names present in the database, without multiples. The new statement would look something like this:

```
SELECT DISTINCT (o.lastName) FROM PersonCMP WHERE o.lastName IS NOT
NULL
```

EJBQL can be a very powerful tool in the development of enterprise applications that use EJBs.

Writing Finders and Selects

When using Finders and Selects with CMP, the method signature will be defined on the home interface, and the query logic will be supplied in the deployment descriptor. This information will be added to the deployment file for an EJB module and will be entered using the deployment descriptor editor in the WebSphere Studio tooling.

Relationships between Entity beans

CMP relationships allow the developer to model data structure and associations in the object-oriented environment present in the application server. By defining relationships between CMPs in the deployment descriptor and creating a supporting database schema, developers can allow the container to manage the operation of a complex group of objects.

Types of relationships

There are many types of relationships, defined with two basic modifiers: cardinality and navigability. Cardinality is the numeric relationship that one object can have with members of its relationship. For example, in different models, a Customer may be associated with zero, one, or many different Addresses, depending on requirements. Navigability is used to describe the "visibility" of the relationship one element has with the member of its association. If the Customer-Address relationship were navigable, one could navigate from an Address to its corresponding Customer. Navigability is directional; it may be possible to navigate from Customer to Address but not back to Customer. It is important to note that for a relationship to exist, it must be navigable in at least one direction.

The operation and database structure required for associations will be determined by these two features. Using different combinations of the two, it is possible to produce many different relationships, each useful in different cases. For associations to work, it is required that there be a supporting database schema. The database would store these relationships using foreign key references. Usually, the child would store the key of its parent (or the multiple would store the key of the singular). In all but one case, this key structure would work.

The first, and perhaps simplest, is a one-to-one relationship. A good example of one-to-one is Employee to Address. Usually, an employee will have a primary mailing address for all company correspondence. This association defines a link from an employee record to an address record in another table. We can define this as a relationship of two EJBs and let the container manage this relationship for us. Because of its singularity, in a one-to-one relationship it is possible for either record to persist the other's reference. This will maintain the relationship between server starts.

To extend this idea, usually a person is employed by only one company, so an employee could have a relationship with a company. This association would allow the relationship of a particular employee record with the record (in another table) of a particular company. It may seem that an employee could have a one-to-one relationship with a company, but that would not be correct.

A much more useful example of Employee to Company is probably one-to-many. In a one-to-one relationship, the company could only have one employee, which is probably a little bit short-sighted. An Employee may work for only one Company, but any Company will most likely have many Employees. In the database, this would be modeled with each Employee having a key to her Company.

The most complex of the associations is the many-to-many relationship. An example of many-to-many is the association of a restaurant with customers. Any Restaurant will probably have many Customers (if it ever expects to have more than one employee, that is), and any customer will probably visit many restaurants. Usually, to support a many-to-many relationship, it is required that there be an intermediate table, every record on this intermediate table will represent a relationship between a particular Restaurant and a particular Customer.

Creating and defining relationships

Relationships are defined as a function of the deployment descriptor editor, but it is also important to construct and map to the schema correctly. This operation will be summarized in the following steps.

The first step is the creation of the relationship. This is done in the deployment descriptor editor. To begin this step, both participants in the relationship must already be created.

After opening the deployment descriptor editor, you must find the Relationships section to begin the creation of an association. The Relationships section will be found in two locations. It can be found on the overview tab, where it will show all relationships (as shown in Figure 6.25).

It can also be found on the Beans tab, where it will show all relationships for a selected bean (shown in Figure 6.26).

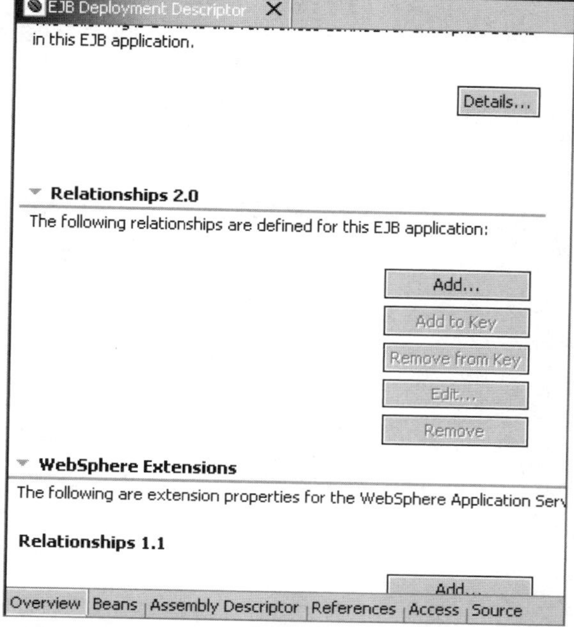

Figure 6.25: Overview tab of EJB deployment descriptor.

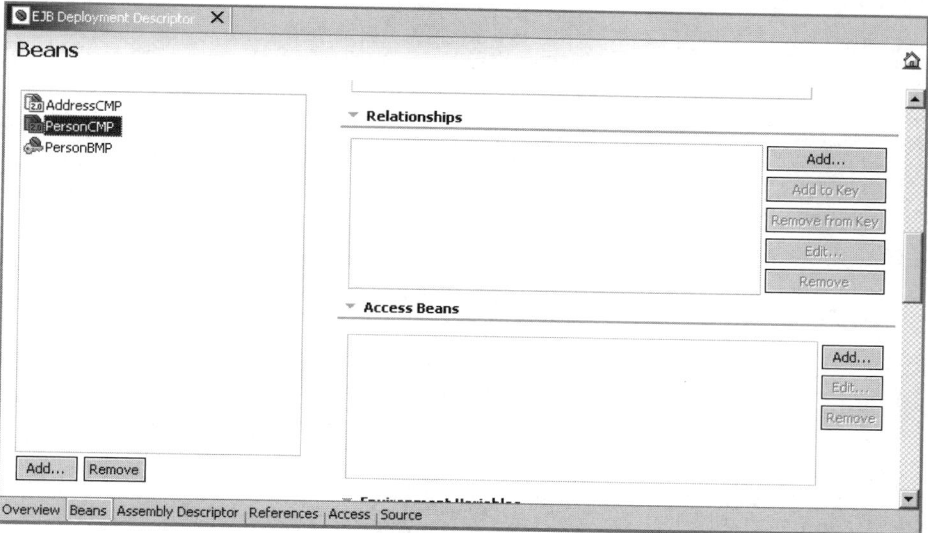

Figure 6.26: Beans tab of EJB deployment descriptor.

Clicking **Add** in either location will begin the process of defining a relationship. Any relationship is defined using two beans (unless a bean type has a relationship with itself). These beans must be in the same EJB module, so the list of beans present in the selection area will represent only the CMP beans available for a relationship in this module. The first step of the process is shown in Figure 6.27.

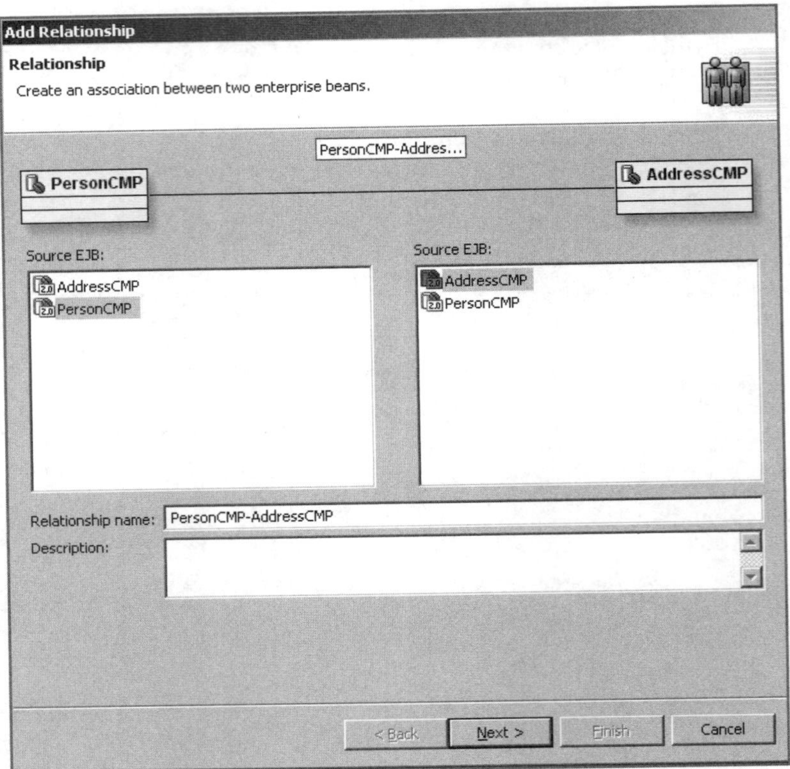

Figure 6.27: Add Relationship wizard: selecting the beans.

After the two participants are selected, it is possible to move to the second step of defining the relationship, shown in Figure 6.28. In this simple example, we will create a one-to-many mapping of Person to Address (a person can have multiple addresses). By selecting a multiplicity of **Many** for Address, we declare that for every one Person, there can be many Addresses. This defines much of the structure of the relationship, because the Address is now required to store the key reference (remember, a child points at its parent).

As we define relationships, we define behavior. The container generates code that supports this structure. Some of this code is present as new methods for working with the "partner" in the relationship. In this example, there are new methods for getting or setting the Addresses for a particular Person and vice versa. These new methods are named using the Role Name provided in this dialog.

The process outlined here will produce a new CMR, or container-managed relationship.

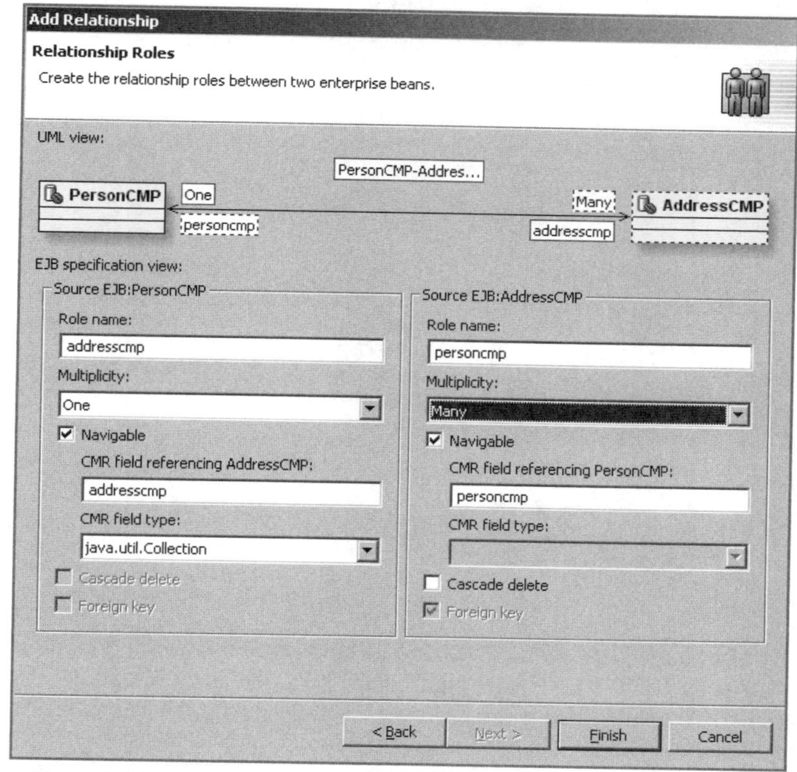

Figure 6.28: Add Relationship wizard: specifying multiplicity.

To support the relationship, it is important that the database have a foreign key reference (a new column) from the Address table to the Person table. It will also be important to map the relationship field (a new field in the EJB) to this new key. This is shown in Figure 6.29.

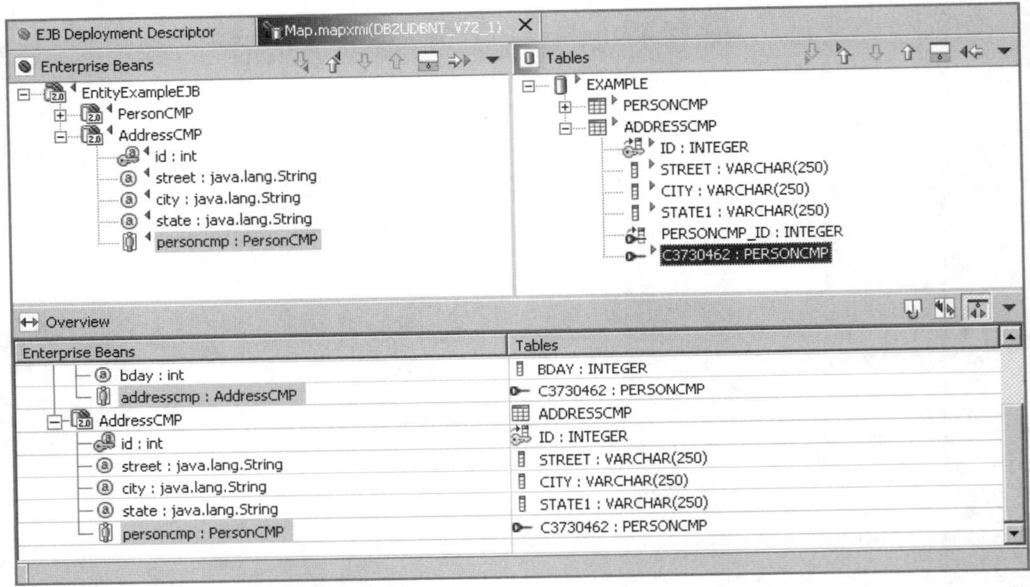

Figure 6.29: Mapping the relationship field to a foreign key.

Relationships can be a very powerful tool in the development of complicated models. They allow a developer the freedom to model an application effectively and work within the constraints of a database.

Summary

The Entity bean is one of the means of persistence and transaction control in a J2EE application. This chapter has covered the details of creating and using an Entity bean.

Entity beans will have the same basic structure as Session beans, but their role in an application is much different. It is expected that Entity beans will be used for persistence in the model, and, as such, their lifecycle was developed to support the requirements of state management and transactional control.

Entity beans are accessed using the interfaces developed for them. Although a container maintains strict control of entity instances and state, the client will have a "view" of the workings of the bean, presented by interfaces. It is expected that Entity beans will use local interfaces almost exclusively, but remote interfaces are possible if required.

In all, Entity beans represent an object-oriented view of the database and should be used as such. A well-developed Entity bean will appear to be, and will represent the function of, records in the database, or the operations to be performed on them, and not much else.

Test yourself

Key terms

Entity bean

Container-Managed Persistence (CMP)

Bean-Managed Persistence (BMP)

finder methods

primary key class

home methods

EJBQL

select methods

CMP relationships

Review questions

1. What type of method is found in the home interface of an Entity bean and not in the home interface of a Session bean?
2. When would you use the ejbPostCreate() method in a bean class?
3. What is the difference between an Entity bean in the pooled state and one that is in the Ready state?
4. If your primary key is only an int, what classes in the standard library can be used for primary key classes? When should you define your own?
5. With Session beans it was necessary to add an ejbCreate() method to the bean class and a create() method to the home interface, even though the SessionBean interface didn't require it. With Entity beans, there is an additional method that is required in the bean class. Which is it? What is required in the home interface as a result?
6. How does the behavior of the remove() method in Entity beans differ from the same method in Session beans?
7. In BMP, when should the developer call the ejbLoad() and ejbStore() methods?

8. Session beans implement Serializable partly so that they can be activated and passivated using secondary storage. Entity beans map to data in persistent storage. What is the purpose of activating and passivating them? Do they need to be Serializable?

9. Consider an application that has an Entity bean representing an Order and an Entity bean representing an OrderItem. When an Order is deleted, all of its associated OrderItem instances should be deleted as well. How can this be implemented?

10. Both Session beans and Entity beans have create() methods in their home interface, and corresponding ejbCreate() methods in the bean classes. How do the return types of these methods differ in the two types of beans?

11. In WebSphere Studio Application Developer, finder methods are not added using the normal wizard used to create the bean itself. How are finder methods added?

12. An application contains four EJB classes. Which should be Entity beans?
    a. TravelAgent
    b. CreditCardValidator
    c. Cruise
    d. Cabin

CHAPTER 7

Message-Driven beans

Mike Brown

Chapter topics

- *A JMS primer*
- *Developing a Message-Driven bean*

Certification objectives

- *Design and develop Message-Driven EJBs*
- *Configure JMS connection factories and destinations*

The Message-Driven bean (MDB) is a new member of the EJB family. It promises to allow application developers to decouple an HTTP-driven application (and its logic) from the request-response paradigm. The Message-Driven bean is a Java Message Service (JMS) message consumer and, as such, is never directly exercised by a client. Instead, the Message-Driven bean works asynchronously with application logic to consume messages that are sent to certain destinations.

A JMS primer

Asynchronous messaging is a new concept to many J2EE application developers. Using messaging for the management of workflow or processes is not a new practice, but the J2EE 1.3 specification offers some new capabilities in the form of the MDB, a JMS message consumer.

Messaging

JMS messaging is the means for robustly delivering and consuming asynchronous messages in a Java environment. It presents a number of APIs as interfaces for working with a messaging service. Product providers are then left to implement these interfaces, producing a messaging provider. JMS is roughly analogous to JDBC for databases, providing a vendor-neutral interface for accessing JMS providers.

For the component developer the focus is on developing JMS clients. There are two types of clients: producers and consumers. Producers create messages and send them to a destination; consumers receive messages and process their contents. It is possible for a client to be both a producer and a consumer, receiving one message and then delivering another.

The producer and consumer are decoupled. The message delivery service takes the message from the producer and sees that it is delivered to the consumer. In this way, a producer can create and send a message, trusting the messaging server to deliver it, without having to pause for delivery (or execution) of the request. For this reason, JMS is considered an asynchronous process; the producer does not block and wait for a response from the consumer.

As Figure 7.1 illustrates, a JMS producer creates the message and sends it to a destination. The consumer, linked to that destination, receives the message while the producer continues with its own execution.

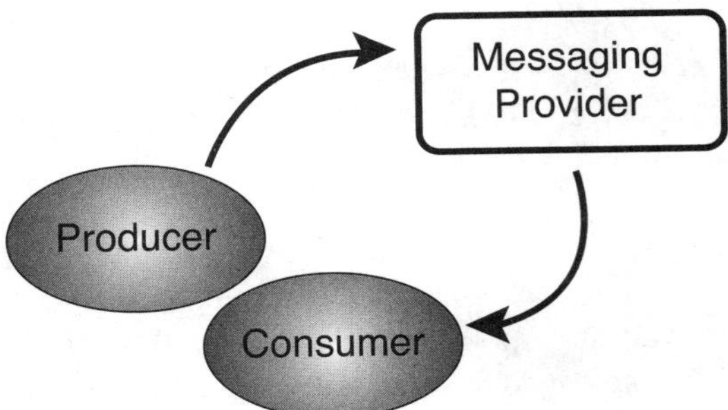

Figure 7.1: JMS messaging.

Destinations

A destination is an abstract item that represents a messaging service established to receive and deliver related messages. Destinations are considered to be administered objects. A system administrator creates the destination and binds it (and a connection factory) into JNDI, allowing clients to use the same service to look the destination up.

There are two standard types of message delivery: topics and queues. Although the specification does not require it, the WebSphere Application Server supports both types.

Basic administration

Messaging is configured in the application server (and the test environment) by adding destinations and connection factories. A destination is a "container" for messages of a certain type. A single messaging provider can support multiple destinations, much as a single database server can support multiple database tables.

To acquire a connection to a JMS provider, a messaging client uses a connection factory. In the current version of JMS, connection factories are specific to server and destination type (one for topics, another for queues).

Both of these resources are bound into JNDI to allow messaging clients to find them when necessary. Figure 7.2 shows a portion of the configuration page for messaging in the WebSphere Test Environment. We will use this JMS page to configure messaging in the WebSphere Studio family of tools.

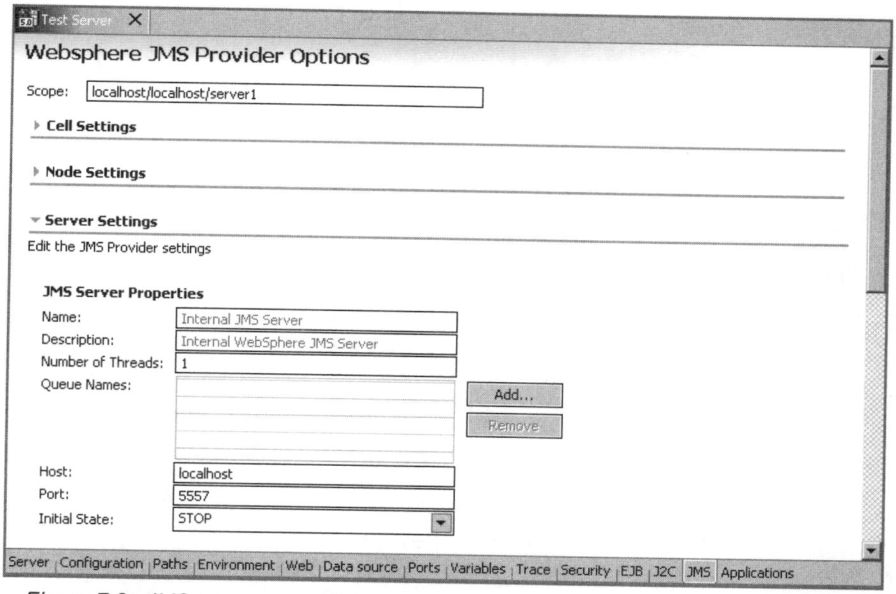

Figure 7.2: JMS server properties.

The first half of the configuration page is for configuring the messaging provider itself. You can see options available for port numbers, threading, and initial state. The second half, shown in Figure 7.3, contains many of the options for configuring destinations and connection factories.

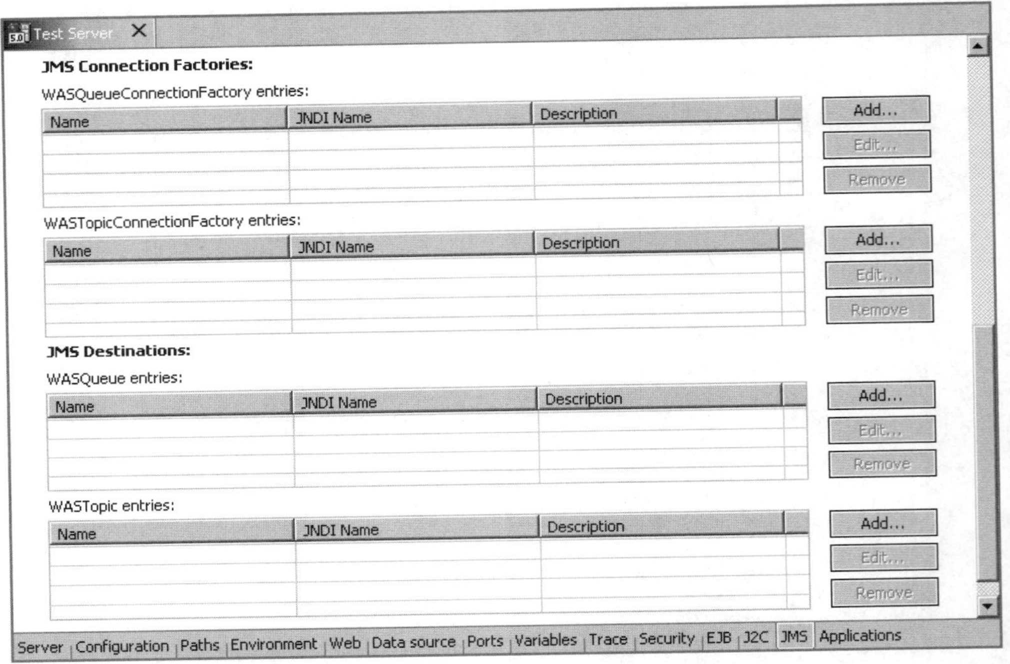

Figure 7.3: Connection factories and destinations.

Notice that there are really two sets of options: connection factories, and destinations. Connection factories are configured to provide a connection to a particular messaging provider and a destination type. Connection factories are similar to datasources in that they represent a pool of connections to this messaging provider. Because of this, a single connection factory can be used to access multiple destinations (as long as the destinations are all of the same type).

Connection factories will each have a JNDI name, which is mandatory, and some other configuration parameters, to establish them as a resource in the environment. In addition to the JNDI name, a connection factory requires a name that is used in the server configuration for symbolic linking. Click the **Add** button to the right of the WASQueueConnectionFactory entries list (see Figure 7.3), and fill in, at a minimum, both the Name and JNDI Name fields, as shown in Figure 7.4.

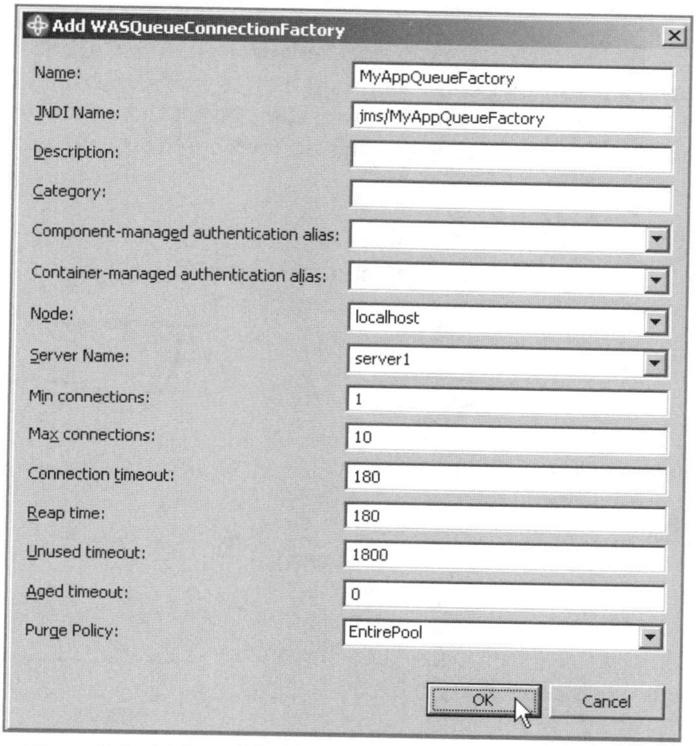

Add WASQueueConnectionFactory

Name: MyAppQueueFactory
JNDI Name: jms/MyAppQueueFactory
Description:
Category:
Component-managed authentication alias:
Container-managed authentication alias:
Node: localhost
Server Name: server1
Min connections: 1
Max connections: 10
Connection timeout: 180
Reap time: 180
Unused timeout: 1800
Aged timeout: 0
Purge Policy: EntirePool
OK Cancel

Figure 7.4: Adding a WebSphere queue connection factory.

A destination, then, is a "bucket" for messages. This container will store messages for the message consumers, based on one of the two messaging types, topic or queue. These containers will also be configured with a JNDI name, which is mandatory, and other administrative options. Like a connection factory, a destination requires a name as well. Select the **Queue Connection Factory** in the JMS Connection Factories list, and then click the **Add** button to the right of the WAS-Queue entries list (see Figure 7.3), and fill in at a minimum, both the Name and JNDI name fields as shown in Figure 7.5

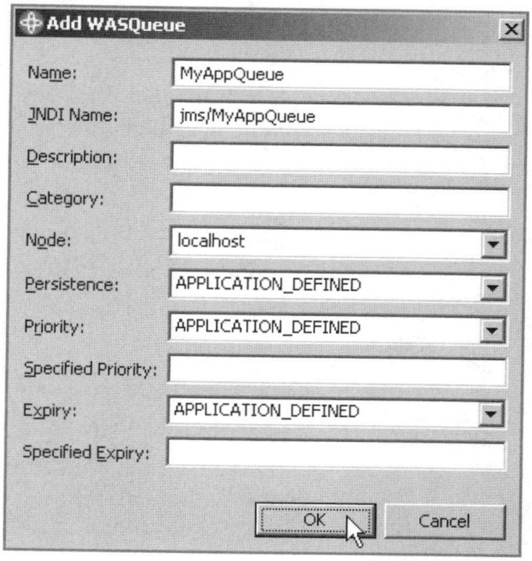

Add WASQueue

Name: MyAppQueue
JNDI Name: jms/MyAppQueue
Description:
Category:
Node: localhost
Persistence: APPLICATION_DEFINED
Priority: APPLICATION_DEFINED
Specified Priority:
Expiry: APPLICATION_DEFINED
Specified Expiry:
OK Cancel

Figure 7.5: Adding a WebSphere queue.

Topics

A topic is much like a subscription to a magazine. Figure 7.6 illustrates this concept. A producer (the magazine publisher) creates the message and delivers it to the destination. Previously, consumers will have subscribed to this topic, indicating their desire to receive the messages sent to this destination. Because of this, this model is often called *pub-sub* (publish-subscribe).

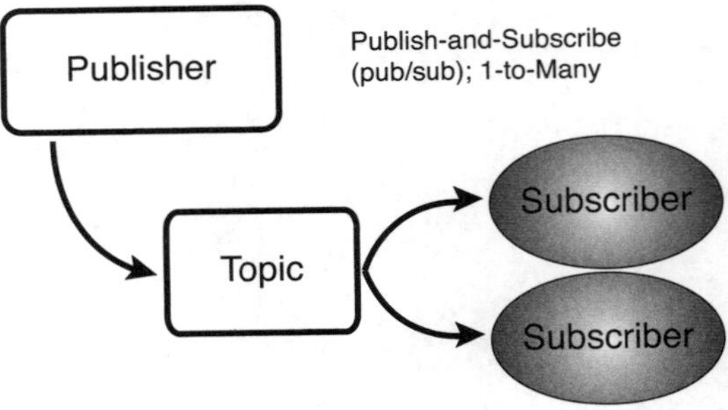

Figure 7.6: Topic message delivery.

With this model it is possible (and very common) for a single message to be delivered to a topic and many copies of that message then delivered from the topic, each to one of the desired consumers. In addition, the message server can be configured to store copies of messages until a consumer becomes available. Such a *durable server* retains these messages until the client (consumer) reconnects. This durability applies to multiple consumers, with a list of messages held and delivered to each consumer when it is available.

Queue

A queue represents the opposite extreme. In the case of a messaging queue, illustrated in Figure 7.7, a single copy of the message is delivered to a single consumer. In this way, it is possible for a critical task to be performed once and only once (like checking out at the grocery store). The message server stores messages in the queue until a consumer is available.

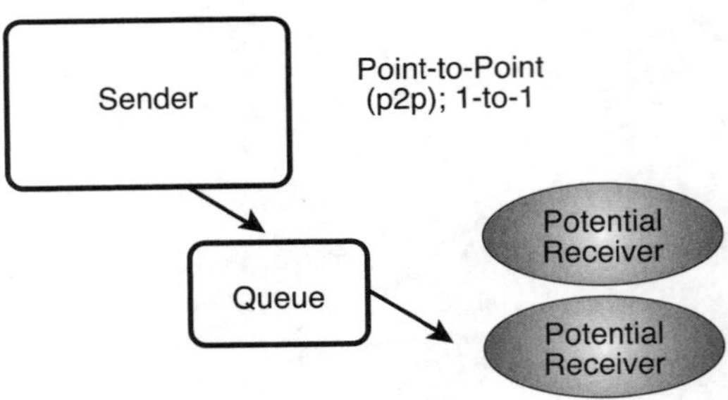

Figure 7.7: Queue message delivery.

Pooling

Because of the way a queue is managed, it is possible for the application server to manage pools of consumers for a particular destination. In much the same way as a pool of stateless Session beans is available to support the clients of an application, the EJB container can manage pools of EJB consumers for any of its queues. In this way, the application server can rapidly handle large queues, with bean instances managed to receive messages as needed.

What is a message?

A message consists of a *header*, which is JMS information, and, optionally, some producer-defined headers, called *properties*. The header is used for delivery and management of a message. A message can also contain a *body*. The makeup of this body depends on the type of message. There are a number of fundamental message types, allowing the component provider a measure of flexibility in designing and using JMS messaging in the application server.

The JMS specification defines five message types: Object Message, Map Message, Text Message, Stream Message, and Byte Message. An Object Message allows the encapsulation of a single (serializable) object, whereas the Map Message allows the creation of name-value maps to encapsulate multiple objects. The Text Message, aptly named, allows the creation of a message that contains a single string, whereas the Byte Message and Stream Message allow the creation of messages that contain "raw" bytes or streams, respectively.

Each message type presents its own interface for working with messages of that type. For example, the Object Message declares the getObject and setObject methods for acquiring or defining the object encapsulated by the message. In addition, it defines the methods necessary to get or set property and header information.

Developing a Message-Driven bean

Message-Driven beans are stateless, transactional objects managed by the EJB Container. They do not present a client view; instead, they are linked to a JMS destination and receive messages from that destination as the messages are delivered by message producers.

The MDB has a very simple lifecycle, much like the lifecycle of the stateless session bean. Figure 7.8 is a diagram of the MDB lifecycle.

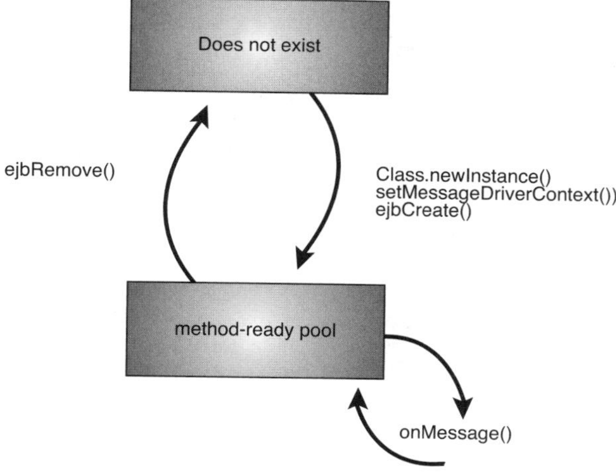

Figure 7.8: MDB lifecycle.

The development of a Message-Driven bean is much simpler than the development of other types of Enterprise JavaBeans. The MDB is written to consume messages from a destination and will never be called directly by a client. For this reason, the MDB is made up of a bean class and its entry in the deployment descriptor. No other developer-supplied elements are required.

The Bean class

Message-Driven beans implement the javax.jms.MessageListener interface and the javax.ejb.MessageDrivenBean interface. The first, MessageListener, declares the onMessage(Message) method. as follows.

```
public interface javax.jms.MessageListener {
    public void onMessage(Message msg);
}
```

The MessageDrivenBean interface, shown in Figure 7.9, declares the lifecycle methods for the MDB.

```
public interface javax.ejb.MessageDrivenBean
{
    public void setMessageDrivenContext(MessageDrivenContext ctx)
        throws javax.ejb.EJBException;
    public void ejbRemove() throws javax.ejb.EJBException;
}
```

Figure 7.9: MessageDrivenBean interface.

In addition, the EJB specification states that there must be a single create method, ejb-Create(), that does not accept any arguments. This method is available to initialize an instance of an MDB and is called by the Container upon creation.

The onMessage() method

The onMessage() method is called by the message server to deliver a message. The logic of the bean will be implemented in this method, and any other "private" or utility method defined on the bean class. An example bean class (and the onMessage() method) is illustrated in Figure 7.10.

```
public class EmployeeAdderBean
    implements javax.ejb.MessageDrivenBean, javax.jms.MessageListener
{
    private MessageDrivenContext fMessageDrivenCtx;

    public MessageDrivenContext getMessageDrivenContext() {
         return fMessageDrivenCtx;
    }

    public void setMessageDrivenContext(MessageDrivenContext ctx) {
        fMessageDrivenCtx = ctx;
    }

    public void ejbCreate() { }

    public void onMessage(javax.jms.Message msg) {
    // get a stateless session bean and work with the model.
    // pull information from the message, and use it to add an employee
    ObjectMessage oMsg = (ObjectMessage) msg;
    try {
        String newEmp = (String) oMsg.getObject();

        EmployeeManagerFacadeHome empFHome = EJBHelper.getEmployeeFacade();

        EmployeeManagerFacade empF = empFHome.create();

        empF.addEmployee(newEmp);

    } catch (JMSException jmsE) {
        // add code here to handle messaging exception
    }
    }

    public void ejbRemove() { }
}
```

Figure 7.10: Implementation of the onMessage() method.

No client interfaces

Because this Enterprise JavaBean has no client visibility, there is no need for the development of client interfaces. However, it is common that an MDB will be a client to other EJBs, with all of the services and functions available to an EJB instance or EJB client.

Using WebSphere Studio Tooling, the creation of an MDB begins with the Enterprise Bean Creation wizard, with the selection of Message-Driven bean, as shown in Figure 7.11.

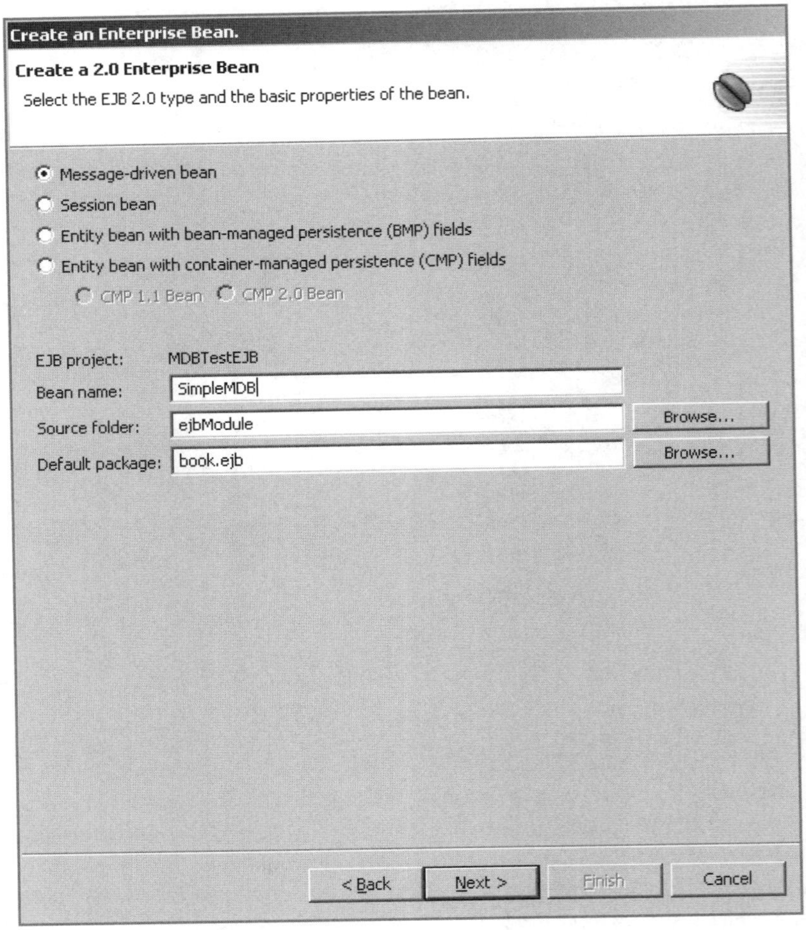

Figure 7.11: Creation of an MDB.

The second page of the Enterprise Bean Creation wizard is where the difference is most apparent. As Figure 7.12 shows, entries are required for the destination type and the ListenerPort (a WebSphere-defined element that indicates a specific message destination).

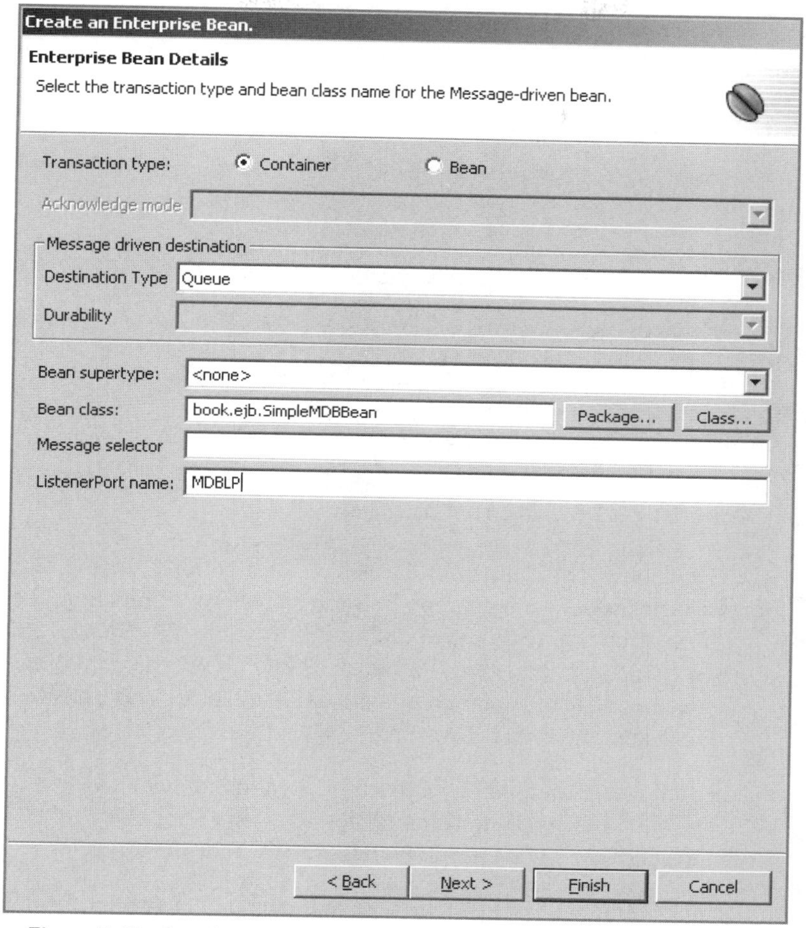

Figure 7.12: Creation of an MDB, continued.

Note that there are no entries required for a client view, or for persistence or instance variables. MDBs are stateless objects and are meant only to consume messages, although they can serve as clients to other EJBs, making modifications to stateful objects with the information contained in the messages they receive.

Deployment descriptor

During MDB creation (using WebSphere Studio Tooling), the developer chooses a destination type and a ListenerPort. This information is added to the bean's entry in the deployment descriptor. An example deployment descriptor is shown in Figure 7.13.

```
<enterprise-beans>
    <message-driven>
    <ejb-name>MessageBean</ejb-name>
    <ejb-class>book.example.SimpleMDBBean</ejb-class>
    <transaction-type>Container</transaction-type>
    <message-selector>MessageType = &quot;Domestic&quot;</message-selector>
    <message-driven-destination>
    <destination-type>javax.jms.Queue</destination-type>
    </message-driven-destination>
    </message-driven>
</enterprise-beans>
```

Figure 7.13: MDB deployment descriptor.

This deployment descriptor defines the destination type and bean class of the MDB. Another piece of information is required for proper function: the ListenerPort. This information is found in the binding information (WebSphere specific) included with the EJB module. The ListenerPort is an abstract item, much like the DataSource, that combines the JNDI information of a connection factory and a destination, allowing the MDB to consume messages from a particular message provider.

In addition to establishing a listening location, the deployment information also makes it possible for an MDB to filter its messages. In effect, this causes the MDB to receive only a subset of the messages delivered to a given destination.

This filtering is handled by query-like elements placed in the deployment descriptor, called *message selectors*. Selectors allow filtering based on criteria listed in the query. The information required for a selector to function is set by the message producer as part of the message's attributes.

Selectors are written to enable filtering based on information contained in the header, but not on the attributes of objects included in the message body. Selectors are written in a version of the SQL, SQL-92. These selectors filter messages delivered to a given consumer.

Summary

The Message-Driven bean is a new component in the EJB specification. It allows the application developer to produce logic that will consume asynchronous messages, opening the way for new means of process workflow and application logic.

Test yourself

Key terms

JMS
Message-Driven beans
synchronous vs. asynchronous
producers and consumers
destination
queue
topic
message provider
connection factory
JMS message
listener port
message selectors

Review questions

1. List the defined types of JMS messages and their purposes.
2. Normal EJBs require two interfaces (home and object) and a bean class. What do MDBs require?
3. MDBs are required to have an ejbCreate() method with no arguments, similar to stateless Session beans. In what other ways are MDBs like stateless Session beans?
4. A point-to-point application refers to a producer and a consumer. Is it possible to have more than one of either?
5. A developer needs to implement remote connectivity in an environment where networking faults are common. Are MDBs useful in this case?
6. Java classes can be written to act as message consumers without being MDBs. Why go to the trouble to create an MDB?

CHAPTER 8

Transactions

Colin Yu

Chapter topics

- *Introduction*
- *Transaction properties*
- *Transaction types*
- *Transaction support in WebSphere Application Server*
- *Transaction isolation*
- *Access intent policies*
- *Best practice of using transactions in Enterprise JavaBeans*

Certification objectives

- *Build EJBs that satisfy transactional requirements*
- *Use JTA to control transaction demarcation*
- *Manipulate transactional behavior of EJBs using deployment descriptors*

Transactions are important for distributed enterprise applications that need to ensure data integrity for concurrent processing and survival of system failure. Support for transactions is a major component of J2EE. The J2EE server implements the necessary low-level transaction protocols between the transaction manager and the resource manager, allowing developers to focus on designing the transaction based on its requirements rather than its implementation.

This chapter introduces basic concepts of transactions including characteristics and types. Next it describes the support for transactions in the J2EE platform, focusing on the transactional models available to Enterprise JavaBeans. The chapter follows with an overview of concurrency problems and illustrates the transactional isolation for Enterprise JavaBeans, which is available in WebSphere Application Server for EJB 2.0–compliant beans. Finally, the "Best Practice" section helps readers further understand transaction handling in J2EE platforms.

Introduction

A typical enterprise application accesses or stores information in an enterprise information system (EIS), such as a database, Java Message Service, or mainframe transaction processing system. Transactions, when used properly, can ensure the information's integrity, accuracy, and reliability, which is critical to an enterprise application and to the success of the business.

In most cases, an enterprise application is distributed and supports multiple users. Handling complex issues such as failure recovery and concurrent process execution in an enterprise application is not a trivial matter. The J2EE platform, by supporting transactions, provides developers with an advanced programming paradigm to write portable and reusable code without worrying about the low-level implementation.

The need for transactions

Transactions are vital because of the necessity of data integrity for concurrent process execution, the importance of failure recovery, and the need for a logical unit of work.

Data integrity would be jeopardized if multiple programs were allowed to simultaneously update the same information. Operations by one program might overwrite the update by another program. For example, two owners of a joint banking account might happen to withdraw money at the same time. Each operation would use the original account balance to subtract the amount of money being withdrawn. After both operations are done, the account balance would result in an uncertain state if no transaction control were used. Transactions are needed to deal with multiple users concurrently modifying data and guarantee that any set of data updated is completely written, with no interleaving of updates.

Also, if a system should fail while processing a business transaction, the affected data might be left partially updated, which is not acceptable for a mission-critical enterprise application. For example, suppose an application is transferring money from one account to another. After the money is debited from the first account, the system crashes because of a power failure. When the system is brought back, the application doesn't remember what logic it was executing before the crash. As a result, the total amount of money in these two accounts is not the same as it was before the failure. In this situation, transactions are necessary to make sure that after recovery the data is in a consistent state.

System failure or system shutdown also might happen after the operations are completed. In this situation, transactions are needed to guarantee that the changes made to the data will survive machine failure or system shutdown.

An application requires a mechanism to conduct a logical unit of work. In the cash transfer example, the credit operation might not complete because of a business logic reason, such as both accounts not being under the same person's name. In this situation, the debit operation should be undone. Transactions are needed to guarantee an all-or-nothing outcome in such circumstances.

Transaction properties

A *transaction* is a logical unit of activity in which multiple updates to resources can be made such that either all or none of the updates are permanent. Transactions share the following properties, collectively known as ACID:

- **Atomicity.** The set of operations contained in a transaction must succeed or fail as a unit. If a single operation cannot be performed, none of the transaction's operations must be performed. The cash transfer example explains the need for atomicity. The transaction must not leave work partially completed.
- **Consistency.** Complete transactional transformations on data elements ensure that data remains consistent from one state to another. In the cash transfer example, because money can be neither created nor destroyed, the accounts should have the same total balance after the money transfer as before.
- **Isolation.** Even though transactions execute concurrently, it appears to each successful transaction that it has executed in a serial schedule with the others, and its intermediate states are transparent to other transactions. In banking, for example, the credit check application shouldn't read uncommitted changes by the cash transfer application.
- **Durability.** Once a transaction commits, the changes it has made to the data must survive any machine failure or system shutdown. In the cash transfer example, after the transaction is completed, even if the system shuts down, the changes to the account balance should be durable and not lost.

Transaction types

There are many different types of transactions, with different levels of complexity and features. The two most popular types are *flat transactions* and *nested transactions*. Currently, the J2EE platform supports only flat transactions, which cannot have any child (nested) transactions.

Flat transactions

A flat transaction is a series of operations that are performed atomically, as a *single unit of work*. After a flat transaction begins, an application can perform different operations, some of which may be persistent and some not. When the transaction comes to an end, the operations will either be all committed or be all rolled back. When a transaction is committed, the changes by the persistent operations are made durable. When a transaction is rolled back, all the changes by the persistent operations will be recovered; it will look like the operations never happened.

Nested transactions

A *nested transaction* occurs when a new transaction is started within the scope of an existing transaction. The new, lower-level transaction is said to be nested within the existing, top-level transaction. Changes made within the nested transaction are invisible to the top-level transaction until the nested transaction is committed. Even then, the changes are not visible outside the top-level transaction until that transaction is committed.

One of the benefits of a nested transaction is that it can roll back without forcing other nested transactions to roll back. This gives the application developer the ability and flexibility to retry the nested transaction. If the nested transaction can be made to succeed, the top-level transaction will commit. If the nested transaction cannot be made to work, the entire transaction is ultimately forced to fail.

However, the implementation of nested transactions is more complex than for flat transactions. This is why J2EE platforms are not required to support nested transactions.

Transaction support in WebSphere Application Server

WebSphere Application Server Version 5 is a J2EE 1.3–compliant application server that implements the necessary low-level transaction protocols, transaction context propagation, and distributed two-phase commit. Similar to JDBC, which provides an abstract implementation to access relational databases, the transaction support in WebSphere Application Server totally abstracts out the low-level transaction. Therefore, application developers can focus on the implementation of business logic at a much higher level, without getting directly involved with the low-level transaction API for the specific underlying transaction system.

WebSphere Application Server supports access to multiple JDBC databases within a single transaction using the two-phase commit protocol. It also supports access to other types of enterprise information systems, such as Java Message Service, mainframe transaction processing systems, and enterprise resource planning systems.

WebSphere Application Server is a transaction manager that supports the coordination of resource managers through the XAResource interface and participates in distributed global transactions with other OTS 1.2–compliant transaction managers, for example, J2EE 1.3 application servers. WebSphere applications can also be configured to interact with databases, JMS queues, and JCA connectors through their local transaction support when distributed transaction coordination is not required.

WebSphere Application Server supports programmatic and declarative transaction demarcation. With the support of programmatic transaction demarcation, which is also called bean-managed transaction demarcation, application developers can use the Java Transaction API (JTA) to control the transaction logic in the component code. That is, application developers are responsible for starting and completing the transaction in the code. With the support of declarative transaction demarcation in enterprise beans, also called container-managed transaction demarcation, WebSphere Application Server is responsible for starting and completing the transaction according to the transaction attributes defined in the deployment descriptor. The only difference between programmatic transaction demarcation and declarative transaction demarcation is the controller of the transaction logic. In both cases, the transaction implementation is on WebSphere Application Server.

An enterprise application is normally composed of a combination of servlets, JavaServer Pages (JSPs), or both, accessing multiple enterprises. Components in an enterprise application have different ways to manage transactions:

- Web components (servlets and JSPs) use bean-managed transaction demarcation.
- A Session bean can either use container-managed transactions or bean-managed transactions.
- Entity beans use container-managed transactions.

Details on managing transactions in an enterprise application are discussed in subsequent sections.

OTS/XA Transaction architecture

XA is a useful specification on its own and has also provided the groundwork for later specifications, such as the Object Transaction Service (OTS), developed by Object Management Group (OMG) as an optional CORBA service, and the transaction model in Enterprise JavaBeans. Many of the definitions in the OTS specification come from the XA specification.

The XA specification describes a model of distributed transactions that delegates the maintenance of the ACID properties to the transaction manager (TM), leaving the application developer free to work on the logic of the application rather than managing distributed transactions. It also describes the interaction with resource manager(s) (RM), such as databases. In the XA model, the application developer uses the RM's native language such as SQL to talk to it, the application developer tells the TM to start and end transactions in another language (not specified), and the TM drives the RM(s) in the resolution of the transaction.

The XA specification also defines the API for this TM-to-RM communication: the XA interface. It is common for database vendors and messaging system vendors to implement the server side of the XA interface to support distributed transactions.

Figure 8.1 illustrates the OTS/XA transaction architecture.

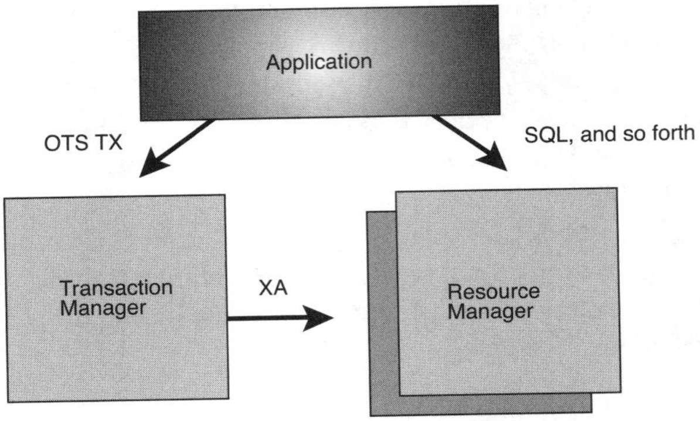

Figure 8.1: OTS/XA transaction architecture.

Java Transaction Service (JTS)

The Java Transaction Service (JTS) is a Java mapping of CORBA OTS. It specifies the implementation of a transaction manager that provides the services and management functions required to support transaction demarcation, transactional resource management, synchronization, and transaction context propagation. It also ensures interoperability between implementations of JTS and interoperability between OTS and JTS. Only system-level vendors—for example, WebSphere Application Server—need to be concerned about JTS.

Java Transaction API (JTA)

On top of JTS, the Java Transaction API (JTA) defines the interfaces between a TM and the parties involved in a distributed transaction system, application, and RM.

JTA has two sets of interfaces. The TransactionManager and XAResource interfaces are low-level APIs between a J2EE server and RMs that application developers don't need to worry about. The interface javax.transaction.UserTransaction is a high-level API used by application developers to demarcate the transaction boundaries in Components, such as for starting a transaction inside a bean, calling other beans also involved in a transaction, and controlling whether the transaction commits or aborts.

WebSphere Application Server supports two ways to begin a JTA transaction. For bean-managed transaction demarcation, a component can obtain the javax.transaction.UserTransaction interface from a JNDI lookup. For container-managed transaction demarcation, a JTA transaction is started automatically by the EJB container.

There are two major reasons to use JTA transactions. First, with JTA transactions, access to multiple EISs (databases, messaging systems, legacy systems, etc.) can be combined into one unit of work (global transaction) without much coding effort, as shown in Figure 8.2. Updates will be either all committed or all rolled back.

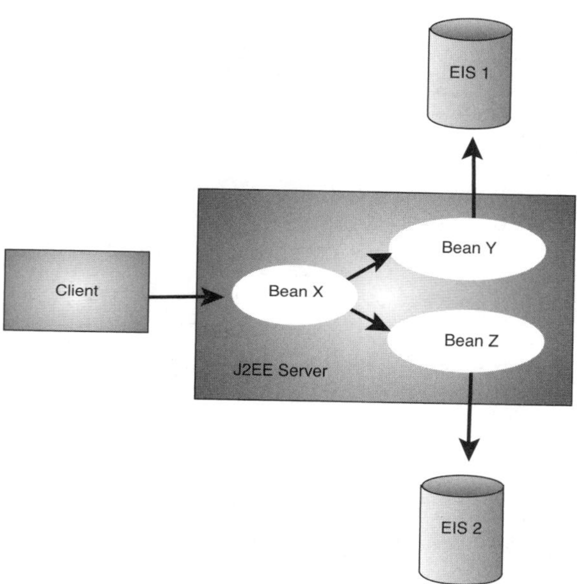

Figure 8.2: Accessing multiple EISs in a global transaction.

A second benefit to using JTA transactions is that the transaction context can be propagated from one component to other components by the containers without requiring any code. As shown in Figure 8.3, the transaction context can be propagated from bean X to bean Y in the same container, or even from bean Y to bean Z in different containers, if appropriate transaction attributes are set for the beans.

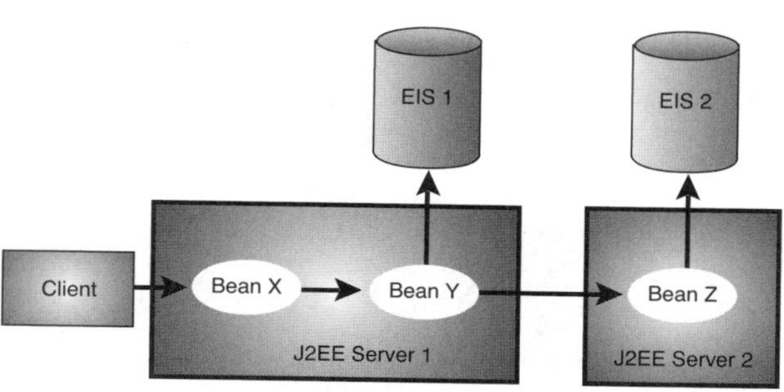

Figure 8.3: Transaction propagation.

The javax.transaction.UserTransaction interface

Application developers can use the javax.transaction.UserTransaction interface to demarcate the transaction programmatically. Figure 8.4 illustrates the interface.

```
public interface javax.transaction.UserTransaction {
public void begin();
public void commit();
public int getStatus();
public void rollback();
public void setRollbackOnly();
public void setTransactionTimeout(int);
}
```

Figure 8.4: The javax.transaction.UserTransaction interface.

The methods begin(), commit(), and rollback() are used to begin a new transaction, commit a transaction permanently, and roll back a transaction in case some problem occurs, respectively.

The method getStatus() is used to retrieve the status of the transaction associated with the current thread. The returned value of this method is one of the constants defined on the javax.transaction.Status interface as follows:

- STATUS_ACTIVE: A transaction is active.
- STATUS_COMMITTED: The last active transaction was committed.
- STATUS_COMMITTING: The last active transaction is committing.
- STATUS_MARKED_ROLLBACK: A transaction is marked for rollback, perhaps by setRollbackOnly().
- STATUS_NO_TRANSACTION: No transaction is active.
- STATUS_PREPARED: A two-phase commit has finished the prepared (first) phase.
- STATUS_PREPARING: A two-phase commit is in the prepared phase.
- STATUS_ROLLEDBACK: The last active transaction was aborted.
- STATUS_ROLLING_BACK: The last active transaction is aborting.
- STATUS_UNKNOWN: The transaction manager has no idea. (Try again later.)

The method setRollabackOnly() is used to force the current transaction to roll back. The method setTransactionTimeout(int) sets the maximum amount of time that a transaction can run before it's aborted to avoid deadlock situations.

Two-phase commit (2PC)

Two-phase commit is a protocol that allows multiple resources to update within a single transaction. It allows the outcome of the transaction to be negotiated by all participants. In phase I, the transaction manager tells the resource managers to prepare to commit and waits for an acknowledgment from each resource manager. If any resource manager in phase I is not ready, the transaction is rolled back and no resource manager commits. If all the RMs are prepared to commit, then in phase II the TM tells the RMs to commit, and every RM commits the update on its own and signals the TM when it is done.

Figure 8.5 illustrates the two-phase commit process.

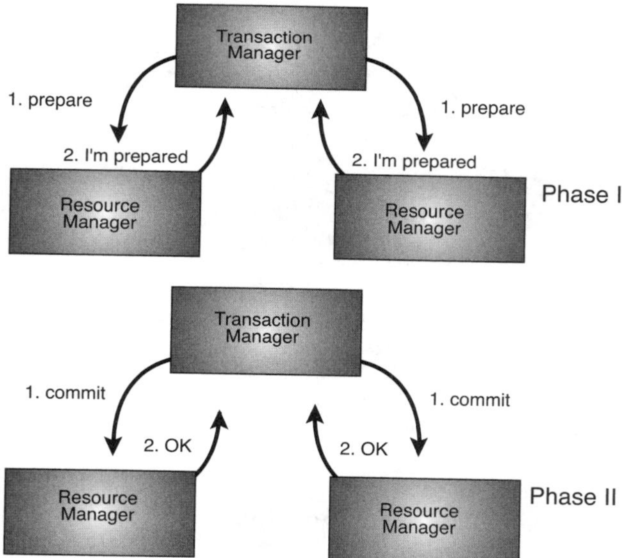

Figure 8.5: The two-phase commit process.

Transactions in Web components

The only choice for Web components to demarcate a transaction is programmatic transaction demarcation. A servlet or a JSP can obtain a UserTransaction object by JNDI lookup and then use the UserTransaction interface to demarcate transactions. Demarcating transactions in a Web component might not be a good choice in a multi-tier application. However, it is still useful in a two-tier application where a Web component needs to directly access EISs under a global transaction.

Before the EJB 1.1 specification, the JNDI location of the UserTransaction interface was not specified. Each EJB container vendor defined it in an implementation-specific manner. WebSphere Application Server Version 4 and later releases bind the UserTransaction interface at the location defined by EJB 1.1, which is java:comp/UserTransaction. That means the UserTransaction interface has been set up in the JNDI ahead of time in WebSphere Application Server Version 5, and no extra effort is needed from the application developer.

The code snippet in Figure 8.6 illustrates how to obtain the UserTransaction object from JNDI lookup and demarcate transactions within a Web component.

```
Context ctx = new InitialContext();
UserTransaction ut=
     (UserTransaction)ctx.lookup("java:comp/UserTransaction");

ut.begin();

try{

  // perform transactional work here

  // commit the transaction
  ut.commit();
} catch (Exception e){

  // perform exception handling work here

  // rollback the transaction
  ut.rollback();
}
```

Figure 8.6: Demarcating transactions in a Web component.

In a multi-tier environment, a servlet normally acts as a controller that deals with user interaction and JSP acts as a dynamic presentation (view) of the application. In this case, demarcating the transaction in a Web component is not recommended. As discussed in the next section, transactional access to enterprise information systems should be delegated to enterprise beans in the EJB tier.

Transactions in Enterprise Beans

In a multi-tier application, Enterprise JavaBeans play an important role for handling transactional work such as accessing a database, sending a message, and calling a program in the legacy system. As discussed in the previous section, an enterprise bean can either choose to demarcate the transaction by itself (bean-managed transaction demarcation) or delegate the work to the container (container-managed transaction demarcation). Enterprise beans declare the transaction demarcation in the deployment descriptor.

Bean-managed transaction demarcation

With bean-managed transaction demarcation, an enterprise bean uses the javax.transaction.UserTransaction interface to explicitly demarcate transaction boundaries.

Bean-managed transaction demarcation is available only for Session beans; an Entity bean must use container-managed transaction demarcation. An Entity bean is prohibited from using getUserTransaction() since EJB 1.1.

An enterprise bean declares bean-managed transaction demarcation by setting the transaction type to **Bean** in the deployment descriptor as follows:

```
<transaction-type>Bean</transaction-type>
```

The code snippet in Figure 8.7 illustrates how to obtain a UserTransaction object from the EJBContext interface and use it to demarcate transactions in an enterprise bean with bean-managed transaction demarcation.

```
UserTransaction ut = ejbContext.getUserTransaction();
try{

  // perform transactional work here

  // commit the transaction
  ut.commit();
} catch (Exception e){

  // perform exception handling work here

  // rollback the transaction
  ut.rollback();
}
```

Figure 8.7: Bean-managed transaction demarcation.

Container-managed transaction demarcation

With container-managed transaction demarcation, the transaction demarcation is delegated to the container, which is responsible for managing the transaction boundaries for the enterprise beans.

In container-managed transaction demarcation, application developers or the application assembler use the deployment descriptor to specify the transaction attributes and the transaction isolation for Enterprise JavaBeans. The transaction attribute defines the transactional requirements, and the transaction isolation determines how transactional reads are isolated. With these two transactional specifiers set in the deployment descriptor, when the bean is deployed, the container will generate the necessary transaction support code. For example, the container will always create a new transaction when the current thread enters a method with transaction attribute RequiresNew.

The advantages of using container-managed transaction demarcation are as follows:

- Application developers are not required to write transaction-specific code in the component. This allows developers to focus on writing the business logic and specify the transaction attributes later on, or leave the job to the application assembler.
- User error from demarcating transactions programmatically can be avoided by having the container take over the responsibility.
- An application assembler that understands the application can customize the transaction attributes in the deployment descriptor without code modification. This leads to more reusable and maintainable code.

Enterprise Beans declare container-managed transaction demarcation by setting the transaction type to container in the deployment descriptor as follows:

```
<transaction-type>Container</transaction-type>
```

How does a bean with container-managed transaction demarcation abort a transaction? The UserTransaction interface offers the rollback() and setRollbackOnly() methods, but that interface is not available to beans with container-managed transactions.

The EJBContext interface also offers a setRollbackOnly() method, and it is available to beans with container-managed transaction demarcation, which gives the beans some control over the transaction. After the setRollbackOnly() of the EJBContext interface is called, the transaction is marked as doomed and the transaction manager will roll back the transaction. The EJBContext interface also offers a getRollbackOnly() method, which returns the state of the transaction. If thetransaction is already aborted or marked for abort, there is no need to call setRollbackOnly(). Figure 8.8 shows an example of aborting a container-managed transaction when an exception occurs.

```
public class SessionEJBBean implements javax.ejb.SessionBean {

        private javax.ejb.SessionContext mySessionCtx;

        public void checkout() {

           try {
                // doing business logic here

                } catch (Exception e) {

                        if (!mySessionCtx.getRollbackOnly())
                                mySessionCtx.setRollbackOnly();
                }
        }
}
```

Figure 8.8: Aborting a container-managed transaction.

Transaction attributes

A *transaction attribute* specifies the transactional requirement for an enterprise bean with container-managed transaction demarcation. There are three guidelines for specifying transaction attributes for enterprise beans:

- All methods in the component (local or remote) interface of a Session bean must have specified transaction attributes.
- Session bean home interface methods should not have transaction attributes.
- All methods in the component (local or remote) and home interfaces of an Entity bean must have specified transaction attributes except for
  - Methods getEJBHome(), getHandle(), getPrimaryKey(), and isIdentical() of the component interface.
  - Methods getEJBMetaData() and getHomeHandle() of the home interface.

If the transaction attribute is set on the bean level, all methods of the bean will have the same transaction attribute. However, it is also possible to set transaction attributes for individual methods.

The following are the six possible values for the transaction attributes. The EJB 2.0 specification strongly recommends using only Required, RequiresNew, and Mandatory for CMP Entity beans that are persisted to a transactional data store (i.e., database).

1. *Required.* With the transaction attribute Required, the container must invoke methods within a transaction context. If the client has a transaction context, it will be propagated to the bean. If not, the container will start a transaction and try to commit the transaction when the method completes.

   The Required value is set for the CMP Entity beans in most cases. One of the reasons for this is that Entity beans perform database updates and are inherently transactional in nature. The other reason is that Entity beans are normally manipulated by Session beans. If the session starts a transaction, the Entity bean should participate in this global transaction for atomic operation. In the cash transfer scenario, you might have Entity beans that represent each of the two accounts. In this case, you want to perform both updates in a single transaction. A possible solution is to develop a Session bean with a business method that starts a transaction and manipulates the Entity beans. The transaction attribute of the Entity beans should be Required in this case.

2. *RequiresNew.* If the transaction attribute is RequiresNew, the container starts a new transaction for the method and tries to commit the transaction when the method completes. If the calling client has a transaction context, the container suspends the association of the transaction context with the current thread and

then starts a new transaction. When the method and the newer transaction complete, the container resumes the suspended transaction.

Use RequiresNew for methods that must be committed regardless of whether the caller's transaction succeeds. An example that illustrates the value of using RequiresNew is a method that performs unconditional logging. Consider the case of a task being performed that may either succeed or fail. If it fails, its transaction is rolled back. Consider further that we require that all attempts to accomplish this particular task be logged. The method that performs the actual logging should be invoked with RequiresNew transaction attribute, so that the logging records are created even if the transaction in which the original task is being performed is rolled back.

3. *NotSupported.* If the transaction attribute is NotSupported, the container must not invoke the methods with a transaction context. If the client has a transaction context, the container suspends the association of the transaction context with the current thread before the Enterprise bean's method is invoked. After the method completes, the container resumes the suspended transaction association.

   Use NotSupported when a method accesses a resource manager that doesn't support two-phase commit. For example, because CICS doesn't support external transaction coordination, the method calling a CICS transaction should use NotSupported as the transaction attribute.

4. *Supports.* If the transaction attribute is Supports, the container must use the client's context for the transaction. If the client has a transaction context, the context is propagated to the enterprise bean method. If not, the method executes without a transaction context.

   Use Supports for methods that either do not update the database or do not require the updates to occur within a transaction. For example, a method that calculates the interest for a mortgage package doesn't care whether it is executing under a transaction context.

5. *Mandatory.* If the transaction attribute is Mandatory, the container must call methods from the transaction context established by the client. If the client has a transaction context, it is propagated to the bean. If not, the container throws javax.transaction.TransactionRequiredException.

   Use Mandatory if you want to make sure that the EJB commits based on the client. If there is an EJB that is writing a record to a database, you may want to make sure that it is always committed within a transaction that may have other resources registered. For example, suppose an employee creation application creates an employee record in the 401(k) system, the insurance system, and the payroll system. You want to ensure that if one of these systems (EJBs) fails, none will get committed. This could be accomplished with Required, but with Mandatory you can make sure that the client always controls the committing and there is the potential for other resources to be coordinated with this one in a transaction.

6. *Never*: If the transaction attribute is Never, the container must call methods without any transaction context established by the client. If the client invokes the EJB method with a transaction context, the container throws a java.rmi.RemoteException. If the client has no transaction context, the container invokes the method without any transaction context.

   There are times when a method doesn't want to participate in a global transaction, such as the one that calls a CICS program. You could use NotSupported, but with Never, you can acknowledge to the client that the execution is not under the transaction context.

Table 8.1 summarizes the effects of each transaction attribute. In the table, T1 and T2 are two different transactions. T1 is a transaction passed with the client request, and T2 is a secondary transaction initiated by the container.

Table 8.1: Summary of transaction attributes and their effects.

Transaction Attribute	Client-Side Transaction	Bean's Transaction
Required	None	T2
	T1	T1
RequiresNew	None	T2
	T1	T2
Supports	None	None
	T1	T1
Mandatory	None	`javax.transaction.TransactionRequiredException`
	T1	T1
NotSupported	None	None
	T1	None
Never	None	None
	T1	`java.rmi.RemoteException`

Specifying transaction attributes in Application Developer

In Application Developer, you can specify the transaction attributes for the Enterprise JavaBean by following these steps:

1. Open the **EJB Deployment Descriptor** in the editor.
2. Click the **Assembly Descriptor** tab.
3. From the Container Transactions section, click the **Add . . .** button as shown in Figure 8.9.

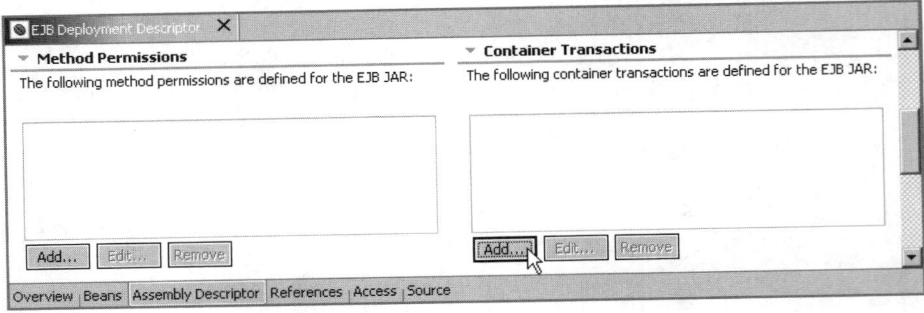

Figure 8.9: The EJB Deployment Descriptor.

4. Select the Enterprise JavaBean from the list as shown in Figure 8.10 and click **Next**.

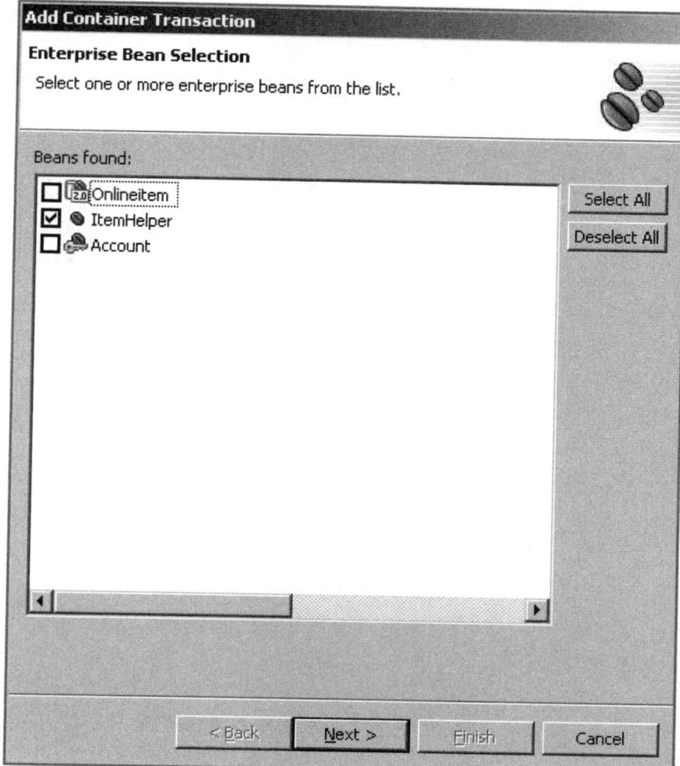

Figure 8.10: Choosing the EJB.

5. Select the transaction attribute from the drop-down list, and then select the methods from the Enterprise JavaBean to associate with this transaction attribute as shown in Figure 8.11.

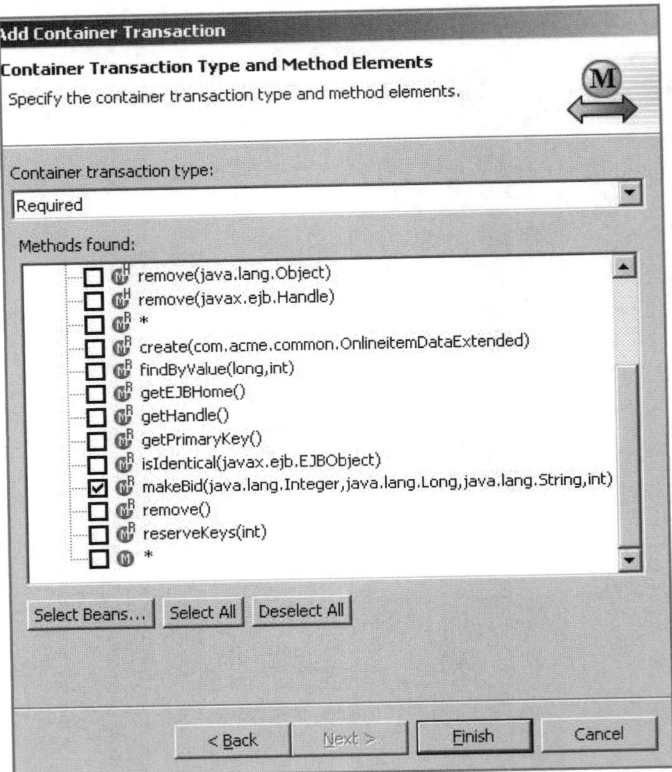

Figure 8.11: Specifying transaction attributes in Application Developer.

6. Click **Finish** and then save the changes by pressing **Ctrl+S**.

Figure 8.11 shows that the makeBid() method of the Session bean ItemHelper has been associated with transaction attribute Required. The * represents all the methods of a certain type—for example, all the methods in the remote interface or all the methods, depending on the small icon on its left.

Figure 8.12 shows that the transaction attribute Required has been selected for Enterprise JavaBean ItemHelper in the deployment descriptor.

```
<assembly-descriptor>
<container-transaction>
                <method>
                        <ejb-name>ItemHelper</ejb-name>
                        <method-intf>Remote</method-intf>
                        <method-name>makeBid</method-name>
                        <method-params>
                        <method-param>java.lang.Integer</method-param>
                        </method-params>
                </method>
                <trans-attribute>Required</trans-attribute>
        </container-transaction>
</assembly-descriptor>
```

Figure 8.12: Deployment descriptor for EJB ItemHelper.

Transactions in application clients

The J2EE platform does not require transaction support in applets and application clients. WebSphere Application Server Version 5 doesn't support UserTransaction in applets and application clients outside the J2EE containers. Applications running in the application client containers can still obtain the UserTransaction interface by a JNDI lookup of java:comp/UserTransaction in WebSphere Application Server Version 5, but this scenario is not supported by IBM even though you might not see any problem. As a result, whether applets and application clients can directly access a UserTransaction object is vendor specific. To ensure portability, applets and application clients should delegate transactional work to enterprise beans.

Transaction isolation

Isolation is important because it guarantees that concurrent users operate independently of one another, even if they are touching the same database data. With WebSphere Application Server, you can control how isolated your transactions are from one another. Choosing the right level of isolation is critical for the robustness and scalability of your deployment.

In an EJB 1.1 module, you can specify isolation at the enterprise bean method level, bean level, or module level. This capability has been removed from the EJB 2.0 modules. You cannot specify the isolation level for EJB 2.0–compliant Entity beans with CMP, which use Access Intent Policies instead.

Concurrency problems

If locking is not available and several users access a database concurrently, problems may occur if their transactions use the same data at the same time. Concurrency problems include

- Lost or buried updates
- Dirty reads
- Unrepeatable reads
- Phantom reads

Lost or buried updates

Lost updates occur when two or more transactions select the same row and then update the row based on the value originally selected. Each transaction is unaware of other transactions. The last update overwrites the updates made by the other transactions, which results in lost data.

For example, two editors make an electronic copy of the same document. Each editor changes the copy independently and then saves the changed copy, thereby overwriting the original document. The editor who saves the changed copy last overwrites the changes made by the first editor. This problem could be avoided if the second editor was prevented from making changes until the first editor had finished.

Dirty reads

A *dirty read* occurs when a second transaction selects a row that is being updated by another transaction. The second transaction is reading data that has not been committed and may be changed by the transaction updating the row.

For example, while an editor is making changes to an electronic document, a second editor takes a copy of the document that includes all the changes made so far and distributes the document to the intended audience. The first editor then decides the changes made are wrong and removes the edits and saves the document. The distributed document contains edits that no longer exist and should be treated as if they never existed. This problem could be avoided if no one was permitted to read the changed document until the first editor determined that the changes were final.

Unrepeatable reads

An *unrepeatable read* occurs when a second transaction accesses the same row several times and reads different data each time. An unrepeatable read is similar to a dirty read in that one transaction is changing the data that a second transaction is reading. However, in an unrepeatable read, the data read by the second transaction was committed by the transaction that made the change. Also, in an unrepeatable read a transaction is doing multiple reads (two or more) of the same row, and each time the information is changed by another transaction—thus the term *unrepeatable read.*

For example, an editor reads the same document twice, but between readings the writer rewrites the document. When the editor reads the document the second time, it has changed; the original read was not repeatable. This problem could be avoided if the editor was allowed to read the document only after the writer had finished writing it.

Phantom reads

A *phantom read* occurs when an insert or delete action is performed against a row that belongs to a range of rows being read by a transaction. The transaction's first read of the range of rows shows a row that no longer exists in the second or succeeding read, as the result of a deletion by a different transaction. Similarly, as the result of an insert by a different transaction, the transaction's second or succeeding read shows a row that did not exist in the original read.

For example, an editor makes changes to a document submitted by a writer, but when the changes are incorporated into the master copy of the document by the production department, they find that new, unedited material has been added to the document by the author. This problem could be avoided if no one could add new material to the document until the editor and production department finished working with the original document.

Isolation level

Transactions not only ensure the full completion (or rollback) of the statements that they enclose, they also isolate the data modified by the statements. The *isolation level* describes the degree to which the data being updated is visible to other transactions.

The isolation level defines how concurrent transactions to an enterprise information system are isolated from one another. Enterprise information systems usually support the following the isolation levels:

- *ReadUncommitted.* This level prevents a transaction from overwriting changes made by other transactions.
- *ReadCommitted.* This level prevents a transaction from reading uncommitted changes by other transactions.
- *RepeatableRead.* This level prevents a transaction from reading uncommitted changes from other transactions. In addition, it ensures that a transaction reading the same data multiple times will receive the same value even if another transaction modifies the data.
- *Serializable.* This level prevents a transaction from reading uncommitted changes from other transactions and ensures that a transaction reading the same data multiple times will receive the same value even if another transaction modifies the data. In addition, it ensures that if a query retrieves a result set based on a predicate condition and another transaction inserts data that satisfies the predicate condition, re-execution of the query will return the same result set.

The various isolation levels and their effects are summarized in Table 8.2.

Note: In this table "No" means a particular condition won't happen and "Yes" means a particular condition may happen. For example, if the isolation level is set to ReadUncommitted, lost updates won't happen but dirty reads, unrepeatable reads, and phantom reads may happen.

Table 8.2: Summary of isolation levels and their effects.

Isolation Level	Lost Update	Dirty Read	Unrepeatable Read	Phantom Read
ReadUncommitted	No	Yes	Yes	Yes
ReadCommitted	No	No	Yes	Yes
RepeatableRead	No	No	No	Yes
Serializable	No	No	No	No

Isolation level and concurrency are closely related. A less restrictive isolation level (such as ReadUncommitted) typically allows greater concurrency, at the expense of more complicated logic to deal with potential data inconsistencies. A useful guideline is to use the most restrictive isolation level provided by an EIS that still allows acceptable performance.

For consistency, all EISs accessed by a J2EE application should use the same isolation level. Currently, the J2EE specification does not define a standard way to set isolation levels when an EIS is accessed under JTA transactions. If a J2EE product does not provide a way to configure the isolation level, the EIS's default isolation level will be used. For most relational databases, the default isolation level is ReadCommitted. WebSphere Application Server supports isolation level for Enterprise JavaBeans as an IBM extension to the J2EE specification.

Do not change the isolation level within a transaction, especially if some work has already been done. In WebSphere Application Server, if a method is called with a different isolation level from that of the first method, the java.rmi.RemoteException exception is thrown.

Specifying isolation levels in Application Developer

In Application Developer, you can specify the isolation level for the Enterprise JavaBean by following these steps (the figures show the deployment descriptor editor for an EJB 1.1 module):

1. Open the **EJB Deployment Descriptor** in the editor.
2. Click the **Access** tab.
3. In the Isolation Level section, click the **Add...** button as shown in Figure 8.13.

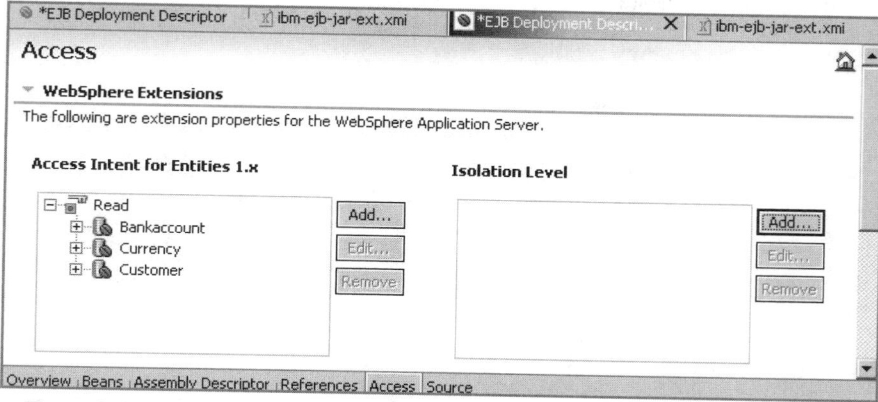

Figure 8.13: Specifying the isolation level in EJB Deployment Descriptor.

4. Select the isolation level as shown in Figure 8.14 and click **Next**.

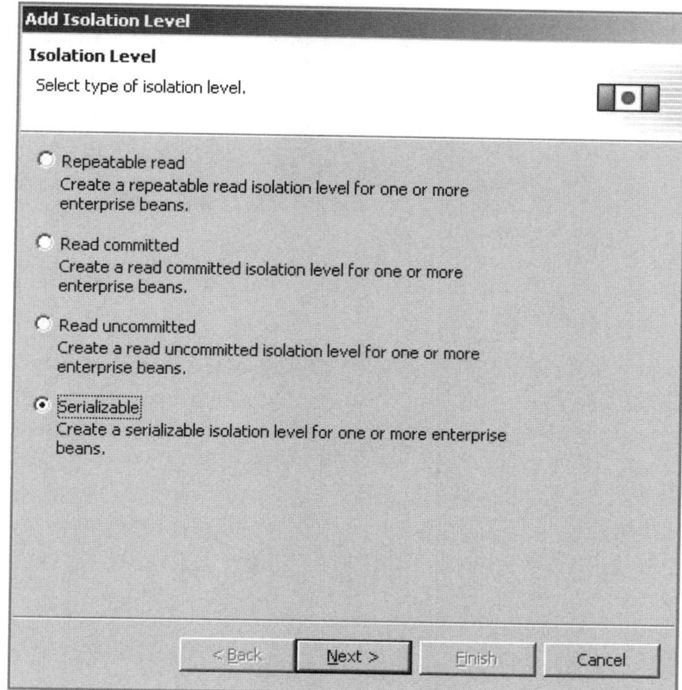

Figure 8.14: Selecting the isolation level.

5. Select the Enterprise JavaBean from the list to associate with this isolation level as shown in Figure 8.15 and click **Next**.

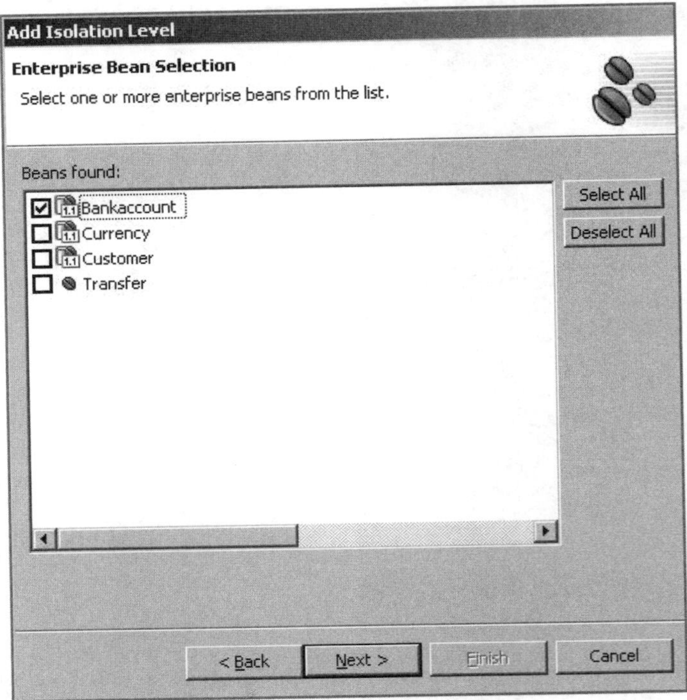

Figure 8.15: Selecting the Enterprise Bean.

6. Specify the methods to associate with this isolation level as shown in Figure 8.16.

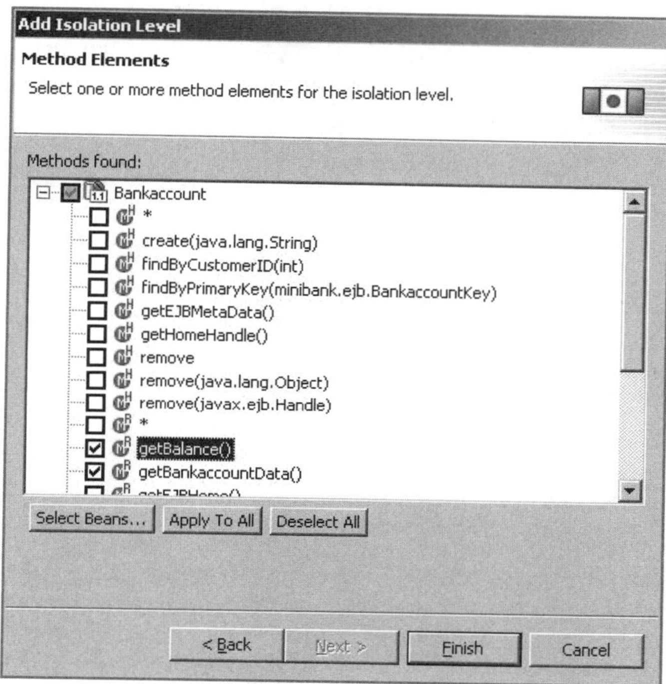

Figure 8.16: Selecting the methods for the isolation level.

7. Click **Finish** and then save the changes by pressing **Ctrl+S**.

Figure 8.17 shows the isolation level attribute for CMP Bankaccount in the IBM deployment descriptor extension.

```
<isolationLevelAttributes xmi:id="IsolationLevelAttributes_1049577990454"
        isolationLevel="SERIALIZABLE">
    <methodElements xmi:id="MethodElement_1049577990454"
        name="getBalance" parms="" type="Remote">
        <enterpriseBean xmi:type="ejb:ContainerManagedEntity"
            href="META-INF/ejb-jar.xml#Bankaccount"/>
    </methodElements>
    <methodElements xmi:id="MethodElement_1049577990455"
        name="getBankaccountData" parms="" type="Remote">
        <enterpriseBean xmi:type="ejb:ContainerManagedEntity"
            href="META-INF/ejb-jar.xml#Bankaccount"/>
    </methodElements>
</isolationLevelAttributes>
```

Figure 8.17: Code illustrating specification of isolation level.

Concurrency control

In addition to isolation level, concurrency control, including locking strategies and access intent modifiers, is supported for EJB 1.1–compliant Entity beans as an IBM extension, to allow the management of contention for data resources.

Locking strategy

One of two locking strategies can be adopted for enterprise beans: pessimistic locking or optimistic locking.

Under the pessimistic locking strategy, locks on a given resource are obtained early in the data access transaction and are not released until the transaction is closed, preventing other clients from updating the resource. The pessimistic locking strategy provides reliable and accurate access to data. However, because it acquires locks for the duration of the transaction, it can lead to high lock contention and thereby degrade performance.

Under the optimistic locking strategy, locks on a given resource are obtained immediately before a read operation and released immediately afterward. Update locks are obtained immediately before an update operation and held until the end of the transaction. The objective of optimistic concurrency is to minimize the time over which a given resource is unavailable for use by other transactions and thus improve the performance. This is especially important for long-running transactions, which under the pessimistic strategy would lock up a resource for unacceptably long periods of time. The basic assumption behind the optimistic locking strategy is that clients will rarely access the same object simultaneously. If this is not true, the performance improvement is undermined.

Whether or not to use optimistic locking depends on the type of transaction. Transactions with a high penalty for failure might be better managed with the pessimistic locking strategy. A high-penalty transaction is one for which recovery would be risky or resource intensive. For low-penalty transactions, it is often worth the risk of failure to gain efficiency through use of the optimistic locking strategy. In general, the optimistic locking strategy is more efficient when update collisions are expected to be infrequent; the pessimistic locking strategy is more efficient when update collisions are expected to occur often.

Following are the steps to configure an EJB 1.1–compliant module to use optimistic locking in Application Developer:

1. Open the **EJB Deployment Descriptor** in the editor.
2. Click the **Beans** tab.
3. From the bean list, highlight the Entity bean to which you want to assign the locking strategy.

4. In the Concurrency Control section, select the option to enable optimistic locking as shown in Figure 8.18.

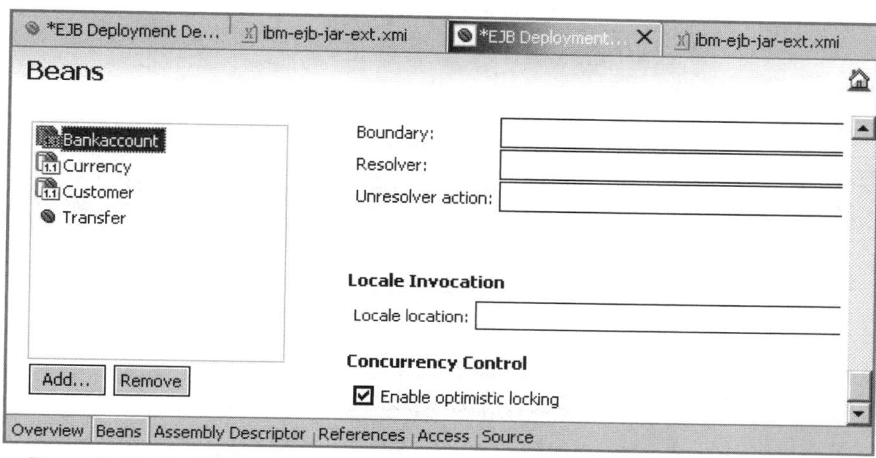

Figure 8.18: Enabling optimistic locking.

5. Save the EJB Deployment Descriptor.

Access Intent

WebSphere also provides extensions to annotate methods defined on an Entity bean's remote and home interfaces using an access intent attribute in the deployment descriptor. Mark a method with the access intent of READ if that method does not update the Entity bean's persistent state. This is called a *READ method*. Mark a method with the access intent of UPDATE if that method updates the Entity bean's persistent state. This is called an *UPDATE method*. The default access intent is UPDATE. The access intent attribute communicates a locking hint to the resource manager. Its use governs whether the SQL FOR UPDATE clause is included in the SELECT statements executed by the Container's persistence manager.

Isolation level, relational resource manager, and access intent work together to influence whether the resource manager can support either a read or an update access by an application.

The following steps are used to configure access intent for EJB 1.1–compliant Entity beans in Application Developer:

1. Open the **EJB Deployment Descriptor** in the editor.
2. Click the **Access** tab.

3. In the Access Intent for Entities 1.x section, click the **Add…** button as shown in Figure 8.19.

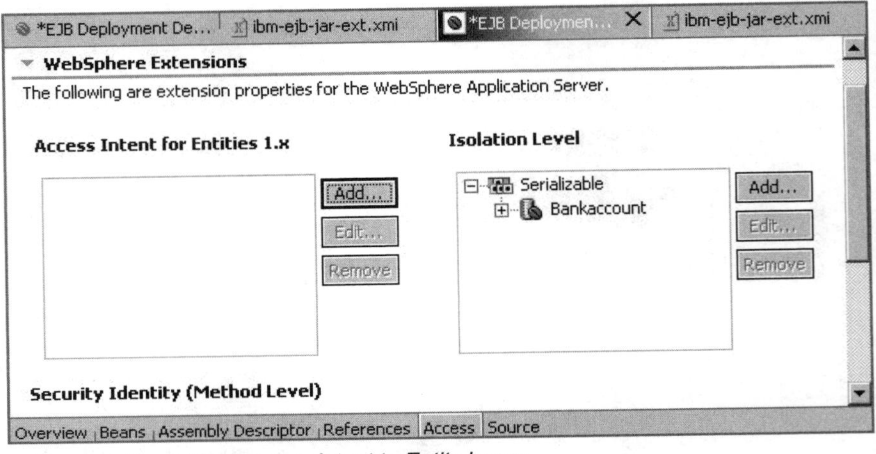

Figure 8.19: Adding access intent to Entity beans.

4. Select the access intent modifier as shown in Figure 8.20 and click **Next**.

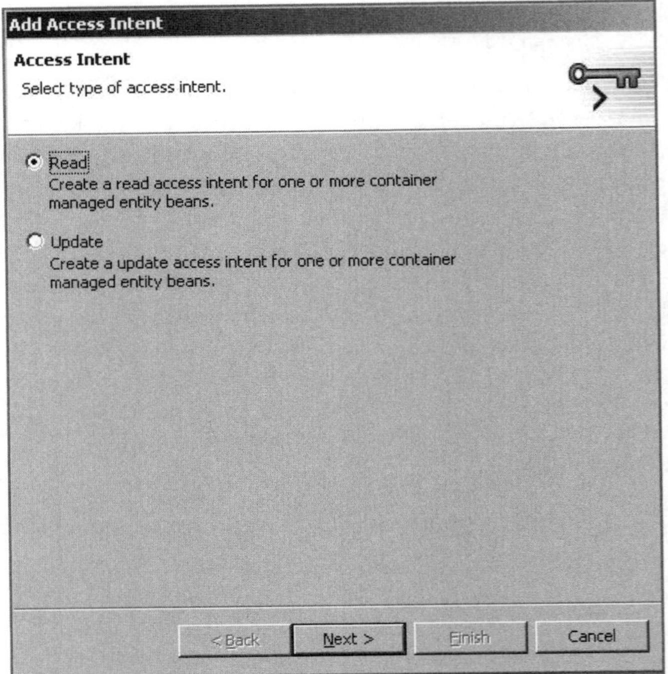

Figure 8.20: Selecting the access intent modifier.

5. Select the bean(s) for this access intent modifier as shown in Figure 8.21 and click **Next**.

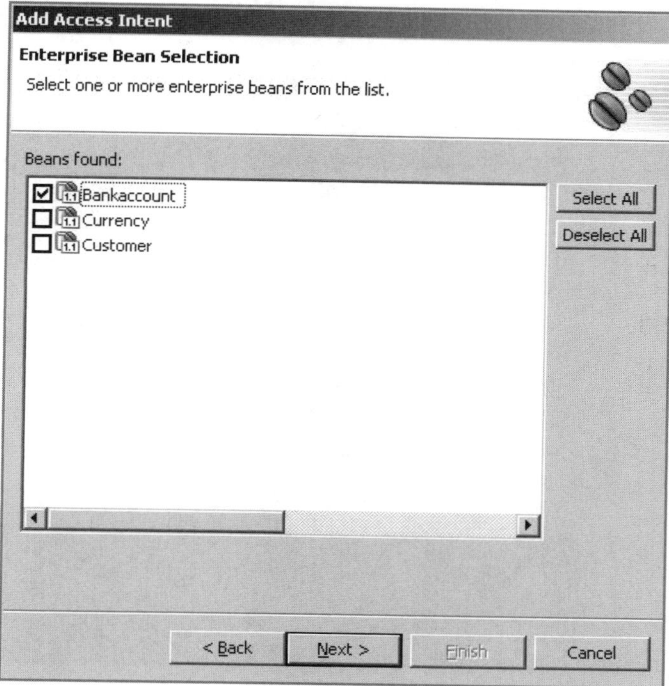

Figure 8.21: Selecting the bean(s) for the access intent modifier.

6. Select the methods of the Entity bean(s) for this access intent modifier as shown in Figure 8.22 and click **Finish**.

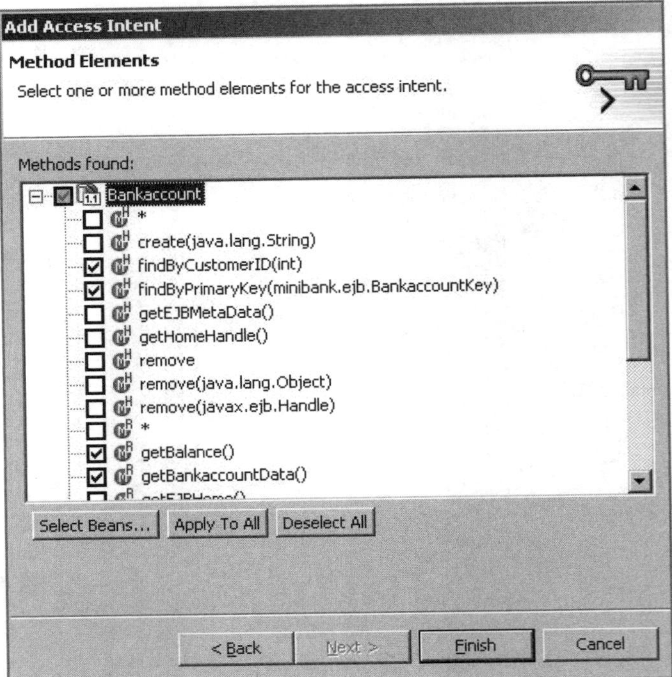

Figure 8.22: Selecting the methods for the access intent modifier.

7. Save the EJB Deployment Descriptor.

Access intent policies

Access intent policies are provided as an IBM extension for EJB 2.0–compliant modules that helps the WebSphere run-time environment manage various aspects of EJB persistence. Access intent policies are specifically designed to supplant the use of isolation level and access intent modifiers in the IBM deployment descriptor extension for EJB 1.1–compliant enterprise beans.

Access intent policies are named and defined at the module level. A module can have one or many such policies. Policies are assigned to individual methods of the declared interfaces of Entity beans and their associated home interfaces. A policy is acted on by the combination of the EJB Container and persistence manager.

WebSphere Application Server provides a set of default access intent policies for EJB 2.0–compliant Entity beans that determine the appropriate isolation level, locking strategy, and access intent used by the WebSphere run-time environment. The various access intent policies and their effects are summarized in Table 8.3. If a method is not configured with an access intent policy, the run-time environment typically uses wsPessimistic-Update-WeakestLockAtLoad by default.

Table 8.3: Summary of access intent policies.

Access Intent Policy	Locking Strategy	Access Intent	Isolation Level
wsPessimisticRead	Pessimistic	read	For Oracle, ReadCommitted; otherwise, RepeatableRead
wsPessimisticUpdate	Pessimistic	update	For Oracle, ReadCommitted; otherwise, RepeatableRead
wsPessimisticUpdate–Exclusive	Pessimistic	update	Serializable
wsPessimisticUpdate–NoCollision	Pessimistic	update	ReadCommitted
wsPessimisticUpdate–WeakestLockAtLoad	Pessimistic	update	RepeatableRead
wsOptimisticRead	Optimistic	read	ReadCommitted
wsOptimisticUpdate	Optimistic	update	ReadCommitted

The following steps are used to configure the access intent policy for EJB 2.0–compliant Entity beans in Application Developer:

1. Open the **EJB Deployment Descriptor** in the editor.
2. Click the **Access** tab.

3. In the Access Intent for Entities 2.x section, click the **Add...** button as shown in Figure 8.23.

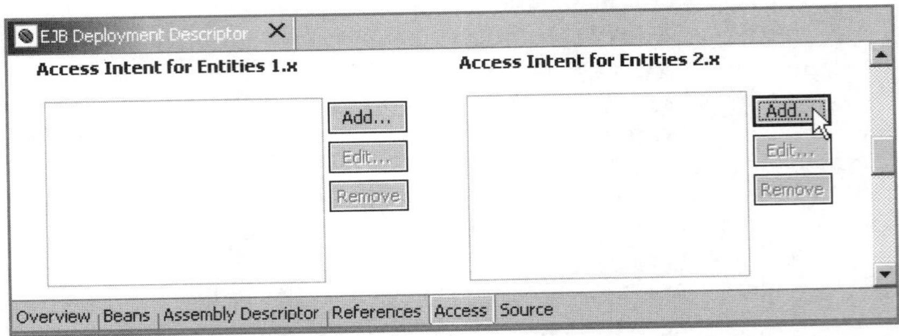

Figure 8.23: Configuring access intent for EJB 2.0–compliant Entity beans.

4. Select one of the access intent policies provided by WebSphere Application Server from the list and give it a name as shown in Figure 8.24. Click **Next**.

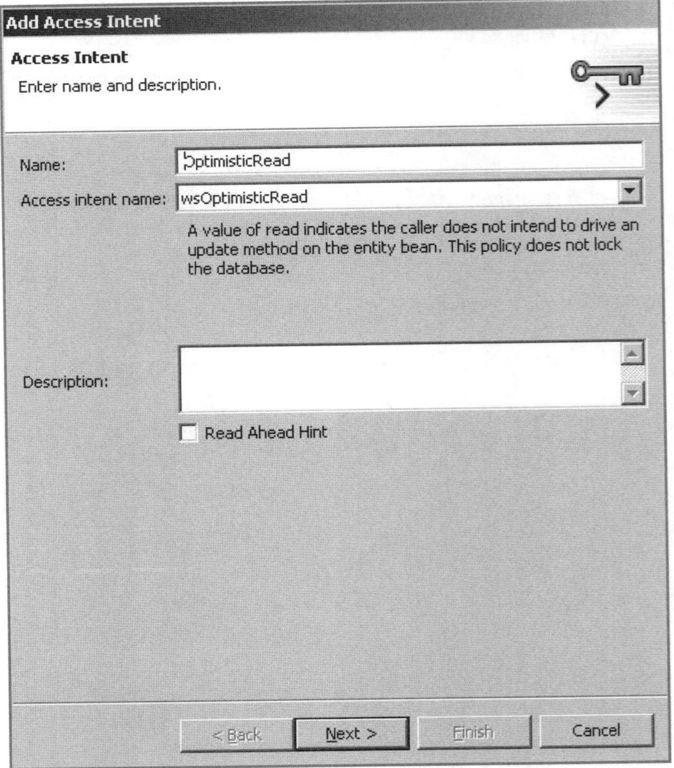

Figure 8.24: Selecting an access intent policy.

5. Select the entity beans to which the access intent policy should apply as shown in Figure 8.25 and click **Next**.

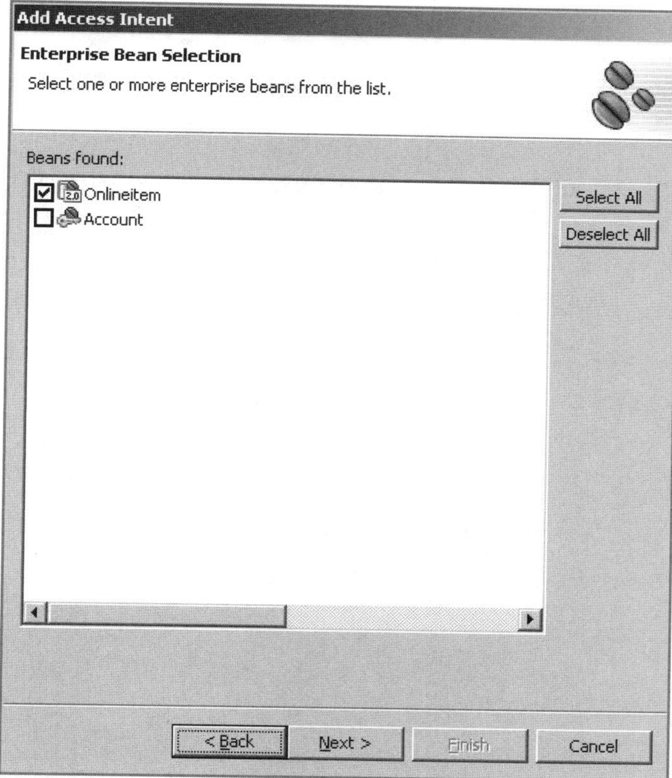

Figure 8.25: Selecting the beans to which the access intent policy should apply.

6. Select the methods to which the access intent policy should apply as shown in Figure 8.26 and click **Finish**.

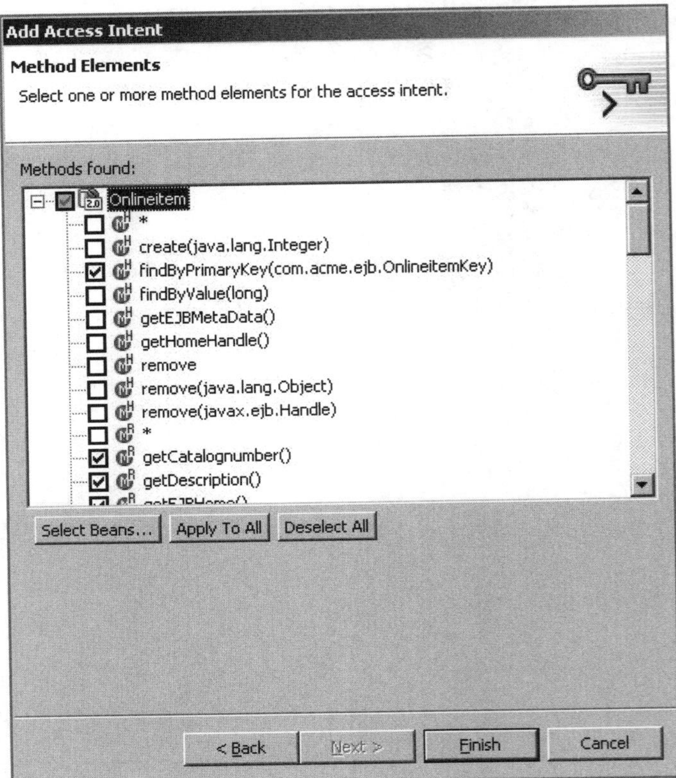

Figure 8.26: Selecting the methods to which the access intent policy should apply.

7. Save the deployment descriptor.

Best practices of using transactions in Enterprise JavaBeans

Controlling transaction from the EJB container is recommended in a multi-tier environment. Servlets and JSP pages in the Web container are mainly responsible for dealing with browser interaction and the presentation aspects of the application. They delegate the user request to the business logic layer, typically implemented by Enterprise JavaBeans, which is the right place to control transactions.

If no Enterprise JavaBean is involved in the application, a servlet should be responsible for controlling transactions as a controller in the Model-View-Controller design pattern. Keep in mind that you can demarcate transaction boundaries programmatically only in a servlet.

Using an application client component in the Application Client container to control transactions is not recommended, because not all application server vendors support this scenario, and the application assemblers have to consider client-side transaction propagation. The server-side components and the client-side components are tightly coupled, and the reusability of the server-side components is reduced.

This section describes the best practice of using transactions in enterprise beans.

Container-managed transaction demarcation versus bean-managed transaction demarcation

The recommended way to manage transactions is through container-managed demarcation. Container-managed demarcation, which demarcates transaction boundaries declaratively, frees the Application Component Provider from the burden of writing additional code to manage transactions explicitly, and helps focus on implementing the core business logic. In addition, the transaction attributes of an Enterprise JavaBean can be switched to a different value in its deployment descriptor by the Application Assembler without any change to existing code, if the business logic changes. This leads to more reusable and maintainable code and reduces the burden of code maintenance on the Application Component Provider. Furthermore, because the container is responsible for managing the transaction boundaries, the likelihood of human error is reduced. In the majority of cases, container-managed demarcation is sufficient and is the most secure, reliable, and efficient way to manage transactions for enterprise applications.

Bean-managed transaction demarcation, which demarcates transaction boundaries programmatically, is only for advanced users who want more control over the workflow. The benefit of programmatic transaction demarcation is that your bean has full control over transaction boundaries. On the other hand, you give up one of the major benefits provided by the J2EE platform. By not relying on the container, application component providers have a greater chance of introducing transactional errors. Keep in mind that bean-managed transaction demarcation is not available for Entity beans.

Encapsulating transactions in the Session bean

In a scenario of cash transfer between banking accounts, you might have Entity beans that represent each of the two accounts, both of which implement a common interface containing debit and credit methods. In order to guarantee the all-or-nothing result during the cash transfer, you want to perform both the debit and credit operations in a single transaction. The solution is to develop a Session bean containing a business method that updates both of the Entity beans within its transaction. The transaction attribute for the transfer method (method-level transaction attribute), or the Session bean (bean-level transaction attribute), should be set to Required, Mandatory, or RequiresNew. In addition, the transaction attribute of each Entity bean, or the debit and credit methods of the Entity beans, must be set to Required, Mandatory, or Supports. In Figure 8.27 the Teller Session bean updates two Entity beans in a single transaction.

```
public class Teller implements SessionBean
{
   private AccountBean checkingAccount;
   private AccountBean savingAccount;

   /**
   * TRANSFER CASH BETWEEN ACCOUNTS*/
   public void transfer()
   {
      checkingAccount.debit( 1000 );
      savingAccount.credit(1000);
   }
   //session bean methods below
}
```

Figure 8.27: Updating two bank accounts in a single transaction.

It is recommended that you avoid accessing EJB entity beans from client or Servlet code. Instead, encapsulate transactions in Session beans and access Entity beans from Session beans. This improves performance in two ways:

- It reduces the number of remote method calls. When a remote client application accesses the Entity bean directly, each getter method is a remote call. A wrapping Session bean can access the Entity bean locally, collect the data in a structure, which it returns by value.
- It provides an outer transaction context for the Entity bean. An Entity bean synchronizes its state with its underlying data store at the completion of each transaction. When the client application accesses the Entity bean directly, each getter method becomes a complete transaction. A store and a load action follow each method. When the Session bean wraps the Entity bean to provide an outer transaction context, the Entity bean synchronizes its state when the outer Session bean reaches a transaction boundary.

Using access intent properly

IBM recommends the following best practices when applying access intent policies to Enterprise JavaBeans methods.

- **Start with defaults.** The default access intent policy (wsPessimisticUpdate-WeakestLockAtLoad) loads persistent data with the weakest lock that is supported by the persistent store (typically a read lock). Updates are allowed, and the database is permitted to undertake lock escalation when necessary. This option generally works best for most EJB application patterns. After your application is built and running, you can more finely tune certain access paths in your application.

- **Don't mix access types.** Avoid using both pessimistic and optimistic policies in the same transaction. For most databases, pessimistic and optimistic policies use different isolation levels. This results in multiple database connections, which prevents you from taking advantage of the performance benefits possible through connection sharing.
- **Access intent for the ejbSelect method must be applied indirectly.** Because ejbSelect methods are not exposed through a home, remote, or local interface, you cannot apply a policy to them directly. An ejbSelect method is called by a home or business method, so apply the appropriate policy to the home or business method that governs the behavior of the ejbSelect method.
- **Take care when applying wsPessimisticUpdate-NoCollision.** This policy does not ensure data integrity. No database locks are held, so concurrent transactions can overwrite each other's updates. Use this policy only if you can be sure that only one transaction will attempt to update persistent store at any given time

Imposing time limits on transactions

A transaction taking longer than expected to complete should be considered to be in an error state. Imposing time limits on transactions is a good practice to discover performance-related error and provide additional speed and certainty.

With container-managed transaction demarcation, the timeout attribute of a transaction can usually be set in the application server as an administrative task. WebSphere Application Server also provides a feature that allows the transaction service to terminate all the transactions associated with a client after the client is inactive for certain time. The following steps show you how to configure the timeout attribute of transactions in WebSphere Application Server.

1. Start the Administrative console.
2. In the navigation pane, select **Servers → Manage Application Servers → *your_app_server***. This displays the properties of the application server *your_app_server* in the content pane.
3. Select the **Transaction Service** tab to display the properties page for the transaction service.
4. Select the **Configuration** tab to display the transaction-related configuration properties.

5. In the "Total transaction lifetime timeout" field, type the number of milliseconds a transaction can execute before it is ended by the transaction service. A value of 0 (zero) indicates that there is no timeout limit.
6. In the "Client inactivity timeout" field, type the number of seconds after which a client is considered inactive and the transaction service ends any transactions associated with that client. A value of 0 (zero) indicates that there is no timeout limit.
7. Click **OK**.
8. Save the server configuration.
9. Stop and then restart the application server.

With bean-managed transaction demarcation, Session EJBs can set a timeout value for a transaction using the setTransactionTimeout() method from theUserTransaction instance acquired from the EJBContext set in the bean. For example:

```
UserTransaction ut = ejbContext.getUserTransaction();
ut.begin();
ut.setTransactionTimeout( 30 ); //set value to 30 seconds
// invoke business functions here
transaction.commit();
```

Summary

Transactions are important to J2EE applications and share these essential characteristics: atomicity, consistency, isolation, and durability. The two common types of transactions are flat transactions and nested transactions. The J2EE platform is required to support flat transactions only.

This chapter describes the transaction model available to each J2EE Component type—applets, application clients, JSPs and servlets, and enterprise beans. An Entity bean must use container-managed transaction demarcation, whereas a Session bean may use either container-managed or bean-managed transaction demarcation. With container-managed transaction demarcation, you specify the transaction attributes in the deployment descriptor.

The J2EE platform provides powerful support for writing transactional applications. It contains the Java Transaction API, which allows applications to access transactions in a manner that is independent of specific implementations and provides a means for declaratively specifying the transactional needs of an application. These capabilities shift the burden of transaction management from J2EE application component providers to J2EE product vendors. Application component providers can thus focus on specifying the desired transaction behavior and rely on a J2EE product to implement the behavior.

Concurrency problems include lost updates, dirty reads, unrepeatable reads, and phantom reads. Configuring the isolation level is a way to avoid these problems.

Specific to Application Developer, this chapter introduced the steps to customize transaction attributes and isolation levels for Enterprise JavaBeans.

Test yourself

Key terms

JTA

JTS

transaction isolation

ACID

atomicity

consistency

isolation

durability

commit

rollback

two-phase commit (2PC)

bean-managed (programmatic) transaction demarcation

Container-managed (declarative) transaction demarcation

OTS

XA

transaction manager (TM)

Resource Manager (RM)

transaction attributes

access intent policies

Review questions

1. Since the container can manage all transactions and can be configured easily using deployment descriptors, why should a developer ever use bean-managed transactions? What's the benefit of having the JTA at all?
2. How can servlets and JavaServer Pages participate in transactions? Can they be configured to do so in the deployment descriptor?
3. What types of Enterprise JavaBeans may use bean-managed transactions?
4. The transaction monitor is provided by the application server, even if the transactions are demarcated programmatically. How does an enterprise bean get access to the container—for example, to acquire a UserTransaction reference?
5. According to the EJB 2.0 specification, CMP Entity beans that are persisted to a transaction data store should use only three of the possible six transaction attributes. Which are they?
6. What's the difference between the transaction attributes Required and Mandatory? Why would you use one over the other?

7. How can applets and application clients participate in transactions?

8. When accessing a method, the container throws a TransactionRequiredException. With which transaction attribute was the method configured?

9. A *system exception* occurs when one of the services supporting an application fails. Examples include a bad JDNI lookup or the inability to get a database connection. Normally the container wraps such an exception inside javax.ejb.EJBException, which is a subclass of java.lang.RuntimeException, and therefore does not need to be declared. Such an exception causes the container to automatically roll back any open transactions. Say your application accesses a database, and if a particular value is incorrect, it throws a custom-made Incorrect ValueException. How do you ensure that any existing transaction is rolled back, assuming you are using container-managed transaction demarcation?

10. Transactions are also available in the JDBC package, where the connection interface provides the methods setAutoCommit(boolean), commit(), and rollback(). This is in contrast to the JTA methods described in this chapter. What advantages do JTA transactions provide?

CHAPTER 9

Security

Colin Yu

Chapter topics

- *Introduction*
- *Security basics*
- *J2EE security*
- *Declarative security for Web modules*
- *Declarative security for EJB modules*
- *Declarative security for applications*
- *Programmatic security*
- *WebSphere security*
- *Configuring WebSphere security*

Certification objectives

- *Access container and server services from enterprise components*
- *Configure resource and security-role references*
- *Deploy enterprise applications into servers*

Security, one of J2EE's many technologies, is always important to Web applications. One of the aspects of security includes security provided by an application server, such as IBM WebSphere Application Server.

This chapter first reviews the fundamental concepts of security, including authentication, authorization, and cryptography, and then explores various concepts of J2EE security, which supports both declarative security models and programmatic security models. This chapter also describes the following:

- How to configure security for J2EE applications with IBM WebSphere Studio Application Developer
- WebSphere extended security architecture and major components
- How to use the IBM WebSphere Application Server Administrative Console to configure WebSphere security, including authentication and authorization mechanisms, user registries, and network security

You may be interested in the introductory topics on SSL (Secure Socket Layer) in the "Security basics" section and on JAAS (Java Authentication and Authorization Service), JSSE (Java Secure Socket Extension), LTPA (Lightweight Third-Party Authentication), and Custom Registry in the "WebSphere security" section. For more information on these topics, refer to the IBM WebSphere Application Server InfoCenter at *http://publib7b.boulder.ibm.com/webapp/wasinfo1/index.jsp*.

Introduction

Enterprise security must be approached from a systemic point of view, which means that all areas of the enterprise infrastructure must be considered together. Those areas include the following:

- Access to the enterprise: Not just Web access, but all types of access, such as Electronic Data Interchange (EDI), must be considered.
- Network security: How to guarantee the confidentiality and integrity of the information must be addressed.
- System security: All platforms in an enterprise should have the same security policy, which is normally called Single sign-on.
- Application security: For example, J2EE security must be provided for the J2EE applications.
- Database and transaction manager security: Because requests move from platform to platform in a J2EE model, it is important to ensure that the database and transaction managers are sensitive to the security context.

The Java security model often places the application programmer in the position of performing security tasks. The J2EE model starts to relegate some of those tasks to the container but still provides the applications programmer with the ability to perform security tasks. The major goals of J2EE security models include the following:

- Support secure application development without knowing how the application servers provide the security service during runtime.

- Reduce the application developer's burden and delegate the responsibility to other roles such as application assembler and application deployer.
- Be policy driven, which isolates the security constraints from the implementation of the application.

WebSphere Application Server Version 5 is a J2EE 1.3-compliant Java application server. It uses a declarative security model in which an application expresses security constraints in a form that is external to the application. This external form of the constraint allows the application to be independent of the chosen security mechanism. The extended security architecture of WebSphere Application Server also allows other security service providers to integrate with the Application Server.

The objective of this chapter is to understand the J2EE security model and security mechanisms of IBM WebSphere Application Server.

Security basics

This section reviews some fundamental concepts of security services and cryptography.

Two fundamental security services are supported by IBM WebSphere Application Server:

- Authentication
- Authorization

Authentication

Authentication is the process of establishing whether a client is valid in a particular context, verifying identity prior to granting access to requested resources. A client can be an end user, a machine, or an application.

The authentication process involves gathering some unique information from the client. There are three major categories of secure authentication used to gather this unique information:

- Knowledge-based—for example, accessing the system with a user name and a password for login, which is compared with the values stored in the system
- Key-based—for example, physical keys, encryption keys, and key cards
- Biometric—use of physiological or behavioral characteristics to verify the identity of an individual, such as fingerprints, voice patterns, or DNA

Authentication mechanisms can combine technologies from these categories. One example is digital certificates, where key-based and knowledge-based authentication are used together.

Authorization

Authorization is the process of checking whether the authenticated user has access to the requested resource. There are two fundamental methods for authorization:

- Access control list (ACL)
- Capability list

Access control list

Each resource has an associated list of users and the users' permissions for that resource (for example, use, read, write, execute, delete, or create). Usually, an access control list specifies a set of roles that are allowed to use a particular resource and also designates the people allowed to play these roles.

For example, in a bank account object (see Table 9.1), we can have different methods (transfer, deposit, getBalance, setInterest, etc.). The access right can be granted on the basis of the roles of the users within the organization. A bank teller can have access to the *getBalance* method but not to *setBalance* method, while a manager can have access to both methods.

Table 9.1: Example of a role access control list.

Resources	Bank teller role	Manager role
GetBalance method	Yes	Yes
SetBalance method	No	Yes

Capability list

Associated with each user is a list of resources and the corresponding privileges held by that user. In this case, the holder is given the right to perform the operation on a particular resource.

When a capability list is used for the bank account object (see Table 9.2), the access right is granted to the user if the resource is listed in the user's capability list.

Table 9.2: Example of a capability list.

Roles	getBalance method	setBalance method
Bank teller role	Yes	No
Manager role	Yes	No

You will find the Tables 9.1 and 9.2 very similar, but the rows and the columns are switched. Actually, this is the difference between the two approaches. We have two sets: roles and resources. In the first case, roles are mapped to resources, while in the second case resources are mapped to roles. Generally, the access control list is chosen because managing security for certain resources is easier and more flexible than mapping resources to roles.

Role-based security

Roles are different levels of security that relate to a specific application. For example, in a banking scenario, employees will be mapped to different roles and then have different access capability. The mapping between users and roles is usually one of these three:

- Users are mapped directly to specific security roles.
- Groups are formed, users are defined as members of a group, and the groups are defined to specific security roles.
- A combination of user/group mapping to security roles is used to handle any exceptions.

Cryptography

The popularity of the Internet makes ways of protecting data and messages from tampering or reading more important. One of the techniques for ensuring privacy of files and communications is *cryptography.*

There are two kinds of cryptography: *symmetric* and *asymmetric*. Symmetric cryptography uses the same key (the secret key) to encrypt and decrypt a message, and asymmetric cryptography uses one key (the public key) to encrypt a message and a different key (the private key) to decrypt it.

Secret-key cryptography

Secret-key cryptography is a symmetric cryptography method that is faster than public-key cryptography. However, it has a considerable disadvantage as well: The same key is needed for encryption and decryption, and both parties must have the same keys. In today's cryptography, the secret keys do not belong to persons but to communication sessions. At the beginning of a session, one of the parties creates a session key and delivers it to the other party; they can then communicate securely. At the end of the session, both parties delete the key, and if they want to communicate again, they must create another key (Figure 9.1).

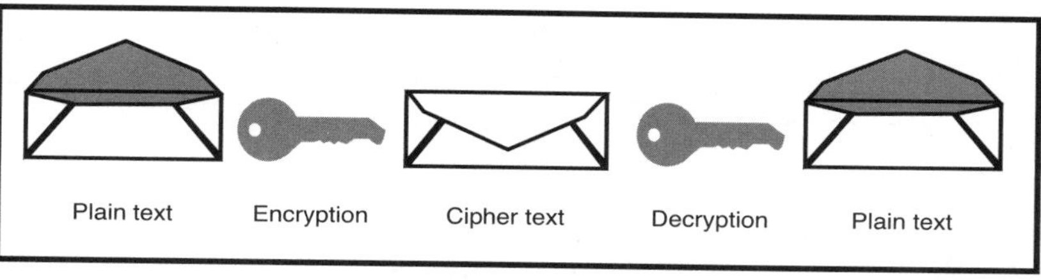

Figure 9.1: Secret-key encryption.

Public-key cryptography

The first imperative of public-key cryptography is the ability to deliver the session keys securely. Public-key cryptography involves the use of different keys for encrypting and decrypting functions. If you encrypt something with Key 1, you can decrypt it only with Key 2, as shown in Figure 9.2.

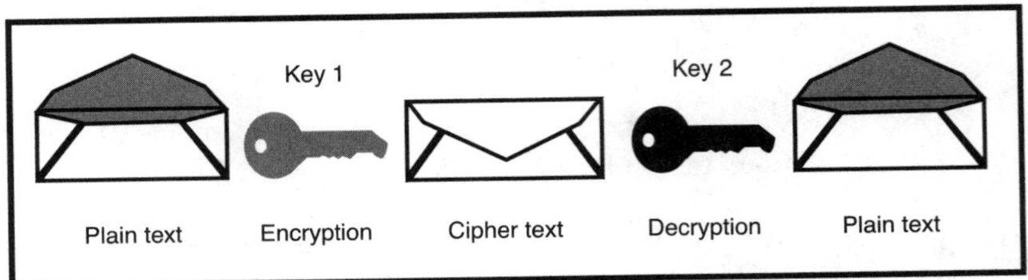

Figure 9.2: Public-key encryption.

This architecture allows the owner of the keys to use one of them as a private key and distribute the other key to the public. Nobody except for the owner of the private key can decrypt the messages that were encrypted by the public key.

Because public-key algorithms are very slow, we usually use the public-key method to deliver the session key, which is a secret key, and use the secret-key algorithms to transmit large amounts of data. This is the concept that Secure Socket Layer (SSL) follows to establish a secure communication.

Besides enabling a secure connection, the public-key algorithm is used for digital signatures, which in turn are used by certificates, both of which will be discussed in the following section.

Digital signature

In a digital world, one often wants to indicate the owner or creator of a document or to signify one's agreement with a document's content. A digital signature is a cryptographic technique for achieving these goals.

Just as with human signatures, digital signing should be done in such a way that digital signatures are verifiable, non-forgeable, and non-repudiable. That is, it must be possible to "prove" that a document signed by an individual was indeed signed by that individual and that only that individual could have signed the document. This proof is easily accomplished with public-key cryptography.

Suppose that Bob wants to sign a "document," m, digitally. To sign this document, Bob simply uses his private key, E_B, to compute $E_B(m)$ as the signature. Suppose Alice has received the document, m, and the signature, $E_B(m)$. She wants to know whether Bob had indeed signed the document and was the only person who could possibly have signed it.

Alice takes Bob's public key, D_B, and applies it to the digital signature, $E_B(m)$, associated with the document m. If the result $D_B(E_B(m)) = m$, it proves that only Bob could have signed the document.

Message digests

We have seen that public-key encryption technology can be used to create a digital signature. Given the overheads of encryption and decryption, signing data via complete encryption/decryption can be superfluous. A more efficient approach, using so-called message digests, can accomplish these same goals without full-message encryption.

A message digest is in many ways like a checksum. Message-digest algorithms take a message, m, of arbitrary length and compute a fixed-length "fingerprint" of the data, known as a message digest, $H(m)$. The message digest protects the data in the sense that if m is changed to m', then $H(m')$ will not match $H(m)$. In our previous sample, rather than having Bob digitally sign the entire message by computing $E_B(m)$, he should be able to sign just the message digest by computing $E_B(H(m))$.

Certificate

One of the principle features of public-key encryption is that it is possible for two entities to exchange secret messages without having to exchange secret keys. Of course, the communicating entities still have to exchange public keys. A user can make his public key publicly available in many ways, for example, by posting the key on his personal Web page, placing the key in a public-key server, or by sending the key to a correspondent by email. A Web commerce site can place its public key on its server in a manner such that browsers automatically download the public key when connecting to the site.

There is, however, a subtle, yet critical, problem with public-key cryptography. How do the entities (users, browsers, etc.) know for sure that they have the public key of the entity with which they are communicating? For example, when Alice is communicating with Bob using public-key cryptography, she needs to know for sure that the public key that is supposed to be Bob's is indeed Bob's.

Binding a public key to a particular entity is typically done by a certification authority (CA), whose job it is to validate identities and issue certificates. VeriSign is a well known CA. A CA has the following roles:

1. A CA verifies that an entity (a person, a company, and so on) is who it says it is.
2. Once the CA verifies the identity of the entity, the CA creates a certificate that binds the public key of the identity to the identity. The certificate contains the public key and globally unique identifying information about the owner of the public key (for example, a human name or an IP address). The certificate is digitally signed by the CA.

The Secure Socket Layer

The Secure Socket Layer (SSL) is a protocol running above TCP/IP that governs the transport and routing of data over the Internet and below the application-layer protocols, such as HTTP, Lightweight Directory Access Protocol (LDAP), and Internet Message Access Protocol (IMAP). It is based on technologies that include certificate, public-key cryptography, and private-key cryptography. It allows the SSL-enabled client and server to authenticate each other and establish safe connections over the Internet.

Let us think about an online shopping scenario. A customer is using a browser to navigate the online categories and wants to make a purchase. She needs to enter her credit card information and send it to the server over the Internet. Certainly she wants to make sure that the confidential information will be sent to the right server. SSL server authentication allows a client (a user or a browser) to confirm a server's identity by verifying the server certificate with the public key of the issuer, a certificate authority.

In the online shopping scenario, the server can optionally make sure the purchase is from a valid customer, from either a username/password combination or a client certificate. Similarly to SSL server authentication, SSL client authentication allows a server to confirm a user's identity with the client certificate. However, in most online shopping cases, SSL client authentication is not necessary. One reason is that not all the clients have their own certificates from a CA. The other reason is that the server can authenticate the clients later with other methods after a SSL connection is set up.

After the server and the client authenticate each other, a secure connection is needed for further communication between the server and the client. All data sent over an encrypted SSL connection is protected, thus providing a high degree of confidentiality. The SSL connection is implemented by public-key cryptography and secret-key cryptography and is created by the following steps, called the SSL handshake:

1. The client creates a *premaster secret key,* encrypts it with the public key obtained from the server certificate, and sends the encrypted premaster secret key to the server.

2. The server receives the encrypted premaster secret key from the client and uses its private key to decrypt the premaster secret key.

3. Both the server and the client generate the *master secret key* from the premaster secret key and then use the master secret key to generate the *session keys,* which are the secret keys used to encrypt and decrypt information exchanged during the SSL session.

4. The server and the client send encrypted messages to each other indicating that the handshake is finished.

J2EE application security

J2EE application security uses role-based security architecture. At development time, application developers determine the security policies for the application by assigning secure resources and methods to certain security roles, for example, managers, employees, or customers. At application assembly time, the security roles are mapped to real users and groups. This two-phase security administration approach allows great flexibility and portability for the application, shown in Figure 9.3.

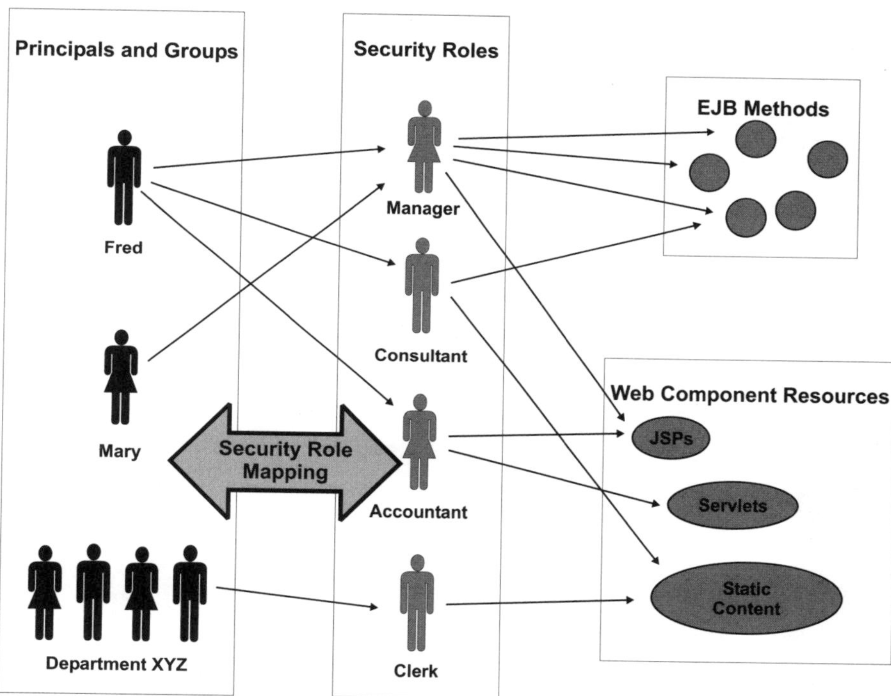

Figure 9.3: J2EE security role mapping.

At runtime, J2EE containers are responsible for enforcing access control secure resources and methods. J2EE containers support two types of security:

- Declarative security
- Programmatic security

This and the following three sections focuse on declarative security, which means that the security polices are defined in an application's deployment descriptor instead of in the application code. It is the responsibility of the application assemblers to define the security roles, access control, and authentication requirements.

Programmatic security allows the application developers to use J2EE API to determine the caller's identity and role, which allows flexible security control to be achieved in application code. Programmatic security will be discussed in more detail in the section titled "Programmatic security."

As discussed in the preceding section, security includes authorization, authentication, and cryptography. A J2EE application may contain Web modules, EJB modules, and application client modules. From the authorization viewpoint, security constraints need to be defined for the security resources and methods in those Web modules and EJB modules. From the authentication viewpoint, the Web modules are responsible for authenticating the clients, probably with the help of user registries and cryptography such as SSL and client certificates. From the role-based security architecture viewpoint, the security roles need to be mapped to real users and groups. A typical process for an application assembler to declare security for a J2EE application will look like this:

For Web modules,

- Defining the authentication method
- Defining the security roles
- Defining the security constraints on Web resource collections
- Defining the security role references for individual servlets/JSPs

For EJB modules,

- Defining security roles
- Assigning method permissions
- Assigning roles for unprotected methods (during application installation time)
- Managing Delegation Policy
- Defining security role references (optional)

For applications,

- Gathering the security roles from all the modules within the application
- Mapping security roles to real users and groups

The following sections will describe security configurations using the aforementioned roadmap.

Declarative security for Web modules

The Web module of an enterprise application is comprised of one or more related servlets, JSPs, and XML and HTML files that can be managed as one integrated unit. This section describes the process and tools of IBM WebSphere Studio Application Developer to configure security for the Web modules of an enterprise application.

Defining the authentication method

The authentication mechanism defines how the user will be authenticated by the Web application. Before any authorization constraint is applied, the user will need to pass the authentication process using a configured mechanism. The servlet specification defines four mechanisms to authenticate users:

- Basic authentication
- Digest authentication
- Client Certificate authentication
- Form-based authentication

Basic authentication

Basic authentication, which is defined in the HTTP 1.0 specification, is the simplest and most commonly used mechanism to protect resources. When a browser requests any of the protected resources, the server sends an Authentication Required HTTP header back to the Web browser, and the browser pops up a little window that asks for a username and password. If the user enters a valid username and password, the server sends the resource.

The following points are advantages of Basic authentication:

- It is very easy to set up.
- All browsers support it.

The following points are disadvantages of Basic authentication:

- It is not secure because the username and password are not encrypted.
- You cannot customize the look and feel of the dialog box presented by the Web browser.

Digest authentication

Digest authentication is the same as Basic authentication except that in this case the password is sent in an encrypted format. IBM WebSphere Application Server Version 5 does not support this option.

Client Certificate authentication

Client Certificate authentication is performed when the SSL connection is established. As was described in the discussion of SSL in the "Security basics" section, a Web container can optionally authenticate the clients with their certificates before an SSL connection between the server and the client is established. The Web container extracts the credentials from the client certificate for future requests from the same client.

The following points are advantages of Client Certificate authentication:

- It is the most secure of the four types.
- All the commonly used browsers support it.

The following points are disadvantages of Client Certificate authentication:

- It requires the client to get a certificate from a CA.
- It is costly to implement and maintain.

Form-based authentication

Form-based authentication is similar to basic authentication; however, instead of using the browser's pop-up dialog box, it uses an HTML form to capture the username and password. Developers must create an HTML page that contains a FORM tag with action attribute *j_security_check* and two fields, *j_username* and *j_password,* that allow the user to enter the username and password. Everything else in the HTML page is customizable. As a result, the developers can control the look and feel of the login page. By default, the values that the user supplies in the form are transmitted in clear text as parameter values in the HTTP request. To secure the user information during transmission, the connection should be encrypted, for example, using SSL.

Form-based authentication works in the following manner:

1. An unauthenticated user requests a resource protected by the Form-based authentication type.
2. The application server redirects the request to the Login Form defined in the Web deployment descriptor.
3. The user enters the user ID and password and submits the form. The action triggers the servlet j_security_check.
4. If the servlet authenticates the user successfully, the originally requested resource is displayed. Otherwise, the error page specified in the deployment descriptor is displayed.

The following points are advantages of Form-based authentication:

- It is very easy to set up.
- All the browsers support it.
- Developers can control the look and feel of the login page.

The following points are disadvantages of Form-based authentication:

- It is not secure because the username and password are not encrypted.
- It should be used only when a session is maintained using HTTPS (HTTP protocol over SSL).

Configuring the authentication method using Application Developer

The authentication method is specified in the deployment descriptor of the Web module. The following steps show how to configure the authentication method using Application Developer.

1. From the Resource Perspective, select the Web project in the J2EE Navigator, expand the tree **Web Content → WEB-INF**, and double-click the file **web.xml**. A Web deployment descriptor opens in a deployment descriptor editor window.
2. Select the **Pages** tab.
3. In the Login section, click the drop-down list of **Authentication method** and select one of the authentication methods.
4. If you choose Basic as the authentication method, you need to provide the Realm name, which is an arbitrary name. If you choose Form as the authentication method, you need to select the Login page and the Error page. The Error Page will be displayed when the authentication fails.
5. Save the deployment descriptor by pressing **Ctrl+S** or selecting **File → Save Web Deployment Descriptor** from the menu.

The code in Figure 9.4 is a web.xml code snippet that shows an authentication mechanism configuration using Form.

```
<login-config>
        <auth-method>FORM</auth-method>
        <form-login-config>
                <form-login-page>login.html</form-login-page>
                <form-error-page>error.html</form-error-page>
        </form-login-config>
</login-config>
```

Figure 9.4: Web module deployment descriptor excerpt illustrating form-based authentication.

Defining security roles

In the Web deployment descriptor web.xml, all security roles used in the Web module must be named, with an optional description. A role is a placeholder; the placeholders are later mapped to real users and groups at application deployment time.

The following steps describe how to create security roles for a Web module using Application Developer:

1. From the Resources Perspective, select the Web project in the J2EE Navigator, expand the tree **Web Content → WEB-INF**, and double-click the file **web.xml**. A Web deployment descriptor opens in a deployment descriptor editor window.
2. Click on the **Security** tab.
3. In the Security Roles section, click **Add**.
4. Change the name of the new added role to the one you want. Optionally, you can give a description to this role.
5. Save the deployment descriptor by pressing **Ctrl+S** or selecting **File → Save Web Deployment Descriptor** from the menu.

The code in Figure 9.5 is a web.xml code snippet that shows that two security roles, Employees and Managers, are defined.

```
<security-role>
      <description>company employees</description>
      <role-name>Employees</role-name>
</security-role>
<security-role>
      <description></description>
      <role-name>Managers</role-name>
</security-role>
```

Figure 9.5: Web module deployment descriptor excerpt illustrating security roles.

Defining security constraints

A Web module may define multiple security constraints. Security constraints declare how the content of the application is protected. For a given security constraint, three characteristics should be defined:

- Web resource collections: A Web resource collection is a set of URL patterns and HTTP methods in the resources the URL patterns represent. A security constraint may have multiple Web resource collections.
- Authorization constraint: An authorization constraint defines the roles that are authorized to access the Web resource collections within the security constraint.

- User data constraint: A user data constraint indicates the transport layer setting needed for client/server communication in order to satisfy a given security constraint. This setting should guarantee either content integrity (preventing tampering in transit) or confidentiality (preventing reading data during transfer). For example, an application may require the use of HTTPS as a means of communication instead of plain HTTP by setting the User Data Constraint to confidentiality. IBM WebSphere Application Server will automatically change the protocol from HTTP to HTTPS when a client accesses the secure resources of this application.

The following steps describe how to create security constraints for a Web module using Application Developer:

1. From the Resources Perspective, select the Web project in the J2EE Navigator, expand the tree **Web Content → WEB-INF**, and double-click the file **web.xml**. A Web deployment descriptor opens in a deployment descriptor editor window.
2. Click on the **Security** tab.
3. Select the **Security Constraints** tab at the top of the editor, then click the **Add** button under the Security Constraints list box. A new item of security constraint appears in the list box. A new item also appears in the list box of the Web Resource Collections section.
4. Select **(New Web Resource Collection)** in the Web Resource Collections section and click the **Edit** button. The Web Resource Collection dialog box opens.
5. In the Name field, enter something meaningful to you.
6. In the HTTP Methods window, check the boxes for the methods that are allowed for this resource collection, for example **POST** and **GET** methods. If you don't choose any method, all the methods are allowed.
7. In the URL Patterns window, enter the URL patterns that represent the Web resources under this collection, for example:

   /*.do

   / home.html

   /news/results.jsp
8. Click **OK** to update the new added item in the Web Resource Collection section. You can add multiple Web resource collections for one security constraint.
9. In the Authorized Roles section, click the **Edit** button. The Define Authorization Constraint dialog window appears.

10. Optionally, you can provide a Description for this authorization constraint. Check the box for the roles that are authorized to access the Web resource collections within the security constraint. Click the **OK** button.
11. Optionally, you can select the User Data Constraint that applies to this security constraint.
12. When you are finished defining other security constraints for this Web project, save the deployment descriptor by pressing **Ctrl+S** or selecting **File → Save Web Deployment Descriptor** from the menu.

The web.xml code snippet in Figure 9.6 shows two security constraints.

```
<security-constraint>
       <web-resource-collection>
              <web-resource-name>HTML pages</web-resource-name>
              <description>Collection of HTML pages</description>
              <url-pattern>/*.html</url-pattern>
              <http-method>GET</http-method>
              <http-method>POST</http-method>
       </web-resource-collection>
       <web-resource-collection>
              <web-resource-name>XML Files</web-resource-name>
              <description>Collecton of XML files</description>
              <url-pattern>/*.xml</url-pattern>
       </web-resource-collection>
       <auth-constraint>
              <description></description>
              <role-name>Employees</role-name>
              <role-name>Managers</role-name>
       </auth-constraint>
</security-constraint>
<security-constraint>
       <web-resource-collection>
              <web-resource-name>Dynamic Pages</web-resource-name>
              <description></description>
              <url-pattern>/*.do</url-pattern>
              <url-pattern>/*.jsp</url-pattern>
              <http-method>POST</http-method>
              <http-method>GET</http-method>
       </web-resource-collection>
       <auth-constraint>
              <description></description>
              <role-name>Managers</role-name>
       </auth-constraint>
</security-constraint>
```

Figure 9.6: Web module deployment descriptor excerpt illustrating security constraints.

Defining security role references for individual servlets/JSPs (optional)

Security role references are used to provide a layer of indirection between security roles named in servletor JSP Java code and security roles that are defined at application assembly time. This allows security role names to be modified without requiring changes in the application code. As you will see from the "Programmatic Security" section later on, the security role references will be used in the method isCallerInRole(String roleName), which is used to determine whether the caller is a member of a particular role.

The following steps describe how to create security role references for a servlet using WebSphere Studio Application Developer. Please note that Application Developer can create only the security role reference with the same name as the security role that it is mapped to. If you need to use particular security role references in your Java code, you need to modify the web.xml file (edit the <role-name> tab, which is under the <security-role-ref> tab) in Application Developer directly or use the Application Assembly Tool to create security role references.

1. From the Resources Perspective, select the Web project in the J2EE Navigator, expand the tree **Web Content → WEB-INF,** and double-click the file **web.xml**. A Web deployment descriptor opens in a deployment descriptor editor window.
2. Click on the **Servlet** tab.
3. From the list box of servlets and JSPs, select the one for which you want to define the constraint.
4. In the Authorized Roles section, click the **Edit** button.
5. From the pop-up dialog, select the roles that are authorized to access this servlet or JSP. Click **OK** to close the dialog.
6. Save the deployment descriptor by pressing **Cntrl+S** or selecting **File → Save Web Deployment Descriptor** from the menu.

The web.xml code snippet in Figure 9.7 shows two role references, Managers and Employes, that are defined for the Servlet ActionServlet.

```
<servlet>
   <servlet-name>ActionServlet</servlet-name>
   <display-name>Action</display-name>
   <servlet-class>cm.test.ActionServlet</servlet-class>
   <init-param>
         <param-name>debug</param-name>
         <param-value>0</param-value>
   </init-param>
   <load-on-startup>2</load-on-startup>
   <security-role-ref>
         <role-name>Employees</role-name>
         <role-link>Employees</role-link>
   </security-role-ref>
   <security-role-ref>
         <role-name>Managers</role-name>
         <role-link>Managers</role-link>
   </security-role-ref>
</servlet>
```

Figure 9.7: Web module deployment descriptor excerpt illustrating security role references for a servlet.

Declarative security for EJB modules

EJBs are J2EE components that implement the business logic of an application. They typically have access to sensitive data. Therefore, assigning the appropriate security policy to EJBs is very critical.

Access control can be applied to individual Session and Entity bean methods so that only callers who are members of the particular security roles can call those methods. Session, Entity, and Message-Driven bean methods can be delegated to execute under the identity of the caller, the EJB server, or a specific security role, which is called Delegation Policy or Run-As Mode Mapping. This section describes the process and tools in IBM WebSphere Studio Application Developer for configuring security for the EJB modules of an enterprise application.

Defining security roles

In the EJB module deployment descriptors ejb-jar.xml, all security roles used in the EJB module must be named, with an optional description. A role is a placeholder that is later mapped to real users and groups at application deployment time.

The following steps describe how to create security roles for an EJB module using Application Developer:

1. From the Resource Perspective, select the EJB project in the J2EE Navigator, expand the tree **ejbModule → META-INF**, and double-click the file **ejb-jar.xml**. The EJB deployment descriptor opens in a Deployment Descriptor editor window.

2. Click the **Assembly Descriptor** tab.

3. Click on the **Add . . .** button under the Security Roles section. Enter a Name and (optionally) a Description and then click **Finish**. Repeat the same step to add all necessary security roles.

4. Save the deployment descriptor by pressing **Ctrl+S** or selecting **File → Save EJB Deployment Descriptor** from the menu.

The ejb-jar.xml code snippet in Figure 9.8 shows that two security roles, Employees and Managers, are defined.

```
<assembly-descriptor>
        <security-role>
                <description>Corporate Managers</description>
                <role-name>Managers</role-name>
        </security-role>
        <security-role>
                <description>Corporate Employees</description>
                <role-name>Employees</role-name>
        </security-role>
</assembly-descriptor>
```

Figure 9.8: EJB module deployment descriptor excerpt illustrating security roles.

Assigning method permissions

Session and Entity bean methods can be secured by assigning appropriate permissions to certain security roles. The method permissions are defined in the EJB deployment descriptor, ejb-jar.xml.

The following steps describe how to assign method permissions for an EJB module using Application Developer:

1. From the Resource Perspective, select the EJB project in the J2EE Navigator, expand the tree **ejbModule → META-INF**, and double-click the file **ejb-jar.xml**. The EJB deployment descriptor opens in a deployment descriptor editor window.

2. Click the **Assembly Descriptor** tab.

3. Click the **Add . . .** button below the Method Permissions section. The Add Method Permissions dialog appears.
4. Select one or more security roles and click **Next**. A list of EJBs should appear.
5. Select one or more EJBs from the list and click **Next**. A list of methods under each EJB you select from the previous step appears.
6. Select one or more methods under each EJB, using the wildcards (*) option if you want to include all methods of a given type (for example, all the methods in the local home interface) or all methods for a given EJB.
7. Click **Finish**.
8. Repeat the steps to create other method permissions.
9. Save the deployment descriptor by pressing **Ctrl+S** or selecting **File → Save EJB Deployment Descriptor** from the menu.

The ejb-jar.xml code snippet in Figure 9.9 shows the method permission for EJB Onlineitem and ItemHelper.

```
<method-permission>
        <role-name>Managers</role-name>
        <role-name>Employees</role-name>
        <method>
        <ejb-name>Onlineitem</ejb-name>
        <method-intf>Home</method-intf>
        <method-name>*</method-name>
        </method>
        <method>
        <ejb-name>Onlineitem</ejb-name>
        <method-intf>Remote</method-intf>
        <method-name>getCatalognumber</method-name>
        <method-params></method-params>
        </method>
        <method>
        <ejb-name>ItemHelper</ejb-name>
        <method-intf>Home</method-intf>
        <method-name>*</method-name>
        </method>
        <method>
        <ejb-name>ItemHelper</ejb-name>
        <method-intf>Remote</method-intf>
        <method-name>*</method-name>
        </method>
</method-permission>
```

Figure 9.9: EJB module deployment descriptor excerpt illustrating method permissions.

Assigning roles to unprotected methods

During application installation, the IBM WebSphere Application Server Administrative Console allows you to specify what method permissions are applied to Session and Entity EJB methods that are not explicitly secured in the deployment descriptor. These unprotected methods can have one of three permissions applied:

- Uncheck: This permission is the default, which indicates that anyone can call these methods.
- Exclude: Nobody can call these unprotected methods.
- Role: Only the members of a specific security role can call these unprotected methods.

Managing delegation policy

When an EJB calls a method in another EJB, the identity of the caller of the first EJB is, by default, propagated to the next. In this way, all EJB methods in the calling chain would see the same principal information. However, in some cases, it is desirable for one EJB to call another with a previously defined identity, for instance, a member of a specific role. One example is the case of a Message-Driven bean's onMessage() method that calls a protected method in a Session bean. The Message-Driven bean's onMessage() method is invoked by the container with no caller identity; therefore, this method cannot call the protected Session bean method. By delegating the onMessage() method to run as a specific role and adding this role to the protected Session bean method's access permissions, the onMessage() method can successfully access the protected method.

Bean-level delegation

The EJB 2.0 specification defines delegation at the EJB bean level using the <run-as> element, which allows the application assembler to delegate all methods of a given bean to run as a member of a specific security role. At deployment time, a real user that is a member of the specified role must be mapped to this role through a process called run-as role mapping. All calls to other EJBs made by the delegated bean will be called using the identity of this mapped user.

Assigning bean-level run-as delegation policies in Application Developer

Method-level delegation policies are defined in the ejb-jar.xml file. The following steps describe how to assign bean-level delegation policies using Application Developer:

1. From the Resource Perspective, select the EJB project in the J2EE Navigator, expand the tree **ejbModule → META-INF**, and double-click the file **ejb-jar.xml**. The EJB deployment descriptor opens in a Deployment Descriptor editor window.

2. Click the **Access** tab.

3. In the Security Identity (Bean Level) box, select the EJB to which you want to assign the delegation policy and click **Add . . . .**
4. Select **Use identity assigned to a specific role (below)**.
5. In the Role Name drop-down box, select the desired role whose identity will be used when the methods of this EJB make a call. The available options for the role name are those you have defined for the EJB module in the "Defining Security Roles" subsection.
6. Enter an optional Role Description.
7. Enter an optional Security identity description.
8. Click **Next**.
9. In the Enterprise Bean Selection dialog, select one or more beans that should use this delegation policy. Click **Finish**.
10. Save the deployment descriptor by pressing **Ctrl+S** or selecting **File → Save EJB Deployment Descriptor** from the menu.

The ejb-jar.xml code snippet in Figure 9.10 assigns a run-as role to Managers for the session EJB ItemHelper.

```
<session id="ItemHelper">
        <ejb-name>ItemHelper</ejb-name>
        <home>com.acme.ejb.ItemHelperHome</home>
        <remote>com.acme.ejb.ItemHelper</remote>
        <ejb-class>com.acme.ejb.ItemHelperBean</ejb-class>
        <session-type>Stateless</session-type>
        <transaction-type>Container</transaction-type>
        <security-identity>
                <description></description>
                <run-as>
                   <description>Run-as corporate managers.</description>
                   <role-name>Managers</role-name>
                </run-as>
        </security-identity>
</session>
```

Figure 9.10: EJB module deployment descriptor excerpt illustrating a run-as role.

Method-level delegation

In addition to the bean-level delegation policy defined by the EJB 2.0 specification, IBM WebSphere Application Server provides the capability to perform method-level EJB delegation. This works in the same way as bean-level delegation, but it can be applied to specific EJB methods rather than to the bean as a whole. This finer degree of delegation granularity allows application assemblers to delegate different methods of the same EJB to different security roles.

In addition, method-level delegation provides an additional delegation option: run as server. This option indicates that the method should make calls to other EJBs using the identity of the Application Server itself.

Assigning method-level run-as delegation policies in Application Developer

Method-level delegation policies are defined in the ibm-ejb-jar-ext.xmi file. The following steps describe how to assign method-level delegation policies using Application Developer:

1. From the Resource Perspective, select the EJB project in the J2EE Navigator, expand the tree **ejbModule → META-INF**, and double-click the file **ejb-jar.xml**. The EJB deployment descriptor opens in a deployment descriptor editor window.
2. Click the **Access** tab.
3. In the Security Identity (Method Level) box, select the EJB to which you want to assign the delegation policy and click **Add . . .** .
4. In the Add Security Identity dialog box, select the desired Run as mode.
5. If you select Use identity assigned to a specific role (below), in the Role name drop-down box, select the desired role whose identity will be used when the EJB methods make calls. The available options for the Role Name are those you have defined for the EJB module in the previous section, "Defining Security Roles." Enter an optional Role Description and an optional Security identity description.
6. Click **Next**.
7. In the Enterprise Bean Selection dialog, select one or more beans containing the methods to which this delegation policy will apply. Click **Next**.
8. In the Method Elements dialog, select the EJB methods to which this delegation policy will be assigned.
9. Click **Finish**.
10. Save the deployment descriptor by pressing **Ctrl+S** or selecting **File → Save EJB Deployment Descriptor** from the menu.

The ibm-ejb-jar-ext.xmil code snippet in Figure 9.11 assigns a Run-as role to Managers for the methods of session EJB ItemHelper.

```
<ejbExtensions xmi:type="ejbext:SessionExtension"
xmi:id="SessionExtension_1046067113393">
    <runAsSettings xmi:id="SecurityIdentity_1046067113403" description="">
      <methodElements xmi:id="MethodElement_1046067113403" name="*"
type="Home">
        <parms xsi:nil="true"/>
        <enterpriseBean xmi:type="ejb:Session" href="META-INF/ejb-
jar.xml#ItemHelper"/>
      </methodElements>
      <methodElements xmi:id="MethodElement_1046067113404" name="findByValue"
parms="long int"
                type="Remote">
        <enterpriseBean xmi:type="ejb:Session" href="META-INF/ejb-
jar.xml#ItemHelper"/>
      </methodElements>
      <runAsMode xmi:type="ejbext:RunAsSpecifiedIdentity"
                xmi:id="RunAsSpecifiedIdentity_1046067113413">
        <runAsSpecifiedIdentity xmi:id="Identity_1046067113413"
roleName="Managers"
              description="Corporate Managers"/>
      </runAsMode>
    </runAsSettings>
    <enterpriseBean xmi:type="ejb:Session" href="META-INF/ejb-
jar.xml#ItemHelper"/>
</ejbExtensions>
```

Figure 9.11: EJB module extension descriptor excerpt illustrating a Run-as role.

Mapping a Run-as role to a real user

A security role is a placeholder for real users and groups; however, for security role delegation, Run-as role should be mapped to a real user from the user registry under this particular security role. For example, if an EJB method runs as Managers role, this Managers Run-as role should be mapped to one user of the Managers security role, even though the Managers security role may have many users and groups.

The mapping is done in the course of installing the application. The application deployer needs to enter the valid username and password of a user in the user registry that is a member of the specified security role.

Defining security role references (optional)

Security role references are used to provide a layer of indirection between security roles named in EJB Java code and security roles that are defined at application assembly time. This layer of indirection allows security role names to be modified without requiring changes in the application code. As you will see from the programmatic security section later on in this chapter, the security role references will be used in the method isCallerInRole(String roleName), which is used to determine whether or not the caller is a member of a particular role.

To link the security role reference to the security role using Application Developer, do the following:

1. From the Resource Perspective, select the EJB project in the J2EE Navigator, expand the tree **ejbModule → META-INF**, and double-click the file **ejb-jar.xml**. The EJB deployment descriptor opens in a deployment descriptor editor window.
2. Click the **References** tab.
3. Select the bean containing the method that calls isCallerInRole(), and click **Add . . . .**
4. In the Add Reference dialog, select **Security Role Reference** and click **Next**.
5. In the Add Security Role Reference dialog, enter the reference's Name. This is the string that is passed to isCallerInRole() in the Java code.
6. Select the desired security role from the Link pull-down menu. Only security roles that have been previously defined in the EJB module are shown in this menu.
7. Optionally, enter a Description for this security role reference.
8. Click **OK** to apply the changes and close the window.

Declarative security for applications

The security roles defined in the Web modules and EJB modules should also be defined at the application level and mapped to real users and groups. The security roles for an application are in the Application Deployment Descriptor application.xml, while the mapping is defined in the ibm-application-bnd.xmi file.

Application Developer provides application assemblers with a simple way to finish this task:

1. From the Resource Perspective, select the enterprise application project, navigate to the application's deployment descriptor file application.xml under the META-INF folder, and double-click it. A deployment descriptor editor window opens.
2. Click the **Security** tab.
3. Click the **Gather . . .** button to import all security roles that have been defined in EJB and Web modules.

4. Select the security role you wish to map, and select one of the following options: Everyone, All authenticated users, or Users/Groups. If you choose Users/Groups, click the appropriate **Add . . .** button and enter the user or group name.

5. Save the deployment descriptor by pressing **Ctrl+S** or selecting **File → Save Application Deployment Descriptor** from the menu.

Programmatic security

J2EE security can be applied declaratively or programmatically. This section focuses on the latter option. Programmatic security can be used by security-aware applications when declarative security alone is not sufficient to express the security model of the application. Using the Java APIs for security can be the way to implement security for the whole application without using the Application Server security functions at all. Programmatic security also gives you the option to implement dynamic security rules for your applications.

WebSphere Application Server provides a security infrastructure for application security that is transparent to the application developer. That is, the developer does not need to code for security, because it will all be handled at deployment and runtime. Nevertheless, if a developer of servlets and EJBs wants greater control of what the end user is allowed to do than is provided by the infrastructure, a few security calls are available.

J2EE security API for EJBs

The EJB 2.0 specification defines two methods in javax.ejb.EJBContext that allow programmatic access to the caller's security context: getCallerPrincipal and isCallerInRole.

getCallerPrincipal()

The getCallerPrincipal method allows the developer to get the name of the current caller. To do this, you need to call getName() on the java.security.Principal object returned by the getCallerPrincipal() method. The Principal.getName() method returns the login name of the user. The code snippet in Figure 9.12 shows how to use getCallerPrincipal method to get the user login name, if the user has been authenticated.If the user has not been authenticated, the string "UNAUTHENTICATED" is returned.

```
EJBContext ejbContext;
...
// get the caller principal
java.security.Principal callerPrincipal =
ejbContext.getCallerPrincipal();
// get the caller's name
String callerName = callerPrincipal.getName();
```

Figure 9.12: Obtaining the client's name from the EJBContext.

isCallerInRole(String roleName)

The isCallerInRole method allows the developer to make additional checks on the authorization rights of a user, which are not possible, or more difficult, to perform through the deployment descriptor of the EJB. The code snippet in Figure 9.13 shows how to use the isCallerInRole method.

```
EJBContext ejbContext;
...
if (ejbContext.isCallerInRole("Managers"))
// Perform some function for which managers are authorized
else
// Throw a security exception
```

Figure 9.13: Programmatic authorization.

J2EE security API for servlet/JSP

The Servlet 2.3 specification defines three methods that allow programmatic access to the caller's security information of HttpServletRequest interface: getRemoteUser, isUserInRole, and getUserPrincipal. Note that the methods getRemoteUser() and getUserPrincipal() return null, even if the user is logged in, unless the Servlet or the JSP itself is secured.

getRemoteUser()

The getRemoteUser method returns a String object containing the user name the client used to log in.

```
String user = request.getRemoteUser()
```

isUserInRole(String roleName)

The isUserInRole method allows the developer to perform additional checks on the authorization rights of a user, which are not possible, or more difficult, to perform through the deployment descriptor of the servlet.

```
if (request.isUserInRole("Manager")) {
// the user is in the manager role
// ...
}
```

getUserPrincipal()

The getUserPrincipal method allows the developer to get the name of the current caller. To do this, you need to call getName() on the java.security.Principal object returned.

```
Principal principal=request.getUserPrincipal();
String username=principal.getName();
```

WebSphere security

As described in the previous sections, a secure application will demand that certain information be presented before responding to a request for service, for example, authentication and authorization. The request for authentication and authorization are described in the deployment descriptor of the Web modules, EJB modules, and applications. As you can see, a secure J2EE application is the service requestor for security.

The J2EE applications are deployed to and executing under an application server, for example, IBM WebSphere Application Server. IBM WebSphere Application Server acts as a bridge between the Security Service Requestors and the Security Service Providers. It is responsible for managing authentication and it collaborates with the authorization engine and the user registry. Its extensible security architecture model allows pluggable authentication mechanisms, authorization mechanisms, and user registries to be the service providers. Furthermore, it supports SSL for secure network connection.

Extensible security architecture model

The diagram in Figure 9.14 presents a general view of the logical layered security architecture model of IBM WebSphere Application Server Version 5.0. The flexibility of that architecture model lies in pluggable modules that can be configured according to the requirements and existing IT resources. The interface layer allows you to connect different modules responsible for authentication, authorization, and user registry.

The pluggable user registry allows you to configure different databases to store user IDs and passwords that are used for authentication.

The pluggable authentication module allows you to choose whether IBM WebSphere Application Server will authenticate the user or will accept the credentials from external authentication mechanisms.

The pluggable authorization interfaces will allow the use of different authorization mechanisms for WebSphere applications. In the current version, JAAS is supported, and Tivoli Access Manager is an external authorization system.

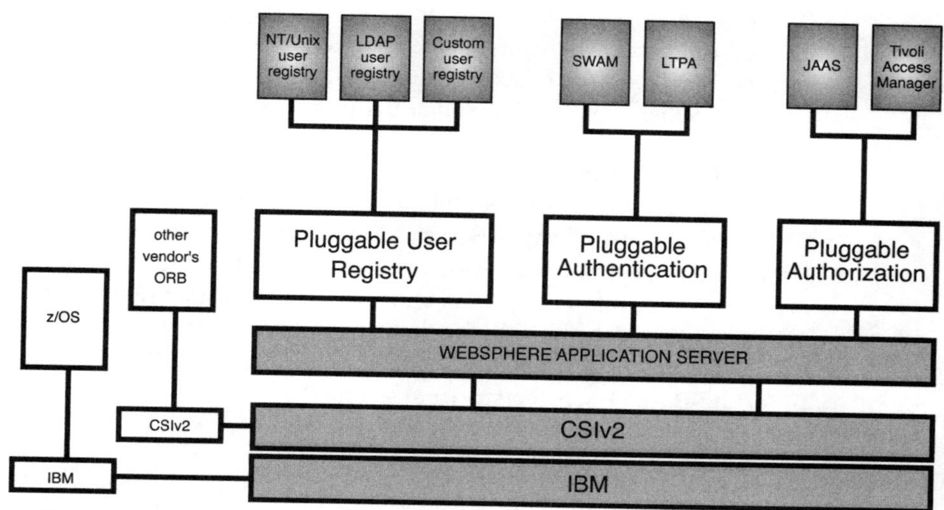

Figure 9.14: IBM WebSphere Application Server Version 5 extensible security architecture.

The following sections introduce these three security components in detail.

User registry

The user registry stores user and group names for authentication and authorization purposes. Authentication mechanisms configured for IBM WebSphere Application Server consult the user registry to collect user-related information when creating credentials, which are then used to represent the user for authorization. The options for user registries include the local operating system user registry, LDAP, and a custom user registry. The WebSphere authentication mechanism cannot be configured to use more than one user registry at a time. Only one active registry is supported, and it is set up when the system administrator configures Global Security settings using the Administration Console.

Local operating system user registry

When this option is chosen, IBM WebSphere Application Server uses the operating system's users and groups for authentication. When configuring IBM WebSphere Application Server on Windows NT or Windows 2000 platforms that are connected to a Windows domain, you should be aware that domain user registry takes precedence over a local machine's user registry.

LDAP user registry

In many cases, the LDAP user registry is recommended as the best solution for large-scale Web implementations. Most of the LDAP servers available on the market are well equipped with security mechanisms that can be used to communicate securely with IBM WebSphere Application Server. IBM WebSphere Application Server supports a few

LDAP servers: IBM SecureWay Directory, Netscape LDAP Server, Lotus Domino LDAP Server, and Microsoft Active Directory. It is also possible to use other LDAP servers. The flexibility of search parameters that an administrator can set up to adapt IBM WebSphere Application Server to different LDAP schemas is considerable.

Custom user registry

This option leaves an open door for any custom implementation of a user registry database. IBM WebSphere Application Server API provides the com.ibm.websphere.security. UserRegistry Java interface, which you should use to write the custom registry. In fact, it is possible to develop integration with any type of custom registry that supports the notion of users and groups by implementing the UserRegistry interface. This interface may be used to access virtually any relational database (JDBC-Based UserRegistry), flat files (File-Based User Registry) and so on.

File-based user registry

IBM WebSphere Application Server provides a file-based registry called FileRegistry. It is not to be used in production environments due to its lack of scalability, but it is included as an example of how a custom registry might operate. The steps to configure the sample FileRegistry will be discussed later in the "Configuring WebSphere security" section.

For details about the UserRegistry interface, refer to the IBM WebSphere Application Server InfoCenter.

Authentication mechanisms

An authentication mechanism defines rules about security information, for example, whether a credential can be forwarded to another Java process and the format in which security information is stored in both credentials and tokens.

Authentication is the process of establishing whether a client is valid in a particular context. A client can be an end user, a machine, or an application. An authentication mechanism in IBM WebSphere Application Server typically collaborates closely with a User Registry. The User Registry is the user's and group's accounts repository that the authentication mechanism consults when performing authentication. The authentication mechanism is responsible for creating a credential, which is an IBM WebSphere Application Server internal representation of a successfully authenticated client user. Not all credentials are created equal. The abilities of the credential are determined by the configured authentication mechanism.

Although IBM WebSphere Application Server provides several authentication mechanisms, only a single "active" authentication mechanism can be configured at once. The active authentication mechanism is selected when the system administrator configures global security.

IBM WebSphere Application Server provides two authentication mechanisms Simple WebSphere Authentication Mechanism (SWAM) and Lightweight Third-Party Authentication (LTPA). These two authentication mechanisms differ primarily in the distributed security features each supports.

Simple WebSphere Authentication Mechanism (SWAM)

The Simple WebSphere Authentication Mechanism is intended for simple, non-distributed, single-Application Server runtime environments. The single-Application Server restriction is due to the fact that SWAM does not support forwardable credentials. This means that if a servlet or EJB in Application Server process 1 invokes a remote method on an EJB living in another Application Server process (process 2), the identity of the caller in Process 1 is not transmitted to process 2. What is transmitted is an unauthenticated credential, which, depending on the security permissions configured on the EJB methods, may cause authorization failures.

Since SWAM is intended for a single-Application Server process, single sign-on (SSO) is not supported. The SWAM authentication mechanism is suitable for simple environments, software development environments, or other environments that do not require a distributed security solution.

SWAM relies on the session ID. It is not as secure as LTPA; therefore, use of SSL with SWAM is strongly recommended.

Lightweight Third-Party Authentication (LTPA)

Lightweight Third-Party Authentication (LTPA) is intended for distributed, multiple Application Servers and machine environments. It supports forwardable credentials and SSO. LTPA is able to support security in a distributed environment through the use of cryptography, which permits LTPA to encrypt, digitally sign, and securely transmit authentication-related data and later decrypt and verify the signature.

LTPA requires that the configured User Registry be a central shared repository such as LDAP or a Windows Domain-type registry.

LTPA enables SSO by use of a transient security cookie. A token called LtpaToken is generated by the authenticating server and encrypted by the LTPA keys that are shared by all the SSO participating servers. The token is issued to the Web user in a transient cookie, which means that the cookie resides in the browser memory instead of the system and expires when the user closes the browser.

Authorization mechanisms

IBM WebSphere Application Server standard authorization mechanisms are based on the J2EE security specification and Java Authentication and Authorization Services (JAAS). JAAS extends the security architecture of the Java 2 Platform with additional support to authenticate and enforce access controls upon users. JAAS programming models allow the developer to design application authentication in a pluggable fashion, which makes the application independent from the underlying authentication and authorization technology.

Java 2 security architecture uses security policy to specify which code (for example, a method invocation that opens a socket) of the application is allowed to execute. Code characteristics, such as a signature, signer ID, or source server, enable the Access Controller within the Java 2 VM to consult policy and decide whether the code will be allowed to invoke a particular method based on the identity of the code. JAAS extends this approach with role-based access control. Permission to invoke a method is granted based not only on the code characteristics but also on the user who is running it. For each authenticated user, a Subject class is created and a set of Principals is included in the subject in order to identify that user. Security policies are granted based on possessed principals.

Configuring WebSphere security

This section describes in further detail the steps necessary to configure security and secure communication between the various components of IBM WebSphere Application Server Version 5. WebSphere allows administration in many different ways, including a good browser-based administrative console, a command line utility called wsadmin, and a programmatic API that allows custom tools development.

This section will focus on using the browser-based administrative console to configure the security for IBM WebSphere Application Server.

Enabling WebSphere Global Security

Global Security specifies the global security configuration for a managed domain and applies to all applications running on IBM WebSphere Application Server. It determines whether security will be applied at all, sets up the user registry against which the authentication will take place, and defines authentication mechanisms, among other things.

The following steps show how to enable WebSphere Global Security through Administrative Console:

1. Start IBM WebSphere Application Server and launch the Administrative Console.
2. After logging in, click the **Security** link in the navigation pane.
3. WebSphere security can be enabled and disabled by selecting the **Global Security Enabled** switch, which is accessed from Administrative Console under **Security → Global Security**.

4. Select an authentication mechanism. WebSphere Application Server supports two authentication mechanisms by default: SWAM and LTPA. SWAM is selected initially. The coming sections will discuss configuring authentication mechanisms in more detail.

5. Select a user registry. WebSphere Application Server supports LocalOS, LDAP, and custom registries. LocalOS is selected initially. The coming sections will discuss configuring user registries in more detail.

6. You have the option to enforce Java 2 Security. For more information on Java 2 Security refer to the official Sun Java site at *java.sun.com/security/index.html*, or to the Java 2 Platform Security Architecture V1.0 paper from Sun.

7. Save the server configuration by clicking the **Save** link at the top of the administrative console.

Configuring a user registry

A brief introduction to the user registry and the options available in IBM WebSphere Application Server is provided in the previous section. This section focuses on how to configure those options from the IBM WebSphere Application Server Administrative Console.

LocalOS

To define IBM WebSphere Application Server's LocalOS configuration, perform the following steps:

1. From the WebSphere Application Server Administrative Console, select **Security → User Registries → Local OS**.

2. Enter a user name and password. This is the identity under which the request is sent to the registry. The LocalOS registry requires an identity for a user that has administrative capabilities, as defined by the LocalOS registry.

3. Click **OK**. (It should not be necessary to set any custom properties for the LocalOS registry.)

4. Save the changes and restart IBM WebSphere Application Server.

LDAP

To define IBM WebSphere Application Server's LDAP configuration, perform the following steps:

1. In the IBM WebSphere Application Server Administrative Console, select **Security → User Registries → LDAP**.

2. Provide the details for the fields in the Configuration panel as follows:

   Server ID: This is the administrator ID in LDAP for IBM WebSphere Application Server.

   Server Password: This is the WebSphere administrator password.

   Type: This is the type of LDAP server.

   Host: Specify the host name of the LDAP server here.

   Port: This is the port number on which the LDAP server is running; by default it is 389.

   Base DN: Specify the base DN of your LDAP configuration here.

   Bind DN: This is the distinguished name for the application server to use to bind to the LDAP server.

   Bind Password: This is the password for the application server to use to bind to the LDAP server.

   Reuse Connection: Generally, this should be selected. In rare situations, such as when you use a router to spray the requests to multiple LDAP servers and this router does not support affinity, disable this checkbox.

3. Click **Apply**.

4. Save the configuration.

Custom registry

To define IBM WebSphere Application Server's Custom Registry configuration, perform the following steps:

1. Open the Custom Registry window in the IBM WebSphere Application Server Administrative Console by selecting **Security → User Registries → Custom**.

2. Enter a user name and password. This is the identity under which the request is sent to the registry.

3. Enter the class name for the custom registry. The supplied sample File-based custom registry is com.ibm.websphere.security.FileRegistrySample. Click **Apply**.

4. Click the **Custom Properties** link and add the properties necessary to initialize the registry (see Table 9.3). These properties will be passed to the initialize method of the custom registry. For the supplied sample file-based custom registry, FileRegistrySample, enter the following properties. (Refer to the IBM WebSphere Application Server InfoCenter for details regarding the format of these files.)

Table 9.3: Properties for initializing custom registry.

Name	Value
UsersFile	users.props
GroupsFile	groups.props

5. Save the configuration.

Configuring an authentication mechanism

You can select SWAM or LTPA as the authentication mechanism. For more information on SWAM and LTPA refer to the section titled "Authentication Mechanisms."

SWAM

As stated previously, SWAM is intended for simple, non-distributed, single-Application Server runtime environments. The single-Application Server restriction is due to the fact that SWAM does not support forwardable credentials.

Using SWAM does not require further configuration for IBM WebSphere Application Server. You can simply select **SWAM** as the authentication mechanism on the Global Security page.

LTPA

Lightweight Third-Party Authentication (LTPA) is intended for distributed, multiple-application server and machine environments. It supports forwardable credentials, and therefore supports single sign-on (SSO). LTPA can support security in a distributed environment through the use of cryptography. LTPA requires that the configured User Registry be a central shared repository such as LDAP, a Windows Domain type registry, or a custom user registry.

If you select LTPA as the authentication mechanism on the Global Security page, you need to follow these steps to further configure LTPA. Importing the LTPA keys into other SSO-enabled servers is beyond the scope of this book; for more information, refer to the IBM WebSphere Application Server InfoCenter.

1. From the IBM WebSphere Application Server Administrative Console, expand the tree **Security → Authentication Mechanisms → LTPA**.
2. Specify the following attributes:

   Password: This is the password to protect LTPA keys. You will need this password in order to import the keys into any other SSO enabled server. Confirm the password by retyping it in the Confirm Password field.

   Timeout: This field specifies the amount of time in minutes for which the LTPA token will be valid without reauthentication.

3. Click **OK** to accept the configuration. You will specify the Key file name after setting up single sign-on attributes.
4. Save the configuration to make the changes effective.
5. Reopen the LTPA configuration page. Configure the Single Sign-On panel by clicking the link **Single sign-on (SSO)** at the bottom of the LTPA page.
6. Select the **Enabled** box, if it is not already selected.
7. Specify the Domain Name. This domain is used when an HTTP cookie is created for SSO and determines the scope to which SSO applies. All SSO-enabled servers must be in the same DNS domain.
8. Click **OK** to approve the changes.
9. Save the configuration to make the changes effective.
10. Reopen the LTPA configuration page. In the LTPA Configuration panel, click the button **Generate Keys**. This button will launch the key generation process in the background. You will be prompted to save the configuration after the process is completed.
11. Save the configuration to have the generated keys stored in the IBM WebSphere Application Server configuration. The keys will appear in the security.xml file.
12. Reopen the LTPA configuration page. Specify the **Key File Name**, which is the name of the file where LTPA keys will be stored when you export them in next step. You need to export the keys in order to enable SSO on another server. Specify the full path name for the key file, for example, *c:\WebSphere\Appserver\etc\SSO_samplekeys*.
13. Click **Export Keys**.
14. Save the server configuration.

Your IBM WebSphere Application Server is now configured to use LTPA authentication mechanism. You will need to log out of the Administrative Console and restart the IBM WebSphere Application Server in order for the changes to take effect.

Configuring JAAS

Java Authentication and Authorization Services (JAAS)

Java Authentication and Authorization Services (JAAS) is a standard extension to the Java 2 SDK v1.3 and it is part of Java 2 SDK v1.4. The current version for JAAS is 1.0. IBM WebSphere Application Server Version 5 also implements and uses JAAS for security purposes. For more information, refer to Sun's Java site *java.sun.com/products/jaas*. The best way to learn JAAS is to start with the sample application that comes with JAAS v1.0.

JAAS for IBM WebSphere Application Server can be configured using the Administrative Console. JAAS provides the pluggable authentication mechanism for IBM WebSphere Application Server.

Application login information

IBM WebSphere Application Server allows you to configure the pluggable authentication module for your application server.

1. Launch the IBM WebSphere Application Server Administrative console and then log in with administrative privileges.
2. Select **Security → JAAS Configuration → Application Logins**.
3. Each login module defines a module class that is the implementation of the JAAS login module itself. Select a login module, WSLogin, for example, and then click the **JAAS Login Modules** link to see the module Classname.
4. When you create your own login module, you will have to create a new entry.
5. The JAAS configuration for the server includes another element: the wsjaas.conf file under the <*WebSphere_root*>\properties directory, where <*WebSphere_root*> is your IBM WebSphere Application Server installation directory. It defines the JAAS login modules for the Java Virtual Machine (JVM) according to the JAAS specification, as in the following example:

```
WSLogin {
 com.ibm.ws.security.common.auth.module.proxy.WSLoginModuleProxy
 required delegate
   =com.ibm.ws.security.common.auth.module.WSLoginModuleImpl;
};
```

6. The preceding example tells the JVM which is the login module for the WSLogin alias. The Java code in the application will refer to this alias to invoke the login module defined for JAAS.
7. There is another configuration file provided for the Java clients: the wsjaas_client.conf file under the <*WebSphere_root*>\properties directory, where <*WebSphere_root*> is your IBM WebSphere Application Server installation directory.

J2C Authentication data entries

J2C Authentication data entries provide an easy way of administering user name and password pairs for authentication purposes for any resources in IBM WebSphere Application Server Version 5. These entries are associated with alias names, where the alias names can be used in the resource definitions to refer to a certain user name and password pair.

The following steps explain how to set up a J2C Authentication data entry using the Administrative Console:

1. Click **Security → JAAS Configuration → J2C Authentication Data**.
2. When you click **New**, the page will appear; specify the user ID and password that may be used by Java 2 Connector or IBM WebSphere Application Server Version 5.0 DataSource.
3. Each user ID and password set is identified by a unique alias name.
4. Save the server configuration.

Configuring network security: Secure Socket Layer

Java Secure Sockets Extension (JSSE)

The SSL implementation used by the application server is the IBM Java Secure Sockets Extension (JSSE). The JSSE is a set of Java packages that enable secure Internet communications. It implements a Java version of the SSL and Transport Level Security (TLS) protocols and includes functionality for data encryption, server authentication, message integrity, and client authentication. Configuring JSSE is very similar to configuring most other SSL implementations (for example, GSKit); however, a few differences are worth noting.

JSSE allows both signer and personal certificates to be stored in a SSL key file, but it also allows a separate file, called a trust file, to be specified. A trust file can contain only signer certificates; therefore, all personal certificates can be stored in an SSL key file and all signer certificates stored in a trust file.

JSSE does not recognize the proprietary SSL key file format that is used by the plug-in (.kdb files); instead, it recognizes standard file formats such as Java Key Store (JKS). As such, SSL key files cannot be shared between the plug-in and application server, and a different implementation of the key management utility (ikeyman) must be used in order to manage application server key and trust files.

Configuring SSL

The first step in configuring SSL is to define an SSL configuration repertoire. A repertoire contains the details necessary for building an SSL connection, such as the location of the key files, their type, and the available ciphers. IBM WebSphere Application Server provides a default repertoire called DefaultSSLSettings.

From the IBM WebSphere Application Server Administrative Console, select **Security/SSL** to see the list of SSL repertoires.

The appropriate repertoire is referenced during the configuration of a service that sends and receives requests encrypted using SSL, such as the Web and EJB containers.

Follow the steps below to configure a new entry in the SSL repertoire:

1. From the SSL Configuration Repertoire page, click **New**.
2. Enter an alias for this configuration; click **OK**.
3. Select the new SSL entry by clicking the link and then click the **Secure Sockets Layer (SSL)** link in Additional Properties. The new configuration details can be entered in the window that appears.
4. Enter the location of the key file name. IBM WebSphere Application Server provides a set of certificates that may be used for testing purposes and a tool called ikeyman to generate a self-signed certificate. For more information, refer to the IBM WebSphere Application Server InfoCenter.
5. Enter the password for the key file.
6. Select the appropriate key type.
7. Enter the location of the trust file name. For more information on generating the trust file for a self-signed certification, refer to the IBM WebSphere Application Server InfoCenter.
8. Enter the password for the trust file.
9. Select the appropriate trust type.
10. If client authentication is supported by this configuration, select the **Client Authentication** box. This will affect only the HTTP and LDAP request. For more details on configuring SSL between the Web server and the application server and configuring SSL between the Java client and the application server, refer to the IBM WebSphere Application Server InfoCenter.
11. The appropriate security level must be set. Valid values are low, medium, and high. Low specifies only digital signing ciphers (no encryption); medium specifies only 40-bit ciphers (including digital signing); high specifies only 128-bit ciphers (including digital signing).
12. If the preset security level does not define the required cipher, it can be manually added to the cipher suite option.
13. Select the **Cryptographic Token** box if hardware or software cryptographic support is available. Refer to the IBM WebSphere Application Server InfoCenter for details regarding cryptographic support.
14. Additional properties can be added by selecting the **Custom Properties** link in the Additional Properties section.

15. Click **OK** to apply the changes.
16. If there are no errors, save the changes to the master configuration and restart IBM WebSphere Application Server.

Summary

The two security services IBM WebSphere Application Server supports are authentication and authorization. Authentication is the process of establishing whether a client is valid in a particular context. Authorization is the process of checking whether the authenticated user has access to the requested resource. There are two fundamental methods for authorization: access control list and capability list. J2EE authorization, which is based on security roles, uses the access control list method. Secure Socket Layer, which is based on public key cryptography and secret key cryptography and certificate, is used for secure communication over the Internet.

J2EE containers are responsible for enforcing access control on components and methods. J2EE containers provide two types of security: declarative security and programmatic security.

With the declarative security model, an application's security policies are expressed in the application deployment descriptor that is external to the application code. In the deployment descriptor of a Web module, the following security constraints can be defined:

- Authentication method with the following options: Basic, Digest, Form-based and Client Certificate
- Security roles
- Security constraints on Web resource collections
- Security role references for individual servlets/JSPs

In the deployment descriptor of an EJB module, the following security constraints can be defined:

- Security roles
- Method permissions
- Roles for unprotected methods
- Delegation policy
- Security role references

In the deployment descriptor of an application, application assemblers can gather the security roles from all the modules within the application and map them to real users and groups

Programmatic security can be used by security-aware applications when declarative security alone is not sufficient to express the security model of the application. The EJB 2.0 specification defines two methods in javax.ejb.EJBContext that allow programmatic access to the caller's security context: getCallerPrincipal() and isCallerInRole(String roleName). The Servlet 2.3 specification defines three methods that allow programmatic access to the caller's security information of the HttpServletRequest interface: getRemoteUser(), isUserInRole(String roleName), and getUserPrincipal().

IBM WebSphere Application Server acts as a bridge between the Security Service Requestors and the Security Service Providers. It is responsible for managing authentication, and it collaborates with the authorization engine and the user registry. Its extensible security architecture model allows pluggable authentication mechanisms, authorization mechanisms, and user registries to be the service providers. IBM WebSphere Application Server supports SSL for secure network connection. The extended security architecture of IBM WebSphere Application Server has three major components: user registry, authentication module, and authorization interfaces.

The pluggable user registry allows you to configure different databases to store user IDs and passwords that are used for authentication. IBM WebSphere Application Server supports three types of user registry: LocalOS, LDAP, and Custom Registry.

The pluggable authentication module allows you to choose whether IBM WebSphere Application Server will authenticate the user or will accept the credentials from external authentication mechanisms. IBM WebSphere Application Server supports two kinds of authentication mechanism: SWAM and LTPA.

The pluggable authorization interfaces will allow the use of different authorization mechanisms for applications. In the current version, JAAS is supported, and Tivoli Access Manager is an external authorization system.

Test yourself

Key terms

authentication

authorization

access control list

capability list

secret key (symmetric) cryptography

public key (asymmetric) cryptography

SSL

digital certificate

digital signature

message digest

certificate authority (CA)

role-based security

HTTPS

security constraints

Web resource collection

authorization constraints

user data constraints

security role references

delegation

user registry

Simple WebSphere Authentication Mechanism (SWAM)

Lightweight Third Party Authentication (LTPA)

Java Authentication and Authorization Services (JAAS)

global security

Java Secure Sockets Extension (JSSE)

Review questions

1. How secure is a simple username/password combination?
2. A Web application uses basic authentication to validate users, and wishes to switch to Form-based authentication. What changes are required?
3. A servlet uses programmatic security checks to see whether a user is in a particular role by writing "if (req.isUserInRole('manager')) . . . ." Unfortunately, this hard-codes the role name "manager" into the servlet. Worse, at the actual deployment location, the equivalent role is instead called "supervisor." What can be done to fix this situation?
4. What's the difference between getUserPrincipal() in the HttpServletRequest class and getCallerPrincipal() in EJBContext?
5. A bank account manager is responsible for all accounts with balances less than $1000. Can declarative security techniques be used to allow this manager to modify only those accounts?
6. Several files are used in the process of setting up security for a J2EE application in WebSphere. Which are they?

C H A P T E R 10

JCA tools and supports

Colin Yu

Chapter topics

- *J2EE Connector Architecture overview*
- *Connection management*
- *Transaction management*
- *Security architecture*
- *Common Client Interface*

Certification objectives

- *Access container and server services from enterprise components*

Since the early 1970s many enterprise information systems (EISs), including legacy systems (for example, IBM CICS and IMS) and enterprise resource planning (ERP) systems (for example, SAP, PeopleSoft, and JD Edwards), have been deployed as business backend infrastructures that provide centralized, highly available, scalable, and secure applications. As more and more businesses move toward delivering Web-based applications over the Internet to customers, employees, and business partners who are normally running in a distributed environment, it becomes very important for businesses to integrate new Web-based applications with existing EISs. One of the goals is to reuse the existing business logic developed in existing EISs. Another important goal is to exploit the enterprise services, including scalability, availability, and security, for the Web-based applications.

Before J2EE Connector Architecture (JCA) specification version 1.0 was formally released by Sun Microsystems in 2001, the Java world had no standard, consistent way to integrate EISs from different suppliers with Web-based applications. Most EIS vendors and application server vendors develop non-standard vendor-specific architectures to provide connectivity between application servers and EIS. For example, the CICS Transaction Gateway (CTG) provides a set of Java API for the programmers to call CICS transactions; SAP has its own implementation of Java Connector; IBM created the Common Connector Framework (CCF) for the application server to interact with the CCF-compliant connectors. As a result, application developers have to use different ways to integrate EISs from different vendors with the Web-based applications, which are not portable across application servers from different vendors. The application code, the application server, and the EIS are actually tightly coupled.

The introduction of the J2EE Connector Architecture, based on technologies of the Java 2 platform, Enterprise Edition (J2EE), defines a standard for integrating the J2EE platform with EISs. It decouples application servers from EISs by defining the system contracts between resource adapters and application servers. EIS vendors no longer need to customize their product to support different application servers, and application server vendors do not need to build specific modules to support a particular EIS. JCA also defines the Common Client Interface (CCI) to enable application components to use a common way to access heterogeneous EISs. In a simple word, JCA allows EIS vendors, application server vendors, and application component providers to focus on their own implementation without paying much attention to the other parties.

WebSphere Application Server Version 5, which supports J2EE 1.3 and JCA 1.0, integrates the tools and runtime for Java Connector Architecture. This chapter provides a high-level overview of the J2EE Connector Architecture. In addition to introducing the key concepts of the architecture and code examples, it describes how to use JCA tools in WebSphere Application Server Version 5 and WebSphere Studio Application Developer Version 5.

J2EE Connector Architecture overview

As described in the previous section, the J2EE Connector Architecture standardizes how the J2EE applications, application server, and EISs work together. That means some common agreement must be achieved, and every party needs to follow the agreement in order to make this happen. The common agreement in JCA consists of system contracts and CCI.

Under JCA, an EIS vendor is required to provide a standard resource adapter, conforming to the system contract for its EIS, that can be plugged into any application server that supports JCA. The resource adapter provides connectivity between the EIS and the application server for the enterprise applications.

On the other hand, an application server vendor that chooses to support JCA, for example, WebSphere Application Server Version 5, must also conform to the system contracts and support the CCI for the application components. It should be able to create seamless connectivity to multiple EISs with the corresponding resource adapters that conform to JCA. As you can see, the relationship between the resource adapters and the application servers is many-to-many.

Figure 10.1 shows how EIS vendors, application servers, and application components work together under JCA. A J2EE-compliant application server has its built-in Connection Manager, Transaction Manager, and Security Manager, which provide application components with an advanced programming paradigm for writing portable and reusable code to handle complex issues such as transaction management without worrying about the low-level implementation. Application components are deployed into containers of the application server, for example, the Web Container and the EJB Container. The EIS vendor provides for its EIS a standard resource adapter, which can be plugged into an application server that supports JCA.

The system contracts, such as transaction management, security management, and connection management, allow the Connection Manager, Transaction Manager, and Security Manager of an application server to use the connection, transaction, and security API that is exposed by the resource adapter and supported by the EIS. These system contracts extend the advanced programming paradigm supported by the application server to the EIS.

The application contract enables the application components to access EISs with Common Client Interface (CCI).

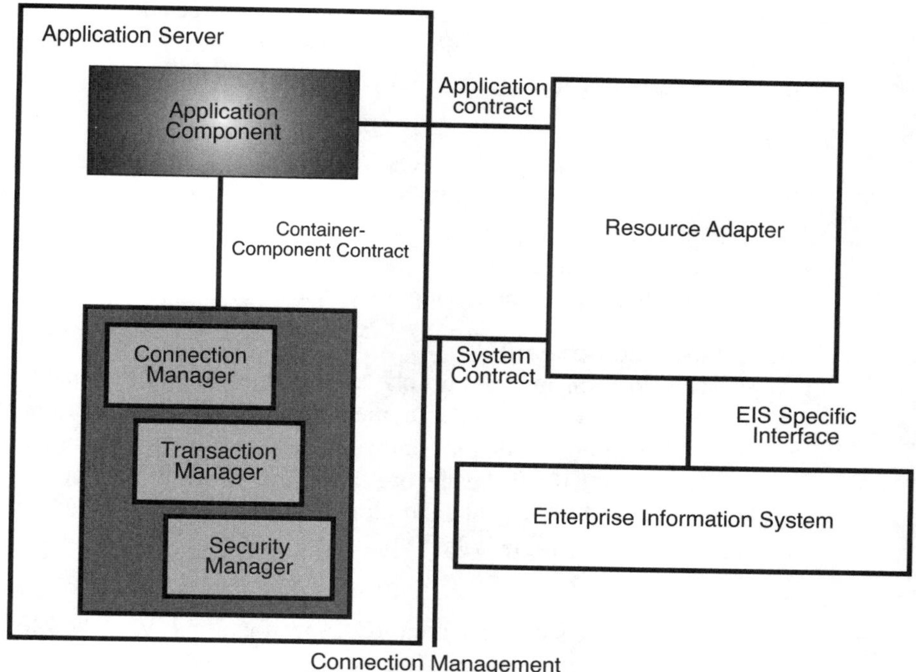

Figure 10.1: J2EE Connector Architecture overview.

The container-component contract between the Application Server and the Application Component is defined in J2EE. It allows an application component to take advantage of the programming paradigm in J2EE platforms.

Components of the J2EE Connector Architecture

The following key terms defined in the JCA specification further explain the major components in JCA described in Figure 10.1.

Enterprise Information System (EIS)

An EIS comprises a company's back-end infrastructure for handling companywide information. An EIS is typically a transaction-processing system, such as IBM CICS and IMS, which we usually call legacy systems, or an ERP system such as SAP, PeopleSoft, and JD Edwards. An EIS can be a database system, for example, IBM DB2, Oracle, or Microsoft SQL Server.

Resource adapter

A resource adapter implements the system contracts to collaborate with the application server to manage transactions, security, and connection pooling. It uses an EIS-specific API to communicate with the EIS. Thus, a resource adapter is specific to an EIS, and each EIS requires just one implementation of a resource adapter, which is created according to the JCA specification. Since the implementation is compliant with the JCA, it is portable across all compliant J2EE servers.

Application server

A J2EE-compliant application server implements the middle tier of the J2EE multi-tier distributed model. It consists a Web container and an EJB container. It provides application components with middleware services for transactions, security, and state maintenance, along with data access and persistence. IBM WebSphere Application Server is one of the J2EE 1.3-compliant application servers.

Application component

Application components are Java classes that implement component methods, JSP page definitions, and any required deployment descriptors. An application component can be a server-side component that is deployed, managed, and executed on an application server, such as an EJB, JSP page, or servlet. It can also be a component executed on the Web-client tier (a browser for example) but made available to the Web client by an application server, for example, a Java applet or DHTML page.

System contracts

The system contracts defined in the JCA specification extend the J2EE programming paradigm, such as transactions, security, and connection pooling, to the EIS tier. Both the application servers and the resource adapters conform to the system contracts. The system contracts are transparent to the application developers. This programming paradigm allows developers to write portable and reusable code to implement the business logic without worrying about the low-level issues related to EIS integration.

The J2EE Connector Architecture Version 1.0 defines the following set of system-level contracts between an application server and a resource adapter. The definition is quoted from the JCA specification:

"A *connection management contract* that enables an application server to pool connections to an underlying EIS, and enables application components to connect to an EIS. This leads to a scalable application environment that can support a large number of clients requiring access to EISs.

A *transaction management contract* between the transaction manager and an EIS that supports transactional access to EIS resource managers. This contract enables an application server to use a transaction manager to manage transactions across multiple resource managers. This contract also supports transactions that are managed internal to an EIS resource manager [local transactions] without the necessity of involving an external transaction manager.

A *security contract* that enables a secure access to an EIS. This contract provides support for a secure application environment that reduces security threats to the EIS and protects valuable information resources managed by the EIS."

Common Client Interface (CCI)

CCI is an abstraction of the interfaces and classes that enable application components to communicate with heterogeneous EIS. Before the CCI, a Java application developer wishing to connect to multiple EISs would have to learn an API specific to each EIS connector. Now, the CCI offers a common API that a resource adapter must implement. Just as JDBC provides an abstract implementation to access relational database, CCI provides an abstract implementation to access EISs.

Transaction-related definitions

The following are the key terms related to transaction management in JCA.

Resource Manager (RM)

A resource manager manages a set of shared EIS resources. Some examples of resource managers are a CICS Transaction Server, an ERP system, and a database system. An application server or a client-tier application needs access to a resource manager to use its managed resources. Resource managers that offer transaction support can be categorized into those that support two-phase coordination (by offering an XAResource interface) and those that support only one-phase coordination (for example, through a LocalTransaction interface).

Transaction manager (TM)

A transaction manager creates and manages transaction objects. It coordinates multiple resource managers in a transaction and participates in distributed global transactions with other transaction managers. WebSphere Application Server acts as a transaction manager, as shown in Figure 10.2. The WebSphere Application Server transaction manager provides coordination, within a transaction, for any number of two-phase capable resource managers. It also enables a single one-phase capable resource manager to be used within a transaction in the absence of any other resource managers, although this is not required in J2EE.

For more information on OTA/XA Transaction Architecture and Java Transaction API (JTA), refer to Chapter 8, "Transactions."

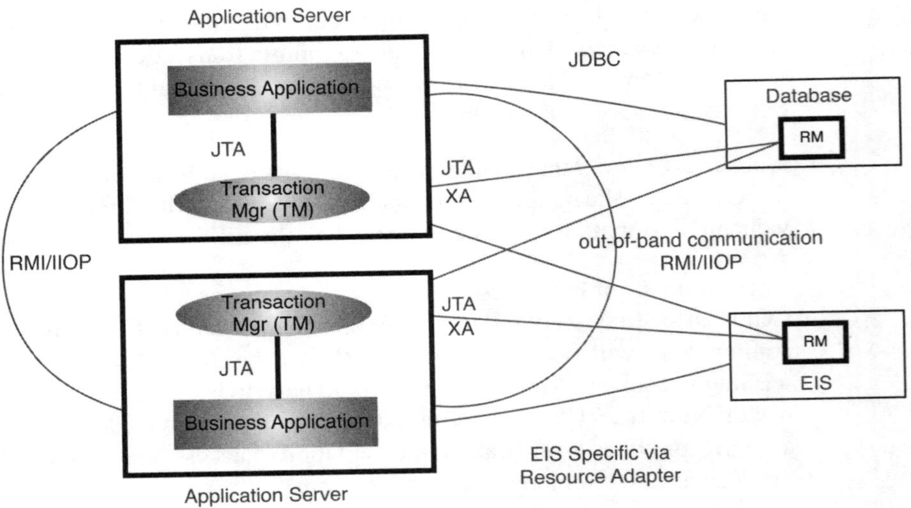

Figure 10.2: Transaction manager and resource manager coordination.

Managed and non-managed environments

There are two types of client access scenarios: *managed* and *non-managed*.

Managed environment

In a managed environment, the application server is responsible for management of the connection object. It allows administrators to configure a Connection Factory object for the application component, for example, an EJB, a servlet, a JSP page, or an application client. When an application component makes a call to the Connection Factory to request a connection, the call is routed to the Connection Manager, which obtains a connection object from the Managed Connection Factory.

Non-managed environment

In a non-managed environment, a client (Java application or Java Applet) directly uses a resource adapter to access the EIS. Instead of relying on the application server as in a managed environment, the client has to use the low-level APIs exposed by the resource adapter to manage connection pooling, security, and transactions.

Connection management

This section discusses the connection management contract under the J2EE Connector Architecture. It also describes how an application component creates and uses connections to an underlying EIS. In particular, it focuses on the programming model under a managed environment and the configuration tasks in WebSphere Studio Application Developer.

Enterprise applications that integrate with EISs run in either a two-tier non-managed environment without an application server involved or a multi-tier managed environment with an application involved. In a non-managed environment, the client application either manages the connection itself or uses the connection pooling provided by the resource adapter. In a multi-tier application environment, the application server implements the connection pooling to access EISs and provides application components (Enterprise JavaBeans, servlets, or JSPs) with connection objects.

WebSphere Application Server Version 5 provides standard support for connection pooling. Connection pooling of expensive connections leads to better scalability and performance in an operational environment. At the same time, WebSphere Application Server keeps this connection pooling support transparent to the application components. That is, it completely handles the connection pooling logic, and application developers do not need to get involved with this issue.

Connection management contract

The connection management contract specifies the support for connection pooling and connection management in JCA. The architecture of the connection management contract in a managed environment is shown with bold flow lines as in Figure 10.3. The four interfaces shown in the resource adapter diagram, ConnectionFactory, Connection, ManagedConnectionFactory, and ManagedConnection, are part of CCI and will be discussed further in a later section titled "Common client interface."

In a managed environment, the administrator of the application server uses the deployment descriptor mechanism to configure the resource adapter and a Connection Factory instance for the application server. Connection Factory is a managed factory object from which an application component requests a connection to the EIS. A later section will describe the configuration tasks in WebSphere Studio Application Developer in detail.

The numbered flows in Figure 10.3 describe how an application component obtains a connection to the EIS with the help of application server and the resource adapter:

1. The application component performs a lookup of a connection factory in the JNDI name space. The connection factory needs to be preconfigured in the JNDI name space. WebSphere Application Server has a built-in JNDI server, and the connection factory instances will be available for application components after the application server starts. After getting a connection factory instance, the application component requests a connection instance from the connection factory instance.

2. The connection factory instance delegates the connection request to the ConnectionManager instance. The ConnectionManager is implemented by the application server vendor. It provides a set of quality of services, including error logging and tracing and connection pool management, to the application components.

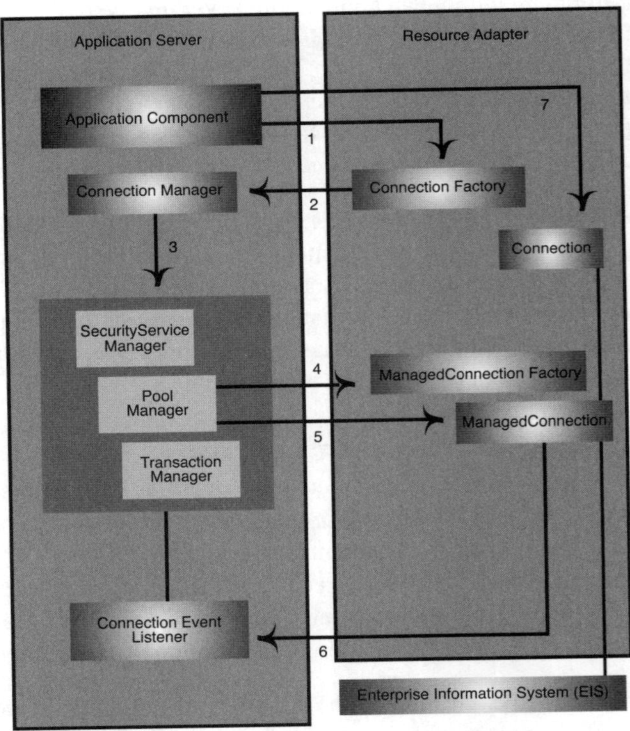

Figure 10.3: Connection management architecture.

3. The ConnectionManager instance, on receiving a connection request from the connection factory, performs a lookup in the connection pool implemented by the application server to check whether any connection instance is available.

4. If there is no connection in the pool is available, the pool manager uses the ManagedConnectionFactory interface implemented by the resource adapter to create a new physical connection to the underlying EIS.

5. If the application server finds an available connection in the pool, it returns this ManagedConnection instance to the ConnectionManager instance. If a new ManagedConnection instance is created in flow 4, the pool manager adds the new ManagedConnection instance to the connection pool and return this newly created ManagedConnection instance to the ConnectionManager instance.

6. The application server registers a ConnectionEventListener with the ManagedConnection instance. The state change of the ManagedConnection instance will notify the application, which manages the connection pooling or handles any error conditions accordingly.

7. The ConnectionManager uses the ManagedConnection instance to get a Connection instance, which acts as an application-level handle to the underlying physical connection. This Connection instance will be returned to and used by the application component to access EIS resources.

Application programming model

An application uses a standard application programming model to call the functions in the EISs after obtaining connections as in Figure 10.3. The following steps are focused on the programming model in a managed environment using an application server, in particular, WebSphere Application Server. For a non-managed environment, the steps look similar, except for the part where the application component gets the connection.

1. During deployment, configure each resource adapter and associated connection factory through the WebSphere Application Server Administrative Console or WebSphere Studio Application Developer Server Configuration Editor.

   For more information, please refer to the sections titled "Adding a resource adapter in Application Developer" and "Configuring a connection factory in Application Developer."

2. Declare a connection factory resource reference (for example, eis/myEIS) in your application component's deployment descriptor (for example, in an ejb-jar.xml file). Bind the reference to a global Java Naming and Directory Interface (JNDI) name defined in Step 1.

   Refer to the section titled "Configuring Connection Factory Resource Reference in Application Developer" for details.

3. Locate the corresponding ConnectionFactory object for the EIS resource adapter using JNDI lookup in your application component during runtime.

4. Get a Connection object to the EIS from the ConnectionFactory object.
5. Create an Interaction object from the Connection object.
6. Create an InteractionSpec object. Set the function to execute in the InteractionSpec object.
7. Create a Record instance for the input and output data used by function.
8. Execute the function through the Interaction object.
9. Process the Record data from the function.
10. Close the Interaction and Connection.

The code snippet in Figures 10.4a and 10.4b show how an application component creates an interaction and executes it on the EIS.

```
javax.resource.cci.ConnectionFactory connectionFactory = null;
javax.resource.cci.Connection connection = null;
javax.resource.cci.Interaction interaction = null;
javax.resource.cci.InteractionSpec interactionSpec = null;
javax.resource.cci.Record inRec = null;
javax.resource.cci.Record outRec = null;

try {
// Perform a JNDI lookup for the ConnectionFactory object

   javax.naming.InitialContext ctx = new
             javax.naming.InitialContext();
   connectionFactory = (javax.resource.cci.ConnectionFactory)
       ctx.lookup("java:comp/env/eis/myEIS");

// create a connection
   connection = connectionFactory.getConnection();

// Create an Interaction and an InteractionSpec
   interaction = connection.createInteraction();
   interactionSpec = new InteractionSpec();
   interactionSpec.setFunctionName("GETCUSTOM");

// Create input record
   inRec = new javax.resource.cci.Record();
// Here add some code to populate the input record

// Execute an interaction
   interaction.execute(interactionSpec, inRec, outRec);

// Process the output...
```

Figure 10.4a: Sample code to call a function in an EIS.

```
} catch (Exception e) {
   // Exception Handling
} finally {
     if (interaction != null) {
          try {
               interaction.close();
          }
          catch (Exception e) {/* ignore the exception*/}
     }
     if (connection != null) {
          try {
               connection.close();
          }
          catch (Exception e) {/* ignore the exception */}
     }
}
```

Figure 10.4b: Sample code to call a function in an EIS.

Adding a resource adapter in Application Developer

Resource adapters are sets of related classes that let an application access a resource, such as data, or an application on an EIS. You can add a resource adapter to Application Developer by following these steps:

1. Create a connector project.
2. Right-click the connector project and choose **Import** from the context menu.
3. Locate the resource adapter archive (.rar file) and then import the .rar file into the connector project.
4. The resource adapter is ready to be used by your applications.

Configuring a connection factory in Application Developer

When working with JCA resource adapters, you have to add an instance of the JCA connection factory and configure its properties. The connection factory provides connections to the EIS on demand. You specify all the information needed by the resource adapter to connect to the particular instance of the EIS. You also specify the JNDI lookup name under which the new connection factory instance would be available to components. With this lookup name, the components can quickly make a connection to the EIS. You can add resource adapters and connection factories on the J2C page of the server configuration editor. To add a connection factory, follow these steps:

1. Expand **Servers** in the Server Configuration view.
2. Double-click your server. An editor opens.

3. Click the **J2C** tab and click **Add** beside the J2C Resource Adapters list table.
4. Select the name of the J2EE resource adapter that you want to create from the Resource Adapter name drop-down list. Click **OK**.
5. Click **Add** beside the J2C Connection Factories list table. In the Create Connection Factory dialog box, enter a name, a JNDI name for the connection factory, and any other values you want for the connection factory. Click OK. You may need to click on another field before you can click **OK**. The JNDI name, for example, eis/mySAP, is a global name for late binding in the EJB or Web deployment descriptor.
6. In the Resource Properties list table, enter the connection properties. For instance, for CICS ECI connection factory, you need to enter the URL of your EIS transaction gateway, the name of your EIS server, and any other required properties in the Value fields.
7. Close the editor and click **Yes** to save the changes.

Configuring a connection factory resource reference in Application Developer

To add a connection factory reference for an EJB, follow these steps:

1. Open the EJB module deployment descriptor.
2. Click on the **References** tab.
3. Select the EJB the reference is created for, and click the **Add** button.
4. Choose EJB resource reference from the pop-up window and click **Next**.
5. Provide a name for the reference, for example, eis/MyEIS, which is used in the Figure 10.5.
6. Select **javax.resource.cci.ConnectionFactory** as the Type.
7. Decide the authentication method, either Container-managed authentication or Component-managed authentication. For more information on authentication methods, please refer to Chapter 9, “Security.” Click **Finish**.
8. Click on the resource reference just created and bind it to a global JNDI name of the connection factory defined in the server configuration, for example, eis/mySAP, as in Figure 10.5.
9. Save the EJB deployment descriptor.

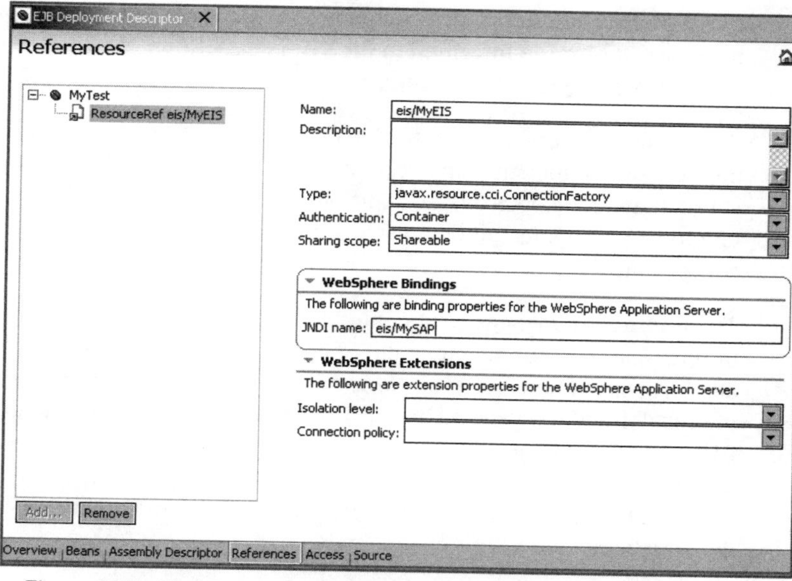

Figure 10.5: Bind the resource reference to a global JNDI name.

Creating a connection factory reference for a servlet in a Web module is a similar process.

Transaction management

This section discussed the transactional support provided by the Java Connector Architecture. Transactional access to EISs is an important requirement for business applications. This section focuses on the transaction model for application developers.

Overview

As in Figure 10.2, when an application component deployed in an application server performs transactional access to multiple resource managers, the transaction manager implemented in the application server takes the responsibility of managing transactions across multiple resource managers.

A resource manager can support two types of transactions: local transactions and XA transactions.

Local transaction

A local transaction is managed internally by a resource manager and does not require coordination by an external manager.

XA transaction

An XA transaction can span multiple resource managers. An XA transaction requires transaction coordination by an external transaction manager. A transaction manager uses a two-phase commit protocol to manage an XA transaction that spans multiple resource managers. For more information on XA Transactions, refer to the section titled "OTS/XA transaction architecture" in Chapter 8.

An application server uses a transaction manager to manage transactions with which an application component can access multiple transactional resource managers. The transaction manager also provides additional low-level services that enable transactional context to be propagated across systems, which are not visible directly to the application components.

The transaction management contract extends the connection management contract and provides support for management of both local transactions (Local Transaction Contract) and XA transactions (XAResource-based Contract). The transaction management contract is defined between an application server and a resource adapter and its underlying EIS resource manager. This contract enables the application server to provide the infrastructure and runtime support for a transaction management. An application component relies on the application server's transaction support for component level transaction demarcation.

The transactions are demarcated either by the container (called container-managed demarcation) or by a component (called bean-managed demarcation). The EJB specification requires an EJB container to support both container-managed and bean-managed transaction demarcation models. The JSP and servlet specifications require a Web container to support bean-managed transaction demarcation. For more information on transaction demarcation, refer to the section titled "Transactions in Enterprise Beans" in Chapter 8.

Transaction management scenarios

The following section uses a set of scenarios to present an overview of the transaction management architecture.

Transactions across multiple two-phase resource managers

As shown in Figure 10.6, both the Transaction Processing (TP) system and the ERP system support XA transactions in this scenario. A servlet invokes EJB X, which accesses transaction programs managed by a TP system, followed by a call to EJB Y which accesses an ERP system. The transaction manager of the application server uses the XAResource interface implemented by the resource adapters to manage and coordinate the transactional access across multiple EIS resource managers. The transaction manager also supports propagation of the transaction context across distributed systems, for example, from the TP System to the ERP System.

The ERP system and the TP system support XA Transactions by implementing an XAResource interface through their resource adapters. The XAResource interface

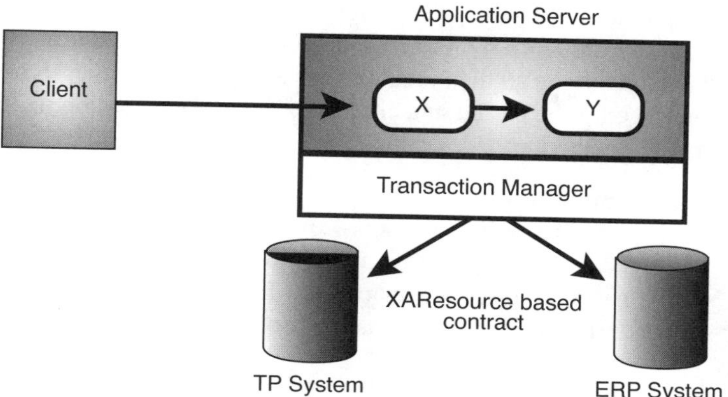

Figure 10.6: Transactions across multiple resource managers that support XA transactions.

enables the two resource managers to participate in transactions that are coordinated by an external transaction manager. When the transaction commits, the transaction manager performs a two-phase commit protocol across the two resource managers, ensuring that all read/write access to resources managed by both the TP system and the ERP system is either entirely committed or entirely rolled back.

Transactions across multiple two-phase resource managers and one one-phase resource manager

Support for this scenario is not required by J2EE or JCA. WebSphere Application Server Enterprise Edition optionally supports this scenario as a value-added feature.

With the Last Participant Support of WebSphere Application Server Enterprise, the transaction manager can coordinate the use of a single one-phase commit (1PC) capable resource with any number of two-phase commit (2PC) capable resources in the same global transaction. At transaction commit, the two-phase commit resources are prepared first using the two-phase commit protocol, and if this is successful, the one-phase commit-resource is then called to commit(one_phase). The two-phase commit resources are then committed or rolled back depending on the response of the one-phase commit resource.

Transactions across multiple one-phase resource managers

Support for this scenario is not required by J2EE or JCA. WebSphere Application Server Enterprise Edition optionally supports this scenario as a value-added feature.

The ActivitySession service of WebSphere Application Server Enterprise provides an alternative unit-of-work (UOW) scope to that provided by global transaction contexts. It is a distributed context that can be used to coordinate multiple one-phase resource managers. The WebSphere EJB container and deployment tooling support ActivitySessions as an extension to the J2EE programming model. EJBs can be deployed with lifecycles that are influenced by ActivitySession context, as an alternative to transaction context. An application can then interact with a resource manager through its LocalTransaction interface for the period of a client-scoped ActivitySession rather than just the duration of an EJB method.

Local transactions

In this scenario, only one resource manager instance participates in a transaction as in Figure 10.7. If an application accesses a single resource manager using an XA transaction, it has a performance overhead compared to using a local transaction because an external transaction manager is required to manage and coordinate XA transactions.

To avoid the overhead of using an XA transaction in a single-resource-manager scenario, the application server may optimize this scenario by using a local transaction instead of an XA transaction. Two options are available for an application server:

- The transaction manager of the application server uses one-phase commit-optimization to coordinate the transaction for this single-resource-manager instance.
- The application server lets the resource manager coordinate this transaction internally without involving an external transaction manager.

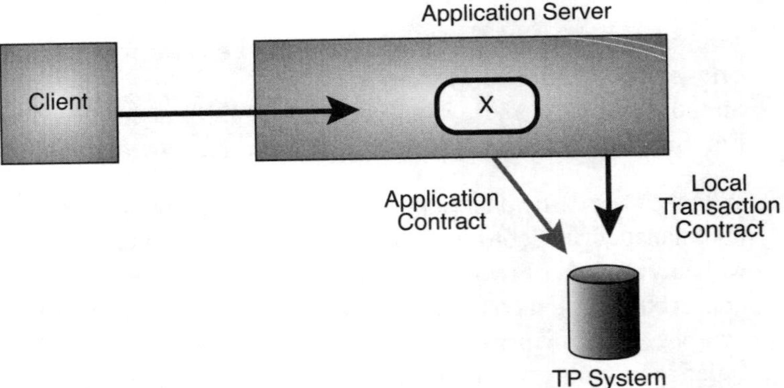

Figure 10.7: Local transaction on a single resource manager.

Developing transactional applications

WebSphere Application Server Version 5 is a J2EE 1.3-compliant application server that implements the necessary low-level transaction protocols, transaction context propagation, and distributed two-phase commit. Similar to JDBC, which provides an abstract implementation to access a relational database, the transaction support in WebSphere Application Server completely abstracts out the low-level transaction. Therefore, application developers can focus on the implementation of business logic at a much higher level, without getting directly involved with the low-level transaction API for the specific underlying transaction system.

For more information on developing transactional applications in the J2EE platform, refer to the sections titled "Transactions in Web components," "Transactions in Enterprise Beans," and "Transactions in application clients" in Chapter 8.

Security architecture

Security is an important requirement for all enterprise applications. The importance of security applications and systems is increasing as more businesses deploy distributed applications and conduct more of their operations over the Internet. It is important for an enterprise to safeguard the sensitive information passed between the Web browsers and Web servers, between the Web servers and the application servers, and between the application servers and connected EISs. Any loss or inaccuracy of information or any unauthorized access to the EIS can be extremely costly to an enterprise.

Chapter 9 describes mechanisms that can be used to protect a system against security threats. The same mechanisms, which include the following examples, can be applied to Enterprise Information Systems:

- Authentication—verifies if a client is valid in a particular context.
- Authorization—determines if a principal is allowed to access a specific EIS resource.
- Security of communication between an application server and an EIS—protects the communication by using Secure Socket Layer (SSL) protocol.

This section focuses on the security management contract, which supports the above security mechanisms and application security model in the Java Connector Architecture.

Security management contract

The J2EE security model defines the security that is applied to client access to the Web tier and then from the Web tier to the EJB tier. JCA defines a security management contract that extends the J2EE end-to-end security model to include support for secure connectivity to EISs.

The JCA security management contract allows support for different security mechanisms to protect an EIS against security threats such as unauthorized access and loss or inaccuracy of information. These mechanisms include authentication, authorization and secure communication links between an application server and an EIS by supporting protocols that provide authentication, integrity, and confidentiality services, such as SSL.

The security management contract is independent of the security mechanism. This means that the application server and EISs can support the security contract regardless of their own different levels of support for security mechanisms. For example, the application server may use basic user password-based authentication while the EIS uses a Kerberos-based end-to-end security environment.

EIS sign-on

This section focuses on EIS sign-on from the perspective of application developers. Before an application component can execute a function in EIS, it has to establish a connection to the EIS under the security context of a resource principal. A principal is an entity that can be authenticated by an authentication mechanism deployed in a system, for example a user. Once the connection is established, all the interactions with the EIS using this connection are executed under the security context of this principal.

There are two choices for conducting EIS sign-on:

- *Container-managed sign-on* allows the deployer to configure the resource principal and EIS sign-on information. For example, the deployer sets a JAAS alias with user name and password in the server configuration for establishing a connection to an EIS instance.
- *Component-managed sign-on* performs sign-on to an EIS by providing explicit resource principal and EIS sign-on information in the code of the application components.

The way to conduct EIS sign-on is specified in the deployment descriptor of the application components. If the <res-auth> element is set to Application, the component code will provide the resource principal and EIS sign-on information to create connections the EIS; if the <res-auth> element is set to Container, the resource principal and EIS sign-on information are set at the application level, normally in the server configuration file, and the application server is responsible for providing the sign-on information when a connection is created.

Container-managed sign-on

In container-managed sign-on the application component lets the container take the responsibility of configuring and managing the EIS sign-on by specifying the <res-auth> element in the deployment descriptor to Container. The container retrieves the security credentials pre-configured by the administrator for establishing a connection to an EIS instance.

Follow these steps to configure container-managed sign-on in WebSphere Studio Application Developer:

1. Expand **Servers** in the Server Configuration view.
2. Double-click your server. An editor opens.

3. Click on the **Security** tab.
4. In the JAAS Authentication Entries section, add a JAAS alias with the username and password by which the application server creates the connections to the EIS.
5. Click on the **J2C** tab and define a J2C connection factory for your EIS. Select the JAAS alias you defined in Step 4 for the Container-managed authentication alias property. For more information on creating a connection factory, refer to the section titled "Configuring a connection factory in Application Developer."
6. Save the server configuration.
7. Open the deployment descriptor of an EJB module or a Web module that contains the application component that needs access to the EIS.
8. Create a resource reference for the application component, such as an EJB or a servlet, that needs a connection to the EIS. Select **Container** as the Authentication type, as in Figure 10.5. For more information on creating resource reference, refer to the section titled "Configuring a connection factory resource reference in Application Developer."
9. Save the deployment descriptor.

At this point, the component can establish a connection to the EIS instance without being concerned about security. The component invokes the getConnection() method on the ConnectionFactory instance and does not need to pass any security-related parameters.

The code snippet in Figure 10.8 shows how to use container-managed sign-on.

```
InitialContext ctx = new InitialContext();

// perform JNDI lookup to obtain a connection factory
javax.resource.cci.ConnectionFactory cf =
            (javax.resource.cci.ConnectionFactory)
            ctx.lookup("java:comp/env/eis/myEIS");

// obtain a connection without passing security information
javax.resource.cci.Connection conn = cf.getConnection();
```

Figure 10.8: Container-managed sign-on.

Component-managed sign-on

With component-managed sign-on, the sign-on information needs to be specified in the component code, and the <res-auth> element in the deployment descriptor needs to be set to Application. Follow these steps to configure component-managed sign-on for an application component.

1. Open the deployment descriptor of the EJB module or a Web module that contains the application component that needs access to the EIS.
2. Create a resource reference for the application component, for example, an EJB or a Servlet, that needs a connection to the EIS. Select **Application** as the Authentication type.
3. Save the deployment descriptor.

At this point, the application component must pass the security information to the ConnectionSpec object implemented by the resource adapter, typically the username and password, and then use the ConnectionSpec object as a parameter of the getConnection() method. The sample code is shown in Figure 10.9.

```
InitialContext ctx = new InitialContext();
// perform JNDI lookup to obtain a connection factory
javax.resource.cci.ConnectionFactory cf =
          (javax.resource.cci.ConnectionFactory)
          ctx.lookup("java:comp/env/eis/myEIS");

// obtain a connection by passing the security information
javax.resource.cci.ConnectionSpec connectionSpec = new
                    com.myeis.ConnectionSpeImpl();
connectionSpec.setUserName("MyUserId");
connectionSpec.setPassword("MyPassword");

// obtain a connection by passing the security information
javax.resource.cci.Connection conn = cf.getConnection(connectionSpec);
```

Figure 10.9: Component-managed sign-on.

Common client interface

The CCI defines a standard client API for application components to access heterogeneous EISs. This section describes the interfaces usually used by the developers.

Connection-related interfaces

Connection-related interfaces are used by application components to obtain physical connections to an EIS. The CCI API provides the following three connection-related interfaces:

ConnectionFactory

The javax.resource.cci.ConnectionFactory interface provides an application component with javax.resource.cci.Connection instance to an EIS. A component looks up a ConnectionFactory instance from the JNDI namespace and then uses it to get a connection to the EIS instance.

The following two methods in the ConnectionFactory interface are usually used by developers. These two methods have been discussed in the section titled "EIS Sign-On."

```
public Connection getConnection()
      throws ResourceException;

public Connection       getConnection(javax.resource.cci.ConnectionSpec
      properties) throws ResourceException;
```

Connection

The javax.resource.cci.Connection interface represents an application-level connection handle to the underlying EIS. The actual physical connection associated with a Connection instance is represented by a ManagedConnection instance.

A component gets a Connection instance by using the getConnection method on a ConnectionFactory instance. A Connection instance may be associated with zero or more Interaction instances.

The following three methods of the Connection interface are usually used by developers.

```
public Interaction createInteraction() throws ResourceException;

public LocalTransaction getLocalTransaction()
      throws ResourceException;

public void close() throws ResourceException;
```

The method createInteraction creates an Interaction instance associated with the Connection instance. An Interaction enables a component to access EIS data and functions.

The method getLocalTransaction returns a LocalTransaction instance that enables a component to demarcate resource manager local transactions.

The method close initiates a close of the connection.

ConnectionSpec

The javax.resource.cci.ConnectionSpec interface provides a means for an application component to pass connection request-specific properties to the ConnectionFactory when making a connection request.

The CCI specification defines a set of standard properties for the ConnectionSpec interface. A resource adapter may define additional properties specific to its underlying EIS.

The following standard properties are defined by the CCI specification for the ConnectionSpec interface:

"UserName—name of the user establishing a connection to an EIS instance Password—password for the user establishing a connection"

Interaction-related interfaces

Interaction-related interfaces enable a component to execute a program or call a business object in an EIS instance. The CCI API defines two interfaces for interactions between an application component and the EIS: Interaction and InteractionSpec.

Interaction

The javax.resource.cci.Interaction interface provides a means for an application component to execute EIS functions, such as a CICS program or a business object in an ERP system.

An Interaction instance supports the following interactions with an EIS instance in CCI specification:

- "An execute method that takes an input Record, an output Record, and an InteractionSpec. This method executes the EIS function represented by the InteractionSpec and updates the output Record.
- An execute method that takes an input Record and an InteractionSpec. This method implementation executes the EIS function represented by the InteractionSpec and produces the output Record as a return value."

```
public boolean execute(InteractionSpec ispec, Record input,
        Record output) throws ResourceException;

public Record execute(InteractionSpec ispec, Record input)
        throws ResourceException;
```

InteractionSpec

The javax.resource.cci.InteractionSpec interface holds properties that an application component uses to interact with an EIS, for example, a CICS transaction name.

The CCI specification defines a set of standard properties for the InteractionSpec interface. A resource adapter may define additional properties specific to its underlying EIS. The following standard properties are defined by the CCI specification for the InteractionSpec interface:

- "FunctionName—a string representing the name of an EIS function. Examples are the name of a transaction program in a CICS system or the name of a business object in an ERP system.

- InteractionVerb—an integer representing the mode of interaction with an EIS instance as specified by the InteractionSpec. The values of interaction verb may be one of the following:
  - SYNC_SEND-The execution of an Interaction performs only a send to the target EIS instance. The input record is sent to the EIS instance without any synchronous response in terms of an output Record or a ResultSet.
  - SYNC_SEND_RECEIVE-The execution of an Interaction sends a request to the EIS instance and receives response synchronously. The input record is sent to the EIS instance with the output received either as a Record or a ResultSet.
  - SYNC_RECEIVE-The execution of an Interaction results in a synchronous receive of an output Record. An example is when a session bean gets a method invocation and it uses this SYNC_RECEIVE form of interaction to retrieve messages that have been delivered to a message queue.
- ExecutionTimeout—an integer representing the number of milliseconds an Interaction waits for an EIS to execute the specified function."

LocalTransaction

The javax.resource.cci.LocalTransaction is used for application-level local transaction demarcation. A LocalTransaction instance is obtained by the getLocalTransaction method in the Connection interface. The following three methods defined in the LocalTransaction interface are self-explained:

```
public void begin() throws ResourceException;
public void commit() throws ResourceException;
public void rollback() throws ResourceException;
```

Data representation-related interfaces

Data representation-related interfaces encapsulate the data structures that an application component uses to interact with an EIS instance, for example, the input and the output of a CICS program. The following five interfaces are defined in CCI specification to represent data.

Record

The javax.resource.cci.Record interface is the base interface for the different kinds of records. Records may be instances of MappedRecord, IndexedRecord, or ResultSet, each of which extends the base Record interface. A Record instance is used as an input or output to the execute methods defined in the Interaction interface.

RecordFactory

RecordFactory is used to create a Record instance.

IndexedRecord

IndexedRecord represents a Record based on the java.util.List interface.

MappedRecord

MappedRecord represents a Record based on the java.util.Map interface.

ResultSet

ResultSet represents tabular data based on the JDBC ResultSet.

Summary

This chapter provided a high-level overview of the Connector architecture and the characteristics of connection management, transaction management, security management, and the common client interfaces.

We've seen in this chapter how an application can create connections to underlying EISs. In a managed environment, the application servers manage connection pooling, thus simplifying connection handling for an application. The connection pooling mechanism, because it is handled by the application server, remains transparent to the application. The connection management contract results in a simplified application-programming model. The contract also serves to increase the scalability of application integration with EISs.

This chapter describes the transactional concepts of the Connector architecture. To guarantee the consistency and integrity of the data, we recommend that any access to an EIS be done under the scope of a transaction.

This chapter explains the support of secure EIS integration provided by the Connector architecture. It introduces an explained the relevant security concepts and terminology. It also describes the types of sign-on to EIS—component- or container-managed—and shows how each such sign-on is handled and the trade-offs of these different approaches.

WebSphere Application Server supports the JCA 1.0 specification. This chapter also gives the steps to add a resource adapter into Application Developer and configure a connection factory in the server configuration.

Test yourself

Key terms

J2EE Connector Architecture (JCA)
enterprise information systems (EIS)
resource adapter
Resource Manager (RM)
transaction manager (TM)
managed environment
Connection
system contracts
Common Client Interface (CCI)
Resource Adapter Archive (RAR)

Review questions

1. What types of systems are good candidates for being accessed by the JCA?
2. Can a call to an EIS system through JCA be enclosed in an XA transaction?
3. What services are provided by the security management contract?
4. What services are provided by the connection contract?
5. Describe a typical process for using resources provided through the Common Client Interface of the JCA.

CHAPTER 11

Profiling analysis tools in WebSphere Studio

Doug Weatherbee

Chapter topics

- *Profiling background and concepts*
- *The Profiling Perspective*
- *Profiling setup procedures*
- *Profiling analysis procedures*

Certification objectives

- *Use tracing and profiling tools to analyze and tune applications*
- *Explain implications of resource management on application design and implementation*
- *Identify misbehaving application components*

WebSphere Studio Application Developer's Profiling Perspective contains a variety of powerful tools that enable you to gather and analyze data about a Java Virtual Machine's runtime behavior. The Profiling perspective helps you to visualize your program execution and explore different patterns within the program. The Profiling tools leverage Sun Microsystems' Java Virtual Machine Profiler Interface (JVMPI).

This chapter begins by discussing the necessary background concepts of the Application Developer Profiling tools before proceeding to outline setup procedures. Part of the background is a description of the IBM Agent Controller and how it facilitates communication between Application Developer Profiling tools and a JVMPI-enabled JVM. The chapter concludes by describing how to use the range of Profiling tools for specific analysis scenarios.

Profiling background and concepts

Application profiling goals

The job of a programmer is usually to write an application that automates a business process. In order to do this, programming languages must bridge two realms: the binary language of machines and the actual world of people and business problems. Programming languages have evolved to the point where object-oriented (OO) languages, such as Java, are closer in design, concept, and syntax to the actual business domain than to the binary workings of machines. OO languages hide the binary runtime characteristics of a computer application. This OO abstraction is, of course, a great benefit for easily designing and coding real-world business processes and use cases. However, from the standpoint of memory- and speed-limited JVMs, computers, and networks, this same abstraction may result in poorly performing, unoptimized, and memory-intensive code simply because programmers cannot understand how their code actually runs.

Moreover, in today's world of large, distributed J2EE Enterprise Applications, building code often involves many developers divided into separate teams, each building numerous Java classes and interfaces that are archived into J2EE modules and finally bundled into the larger Enterprise Application. As coders, our primary focus is first to write code that meets the functional requirements of our use cases. But once we've accomplished this, how do we dig deeper into the performance of our code when one use case can involve dozens of classes produced by many separate developers? The functional requirements of the use case may be examined and met through unit and integration testing. However, testing functional requirements doesn't mean testing code performance.

The profiling tools in Application Developer enable you to measure, organize, and visually display information about the actual runtime behavior of code inside a JVM. Profiling is not concerned with testing business functional requirements of your code. On the contrary, profiling helps you more fully understand the design and performance of your code. The JVM may be a stand-alone Java application, a WebSphere Application Server, another JVMPI-enabled application server, or a collection of JVMPI application servers. Measuring and organizing information about the runtime behavior of your code will create a deeper comprehension of your Java program. The Application Developer Profiler will help you identify code bottlenecks, monitor JVM garbage collection, and locate memory leaks and memory-intensive class instances in your code. Two new features of Application Developer Version 5 are the addition of profiling tools that enable pattern identification and application flow to be displayed visually through Unified Modeling Language (UML) Sequence Diagrams and the ability to profile applications deployed across servers in distributed environments.

Code bottlenecks

Often, somewhere in the collection of classes and interfaces implementing a completed use case are methods with excessive execution times, resulting in performance bottlenecks. For example, imagine you are responsible for coding the controller layer of an application and are given a prebuilt utility JAR and EJB JAR that will handle the location and retrieval of data. You construct a controller servlet that makes a single method call to a prebuilt helper class in the utility JAR. The helper class in turn makes a call to the remote interfaces of an Entity EJB. The helper class calls several accessor methods of the Entity EJB. Performance is fine as long as you run the servlet, the helper class, and the Entity EJB in the same server JVM, because WebSphere transforms the remote EJB calls to local intra-JVM calls. However, in production environments the Web module and EJB Modules may be deployed on separate application server JVMs. Suddenly, your servlet's simple call to one method in the helper class takes a long time, because it actually results in round tripping or several inter-JVM network calls. Application Developer Profiling enables you to identify these types of bottlenecks in your code. Other causes of poorly performing methods with long execution times could be excessively layered applications or unknown, large synchronized code blocks. The Application Developer Profiling Perspective provides several tools that aid in identifying specific methods that simply take too long.

Memory leaks and garbage collection

Memory leaks were often a problem for C++ developers, because they had to write code to explicitly manage allocation and deallocation of memory. Neglecting to release the instances created a memory leak that eventually could bring down the application. A major improvement of Java was the addition of automatic garbage collection. The scope of an object determines when it is automatically marked for garbage collection. This feature can, however, lull developers into the mistake of thinking that J2EE Java applications cannot have memory leaks. Memory leaks in J2EE applications do occur. For instance, consider excessive object allocation to a long-lived HTTPSession. Objects placed into the HTTPSession do not get garbage-collected until the HTTPSession is garbage-collected. The Application Developer Profiling tools allow you to run and view JVM garbage collection and can identify object instances still active in the JVM memory after garbage collection has occurred. Moreover, the tools will report on the size of object instances running in memory.

Pattern identification

When you are beginning to profile a large amount of code, it is important not to get bogged down in the details immediately. First, you must identify from a high level the general flow of your application as a request makes its way through the many classes that make up the controller, model, and view layers of your Enterprise Application. You are looking for high-level runtime patterns in your application that will point to potential problem areas in specific parts of your code. The Application Developer Sequence Diagram tool is key to identifying these runtime patterns.

Distributed J2EE profiling

J2EE Enterprise Applications typically do not run inside one JVM but rather are deployed on multiple application servers across multiple machines. This presents a problem for the traditional form of profiling that focuses on a single JVM. Distributed application profiling requires a profiling tool that can dynamically connect or attach to new JVMs as remote method invocations, for example to EJBs, are being made. The Application Developer J2EE Request Profiling Agent is designed specifically for profiling distributed J2EE applications.

Architecture

To profile a JVM successfully, several parts of a profiling architecture must be in place. Sun Microsystems' JVMPI document outlines an emerging standardized approach to building JVMs for profiling. Application Developer uses the JVMPI in its profiling architecture with the Java Profiling Agent and extends it by providing the J2EE Request Profiler. In addition, IBM has produced the Agent Controller, which acts as a bridge between the Application Developer Profiler and JVMs.

Sun's Java Virtual Machine Profiling Interface

The Application Developer Profiling tools leverage Sun Microsystems JVMPI document. The JVMPI is not yet a final standard profiling interface but rather, according to the JVMPI, "an experimental feature in the JDK 2" (Java Virtual Machine Profiling Interface, Sun Microsystems, Dec. 7, 2002). Profiling tools such as Application Developer's Profiling Perspective indirectly leverage interface methods outlined in the JVMPI to display code execution statistics and information about JVMs. The JVMPI identifies a range of methods that enable two-way communication and data exchange between a JVM and an in-process Profiling Agent. The JVM can send events to the Profiling Agent signaling thread creation, heap allocation, and other runtime activities. In turn, the in-process Profiling Agent can request further detailed data about these runtime activities. Generally, the data that the IBM implementation of the Profiling Agent returns consists of XML fragments. Although not yet an official standard, JVM vendors, such as IBM, that have implemented the JVMPI have provided a window into their JVMs for early adopting profiling technologies.

Application Developer profiling architecture

A complete end-to-end Application Developer profiling architecture includes the Profiling Client Tool (Application Developer), the IBM Agent Controller, the JVM in-process Profiling Agent, and the JVM itself. The architecture is displayed in Figure 11.1:

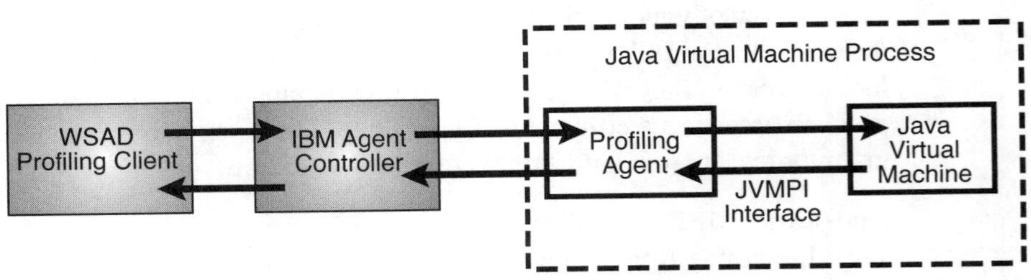

Figure 11.1: Application Developer Profiling architecture.

The Profiling Agent resides in process with the JVM and, as discussed previously, gathers data about the JVM through a variety of JVMPI-defined methods. The IBM Agent Controller provides the bridge between the in-process Profiling Agent and the Application Developer Profiling Client application. The Application Developer Profiling Client application consumes the XML fragments it receives from the Profiling Agent via the Agent Controller and assembles and displays the information in a variety of Application Developer Profiling Perspective views.

Note: The profiling data is not automatically returned from the Profiling Agent via the Agent Controller to the Application Developer Profiling Client. You must explicitly "refresh" your profiling data in the Application Developer Profiling Client. Refreshing results in Application Developer sends a message to the Agent Controller, which in turn requests updated profiling data from the in-process Profiling Agent. This is done for performance reasons. A constant exchange of profiling data between the in-process Profiling Agent and Application Developer would result in poor Workbench performance.

Java Profiling Agent

The Java Profiling Agent is a code library included in the IBM JDK 2 that follows the interface guidelines of the JVMPI. When the IBM JVM is started, the Profiling Agent attaches itself to the newly started JVM and, when requested by the IBM Agent Controller, returns execution information to the Profiling Client in the form of XML fragments. Although running in process, the Profiling Agent does not automatically start with a JVM. In order to start the Profiling Agent, the JVM must be invoked using the -XrunpiAgent Java option. The full syntax of the -XrunpiAgent Java option is

```
java -XrunpiAgent[:agent_parm=value[,agent_parm=value]*]
```

The *agent_parm* can be one of four possibilities: *server*, *filters*, *file*, or *help*.

- The server agent_parm can have one of four values: *enabled*, *standalone*, *controlled*, or *application*.
  - *enabled*—This is the default for the -XrunpiAgent Java option, and it is the most common way to use the Profiling Agent in conjunction with Application Developer. In fact, when you start an internal Application Developer WebSphere Test Server in profile mode (**Servers → Profile**), Application Developer automatically passes the -XrunpiAgent Java option to the starting Test Server. The Profiling Agent is alive in the background of the JVM, but does not utilize process resources until Application Developer connects to it via the Agent Controller and requests the Agent to start monitoring program execution. When the Agent starts monitoring, it keeps track of program

execution and, upon a further request from the workbench, will send that data to the Application Developer profiling client, again via the Agent Controller.

- *controlled*—The Profiling Agent is loaded first in the process and stops the application code from running until the Application Developer profiling client attaches to the Profiling Agent and requests the Agent to start monitoring.
- *application*—The Java Profiling Agent is loaded in a similar manner to *enabled* but collects profiling data only when both the application code requests that the profiling agent start profiling (using the *com.ibm.etools.logging.tracing.agent.Profiler* class, located in <IBM Agent Controller install directory>/lib/logutil.jar) and the Application Developer Profiling Client requests that the Profiling Agent start monitoring.
- *standalone*—The Profiling Agent runs in a stand-alone mode and thus prevents an Application Developer Profiling Client from connecting to it. Any configuration information must be provided in a configuration file whose name is the value of the filter agent_parm. The output of profiling data must be sent to an XML file whose name is the value of the file agent_parm.

- The filters agent_parm, whose value is the name of a filter configuration file, is used only when server=standalone is specified. The filters configuration file has an extension of .txt and contains "pattern mode" pairs. A pattern is usually a Java package or class name, and the mode identifies whether to INCLUDE or EXCLUDE the pattern when profiling data is collected. An asterisk [*] can be used as a wildcard once in a pattern, at either the beginning or end of the string. The default is filters.txt if not specified.
- The file agent_parm, whose value is the name of an output file, is also used only when server=standalone is specified. The output file has an extension of .trcxml and will be a complete XML document containing all the profiling data output of the Profiling Agent. The default is trace.trcxml if not specified.
- The help agent_parm displays a list of the available Profiling Agent options using stdout.

Examples:

```
Java -XrunpiAgent
```

In this example the default is used (server=enabled).

```
Java -XrunpiAgent:server=standalone
```

In this example the defaults are used (filters=filters.txt and file=trace.trcxml).

```
java -XrunpiAgent:server=standalone,filters=myFilters.txt,file=
myProfilingOutput.trcxml
```

In this example server, filters, and file options are all provided.

As you will see later in the chapter, a non-Application Developer stand-alone WebSphere Application Server process does not automatically start a Java Profiling Agent. Rather, you must configure the WebSphere Server's Process Definition to have a Generic JVM Argument of -XrunpiAgent. This will be discussed in detail later in the chapter.

J2EE Request Profiler

The J2EE Request Profiler is somewhat similar to the Java Profiling Agent in that it gathers program execution data, but its scope is much narrower. The J2EE Request Profiler is a WebSphere Server Profiling Agent that focuses on tracking requests made from one WebSphere Server to another, usually to and from servlets or JSP pages in Web containers and EJBs in EJB containers. For example, in modern clustered J2EE environments, application code from one WebSphere server may make remote procedure calls to EJBs residing in another WebSphere Server running on another node. In this example, the first WebSphere Server would have a J2EE Request Profiler running in process and the second WebSphere Server would have a second J2EE Request Profiler running in process. Both J2EE Request Profilers would be collecting profiling data about incoming remote requests.

Like the Java Profiling Agent, which requires the -XrunpiAgent Java option, the J2EE Request Profiler requires a JVM environment variable of -DPD_DT_ENABLED=true. When you start an internal Application Developer WebSphere Test Server in profile mode (**Servers → Profile**), Application Developer automatically passes the -DPD_DT_ENABLED=true environment variable to the starting Test Server. However, when working with a non-Application Developer stand-alone WebSphere Server, you are required to start the J2EE Request Profiler explicitly by configuring the Server's Process Definition to have a Generic JVM Argument of -DPD_DT_ENABLED=true. Once you have done this on your stand-alone WebSphere Servers, an Application Developer Profiler can dynamically attach to remote WebSphere Servers as remote procedure calls are made at run time. As long as you enable the J2EE Request Profiler on all your servers in a given cluster, you can, in effect, follow and profile your program execution across JVMs as it happens without prior knowledge of the remote calls. You must, however, have the IBM Agent Controller installed and running on all the server machines where the Application Developer Profiling Client is attaching to either the J2EE Request Profiler or Profiling Agent.

IBM Agent Controller

As you may have concluded from the previous discussion, the IBM Agent Controller (AC) is a daemon process that provides a bridge between the Java Profiling Agent and J2EE Request Profiler, and the Application Developer Profiling Client. It transfers the data and information between these applications and in some cases allows Application Developer to start and stop other applications, such as WebSphere Application Server. The AC plays a part in several important Application Developer functions, such as enabling Application Developer to Profile stand-alone Java applications and J2EE applications running inside of WebSphere Application Server. Application Developer also uses the AC to import WebSphere Application Server logs and logs other than the Application Developer LoggingUtil.log (default created log in the *workspace\metadata* directory). Application Developer can use the AC to create, deploy, control, and debug a remote WebSphere Application Server instance. The AC enables the workbench to run various Application Developer Component Testing frameworks against both Java applications residing locally in the workbench and remotely deployed J2EE applications on WebSphere Application Server.

In Application Developer Version 4, the IBM Agent Controller was automatically installed with Application Developer. This is not the case with Application Developer Version 5. You must explicitly install the AC by selecting the Install IBM Agent Controller menu option of Application Developer Version 5 install CD.

Note: Application Developer Versions 4 and 5 have different versions of the AC. In order for profiling to work, your Application Developer and AC versions must be the same.

As stated previously, you must install the AC on all machines with WebSphere Servers that you intend to profile. This rule also applies to the Application Developer internal WTE Servers. You must install the AC on the same machine as Application Developer in order to profile an Application Developer WTE Server. If you already have Application Developer Version 4 installed, you must uninstall the earlier AC version and then install the Application Developer Version 5 AC.

The AC configuration file, serviceconfig.xml, located in the <IBM Agent Controller install directory>/config directory, contains a listing of JVM applications it can connect to. The AC installation program automatically configures the Application Developer internal WTE Servers but not necessarily remote stand-alone WebSphere Servers. If WebSphere Application Server is installed on a machine before the AC is installed, the AC installation program will perform an automatic configuration similar to an internal

Application Developer WTE Server. However, if you install the AC prior to installing WebSphere, you must manually add the WebSphere installation directory path to the AC serviceconfig.xml. Review the AC Installation Guide on the Application Developer Version 5 install CD for more information.

The AC is started in various ways depending on the operating system. On Linux, AIX, and Solaris, use the RAStart.sh and RAStop.sh, located in the <IBM Agent Controller install directory>/bin directory, to start and stop the AC, respectively. On a Windows platform the AC is registered as a Windows Service and can be started and stopped using the Services application. The AC default external communication port is 10002. This is the default port the Application Developer Profiling client uses when connecting to a remote AC residing on a separate host. For security reasons, you may change the AC default communication port, which is defined in the serviceconfig.xml configuration file. You must then also change the Application Developer Profiling preference to match the updated AC port. This will be discussed later in the chapter.

Note: Since the AC opens and listens on a port, for security reasons it is highly recommended that it be installed behind a firewall. During the AC installation, you are also prompted with choices regarding security restrictions, such as limits on hostnames the AC will communicate with. A complete discussion of the AC installation process is beyond the scope of this book. See the Installation Guide on the Application Developer version 5 CD for more information.

The Profiling Perspective

This section of the chapter will describe the range of views available in the Application Developer Profiling Perspective and outline the Workbench Profiling-related preferences that can be set in Application Developer.

Profiling Monitor view

The Profiling Monitor view is a type of navigational view located in the top left corner of the Profiling Perspective of Application Developer. It displays five types of objects: project, monitor, host, process, and agent. Of these, a project is the only Profiling Monitors view resource that is not specifically a profiling resource. In contrast, Application Developer creates the profiling-specific monitor, host, process, and agent under a project of your choice when you start a profiling session. Each profiling object exists in an aggregated tree with the monitor at the root and then the host, process, and agent. (See Figure 11.2.)

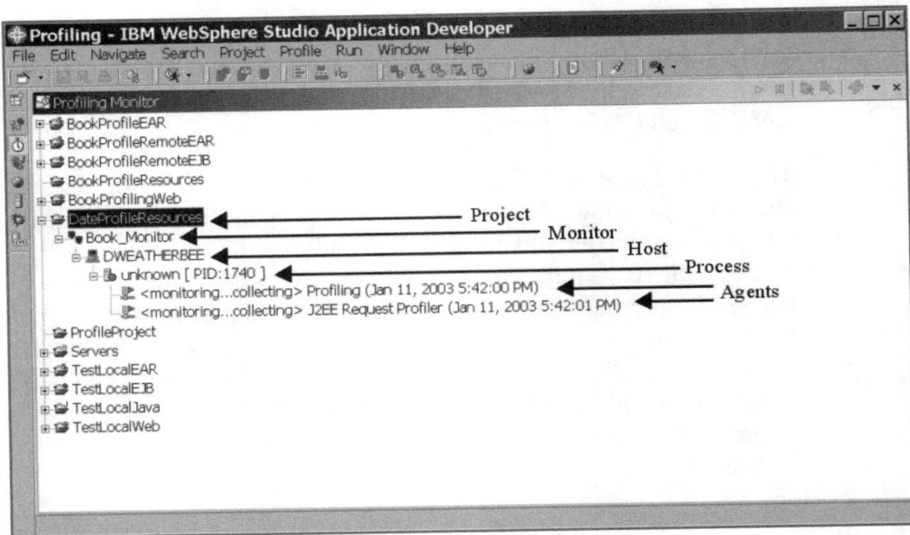

Figure 11.2: Profiling Monitor.

Each profiling object contains information that is scoped to the type of resource it represents and what that resource contains. For example, you can view the data of multiple profiling processes and agents running on a specific server machine by selecting the host object in the Monitors view. A great feature of the Application Developer Profiler is that you can save the profiling data collected and categorized by these profiling objects as XMI files. XMI files are a type of XML document designed to contain metadata or configuration information. Saved profiling XMI files can be used to review profiling data long after the profiling session and the test servers have been stopped.

Monitors

A monitor is the highest profiling object in the Monitors view hierarchical tree. It can contain profiling data that spans several nodes in a distributed application server cluster. During the later stages of testing and profiling you may want to gather and analyze profiling data on the behavior of your Enterprise Application in a distributed environment. You can deploy your Enterprise Applications to multiple nodes and application servers and use the Application Developer Profiler and the J2EE Request Profiler to produce data tracking program execution across JVMs. The monitor in the Monitors view represents the application behavior across that collection of distributed nodes and JVMs. Multiple-node profiling data displayed at the monitor level will be totaled or aggregated.

Monitors are not visible in the Profiling Monitor view by default, so you will have to go to the Application Developer Profiling preferences and explicitly set the Workbench to display them (**Window → Preferences → Profiling and Logging → Profiling Monitor View → Monitor** checkbox).

Hosts

Host profiling objects represent physical machines or machine execution partitions. When you attach the Application Developer Profiler to a host you must supply either the host IP address or hostname. Application Developer uses the IP address or hostname you supply as the host display name in the Profiling Monitors view. Directly under a host in the Monitors view containment tree you will find specific JVM processes that are profiled. You can have multiple hosts with the same name in the Monitors view because Application Developer uses the entire path of profiling objects for unique identification.

Processes

A Process in the Monitors view represents a running JVM. You will see one Process per server when profiling a WebSphere Application Server JVM. When profiling a Java Application, you may have one Process or several Processes for code executing in a multitasking Java program. Directly under Process in the Monitors view you will find Agents. The Process name can take two forms depending on how the JVM it represents is started.

If you start the Process from the Application Developer Workbench, then the name of the Java class you started along with its OS Process Identifier will be used as the Process name. For example, using the Workbench to start a Java Application by running a StartHere.class will result in a Process name similar to "StartHere [PID:1862]". If you attach the Application Developer profiler to an already running JVM, the Process name will include the word "java" and the OS Process Identifier. The latter is how a Process name is created when profiling a WebSphere Application Server JVM. For example, the Process name would look similar to "java [PID: 1862]".

Agents

Agents are a visual representation of the Java Profiling Agent and J2EE Request Profiler running inside the JVM process. As described in the previous sections, the Java Profiling Agent and J2EE Request Profiler are mechanisms used to collect profiling data from a JVM. Agents by default in the Profiling Monitor view are not automatically monitoring JVM program execution. You must start an Agent's monitoring after you have connected or attached to the JVM. Starting an Agent monitoring in Application Developer sends a message to the actual Profiling Agent or J2EE Request Profiler running inside the JVM process to begin collecting profiling data.

Profiling Console view

The Profiling Console view will display output data or error messages from a profiled stand-alone JVM. The view has basic text-editing functions, such as copy, paste, and go to line.

Statistical profiling views

There are several statistical profiling views in Application Developer, including Package Statistics, Class Instance Statistics, Class Method Statistics, Method Statistics, and Instance Statistics Views. They all present profiling data in tabular form with program execution displayed as a range of numerical values organized by columns and rows.

Time measurement in the statistical views

There are two units of time measurement in the statistical views, called Base Time and Cumulative Time. Base Time measures the time a specific method takes to execute excluding the execution times of methods it invokes. For example, in the method shown in Figure 11.3, methodA, the time spent executing the for loop is reflected in Base Time while the time spent executing methodB is ignored:

```
public void methodA()
{
   //methodB() execution time is ignored
Counter count = methodB();

for (i=0; i<count.lenth(); i++)
{
          //do something
}
}
```

Figure 11.3: Base Time and Cumulative Time.

In contrast, Cumulative Time reflects the execution time of the originating method and the methods it calls. In this example, both methodA and methodB execution times are reflected in the Cumulative Time. In addition, any methods methodB calls are included, and so on until the end of this method execution stack is reached. You should be aware that the Cumulative Time total will include time spent executing recursive or looped method calls. Time spent in recursive method calls will not be subtracted from the Cumulative Time counter.

Note: Time, regardless of whether it is Base or Cumulative, is calculated as clock time rather than CPU (processor) time. That is, the time the CPU spends on its activities, such as thread and process context switches, is not included because these activities are not directly related to your program code performance and will vary from machine to machine.

Package Statistics view

The Package Statistics view is new to Application Developer Version 5 and displays application class information organized and grouped by the containing Java packages. Viewing profiling data at the level of Java packages rather than individual classes is very useful during the initial stages of tracking down problematic areas in your code. Once you have used the Package Statistics view to identify problems at the package level, you can stay within the view, drilling down a tree to specific classes, or switch to other views for further investigation into method data. A great feature of the Application Developer profiling tools is the class selection synchronization between the views. For example, if you select a certain class in the Package Statistics view and switch to the Class Method Statistics view for further investigation, the same class will be selected and highlighted in the new view. The Package Statistics view by default includes the following column headers:

- Package—This column displays the Java package name, in ascending or descending order. You can expand the package tree to show the contained classes. As stated previously, it is very common to begin by examining package statistics first to locate problem areas and then drilling down the tree to locate the specific class causing the problem.
- New Occurrence—This small column, just to the right of the Packages column, flags classes that have been created since the last profiling information of your application was retrieved or refreshed. New Occurrences are identified by yellow diamond-shaped icons appearing in the small column.
- Base Time—This column displays the Base Time as described in the earlier section, "Time measurement in the statistical views."
- Cumulative Time—This column contains the Cumulative Time as described in the earlier section "Time measurement in the statistical views."
- Calls—This column displays the total number of method calls made on the selected package or class.
- Live Instances—This column displays the number of current object instances still active in memory.
- Active Size—This column displays the total size of the live instances.

Column cells that contain numerical data may sometimes have delta icons displayed. Delta icons indicate that since you have last refreshed or retrieved your profiling data, the highlighted cell value has either increased or decreased.

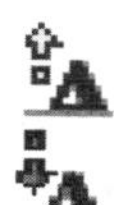

- A delta icon with a yellow up arrow signals an increase in the cell value.
- A delta icon with a blue down arrow signals a decrease in the cell value.

The Package Statistics view by default does not include the following column header:

- Total Instances—This column, when displayed, contains the total number of object instances still active in the JVM and destroyed by garbage collection.

The rows of data in the Package Statistics view are by default sorted in ascending alphabetic order by package name under the Package header. Under each package tree the classes are also by default sorted in ascending alphabetic order. You can customize the view sort order by selecting the header of any column. Selecting any column header that contains strings, such as Package Name, sorts the table by that column alphabetically. Selecting any column header that contains numerical data, such as Base Time, sorts the table by that column's numerical value. If you click a column header more than once you can reverse the sort order from ascending to descending. The most recently sorted column header title will have a prefix “<” if the column is sorted in ascending order and “>” if the column is sorted in descending order. You can choose to add or subtract columns from the view by using the Choose Column dialog. It can be accessed through a pop-up menu by right-clicking **View** and selecting **Choose Columns**. The Dialog also allows you to change the order in which the columns are displayed in the View table. (See Figure 11.4.)

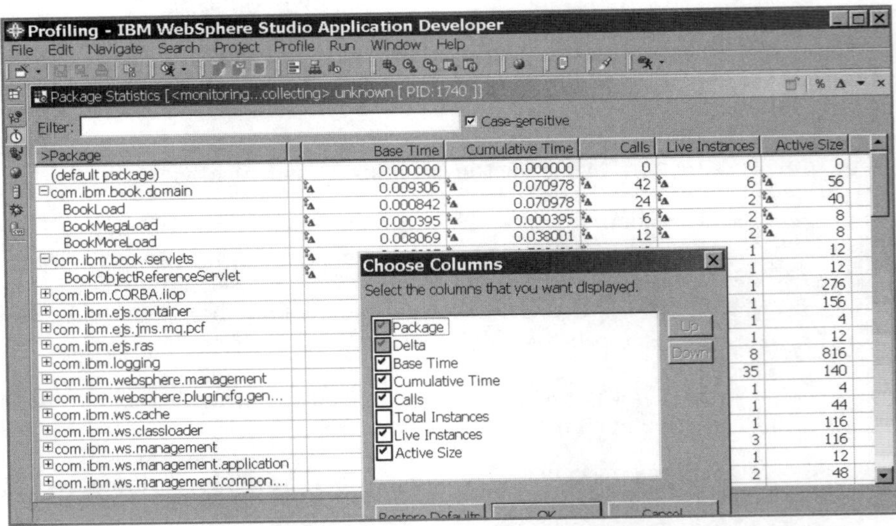

Figure 11.4: Package Statistics view default columns and Choose Columns dialog.

The view also has a small toolbar located in the top right corner that contains Open Source, Show Percentage, and Show Delta Columns buttons. As well, by using the drop-down arrow you can choose from the menu to Exclude Old and Unchanged data. Figure 11.5 shows the location of the Package Statistics view toolbar.

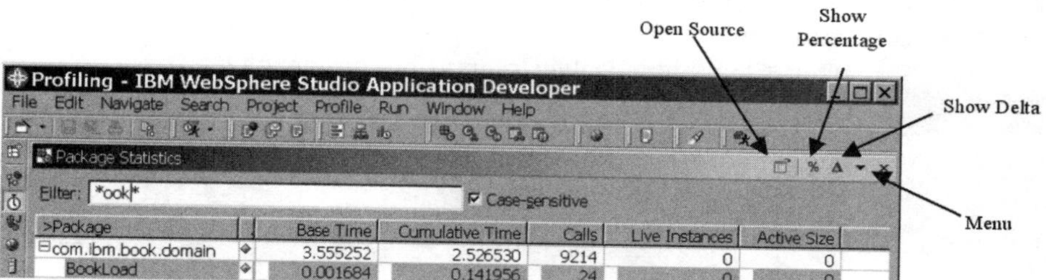

Figure 11.5: Package Statistics view toolbar.

The functions of the buttons and menu are as follows:

- Open Source—You can use this button to open the source code of a class or method you have selected in the view. This is very useful when you have used the Profiling tools to identify a poorly performing class and want to investigate and edit the source code. In order for this to work, the source code must be loaded into a project in the Application Developer Workbench.
- Show Percentage—This button enables you to change the column values from numbers to percentages and back to numbers. It is useful for comparing the percentage breakdown of column data of one package or class against another.
- Show Delta Columns—This button adds an extra column for each numerical or percentage column in the Package Statistics view. The extra columns include the delta increase or decrease change in value since the last refresh of the profiling data.
- Menu → Exclude → Old or Menu → Exclude → Unchanged—These menu items allow you to exclude either old data or data that is unchanged since the last time you refreshed your profiling data. As described above, data that is new since the last refresh is indicated by the yellow New Occurrence diamond icon.

In addition to the above toolbar and menu items, the Package Statistics view has a Filter field located across the top left. Here you enter string patterns including full or partial package names and one or more wildcard characters of * to short list a certain package or group of packages. For example, "com.ibm.book*" gives you a short list of only packages beginning with "com.ibm.book" such as "com.ibm.book.servlets." Using the * character at the beginning of a filter pattern such as "*book.domain" affects only packages such as "com.ibm.book.domain." After typing the string pattern into the Filter field you must press **Enter** to activate the short list. If you require a case-sensitive filter, you simply check the **Case-sensitive** check box to the right of the Filter field. You can also use the wildcard character twice in a Filter, at the beginning and end of your string pattern. In Figure 11.6, a Filter pattern of "*book*" is used to short list only packages containing "book." Figure 11.6 also displays the Profiling Statistics view with the Show Percentages and Show Delta Columns buttons enabled.

Profiling - IBM WebSphere Studio Application Developer

File Edit Navigate Search Project Profile Run Window Help

Package Statistics [<monitoring...collecting> unknown [PID:1740]]

Filter: *book* ☑ Case-sensitive

>Package	Base Time	Delta:Base Time	Cumulative Time	Delta:Cumulative Time	Calls	Delta:C...
com.ibm.book.domain	0.0234%	0.0232%	0.0249%	0.0235%	12.18...	12.07.
BookLoad	0.0000%	0.0000%	0.0014%	0.0000%	0.063...	0.000.
BookMegaLoad	0.0000%	0.0000%	0.0000%	0.0000%	0.015...	0.000.
BookMoreLoad	0.0002%	0.0000%	0.0007%	0.0000%	0.031...	0.000.
BookQuestion	0.0232%	0.0000%	0.0235%	0.0000%	12.07...	0.000.
com.ibm.book.jdbc	0.0729%	0.0000%	0.8376%	0.0000%	0.007...	0.000.
BookQuestionDAO	0.0729%	0.0000%	0.8376%	0.0000%	0.007...	0.000.
com.ibm.book.servlets	0.0021%	0.0017%	0.8866%	0.8569%	0.045...	0.013.
BookObjectReferenceServlet	0.0003%	0.0000%	0.0297%	0.0000%	0.031...	0.000.
BookProfilingServlet	0.0017%	0.0000%	0.8569%	0.0000%	0.013...	0.000.
com.ibm.book.utilities	0.0004%	0.0000%	0.2546%	0.0000%	0.013...	0.000.
BookDataSource	0.0000%	0.0000%	0.2546%	0.0000%	0.005...	0.000.
BookHelperJNDI	0.0004%	0.0000%	0.0164%	0.0000%	0.007...	0.000.

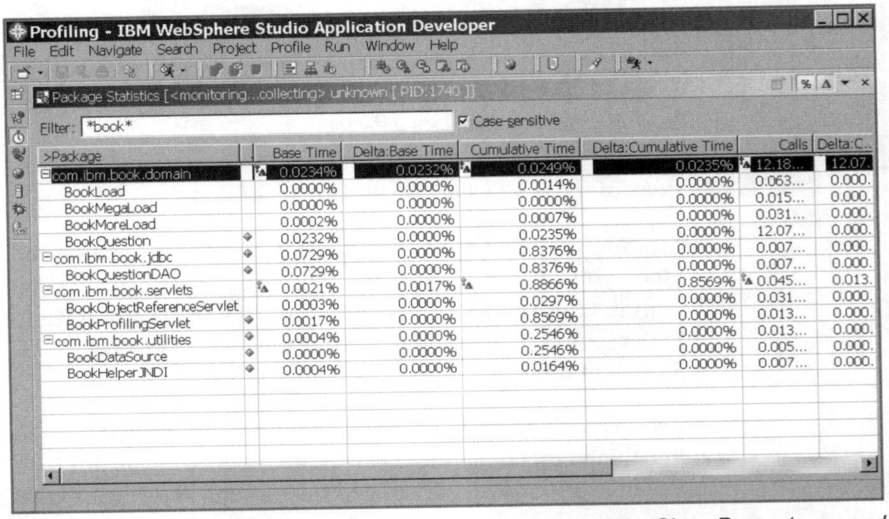

Figure 11.6: Profiling Statistics view with Filter pattern and the Show Percentages and Show Delta Columns buttons enabled.

Class Method Statistics view

The Class Method Statistics view is similar in tabular layout to the Package Statistics view, but it displays method data organized and grouped by classes. You will often use the Class Method Statistics view to investigate method statistics after first identifying problematic packages and classes in the Package Statistics view. To view method data of a specific class, drill down the tree in the Class Name column. Figure 11.7 displays the Class Method Statistics view with the BookLoad and BookObjectReferenceServlet classes expanded to show their underlying methods.

The Class Method Statistics view by default includes the following column headers:

- Class Names—This column displays the class name in ascending or descending order. You can expand the class name tree to show the contained methods. As stated previously, it is very common to begin by locating package problems in the Package Statistics view first and then switching to the Class Method Statistics view to examine problem classes and methods more deeply.

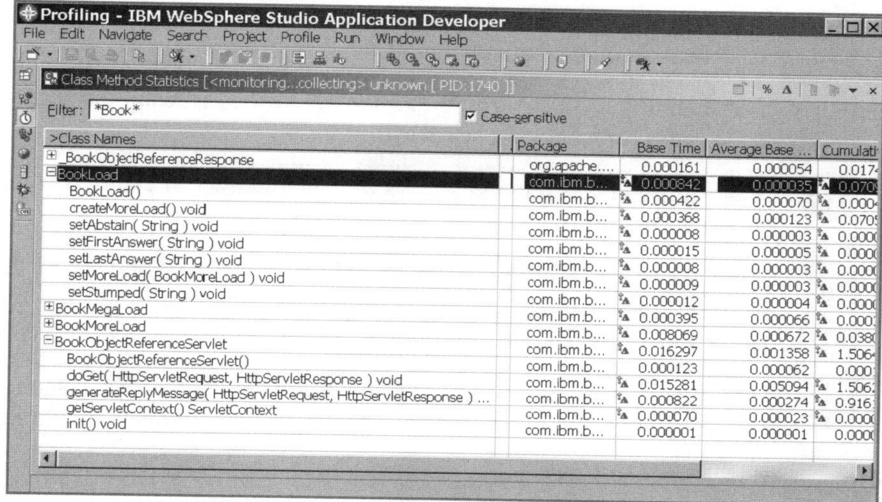

Figure 11.7: Class Method Statistics view with class name tree expanded showing methods.

- New Occurrence—This is a small column just to the right of the Class Names column that flags classes that have been created or methods that have been newly invoked since the last profiling information of your application was retrieved or refreshed. New occurrences are identified by golden diamond-shaped icons appearing in the small column. Figure 11.8 shows that the BookObjectReferenceServlet.doPost() method was newly invoked since the profiling data was last refreshed.

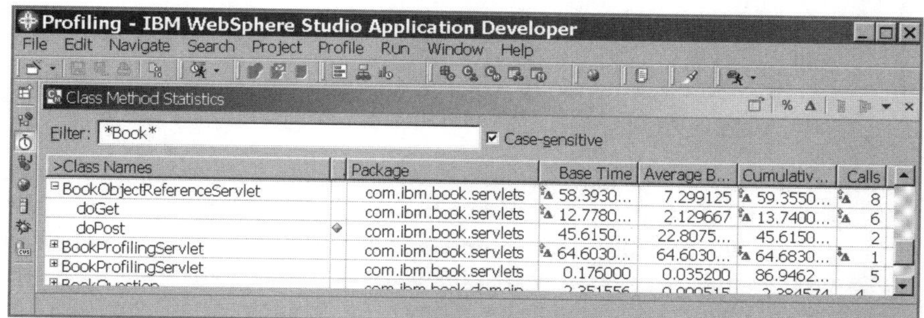

Figure 11.8: Example of New Occurrence of doPost method.

- Base Time—Base Time is described in the section “Time measurement in the statistical views.”

- Average Base Time—This column displays the average Base Time of calls made on a method or the total calls made on a class.
- Cumulative Time—Cumulative Time is described in the section "Time measurement in the statistical views."
- Calls—This column displays the total number of calls made on the selected method or class.

As in the Package Statistics view, column cells that contain numerical data may sometimes have delta icons displayed. The Class Method Statistics view by default does not include the following column headers:

- Total Instances—This column, when displayed, contains the total number of object instances still active in the JVM and destroyed by garbage collection.
- Collected—This column, when displayed, contains the number of object instances garbage collected.
- Live Instances—This column, when displayed, contains the number of current object instances still active in the JVM memory.
- Active Size—This column, when displayed, contains the total size in bytes of the live instances.
- Instance Size—This column, when displayed, contains the size in bytes of an instance.

The rows of data in the Class Method Statistics view are by default sorted in ascending alphabetic order by the Class Names header. Under each class tree the methods are also by default sorted in ascending alphabetic order, with the exception that the class constructor method is listed first. As in the Package Statistics view, you can customize the view sort order by selecting the header of any column. To add, remove, or reorder the view columns, you use the **Choose Column** dialog. It can be accessed through a pop-up menu by right-clicking the view and selecting **Choose Columns**.

The view has a small toolbar located in the top right corner that contains the Open Source, Show Percentage, and Show Delta Columns buttons and the Exclude menu. Their functionality is the same as the corresponding buttons and menu items in the Package Statistics view. However, the Class Methods Statistics view toolbar contains two additional buttons enabling you to switch from the Class Methods Statistics view to the Method Execution and Invocation views. These views visually display method execution and invocation data. You must first select the method in the table you want to display visually and then select one of the buttons. The Method Execution and Method Invocation graphical views will be discussed later in the chapter. Figure 11.9 shows the location of the Method Execution and Invocation buttons.

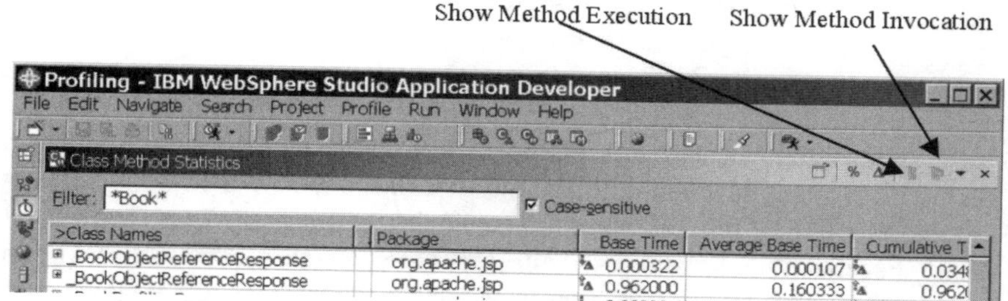

Figure 11.9: Class Method Statistics view Method Execution and Invocation buttons.

Method Statistics view

The Method Statistics view is very similar to the Class Method Statistics view but without the default sort order by Class Names column. The view's default sort order is the first column, Method Names. The view does, however, contain Class Names as the second column in case you need to identify your method's class context. The Method Statistics view does not include as many data columns as the Class Method Statistics view but rather focuses on presenting a few key statistics of methods in your application. The columns available and, by default, shown in this view are Method Names, Class Names, New Occurrence, Base Time, Average Base Time, and Cumulative Time. As in the Package and Class Method Statistics views, column cells that contain numerical data may sometimes have delta icons displayed. The view has a small toolbar located in the top right corner that contains the Open Source, Show Percentage, Show Delta Columns, Show Method Execution, and Show Method Invocation buttons and the Exclude menu. Their functionality is the same as that of the corresponding buttons and menu items in the Class Methods Statistics view. Figure 11.10 exhibits the Method Statistics view with the doGet method of the BookProfilingServlet selected.

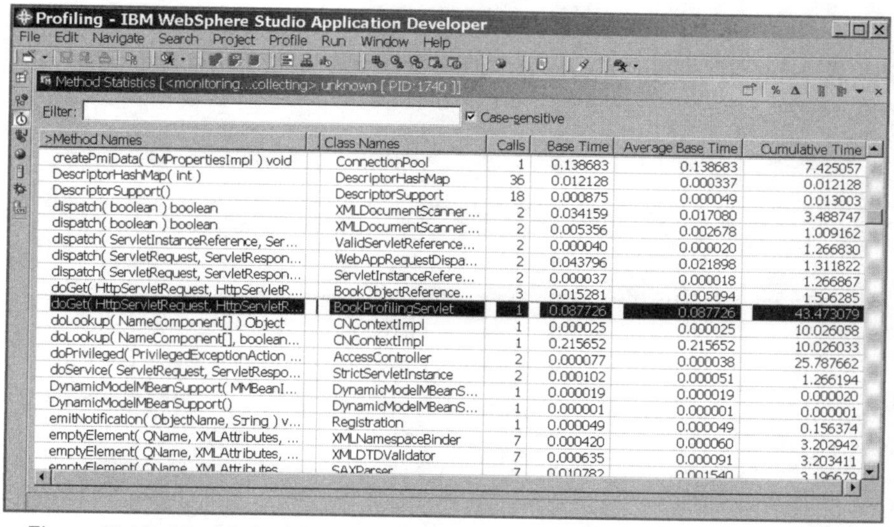

Profiling - IBM WebSphere Studio Application Developer

File Edit Navigate Search Project Profile Run Window Help

Method Statistics [<monitoring...collecting> unknown [PID:1740]]

Filter: Case-sensitive

>Method Names	Class Names	Calls	Base Time	Average Base Time	Cumulative Time
createPmiData(CMPropertiesImpl) void	ConnectionPool	1	0.138683	0.138683	7.425057
DescriptorHashMap(int)	DescriptorHashMap	36	0.012128	0.000337	0.012128
DescriptorSupport()	DescriptorSupport	18	0.000875	0.000049	0.013003
dispatch(boolean) boolean	XMLDocumentScanner...	2	0.034159	0.017080	3.488747
dispatch(boolean) boolean	XMLDocumentScanner...	2	0.005356	0.002678	1.009162
dispatch(ServletInstanceReference, Ser...	ValidServletReference...	2	0.000040	0.000020	1.266830
dispatch(ServletRequest, ServletRespon...	WebAppRequestDispa...	2	0.043796	0.021898	1.311822
dispatch(ServletRequest, ServletRespon...	ServletInstanceRefere...	2	0.000037	0.000018	1.266867
doGet(HttpServletRequest, HttpServletR...	BookObjectReference...	3	0.015281	0.005094	1.506285
doGet(HttpServletRequest, HttpServletR...	BookProfilingServlet	1	0.087726	0.087726	43.473079
doLookup(NameComponent[]) Object	CNContextImpl	1	0.000025	0.000025	10.026058
doLookup(NameComponent[], boolean...	CNContextImpl	1	0.215652	0.215652	10.026033
doPrivileged(PrivilegedExceptionAction ...	AccessController	2	0.000077	0.000038	25.787662
doService(ServletRequest, ServletRespo...	StrictServletInstance	2	0.000102	0.000051	1.266194
DynamicModelMBeanSupport(MMBeanI...	DynamicModelMBeanS...	1	0.000019	0.000019	0.000020
DynamicModelMBeanSupport()	DynamicModelMBeanS...	1	0.000001	0.000001	0.000001
emitNotification(ObjectName, String) v...	Registration	1	0.000049	0.000049	0.156374
emptyElement(QName, XMLAttributes, ...	XMLNamespaceBinder	7	0.000420	0.000060	3.202942
emptyElement(QName, XMLAttributes, ...	XMLDTDValidator	7	0.000635	0.000091	3.203411
emptyElement(QName, XMLAttributes	SAXParser	7	0.010782	0.001540	3.196679

Figure 11.10: The Method Statistics view.

Class Instance Statistics view

The Class Instance Statistics view organizes and displays information about all the instantiated class instances in your application at runtime. This view is very useful in understanding the number of object instances the JVM creates during the execution of a particular application use case or scenario. You can also use the view to identify the memory footprint in bytes of an individual instance or the total of a category of class instances. By default the Class Instances Statistics view displays the Class Names, New Occurrences, Package, Total Instances, Collected, Live Instances, Active Size, and Instance Size columns. The default sort order is by the Class Names column. However, Class Names is a tree that can be expanded to show all the instances of the class type that have been created in memory, including instances no longer active in the JVM memory because they have been garbage-collected. Each class instance under the Class Name will be numbered in order of creation starting with 1. For example, a Class Name could be BookLoad, and the class instances would be BookLoad.1, BookLoad.2, BookLoad.3, etc. Figure 11.11 presents the view with the default columns and a Filter pattern of Book*.

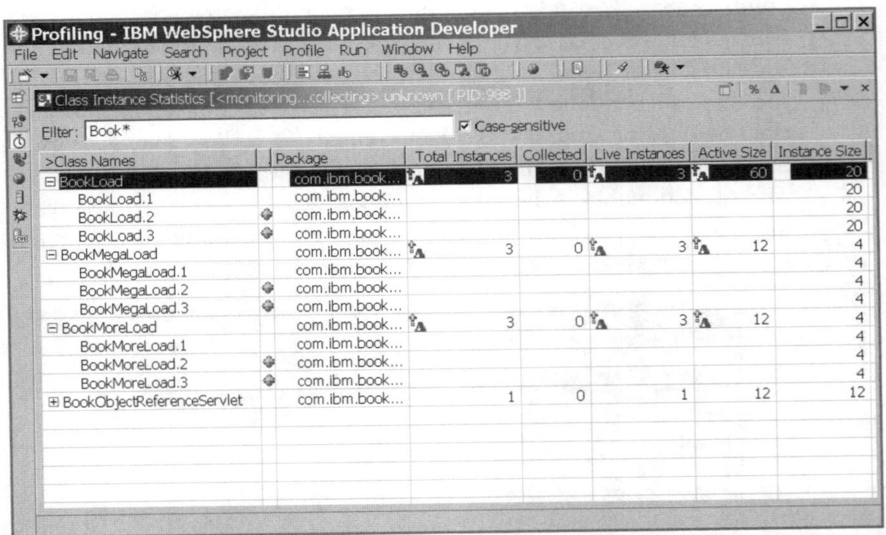

Figure 11.11: The Class Instance Statistics view with default columns and filter pattern.

As in other statistical views, utilizing the Choose Columns dialog, you can add the Base Time, Cumulative Time, and Calls columns to the table and also reorder or remove columns already present in the view. This view includes the same toolbar located in the top right corner with the Open Source, Show Percentage, and Show Delta Columns; the Show Method Execution and Show Method Invocation buttons; and the Exclude menu.

By adding and reordering column headers and using the Show Delta button you can use this view to examine instances destroyed through garbage collection. Figure 11.12 shows that three instances each of the BookLoad, BookMegaLoad, and BookMoreLoad; 913 instances of BookQuestion; and one instance of BookQuestionDAO have been garbage-collected (the Collected column). The Live Instances column displays that, of this group of classes filtered by, currently the only Live Instances in memory are two Servlets and two jspServlets (the first two rows of Class Names ending in Response). By examining the Delta:Collected column, you can determine how many of the three BookLoad class instances were collected since the last time this view's profiling data was refreshed.

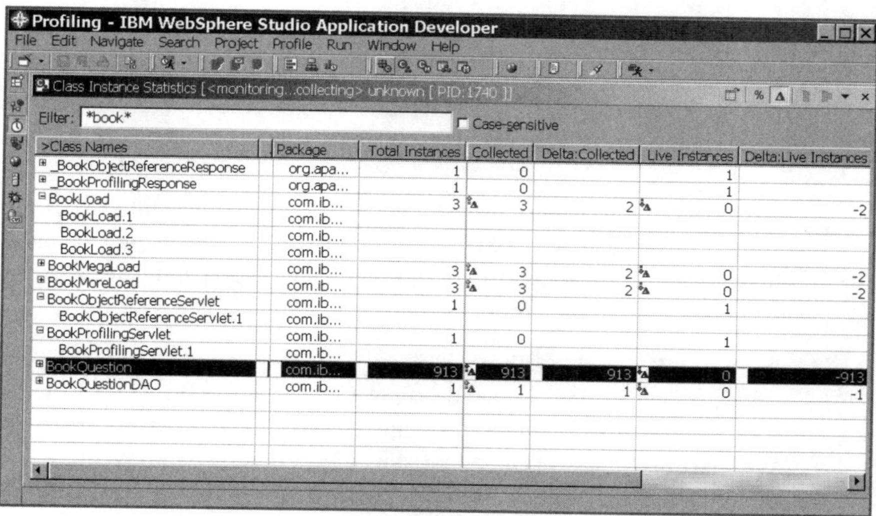

Figure 11.12: Class Instance Statisitics view and garbage collection.

In the following figure, Figure 11.13, the same group of classes is shown with a different set of Class Instance Statistics view columns. The Delta:Active Size column displays how much memory was released when garbage collection destroyed the BookLoad, BookMegaLoad, BookMoreLoad, BookQuestion, and BookQuestionDAO instances.

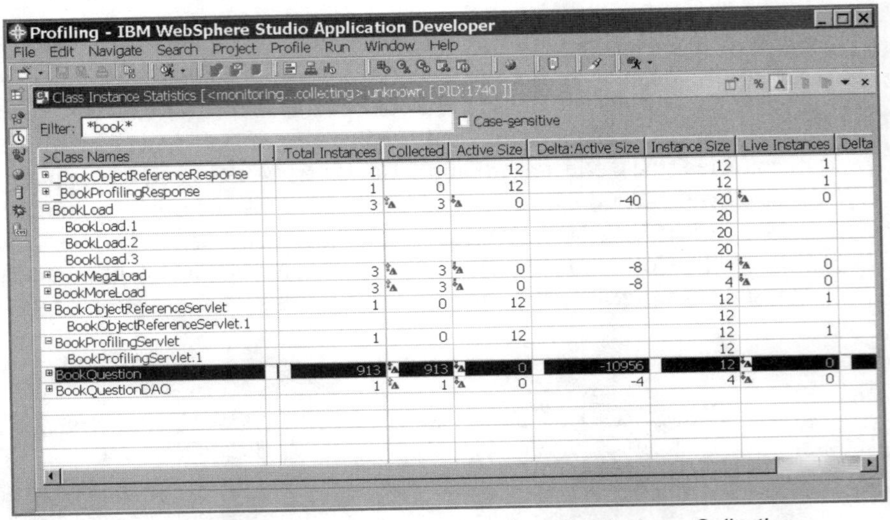

Profiling - IBM WebSphere Studio Application Developer

File Edit Navigate Search Project Profile Run Window Help

Class Instance Statistics [<monitoring...collecting> unknown [PID:1740]]

Filter: *book* Case-sensitive

>Class Names	Total Instances	Collected	Active Size	Delta:Active Size	Instance Size	Live Instances	Delta
_BookObjectReferenceResponse	1	0	12		12	1	
_BookProfilingResponse	1	0	12		12	1	
BookLoad	3	3	0	-40	20	0	
BookLoad.1					20		
BookLoad.2					20		
BookLoad.3					20		
BookMegaLoad	3	3	0	-8	4	0	
BookMoreLoad	3	3	0	-8	4	0	
BookObjectReferenceServlet	1	0	12		12	1	
BookObjectReferenceServlet.1					12		
BookProfilingServlet	1	0	12		12	1	
BookProfilingServlet.1					12		
BookQuestion	913	913	0	-10956	12	0	
BookQuestionDAO	1	1	0	-4	4	0	

Figure 11.13: Delta of Instance Memory Allocation after Garbage Collection.

This information is very useful when you want to pinpoint classes that consume large amounts of memory. Furthermore, because the instances of each class type are numbered, such as BookLoad.1, BookLoad.2, etc., you can locate a specific instance of a class causing the memory problem.

Instance Statistics view

The Instance Statistics view presents data similar to the Class Instance Statistics view in a slightly different manner. It organizes and sorts data by the Instance Name column. Whereas the Class Instance Statistics view sorts by Class Name with an expanded tree displaying actual object instances, the Instance Statistic view simply sorts by Instance Name. If more than one instance was created in memory, such as BookLoad in Figure 11.14, each instantiated instance is assigned a number, beginning with 1. The numbers are then used to sort in ascending order the multiple BookLoad instances.

By default the Instances Statistics view displays the Instance Name, New Occurrences, Package, Collected, Base Time, Cumulative Time, Instance Size, and Calls columns. These are the only available columns in this view. As in other Statistical views, you can remove or reorder the default columns. You will also notice that the Toolbar located at the top right corner of the view does not include the Show Method Execution and Show Method Invocation buttons. Otherwise the toolbar buttons and menu items, as well as the Filter pattern text field, are the same as in other Statistical Views.

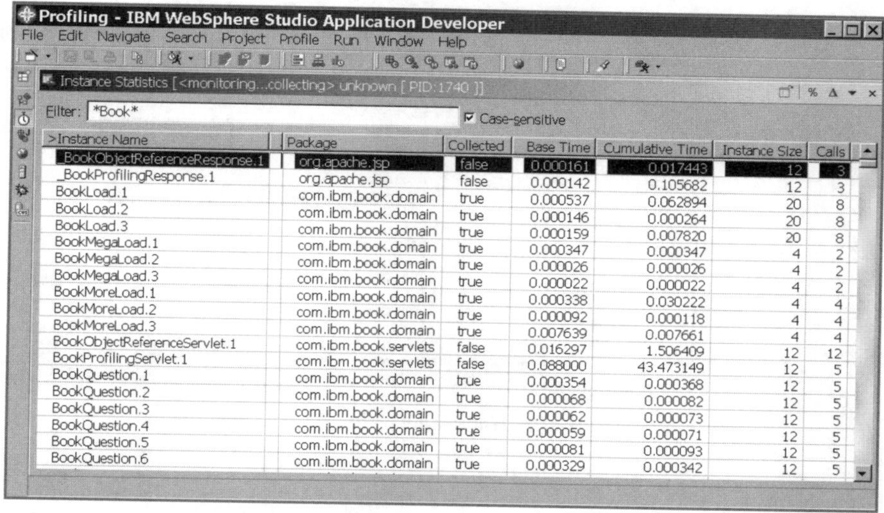

>Instance Name	Package	Collected	Base Time	Cumulative Time	Instance Size	Calls
_BookObjectReferenceResponse.1	org.apache.jsp	false	0.000161	0.017443	12	3
_BookProfilingResponse.1	org.apache.jsp	false	0.000142	0.105682	12	3
BookLoad.1	com.ibm.book.domain	true	0.000537	0.062894	20	8
BookLoad.2	com.ibm.book.domain	true	0.000146	0.000264	20	8
BookLoad.3	com.ibm.book.domain	true	0.000159	0.007820	20	8
BookMegaLoad.1	com.ibm.book.domain	true	0.000347	0.000347	4	2
BookMegaLoad.2	com.ibm.book.domain	true	0.000026	0.000026	4	2
BookMegaLoad.3	com.ibm.book.domain	true	0.000022	0.000022	4	2
BookMoreLoad.1	com.ibm.book.domain	true	0.000338	0.030222	4	4
BookMoreLoad.2	com.ibm.book.domain	true	0.000092	0.000118	4	4
BookMoreLoad.3	com.ibm.book.domain	true	0.007639	0.007661	4	4
BookObjectReferenceServlet.1	com.ibm.book.servlets	false	0.016297	1.506409	12	12
BookProfilingServlet.1	com.ibm.book.servlets	false	0.088000	43.473149	12	5
BookQuestion.1	com.ibm.book.domain	true	0.000354	0.000368	12	5
BookQuestion.2	com.ibm.book.domain	true	0.000068	0.000082	12	5
BookQuestion.3	com.ibm.book.domain	true	0.000062	0.000073	12	5
BookQuestion.4	com.ibm.book.domain	true	0.000059	0.000071	12	5
BookQuestion.5	com.ibm.book.domain	true	0.000081	0.000093	12	5
BookQuestion.6	com.ibm.book.domain	true	0.000329	0.000342	12	5

Figure 11.14: Instance Statistics view.

Graphical profiling views

The five graphical profiling views in Application Developer are the Heap, Object Reference, Method Execution, Method Invocation, and Execution Flow views. They present profiling data in a variety of visual forms.

Heap view

The Heap view is very useful in graphically comparing the memory size of objects or performance time of methods in your application. It uses a combination of a Class List, Histogram, View Status Line, and Slide Bar to present profiling data visually. Figure 11.15 highlights the four Heap view areas.

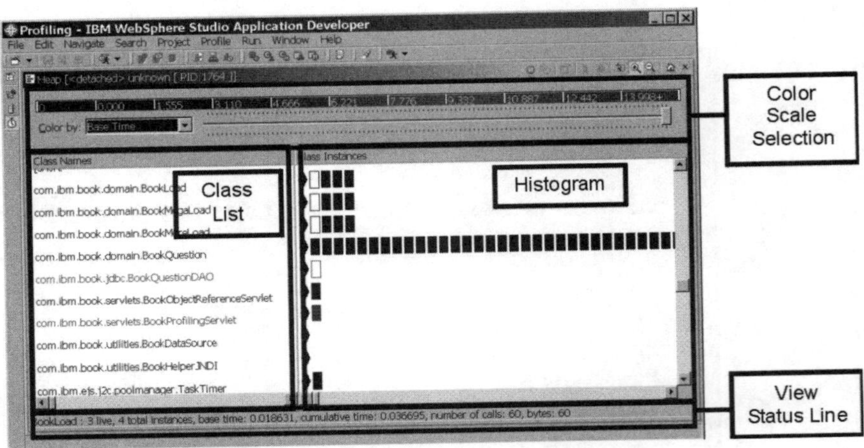

Figure 11.15: The Heap view with areas highlighted.

By default, the Class List area is sorted alphabetically by package name, although by using the pop-up menu, you can sort the list by class name and choose to view class names with or without package names. If you have arrays in your application, they will be listed as [array type].

The Color Scale Selection area includes the Color by field, the Slide Bar, and across the top, the Color Legend. The “Color by” field filters the type of data displayed in the Histogram area by the following criteria: Base Time, Cumulative Time, Number of Calls, Number of Threads, Active Memory, and Total Memory. The first four criteria measurements are the same as described in the Statistical views section of the chapter. Active Memory tracks object instances currently in memory, whereas Total Memory measures all instances currently in memory and instances previously garbage collected. You can use only one “Color by” selection at a time to display visually in the Histogram. As you drag the Slide Bar from right to left, the colors of objects displayed in the Histogram change according to the Color Legend. The Color Legend values are a color-coded numerical gauge for the type of filter selected in the “Color by” field. By default, the Color Legend starts from the left with a value of 0 and a color of black and as you move right, increases numerically, and changes from blue to purple, orange, and finally, red. Figure 11.16 outlines the color variations of the Color Legend.

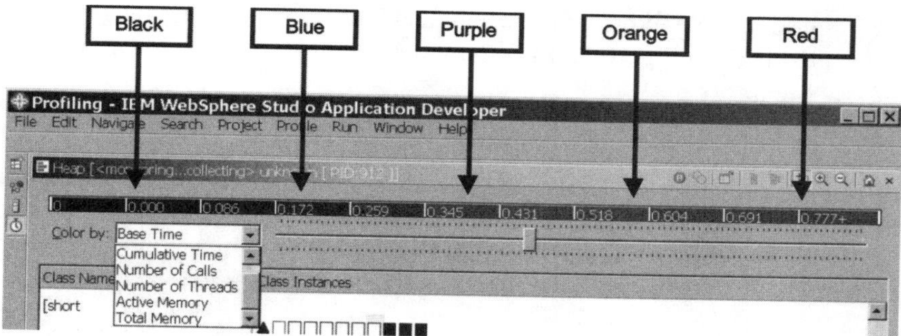

Figure 11.16: Color variations of the Heap view Color Legend.

The Histogram area can display either objects or methods. The View toolbar located at the top right includes, first, a Method button and, second, an Object button. Usually the Heap view will open in Object mode, as presented in Figure 11.17.

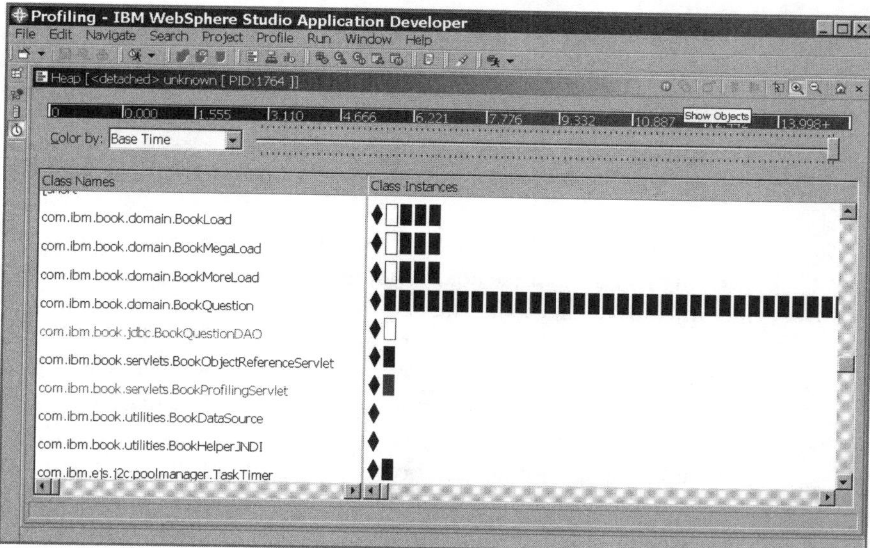

Figure 11.17: The Heap view histogram in Object mode.

In Object mode, the histogram displays diamond and rectangle rows corresponding to classes in the Class List. Diamonds simply represent the class objects of a given class. Rectangles, on the other hand, represent individual instances of a class when you select either Base Time, Cumulative Time, Number of Calls, or Number of Threads in the "Color by" field. Rectangles and diamonds appearing as outlines rather than solid color-filled shapes represent class objects and instances that have been reclaimed through garbage collected. If you choose Active Memory or Memory Total in the "Color by" field, each class will have one rectangle of varying horizontal length depending upon its total data value. Figure 11.18 displays an example of this using a "Color by" filter of Active Memory.

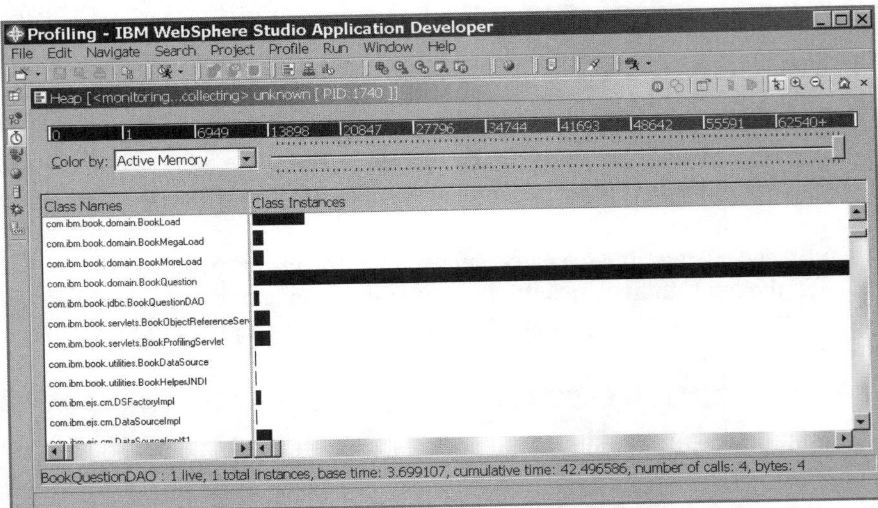

Figure 11.18: "Color by" filter of Active Memory.

When using Active Memory and Total Memory, the horizontal size of a class's rectangle can seem to contradict the color-coding of the Color Legend. In the preceding figure, you might think that the long horizontal rectangle would be orange or red, indicating its value to be large according to the Color Legend. In fact, the color of the rectangle is blue, indicating a small value. This is because the color of the rectangle indicates the average size of all instances (small number = low Color Legend color). In contrast, the horizontal length of the rectangle reflects the total number of all instances (large number = long horizontal rectangle). Furthermore, the color of class name in the Class List represents the total memory size of all of its instances. Although each instance of the class has a small memory size (blue horizontal rectangle), the fact that there are so many instances (long length of the horizontal rectangle) results in large memory size when all instances are combined (orange or red Class List class name). Figure 11.19 presents this visually.

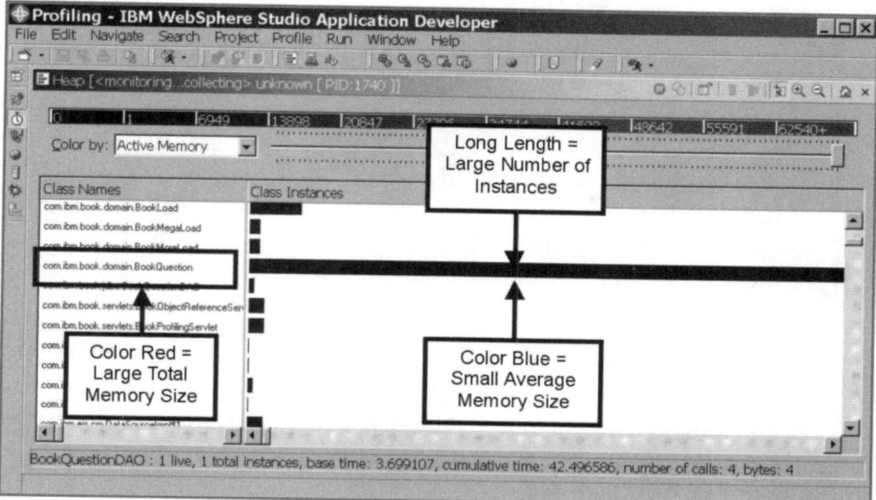

Figure 11.19: Heap view Active and Total Memory explained.

Selecting the Method button will change the histogram to Method mode, as displayed in Figure 11.20.

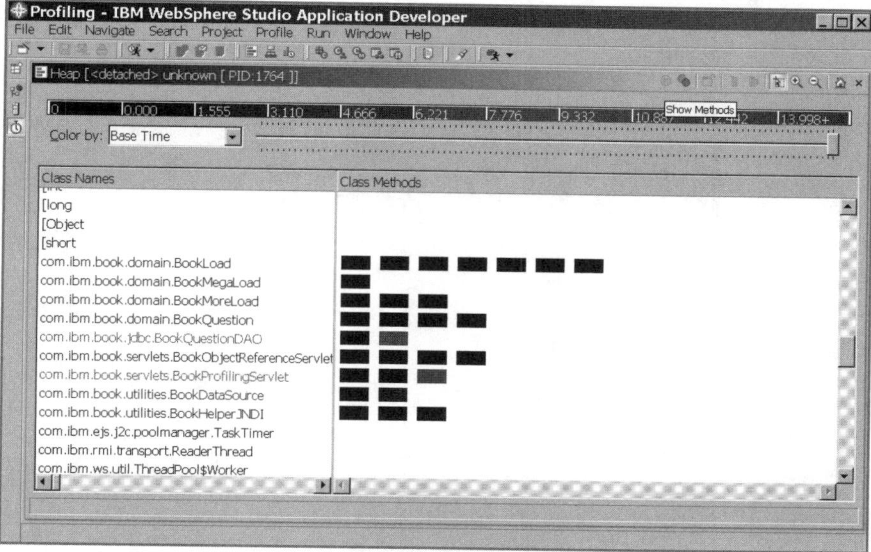

Figure 11.20: The Heap view histogram in Method mode.

In Method mode, the rectangles represent the invoked methods of the corresponding classes in the Class List.

Hovering your mouse over the specific instances, classes, and methods in the histogram area triggers a display of related information in the View Status line, located along the bottom of the Heap view. When you select the diamond-shaped class objects the view Status line displays the class name, base time, cumulative time, number of method calls, and size in bytes. When you hover over the rectangle-shaped instances, the Status line will list class name, instance numerical ID, the Process ID of the JVM that created the instance, base time, cumulative time, total number of calls, and the size of the instance in bytes. When using the histogram in Method mode, hovering over the rectangle-shaped methods will display the class and method name, base time, cumulative time, and the total number of method calls.

When you select a specific method rectangle in the histogram, the Heap view toolbar includes two buttons that enable you to switch to the Method Invocation and Method Execution views on your highlighted method. The Toolbar also includes View Source, Zoom In, Zoom Out, and Refresh Views buttons.

Object Reference view

The Object Reference view displays references to and from objects. Objects that have references to them by other objects cannot be garbage-collected and, therefore, remain in memory indefinitely or until those references are released. Unreleased references in your code can lead to an application memory leak, a situation in which increasingly large numbers of referenced objects accumulate, to a point where the JVM can no longer function. The Object Reference view is designed to help you track down these references in your application. Figure 11.21 shows the Object Reference view.

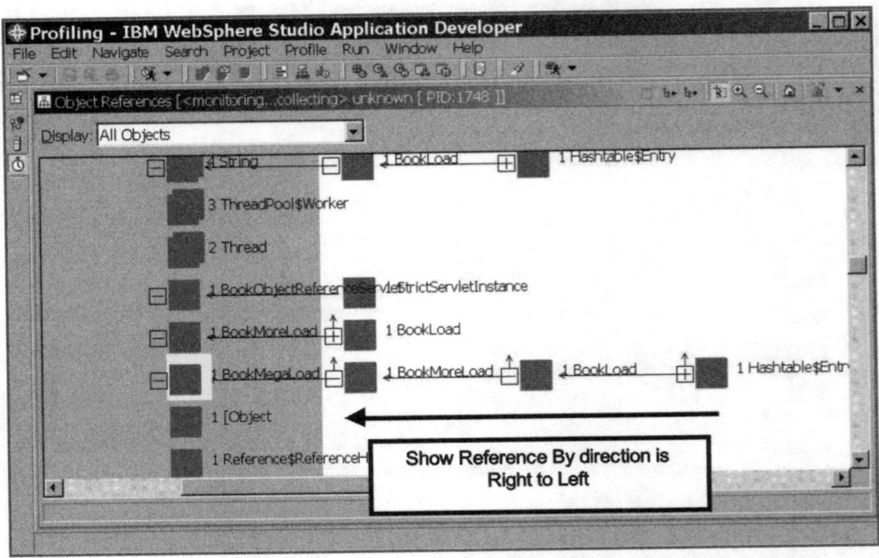

Figure 11.21: Object Reference view with Show Reference By option selected.

In Figure 11.21, the view has a gray area located on the left displaying a base set of objects. Each single object is represented by a single square, and multiple instances of objects are displayed as two squares. To the right of the gray area are objects that have reference arrow lines connecting back to the base set of objects. An object in the gray area may also appear to the right, as it also may have references to other gray area objects. By default, the Object Reference view displays references as directional arrow lines pointing from the right to the left. This setting is called Show Reference By. You can change the reference lines to the opposite direction, left to right, by selecting the Show Reference To item in the toolbar. Figure 11.22 displays the Show Reference To setting.

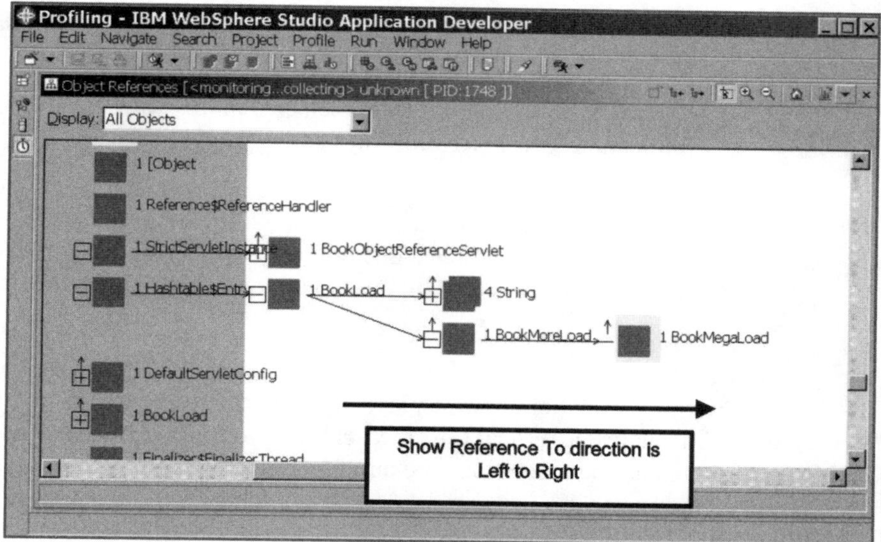

Figure 11.22: Object Reference view with Show Reference To option selected.

When the view is first opened, not all of the reference arrow lines and objects will be displayed. You may need to expand the plus sign located immediately to the left of the Object box to view the reference arrow line and the referenced object. The Expand and Collapse buttons on the View toolbar can also be used.

There are times when you will want to understand when a period of activity in your application, such as a payment transaction, creates new referenced objects but does not release them when completed. To do this, you need to set a marker indicating those objects created and referenced before the transaction begins. The Collect Object References button on the Profile Monitors view or the Workbench Profile → Collect Object References menu item sets that marker. When the period of transaction activity has concluded, your next refresh of the profiling data in the Object Reference view will include both old and new objects. Old objects will have their class names displayed in red, whereas newly created objects will have their class names displayed in black.

When you work with a large number of objects and you want to restrict the view's display to include only a subset of your application's created object, you use the Display field. The view's Display field, located at the top left, filters the display of objects. It has the following settings:

- All Objects—There are no restrictions on displaying objects.
- Non-JDK and Non-Array Objects—All objects are displayed except arrays and classes in packages beginning with sun* or java*.
- New Objects—Only newly created and referenced objects are displayed.
- New Non-JDK and Non-Array Objects—Newly created objects are displayed except for arrays and classes in packages beginning with sun* or java*.
- Selected Type—Only the object selected in this view or one of the other Application Developer Profiling views is displayed.

Finally, when you want to find out a little more information about objects displayed in the Object Reference view, you should check the View Status line. When you point to the class with your mouse, the Status line will display the number of object instances, class name, total memory consumed by the objects, and number of references to it.

Method Execution view

The Method Execution view displays method execution patterns, much like a UML diagram, but against a vertical time measure. Methods are represented as vertical bars; the longer the bar, the longer the time duration of the method. Figure 11.23 is an example of the Method Execution view.

To open this view, select a method in the Class Methods Statistics, Methods Statistics, or Heap view–Method Mode, and using the pop-up menu, select **Show Method Execution**. In Figure 11.23, the view shows the method execution beginning with the doGet() of the BookObjectReferenceServlet. The doGet() is represented by the first vertical bar. Pointing the mouse to the vertical bar will display in the View Status line the class name and method, cumulative time, and number of times the method has been invoked.

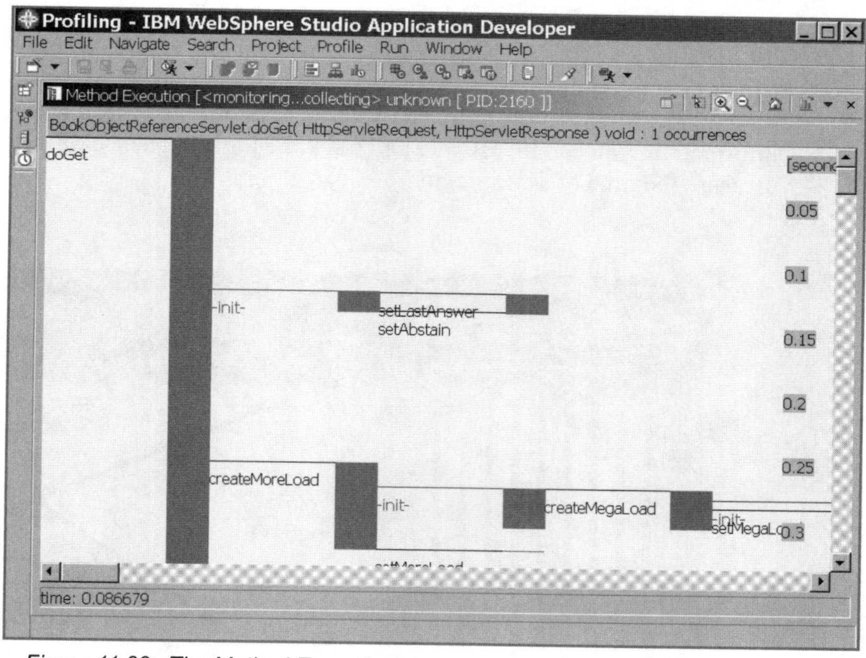

Figure 11.23: The Method Execution view.

Figure 11.23 displays a simple series of method calls. In larger, more complex applications, the Method Execution view is very useful in discovering execution patterns. Figure 11.24 displays the method execution of a classic Model-View-Controller (MVC) architecture Web site built using servlets, JSP pages, and classes. The data displayed in the view represents method execution of a browser-based user logging into a Web site. The first vertical bar on the left side of the view represents the doPost method of the Controller servlet. The remaining vertical bars represent method calls from the servlet to the Model classes involved in a JDBC database lookup and authentication of the user (the upper group of bars) and the forward method call to the View JSP page responsible for creating a response HTML page (the lower group of bars). This complex Web application uses more than one servlet, one JSP page, and one model class to accomplish the login task. Using the Zoom In and Zoom Out toolbar buttons along with the Status line information, you can investigate and track the login sequence of method calls and also measure the time of a user login.

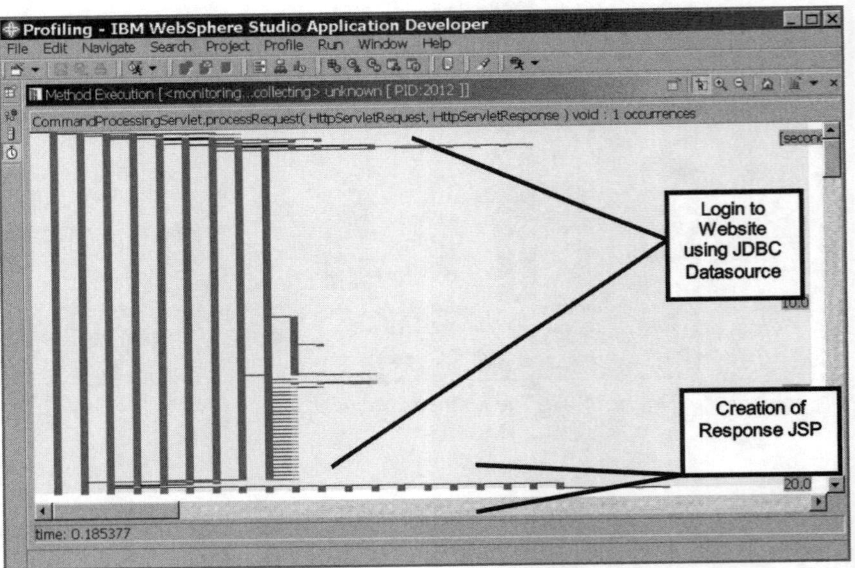

Figure 11.24: Method Execution view of complex Web site login.

Method Invocation view

The Method Invocation view displays profiling data in the same manner as the previous Method Execution view but with the addition of navigation buttons to the View toolbar. Figure 11.25 highlights the navigation toolbar buttons of the Method Invocation view.

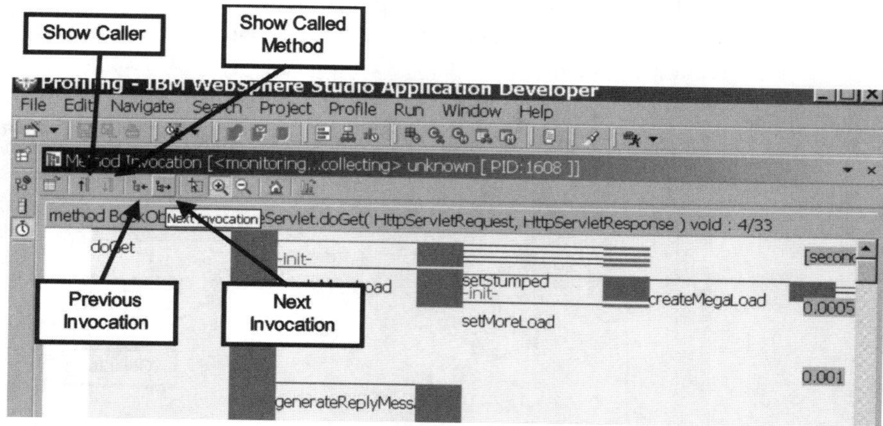

Figure 11.25: Method Invocation view navigation toolbar buttons.

The Show Caller and Show Called Method buttons are used to navigate forward and backward through the method invocation stack. The Previous Invocation and Next Invocation buttons are used to cycle through several invocations of the same method. In the previous example the doGet() has been invoked 33 times, and we are viewing the fourth invocation of the method. This information is displayed as “4/33” in the view’s secondary title bar immediately under the Toolbar.

Sequence Diagram Profiling tools

The Sequence Diagram Profiling tools are new to Application Developer Version 5. They translate profiling data into UML sequence diagrams. The Sequence Diagram Profiling tools are extremely useful in identifying runtime sequence patterns in your application and also for verifying actual sequence diagrams against design time sequence diagrams. The tools include the Sequence Diagram view, the Sequence Diagram Overview, and the Execution Table view.

Sequence Diagram view

The Sequence Diagram view, shown in Figure 11.26, displays profiling data as a UML sequence diagram. Sequence diagrams display objects as boxes resting on top of dashed vertical lines. The dashed vertical lines are called lifelines and represent the lifespan of an object instance. Along parts of the lifelines are vertical outlined bars representing individual methods. When more than one method is called from within one object instance, the vertical outlined bar is sectioned. Each section of the method bar represents a different instance method.

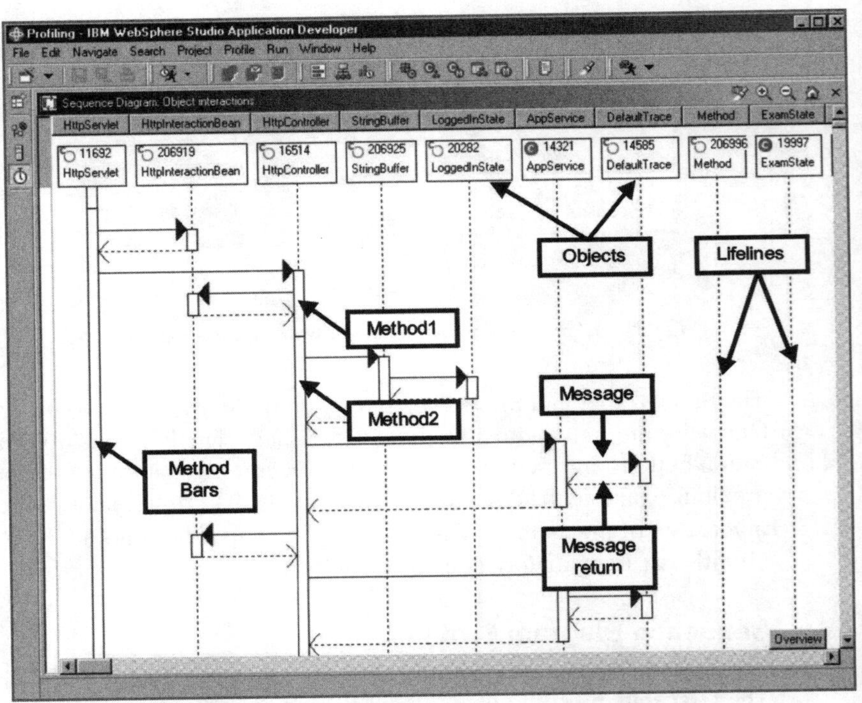

Figure 11.26: The Sequence Diagram view.

Figure 11.26 also highlights the interactions between the object instances as message and message return arrow lines. UML message arrows represent a call from the originating method to the destination method. Message return arrows simply represent the method return.

Usually, a UML Sequence Diagram presents only object interactions. The Application Developer Sequence Diagram view, however, extends Sequence Diagrams to include interactions between separate threads, JVM processes, and even network interactions between separate hosts. Application Developer extends Sequence Diagrams because of the requirement of profiling large, distributed J2EE applications. In order to display these various interactions, there are several different types of Application Developer Sequence Diagram views:

- Object Interaction—This Sequence Diagram is displayed in Figure 11.26. It displays method interactions between all the created object instances in your application. For example, if a running application code creates two instances of the Customer class during a single use case, both Customer object instances will be displayed at the top of Diagram as two separate object boxes. You will be able to see the interactions of both object instances separately, each with its own lifeline and outlined method bar.
- Class Interaction—The Class Interaction Sequence Diagram looks almost exactly the same as the Object Interaction Diagram except that it displays only one box for each class type used in your application. So in the example just described, where two Customer object instances are displayed in the Object Interaction Sequence Diagram, only one Customer class instance will be presented in the Class Interaction Sequence Diagram. All interactions with the class Customer, regardless of whether there is more than one created object instance, are displayed in relation to the single Class box, its lifeline, and its method bar.
- Thread Interaction—This Diagram displays thread interactions in your application. Sometimes you may have several concurrent threads created and running in a stand-alone Java application or want to view your Web Container transport threads. The Thread Interaction Sequence Diagram will display each thread as a thread box along the top of the view (similar to the Object and Class boxes). Each thread box will have its own lifeline and method bar. The method bar will indicate which Object Methods are executing in that specific thread.
- Process Interaction—The Process Interaction Sequence Diagram utilizes the J2EE Request Profiler to display interactions between different WebSphere Servers. Each WebSphere JVM is assigned a Process box along the top of the Diagram. The lifelines display bars representing servlets, JSP pages, and EJBs. Interactions between the JVM processes are shown as message and message return arrows. This is very useful in understanding the execution patterns of distributed J2EE applications.
- Host Interaction—The Host Interaction Sequence Diagram is primarily of use to system and network administrators needing to understand the network interaction between various machines.

It is important to understand the hierarchy of the Profiling Monitor view as it relates to each of the Sequence Diagrams. In order to open any of the Diagrams, you must choose a Monitor, Host, Process, or Agent in the Profiling Monitor view. You may remember from the earlier discussion that the Monitor view displays these as a tree hierarchy with Monitors at the top and Agents on the bottom. To open one of the Sequence Diagrams, you must select one of the Profiling Monitor view tree items and choose Show View from the pop-up menu. Depending on where you are in the tree, you will be given certain Sequence Diagrams to choose from. For example, if you would like to view interactions between HostA and HostB, you would have to select a monitor that contains both HostA and HostB. You cannot choose an Agent and view the Host Interaction Sequence Diagram. The nested tree structure of the Profiling Monitor view matters. The tree determines the scope of the Sequence Diagram data. An easy way to always choose the correctly scoped item in the Profiling Monitor view is to select the monitor and choose Show View from the pop-up menu. The pop-up menu will always display all the Sequence Diagram choices. Caution is sometimes needed when doing this because you may not want to view data from more than one JVM. In that case you can drill down the tree and select a more tightly scoped Profiling Monitor view item. This will restrict the profiling data that can be displayed and make your Object and Class Interaction Sequence Diagrams readable.

Time in the Sequence Diagram view

Time in the Sequence Diagram is not related to the vertical length of the timelines. The length of timelines and method bars depends on the amount of diagram space required to display the downstream interactions. The more interactions, generally, the longer the vertical length of a timeline. Time in the Sequence Diagram is measured and displayed using a color-coded Time vertical bar located on the far left side of the view. (See Figure 11.27)

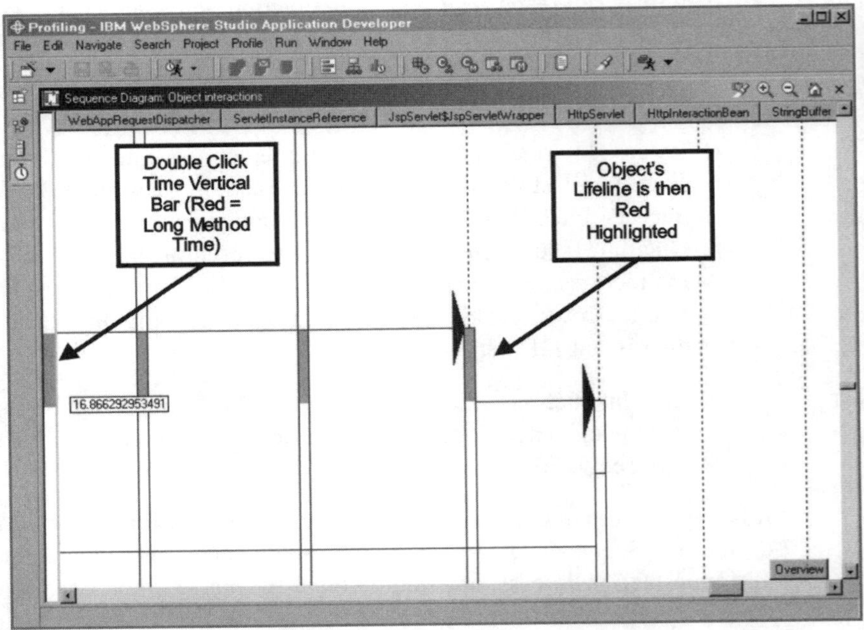

Figure 11.27: Time on the Sequence Diagram.

The Time vertical bar signals longer periods of time with varying intensities of the color red. The longer a particular event or method takes (or thread or host interaction, etc.) the darker the color red in the corresponding section of the Time vertical bar. As you scroll down a large Sequence Diagram, you will see red sections of the Time vertical bar. Double-clicking red sections of the bar creates red sections in the corresponding horizontally located method bars. Scroll to the right until you find the problematic event or method. As you can see in the figure, hovering over the Time vertical bar will produce a pop-up box containing the time interval in seconds.

Sequence Diagram Overview

Another great feature of all the Sequence Diagrams is the Sequence Diagram Overview. Often your code interactions cannot be contained within the Sequence Diagram view. The Overview enables you to work with these very large Sequence Diagrams. Each Sequence Diagram view has an Overview button located on the lower right corner. Clicking the button activates the Overview pop-up window. The window displays a scaled-down version of all the interaction sequences loaded into the view but not visible. (See Figure 11.28)

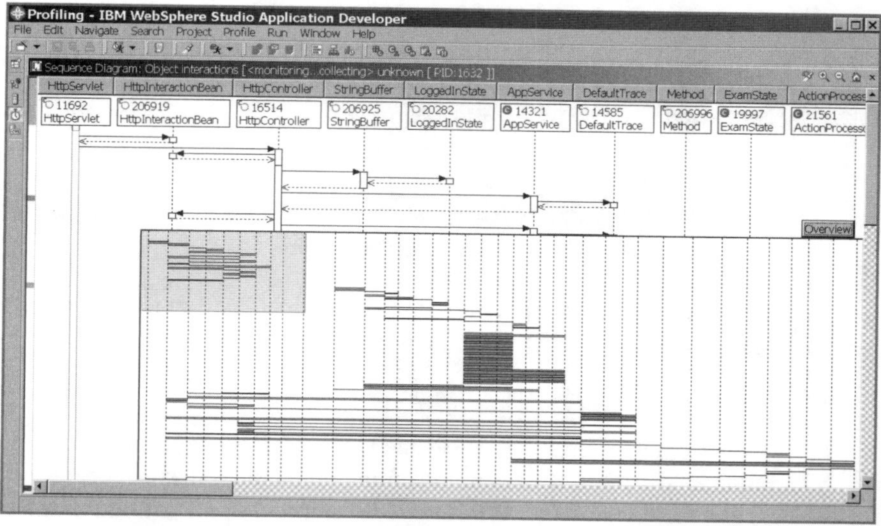

Figure 11.28: The Sequence Diagram Overview.

The Overview window includes a translucent red rectangle (in Figure 11.28, located in the top right corner of the Overview window) that represents the main screen of the Sequence Diagram View. As you drag the translucent red rectangle, the underlying main screen of sequence diagram changes position accordingly. You can also double-click anywhere in the Overview to reposition the main screen.

Execution Table view

The Execution Table view presents the same information displayed in the Sequence Diagram but in a tabular format. Figure 11.29 is an example of the view.

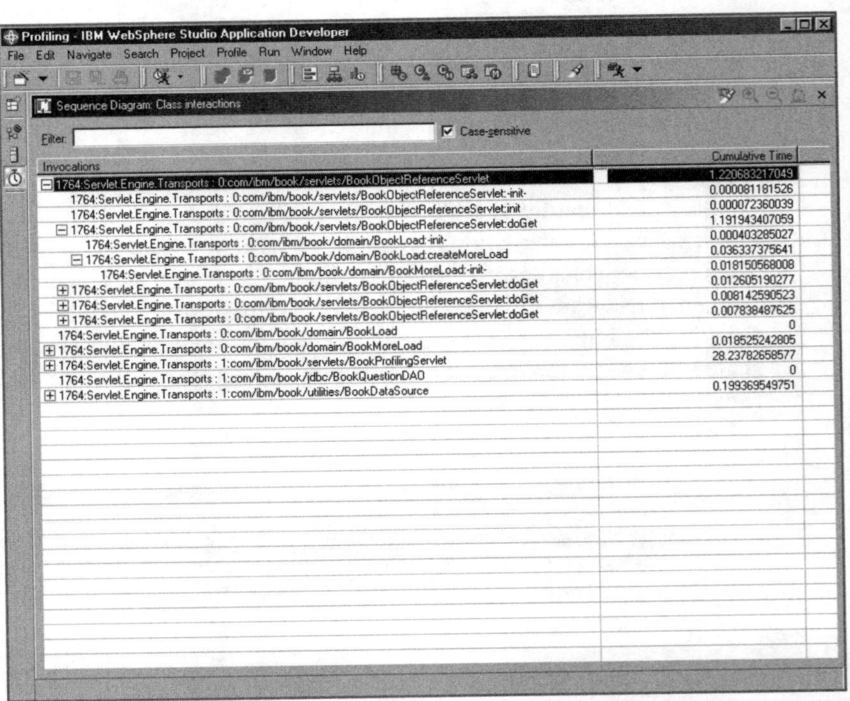

Figure 11.29: The Execution Table view.

To open the Execution Table view, right-click any Sequence Diagram view and select Show Execution Table from the pop-up menu.

Profiling preferences

The Profiling preferences are located in the same location as other Application Developer preferences. There are several Profiling preferences that can be customized. In order to access them, you select **Window → Preferences → Profiling and Logging**. Changes made to the Profiling preferences are applied to all profiling resources and sessions.

Profiling and Logging

The Profiling and Logging Preferences window contains the "Enable profiling" check box, which is enabled by default. There is also an "Enable logging" check box, which is not enabled. Logging is discussed later in the chapter. Profiling tips can be displayed during a profiling session by selecting the "Show profiling tips" check box. You can also alter the default profiling project name. The value entered here will appear in the Attach to Java Process wizard (used to begin a profiling session and discussed later). The port used by Application Developer to connect to the IBM Agent Controller is configured in the "Agent Controller local port" text field. The default port is 10002. This is also the default listening port of the IBM Agent Controller. If you change the Agent Controller's listening port, you must also change the Agent Controller local port in the Application Developer Profiling and Logging Preferences window to a corresponding value. The Profiling and Logging Preferences window is the top of a tree of profiling-related windows. The leaf windows are Hosts, Monitors View, Profiling, Graph Colors, and Sequence Diagram.

Hosts

The Hosts preferences window displays a profiling default machine of localhost. If you will be using Application Developer to profile applications commonly running on certain remote machines, you could add the machine hostnames here. Hosts listed here will be automatically listed for you when you set up a profiling session.

Profiling Monitor view

By default, the Profiling Monitor view displays processes and profiling agents. You can use the Monitors View Preferences window to add folders, monitors, and hosts as well as remove any of the defaults. Note that settings in the Monitors View Preferences window can be overridden on any specific Profiling Monitors view by selecting the View Menu button and adding and removing any of the resources from the view. Changes made on specific Profiling Monitors views will apply only to those specific views.

Profiling

The Profiling Preferences window contains two tabbed subwindows: Filters and Options. Filters are string patterns used to include and exclude classes and instances during a profiling session. These patterns determine the information collected about classes in your application. If there were no filters applied during a profiling session, every application class and instance, including WebSphere runtime classes, would be included in the profiling data sent to Application Developer. A discussion of Profiling Filters and Filter Sets and how to create them will be addressed later in the chapter. If you repeatedly profile certain classes and packages in your application code, you may want to create custom Filter Sets in the Filter tab.

The Options tab allows you to adjust the amount of profiling information you collect based on time and the number of method invocations made in your application. You can also collect information beyond your filter patterns to include boundary classes. For example, you could create a filter pattern that includes "com.ibm.book.LoginServlet" and also specify that you would like to include boundary classes to a depth of 1. This would result in a collection and reporting of all class instances directly called by a method in your servlet. Selecting the "Collect instance-level information" check box enables the Heap, Object Reference, Class Instance Statistics, and Instance Statistics views. If you do not select the "Collect instance-level information" check box, these views will not be available during your profiling session.

Graph Colors

Under the Profiling Preferences window is the Graph Colors Preference window. It contains the default colors of the graphical profiling views, such as the Heap and Object Reference views. You can alter these defaults at any time.

Sequence Diagram

The Sequence Diagram Preferences window simply allows you to hide or display any self-referencing calls when using the various Sequence Diagram views.

Profiling setup procedures

Having discussed the architecture and the various profiling tools in Application Developer, this section will outline how you setup and start a profiling session.

Setting profiling filters

As described in the previous section in connection with the Profiling Preferences window, profiling filters are string patterns used to include and exclude classes and instances during a profiling session.

What are filters?

Filter patterns determine the information collected about classes and instances running in your JVM application. If there were no filters applied during a profiling session, every application class and instance, including the JDK and WebSphere runtime classes, would be included in the profiling data sent to the Application Developer profiling client. In Application Developer Version 5, filters are grouped into Sets. A Filter Set includes a list of package, class, and method names, each associated with a filter rule of INCLUDE or EXCLUDE. In order to collect and view profiling data on the calculate() method of the com.ibm.book.ProcessOrder, the filter string would be constructed as described in Table 11.1:

Table 11.1: Construction of a filter string.

Package or Class	Method Name	Filter Rule
com.ibm.book.ProcessOrder	calculate	INCLUDE

A wildcard of * can be used with package, class, and method names. Therefore, you could use the format in Table 11.2 to capture the same information about the calculate() method of the com.ibm.book.ProcessOrder:

Table 11.2: Filter string with Wildcard.

Package or Class	Method Name	Filter Rule
com.ibm.book*	*	INCLUDE

Application Developer includes some sample Filter Sets for stand-alone Java applications and WebSphere-hosted applications. The order of the filter strings listed within a specific Filter Set is important when you want to profile a specific "subpackage" but not the "parent" package. For example, in order to profile the package com.ibm.book.* and not com.ibm.* you have to INCLUDE it in the list before you EXCLUDE com.ibm.*, as shown in Table 11.3.

Table 11.3: Order of inclusions and exclusions in a Filter Set.

Package or Class	Method Name	Filter Rule
com.ibm.book.*	*	INCLUDE
. . .	. . .	. . .
com.ibm.*	*	EXCLUDE
. . .	. . .	. . .

Creating Filter Sets in Application Developer Preferences

You can create custom Filter Sets in the Application Developer's Profiling Preferences. In the Profiling Preferences window Filters tab, click the **Add** button next to the "Select a filter set:" listbox, as shown in Figure 11.30.

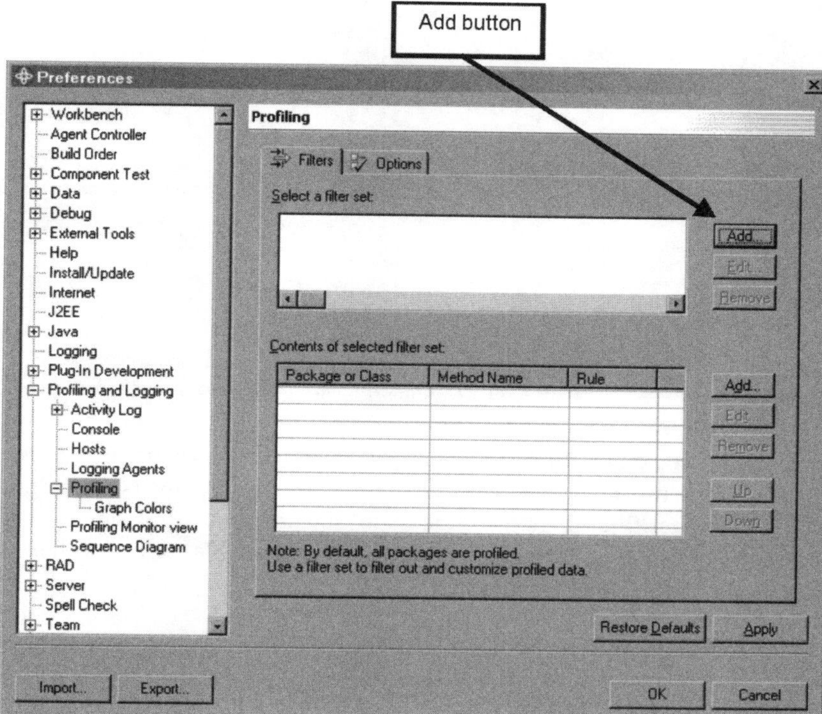

Figure 11.30: Select the Add button to create a Custom Filter Set.

When the Add Filter Set dialog appears, enter a Filter Set Name and click the **OK** button. The Name is then listed in the "Select a filter set:" list box. Ensure that the newly created Filter Set is selected and click the **Add:** button of the "Contents of selected filter set:" table. The Add Filter dialog appears. Enter a package or class name, a method name, and whether you want to INCLUDE or EXCLUDE this filter pattern. Select the **OK** button of the Add Filter dialog to complete the creation of the new filter pattern. Figure 11.31 displays this workbench Preference window.

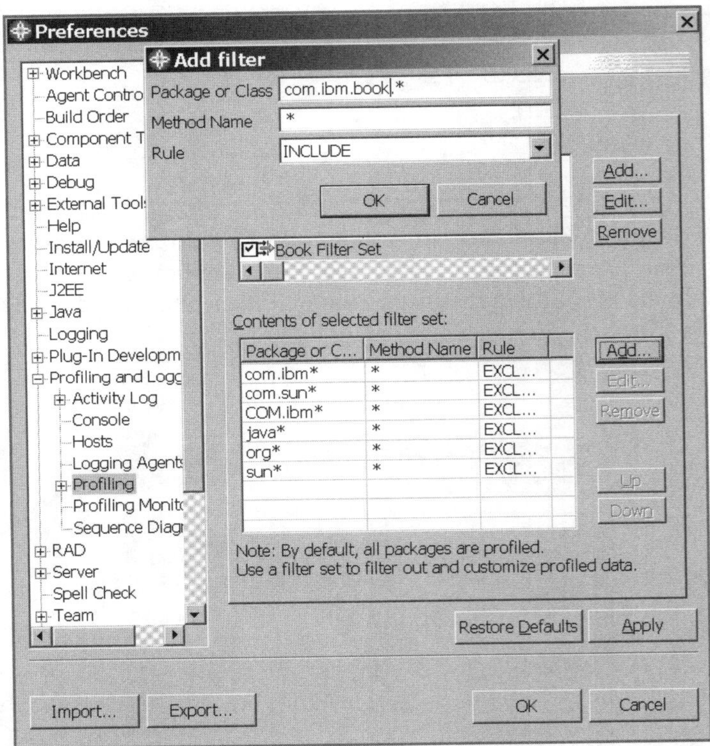

Figure 11.31: Adding a filter pattern to a Filter Set.

Creating a new filter pattern in the Filter Set places the filter pattern at the top of the "Contents of selected filter set:" table. Make sure this is the correct position relative to the other filter patterns of the table (see previous discussion of filter pattern orders). The newly created Filter Set is now globally available for use with any Application Developer Profiling Session.

Creating filters during Profiler attaching

You can also create Filter Sets and filter patterns during each specific profiling session. The Filter Sets and patterns created during a specific profiling session cannot be used for other profiling sessions. Figure 11.32 includes the Profiling Filters page of an Attach to Remote Java Process wizard.

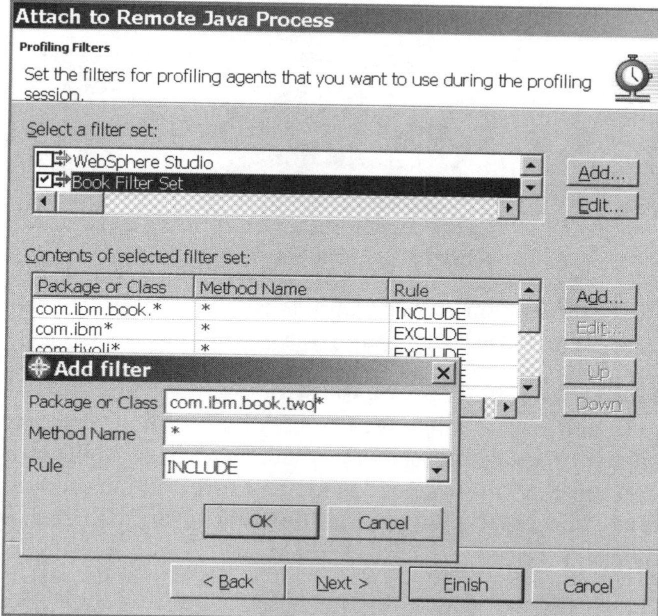

Figure 11.32: Setting Filter Sets and patterns during profiling session.

The Profiling Filters page of the Attach to Remote Java Process wizard is used in exactly the same way as the Application Developer Profiling Preferences as described previously. The difference is that the resulting Filter Sets and patterns created through Application Developer Preferences are available and reusable by all profiling sessions, whereas sets created during the setup of a profiling session can be used only for that specific session.

Profiling WebSphere applications

In order to start a profiling session in Application Developer, the Profiling Perspective must be active. You can initiate a profiling session from any other Application Developer Perspective, but the workbench will automatically switch to the Profiling Perspective as soon as the profiling session is begun. As described in earlier sections of this chapter, you can profile a stand-alone Java application or a WebSphere Application Server JVM. JVMs can run either locally on the same machine as Application Developer or remotely. Whether the JVM you intend to profile is local or remote, the IBM Agent Controller must be installed and running on the same machine as the profiled JVM. Generally,

Application Developer includes two types of Profiling Wizards: the Launch Java Process and the Attach to Java Process wizards. Each wizard can be used locally or remotely. To start either wizard, you must click the Profile button. Figure 11.33 displays the location of the Profile button.

Figure 11.33: The Profile button.

The Profile button is, by default, located on the workbench toolbar in the Profile, Web, J2EE, Java, Server, and Debug Perspectives.

Launching a Java process for profiling

To launch a stand-alone Java process for profiling, you must have a Java application containing a class with a main() method, either in an Application Developer project or on the local machine file system. Using the Profile button drop-down menu, select **Launch → Java Process**. The Launch Java Process wizard will open on the Select Class Page (see Figure 11.34):

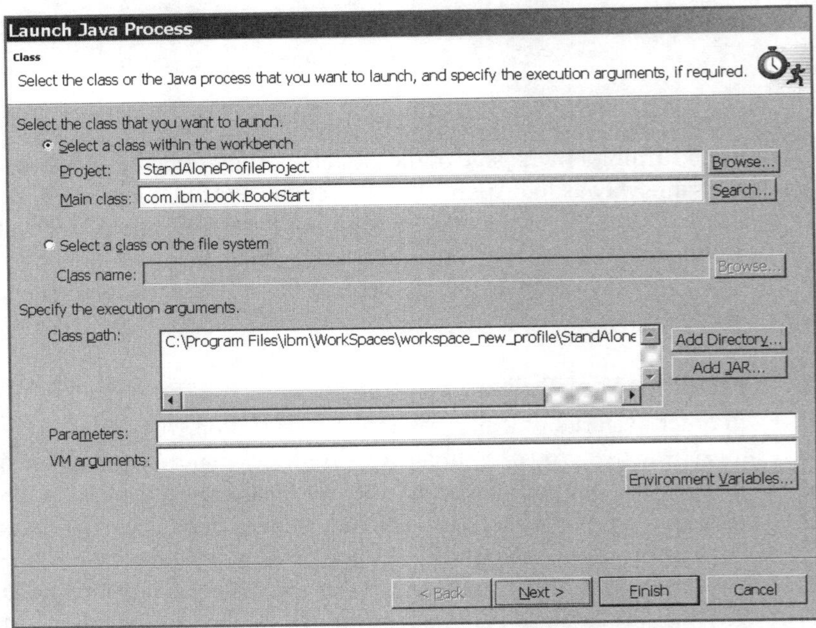

Figure 11.34: Launch Java Process wizard—Class page.

The Class page of the wizard allows you select a main() method class in a Workbench project or on the file system. You can also set the runtime classpath and input Virtual Machine arguments using this wizard page. Clicking the Next button opens the Destination page of the wizard, as shown in Figure 11.35:

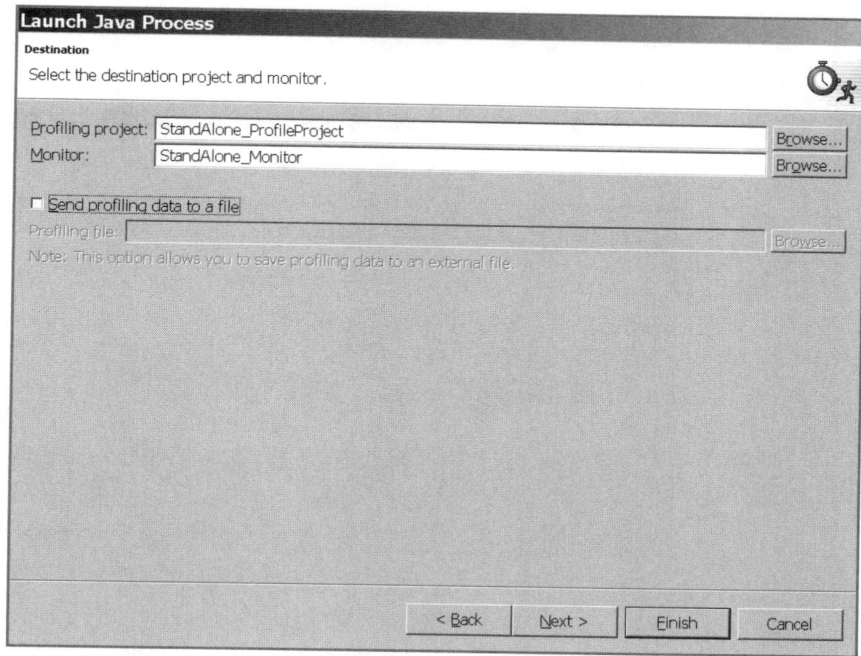

Figure 11.35: Launch Java Process wizard—Destination page.

The Destination page of the wizard includes text boxes for defining the Profiling Project and Monitor names. You can also send the profiling data to an external XML profile trace file with an extension of .trcxml.

Note: When very large amounts of profiling data are being generated by the JVM Profiling Agent, the Application Developer JVM Profiling Client can run slowly. If you send the profiling data to an external file, your profiling session can run much faster. Streaming profiling data to a file will always be faster than streaming to a profiling client. After you run your profiling session in Application Developer, you can import the external .trcxml into Application Developer and review the profiling data without Application Developer performance degradation.

Clicking the Next button of the wizard opens the Profiling Filters page, as shown in Figure 11.36:

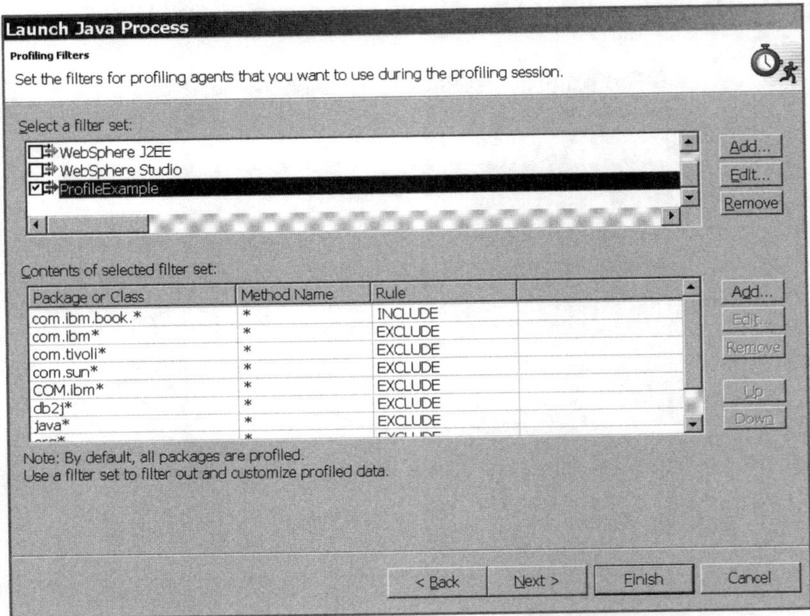

Figure 11.36: Launch Java Process wizard, Profiling Filters page.

The Profiling Filters page of the wizard is described in the earlier section "Creating filters during Profiler attaching." The resulting Filter Sets and patterns created in the wizard can be used only for this specific launched profiling session. Clicking the Next button opens the Profiling Options page of the wizard, as shown in Figure 11.37:

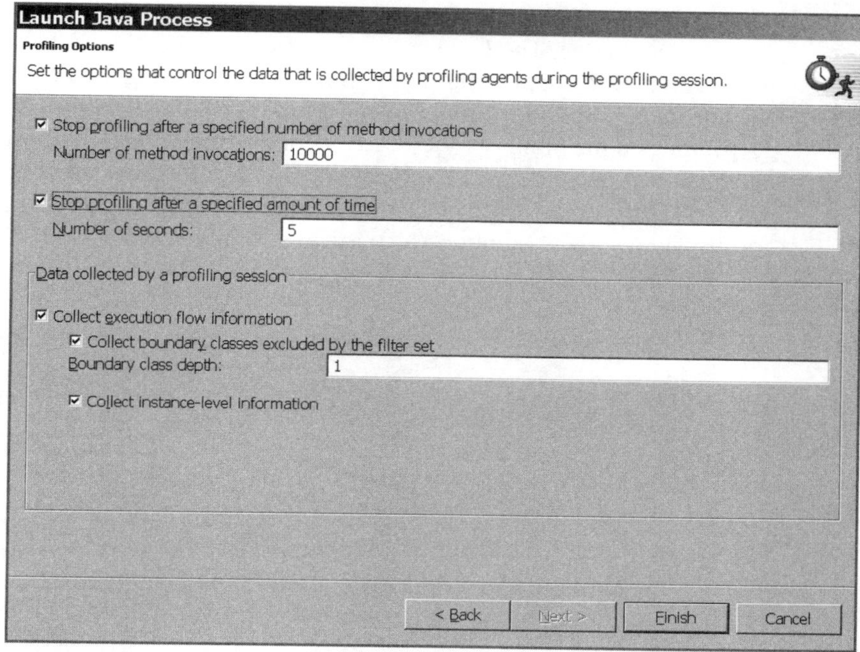

Figure 11.37: Launch Java Process wizard, Profiling Options page.

The Profiling Options page of the wizard includes check boxes and associated text boxes for stopping a profiling session after a specified number of method invocations in your profiled JVM or an elapsed number of seconds. In the "Data collected by a profiling session" section of the page, you can specify that boundary classes outside your INCLUDE filtered packages and classes can be included in the profiling data. You can specify the depth of classes outside your INCLUDE filtered packages and classes in the "Boundary class depth:" text box. By default, a boundary class depth of 1 is included. You can eliminate the boundary class depth by deselecting the "Collect boundary . . ." check box. If you select the "Collect instance-level information" check box, the Profiling Session will gather profiling data required by the Heap, Object Reference, Class Instance Statistics, and Instance Statistics views.

Note: If you do not select the "Collect instance-level information" check box, the Heap, Object Reference, Class Instance Statistics, and Instance Statistics views will be disabled when reviewing the Profiling Data.

Finally, you launch and profile your stand-alone Java application by clicking the wizard's **Finish** button. The Launch Java Process wizard will launch the Java application JVM using the -XrunpiAgent Java option, thereby starting the JVM in profile mode. The wizard also creates a Profiling Project, a Monitor, a Host, a Process, and an Agent. Depending on the Monitors View settings of Profiling Preferences (see the earlier section on this topic), Application Developer displays all or various combinations of these profiling objects in the Profiling Monitor. Figure 11.38 is an example of the Profiling Monitor displaying a new Monitor, Host, Process, and Profiling Agent.

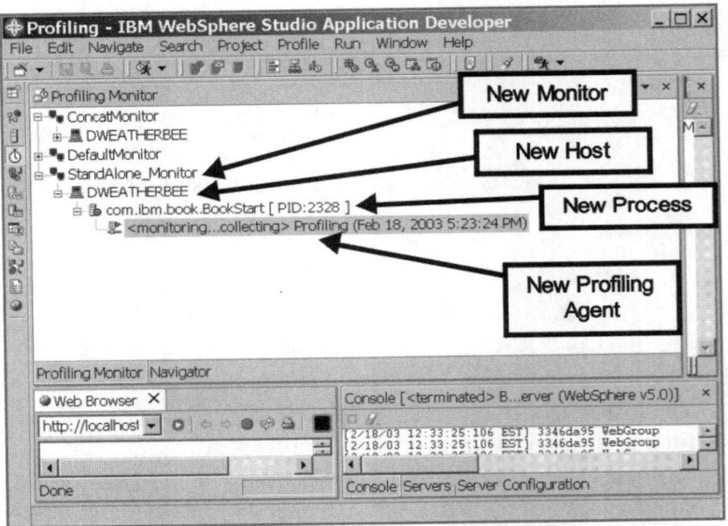

Figure 11.38: Profiling Monitor displaying new Monitor, Host, Process, and Profiling Agent.

There are several ways to display the profiling data in the various statistical, graphical, and Sequence Diagram views. In the Profiling Perspective, you can use the various Profiling View buttons located on Application Developer's toolbar. Figure 11.39 identifies the buttons on the toolbar.

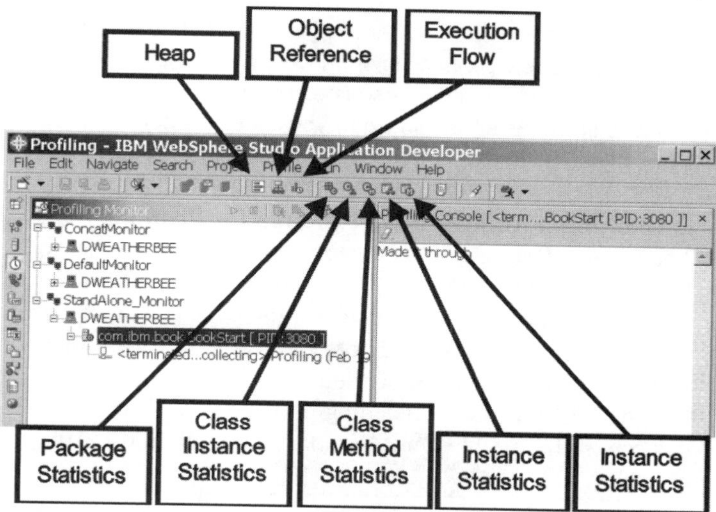

Figure 11.39: Profiling view toolbar buttons.

You can also choose one of the profiling objects in the Profiling Monitor and, using the profiling object's context menu, select Show View. Figure 11.40 displays the profiling object's Show View menu item.

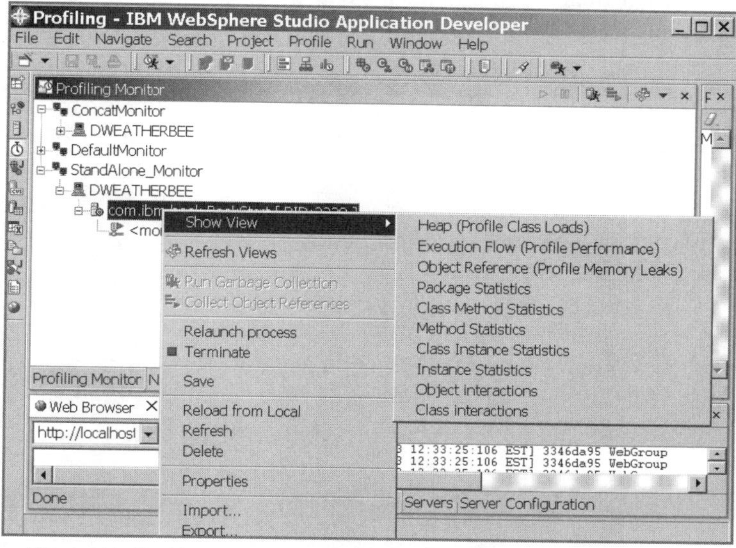

Figure 11.40: Using the Profiling Object's Show View menu item.

Note: As described in earlier sections of this chapter, each profiling object in the Profiling Monitor contains information that is scoped to the type of resource it represents and what that resource contains. The scope of the profiling data displayed in whatever profiling view you choose is determined by the selected profiling object in the Profiling Monitor.

Launching a Remote Java Process for Profiling

The Launch Remote Java Process wizard is very similar to the previously described Launch Java Process wizard. The Remote wizard, however, has an initial page that the local wizard does not have. The Remote wizard's first page, the Host page, asks you to identify the remote host and port you would like to connect to. The remote host is where your stand-alone Java application class resides, and the remote port identifies the remote host Agent Controller's listening port. You may remember from the chapter's initial discussion of the Agent Controller that its default port is 10002.

Note: In order to launch and profile your stand-alone Java application remotely, the IBM Agent Controller must be installed and running on the same remote host as the Java application. There are several installation versions of AC for most major OS platforms. Check Application Developer's installation CD for more information.

The Host page of the Launch Remote Java Process wizard is displayed in Figure 11.41.

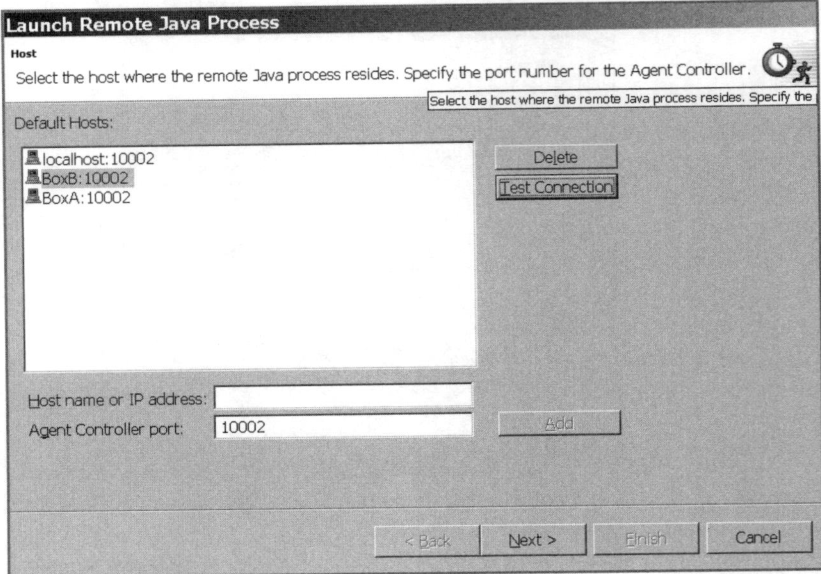

Figure 11.41: Launch Remote Java Process Host page.

By default, the Host page will include localhost:10002. You can use the Host page to create additional host:port combinations and test Application Developer's connection to the running remote Agent Controller.

Attach to Java Process: Application Developer WebSphere Test Environment

To profile a J2EE application running in the Application Developer WebSphere Test Environment Server, you can use the Attach to Java Process wizard. Before activating the wizard you must first start the IBM Agent Controller and then your WebSphere Test Environment Server in Profile mode. Starting your WebSphere Test Environment Server in Profile mode can be done in two ways. Select a Web module or EJB module component and, using its context menu, select **Profile on Server**. The Server Selection wizard starts by presenting you with a choice to create a new server or use an existing Test Server configuration. Either choice will start the server in profile mode by automatically using the -XrunpiAgent (Java Profiling Agent) and -DPD_DT_ENABLED=true (J2EE Request Profiler) Java options on server startup. A second way to start a WebSphere Test Environment Server is to use the Servers view. You must first have created a Server Configuration prior to using the Server view for startup. Select the **WebSphere Test Environment Server** in the Servers view list and, using the context menu, select **Profile**. This will start the server in Profile mode by automatically using the -XrunpiAgent and -DPD_DT_ENABLED=true Java options on server startup. Regardless of which method you use, the Status column of the Servers view will indicate that the server is running in Profile mode. Figure 11.42 highlights a server started in Profile mode.

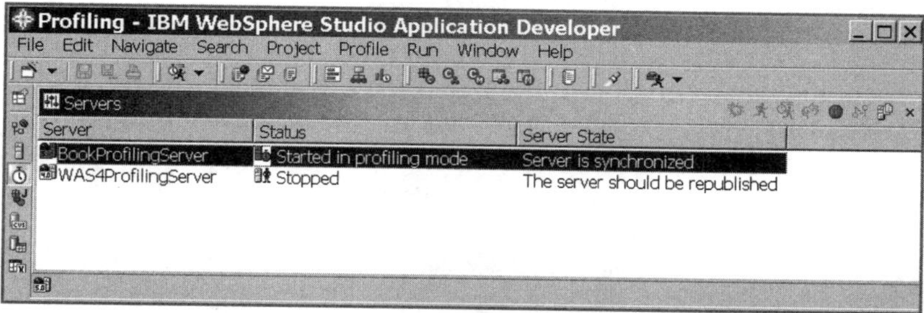

Figure 11.42: WebSphere Test Enviroment Server started in Profile mode.

Once a WebSphere Test Environment Server is started in Profile mode, using the Profile button drop-down menu, select **Attach → Java Process**. The Attach to Java Process wizard will open on the Agents page, as shown in Figure 11.43.

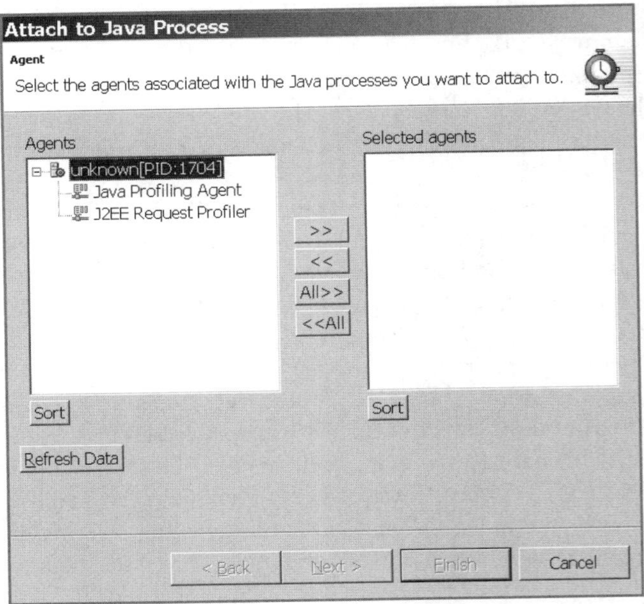

Figure 11.43: Attach Java Process wizard Agents page.

Note: It is possible to use the Attach to Remote Process wizard to connect to an Application Developer WebSphere Test Environment Server running on a remote machine. The Attach to Remote Process wizard would first present the Host page, requesting the remote host name and connection port. A more likely scenario of remotely profiling an application server would be remotely running WebSphere Application Server independent of Application Developer. This is described in the next section.

The Attach to Java Process wizard's Agents Page presents you with a list, located on the left side, of the JVM processes running in Profile Mode on your machine. In Figure 11.43, the "unknown[PID: 1704]" represents the WebSphere Test Environment Server started in Profile Mode. If you do not see any JVM processes in the left-side Agents list box, select the **Refresh Data** button. This will force Application Developer to reconnect to the IBM Agent Controller running locally on your machine. If you still do not see any JVM processes listed, check that the IBM Agent Controller is started and that your WebSphere Test Environment Server is started in Profile mode. In order to attach successfully to your Server, in the Agents list box, select the JVM process and using the Arrow buttons move the JVM process to the right-side Selected Agents list box. Figure 11.44 displays the aforementioned JVM process "unknown[PID: 1704]" moved to Selected Agents list box.

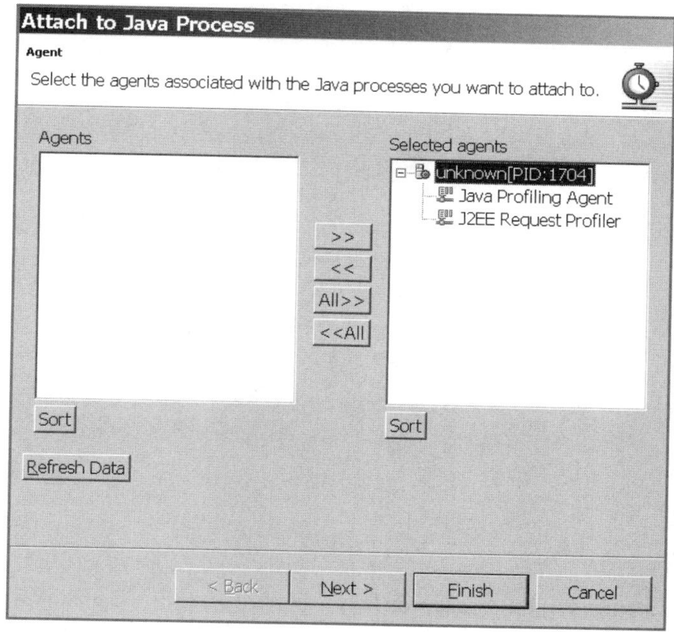

Figure 11.44: JVM process moved to Selected Agents.

Note: The two previous figures include an expanded JVM process displaying both the Java Profiling Agent and J2EE Request Profiler. You can select either one of the Agents depending on whether you require single (Java Profiling Agent) or distributed (J2EE Request Profiler) WebSphere JVM profiling (see the earlier section for more information). If you require single in-depth and distributed profiling, you can include both Agents.

Selecting the Next button opens the Destination page of the wizard, as shown in Figure 11.45:

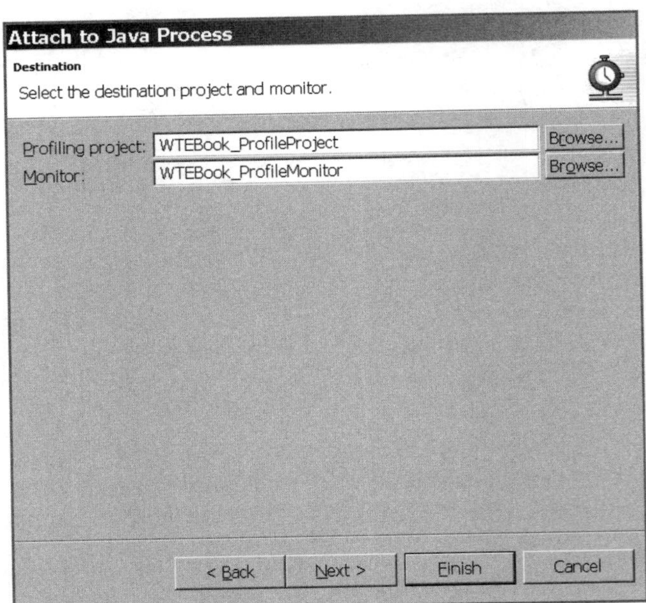

Figure 11.45: Attach to Java Process wizard Destination page.

In contrast to the Launch Java Process wizard, the Destination page of the Attach wizard does not allow you to send the profile data to a file. The Attach wizard allows you only to create or reuse a Profile Project and Monitor.

Note: If you want to send your profiling data to an external file, you must wait until after you have clicked the Finish button of the Attach wizard. In the Profiling Monitor you must then select the Properties context menu item of either the Java Profiling Agent or J2EE Request Profiler. The resulting Properties dialog allows you to send the Agent profiling data to an external file.

Clicking the **Next** button of the wizard opens the Profiling Filters page. The Attach wizard Profiling Filters page displays the same information as the corresponding page in the Launch wizard. The Profiling Filters page allows you to create or reuse Filter Sets for your WebSphere Test Environment profiling session. Clicking the **Next** button of the Profiling Filters page opens the Profiling Options page. Exactly the same as its counterpart in the Launch wizard, the Profiling Options page of the Attach wizard includes check boxes and associated text boxes for stopping a profiling session after a specified number of method invocations in your profiled JVM or an elapsed number of seconds. In the "Data collected by a profiling session" section of the page, you can specify boundary classes outside your INCLUDE filtered packages and classes that can be included in the profiling data. If you select the "Collect instance-level information" check box, the profiling session will gather profiling data required by the Heap, Object Reference, Class Instance Statistics, and Instance Statistics views. Clicking the **Finish** button will attach Application Developer as a Profiling Client, via the IBM Agent Controller, to the local WebSphere Test Environment Server running in Profile mode.

Note: When clicking the Finish button of either the Attach to Java Process or the Attach to Remote Java Process wizard, you will be prompted, by default, with a Profiling Tips dialog. Figure 11.46 displays the dialog. The Profiling Tips dialog informs you that you must "switch on" the JVM Process Java Profiling Agent and J2EE Request Profiler by using the context menu of the Agents and selecting Start Monitoring. Unless you start Agent monitoring, Application Developer cannot collect profiling data. You can click the OK button of the dialog.

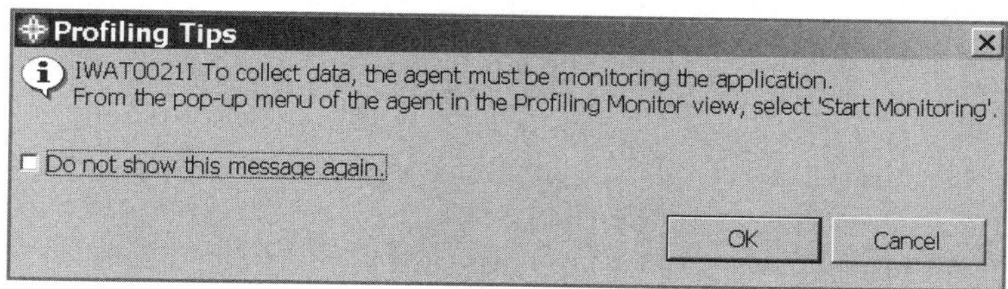

Figure 11.46: Profiling Tips dialog.

Similar to the Launch wizards, the Attach wizard also creates a Profiling Project, a Monitor, a Host, a Process, and Agent(s). Depending on the Monitors view settings of Profiling Preferences, Application Developer displays all or various combinations of these profiling objects in the Profiling Monitor. Figure 11.47 is an example of the Profiling Monitor displaying a new Monitor, Host, Process, Java Profiling Agent, and J2EE Request Profiler. Notice that the Java Profiling Agent and J2EE Request Profiler indicate that they are "attached." Figure 11.47 displays the Agents with a status of "attached."

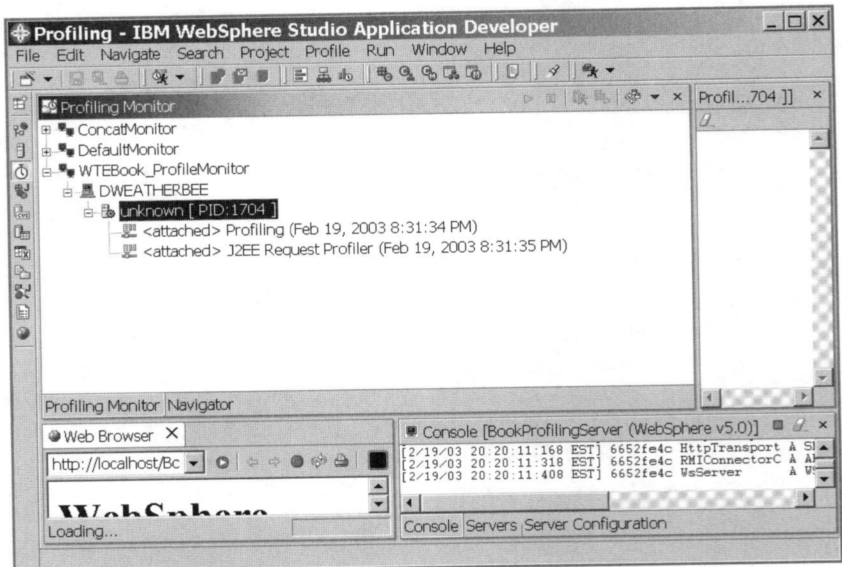

Figure 11.47: Java Profiling Agent and J2EE Request Profiler with status of "attached."

As the Profiling Tips dialog informed us, in order actually to collect profiling data on code running in your server you must select the Agents context menu choice Start Monitoring. Once the Agents are monitoring and collecting profiling data on your WebSphere Test Environment Server, you must generate some activity on your WebSphere-hosted code. This may mean that you surf to a servlet or JSP page or use Application Developer's Universal Test Client to invoke an EJB. After utilizing the Web and EJB components, you should open the statistical, graphical, and Sequence Diagram views to examine the profiling data generated by your activities. Figure 11.48 displays the Agents with a Status of "monitoring . . . collecting."

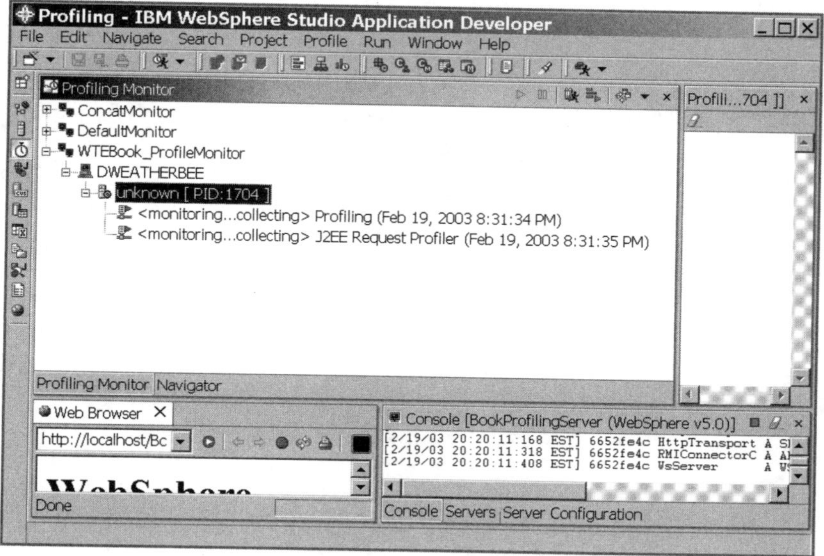

Figure 11.48: Java Profiling Agent and J2EE Request Profiler with status of "monitoring . . . collecting."

Attach to Java Process: Independent WebSphere Application Server

An independent, non-Application Developer WebSphere Application Server process does not automatically start a Java Profiling Agent or J2EE Request Profiler. As discussed in earlier sections of the chapter, -XrunpiAgent enables the JVMPI Profiling Agent and -DPD_DT_ENABLED=true enables the IBM WebSphere-specific J2EE Request Profiler. When you start a WebSphere Test Environment Server in Profile Mode (**Servers → Profile**), Application Developer automatically passes the JVM argument of -XrunpiAgent -DPD_DT_ENABLED=true to the starting Test Server. You do not have to worry about passing the JVM argument yourself.

However, when working with an independent WebSphere Application Server, you must configure the WebSphere Server's Process Definition to have a Generic JVM argument of -XrunpiAgent -DPD_DT_ENABLED=true. Figure 11.49 highlights the Generic JVM arguments location in the WebSphere Application Server Administration Console.

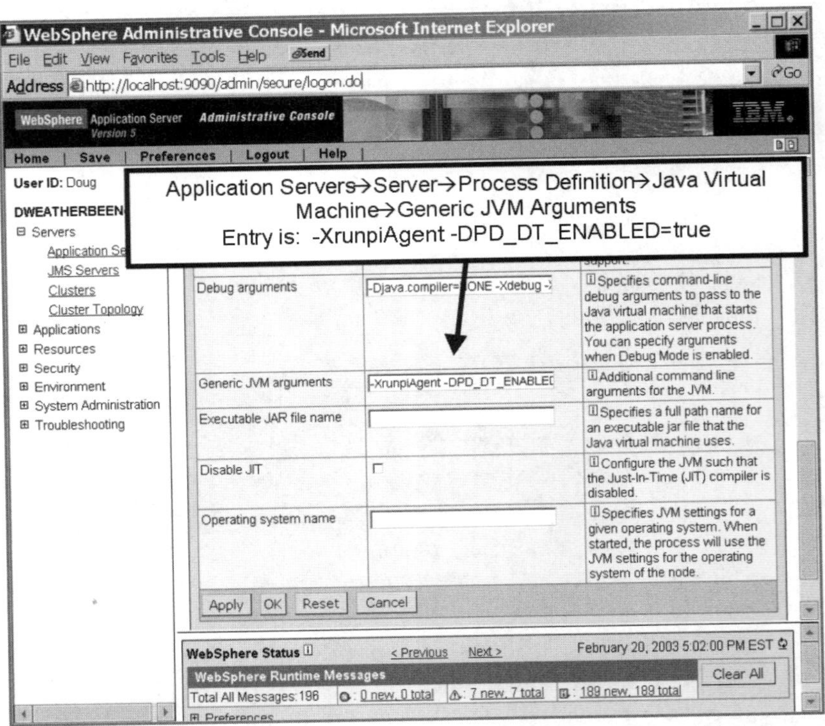

Figure 11.49: Generic JVM argument location in the WebSphere Application Server Administration Console.

To configure profiling related JVM arguments in the WebSphere Application Server, use the Administration Console and select **Servers → Application Servers →** *YourServer* **→ Process Definition → Java Virtual Machine → Generic JVM Arguments** and enter **-XrunpiAgent -DPD_DT_ENABLED=true**. You must then ensure that the IBM Agent Controller is installed and running on the same machine as your profile-enabled WebSphere Application Server. Then start, or restart, the profile-enabled WebSphere Application Server.

Once an independent WebSphere Application Server is started, use the Application Developer Profile button drop-down menu and select **Attach → Java Process** (Application Developer and WebSphere running on same machine) or **Attach → Remote Process** (Application Developer and WebSphere running on different machines). Depending on your choice, the Attach to Java Process or Attach to Remote Java Process wizard appears. Use the wizard as described previously to attach Application Developer to the independent WebSphere Application Server.

Saving profiling resource data in Application Developer

Profiling data is not automatically saved unless you either send it to an external file, as described in earlier sections of this chapter, or explicitly save it in a workbench project folder. Once the profiling data is saved, you can review the data at a later time. This is sometimes very useful, because a live profiling session can slow Application Developer's performance in rendering the data in the various Profiling views. Viewing saved profile data after a profiling session has been terminated can improve workbench performance. You can also transfer the saved data to other computers for reviewing. On the other hand, if the application you are profiling generates a large amount of profiling data, saving this data can take some time and produce large XML profiling documents.

Each profiling object visible in the Profiling Monitor view—Monitor, Host, Process, Java Profiling Agent, and J2EE Request Profiler—represents profiling data that can be saved to a workbench project. You explicitly save the profiling data by using the **Save** context menu item. The profiling data will be stored in the Profiling Project you identified in the Destination page of either the Launch or the Attach wizard. The profiling objects each have a corresponding *.xmi file. Table 11.4 identifies the specific files for each profiling object:

Table 11.4: File extensions for profiling objects.

Profiling Object	File Extension
Monitor	.trcmxmi
Host	.trcnxmi
Process	.trcpxmi
Agent	.trcaxmi

Profiling analysis procedures

This final section of this chapter outlines some procedures you can use to gather and analyze profiling data. The procedures assume that you have successfully set up a profiling session using either the Launch or Attach wizard, that your Java Profiling Agent and/or J2EE Request Profiler are monitoring and collecting profiling data from your JVM, and finally, that you have generated some activity on your running application.

Identifying performance bottlenecks in your code

Often, somewhere in the collection of classes and interfaces implementing a completed use case, are methods with excessive execution times, resulting in performance bottlenecks. These methods may not be the actual performance bottleneck but may be calling other methods that spend a long time on the stack. There are several views that help you pinpoint the specific problematic methods. These views are the Class Method Statistics, Method Statistics, Heap, and Execution views.

Class Method Statistics view

Using the Class Statistics view, you can use the following steps to locate performance bottlenecks in your code:

1. Select a profiling object in the Profiling Monitor view.
2. From the profiling object's context menu, select **Show View → Class Method Statistics**. The view should open.
3. By default, the Base Time and Cumulative Time columns should appear in the view. If they do not, use the Choose Columns dialog to add the columns to the view.
4. Sort the table by the Cumulative Time column. The Class Names column should now be sorted with the slowest-performing class listed at the top. "Open" the slowest-performing class using the plus sign next to the name of the class. The methods of the class should now be visible.
5. Now sort the table by the Base Time column. Under the Class Names the methods will now be ordered by base time. You can now locate the methods with long execution times.
6. If you select a method in the table and use the View Open Source button, you can further investigate the specific code causing the performance problem. You have used the Workbench Profiling tools to locate the problematic code. By examining the actual source code, you can determine the problem and take corrective action.

Method Statistics view

Using the Method Statistics view, you can use the following steps to locate performance bottlenecks in your code:

1. Select a profiling object in the Profiling Monitor view.
2. To open the Method Statistics view, from the profiling object's context menu select **Show View → Method Statistics**.
3. By default, the Base Time and Cumulative Time columns should appear in the view. If they do not, use the Choose Columns dialog to add the columns to the view.
4. Sort the table by the Base Time column. The Method Names column should now be sorted with the slowest-performing methods listed at the top.

5. If you select a method in the table and use the View Open Source button, you can further investigate the specific code causing the performance problem. You have used the Workbench Profiling tools to locate the problematic code. By examining the actual source code, you can determine the problem and take corrective action.

Heap view

Using the Heap view, you can use the following steps to locate performance bottlenecks in your code:

1. Select a profiling object in the Profiling Monitor view.
2. To open the Heap view, from the profiling object's context menu select **Show View → Heap**.
3. Make sure the Heap view is in Method mode by selecting the Method Mode button on the view toolbar.
4. Select **Base Time** from the **Color** by field.
5. Move the Slide Bar from right to left until you can see a change in the color of the rectangles that represent methods from black to orange or red.
6. Select the method rectangle that has changed from the color black to orange or red. The orange or red method rectangle represents a time-consuming method that may require optimization.
7. With the method rectangle selected, use the View Open Source button to investigate further the specific code causing the performance problem. You have used the Workbench Profiling tools to locate the problematic code. By examining the actual source code, you can determine the problem and take corrective action.

Execution Flow view

Using the Execution Flow view, you can use the following steps to locate performance bottlenecks in your code:

1. Select a profiling object in the Profiling Monitor view.
2. From the profiling object's context menu select **Show View → Execution Flow**. The view should open.
3. The Execution Flow view has a vertical time measurement bar located on the right side of the view. The longer this bar is for a method, the longer the method's execution time.
4. You may need to use the View Zoom In button to locate specific methods in your code for review and comparison with the time measurement bar.

Measuring garbage collection

Java garbage collection is usually automatically handled by a JVM. Generally, the more objects created in a JVM, the more garbage collection has to run. Although necessary, performing garbage collection uses JVM resources and impairs application performance. Understanding what object instances are disposed of or ignored during garbage collection can be useful in optimizing application performance by reducing unnecessary object creation. There are several views that help you examine garbage collection. The views are the Class Instance Statistics, Heap, and Execution Flow Views.

Class Instance Statistics view

Using the Class Instance Statistics view, you can use the following steps to examine the most frequently used garbage collection class instances in your code:

1. Select a profiling object in the Profiling Monitor view.
2. From the profiling object's context menu select **Show View → Class Instance Statistics**. The view should open.
3. By default, the Collected column does not appear in the Class Instance Statistics view. You may therefore have to add the column using the view's Choose Columns dialog.
4. You can sort the table by the Collected column to highlight the most frequently garbage collected Class instances.

Note: If garbage collection has not yet occurred, you can explicitly perform it and then view the object instances disposed of. The Profiling Monitor view has a Run Garbage Collection button. You could also select the **Process Profiling** object in the Profiling Monitor and, using the context menu, select **Run Garbage Collection**. Because the Run Garbage Collection button/menu item is associated with the Profiling Monitor view, you can explicitly run garbage collection regardless of which profiling view you have opened.

Heap view

Using the Heap view, you can use the following steps to examine the class instances destroyed by garbage collection:

1. Select a profiling object in the Profiling Monitor view.
2. From the profiling object's context menu select **Show View → Heap**. The view should open.

3. Make sure the Heap view is in Object mode.

4. The Heap view represents class instances that have been garbage-collected as empty rectangles.

5. Hover your mouse over any of the empty rectangles to get the time in which garbage collection occurred for that specific object instance. The information is presented in the Heap view Status line.

6. Use the **Run Garbage Collection** function if needed.

Execution Flow view

Using the Execution Flow view, you can use the following steps to examine the frequency of garbage collection running against your application code:

1. Select a profiling object in the Profiling Monitor view.

2. From the profiling object's context menu select **Show View → Execution Flow**. The view should open.

3. On the far left side of the view is the Garbage Collected column represented by the acronym GC. When the JVM performs garbage collection, a horizontal line will be placed in the column. When you load your application with activity, you can monitor the frequency of garbage collection using this approach. Remember to use the view's **Refresh Views** button to update the profiling data displayed in the view.

Locating Classes with high memory usage

Closely associated with garbage collection is creation of memory-intensive object instances. The larger the memory footprint of your object instances, generally, the greater the frequency of JVM garbage collection. In addition, memory-intensive objects placed into the HTTPSession hash impair the performance of Application Server session clustering. Two views that help you identify classes with high memory usage are the Class Instance Statistics and Heap views.

Class Instance Statistics view

Using the Class Instance Statistics view, you can use the following steps to locate class instances with high memory usage:

1. Select a profiling object in the Profiling Monitor view.

2. From the profiling object's context menu select **Show View → Class Instance Statistics**. The view should open.

3. By default, the Active Size and Instance Size columns should appear in the view. If they do not, you will have to add the columns using the view's Choose Columns dialog.

4. You can sort the table by either the Active Size (total of all instances in memory of this class type) or Instance Size (average size of instances of this class type). The classes with either the greatest Active Size or Instance Size represent the most memory-intensive classes running in your application.

Heap view

Using the Heap view, you can use the following steps to locate class instances with high memory usage:

1. Select a profiling object in the Profiling Monitor view.
2. To open the Heap view, from the profiling object's context menu select **Show View → Heap**.
3. Make sure the Heap view is in Object mode.
4. In the Color Scale Selection area, select **Active Memory** in the Color by: field.
5. Adjust the slider bar from right to left and note whether any classnames in the Class List area (left area of View) change from black or blue to orange or red. The color of the classnames in the Class List area signals the total size of all instances of that classtype.
6. Also, while adjusting the slider bar, note whether any of the horizontal rectangles in the histogram change from black or blue to orange or red. Each horizontal rectangle represents the class that is to the immediate right. The colors of the horizontal rectangles in the histogram represent the average size of the instances of that class type. Any orange or red horizontal rectangles signal high average sizes of those instances.

Summary

The Profiling tools in Application Developer enable you to measure, organize, and visually display information about the runtime behavior of code inside a JVM. The chapter has presented the information on Application Developer's Profiling tools by first presenting the goals of profiling and the profiling architecture on which Application Developer is built. The discussion then focused on the many tools inside of Application Developer's Profiling Perspective before moving on to describe how to use those tools to set up a Profiling Session. Finally the chapter provided a series of Application Developer profiling procedures you can use to understand and optimize your program code.

Test yourself

Key terms

Java Virtual Machine Profiler Interface (JVMPI)

profile

IBM Agent Controller (AC)

memory leak

Java Profiling Agent

profiling client

J2EE Request Profiler

monitor

Process object

process

agent

host

Base Time

Cumulative Time

filters

Sequence Diagram

Review questions

1. What flag is sent to the JRE to tell it to collect profiling data and return it to the Agent Controller?
2. How can basic profiling be done without a mechanism like the JVMPI?
3. What is the purpose of the Object Reference view?
4. Profiling information is not automatically updated by Application Developer. Instead, the user needs to refresh the data by clicking a button. Why not update automatically?
5. Describe the hierarchy among monitors, hosts, processes, and agents.
6. When the Sequence Diagram view is generated during profiling, what is the source of the profiling data?

CHAPTER 12

Implementing clients

Gene Van Sant

Chapter topics

- *J2EE components and containers*
- *J2EE Enterprise container clients*
- *J2EE Web container clients*
- *J2EE Application Client container clients*
- *WebSphere client models*
- *Web Services clients*
- *Best practices*

Certification objectives

- *Implement Java clients calling EJBs*
- *Implement Java clients calling Web Services*
- *Implement mechanisms that support loose coupling between clients and components*

Even a moderate amount of experience designing software systems typically leads to an acceptance of one of the industry's mantras: separation of concerns. Good separation of concerns calls for chopping a system into components and making sure the components concentrate on what they do best, not on each other. Yet each refining chop to the system causes complexity to emerge by exposing details. Taming this complexity by knowing where to chop and what to do with the exposed details has become likened to a quest for the Holy Grail. Decades of failure attest to the folly of underestimating the undertaking. Most solution designers have now learned that chopping something into bits dramatically increases its complexity.

Whereas many proposed technologies continue to end in disillusionment, a new hope arises from J2EE. J2EE components continue to offer a tractable solution, even as new requirements hit the market. J2EE suggests reasonable chopping points and provides standards for dealing with the exposed details. J2EE services handle many of these details yet expose to J2EE clients the details they need. A J2EE client always invokes J2EE services to access a J2EE component. Whereas other chapters discuss getting various J2EE components to talk or listen to other systems, this chapter focuses on talking to J2EE components. Though conceptually simple, this topic merits its own chapter because of the inherent complexity of integrating the many different types of components and forms of access that exist.

J2EE components and containers

N-tier architectures require that components in the different tiers access components in other tiers. Application clients reside in the first tier, but components in all tiers become clients in the context of each request that they make to other components. Suitable access mechanisms provide a degree of location and interaction transparency, facilitating connections by helping to locate components and allowing components to communicate.

This chapter distinguishes between clients, components, J2EE clients, and J2EE components. Clients access components. J2EE clients access J2EE components. In addition, each component or J2EE component may itself act as a client or J2EE client. By definition, all J2EE components reside inside J2EE containers, whereas all components reside outside of J2EE containers. Both clients and J2EE clients may live inside or outside of J2EE containers.

Typical distributed systems support various mechanisms for discovery of the distributed environment, joining components to the environment, and looking up components in the environment. Different types of J2EE components use different mechanisms. J2EE clients must interact with the J2EE services supporting the mechanisms appropriate to the J2EE component they access. The details of how to perform the access depend on where the J2EE client and the J2EE component reside, and what service restrictions apply. J2EE clients residing outside J2EE containers may require extensive programming and configuration. Placing J2EE clients inside J2EE containers makes them J2EE components as well, simplifying access to other J2EE components.

J2EE components

J2EE specifies services that support several types of components and communications. The specification provides for both declarative and programmatic control of these services. A J2EE container represents a logical construct of services for which J2EE specifies standard declarative controls. J2EE components residing inside J2EE containers may make use of declarations to control the services implicitly, or they may use programming to control them explicitly.

Figure 12.1 shows the types of components that exist. Although all components may act as clients to other components, only requests to J2EE components make the requesting component a J2EE client. Some J2EE components specialize as clients to other system components in a J2EE application. All J2EE clients make requests to J2EE servers running the services supporting the J2EE containers in which the J2EE components that they access reside. This allows the services to maintain full control by implementing the J2EE components' declarative directives and enforcing the J2EE components' declarative policies. No client may ever access J2EE components directly. J2EE components may access other components either directly or through the services defined by their J2EE container. Good J2EE components typically avoid accessing other components directly.

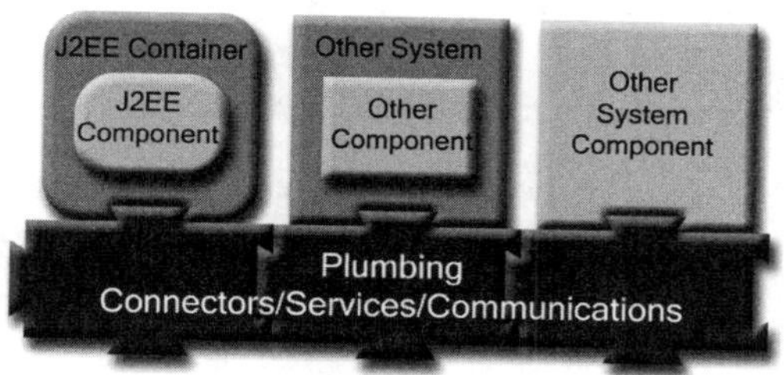

Figure 12.1: Types of components.

Recall that J2EE defines four different J2EE containers that support four fundamental types of J2EE components: Application Client, Web, Enterprise, and Resource Adapter. J2EE application client components specialize in accessing J2EE Enterprise components. J2EE Enterprise components specialize in accessing other system components and accessing other J2EE Enterprise components. J2EE Web components serve as the glue that facilitates access to J2EE Enterprise components from other system components. J2EE Resource Adapter components serve as the glue that facilitates access to other system components from J2EE Enterprise components. Although J2EE application client components and J2EE Web components may access other system components, such access makes them fat clients because the containers they live in offer only limited services for such access. Good clients perform access to other system components from inside a J2EE Enterprise container.

Usage of the terms *thin, thick,* and *fat* merits some clarification here. The term *thin* indicates no direct control of application logic and data. The term *thick* indicates control of application logic and data using the appropriate services. The term *fat* indicates the bad practice of controlling application logic and data with insufficient usage of appropriate services.

J2EE component references

As J2EE components, J2EE clients access four types of references: Enterprise JavaBean (EJB) references, resource manager connection factory references, resource environment references, and UserTransaction references. These references allow J2EE components to reveal their dependencies declaratively, which avoids hard coding and allows for loose coupling between J2EE applications and their operational environments. The chapter on deployment covers references in more detail, but this chapter introduces them from the client's perspective.

This chapter covers EJB references and UserTransaction references later, but the other two types of references merit distinction right away. J2EE defines resource manager connection factory references and resource environment references for use by J2EE components to access external resources. Figure 12.2 shows an example of a resource manager connection factory reference used to connect to an external resource.

```
<resource-ref id="IngasBeer">
  <description>Beer resource for Inga the beer monger</description>
  <res-ref-name>beer/beerCellar</res-ref-name>
  <res-type>com.acme.BeerConnectionFactory</res-type>
  <res-auth>Container</res-auth>
  <res-sharing-scope>Shareable</res-sharing-scope>
</resource-ref>
```

Figure 12.2: A resource manager connection factory reference deployment descriptor.

Figure 12.3 shows an example of a resource environment reference used to access externally administered components.

```
<resource-env-ref id="SvensBeer">
  <description>Beer resource for Sven the beer drinker</description>
  <resource-env-ref-name>beer/beerMonger</resource-env-ref-name>
  <resource-env-ref-type>com.acme.BeerConnection</resource-env-ref-type>
</resource-env-ref>
```

Figure 12.3: A resource environment reference deployment descriptor.

Within the difference lies the potential for one of J2EE's greatest enigmas. A J2EE component declares a resource manager connection factory reference when it wants to perform tight access on an external resource using local declarative control of services. A J2EE component typically declares a resource environment reference when it wants to perform loose access on an external resource that the services already manage. A resource manager connection factory reference resolves to a factory that creates connections to a resource, whereas a resource environment reference resolves to an actual resource. Usage of the terms *tight access* and *loose access* merit some clarification here. Tight access indicates an access model usually appropriate for thick clients, where the application controls the resource. Loose access indicates and access model usually appropriate for thin clients, where the operational environment controls the resource.

The descriptor snippets seen in Figures 12.2 and 12.3 represent resources accessed by the two components Inga and Sven. In this example, Inga accesses the resource manager connection factory reference IngasBeer, which uses all sorts of fancy services to obtain the shareable resource beer. In fact, vendors of these services typically extend the descriptors to provide additional service customization. Sven, on the other hand, accesses the resource environment reference SvensBeer, which simply provides the resource. Note that these references provide a layer of abstraction between the Sven and Inga implementations and the actual resource. This abstraction allows for the separation of the application from the operational environment. The chapter on deployment shows how the services map Inga's beer/beerCellar reference and Sven's beer/beerMonger reference to resources in the operational environment.

Figure 12.4 shows an example of a vendor extension to a resource manager connection factory reference. Inga might indicate that she wants exclusive access while pouring beer by setting the isolationLevel to TRANSACTION_SERIALIZABLE. She might also indicate her eagerness to pour beer by setting connectionManagementPolicy to Aggressive.

```
<resourceRefExtensions xmi:id="IngasBeerExtension"
    isolationLevel="TRANSACTION_SERIALIZABLE"
    connectionManagementPolicy="Aggressive">
  <resourceRef href="inga.xml#IngasBeer"/>
</resourceRefExtensions>
```

Figure 12.4: Resource manager connection factory reference descriptor extension.

The tight resource integration achieved using resource manager connection factory references makes J2EE components thick clients and gives them the potential to get fat. The loose resource coupling achieved using resource environment references helps make J2EE components thin clients. As stated in the introduction, this chapter primarily concerns itself with how a thin client component such as Sven accesses beer and not how a component such as Inga accesses beer. The chapters on Enterprise components focus on how Inga accesses beer. This chapter focuses on Sven as a thin client and not on a Sven client that gets fat without any Inga around.

Although the conceptual difference between these two types of references remains fairly clear, their operational behavior makes them less trivial to understand. How the references get resolved at runtime depends on the type of reference and the type of J2EE container from which the J2EE component makes the reference. For instance, if a J2EE component looks up a resource manager connection factory using a resource manager connection factory reference from a J2EE Web container or J2EE Enterprise container, WebSphere Application Server resolves the reference by looking up the connection information using the Java Naming and Directory Interface (JNDI). If the J2EE component performs the lookup from a J2EE Application Client container, WebSphere Application Client resolves the reference by reading resource declarations packaged with the application. If the J2EE component looks up the same resource manager connection factory using a resource environment reference, both WebSphere Application Server and WebSphere Application Client resolve the reference by looking up the connection information in JNDI. In this case, either the resource manager connection factory provides default values for res-auth, res-sharing-scope, and its extensions, or it refuses to create the connection without the values. If any component chooses to look up the resource manager connection factory directly from JNDI, it loses the benefits of either type of reference.

Services configuration

Configuration control of the services occurs in three basic ways: bootstrap, application startup, and dynamic. Recall that bootstrap means at server startup, application startup means when the application gets started within the already running server, and dynamic means while the application runs. Bootstrapping allows complete control of the services, but applications may not have the privilege to bootstrap. All applications get some dynamic control of the services through application programming interfaces (APIs). J2EE dramatically simplifies control of the services by allowing J2EE applications to control the services declaratively both at application startup and dynamically using deployment descriptors. J2EE components use different deployment descriptors depending on the J2EE container they reside in. Just as a compiler validates API controls, a deployment descriptor validator validates the deployment descriptor controls.

This chapter provides details on service configuration, but it may help to list some concrete examples now. Use of bootstrap options may take place on the command line like this:

```
java -Djava.naming.provider.url=corbaloc:iiop:loofa.com:2809 ...
```

Alternatively, applications may configure service property files, such as sas.client.props, by placing parameters in them such as

```
com.ibm.CORBA.authenticationTarget=BasicAuth
```

Of course, applications may still use APIs to configure services programmatically, as the following example illustrates:

```
properties.put("com.ibm.CORBA.loginPassword", password);
javax.naming.Context ic = new javax.naming.InitialContext(properties);
```

Finally, J2EE provides declarative support for configuring services using deployment descriptors. An entry in a deployment descriptor typically looks something like this:

```
<resource-ref>
  <res-ref-name>BeerQueue</res-ref-name>
  <res-type>javax.jms.Queue</res-type>
  <res-auth>Container</res-auth>
</resource-ref>
```

The overall approach to configuring the services results from thoughtful design and a share of history. For instance, applications typically want to enforce a security policy at bootstrap yet provide a password at runtime. Application components residing inside J2EE containers make use of both programmatic APIs and declarative deployment descriptors. Application components residing outside of J2EE containers make use of properties and programmatic APIs to roll their own containers. Ideally, applications make use of J2EE containers where possible and perform as much configuration as possible in the J2EE deployment descriptors.

JRE configuration

Performing the appropriate configurations sometimes requires changes to the Java Runtime Environment (JRE). The Java platform allows for extending and modifying the services available to applications running in a JRE. Optional packages, formerly known as standard extensions, allow for the extension of the JRE using implementations of standard, open APIs. In addition, defining the location of Java bootstrap code allows for overriding existing JRE API implementations.

The Java platform provides control of the JRE via options on the command line or through the Java Native Interface (JNI) invocation API. The command line option for extending the JRE with optional packages follows:

```
-Djava.ext.dirs=<extension directories separated by ;>
```

The command line option for prepending the bootstrap code to override the existing JRE API implementations follows:

```
-Xbootclasspath/p:<directories and zip/jar files separated by ;>
```

JNI allows other languages, such as C and Perl, to control the JRE completely and wrap Java applications so that they appear native in other environments.

J2EE Enterprise container clients

J2EE Enterprise containers provide application components with the highest level of services and typically host the core of J2EE applications. Recall that the Enterprise container supports three fundamental types of components, called Enterprise JavaBeans (EJBs): the Session EJB, the Entity EJB, and the Message-Driven EJB. Clients must interact with Session and Entity EJBs in a synchronous manner, whereas Message-Driven EJBs support an asynchronous access model. Session and Entity EJBs provide authentication and authorization controls, but Message-Driven EJBs provide no such controls. This naturally puts them in two separate categories, because the clients to each must interact with a distinct set of services. EJB clients may also combine multiple requests into a single logical unit of work using transactions.

Clients to Session EJBs and Entity EJBs

The most flexible form of component access uses an Object Request Broker (ORB). ORBs enable components to communicate with each other by connecting components that make requests (clients) with components that service requests (servers). Enabling security in the ORB activates services that ensure the confidentiality, authenticity, and authorization of the access.

The client component must first locate the ORB by acquiring an InitialContext using the Java Naming and Directory Interface (JNDI) API. The client component may then use the InitialContext to obtain a proxy to a server component. The client component uses this proxy to communicate with the server component. Remember that communications always occur via a proxy, allowing the J2EE services to maintain full control.

Access from J2EE components: declarative

J2EE encourages the use of other J2EE components to access J2EE Enterprise components (EJBs). All J2EE components provide a declarative mechanism in their deployment descriptors to facilitate EJB access. These deployment descriptors reveal the J2EE component's access dependencies to the J2EE container, allowing seamless integration with the services and proper deployment. Think of it as type safety and design validation on the enterprise integration scale. All J2EE components may declare access to EJB remote interfaces, as in Figure 12.5.

```
<ejb-ref id="EjbRef_1">
  <ejb-ref-name>ejb/App</ejb-ref-name>
  <ejb-ref-type>Session</ejb-ref-type>
  <home>com.loofa.AppHome</home>
  <remote>com.loofa.App</remote>
  <ejb-link>AppEJB.jar#App</ejb-link>
</ejb-ref>
```

Figure 12.5: EJB remote access declaration for all J2EE components.

Only Web and Enterprise components may declare access to EJB local interfaces, as shown in Figure 12.6. This restriction exists by design, because local interfaces primarily support tight aggregation relationships hidden from the client.

```
<ejb-local-ref id="EJBLocalRef_1">
  <description>Local reference to Beer Entity EJB</description>
  <ejb-ref-name>ejb/Beer</ejb-ref-name>
  <ejb-ref-type>Entity</ejb-ref-type>
  <local-home>com.loofa.BeerLocalHome</local-home>
  <local>com.loofa.BeerLocal</local>
  <ejb-link>Beer</ejb-link>
</ejb-local-ref>
```

Figure 12.6: EJB local access declaration for J2EE Web components and J2EE Enterprise components.

WebSphere Application Server resolves these references at runtime using additional binding declarations. These bindings look different depending on the J2EE container the J2EE client component resides in. Figure 12.7 shows a binding declaration for J2EE application client components in a WebSphere Application Client.

```
<ejbRefs xmi:id="EjbRefBinding_1" jndiName="ejb/com/loofa/AppHome">
  <bindingEjbRef href="META-INF/application-client.xml#EjbRef_1"/>
</ejbRefs>
```

Figure 12.7: J2EE application client component EJB client binding for WebSphere Application Client.

Figure 12.8 shows a binding declaration for J2EE Web and Enterprise Components in a WebSphere Application Server.

```
<ejbRefBindings xmi:id="EjbRefBinding_1"
    jndiame="ejb/com/loofa/AppHome">
  <bindingEjbRef href="WEB-INF/web.xml#EjbRef_1"/>
</ejbRefBindings>
```

Figure 12.8: J2EE Web component and J2EE Enterprise component EJB client binding for WebSphere Application Server.

WebSphere Studio Application Developer reduces these configurations to a trivial task by providing dialogs for editing and validating all these deployment descriptors. The dialogs may look slightly different from each other, but they all edit J2EE component references to EJBs. Figure 12.9 shows the dialog for editing EJB references in a J2EE application client component's deployment descriptor.

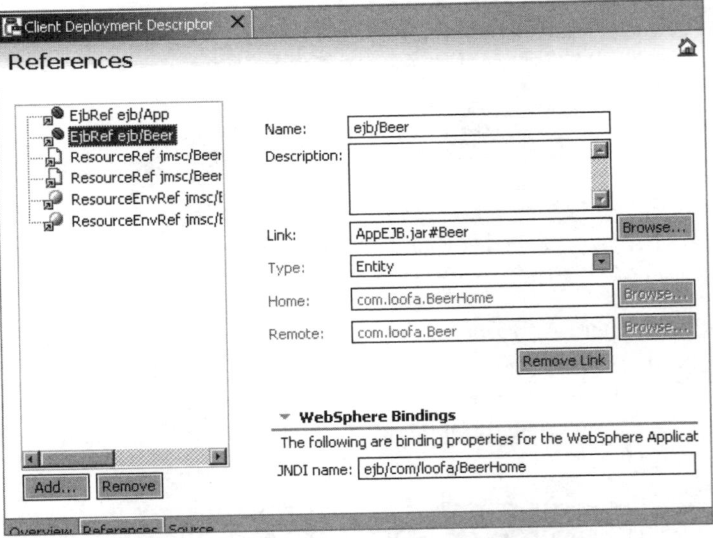

Figure 12.9: EJB references for a J2EE application client component.

Figure 12.10 shows the dialog for editing EJB references in a J2EE Web component's deployment descriptor.

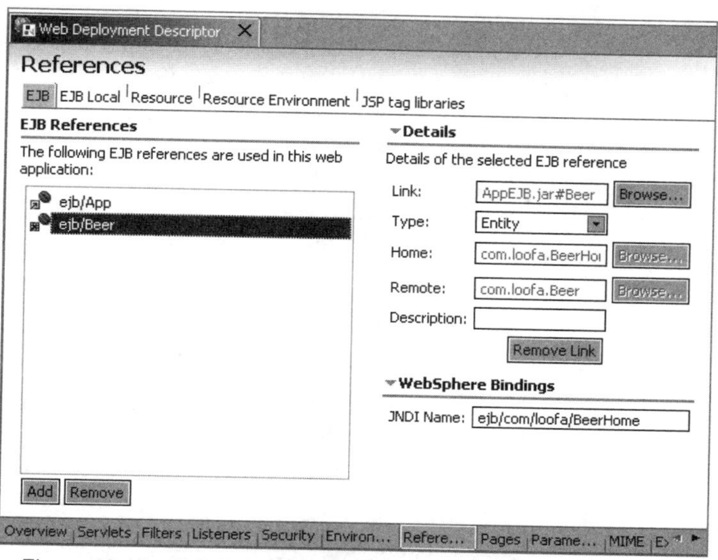

Figure 12.10: EJB References for a J2EE Web Component.

Figure 12.11 shows the dialog for editing EJB references in a J2EE Enterprise component's (EJB's) deployment descriptor.

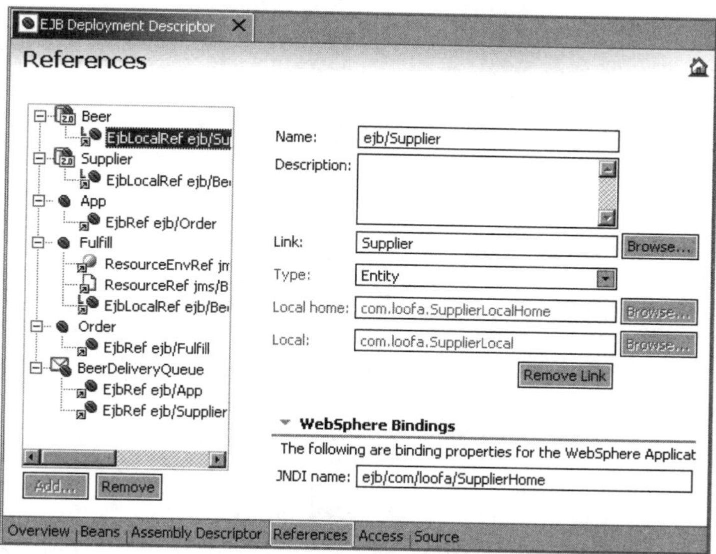

Figure 12.11: EJB references for a J2EE Enterprise component (EJB).

Access from J2EE components: programmatic

EJB clients residing in J2EE containers (J2EE components) have a simple programmatic access model because the J2EE container handles the ORB configuration details. J2EE components acquire a reference to the default ORB InitialContext as follows:

```
Context context = new InitialContext();
```

Sometimes the EJB client must make use of ORB services other than the preconfigured ones, or the client may not reside in a preconfigured J2EE container. In such cases, the EJB client configures the services using dynamic properties, either at bootstrap or at runtime. Figure 12.12 shows how an EJB client acquires a dynamically configured InitialContext.

```
Properties properties = new Properties();
// Set the properties used by JNDI to create the initial context
properties.put(
  Context.INITIAL_CONTEXT_FACTORY,
  "com.ibm.websphere.naming.WsnInitialContextFactory");
// Specify the location of the bootstrap server
properties.put(
  javax.naming.Context.PROVIDER_URL,
  // supported as legacy but obsoleted
  // "iiop://loofa.com:2809"
  "corbaloc:iiop:loofa.com:2809");
// get access to the JNDI namespace
Context context = new InitialContext(properties);
```

Figure 12.12: Acquiring a dynamically configured InitialContext at runtime using properties.

Once the client acquires the InitialContext, it uses it to access the EJB. Figure 12.13 shows how an EJB client correctly accesses an EJB with a local interface.

```
try {
  Context jndiContext = new InitialContext();
  BeerLocalHome beerLocalHome =
    (BeerLocalHome) jndiContext.lookup("java:comp/env/ejb/Beer");
  BeerLocal beerLocal = beerLocalHome.findByPrimaryKey("Loofa Brew");
  int price = beerLocal.getPrice();
  System.out.println("Loofa Brew price: " + price);
} catch (NamingException e) {
  e.printStackTrace(System.err);
} catch (FinderException e) {
  e.printStackTrace(System.err);
}
```

Figure 12.13: Calling an EJB from a J2EE component using a local interface.

Client programs that want to interoperate with other EJB container implementations must perform type narrowing of the client-side representations of the home and remote interfaces. Figure 12.14 shows how an EJB client correctly accesses an EJB with a remote interface.

```
try {
  Context jndiContext = new InitialContext();
  AppHome appHome =
    (AppHome) PortableRemoteObject.narrow(
      jndiContext.lookup("java:comp/env/ejb/App"),
      AppHome.class);
  App app =
    (App) PortableRemoteObject.narrow(appHome.create(), App.class);
  String response = app.processRequest("Loofa Brew");
  System.out.println("... got response: " + response);
} catch (RemoteException e) {
  e.printStackTrace(System.err);
} catch (NamingException e) {
  e.printStackTrace(System.err);
} catch (CreateException e) {
  e.printStackTrace(System.err);
}
```

Figure 12.14: Calling an EJB from a J2EE component using a portable remote interface.

EJB clients often benefit from making use of a subcontext of the InitialContext which avoids much of the clutter brought on by unwieldy namespaces. EJB clients residing in J2EE Containers make use of the java:comp/env Environment Naming Context (ENC) as a best practice. Use of the ENC avoids conflicts and makes applications much easier to configure, so good clients avoid using straight JNDI lookups. Figures 12.15a and 12.15b show how an EJB client accesses EJBs using a subcontext.

```
try {
  Context jndiContext = new InitialContext();
  Context context = (Context) jndiContext.lookup("java:comp/env/ejb");
  AppHome appHome =
    (AppHome) PortableRemoteObject.narrow(
      context.lookup("App"),
      AppHome.class);
  App app =
    (App) PortableRemoteObject.narrow(appHome.create(), App.class);
  String response = app.processRequest("Loofa Brew");
  System.out.println("... got response: " + response);
```

Figure 12.15a: Calling an EJB from a J2EE component using an ENC subcontext.

```
} catch (RemoteException e) {
  e.printStackTrace(System.err);
} catch (NamingException e) {
  e.printStackTrace(System.err);
} catch (CreateException e) {
  e.printStackTrace(System.err);
}
```

Figure 12.15b: Calling an EJB from a J2EE component using an ENC subcontext.

EJB clients may wish to make use of straight JNDI lookups at times. A J2EE component that circumvents the ENC like this follows the bad practice of hard coding. Figure 12.16 shows an EJB client performing a straight JNDI lookup.

```
try {
  java.util.Properties properties = new java.util.Properties();
  properties.put(
    Context.INITIAL_CONTEXT_FACTORY,
    "com.ibm.websphere.naming.WsnInitialContextFactory");
  properties.put(
    Context.PROVIDER_URL,
    // supported as legacy but obsoleted
    // "iiop://loofa.com:2809"
    "corbaloc:iiop:loofa.com:2809");
  Context jndiContext = new InitialContext(properties);
  AppHome appHome =
    (AppHome) PortableRemoteObject.narrow(
      jndiContext.lookup("ejb/com/loofa/AppHome"),
      AppHome.class);
  App app =
    (App) PortableRemoteObject.narrow(appHome.create(), App.class);
  String response = app.processRequest("Loofa Brew");
  System.out.println("AppJC: got response: " + response);
} catch (RemoteException e) {
  e.printStackTrace(System.err);
} catch (NamingException e) {
  e.printStackTrace(System.err);
} catch (CreateException e) {
  e.printStackTrace(System.err);
}
```

Figure 12.16: EJB client making a JNDI lookup outside of ENC.

Lastly, EJB clients may follow another bad practice and access EJBs directly via a full JNDI name, as shown in Figure 12.17.

```
try {
  Context jndiContext = new InitialContext();
  AppHome appHome =
    (AppHome) PortableRemoteObject.narrow(
      jndiContext.lookup(
          // supported as legacy but obsoleted
          // "iiop://loofa.com:2809/ejb/com/loofa/AppHome"
          "corbaname:iiop:loofa.com:2809#ejb/com/loofa/AppHome"),
        AppHome.class);
  App app =
    (App) PortableRemoteObject.narrow(appHome.create(), App.class);
  String response = app.processRequest("Loofa Brew");
  System.out.println("AppJC: got response: " + response);
} catch (RemoteException e) {
  e.printStackTrace(System.err);
} catch (NamingException e) {
  e.printStackTrace(System.err);
} catch (CreateException e) {
  e.printStackTrace(System.err);
}
```

Figure 12.17: EJB client making a direct JDNI lookup outside of ENC.

Access from J2EE components: operational

J2EE Web components and J2EE Enterprise components get run by their respective J2EE containers, which involves installing and configuring an Application Server. J2EE application client components run in an Application Client container. An example of launching a J2EE application client component from an operating system shell using the WebSphere Application Client follows:

```
launchClient App.ear -CCjar=AppJAC.jar
```

J2EE application client components also run easily within WebSphere Studio Application Developer. Figure 12.18 shows a WebSphere Studio Application Developer launch configuration for a J2EE application client component.

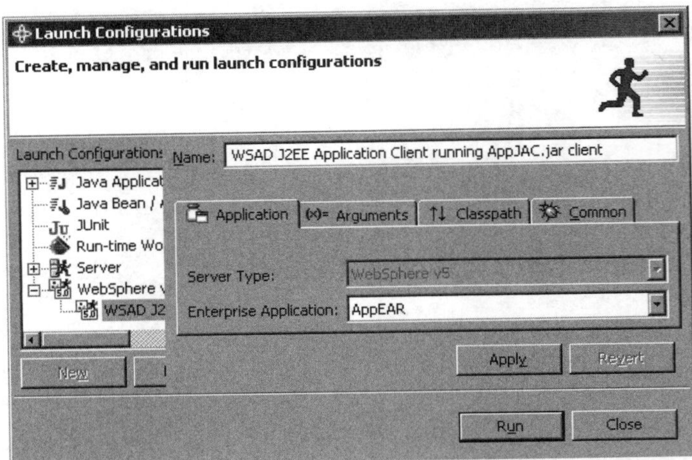

Figure 12.18: Launching a J2EE application client component in WebSphere Studio Application Developer.

Figure 12.19 shows the settings in a WebSphere Studio Application Developer launch configuration to launch a specific J2EE application client component in verbose mode.

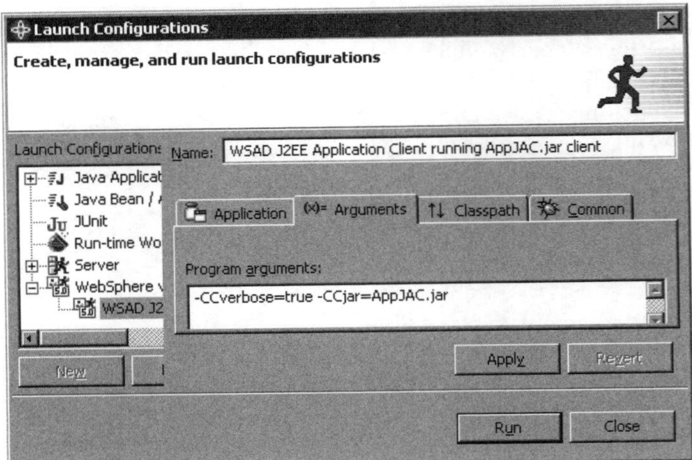

Figure 12.19: Launching a specific J2EE application client component in verbose mode in WebSphere Studio Application Developer.

Rolling your own access client

Enterprise programming gets harder when code runs outside of J2EE containers. Mechanisms exist in the Java platform to support integration between different versions and editions of Java from different vendors. However, vendors support only some combinations in practice. IBM provides a number of service libraries that enable different JREs with WebSphere Application Client J2EE services. If clients choose to run outside of J2EE containers, they must configure the services themselves.

EJB clients running in a JRE outside of a J2EE container require a certain amount of bootstrapping to enable the services needed to communicate with WebSphere EJBs. EJB clients require different WebSphere services depending on the base JRE they wish to modify. Figure 12.20 shows the JRE overrides and extensions necessary for an IBM standard JRE (J2SE) to run a WebSphere EJB client.

```
set WAS_HOME=C:\Program Files\IBM\WebSphere Studio\runtimes\base_v5
set JAVA_JRE=%WAS_HOME%\Java\jre
set JMS_PATH=C:\Program Files\IBM\WebSphere MQ\Java\lib
set WAS_EXT_DIRS=%JAVA_JRE%\lib\ext;%JAVA_JRE%\lib;%WAS_HOME%\classes;%WAS_
HOME%\lib;%WAS_HOME%\lib\ext;%WAS_HOME%\properties;%JMS_PATH%
set WAS_BOOTCLASSPATH=%JAVA_JRE%\lib\ext\ibmorb.jar;%WAS_HOME%\properties

"%JAVA_JRE%\bin\java" -Xbootclasspath/p:"%WAS_BOOTCLASSPATH%" -Djava.ext.di
rs="%WAS_EXT_DIRS%" -Dserver.root="%WAS_HOME%" com.loofa.AppJC
```

Figure 12.20: Using an IBM J2SE JRE to run the WebSphere EJB client outside of a J2EE container.

Figure 12.21 shows the JRE overrides and extensions necessary for a Sun standard JRE (J2SE) to run a WebSphere EJB client.

```
set WAS_HOME=C:\Program Files\WebSphere\AppClient
set JAVA_JRE=C:\Program Files\JavaSoft\JRE\1.3.1_03
set JMS_PATH=C:\Program Files\IBM\WebSphere MQ\Java\lib
set WAS_EXT_DIRS=%WAS_HOME%\java\jre\lib\ext;%WAS_HOME%\classes;%WAS_HOME%\
lib;%WAS_HOME%\lib\ext;%WAS_HOME%\java\lib;%WAS_HOME%\java\jre\lib;%WAS_HOM
E%\properties;%JAVA_JRE%\lib;%JAVA_JRE%\lib\ext;%JMS_PATH%
set WAS_BOOTCLASSPATH=%WAS_HOME%\java\jre\lib\ext\ibmorb.jar;%WAS_HOME%\jav
a\jre\lib\ext\ibmext.jar;%WAS_HOME%\java\jre\lib\ext\ibmjcefw.jar;%WAS_HOME
%\java\jre\lib\ext\ibmjceprovider.jar;%WAS_HOME%\java\jre\lib\ext\iwsorbuti
l.jar;%WAS_HOME%\java\jre\lib\ext\ibmjlog.jar;%WAS_HOME%\java\jre\lib\ext\i
bmjsse.jar;%WAS_HOME%\java\jre\lib\ext\ibmpkcs.jar;%WAS_HOME%\properties

"%JAVA_JRE%\bin\java" -Xbootclasspath/p:"%WAS_BOOTCLASSPATH%" -Djava.ext.di
rs="%WAS_EXT_DIRS%" com.loofa.AppJC
```

Figure 12.21: Using a Sun J2SE JRE to run the WebSphere EJB client outside of a J2EE container.

A client may also choose to perform some of the configuration programmatically, or it may get bootstrapped with all the information it needs by adding more command arguments during launch. Figure 12.22 shows the command arguments necessary to configure default ORB settings at bootstrap.

```
-Djava.naming.provider.url=corbaloc:iiop:loofa.com:2809 -Djava.naming.facto
ry.initial=com.ibm.websphere.naming.WsnInitialContextFactory -Dcom.ibm.CORB
A.ConfigURL=file:sas.client.props
```

Figure 12.22: Additional bootstrap ORB configuration options for an EJB client.

The programmatic approach allows EJB clients to implement the amount of dynamic configuration they need at runtime. Figure 12.23 shows an EJB client configuring the ORB programmatically at runtime.

```
try {
  java.util.Properties properties = new java.util.Properties();
  properties.put(
    "java.naming.provider.url",
    // supported as legacy but obsoleted
    // "iiop://loofa.com:2809"
    "corbaloc:iiop:loofa.com:2809");
  properties.put(
    "java.naming.factory.initial",
    "com.ibm.websphere.naming.WsnInitialContextFactory");
  properties.put("com.ibm.CORBA.loginUserid", "dude");
  properties.put("com.ibm.CORBA.loginPassword", "2beer!2be");
  Context context = new InitialContext(properties);
  AppHome appHome = (AppHome) context.lookup("ejb/com/loofa/AppHome");
  App app = appHome.create();
  String response = app.processRequest("Loofa Brew");
  System.out.println("AppJC: got response: " + response);
} catch (RemoteException e) {
  e.printStackTrace(System.err);
} catch (NamingException e) {
  e.printStackTrace(System.err);
} catch (CreateException e) {
  e.printStackTrace(System.err);
}
```

Figure 12.23: Typical programmatic ORB configuration by an EJB client.

By rolling all of the required services together and calling the appropriate WebSphere launch sequence, the EJB client becomes a J2EE application client component. Figure 12.24 shows how to launch a WebSphere Application Client to run a J2EE application client component.

```
set WAS_HOME=C:\IBMWASJAC\Program Files\WebSphere\AppClient
set JAVA_JRE=%WAS_HOME%\java\jre
set JAVA_JDK=%WAS_HOME%\java
set JMS_PATH=C:\Program Files\IBM\WebSphere MQ\Java\lib

set WAS_EXT_DIRS=%JAVA_JRE%\lib;%WAS_HOME%\classes;%WAS_HOME%\lib;%WAS_HOME
%\lib\ext;%WAS_HOME%\web\help;%JMS_PATH%
set WAS_CLASSPATH=%WAS_HOME%\properties;%WAS_HOME%\lib\bootstrap.jar;%WAS_H
OME%\lib\lmproxy.jar
set WAS_BOOTCLASSPATH=%JAVA_JRE%\lib\ext\ibmorb.jar;%WAS_HOME%\properties

"%JAVA_JRE%\bin\java" -Xbootclasspath/p:"%WAS_BOOTCLASSPATH%" -Dws.ext.dirs
="%WAS_EXT_DIRS%" -classpath "%WAS_CLASSPATH%" -Dws.output.encoding=console
 -Dcom.ibm.CORBA.ConfigURL="file:%WAS_HOME%/properties/sas.client.props" -D
com.ibm.SOAP.ConfigURL="file:/%WAS_HOME%/properties/sas.client.props" -Dcom
.ibm.CORBA.RasManager=com.ibm.websphere.ras.WsOrbRasManager -Dwas.install.r
oot="%WAS_HOME%" -Djava.security.auth.login.config="%WAS_HOME%\properties\w
sjaas_client.conf" -Dcom.ibm.CORBA.BootstrapHost=loofa.com -Dcom.ibm.CORBA.
BootstrapPort=2809 -Djava.naming.factory.initial=com.ibm.websphere.naming.W
snInitialContextFactory com.ibm.ws.bootstrap.WSLauncher com.ibm.websphere.c
lient.applicationclient.launchClient App.ear
```

Figure 12.24: Launching a J2EE application client component using WebSphere services.

Note that in order for Sun JREs to work with the IBM services, the Sun JRE must see the IBM ORB properties. Sun's JRE security must also contain additional IBM configuration. The WebSphere Pluggable Client install performs these configurations automatically. The following properties file snippets illustrate how to perform the configurations manually.

First, Sun's JRE must contain some IBM security configuration. Figure 12.25 shows typical modifications to the Sun Java security properties file.

```
C:\Program Files\JavaSoft\JRE\1.3.1_03\lib\security\java.security
#comment Sun's provider out
#security.provider.2=com.sun.rsajca.Provider
#and add IBM's
security.provider.2=com.ibm.crypto.provider.IBMJCE
security.provider.3=com.ibm.jsse.IBMJSSEProvider
security.provider.4=com.ibm.security.cert.IBMCertPath
```

Figure 12.25: Typical configuration changes to the Sun JRE Java security properties.

Second, IBM's ORB properties file must replace the default Sun ORB properties file to tell the Sun JRE about IBM's ORB. Figure 12.26 shows typical configuration properties for IBM's ORB.

```
C:\Program Files\JavaSoft\JRE\1.3.1_03\lib\orb.properties
# IBM JDK properties
org.omg.CORBA.ORBClass=com.ibm.CORBA.iiop.ORB
org.omg.CORBA.ORBSingletonClass=com.ibm.rmi.corba.ORBSingleton
javax.rmi.CORBA.StubClass=com.ibm.rmi.javax.rmi.CORBA.StubDelegateImpl
javax.rmi.CORBA.PortableRemoteObjectClass=com.ibm.rmi.javax.rmi.PortableRem
oteObject
javax.rmi.CORBA.UtilClass=com.ibm.ws.orb.WSUtilDelegateImpl
com.ibm.CORBA.iiop.SubcontractInit=com.ibm.ws.orb.WSSubcontractInitImpl

# WS Plugins
com.ibm.CORBA.ORBPluginClass.com.ibm.ejs.jts.jts.JtsPlugin
com.ibm.CORBA.ORBPluginClass.com.ibm.ws.wlm.client.WLMClient
com.ibm.CORBA.ORBPluginClass.com.ibm.ws.orbimpl.transport.WSTransport
com.ibm.CORBA.ORBPluginClass.com.ibm.ws.orbimpl.WSORBPropertyManager
com.ibm.CORBA.ORBPluginClass.com.ibm.ISecurityUtilityImpl.SecurityPropertyM
anager
com.ibm.CORBA.ORBPluginClass.com.ibm.ws.orb.WSSubcontractInitImpl

# WS Interceptors
org.omg.PortableInterceptor.ORBInitializerClass.com.ibm.ejs.jts.jts.ClientI
nterceptor
org.omg.PortableInterceptor.ORBInitializerClass.com.ibm.ejs.ras.RasContextS
upport
org.omg.PortableInterceptor.ORBInitializerClass.com.ibm.ISecurityLocalObjec
tBaseL13Impl.ClientRIWrapper
org.omg.PortableInterceptor.ORBInitializerClass.com.ibm.ws.activity.Activit
yServiceClientInterceptor
org.omg.PortableInterceptor.ORBInitializerClass.com.ibm.ISecurityLocalObjec
tBaseL13Impl.CSIClientRI
org.omg.PortableInterceptor.ORBInitializerClass.com.ibm.debug.olt.ivbtrjrt.
OLT_RI
org.omg.PortableInterceptor.ORBInitializerClass.com.ibm.ws.wlm.client.WLMCl
ientInitializer

# WS ORB & Plugins properties
com.ibm.ws.orb.transport.ConnectionInterceptorName=com.ibm.ISecurityLocalOb
jectBaseL13Impl.SecurityConnectionInterceptor
com.ibm.CORBA.enableLocateRequest=true
com.ibm.ws.orb.transport.WSSSLClientSocketFactoryName=com.ibm.ws.security.o
rbssl.WSSSLClientSocketFactoryImpl
com.ibm.CORBA.ORBCharEncoding=UTF8
```

Figure 12.26: IBM's ORB.properties.

Security configurations on the client enable the creation of a confidential authenticated connection with an authenticated server. EJB clients must configure the Secure Association Services (SAS) / Common Security Interoperability version 2 (CSIv2) services. CSIv2 replaces SAS although IBM still supports SAS. Figures 12.27a, b, c, d, and e reproduce the properties file in its entirety. IBM has commented it exceptionally well to make it self-explanatory.

```
###############################################################################
#
#                          SAS Properties File
#
#  This file contains properties that are used by the Secure Association
#  Services (SAS) component of the WebSphere Application Server product.
#  SAS executes on WebSphere java servers and client systems with java
#  applications that access WebSphere servers.
#
#  ** SAS/CSIv2 Trace Instructions **
#
#  Note:  To enable logging of trace on the application client, add the
#  following property to the startup script: -DtraceSettingsFile=filename.
#  Do not specify filename as a fully qualified path and filename, just
#  specify the filename.  The file must exist in the classpath to be
#  loaded. A sample file is provided in
#    <was_root>/properties/TraceSettings.properties.
#
#  There are two related functions provided by this file:
#
#    1.traceFileName property
#      This should be set to the fully qualified name of a file to which
#      you want output written. For example,
#      traceFileName=c:\\MyTraceFile.log. This property must be
#      specified, otherwise no visible output is generated.
#    2.Trace string
#      To enable SAS/CSIv2 trace, specify the trace string:
#      SASRas=all=enabled
#
#  If you only want to trace specific classes, you can specify a
#  trace filter by adding the property
#  com.ibm.CORBA.securityTraceFilter=<comma-separated class names>
#
#  Example:
#    com.ibm.CORBA.securityTraceFilter=
#    SecurityConnectionInterceptor, CSIClientRI, SessionManager
#
#  ** Encoding Passwords in this File **
#
```

Figure 12.27a: The available security configuration parameters in IBM's sas.client.props.

```
#  The PropFilePasswordEncoder utility may be used to encode passwords in a
#  properties file. To edit an encoded password, replace the whole password
#  string (including the encoding tag {...}) with the new password and then
#  encode the password with the PropFilePasswordEncoder utility. Refer to
#  product documentation for additional information.
#
###########################################################################

#------------------------------------------------------------------------
# Client Security Enablement
#
# - security enabled status  ( false, true [default] )
#------------------------------------------------------------------------
com.ibm.CORBA.securityEnabled=true

#------------------------------------------------------------------------
# RMI/IIOP Authentication Protocol (sas, csiv2, both [default])
#
# Specify "both" when communicating with 5.0x and previous release servers.
# Specify "csiv2" when communicating with only 5.0x servers.
# Specify "sas" when communicating with only previous release servers.
#------------------------------------------------------------------------
com.ibm.CSI.protocol=both

#------------------------------------------------------------------------
# Authentication Configuration
#
# - authenticationTarget
#     (BasicAuth [default], this is the only supported selection
#      on a pure client for this release.  This is for message
#      layer authentication only, SSL client certificate authentication
#      is configured below under CSIv2 configuration.)
# - authenticationRetryEnabled
#     (enables authentication retries if login fails when
#      loginSource=prompt or stdin)
# - authenticationRetryCount
#     (the number of times to retry)
# - source
#     (prompt [default], properties, keyfile, stdin, none)
# - timeout
#     (prompt timeout, specified in seconds, 0 min to 600 max
#     [default 300])
# - validateBasicAuth
#     (determines if immediate authentication after uid/pw login,
#      or wait for method request to send uid/pw to server,
#      setting this to false gives the previous release behavior.)
```

Figure 12.27b: The available security configuration parameters in IBM's sas.client.props.

```
# - securityServerHost
#      (when validateBasicAuth=true, this property might need to be set
#       in order for security code to lookup SecurityServer.  Needs to
#       be set to any running WebSphere server host in the cell you are
#       authenticating to.
# - securityServerPort
#      (when validateBasicAuth=true, this property might need to be set
#       in order for security code to lookup SecurityServer.  Needs to
#       be set to the bootstrap port of the host chosen above.
# - loginUserid
#      (must be set if login source is "properties" )
# - loginPassword
#      (must be set if login source is "properties" )
# - principalName
#      (format: "realm/userid", only needed in cases where realm
#       is required. Typically the realm is already provided by the
#       server via the IOR and this property is not necessary).
#
#------------------------------------------------------------------------
com.ibm.CORBA.authenticationTarget=BasicAuth
com.ibm.CORBA.authenticationRetryEnabled=true
com.ibm.CORBA.authenticationRetryCount=3
com.ibm.CORBA.validateBasicAuth=true
com.ibm.CORBA.securityServerHost=
com.ibm.CORBA.securityServerPort=
com.ibm.CORBA.loginTimeout=300
com.ibm.CORBA.loginSource=prompt

# RMI/IIOP user identity
com.ibm.CORBA.loginUserid=
com.ibm.CORBA.loginPassword=
com.ibm.CORBA.principalName=

#------------------------------------------------------------------------
# CSIv2 Configuration (see InfoCenter for more information on these
# properties).
#
# This is where you enable SSL client certificate authentication. Must also
# specify a valid SSL keyStore below with a personal certificate in it.
#------------------------------------------------------------------------

# Does this client support stateful sessions?
com.ibm.CSI.performStateful=true

# Does this client support/require BasicAuth (userid/password) client
# authentication?
com.ibm.CSI.performClientAuthenticationRequired=false
com.ibm.CSI.performClientAuthenticationSupported=true
```

Figure 12.27c: The available security configuration parameters in IBM's sas.client.props.

```
# Does this client support/require SSL client authentication?
com.ibm.CSI.performTLClientAuthenticationRequired=false
com.ibm.CSI.performTLClientAuthenticationSupported=false

# Note: You can perform BasicAuth (uid/pw) and SSL client authentication
# (certificate) simultaneously, however, the BasicAuth identity will
# always take precedence at the server.

# Does this client support/require SSL connections?
com.ibm.CSI.performTransportAssocSSLTLSRequired=false
com.ibm.CSI.performTransportAssocSSLTLSSupported=true

# Does this client support/require 40-bit cipher suites when using SSL?
com.ibm.CSI.performMessageIntegrityRequired=true
com.ibm.CSI.performMessageIntegritySupported=true
# Note: This property is only valid when SSL connections are supported
# or required.

# Does this client support/require 128-bit cipher suites when using SSL?
com.ibm.CSI.performMessageConfidentialityRequired=false
com.ibm.CSI.performMessageConfidentialitySupported=true
# Note: This property is only valid when SSL connections are supported
# or required.

#-------------------------------------------------------------------------
# SSL Configuration
#
# - protocol
#     (SSL [default], SSLv2, SSLv3, TLS, TLSv1)
# - keyStoreType
#     (JKS [default], JCEK, PKCS12)
# - trustStoreType
#     (JKS [default], JCEK, PKCS12)
# - keyStore and trustStore
#     (fully qualified path to file)
# - keyStoreClientAlias
#     (string specifying ssl certificate alias to use from keyStore)
# - keyStorePassword and trustStorePassword
#     (string specifying password - encoded or not)
# - cipher suites
#     (refer to InfoCenter for valid ciphers)
#
#    com.ibm.ssl.enabledCipherSuites=enabled_cipher_suites
#
#    Note: The com.ibm.ssl.enabledCipherSuites property defines the cipher
#          suites used for the SSL session. If this property is defined, it
#          overrides the default cipher suites defined for the specified
#          QOP.
#
#-------------------------------------------------------------------------
```

Figure 12.27d: The available security configuration parameters in IBM's sas.client.props.

```
com.ibm.ssl.protocol=SSL
com.ibm.ssl.keyStoreType=JKS
com.ibm.ssl.keyStore=C:/WebSphere/AppClient/etc/DummyClientKeyFile.jks
com.ibm.ssl.keyStorePassword={xor}CDo9Hgw\=
com.ibm.ssl.trustStoreType=JKS
com.ibm.ssl.trustStore=C:/WebSphere/AppClient/etc/DummyClientTrustFile.jks
com.ibm.ssl.trustStorePassword={xor}CDo9Hgw\=

#-----------------------------------------------------------------------
# Quality of Protection for the IBM protocol
#
# - perform  ( high [default], medium, low )
#-----------------------------------------------------------------------
com.ibm.CORBA.standardPerformQOPModels=high

#-----------------------------------------------------------------------
# CORBA Request Timeout
#    (used when getting NO_RESPONSE exceptions, typically during
#     high-stress loads.  Specify on all processes involved in the
#     communications.)
#
# - timeout
#      (specified in seconds [default 180], 0 implies no timeout)
#
#     com.ibm.CORBA.requestTimeout=180
#-----------------------------------------------------------------------
com.ibm.CORBA.requestTimeout=180
```

Figure 12.27e: The available security configuration parameters in IBM's sas.client.props.

Launching these configurations from inside WebSphere Studio Application Developer requires creating a launch configuration for a Java application, selecting a JRE, and configuring the Java virtual machine (JVM) arguments manually in the arguments tab or using the tool on the classpath tab. Figure 12.28, Figure 12.29, and Figure 12.30 show the launch configuration, selected JRE, and JVM arguments for rolling your own EJB client on a Sun J2SE JRE in WebSphere Studio Application Developer.

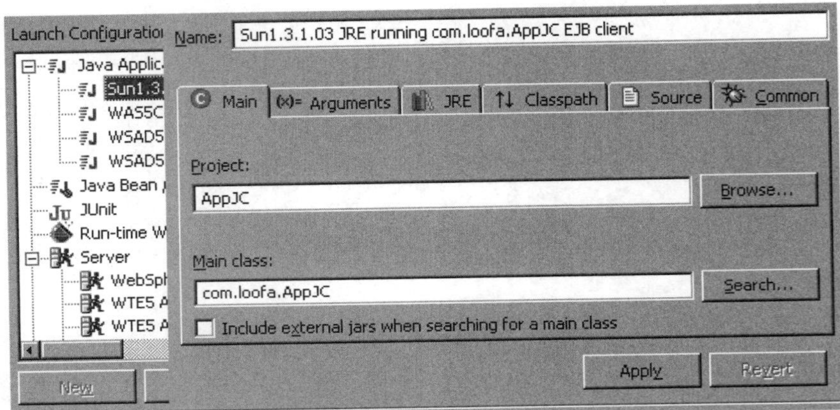

Figure 12.28: Launching a "roll your own" EJB client inside WebSphere Studio Application Developer.

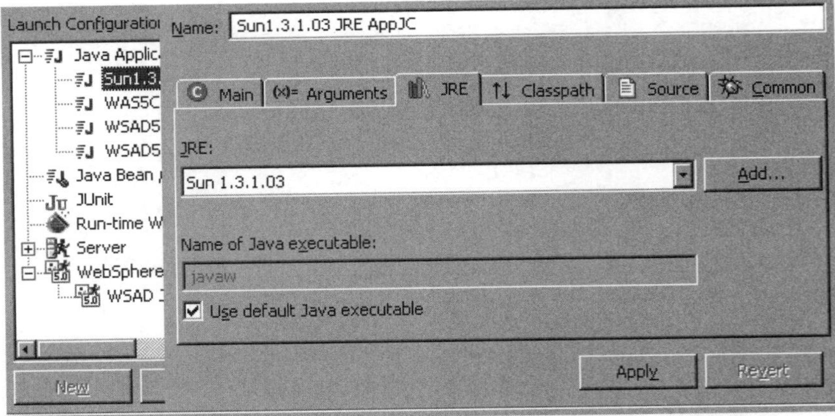

Figure 12.29: Selecting a JRE for a "roll your own" EJB client inside WebSphere Studio Application Developer.

Figure 12.30: Setting the VM arguments for a "roll your own" EJB client inside WebSphere Studio Application Developer.

Clients to Message-Driven EJBs

J2EE provides access to Message-Driven EJBs (MDBs) via the standard Java Messaging Service (JMS) API. The J2EE 1.4 specification provides more extensive declarative support for clients of MDBs in future releases.

JMS clients may access two forms of message destinations. They either send a message to a queue or publish a message to a topic. A queue provides asynchronous, assured, once-and-only-once delivery to a destination. A topic provides the same delivery, but to multiple destinations. JMS clients remain blissfully unaware of what happens to the data and where it ends up. In fact, one of the biggest benefits of messaging services lies in their ability to perform data filtering, translation, and routing.

Although thin messaging clients usually make a better solution, sometimes solutions require a thick messaging client. The need for asynchronous assured delivery often arises when clients have unreliable access to other components. This justifies using a thick client. Thick messaging clients require more information at deploy time than do thin messaging clients, because they need to configure a queue in the operational environment.

The operational environment actually determines whether the client has thin or thick access by providing local or remote queue access. JMS clients may declaratively configure local messaging using resource manager connection factory references, or they may access remote configurations using resource environment references.

Access from J2EE components: declarative

J2EE components that access MDBs (JMS) may treat them like a reference to any other external resource by using resource manager connection factory references. Accessing JMS from J2EE components in this manner gives clients a great deal of declarative control to administer the JMS resource locally. Remember that standard J2EE descriptors tell the services how to handle the authentication and sharing of external resources. In addition, WebSphere provides some heuristic descriptors for resource isolation level and connection management policy. Figures 12.31 and 12.32 show declarative access to JMS queues or topics using resource manager connection factory references.

```
<resource-ref id="ResourceRef_1">
  <description></description>
  <res-ref-name>jms/MQCF</res-ref-name>
  <res-type>javax.jms.QueueConnectionFactory</res-type>
  <res-auth>Application</res-auth>
  <res-sharing-scope>Unshareable</res-sharing-scope>
</resource-ref>
<resource-ref id="ResourceRef_2">
  <description></description>
  <res-ref-name>jms/MQ</res-ref-name>
  <res-type>javax.jms.Queue</res-type>
  <res-auth>Application</res-auth>
  <res-sharing-scope>Unshareable</res-sharing-scope>
</resource-ref>
```

Figure 12.31: JMS queue access using a resource manager connection factory reference from a J2EE component.

```
<resource-ref id="ResourceRef_1">
  <description></description>
  <res-ref-name>jms/MTCF</res-ref-name>
  <res-type>javax.jms.TopicConnectionFactory</res-type>
  <res-auth>Application</res-auth>
  <res-sharing-scope>Shareable</res-sharing-scope>
</resource-ref>
<resource-ref id="ResourceRef_2">
  <description></description>
  <res-ref-name>jms/MT</res-ref-name>
  <res-type>javax.jms.Topic</res-type>
  <res-auth>Application</res-auth>
  <res-sharing-scope>Shareable</res-sharing-scope>
</resource-ref>
```

Figure 12.32: JMS topic access using a resource manager connection factory reference from a J2EE component.

In J2EE, the res-auth descriptor specifies whether the J2EE container authenticates to the resource or the J2EE application performs the authentication programmatically. The res-sharing-scope descriptor specifies whether the resource allows Shareable or Unshareable connections. Figure 12.33 shows the additional WebSphere descriptors isolationLevel and connectionManagementPolicy, which allow the application to make tradeoffs between concurrency and transactional success rates.

```
<resourceRefExtensions xmi:id="ResourceRefExtension_1"
    isolationLevel="TRANSACTION_SERIALIZABLE"
    connectionManagementPolicy="Aggressive">
  <resourceRef href="META-INF/ejb-jar.xml#ResourceRef_1"/>
</resourceRefExtensions>
```

Figure 12.33: WebSphere extension descriptors for JMS resource isolation level and connection management.

JMS clients declaring access to JMS with resource manager connection factory references must have all references resolved locally. J2EE Web components and J2EE Enterprise components have their resource manager connection factory references resolved by administering the Application Server in which they run. J2EE Application Clients components have their resource manager connection factory references resolved by administering the J2EE Application Client container in which they run. Figures 12.34a and 12.34b show typical resource definitions in client-resource.xmi used by WebSphere Application Client to resolve resource manager connection factory references for J2EE Application Client components.

```
<resources.jms:JMSProvider
  xmi:id="JMSProvider_2"
  name="WebSphere JMS Provider"
  description="Default - cannot be changed">
  <classpath>C:\Program Files\IBM\WebSphere MQ\Java\lib\com.ibm.mq.jar;
   C:\ProgramFiles\IBM\WebSphere MQ\Java\lib\com.ibm.mqbind.jar;
   C:\Program Files\IBM\WebSphere MQ\Java\lib\com.ibm.mqjms.jar
  </classpath>
  <factories
    xmi:type="resources.jms.internalmessaging:WASQueueConnectionFactory"
    xmi:id="WASQueueConnectionFactory_1"
    name="BeerDeliveryQueueConnectionFactory"
    jndiName="jmsc/BeerDeliveryQueueConnectionFactory"
    description="" node="localhost" serverName="server1">
    <propertySet xmi:id="J2EEResourcePropertySet_1" />
  </factories>
```

Figure 12.34a: Resolving JMS client resource manager connection factory references for a J2EE application client component.

```
  <factories
    xmi:type="resources.jms.internalmessaging:WASQueue"
    xmi:id="WASQueue_1" name="BeerDeliveryQueue"
    jndiName="jmsc/BeerDeliveryQueue"
    description=""
    persistence="APPLICATION_DEFINED"
    priority="APPLICATION_DEFINED"
    expiry="APPLICATION_DEFINED">
    <propertySet xmi:id="J2EEResourcePropertySet_2" />
  </factories>
</resources.jms:JMSProvider>
```

Figure 12.34b: Resolving JMS client resource manager connection factory references for a J2EE application client component.

J2EE components may also access MDBs (JMS) as references to administered components. Accessing JMS from J2EE components in this manner allows the declarative control of the services to occur elsewhere. Figures 12.35 and 12.36 show declarative access to JMS queues or topics using resource environment references.

```
<resource-env-ref id="ResourceEnvRef_1">
  <description></description>
  <resource-env-ref-name>jms/MQCF</resource-env-ref-name>
  <resource-env-ref-type>javax.jms.QueueConnectionFactory
  </resource-env-ref-type>
</resource-env-ref>
<resource-env-ref id="ResourceEnvRef_2">
  <description></description>
  <resource-env-ref-name>jms/MQ</resource-env-ref-name>
  <resource-env-ref-type>javax.jms.Queue</resource-env-ref-type>
</resource-env-ref>
```

Figure 12.35: JMS queue access using a resource environment reference from a J2EE component.

```
<resource-env-ref id="ResourceEnvRef_1">
  <description></description>
  <resource-env-ref-name>jms/MTCF</resource-env-ref-name>
  <resource-env-ref-type>javax.jms.TopicConnectionFactory
  </resource-env-ref-type>
</resource-env-ref>
<resource-env-ref id="ResourceEnvRef_2">
  <description></description>
  <resource-env-ref-name>jms/MT</resource-env-ref-name>
  <resource-env-ref-type>javax.jms.Topic</resource-env-ref-type>
</resource-env-ref>
```

Figure 12.36: JMS topic access using a resource environment reference from a J2EE component.

JMS clients declaring access to JMS with resource environment references must have all references resolved using bindings to administered components, such as those shown for EJB clients in Figures 12.7 and 12.8.

Finally, JMS clients may mix resource manager connection factory references and resource environment references in any combination to suit their needs. For instance, JMS clients that wish to perform local administration of JMS connections to remotely administered JMS queues may use resource manager connection factory references to get connections and resource environment references to get queues, as shown in Figure 12.37. J2EE applications typically use this method.

```
<resource-ref id="ResourceRef_1">
  <description></description>
  <res-ref-name>jms/MQCF</res-ref-name>
  <res-type>javax.jms.QueueConnectionFactory</res-type>
  <res-auth>Application</res-auth>
  <res-sharing-scope>Unshareable</res-sharing-scope>
</resource-ref>
<resource-env-ref id="ResourceEnvRef_2">
  <description></description>
  <resource-env-ref-name>jms/MQ</resource-env-ref-name>
  <resource-env-ref-type>javax.jms.Queue</resource-env-ref-type>
</resource-env-ref>
```

Figure 12.37: JMS queue access using local connection administration to a remotely administered queue.

WebSphere Studio Application Developer facilitates writing the resource manager connection factory references and resource environment references for JMS clients that reside in J2EE containers. Figures 12.38 and 12.39 show the dialogs used to declare the connection and queue shown in Figure 12.37 for a J2EE application client component. Other J2EE components have similar dialogs, which Chapter 13 covers in detail. Note that Figure 12.39 shows a JNDI binding but Figure 12.38 shows none, since the resource exists locally. Also note that J2EE application client components' locally administered resources require manual declaration in client-resource.xmi, as shown previously in Figure 12.34.

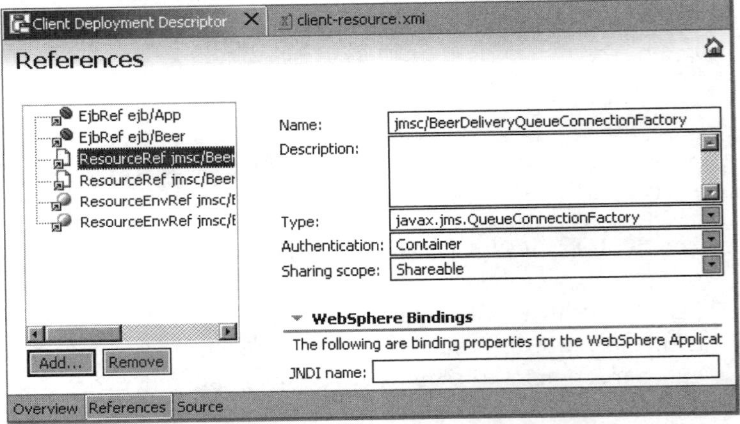

Figure 12.38: JMS client resource manager connection factory reference for a J2EE application client component.

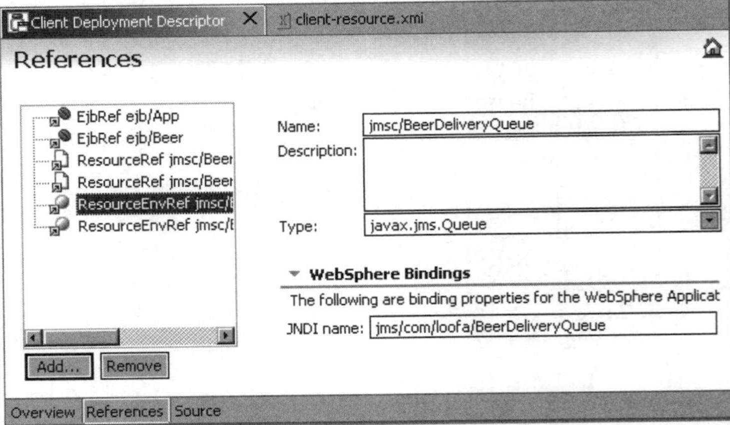

Figure 12.39: JMS client resource environment reference for a J2EE application client component.

Access from J2EE components: programmatic

The programmatic portion of the J2EE component has no dependency on whether the declarative portion defines access via a resource manager connection factory reference or a resource environment reference to an administered component. J2EE provides this independence by design.

To send a message to a queue, JMS clients perform the following steps, as shown in Figure 12.40:

1. Locate the factory and the queue via the JNDI API.
2. Use the factory to create a connection.
3. Establish a session using the connection.
4. Use the session to create a sender and a message.
5. Use the sender to send the message.
6. Make sure they close their connections.

```
QueueConnection queueConnection = null;
try {
  Context jndiContext = new InitialContext();
  QueueConnectionFactory queueConnectionFactory =
    (QueueConnectionFactory) jndiContext.lookup("java:comp/env/jms/MQCF");
  Queue queue = (Queue) jndiContext.lookup("java:comp/env/jms/MQ");
  queueConnection = queueConnectionFactory.createQueueConnection();
  QueueSession queueSession =
    queueConnection.createQueueSession(false, Session.AUTO_ACKNOWLEDGE);
  QueueSender queueSender = queueSession.createSender(queue);
  TextMessage textMessage = queueSession.createTextMessage();
  textMessage.setText("hey dude ...");
  queueSender.send(textMessage);
} catch (NamingException e) {
  e.printStackTrace(System.err);
} catch (JMSException e) {
  e.printStackTrace(System.err);
} finally {
  if (queueConnection != null) {
    try {
      queueConnection.close();
    } catch (JMSException e) {
      e.printStackTrace(System.err);
    }
  }
}
```

Figure 12.40: JMS client accessing a queue from a J2EE component.

To publish a message to a topic, JMS clients follow the same procedure but access a different API, as shown in Figure 12.41.

```
TopicConnection topicConnection = null;
try {
  Context jndiContext = new InitialContext();
  TopicConnectionFactory topicConnectionFactory =
    (TopicConnectionFactory) jndiContext.lookup("java:comp/env/jms/MTCF");
  Topic topic = (Topic) jndiContext.lookup("java:comp/env/jms/MT");
  topicConnection = topicConnectionFactory.createTopicConnection();
  TopicSession topicSession =
    topicConnection.createTopicSession(false, Session.AUTO_ACKNOWLEDGE);
  TopicPublisher topicPublisher = topicSession.createPublisher(topic);
  TextMessage message = topicSession.createTextMessage();
  message.setText("hey dude ...");
  topicPublisher.publish(message);
} catch (NamingException e) {
  e.printStackTrace(System.err);
} catch (JMSException e) {
  e.printStackTrace(System.err);
} finally {
  if (topicConnection != null) {
    try {
      topicConnection.close();
    } catch (JMSException e) {
      e.printStackTrace(System.err);
    }
  }
}
```

Figure 12.41: JMS client accessing a topic from a J2EE component.

Rolling your own access client

JMS clients not residing in J2EE containers have the same special considerations for accessing the JNDI API as do the EJB clients discussed earlier. They may not use local deployment descriptors to administer the connections, queues, and topics. They must look up the administered components from the regular JNDI namespace, as shown in Figure 12.42, rather than look them up in the Environment Naming Context (ENC) as J2EE components do.

```
QueueConnectionFactory queueConnectionFactory =
  (QueueConnectionFactory) jndiContext.lookup("jms/app/MQCF");
Queue queue = (Queue) jndiContext.lookup("jms/app/MQ");
...
TopicConnectionFactory topicConnectionFactory =
  (TopicConnectionFactory) jndiContext.lookup("jms/app/MTCF");
Topic topic = (Topic) jndiContext.lookup("jms/app/MT");
```

Figure 12.42: JMS topic and queue access from outside a J2EE container.

Enabling a client's JRE with JMS services requires some of the configuration already covered for rolling your own EJB client. JMS clients extend their JREs with the WebSphere MQ libraries as follows:

```
-Djava.ext.dirs="...C:\Program Files\IBM\WebSphere MQ\Java\lib;..."
```

Clients may access JMS without using JNDI, but using JMS in this manner makes clients fat.

Client transactions

Implementing transactions in a distributed system has proven through time to present the most daunting task in systems integration efforts. Competing technologies offer little alternative to J2EE's support for distributed transactions. Clients may combine as many XA interface compliant resources as they wish in a logical unit of work (LUW). The J2EE services issue a two-phase commit (2PC) on the client's behalf.

Whenever clients access XA interface compliant external resources, they may combine multiple requests to multiple components in a single transaction, where either all or none of the changes they make get committed. J2EE components have access to two bindings in the java:comp context: env for the environment naming context (ENC), and UserTransaction for the transaction context. Clients running in J2EE Web components and J2EE Enterprise components that manage their own transactions may use the transaction from this binding, as shown in Figures 12.43a and 12.43b.

```
try {
  Context jndiContext = new InitialContext();
  Context envContext = (Context) jndiContext.lookup("java:comp/env");

  UserTransaction transaction =
    (UserTransaction) jndiContext.lookup("java:comp/UserTransaction ");

  QueueConnection queueConnection = null;
  QueueConnectionFactory queueConnectionFactory =
    (QueueConnectionFactory) envContext.lookup(
      "jms/BeerDeliveryQueueConnectionFactory");
  Queue queue = (Queue) envContext.lookup("jms/BeerDeliveryQueue");
  queueConnection = queueConnectionFactory.createQueueConnection();
  QueueSession queueSession =
    queueConnection.createQueueSession(
      false,
      Session.AUTO_ACKNOWLEDGE);
  QueueSender queueSender = queueSession.createSender(queue);

  BeerHome beerHome = (BeerHome) envContext.lookup("ejb/Beer");
  Beer beer = beerHome.findByPrimaryKey("Loofa Brew");

  transaction.begin();
  beer.setPrice(0);
  TextMessage textMessage = queueSession.createTextMessage();
  textMessage.setText("deliver my beer dude");
  queueSender.send(textMessage);
  transaction.commit();

} catch (RemoteException e) {
  e.printStackTrace(System.err);
} catch (NamingException e) {
  e.printStackTrace(System.err);
} catch (JMSException e) {
  e.printStackTrace(System.err);
} catch (FinderException e) {
  e.printStackTrace(System.err);
```

Figure 12.43a: Using a transaction in a J2EE Web or Enterprise component.

```
} catch (NotSupportedException e) {
  e.printStackTrace(System.err);
} catch (SystemException e) {
  e.printStackTrace(System.err);
} catch (RollbackException e) {
  e.printStackTrace(System.err);
} catch (HeuristicMixedException e) {
  e.printStackTrace(System.err);
} catch (HeuristicRollbackException e) {
  e.printStackTrace(System.err);
}
```

Figure 12.43b: Using a transaction in a J2EE Web or Enterprise component.

J2EE application client components may also perform transactions, but they must access the transaction directly through JNDI as follows:

```
UserTransaction transaction =
  (UserTransaction) jndiContext.lookup("jta/usertransaction");
```

Access beans

Access beans generated by WebSphere Studio Application Developer provide a quick way to implement typical mechanisms to facilitate EJB access. They come in three flavors: Data Class (DCAB), Copy Helper (CHAB), and JavaBean Wrapper (JWAB).

This section discusses each Access bean in more detail, but it may be helpful to give an overview first. Table 12.1 summarizes the general characteristics of the available Access bean types. It shows whether or not EJB clients can use the Access bean to access the remote or local interface of a Session or Entity EJB. The Cardinality column indicates whether one or more Access beans may coexist for an EJB. The Caching column shows whether the Access bean caches data for Entity EJB clients.

Table 12.1: Summary of Access bean types.

Type	Remote	Local	Entity	Session	Cardinality	Caching	Factory
DCAB	Y	Y	Y	N	1..*n*	...	Y
JWAB	Y	N	Y	Y	1..1	N	Y
CHAB	Y	N	Y	N	1..1	Y	Y

All Access beans have the great benefit of offering a quick solution, yet this may come at the ominous price of a poor solution. JWABs for Entity EJBs in particular have the potential to make a poor solution. They access Entity EJBs remotely, which rarely makes good practice because every access to the JWAB may result in a database transaction. CHABs fix this problem by caching changes locally until the client issues a commit. However, solutions generally should avoid zealous access to Entity EJBs from outside the Enterprise container.

Access bean factory classes and DCABs offer the most modern design pattern. They use EJBs as designed, without an additional proxy. EJB clients use the factories to delegate some of the EJB programming complexity. EJB clients may also use DCABs to reduce the number of requests they make to an Entity EJB. This reduces time complexity and makes life easier for the transaction service.

Figure 12.44 shows how to tell WebSphere Studio Application Developer to generate Access beans.

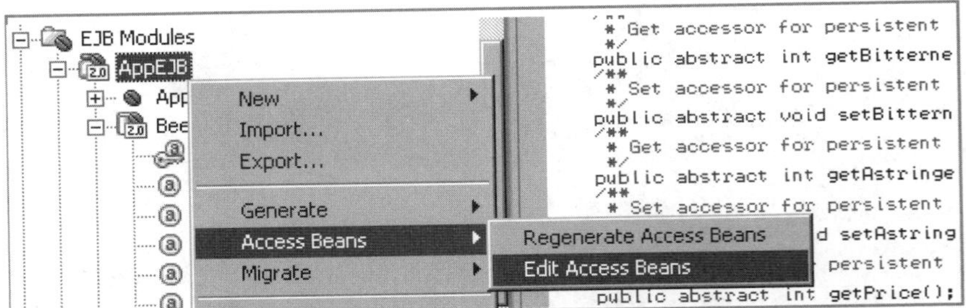

Figure 12.44: Telling WebSphere Studio Application Developer to generate Access beans.

Access bean factories

All Access bean types provide factory classes that facilitate EJB access. An EJB client may use the factory class with its default values or it may choose to supply its own values. Figure 12.45 shows an EJB client using a factory class with its default ORB configuration.

```
try {
  AppFactory appFactory = new AppFactory();
  App app = appFactory.create();
  app.processRequest("Loofa Brew");
} catch (RemoteException e) {
  e.printStackTrace(System.err);
} catch (CreateException e) {
  e.printStackTrace(System.err);
}
```

Figure 12.45: EJB client using an Access bean factory class with default JNDI values.

Figure 12.46 shows an EJB client using a factory class with custom values for the Initial Context Factory Name, the Initial Context Provider URL, and the JNDI Name.

```
try {
  AppFactory appFactory = new AppFactory();
  appFactory.setInitialContextFactoryName(
    "com.ibm.websphere.naming.WsnInitialContextFactory");
  appFactory.setInitialContextProviderURL(
    "corbaloc:iiop:loofa.com:2809");
  appFactory.setJNDIName("ejb/com/loofa/AppHome");
  App app = appFactory.create();
  app.processRequest("Loofa Brew");
} catch (RemoteException e) {
  e.printStackTrace(System.err);
} catch (CreateException e) {
  e.printStackTrace(System.err);
}
```

Figure 12.46: EJB client using an Access bean factory class with custom JNDI values.

Data Class Access beans

Data Class Access beans (DCABs), also known as DataClasses, provide separate, thin data classes that maintain copies of subsets of an Entity EJB's data. These copies keep track of changes to their data and know how to synchronize the changes with the actual Entity EJB. DCABs also provide factories for accessing Entity EJBs. DCABs provide Entity EJB clients with a mechanism to cache a copy of an Entity EJB's data locally. Any Entity EJB may have many associated DCABs containing subsets of data that suit various Entity EJB client needs. Figure 12.47 shows some DCABs in WebSphere Studio Application Developer's EJB Deployment Descriptor editor.

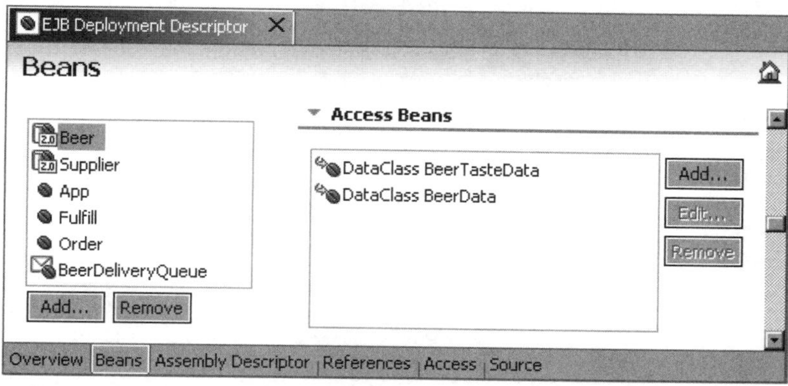

Figure 12.47: DCABs in EJB Deployment Descriptor Access beans view.

Figure 12.48 shows an Entity EJB's interface before and after generating a few DCABs. Note the extra sets of methods generated for getting, setting, and synchronizing related aggregations of data.

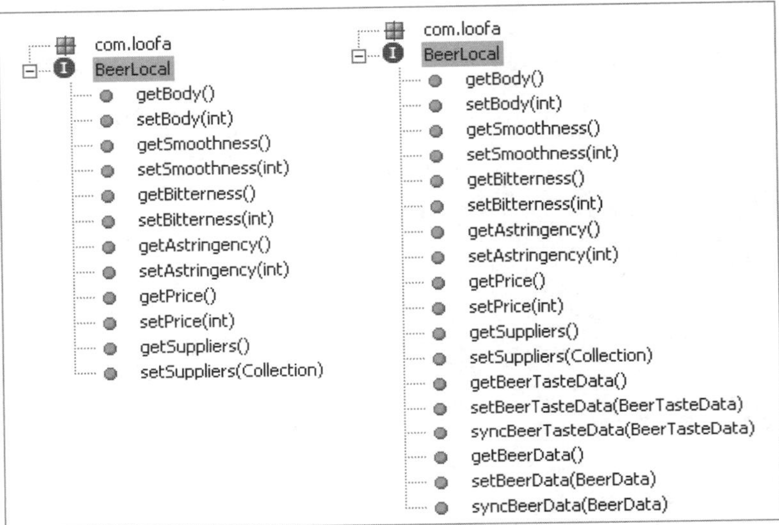

Figure 12.48: Entity EJB before and after generating some Data Class Access beans.

Figure 12.49 shows an Entity EJB client using a DCAB to set some data. The Entity EJB client makes only one call to the Entity EJB instead of the multiple calls required without the use of the DCAB.

```
try {
  BeerFactory beerFactory = new BeerFactory();
  beerFactory.setInitialContextFactoryName(
    "com.ibm.websphere.naming.WsnInitialContextFactory");
  beerFactory.setInitialContextProviderURL(
    "corbaloc:iiop:loofa.com:2809");
  beerFactory.setJNDIName("ejb/com/loofa/BeerHome");
  Beer beer = beerFactory.findByPrimaryKey("Loofa Brew");
  BeerTasteData beerTasteData = beer.getBeerTasteData();
  beerTasteData.setAstringency(24);
  beerTasteData.setBitterness(34);
  beer.syncBeerTasteData(beerTasteData);
} catch (RemoteException e) {
  e.printStackTrace(System.err);
} catch (FinderException e) {
  e.printStackTrace(System.err);
}
```

Figure 12.49: EJB client using a Data Class Access bean (DCAB) from an Entity EJB client.

JavaBean Wrapper Access beans

JavaBean Wrapper Access beans (JWABs), also known as Type1AccessBeans, provide a mechanism for clients to access remote interfaces of both Session and Entity EJBs via a generated proxy. Any EJB with a remote interface may have a JWAB. Figure 12.50 shows a JWAB in WebSphere Studio Application Developer's EJB Deployment Descriptor editor.

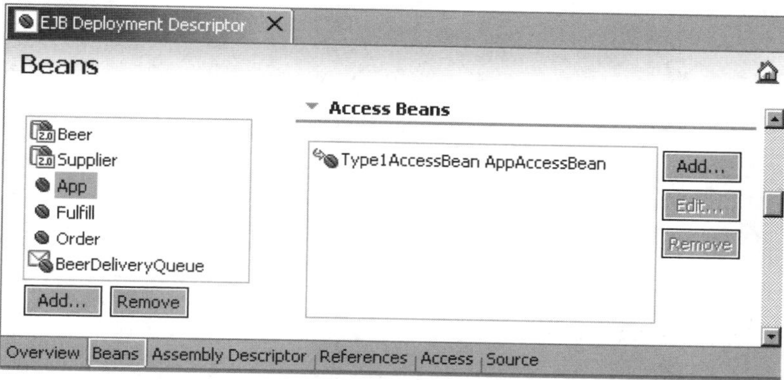

Figure 12.50: JWAB in EJB Deployment Descriptor Access beans view.

Figure 12.51 shows an EJB client using a JWAB to access an EJB. Note that the EJB client needs only to create a JWAB to access the EJB, but it may also configure some custom ORB properties.

```
try {
  // optionally set some custom configuration properties
  AppAccessBean.setInit_GlobalNameServiceTypeName(
    "com.ibm.websphere.naming.WsnInitialContextFactory");
  AppAccessBean.setInit_GlobalNameServiceURLName(
    "corbaloc:iiop:loofa.com:2809");
  AppAccessBean appAccessBean = new AppAccessBean();
  appAccessBean.processRequest("Loofa Brew");
} catch (RemoteException e) {
  e.printStackTrace(System.err);
} catch (NamingException e) {
  e.printStackTrace(System.err);
} catch (CreateException e) {
  e.printStackTrace(System.err);
}
```

Figure 12.51: EJB client using a JavaBean Wrapper Access bean (JWAB).

Copy Helper Access beans

Copy Helper Access beans (CHABs), also known as Type2AccessBeans, provide a mechanism for clients to access remote interfaces of Entity EJBs via generated proxies that cache the EJB's data locally. Only Entity EJBs with remote interfaces may have a CHAB. Figure 12.52 shows an Entity EJB client using a CHAB to set data locally before making the commit call that sets the data in the actual Entity EJB.

```
try {
  BeerAccessBean beerAccessBean = new BeerAccessBean();
  // optionally set some custom configuration properties
  beerAccessBean.setInit_GlobalNameServiceTypeName(
    "com.ibm.websphere.naming.WsnInitialContextFactory");
  beerAccessBean.setInit_GlobalNameServiceURLName(
    "corbaloc:iiop:loofa.com:2809");
  beerAccessBean.setInit_JNDIName("ejb/com/loofa/BeerHome");
  beerAccessBean.setInit_primaryKey("Loofa Brew");
  beerAccessBean.setAstringency(89);
  beerAccessBean.setPrice(34);
  beerAccessBean.commitCopyHelper();
} catch (RemoteException e) {
  e.printStackTrace(System.err);
} catch (NamingException e) {
  e.printStackTrace(System.err);
} catch (CreateException e) {
  e.printStackTrace(System.err);
} catch (FinderException e) {
  e.printStackTrace(System.err);
}
```

Figure 12.52: EJB client using a Copy Helper Access bean (CHAB).

J2EE Web container clients

Because so many existing applications only support access via Web protocols, many components may need to access other components using Web protocols. The chapters on J2EE Web components cover details on accessing J2EE Web components from browsers and other J2EE Web components. J2EE application client components and J2EE Enterprise components must roll their own access to Web components (components accessible via Web protocols, whether J2EE or otherwise).

Access to Web components requires only a standard JRE (J2SE). Web clients use standard JRE communications APIs to perform the access. Figure 12.53 shows a Web client accessing a Web component.

```
try {
  // create a URLConnection to the Web Component
  URL url = new URL("http://loofa.com/AppWeb/AppServlet");
  URLConnection con = url.openConnection();
  con.setUseCaches(false);
  // set a header
  con.setRequestProperty("headerName", "headerValue");
  // create the input stream
  BufferedReader in =
    new BufferedReader(new InputStreamReader(con.getInputStream()));
  //display the document
  String data = in.readLine();
  while (data != null) {
    System.out.println(data);
    data = in.readLine();
  }
  in.close();
} catch (MalformedURLException e) {
  e.printStackTrace(System.err);
} catch (IOException e) {
  e.printStackTrace(System.err);
}
```

Figure 12.53: Web component access from a Java client.

J2EE Application Client container clients

The technologies covered so far require clients to poll servers for information. Polling technology may prove inadequate for solutions in which clients spend time waiting for different things to happen. Such solutions may opt for the server to post information to the client. Therefore, in addition to making requests to other J2EE components or services, J2EE application client components may wish to service requests. No declarative mechanism exists in J2EE 1.3 to enable a J2EE application client component to receive requests. However, with a little effort, J2EE application client components can use the existing Java Messaging Service (JMS) or Object Request Broker (ORB) services to achieve this.

Access using JMS

Using JMS to asynchronously receive information posted to J2EE application client component involves implementing a listener and attaching it to a queue or a topic. In this manner J2EE application client components, like any other Java client, may listen for messages from queues, and may also listen for messages from topics to which they subscribe. This allows clients to access J2EE application client components similarly to how they access MDBs.

Regardless of whether the J2EE application client component wishes to listen to a queue or a topic, it must implement a listener, as shown in Figure 12.54.

```
private class MListener implements MessageListener {
  public void onMessage(Message message) {
    try {
      System.out.println("got: " + ((TextMessage) message).getText());
    } catch (JMSException e) {
      e.printStackTrace(System.err);
    }
  }
}
```

Figure 12.54: A client JMS listener.

Depending on whether the client wishes to listen to a queue or a topic, it uses a similar procedure but different JMS API. When listening to a topic, it may choose to subscribe in a durable or nondurable manner. Durable subscriptions have the benefit of outliving connections, allowing the client to receive all messages from the time they subscribe until they unsubscribe, whether or not they remain connected for the duration of the subscription. If a client disconnects or loses a connection while having a durable subscription, the messages get persisted until the client reconnects. This technology requires the client to identify itself with a unique identifier while subscribing. Figures 12.55a and 12.55b show a client making a durable subscription to a JMS topic.

```
public void subscribe() {
  try {
    Context jndiContext = new InitialContext();
    TopicConnectionFactory topicConnectionFactory =
      (TopicConnectionFactory)
      jndiContext.lookup("java:comp/env/jms/MTCF");
    topicConnection = topicConnectionFactory.createTopicConnection();
    topicSession = topicConnection.createTopicSession(false,
      Session.AUTO_ACKNOWLEDGE);
    Topic topic = (Topic) jndiContext.lookup("java:comp/env/jms/MT");
    topicSubscriber = topicSession.createDurableSubscriber(topic, "subId");
    topicSubscriber.setMessageListener(new MListener());
    topicConnection.start();
  } catch (NamingException e) {
    e.printStackTrace(System.err);
  } catch (JMSException e) {
    e.printStackTrace(System.err);
  }
}
```

Figure 12.55a: A durable subscriber client to a JMS topic.

```
public void unsubscribe() {
  try {
    topicSubscriber.close();
    topicSession.unsubscribe("subId");
    topicSession.close();
    topicConnection.close();
  } catch (JMSException e) {
    e.printStackTrace(System.err);
  }
}
```

Figure 12.55b: A durable subscriber client to a JMS topic.

A client uses a nondurable subscription if it wishes to receive only messages published during the connection period. A nondurable subscription requires no unique identifier while subscribing. Figure 12.56 shows a client making a nondurable subscription to a JMS topic.

```
public void subscribe() {
  try {
    Context jndiContext = new InitialContext();
    TopicConnectionFactory topicConnectionFactory =
      (TopicConnectionFactory)
      jndiContext.lookup("java:comp/env/jms/MTCF");
    topicConnection = topicConnectionFactory.createTopicConnection();
    topicSession = topicConnection.createTopicSession(false,
      Session.AUTO_ACKNOWLEDGE);
    Topic topic = (Topic) jndiContext.lookup("java:comp/env/jms/MT");
    topicSubscriber = topicSession.createSubscriber(topic);
    topicSubscriber.setMessageListener(new MListener());
    topicConnection.start();
  } catch (NamingException e) {
    e.printStackTrace(System.err);
  } catch (JMSException e) {
    e.printStackTrace(System.err);
  }
}

public void unsubscribe() {
  try {
    topicSubscriber.close();
    topicSession.close();
    topicConnection.close();
  } catch (JMSException e) {
    e.printStackTrace(System.err);
  }
}
```

Figure 12.56: A nondurable subscriber client to a JMS topic.

Finally, clients may listen for messages from queues, though typical solution design considerations make this a rare case. Applications typically use MDBs to listen to queues and process business logic as opposed to client logic. Figure 12.57 shows a client listening for messages on a queue.

```
public void subscribe() {
  try {
    Context jndiContext = new InitialContext();
    QueueConnectionFactory queueConnectionFactory =
      (QueueConnectionFactory)
      jndiContext.lookup("java:comp/env/jms/MQCF");
    queueConnection = queueConnectionFactory.createQueueConnection();
    queueSession = queueConnection.createQueueSession(false,
      Session.AUTO_ACKNOWLEDGE);
    Queue queue = (Queue) jndiContext.lookup("java:comp/env/jms/MQ");
    queueReceiver = queueSession.createReceiver(queue);
    queueReceiver.setMessageListener(new MListener());
    queueConnection.start();
  } catch (NamingException e) {
    e.printStackTrace(System.err);
  } catch (JMSException e) {
    e.printStackTrace(System.err);
  }
}

public void unsubscribe() {
  try {
      queueReceiver.close();
      queueSession.close();
      queueConnection.close();
  } catch (JMSException e) {
    e.printStackTrace(System.err);
  }
}
```

Figure 12.57: A receiver client for a JMS queue.

Access using the ORB

Using the ORB to allow clients to access a J2EE application client component involves programmatically performing some of the same tasks that J2EE Enterprise containers perform for EJBs. The J2EE application client component must create a remote object, export it, and register it with JNDI or otherwise publish it. This allows clients to access J2EE Application Clients components similarly to how they access EJBs.

First, the J2EE application client component must define a remote interface to declare the access methods available to its clients. An example of a remote interface for an ORB proxy follows:

```
public interface Listener extends Remote {
  public void processRequest(String message) throws RemoteException;
}
```

The J2EE application client component then implements the remote interface with the appropriate behavior:

```
public class ListenerImplementation implements Listener {
  public void processRequest(String message) {
    System.out.println("JACS client said: " + message);
  }
}
```

The J2EE application client component must also create the necessary ORB code using the remote method invocation compiler (rmic) as follows:

```
rmic -keep -iiop ListenerImplementation
```

At runtime, the J2EE application client component must export its listener component. It may give other clients access to the listener component either by registering it in the JNDI namespace or by calling another component's registration method. Figure 12.58 shows a component exporting and registering its listener remote interface.

```
Listener listener = new ListenerImplementation();
try {
  Context context = new InitialContext();
  PortableRemoteObject.exportObject(listener);
  // register with JNDI
  context.rebind("client/listener42", listener);
  // or call another component and pass the remote reference
  someEJayBee.talkToMe(listener);
} catch (NamingException e) {
    e.printStackTrace(System.err);
} catch (RemoteException e) {
    e.printStackTrace(System.err);
}
```

Figure 12.58: J2EE application client component registering a listener remote interface.

Available client models

Up until this point this chapter describes clients in terms of the J2EE components that they access. The focus now turns to the clients themselves. Of the overwhelming combinations of access technologies that exist, IBM provides a few common client environments for installation. They include J2EE Application Client, ActiveX to EJB bridge, Applet Client, Thin Application Client, and Pluggable Application Client.

WebSphere J2EE Application Client provides the simplest way for clients to run J2EE Application Client containers. It installs all the necessary services and configures the client system to launch J2EE application client components.

WebSphere ActiveX to EJB bridge allows ActiveX programs to access EJBs using WebSphere-provided ActiveX automation objects. WebSphere achieves this by JRE enabling any ActiveX automation container, such as Visual Basic, VBScript, and Active Server Pages (ASP). Clients can use the bridge to provide access directly to application clients or to extend access through other services.

WebSphere Applet Client provides a JRE plugin for browsers, simplifying the task of configuring a browser JRE to access J2EE Enterprise components. The client needs only to run the WebSphere Applet Client installation and perform minimal plugin configuration.

WebSphere Thin Application Client provides clients with enough services to access J2EE components, but lacks the full support of a J2EE Application Client container. The chapter discusses this in more detail in the "roll your own access" sections. WebSphere can install the appropriate services and simplify the configuration.

WebSphere Pluggable Application Client supports installing the Thin Application Client to run with other vendor JREs. The installation checks to make sure the client already has a supported JRE installed. IBM currently supports Sun JRE versions 1.3.1_03, 1.3.1_04, 1.3.2_01, and 1.3.3_01. Clients may experience limited success with other JREs.

Web Services clients

As many in the industry herald the arrival of Web Services as an incredible innovation, J2EE contents itself with a somber nod and dutiful adaptation of existing J2EE services. Naturally, this causes concerns over the extent to which existing J2EE services might need enhancement. To this end, IBM leads an effort to standardize Web Services for J2EE; refer to Java Specification Request (JSR) 109, currently in its final stages. Web Services clients merit a place alongside J2EE component clients in this chapter due to limited similarities in the technologies. Both provide mechanisms for *distributing* a system. J2EE, however, offers the bulk of its services to the *concerns* that arise in distributed systems, namely those arising in systems integration.

Much like a client to an EJB, a Web Service client must first locate a Web Service and then talk to it. However, whereas EJB clients reference EJBs by name, Web Services clients have the greatly touted benefit of not requiring a particular Web Service name. An EJB client finds an EJB by name, but a Web Service client might find a Web Service by description. Recall that a J2EE Enterprise container binds an EJB in a persistent naming service via JNDI. Similarly, a Web Service provider publishes a Web Service to a Web Service broker via Universal Description Discovery and Integration (UDDI). The big difference lies in what gets bound or published for clients to see. EJB clients see an EJB interface. Web Services clients see Web Services Description Language (WSDL).

While the industry deliberates over details on how J2EE services might best aid in the deployment, lookup, and invocation of Web Services, WebSphere Application Server supports the basic requirements. WebSphere Application Server and WebSphere Studio Application Developer currently provide support for exposing J2EE components as Web Services and using proxies to simplify client access to Web Services.

This section details how to read a Web Service's WSDL manually and use Simple Object Access Protocol (SOAP) to talk to it. It also shows how to use WebSphere Studio Application Developer to automate this task. Clients use either SOAP Remote Procedure Call (RPC) or SOAP Document Exchange to send messages to the Web Service. In SOAP RPC, the message invokes an operation and provides its arguments. In SOAP Document Exchange, the message carries a document that the recipient must interpret.

SOAP RPC clients

Clients must make an RPC call if they want to call an operation in WSDL that uses a SOAP RPC binding. The client must obtain all the appropriate information from WSDL to make the call. The following snippets provide an indication of how the WSDL maps to the Web Service SOAP RPC client code. Figures 12.59a and 12.59b show some WSDL for a quote RPC Web Service. The important information needed by a client to make a call to it appears in bold.

```
<?xml version="1.0" encoding="UTF-8"?>
<wsdl:definitions
  name="QuoteServiceRPC"
  targetNamespace="http://loofa.com/QuoteServiceRPC"
  xmlns:loofa="http://loofa.com/QuoteServiceRPC"
  xmlns:soap="http://schemas.xmlsoap.org/wsdl/soap/"
  xmlns:wsdl="http://schemas.xmlsoap.org/wsdl/"
  xmlns:xsd="http://www.w3.org/1999/XMLSchema">
  <wsdl:message name="quoteRequestMessage">
```

Figure 12.59a: Web Service WSDL for RPC.

```
    <wsdl:part name="genre" type="xsd:string" />
  </wsdl:message>
  <wsdl:message name="quoteResponseMessage">
    <wsdl:part name="quote" type="xsd:string" />
  </wsdl:message>
  <wsdl:portType name="QuotePortType">
    <wsdl:operation name="getQuote" parameterOrder="genre">
      <wsdl:input name="getQuoteRequest"
        message="loofa:quoteRequestMessage" />
      <wsdl:output name="getQuoteResponse"
        message="loofa:quoteResponseMessage" />
    </wsdl:operation>
  </wsdl:portType>
  <wsdl:binding name="QuoteBinding" type="loofa:QuotePortType">
    <soap:binding style="rpc"
      transport="http://schemas.xmlsoap.org/soap/http" />
    <wsdl:operation name="getQuote">
      <soap:operation soapAction="" style="rpc" />
      <wsdl:input name="getQuoteRequest">
        <soap:body
          encodingStyle="http://schemas.xmlsoap.org/soap/encoding/"
          namespace="http://loofa.com/QuoteServiceRPC"
          parts="genre" use="encoded" />
      </wsdl:input>
      <wsdl:output name="getQuoteResponse">
        <soap:body
          encodingStyle="http://schemas.xmlsoap.org/soap/encoding/"
          namespace="http://loofa.com/QuoteServiceRPC" use="encoded" />
      </wsdl:output>
    </wsdl:operation>
  </wsdl:binding>
  <wsdl:service name="QuoteServiceRPC">
    <wsdl:port name="QuotePort" binding="loofa:QuoteBinding">
      <soap:address
        location="http://loofa.com:80/WebServices/RPCRouter" />
    </wsdl:port>
  </wsdl:service>
</wsdl:definitions>
```

Figure 12.59b: Web Service WSDL for RPC.

The Web Service SOAP RPC client uses information taken from WSDL to access the Web Service. Figure 12.60 shows a Web Service SOAP RPC client requesting a literary quote from the quote Web Service defined in Figure 12.59. The Web Service SOAP RPC client code that comes directly from the WSDL appears in bold.

```
package com.loofa;
import java.net.MalformedURLException;
import java.net.URL;
import java.util.Vector;

import org.apache.soap.Constants;
import org.apache.soap.SOAPException;
import org.apache.soap.rpc.Call;
import org.apache.soap.rpc.Parameter;
import org.apache.soap.rpc.Response;

public class QuoteServiceRPCClient {
  public static void main(String args[]) {
    Call call = new Call();
    call.setMethodName("getQuote");
    call.setEncodingStyleURI(Constants.NS_URI_SOAP_ENC);
    call.setTargetObjectURI("http://loofa.com/QuoteServiceRPC");
    Vector params = new Vector();
    params.addElement(
      new Parameter(
        "genre",
        java.lang.String.class,
        "literary",
        Constants.NS_URI_SOAP_ENC));
    call.setParams(params);
    try {
      Response response =
        call.invoke(
          new URL("http://loofa.com:80/WebServices/RPCRouter"), "");
      System.out.println(
        "quote: " + response.getReturnValue().getValue());
    } catch (MalformedURLException e) {
      e.printStackTrace(System.err);
    } catch (SOAPException e) {
      e.printStackTrace(System.err);
    }
  }
}
```

Figure 12.60: Web Service SOAP RPC client.

Executing the Web Service SOAP RPC client in Figure 12.60 causes the SOAP engine to generate the expected Web Service SOAP RPC request shown in Figure 12.61.

```
POST /WebServices/RPCRouter HTTP/1.0
Host: loofa.com:80
Content-Type: text/xml; charset=utf-8
Content-Length: 468
SOAPAction: ""

<?xml version='1.0' encoding='UTF-8'?>
<SOAP-ENV:Envelope
  xmlns:SOAP-ENV="http://schemas.xmlsoap.org/soap/envelope/"
  xmlns:xsi="http://www.w3.org/2001/XMLSchema-instance"
  xmlns:xsd="http://www.w3.org/2001/XMLSchema">
  <SOAP-ENV:Body>
    <ns1:getQuote xmlns:ns1="http://loofa.com/QuoteServiceRPC"
      SOAP-ENV:encodingStyle="http://schemas.xmlsoap.org/soap/encoding/">
      <genre xsi:type="xsd:string">literary</genre>
    </ns1:getQuote>
  </SOAP-ENV:Body>
</SOAP-ENV:Envelope>
```

Figure 12.61: Generated request from the Web Service SOAP RPC client.

Finally, the SOAP engine translates the response for the Web Service SOAP RPC client. The Web Service SOAP RPC client receives the response shown in Figures 12.62a and 12.62b.

```
HTTP/1.1 200 OK
Server: WebSphere Application Server/5.0
Set-Cookie: JSESSIONID=0000FRLSABSEDWE2IHRUYSNFYJY:-1;Path=/
Cache-Control: no-cache="set-cookie,set-cookie2"
Expires: Thu, 01 Dec 1994 16:00:00 GMT
Content-Type: text/xml; charset=utf-8
Content-Length: 531
Content-Language: en-US
Connection: close

<?xml version='1.0' encoding='UTF-8'?>
<SOAP-ENV:Envelope
  xmlns:SOAP-ENV="http://schemas.xmlsoap.org/soap/envelope/"
  xmlns:xsi="http://www.w3.org/2001/XMLSchema-instance"
  xmlns:xsd="http://www.w3.org/2001/XMLSchema">
  <SOAP-ENV:Body>
```

Figure 12.62a: Response to the Web Service SOAP RPC client.

```
    <ns1:getQuoteResponse
      xmlns:ns1="http://loofa.com/QuoteServiceRPC"
      SOAP-ENV:encodingStyle="http://schemas.xmlsoap.org/soap/encoding/">
      <return xsi:type="xsd:string">
        Men are jerks, women are psychotic -- Kurt Vonnegut
      </return>
    </ns1:getQuoteResponse>
  </SOAP-ENV:Body>
</SOAP-ENV:Envelope>
```

Figure 12.62b: Response to the Web Service SOAP RPC client.

SOAP Document Exchange clients

Clients must send a message and receive a response if they want to use an operation in WSDL that uses a SOAP Document Exchange binding. Just as with SOAP RPC, clients obtain all the appropriate information from WSDL to make the exchange. The following snippets provide an indication of how the WSDL maps to the Web Service SOAP Document Exchange client code. Figures 12.63a and 12.63b show some WSDL for a quote Document Exchange Web Service. The important information needed by a client to make a call to it appears in bold.

```
<?xml version="1.0" encoding="UTF-8"?>
<wsdl:definitions name="QuoteServiceDEX"
targetNamespace="http://loofa.com/QuoteServiceDEX"
xmlns:loofa="http://loofa.com/QuoteServiceDEX"
xmlns:xsd="http://www.w3.org/1999/XMLSchema"
xmlns:soap="http://schemas.xmlsoap.org/wsdl/soap/"
xmlns:wsdl="http://schemas.xmlsoap.org/wsdl/">
  <wsdl:types>
    <xsd:schema xmlns:xsd="http://www.w3.org/2001/XMLSchema"
      elementFormDefault="qualified"
      targetNamespace="http://loofa.com/QuoteServiceDEX">
      <xsd:element name="quoteRequest">
        <xsd:complexType>
          <xsd:sequence>
           <xsd:element name="genre" type="xsd:string" />
          </xsd:sequence>
        </xsd:complexType>
      </xsd:element>
      <xsd:element name="quoteResponse">
        <xsd:complexType>
          <xsd:sequence>
```

Figure 12.63a: Web Service WSDL for Document Exchange.

```
            <xsd:element name="quote" type="xsd:string" />
          </xsd:sequence>
        </xsd:complexType>
      </xsd:element>
      <xsd:element name="string" nillable="true" type="xsd:string" />
    </xsd:schema>
  </wsdl:types>
  <wsdl:message name="quoteRequestMessage">
    <wsdl:part name="body" element="loofa:quoteRequest" />
  </wsdl:message>
  <wsdl:message name="quoteResponseMessage">
    <wsdl:part name="body" element="loofa:quoteResponse" />
  </wsdl:message>
  <wsdl:portType name="QuotePortType">
    <wsdl:operation name="getQuote">
      <wsdl:input message="loofa:quoteRequestMessage" />
      <wsdl:output message="loofa:quoteResponseMessage" />
    </wsdl:operation>
  </wsdl:portType>
  <wsdl:binding name="QuoteBinding" type="loofa:QuotePortType">
    <soap:binding style="document"
      transport="http://schemas.xmlsoap.org/soap/http" />
    <wsdl:operation name="getQuote">
      <soap:operation
        soapAction="http://loofa.com/QuoteServiceDEX"
        style="document" />
      <wsdl:input>
        <soap:body use="literal" />
      </wsdl:input>
      <wsdl:output>
        <soap:body use="literal" />
      </wsdl:output>
    </wsdl:operation>
  </wsdl:binding>
  <wsdl:service name="QuoteServiceDEX">
    <wsdl:port name="QuotePort" binding="loofa:QuoteBinding">
      <soap:address
        location="http://loofa.com:80/WebServices/DEXRouter" />
    </wsdl:port>
  </wsdl:service>
</wsdl:definitions>
```

Figure 12.63b: Web Service WSDL for Document Exchange.

Just as with an RPC Web Service, a Web Service SOAP Document Exchange client uses information taken from WSDL to access the Web Service. Figures 12.64a and 12.64b show a Web Service SOAP Document Exchange client requesting a literary quote from the quote Web Service in Figure 12.63. The Web Service SOAP Document Exchange client code that comes directly from the WSDL appears in bold.

```
package com.loofa;
import java.io.ByteArrayInputStream;
import java.io.IOException;
import java.net.MalformedURLException;
import java.net.URL;
import java.util.Vector;

import javax.xml.parsers.DocumentBuilderFactory;
import javax.xml.parsers.FactoryConfigurationError;
import javax.xml.parsers.ParserConfigurationException;

import org.apache.soap.Body;
import org.apache.soap.Envelope;
import org.apache.soap.SOAPException;
import org.apache.soap.messaging.Message;
import org.apache.xml.serialize.TextSerializer;
import org.w3c.dom.Document;
import org.w3c.dom.Element;
import org.xml.sax.SAXException;

public class QuoteServiceDEXClient {
  public static void main(String args[]) {
    try {
      String cannedRequest =
        "<quoteRequest xmlns=\"http://loofa.com/QuoteServiceDEX\">" +
        "  <genre>literary</genre>" +
        "</quoteRequest>";

      // create message envelope and body
      Envelope outEnvelope = new Envelope();
      Body outBody = new Body();
      Document doc =
        DocumentBuilderFactory.newInstance().newDocumentBuilder().parse(
          new ByteArrayInputStream(cannedRequest.getBytes()));
      Vector vector = new Vector();
      vector.add(doc.getDocumentElement());
      outBody.setBodyEntries(vector);
      outEnvelope.setBody(outBody);

      // create and send message
      Message message = new Message();
      URL url = new URL("http://loofa.com:80/WebServices/DEXRouter");
      message.send(url, "", outEnvelope);
```

Figure 12.64a: Web Service SOAP Document Exchange client.

```
      // receive response envelope
      Envelope inEnvelope = message.receiveEnvelope();
      Body inBody = inEnvelope.getBody();
      java.util.Vector v = inBody.getBodyEntries();
      Element element = (Element) v.firstElement();
      TextSerializer textSerializer = new TextSerializer();
      textSerializer.setOutputByteStream(System.out);
      textSerializer.serialize(element);
    } catch (MalformedURLException e) {
      e.printStackTrace(System.err);
    } catch (SAXException e) {
      e.printStackTrace(System.err);
    } catch (IOException e) {
      e.printStackTrace(System.err);
    } catch (ParserConfigurationException e) {
      e.printStackTrace(System.err);
    } catch (FactoryConfigurationError e) {
      e.printStackTrace(System.err);
    } catch (SOAPException e) {
      e.printStackTrace(System.err);
    }
  }
}
```

Figure 12.64b: Web Service SOAP Document Exchange client.

Executing the Web Service SOAP Document Exchange client in Figure 12.64 causes the SOAP engine to generate the expected Web Service SOAP Document Exchange request shown in Figure 12.65.

```
POST /WebServices/DEXRouter HTTP/1.0
Host: loofa.com:9080
Content-Type: text/xml; charset=utf-8
Content-Length: 384
SOAPAction: ""

<?xml version='1.0' encoding='UTF-8'?>
<SOAP-ENV:Envelope
  xmlns:SOAP-ENV="http://schemas.xmlsoap.org/soap/envelope/"
  xmlns:xsi="http://www.w3.org/2001/XMLSchema-instance"
  xmlns:xsd="http://www.w3.org/2001/XMLSchema">
  <SOAP-ENV:Body>
    <quoteRequest xmlns="http://loofa.com/QuoteServiceDEX">
      <genre>literary</genre>
    </quoteRequest>
  </SOAP-ENV:Body>
</SOAP-ENV:Envelope>
```

Figure 12.65: Generated request from the Web Service SOAP Document Exchange client.

Finally, the SOAP engine translates the response for the Web Service SOAP Document Exchange client. The Web Service SOAP Document Exchange client receives the response shown in Figure 12.66.

```
HTTP/1.1 200 OK
Server: WebSphere Application Server/5.0
Set-Cookie: JSESSIONID=0000PFVAQBGM2OAEAAMP2IMZG0I:-1;Path=/
Cache-Control: no-cache="set-cookie,set-cookie2"
Expires: Thu, 01 Dec 1994 16:00:00 GMT
Content-Type: text/xml
Content-Length: 458
Content-Language: en-US
Connection: close

<?xml version="1.0" encoding="UTF-8"?>
<SOAP-ENV:Envelope
  xmlns:SOAP-ENV="http://schemas.xmlsoap.org/soap/envelope/"
  xmlns:xsd="http://www.w3.org/2001/XMLSchema"
  xmlns:xsi="http://www.w3.org/2001/XMLSchema-instance">
  <SOAP-ENV:Body>
    <quoteResponse xmlns="http://loofa.com/QuoteServiceDEX">
      <quote>
        I am afraid we are not rid of God because we still have
        faith in grammar -- Friedrich Nietzsche
      </quote>
    </quoteResponse>
  </SOAP-ENV:Body>
</SOAP-ENV:Envelope>
```

Figure 12.66: Response to the Web Service SOAP Document Exchange client.

Web Service client proxies

WebSphere Studio Application Developer greatly simplifies the task of creating Web Service clients. It reads a Web Service's WSDL and generates a proxy for Web Service clients to use. Simply select the WSDL source of the Web Service and tell WebSphere Studio Application Developer to generate a proxy, as shown in Figure 12.67.

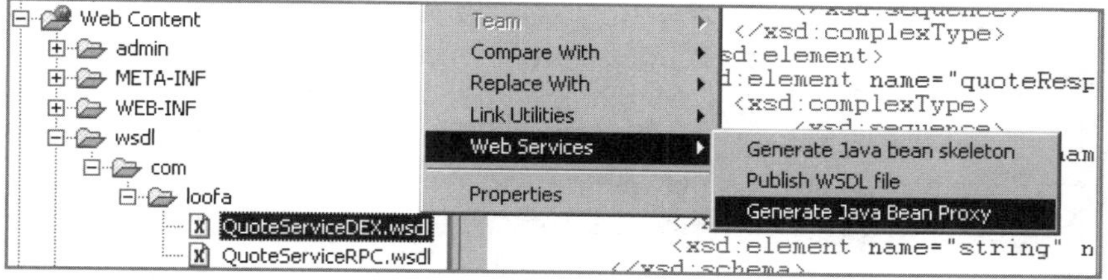

Figure 12.67: Telling WSAD to generate a Web Service Proxy.

The generated proxies perform the same tasks as the code written earlier. Web Service clients use the proxies differently depending on whether the Web Service binds as RPC or Document Exchange. Figure 12.68 shows a client using a proxy to access a RPC Web Service. Figure 12.69 shows a client using a proxy to access a Document Exchange Web Service.

```
public static void main(String args[]) {
  QuoteServiceRPCProxy p = new QuoteServiceRPCProxy();
  try {
    String quote = p.getQuote("literary");
    System.out.println("quote: " + quote);
  } catch (Exception e) {
    e.printStackTrace(System.err);
  }
}
```

Figure 12.68: Using the Web Service RPC proxy.

```
public static void main(String args[]) {
  QuoteServiceDEXProxy p = new QuoteServiceDEXProxy();
  QuoteRequestElement request = new QuoteRequestElement();
  request.setGenre("literary");
  try {
    QuoteResponseElement response = p.getQuote(request);
    System.out.println("quote: " + response.getQuote());
  } catch (Exception e) {
    e.printStackTrace(System.err);
  }
}
```

Figure 12.69: Using the Web Service Document Exchange proxy.

Best practices

The more services a client interacts directly with, the more complex the client becomes, eventually earning the moniker of fat client. J2EE attempts to manage this complexity by relegating the fat client to a J2EE container, where it must take the form of a J2EE component. The J2EE container provides the J2EE component with standard seamless integration of the services and offers it the ability to interact with the services declaratively as well as programmatically. However, rarely will a single J2EE component suit the client best, so it gets chopped here and there to make it suitable to one or more J2EE components. Chopping the client up in this manner separates its concerns to suit the J2EE services.

Solution designers must balance the temptation to chop a solution into bits with the need to have components that provide function. Remember that each chop to a system exposes details, leading to increased complexity. The key to success lies in exposing the necessary details to plug into the right services.

Solution designers distinguish between functional and nonfunctional concerns. The burden lies on the solution designer to align each chop with a separation of these concerns. Traditional solution designs usually chop along the lines separating a solution's functional concerns. However, the key to a successful solution design lies in the ability to avoid chopping through nonfunctional concerns. This ability comes with the intimate understanding of the underlying services gained through experience. In fact, a solution that makes the best use of available services may appear a bit awkward at first.

Take Christian's BierHaus for instance. Christian's BierHaus illustrates the difference between functional and nonfunctional concerns. It also provides a familiar setting to introduce a few best practices.

Christian's BierHaus has very simple functional concerns. Qualified customers may request and consume beer. Customers must pay for the beer before they leave. When Sven raises a brow, Inga knows to get a beer. As Olaf watches Inga's antics at the head of the steps, he knows to conjure up some brew. Sven has little concern for Olaf's beer cellar, and Olaf has even less for Sven's furrowed brow. Neither Inga nor Olaf shows any concern for how Brutalix gets Sven to fork over his shekels. Or so it seems to the casual observer. In truth, a veritable symphony takes place the moment Sven raises a brow.

Nonfunctional concerns make or break Christian's BierHaus. How long must a customer wait for a beer? How well can a customer rely on getting a beer once they request it? Can a customer count on the availability of beer? Can Christian manage the process? How many customers get away without paying, or pay too much? How many unqualified customers quaff his beer? Et cetera. Christian wants the beer to flow smoothly, regardless of the new magistrate, the carnival rolling through, or Olaf taking leave of his senses, so he hires only the best staff from top-notch Swiss hotel schools that execute the underlying services flawlessly. These nonfunctional concerns have become known as "ilities": adaptability, affordability, agility, availability, capacity, complexity, composability, debuggability, evolvability, extensability, flexibility, interoperability, maintainability, manageability, performance, portability, predictability, quality, reliability, reusability, scalability, security, simplicity, survivability, testability, understandability, usability, and so forth.

Successful solution designs separate the solution concerns and align the components with the appropriate services. Some best practices have precipitated over time, but take heed that without moderation, best practices always tend to degenerate to worst practices. The use of one best practice tends to have a cascading effect, causing the need for other best practices, which may in some cases overcomplicate the solution.

Isolate data

Christian's BierHaus: As Jack swaggers into Christian's and hollers at Inga, he adds a discordant note to the dignified tone of the establishment, but Inga can readily adapt to this new data without convening in the cellar with Olaf.

Issue: Exposing data structures between different tiers increases complexity. Though this complexity may not appear in a simple system, it appears dramatically by tightly coupling the different tiers of a solution as it tries to flex to meet new requirements.

Best Practice: Consider creating separate data structures for different interactions between tiers. Isolating data in this fashion loosely couples the tiers, which enables better reuse. As new tiers appear on the scene, existing tiers meet their needs more readily.

Figures 12.70 and 12.71 show the difference between this loose and tight coupling. Note that EyeBrowRequest tightly couples the client with the component it accesses, assuming that different clients make requests differently. The section titled "Avoid chatter" discusses the case where the whole village might order beer using their eyebrows as a standard.

```
public BeerOrder(EyeBrowRequest request){
  quantity = Integer.valueOf(request.getParameter("number")).intValue();
  item = request.getParameter("type");
}
```

Figure 12.70: Tightly coupled client.

```
public BeerOrder(int quantity, String item){
  this.quantity = quantity;
  this.item = item;
}
```

Figure 12.71: Loosely coupled client.

Chief improvements in the "ilities" are debuggability, flexibility, maintainability, reusability, security, and testability.

Centralize control

Christian's BierHaus: With each new magistrate comes the latest decrees and levies, so Brutalix and the rest of the confused staff have only words of praise when Guido comes on board to make sense of the magistrate's endless rants and regulations.

Issue: Distributing control logic across multiple client requests increases complexity. This complexity typically appears in the form of a maintenance nightmare, as a minute change to the system causes it to collapse.

Best Practice: Consider introducing an appropriate J2EE component as a logical control center for the client requests. Centralizing the logic exposes the true nature of the beast. This exposure allows changes to result in predictable outcomes.

Figures 12.72 and 12.73 show the difference between disparate logic and centralized logic. Note that Brutalix's logic for who gets beer differs radically from Inga's. Christian gets better control of the process by allowing Guido to make all the decisions on Brutalix's and Inga's behalf.

```
public class Brutalix {
  public boolean isAuthorized(Customer customer) {
    return (motherKnows(customer) || hasShekels(customer) ... );
  }
}
public class Inga {
  public boolean isAuthorized(Customer customer) {
    return (!hasBeer(customer) && !passedOut(customer) ... );
  }
}
```

Figure 12.72: Disparate logic.

```
public class Brutalix {
  public boolean isAuthorized(Customer customer) {
    return guido.grantAccess(customer);
  }
}
public class Inga {
  public boolean isAuthorized(Customer customer) {
    return guido.grantBeer(customer);
  }
}
```

Figure 12.73: Centralized logic.

Chief improvements in the "ilities" are debuggability, flexibility, maintainability, reliability, reusability, security, and testability.

Delegate

Christian's BierHaus: Guido seems noticeably rough at applying the special guidelines extended to families of the rotating magistrates, so Christian appoints Hella as dignitary legate.

Issue: Centralizing control creates large cumbersome components that result in increased complexity. Maintainability suffers with a notable increase in testing and debugging difficulties.

Best Practice: Use centralized controllers to initiate requests, but delegate the requests as commands to other specialized controllers. Delegating control separates related logic, localizing changes to the system. Localizing changes simplifies unit testing, debugging, and maintenance, thereby increasing reliability.

Figures 12.74 and 12.75 show how components can delegate related logic to other components. Guido's logic gets strange and unmanageable, so Christian simplifies matters by delegating the BierHaus's separate business logic to both Hella and Guido.

```
public Guido {
  public boolean grantAccess(Customer customer) {
    return ((isMagistrate(customer) || knowsMagistrate(customer) ... ) ||
             (motherKnows(customer) || hasShekels(customer) && ... ));
  }
  public boolean grantBeer(Customer customer) {
    return ((knowsMagistratesName(customer) || ... ) ||
            (!hasBeer(customer) && !passedOut(customer) && ... ));
  }
}
```

Figure 12.74: Large, cumbersome centralized controller.

```
public Christian {
  public boolean grantAccess(Customer customer) {
    return (hella.grantAccess(customer) || guido.grantAccess(customer));
  }
  public boolean grantBeer(Customer customer) {
    return (hella.grantBeer(customer) || guido.grantBeer(customer));
  }
}
```

Figure 12.75: Centralized controller delegating to other controllers.

Chief improvements in the "ilities" are debuggability, maintainability, and testability.

Maintain state

Christian's BierHaus: Customers tend to repeat requests for beer politely and unwittingly as a reflex to the mere sight of an empty stein, so Inga and the new hire, Hans, throw coasters down to keep track.

Issue: Many clients lie outside of an application's control, making the application unnecessarily complex. Applications that blindly follow a client request may fail to meet functional requirements, with unpredictable results.

Best Practice: Maintain state in a J2EE component. Applications fully control the state of J2EE components. Applications with controlled states behave predictably.

Figures 12.76 and 12.77 show how a component adds state to an incoming request. Adding state to the incoming request allow Inga and Hans to have actual conversations with customers rather than blindly carrying out their orders.

```
public class Inga extends HttpServlet {
  public void processRequest(
    HttpServletRequest request,
    HttpServletResponse response) {
    int req = Integer.valueOf(request.getParameter("request")).intValue();
    // uncontrolled request
    CommandProcessor.execute(req);
}
```

Figure 12.76: No state management.

```
public class Inga extends HttpServlet {
  public void processRequest(
    HttpServletRequest request,
    HttpServletResponse response) {
    HttpSession session = request.getSession();
    int state = ((Integer) session.getAttribute("state")).intValue();
    int req = Integer.valueOf(request.getParameter("request")).intValue();
    if (StateMachine.isValidTransition(state, req)) {
      // good request
      CommandProcessor.execute(req);
      int nextState = StateMachine.nextState(state, req);
      session.setAttribute("state", new Integer(nextState));
    } else {
      // bad request
    }
  }
```

Figure 12.77: Storing the state in a J2EE Component.

Chief improvements in the "ilities" are predictability and reliability.

Avoid chatter

Christian's BierHaus: The staff communicates concisely, using written orders if necessary, so that they remain available to customers even when the place gets jammed.

Issue: Extensive interaction between distributed components increases time complexity. Applications with time complexity may not meet performance requirements and may suffer from poor scalability and availability.

Best Practice: Minimize distribution cross-section time complexity. Components requiring extensive interaction defeat the purpose of separating them. Good distribution isolates time complexity rather than exposing it, minimizing component interaction. Less chatter in a distributed system increases performance, and also leads to better scalability and availability.

Figures 12.78 and 12.79 show how components can communicate tersely, using commands to minimize chatter. Inga and Hans spend less time talking to Olaf if they avoid elaborate conversations by using simple commands.

```
public class Olaf {
  public void setQuantitiy(int quantity) {
    ...
  }
  public void setItem(String item) {
    ...
  }
  public void processOrder() {
    ...
  }
}
```

Figure 12.78: Large distribution cross-section.

```
public class Olaf {
  public void processCommand(OrderCommand orderCommand) {
    ...
  }
}
```

Figure 12.79: Small distribution cross-section.

Chief improvements in the “ilities” are availability, performance, and scalability.

Summary

Remember that J2EE offers the bulk of its services to the systems integration concerns that arise in distributed systems. Client access represents the front line of this integration. Although J2EE addresses many of these integration concerns with its services, a client component out of harmony with the services can devastate an entire solution. Today's e-business solutions have complex functional requirements accompanied by a list of "ilities" that seem almost impossible to meet. Sometimes they make about as much sense as making contact with the supreme Martian chicken. The client might dictate that it needs a spacesuit, yet the overall solution design might dictate that the client wear a chicken costume. A good solution gives clients access to the services they need and it avoids imposing unreasonable services on clients. It also avoids allowing clients access to unreasonable services and it imposes needed services on clients. Many, but not all, client components benefit from residing in a J2EE container.

Many design problems reveal themselves only when an application submits its components to the true test of talking to each other. This teaches the solutions designer how J2EE services address nonfunctional requirements. This experience remains essential because J2EE provides specifications for what services look like and do, but few standards defining how well the services work.

This chapter discussed how to implement clients in a distributed system. As J2EE components, clients buy into a layer of abstraction. This layer of abstraction allows J2EE implementations to offer their services and allows the forging of these services to extend well beyond the J2EE component's implementation. The next chapter addresses the deployment of J2EE components in an operational environment.

Test yourself

Key terms

Access beans

Data Class Access bean (DCAB)

Object Request Broker (ORB)

Java Naming and Directory Interface (JNDI)

Copy Helper Access bean (CHAB)

Web Services

JavaBean Wrapper Access bean (JWAB)

Universal Description, Discovery, and Integration (UDDI)

bootstrap control of services

Simple Object Access Protocol (SOAP)

declarative control of services

Web Services Description Language (WSDL)

dynamic control of services

Review questions

1. What types of Access beans does WebSphere Studio Application Developer provide? What type supports the best practices?
2. How does an EJB client typically access an EJB?
3. Differentiate between a resource manager connection factory reference and a resource environment reference. Why would a client use each?
4. What does the client obtain from an InitialContext?
5. When acquiring a home interface to an EJB, the client does a JNDI lookup and then invokes static method PortableRemoteObject.narrow(Object, Class) to cast to the home interface type. Why go through the narrow() method instead of simply casting the reference directly?
6. Can J2EE application client components also service requests from other J2EE components? How?

CHAPTER 13

Packaging and deployment

Gene Van Sant

Chapter topics

- *Naming*
- *Deployment descriptors*
- *References*
- *Security*
- *Packaging*
- *Installing*

Certification objectives

- *Assemble Web components, EJB components, and client application components into enterprise applications*
- *Deploy enterprise applications into servers*
- *Configure resource and security-role references*

The brief history of dealing with full software lifecycles has resulted in a separation of software lifecycle roles. Although these roles have proven essential to the success of software solutions by allowing each role to thrive in its own environment, the separation also causes a schism between roles. Poor integration of analysis, design, development, packaging, deployment, administration, maintenance, and other roles invariably leads to delays in the software lifecycle. As the sun continues to set on inefficient software lifecycle methodologies, so it must set on the strict isolation of roles. The schism between roles calls desperately for a force that might somehow bind them together. J2EE specifies standards that provide a blueprint for binding the different lifecycle roles to a single contract.

Mechanisms to aid in the delivery of software solutions improve vastly over the years, yet the information revolution still wields the equivalent of Stone Age tools. The tools of today's bitsmith range from programming languages that allow the fine-tuning of each individual bit to tools that deliver massive prefabricated symphonies of bits. As tools rapidly evolved from first-generation language (1GL) machine coding, to 2GL assembler, to 3GL programming, to 4GL scripting, the world expected 5GL, and Japan even promised it. The evolutional complexity of these tools reached a critical mass when 5GLs failed to deliver.

J2EE takes a new approach. Whereas other systems tend to focus strictly on programmatic, scriptive, declarative, or configurative tooling, J2EE blends them together as appropriate. While throwing a bag of tools together may not seem very innovative, J2EE does more by specifying standards that provide a roadmap capable of successfully federating proven technologies. The bulk of J2EE focuses on describing standards for *proven* technologies rather than prescribing standards for vaporware. Tasks suited best for programmatic tooling use Java. Tasks suited best for other tooling use XML. J2EE often combines the tooling.

Figure 13.1 shows the fuzzy relationships between different roles. The Application Component Provider role creates components in a development environment. The Administrator role runs them in an operational environment. Between the two lie packaging and deployment. The term *packaging* refers to the process of assembling modules from components and applications from modules. The term *deployment* refers to customizing and installing applications in an operational environment.

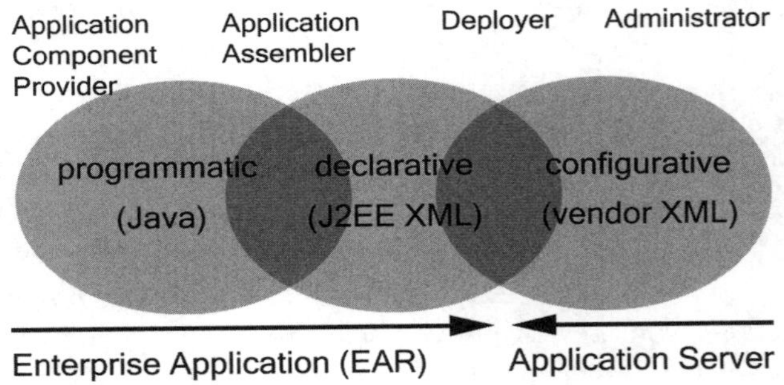

Figure 13.1: Role integration and tooling.

The standards that J2EE specifies to help integrate these roles introduce a great deal of overlap in role responsibilities and tooling. This overlap provides an agile environment for software solutions, yet it presents a challenge to traditional software methodologies. This chapter helps illuminate areas where role responsibilities and tooling overlap, yet it stops short of discussing the technologies and tooling covered in other chapters.

Naming

All J2EE components have access to a naming environment from which to look up other components, external resources, and configuration information by name. This naming environment allows the loose coupling of J2EE components from their behavioral parameters, external resources, and each other. The Application Component Provider role must reveal these dependencies by name in deployment descriptors and use the Java Naming and Directory Interface (JNDI) API to look them up by name from the Environment Naming Context (ENC). The Application Assembler role and Deployer role must resolve these named dependencies.

Figure 13.2 shows how a J2EE component uses its ENC to perform a lookup by name. In this case it uses the value of maxCats to customize its behavior. The next section, on deployment descriptors, discusses how the value actually gets resolved for the J2EE component.

```
try {
  Context jndiContext = new InitialContext();
  Context enc = (Context) jndiContext.lookup("java:comp/env");
  Integer maxCats = (Integer) enc.lookup("maxCats");
  System.out.println("maximum cats allowed in a bag: " + maxCats);
} catch (NamingException e) {
  e.printStackTrace(System.err);
}
```

Figure 13.2: J2EE component using ENC to perform a lookup.

J2EE recommends that applications use standard subcontexts of ENC for resources: java:comp/env/eis for connectors, java:comp/env/ejb for EJBs, java:comp/env/jdbc for data sources, java:comp/env/jms for JMS, java:comp/env/mail for mail sessions, java:comp/env/url for URLs, and so forth.

Deployment descriptors

One of the most pronounced limitations of conventional software systems lies in their isolation of development from other lifecycle roles. All too often, minute changes in requirements cause complex system changes. J2EE helps solve this limitation by turning programming into both a programmatic and a declarative task. A good J2EE component uses the proper proportions of both programmatic and declarative tooling.

J2EE defines deployment descriptors that provide the necessary declarative mechanism to bind the development role to other lifecycle roles. Effective use of these deployment descriptors ensures the proper integration between the lifecycle roles. Using WebSphere Studio Application Developer simplifies deployment by providing dialogs for editing and validating these deployment descriptors.

J2EE defines its deployment descriptors using XML Document Type Definitions (DTDs) located at *java.sun.com/dtd/*. In a DTD, each <!Element> construct declares a valid named element. Parentheses enclose a list of child elements for the element. Each element in the list may have an occurrence operator following it. Elements not followed by an occurrence operator must appear exactly once (one occurrence). Elements followed by ? must appear once or not at all (zero or one occurrence). Elements followed by + must appear at least once (one or more occurrences). Elements followed by * may appear any number of times or not at all (zero or more occurrences). So, a declaration for a dog element that has a name, might have a description, and could have any number of puppies looks like this:

```
<!ELEMENT dog (name, description?, guardian+, puppy*)>
```

References

Central to all J2EE components, references provide the mechanism for components to reveal their required resources. Good J2EE components declaratively reveal all resources that they consume programmatically. This improves component flexibility by exposing required resources. It also avoids the bad practice of *hard coding*, which refers to performing declarative programming using programmatic tooling. Good J2EE components declare references in XML and program access to the references in Java. This allows for the customization of components to occur without programmatic tooling.

J2EE specifies env-entry, resource-ref, resource-env-ref, ejb-ref, and security-role-ref deployment descriptors to reveal a J2EE component's programmatic references to declarative tooling. The Application Component Provider role uses these deployment descriptors to define named references in the J2EE component's code, to describe them, and to reveal the nature of their expected attributes. The J2EE component code accesses these references from the java:comp/env context (ENC). The Application Assembler role uses these deployment descriptors to define meaningful values for the named reference attributes that concern the application. The Deployer role uses these deployment descriptors to define operational values for the named reference while deploying the J2EE components in an operational environment. The Administrator role may also define operational values for the named references while administering the J2EE components in an operational environment. WebSphere Application Server allows the Deployer role and the Administrator role to resolve many of these references with JNDI names. The Administrator role must ensure that appropriate values in the operational environment get published to the correct JNDI name for the application.

When used together with the ENC these references allow the loose coupling or tight coupling of J2EE components from their behavioral parameters, external resources, and other J2EE components. A J2EE component becomes loosely coupled to a resource when it accesses references that allow the operational environment to maintain control of the resource. A J2EE component becomes tightly coupled to a resource when it accesses references that allow it to take control of the resource.

Environment entries

The Application Component Provider role uses environment entry references to reveal behavior customization values required by a J2EE component. Environment entry references provide the declarative support necessary to allow the configuration of J2EE components for particular applications. J2EE defines an environment entry as follows:

```
<!ELEMENT env-entry (description?, env-entry-name, env-entry-type,
  env-entry-value?)>
```

Each env-entry element must contain an env-entry-name and an env-entry-type and may optionally contain a description and an env-entry-value. The env-entry-name defines the name used in a J2EE component's code. Code accesses this name from the java:comp/env context (ENC). The env-entry-type reveals the Java type expected by the component code. The env-entry-value defines a value for the environment entry reference. Figure 13.3 shows the env-entry used by the code in Figure 13.2.

```
<env-entry>
  <description>
    The maximum number of cats allowed in a bag
  </description>
  <env-entry-name>maxCats</env-entry-name>
  <env-entry-type>java.lang.Integer</env-entry-type>
  <env-entry-value>42</env-entry-value>
</env-entry>
```

Figure 13.3: Environment entry deployment descriptor.

The Application Assembler role uses these references to define values appropriate to a particular application. The Deployer role uses these references to define values appropriate to a particular operational environment.

Figure 13.4 through Figure 13.6 show the WebSphere Studio Application Developer dialogs for defining environment entry references for J2EE components.

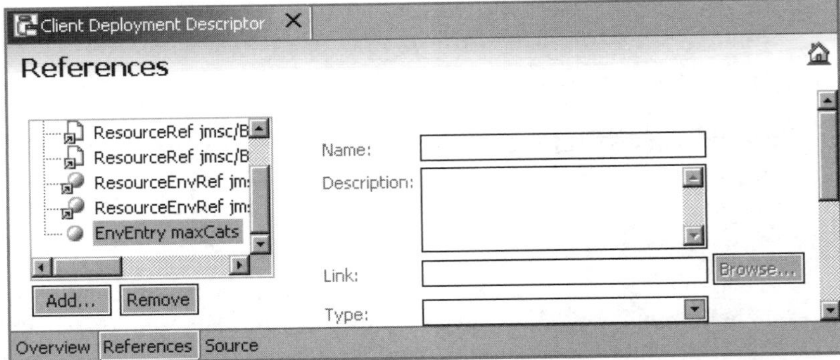

Figure 13.4: Defining a J2EE Application Client component environment entry in WebSphere Studio Application Developer.

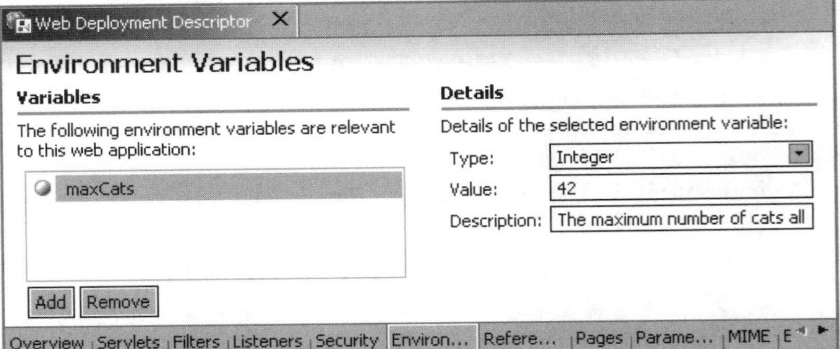

Figure 13.5: Defining a J2EE Web component environment entry in WebSphere Studio Application Developer.

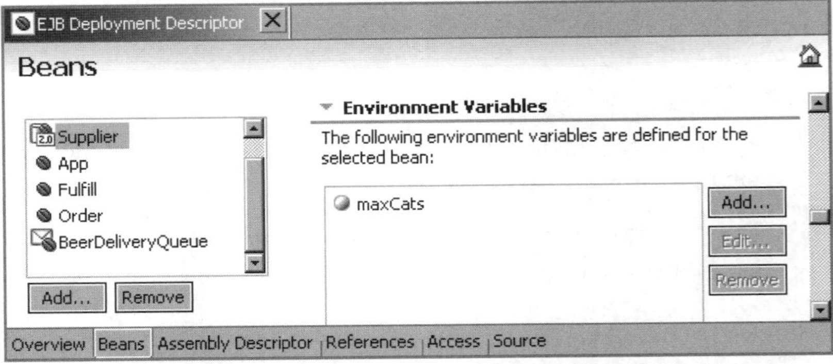

Figure 13.6: Defining a J2EE Enterprise component environment entry in WebSphere Studio Application Developer.

Resource manager connection factory references

The Application Component Provider role uses resource manager connection factory reference deployment descriptors to reveal external resource manager connections required by a J2EE component. J2EE components use these references to achieve tight coupling with external resources using local declarative service controls. J2EE defines a resource manager connection factory reference as follows:

```
<!ELEMENT resource-ref (description?, res-ref-name, res-type, res-auth,
  res-sharing-scope?)>
```

Each resource-ref element must contain a res-ref-name, a res-type, and a res-auth element and may optionally contain a description and a res-sharing-scope element. The res-ref-name defines the name used in a J2EE component's code. Code accesses this name from the java:comp/env context (ENC). The res-type reveals the Java type expected by the component code. The res-auth reveals whether the J2EE component performs the sign-on or the J2EE container performs the sign-on on the J2EE component's behalf. A res-auth value of Application indicates that the code performs a programmatic sign-on. A res-auth value of Container indicates that the Deployer role must provide authentication information for the sign-on. The Application Component Provider role sets res-sharing-scope to Shareable or Unshareable to reveal whether or not the code intends to share connections to the resource. The res-sharing-scope defaults to Shareable. Figure 13.7 shows an example.

```
<resource-ref id="ResourceRef_1">
  <description>Beer needing delivery</description>
  <res-ref-name>jms/BeerDeliveryQueueConnectionFactory</res-ref-name>
  <res-type>javax.jms.QueueConnectionFactory</res-type>
  <res-auth>Container</res-auth>
  <res-sharing-scope>Shareable</res-sharing-scope>
</resource-ref>
```

Figure 13.7: Resource manager connection factory reference deployment descriptor.

WebSphere provides additional elements for resource manager connection factory reference deployment descriptors, shown in Figure 13.8. These elements provide the ability to make a trade-off between the accuracy of data that clients see and the concurrency of client accesses, as discussed in Chapter 8.

```
<resourceRefExtensions xmi:id="ResourceRefExtension_1"
    isolationLevel="TRANSACTION_NONE"
    connectionManagementPolicy="Aggressive">
  <resourceRef href="META-INF/ejb-jar.xml#ResourceRef_1"/>
</resourceRefExtensions>
```

Figure 13.8: Resource manager connection factory reference WebSphere extension.

These references provide the Application Assembler role with the ability to package both standard and extended meta data regarding the resource together with an application. The Deployer role must resolve these references to factories that create connections to a resource in the operational environment. For a J2EE Application Client component, the Deployer role must add appropriate definitions to resource.xmi for WebSphere Application Client, as shown in Figure 12.34. For a J2EE Web component or a J2EE Enterprise component in WebSphere Application Server, the Deployer role must resolve these references using published JNDI names that point to the appropriate definitions in the operational environment, as shown in Figure 13.9. The Administrator role makes sure the appropriate operational environment information gets published in JNDI.

```
<resRefBindings xmi:id="ResourceRefBinding_1"
  jndiName="jms/com/loofa/BeerDeliveryQueueConnectionFactory">
  <bindingResourceRef href="META-INF/ejb-jar.xml#ResourceRef_1"/>
</resRefBindings>
```

Figure 13.9: Resource manager connection factory reference WebSphere binding.

Figure 13.10 through Figure 13.12 show the WebSphere Studio Application Developer dialogs for defining resource manager connection factory references for J2EE components.

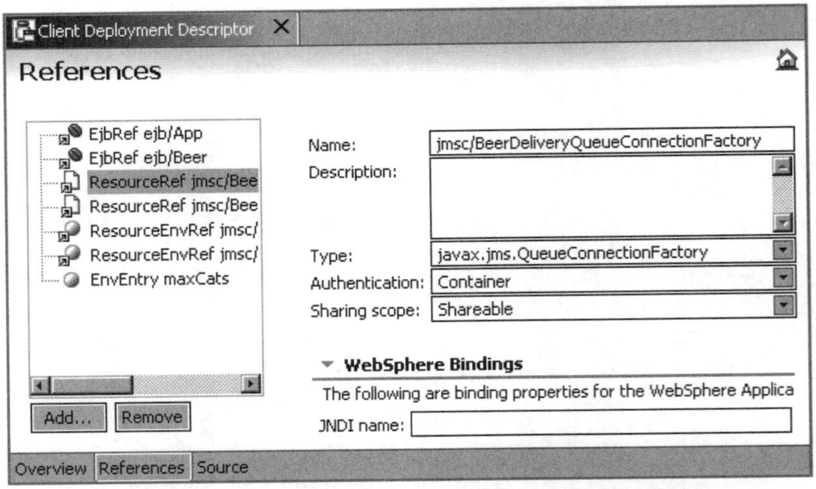

Figure 13.10: Defining a J2EE Application Client component resource manager connection factory reference in WebSphere Studio Application Developer.

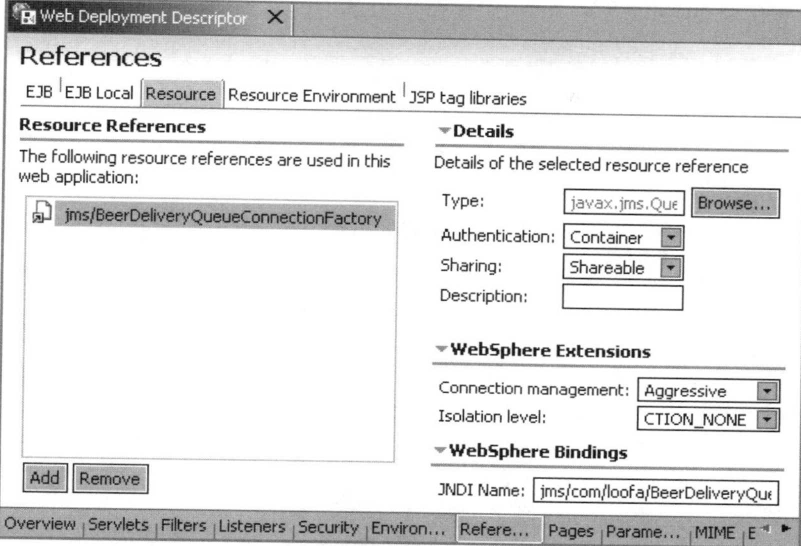

Figure 13.11: Defining a J2EE Web component resource manager connection factory reference in WebSphere Studio Application Developer.

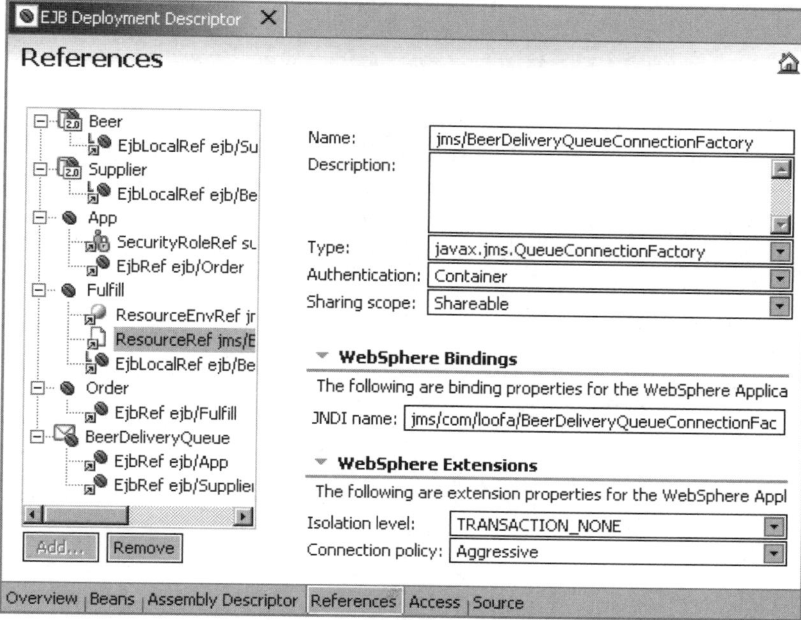

Figure 13.12: Defining a J2EE Enterprise component resource manager connection factory reference in WebSphere Studio Application Developer.

Resource environment references

The Application Component Provider role uses resource environment reference deployment descriptors to reveal administered components required by a J2EE component. J2EE components use these references to achieve loose coupling from external resources that services already manage. J2EE defines a resource environment reference as follows:

```
<!ELEMENT resource-env-ref (description?, resource-env-ref-name,
  resource-env-ref-type)>
```

Each resource-env-ref element must contain a resource-env-ref-name and a resource-env-ref-type and may optionally contain a description. The resource-env-ref-name defines the name used in a J2EE component's code. Code accesses this name from the java:comp/env context (ENC). The resource-env-ref-type reveals the Java type expected by the component code. Figure 13.13 shows an example.

```
<resource-env-ref id="ResourceEnvRef_1">
  <description>Beer needing delivery</description>
  <resource-env-ref-name>jms/BeerDeliveryQueue</resource-env-ref-name>
  <resource-env-ref-type>javax.jms.Queue</resource-env-ref-type>
</resource-env-ref>
```

Figure 13.13: Resource environment reference deployment descriptor.

These references provide the Application Assembler role with the ability to package type meta data regarding the resource together with the application. The Deployer role must resolve these references to actual resources in the operational environment. For J2EE components in WebSphere Application Server, the Deployer role must resolve these references using a JNDI name that points to the appropriate definitions published in JNDI, as shown in Figure 13.14. The Administrator role makes sure that the administered components get published in JNDI.

```
<resourceEnvRefBindings xmi:id="ResourceEnvRefBinding_1"
  jndiName="jms/com/loofa/BeerDeliveryQueue">
  <bindingResourceEnvRef href="META-INF/ejb-jar.xml#ResourceEnvRef_1"/>
</resourceEnvRefBindings>
```

Figure 13.14: Resource environment reference WebSphere binding.

Figure 13.15 through Figure 13.17 show the WebSphere Studio Application Developer dialogs for defining resource environment references for J2EE components.

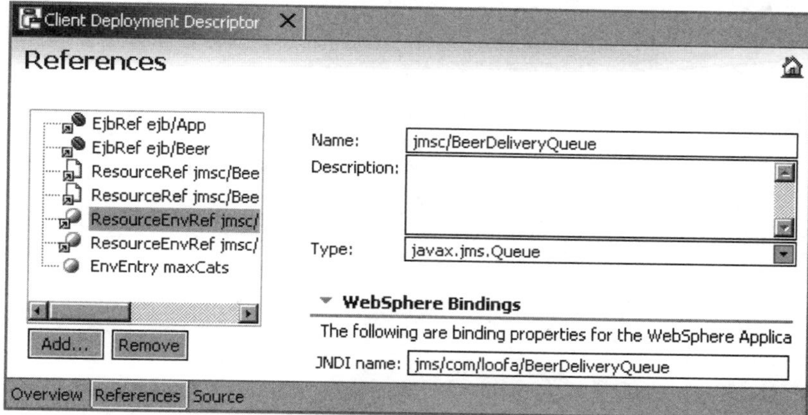

Figure 13.15: Defining a J2EE Application Client component resource environment reference in WebSphere Studio Application Developer.

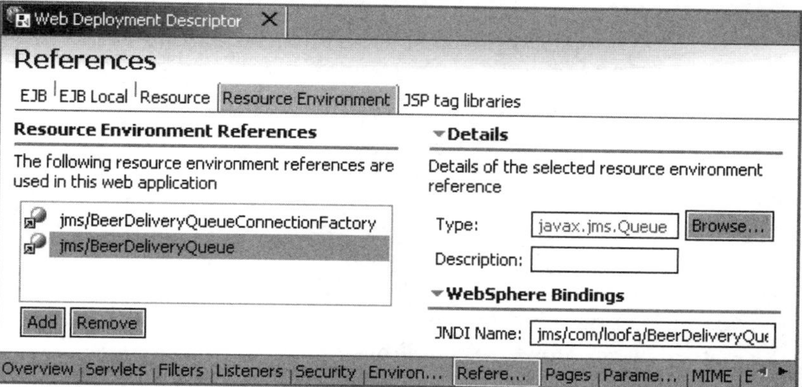

Figure 13.16: Defining a J2EE Web component resource environment reference in WebSphere Studio Application Developer.

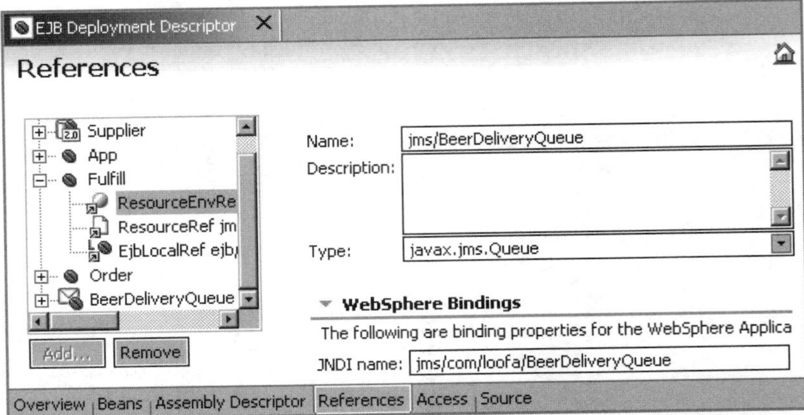

Figure 13.17: Defining a J2EE Enterprise component resource environment reference in WebSphere Studio Application Developer.

EJB references

The Application Component Provider role uses EJB reference deployment descriptors to reveal EJBs accessed by a J2EE component. Since these references declare a *remote* interface, J2EE components residing in all J2EE containers may declare them. J2EE defines an EJB reference as follows:

```
<!ELEMENT ejb-ref (description?, ejb-ref-name, ejb-ref-type,
  home, remote, ejb-link?)>
```

J2EE requires that Enterprise containers also support access to local EJBs and recommends that Web containers support such access. WebSphere Application Server provides support for both. The Application Component Provider role uses EJB local reference deployment descriptors to reveal local EJBs accessed by a J2EE component. Since these references declare *local* interfaces, only J2EE components residing in Web containers and Enterprise containers in the same JVM as the EJB may declare them. J2EE defines an EJB local reference as follows:

```
<!ELEMENT ejb-local-ref (description?, ejb-ref-name, ejb-ref-type,
  local-home, local, ejb-link?)>
```

For both EJB references and EJB local references, each ejb-ref element must contain an ejb-ref-name, an ejb-ref-type, a home, and a remote and may optionally contain an ejb-link and a description. The ejb-ref-name defines the name used in a J2EE component's code. Code accesses this name from the java:comp/env context (ENC). The ejb-ref-type reveals the EJB type expected by the component code by setting it to Entity or Session. The home and remote reveal the Java type expected by the component code for each. The ejb-link declares where to locate the EJB. Figure 13.18 and Figure 13.19 show examples of each.

```
<ejb-ref id="EjbRef_1">
  <ejb-ref-name>ejb/App</ejb-ref-name>
  <ejb-ref-type>Session</ejb-ref-type>
  <home>com.loofa.AppHome</home>
  <remote>com.loofa.App</remote>
  <ejb-link>AppEJB.jar#App</ejb-link>
</ejb-ref>
```

Figure 13.18: EJB remote access declaration for all J2EE containers.

```
<ejb-local-ref id="EJBLocalRef_1">
  <description>Local reference to Beer Entity EJB</description>
  <ejb-ref-name>ejb/Beer</ejb-ref-name>
  <ejb-ref-type>Entity</ejb-ref-type>
  <local-home>com.loofa.BeerLocalHome</local-home>
  <local>com.loofa.BeerLocal</local>
  <ejb-link>Beer</ejb-link>
</ejb-local-ref>
```

Figure 13.19: EJB local access declaration for Web containers and Enterprise containers.

The Deployer role must resolve all EJB references to actual EJBs in the operational environment. In WebSphere Application Server the Deployer role must resolve these references using JNDI names that point to the appropriate EJBs published to JNDI. These bindings look different depending on the J2EE container the component resides in. Figure 13.20 shows the bindings for WebSphere Application Client. Figure 13.21 shows the bindings for WebSphere Application Server. The Deployer role and the Administrator role must also make sure the EJBs get published to JNDI with the correct name.

```
<ejbRefs xmi:id="EjbRefBinding_1" jndiName="ejb/com/loofa/AppHome">
  <bindingEjbRef href="META-INF/application-client.xml#EjbRef_1"/>
</ejbRefs>
```

Figure 13.20: WebSphere Application Client EJB client binding.

```
<ejbRefBindings xmi:id="EjbRefBinding_1" jndiName="ejb/com/loofa/
AppHome">
  <bindingEjbRef href="WEB-INF/web.xml#EjbRef_1"/>
</ejbRefBindings>
```

Figure 13.21: WebSphere Application Server EJB client binding.

Figure 13.22 through Figure 13.24 show the WebSphere Studio Application Developer dialogues for defining local and remote EJB references for J2EE components. J2EE Application Client components may define only remote EJB references.

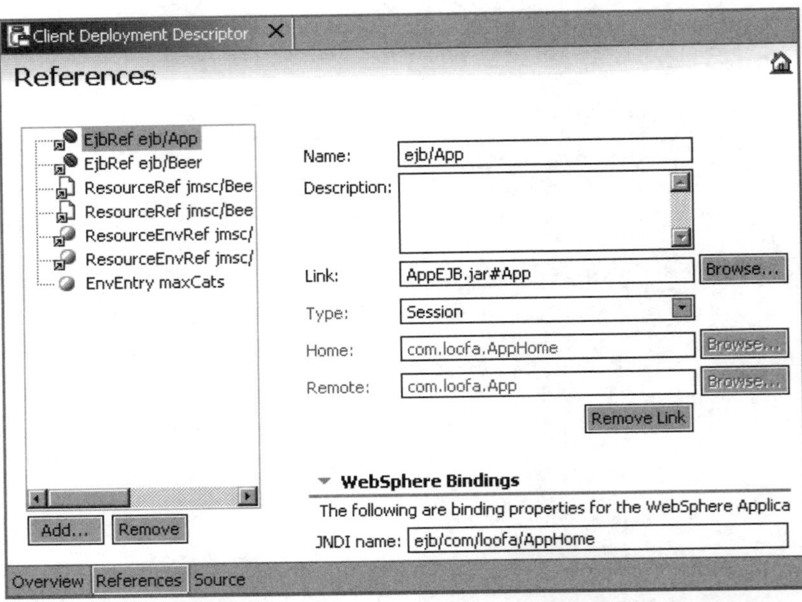

Figure 13.22: Defining a J2EE Application Client component EJB reference in WebSphere Studio Application Developer.

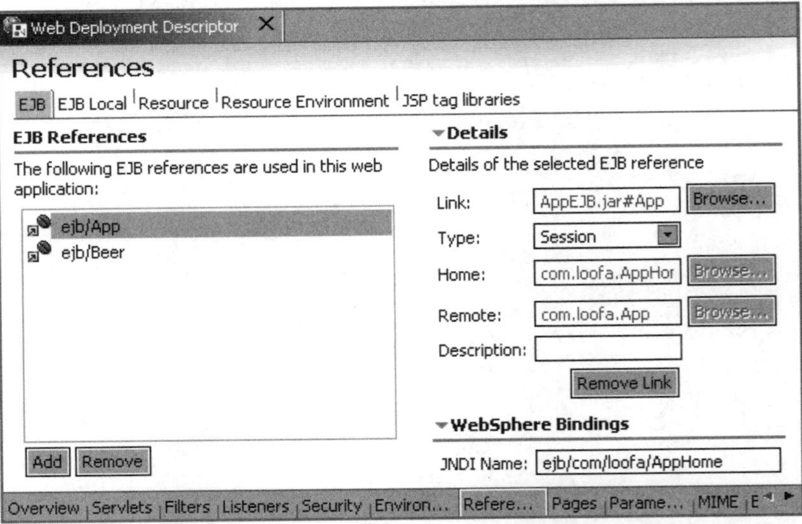

Figure 13.23: Defining a J2EE Web component EJB reference in WebSphere Studio Application Developer.

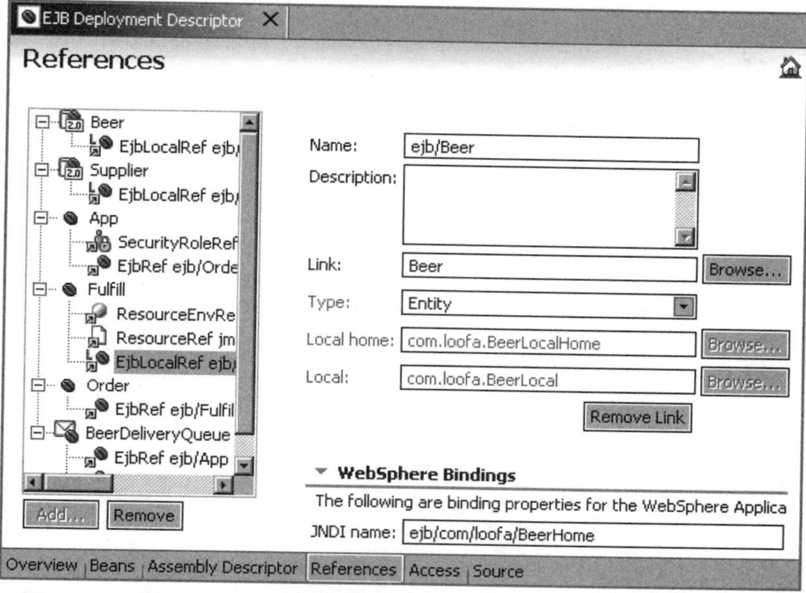

Figure 13.24: Defining a J2EE Enterprise component EJB reference in WebSphere Studio Application Developer.

Security role references

The Application Component Provider role uses security role references to reveal security roles required by a J2EE component. The Application Assembler role uses them to optionally define mappings to different security roles defined declaratively. J2EE defines a security role reference as follows:

```
<!ELEMENT security-role-ref (description?, role-name, role-link?)>
```

Each security-role-ref element must contain a role-name and may optionally contain a role-link and a description. The role-name defines the name used in the J2EE component's code. Either this role-name must appear in a security-role (see the following section on "Security"), or the role-link element must map it to a different role-name that appears in a security-role. Figure 13.25 shows an example.

```
<security-role-ref>
  <role-name>supplier</role-name>
  <description>Supplier that sells us beer</description>
  <role-link>beerSupplier</role-link>
</security-role-ref>
```

Figure 13.25: Security role reference deployment descriptor.

Figure 13.26 and Figure 13.27 show the WebSphere Studio Application Developer dialogues for defining security role references for J2EE Web components and J2EE Enterprise components. J2EE Application Client components may not define security role references. The J2EE Web component reference comes from modifying the source.

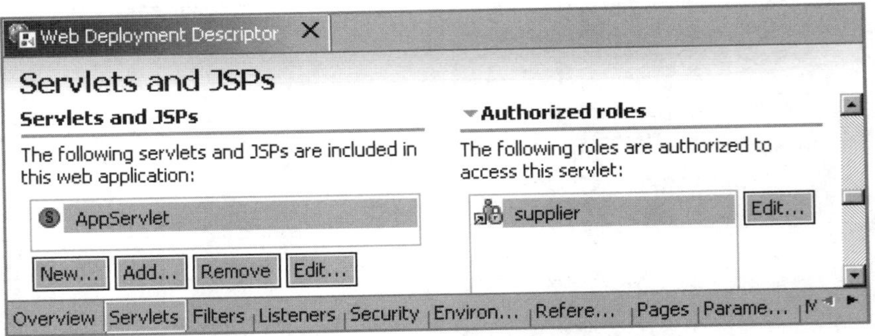

Figure 13.26: Defining J2EE Web component security role references in WebSphere Studio Application Developer.

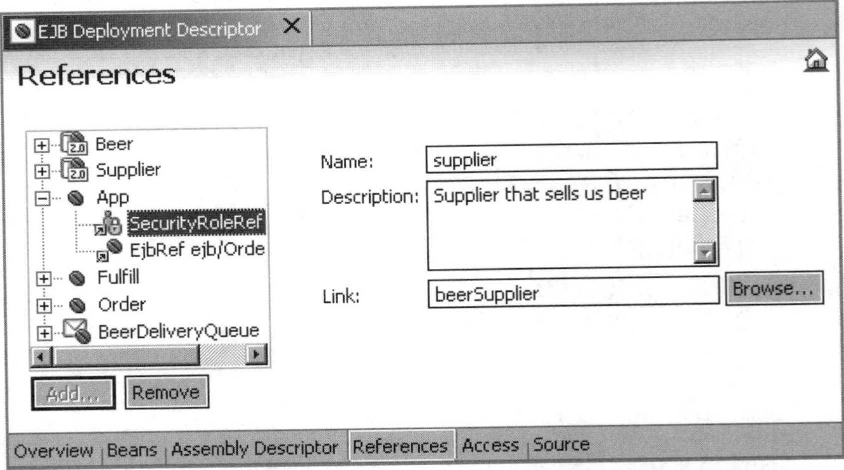

Figure 13.27: Defining J2EE Enterprise component security role references in WebSphere Studio Application Developer.

Security

The benefits of using deployment descriptors as a common contract for the different lifecycle roles reveal themselves exceptionally well in J2EE security. Security pervades all lifecycle roles, and each role benefits clearly from the degrees of separation between programming and operational aspects of security. Application programmers seldom have a desire to perform operational security administration, and operational security administrators care little for the underlying programming, yet successful security implementations must bind all lifecycle roles to the same monolithic security model.

Recall that security involves aspects of confidentiality, integrity, authentication, authorization, accountability, and auditing. The technologies specified in J2EE and provided by WebSphere Application Server address each of these areas yet minimize the need for configuration. For authentication, J2EE applications declare security roles that access the application. For authorization, J2EE applications declare permission constraints to control access to application components based on the security roles. They may also define the confidentiality and integrity by which some components communicate.

The Application Component Provider and Application Assembler reveal the application's expected security roles and permission constraints using deployment descriptors. The Deployer must map these security roles to principals in the operational environment. The Administrator establishes these principals in the operational environment.

Authentication and roles

J2EE specifies security role deployment descriptors used for mapping authenticated principals to authorization permissions. Application Component Providers must declaratively reveal the roles they expect. Application Assemblers must define security roles for the J2EE components and gather these roles to reveal them for the entire application. Administrators must ensure that authenticated principals assume a role when accessing the application.

The Application Component Provider role and the Application Assembler role use security role deployment descriptors to reveal security roles expected either programmatically or declaratively in a J2EE application. J2EE defines a security role as follows:

```
<!ELEMENT security-role (description?, role-name)>
```

Each security-role element must contain a role-name and may optionally contain a description. The role-name defines the name used programmatically in a J2EE component's code or declaratively in a J2EE component's security constraint deployment descriptors. Figure 13.28 shows an example (compare Figure 13.25).

```
<security-role>
  <role-name>beerSupplier</role-name>
  <description>Suppliers that sell us beer</description>
</security-role>
```

Figure 13.28: Security role deployment descriptor.

Figure 13.29 and Figure 13.30 show the WebSphere Studio Application Developer dialogues for defining security roles for J2EE Web components and J2EE Enterprise components. J2EE Application Client components may not define security roles.

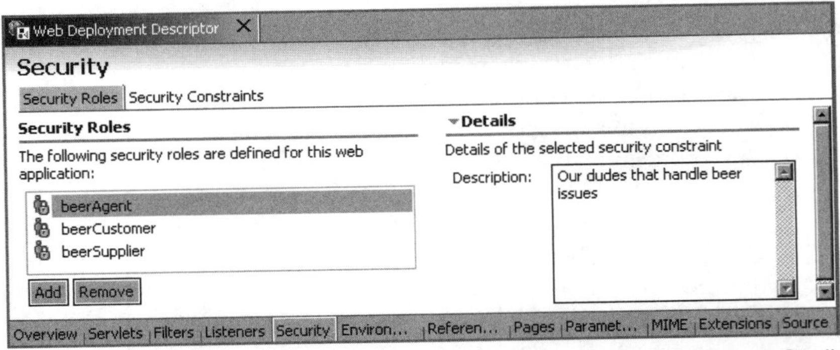

Figure 13.29: Defining J2EE Web component security roles in WebSphere Studio Application Developer.

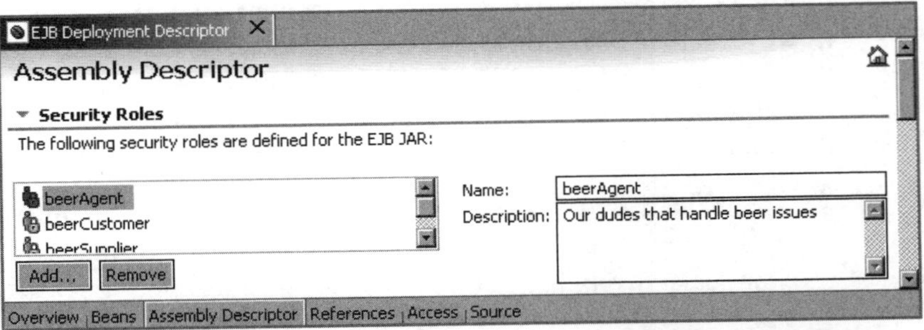

Figure 13.30: Defining J2EE Enterprise component security roles in WebSphere Studio Application Developer.

The Application Assembler role must also define security roles for the entire application in the J2EE application deployment descriptor. Figure 13.31 shows an example of a J2EE application's security roles.

```
<security-role id="SecurityRole_1">
  <description>Suppliers that sell us beer</description>
  <role-name>beerSupplier</role-name>
</security-role>
<security-role id="SecurityRole_2">
  <description>Customers that buy our beer</description>
  <role-name>beerCustomer</role-name>
</security-role>
<security-role id="SecurityRole_3">
  <description>Our dudes that handle beer issues</description>
  <role-name>beerAgent</role-name>
</security-role>
```

Figure 13.31: J2EE application security role deployment descriptors.

The Deployer role must create authorizations that map the J2EE application's security roles to security roles in the operational environment. Applications running in WebSphere Application Server may bind their roles to everyone, all authenticated users, or specific users or groups. Figure 13.32 shows an example of WebSphere security role bindings.

```
<authorizationTable xmi:id="AuthorizationTable_1">
  <authorizations xmi:id="RoleAssignment_1">
    <users xmi:id="User_1" name="sven"/>
    <users xmi:id="User_2" name="olaf"/>
    <role href="META-INF/application.xml#SecurityRole_1"/>
  </authorizations>
  <authorizations xmi:id="RoleAssignment_2">
    <specialSubjects xmi:type="applicationbnd:AllAuthenticatedUsers"
      xmi:id="AllAuthenticatedUsers_1" name="AllAuthenticatedUsers"/>
    <role href="META-INF/application.xml#SecurityRole_2"/>
  </authorizations>
  <authorizations xmi:id="RoleAssignment_3">
    <users xmi:id="User_1" name="sven"/>
    <role href="META-INF/application.xml#SecurityRole_3"/>
    <groups xmi:id="Group_1" name="beerSuppliers"/>
  </authorizations>
</authorizationTable>
```

Figure 13.32: WebSphere J2EE application security role bindings.

Table 13.1 shows the meaning of these security role bindings. Each operational role appearing in the left column maps to a security role in the J2EE application shown in the first row. Note that sven has authorization as both beerAgent and beerSupplier.

Table 13.1: WebSphere J2EE Application Authorization Summary.

	RoleAssignment_1 beerAgent	**RoleAssignment_2 beerCustomer**	**RoleAssignment_3 beerSupplier**
Group_1 beerSuppliers			Authorized
AllAuthenticatedUsers		Authorized	
User_1 sven	Authorized		Authorized
User_2 olaf	Authorized		

Figures 13.33 through Figure 13.35 show the Security tab of the Application Deployment Descriptor dialog in WebSphere Studio Application Developer. This tab provides the ability to define security roles for the J2EE application. It also enables the binding of these roles in WebSphere Application Server. Figure 13.33 shows how to use WebSphere Studio Application Developer to define a binding that ties one of a J2EE application's security roles to all authenticated WebSphere Application Server users.

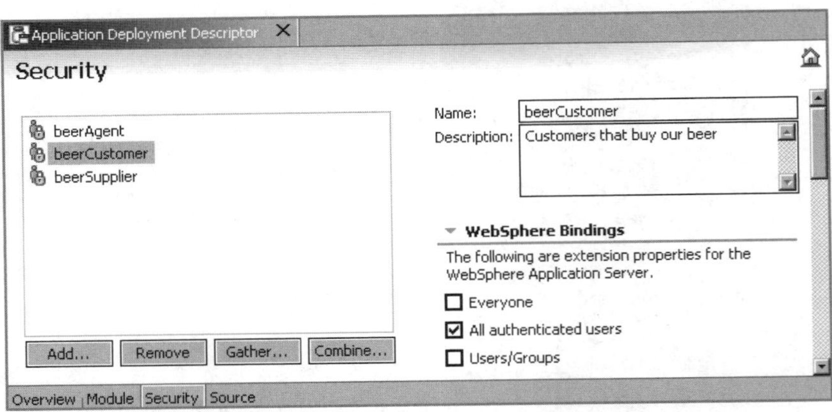

Figure 13.33: Defining a J2EE application security role binding for all authenticated WebSphere Application Server users in WebSphere Studio Application Developer.

Figure 13.34 shows how to use WebSphere Studio Application Developer to define a binding that ties one of a J2EE application's security roles to a set of WebSphere Application Server users.

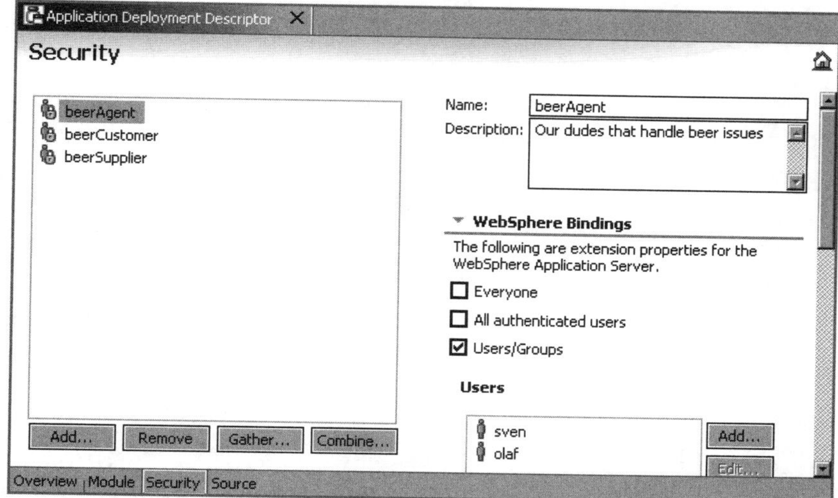

Figure 13.34: Defining a J2EE application security role binding for a set of WebSphere Application Server users in WebSphere Studio Application Developer.

Figure 13.35 shows how to use WebSphere Studio Application Developer to define a binding that ties one of a J2EE application's security roles to a set of WebSphere Application Server users and groups.

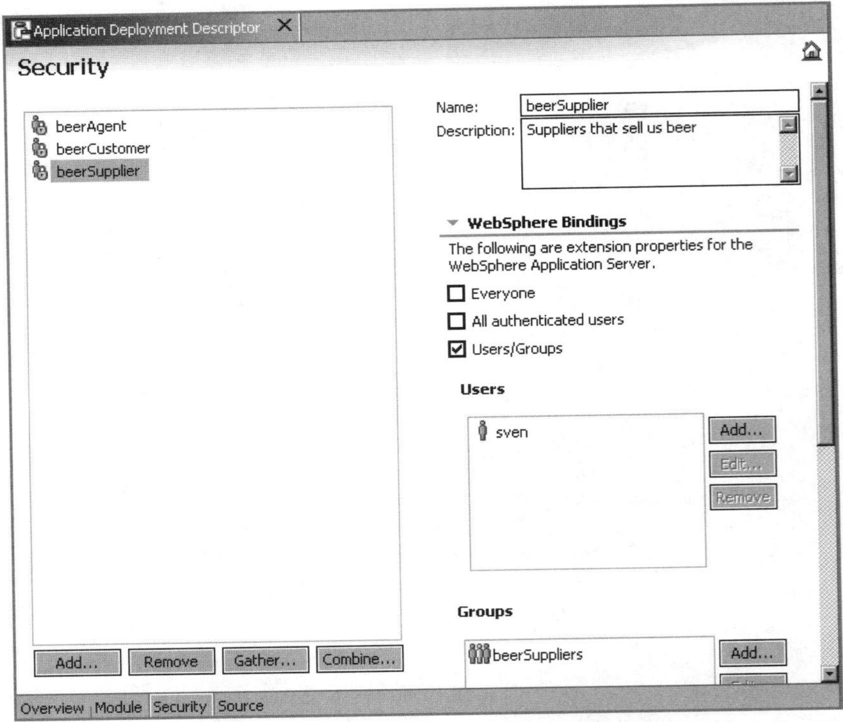

Figure 13.35: Defining a J2EE application security role binding for a set of WebSphere Application Server users and groups in WebSphere Studio Application Developer.

Authorization and access controls

J2EE specifies access controls differently based on J2EE component type. Access control occurs either programmatically or declaratively. Web containers provide coarse authorization based on resource requests. Enterprise containers provide more finely grained authorization based on both the J2EE component and the method servicing the request.

The Application Assembler and Deployer roles use security constraint deployment descriptors to enforce integrity, confidentiality, and authorization aspects of security on Web component access. J2EE defines a security constraint as follows:

```
<!ELEMENT security-constraint (display-name?, web-resource-collection+,
  auth-constraint?, user-data-constraint?)>
<!ELEMENT web-resource-collection (web-resource-name, description?,
  url-pattern*, http-method*)>
<!ELEMENT auth-constraint (description?, role-name*)>
<!ELEMENT user-data-constraint (description?, transport-guarantee)>
```

Each security-constraint element must contain one or more web-resource-collections and may optionally contain a display-name, an auth-constraint, and a user-data-constraint. The web-resource-collection defines a set of resources and access methods to which the constraint applies. These resource collections map to actual Web components in the servlet deployment descriptor. The auth-constraint defines access authorization either by listing a set of declared security-roles or by implying all declared security-roles using *. The user-data-constraint defines access integrity and confidentiality by setting the transport-guarantee element to NONE, INTEGRAL, or CONFIDENTIAL. Figure 13.36 shows an example.

```
<security-constraint>
  <web-resource-collection>
    <web-resource-name>supplierStuff</web-resource-name>
    <description>collection of resources for suppliers</description>
    <url-pattern>/WebApp</url-pattern>
    <http-method>GET</http-method>
  </web-resource-collection>
  <auth-constraint>
    <description>authorized roles for supplier access</description>
    <role-name>beerSupplier</role-name>
    <role-name>beerAgent</role-name>
  </auth-constraint>
  <user-data-constraint>
    <transport-guarantee>INTEGRAL</transport-guarantee>
  </user-data-constraint>
</security-constraint>
```

Figure 13.36: J2EE Web container security constraint deployment descriptor.

Figure 13.37 shows the WebSphere Studio Application Developer dialog for defining authorization permissions for J2EE Web components.

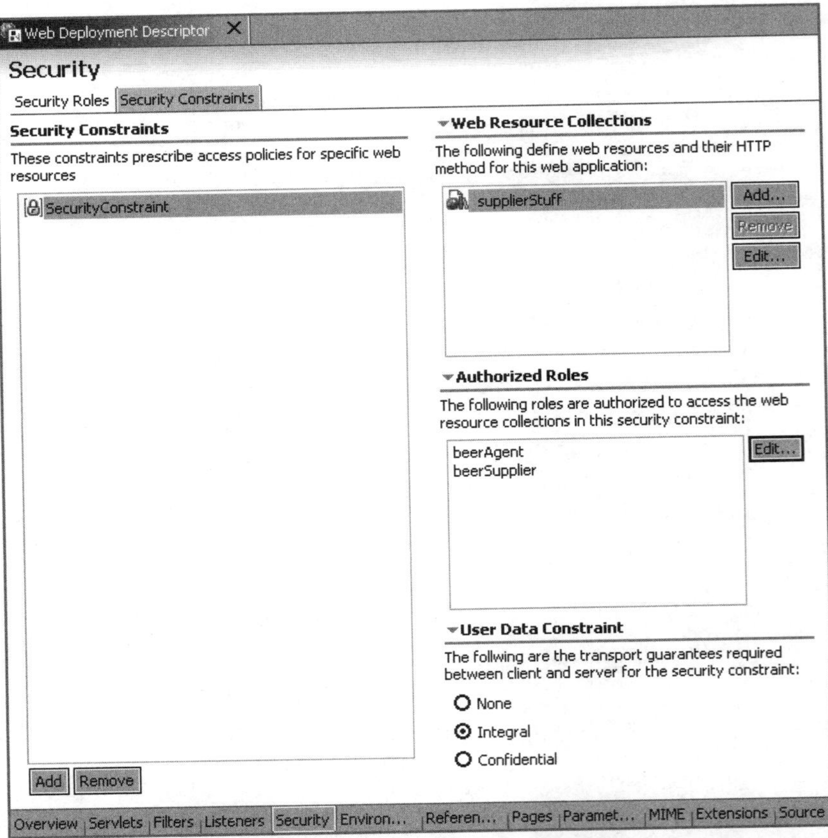

Figure 13.37: Defining J2EE Web component authorization in WebSphere Studio Application Developer.

The Application Assembler and Deployer roles use method permission deployment descriptors to enforce authorization on J2EE Enterprise component access. J2EE defines a method permission as follows:

```
<!ELEMENT method-permission (description?, (role-name+|unchecked),
  method+)>

<!ELEMENT method (description?, ejb-name, method-intf?, method-name,
  method-params?)>

<!ELEMENT method-params (method-param*)>
```

Each method-permission element must contain one or more methods, must also contain either unchecked or one or more role-names, and may optionally contain a description. The methods define which EJB methods the authorization applies to. The role-name defines which declared security-roles have authorization to access the EJB methods. Figure 13.38 shows an example.

```
<method-permission>
  <role-name>aRole</role-name>
  <method>
    <ejb-name>App</ejb-name>
    <method-name>*</method-name>
  </method>
</method-permission>
```

Figure 13.38: J2EE Enterprise container method permission deployment descriptor.

The Application Assembler and Deployer roles use exclude list deployment descriptors to deny access to EJB methods regardless of method permissions. J2EE defines an exclude list as follows:

```
<!ELEMENT exclude-list (description?, method+)>
```

Each exclude-list element must contain one or more methods and may optionally contain a description. The methods define which EJB methods to deny access to. Figure 13.39 shows an example.

```
<exclude-list>
  <method>
    <ejb-name>Beer</ejb-name>
    <method-intf>Remote</method-intf>
    <method-name>setPrice</method-name>
    <method-params>
      <method-param>int</method-param>
    </method-params>
  </method>
</exclude-list>
```

Figure 13.39: J2EE Enterprise container exclude list deployment descriptor.

Figure 13.40 shows the WebSphere Studio Application Developer dialog for defining authorization permissions for J2EE Enterprise components.

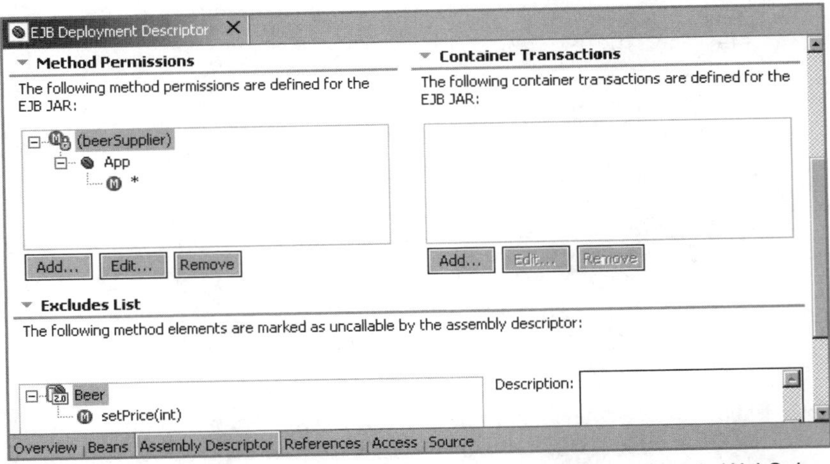

Figure 13.40: Defining J2EE Enterprise component authorizations in WebSphere Studio Application Developer.

Packaging

Recall that J2EE containers represent logical constructs of services for which J2EE specifies standard declarative controls. Recall that J2EE components residing in these containers exist as independent units of software function that declare all of their dependencies explicitly via deployment descriptors. A deployment module provides the packaging structure to hold all aspects of J2EE component implementation necessary for deployment in J2EE containers. J2EE specifies deployment modules for each J2EE container. J2EE applications contain one or more deployment modules. The Application Assembler role performs the packaging of a J2EE application by assembling J2EE components into deployment modules for the necessary J2EE containers and assembling these deployment modules into J2EE applications.

Figure 13.41 shows a J2EE application's components and modules. It shows J2EE components packaged into the four types of J2EE deployment modules: the application client module, the Web module, the EJB module, and the resource adapter module.

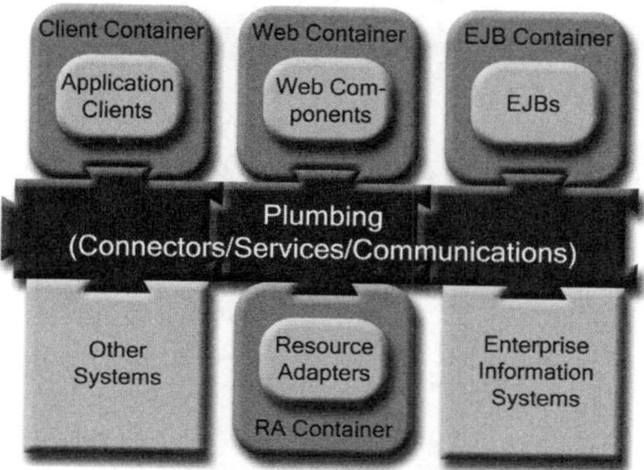

Figure 13.41: A J2EE application.

In addition to the deployment descriptors for references and security already discussed, J2EE specifies deployment descriptors specific to the different services provided by each J2EE container. This chapter provides only a summary of the deployment descriptors for each module, since the chapters specific to the different J2EE components cover these deployment descriptors in more detail.

Figures 13.42 through Figure 13.45 show the deployment descriptor definitions for each of the four different J2EE containers. Figure 13.46 shows the deployment descriptor definition for the J2EE Application that ties them all together.

```
<!ELEMENT application-client (icon?, display-name, description?,
  env-entry*, ejb-ref*, resource-ref*, resource-env-ref*,
  callback-handler?)>
```

Figure 13.42: J2EE Application Client module deployment descriptor definition.

```
<!ELEMENT web-app (icon?, display-name?, description?, distributable?,
  context-param*, filter*, filter-mapping*, listener*, servlet*,
  servlet-mapping*, session-config?, mime-mapping*, welcome-file-list?,
  error-page*, taglib*, resource-env-ref*, resource-ref*,
  security-constraint*, login-config?, security-role*, env-entry*,
  ejb-ref*,  ejb-local-ref*)>
```

Figure 13.43: J2EE Web module deployment descriptor definition.

```
<!ELEMENT ejb-jar (description?, display-name?, small-icon?, large-icon?,
  enterprise-beans, relationships?, assembly-descriptor?,
  ejb-client-jar?)>
```

Figure 13.44: J2EE Enterprise module deployment descriptor definition.

```
<!ELEMENT connector (display-name?, description?, icon?, vendor-name,
  spec-version, eis-type, version, license?, resourceadapter)>
```

Figure 13.45: J2EE Resource Adapter module deployment descriptor definition.

```
<!ELEMENT application (icon?, display-name, description?, module+,
  security-role*)>
<!ELEMENT module ((connector | ejb | java | web), alt-dd?)>
```

Figure 13.46: J2EE Application deployment descriptor definition.

Figures 13.47a and 13.47b show a J2EE application deployment descriptor defining an application that contains four separate modules and three security roles. This section discusses the modules contained within the application. The previous section on security covered the security roles.

```
<?xml version="1.0" encoding="UTF-8"?>
  <!DOCTYPE application PUBLIC
  "-//Sun Microsystems, Inc.//DTD J2EE Application 1.3//EN"
  "http://java.sun.com/dtd/application_1_3.dtd">
  <application id="Application_ID">
  <display-name>AppEAR</display-name>
  <module id="JavaClientModule_1">
    <java>AppJAC.jar</java>
  </module>
  <module id="WebModule_1">
    <web>
      <web-uri>AppWEB.war</web-uri>
      <context-root>AppWEB</context-root>
    </web>
  </module>
  <module id="EjbModule_1">
    <ejb>AppEJB.jar</ejb>
  </module>
  <module id="ConnectorModule_1">
    <connector>AppCON.jar</connector>
  </module>
```

Figure 13.47a: J2EE Application deployment descriptor.

```
    <security-role id="SecurityRole_1">
      <description>Our dudes that handle beer issues</description>
      <role-name>beerAgent</role-name>
    </security-role>
    <security-role id="SecurityRole_2">
      <description>Customers that buy our beer</description>
      <role-name>beerCustomer</role-name>
    </security-role>
    <security-role id="SecurityRole_3">
      <description>Suppliers that sell us beer</description>
      <role-name>beerSupplier</role-name>
    </security-role>
  </application>
```

Figure 13.47b: J2EE Application deployment descriptor.

The following figures show the packaging structures of a J2EE application. J2EE uses a standard archive format to package all of an application's resources. Each archive contains a meta information directory, which contains a manifest file and other meta data files.

Figure 13.48 shows a simple Java Archive (JAR). Note that the META-INF/ MANIFEST.MF file appears first, followed by the contents of the archive. All meta information for the archive goes in the META-INF directory.

```
AppJ.jar
+---META-INF
|   +---MANIFEST.MF
+---com
    +---loofa
        +---Utility.class
```

Figure 13.48: Java Archive (JAR) structure.

The manifest file typically contains a list of name-value pairs describing the archive. The manifest file may also contain a list of digitally signed files in the archive. Figure 13.49 shows an example of a manifest file that shows who created the archive and its build level. It also contains a digital signature for the com.loofa.Utility class so that systems that use the class can rely on the authenticity of its author and the integrity of its contents.

```
Manifest-Version: 1.0
Created-By: 1.3.1 (Loofa)
Implementation-Vendor: Loofa
Implementation-Vendor-Id: com.loofa
Build-Level: 030602

Name: com/loofa/Utility.class
Digest-Algorithms: SHA MD5
SHA-Digest: qDcdbj5rD5hvk4Quzsc3l/5nCYc=
MD5-Digest: f/ZEC8C6tlqHO/GukXcBAA==
```

Figure 13.49: JAR manifest file.

Figure 13.50 shows a J2EE Enterprise Archive (EAR). It contains one or more modules, the application deployment descriptor, and the IBM bindings.

```
AppEAR.ear
+---META-INF
|   +---MANIFEST.MF
|   +---application.xml
|   +---ibm-application-ext.xmi
+---AppJAC.jar
+---AppWEB.war
+---AppEJB.jar
+---AppCON.rar
+---AppJ.jar
```

Figure 13.50: J2EE Enterprise Archive (EAR) structure.

Figure 13.51 shows a J2EE Application Client Java Archive (Application Client JAR). It contains the J2EE Application Client component code, the application client deployment descriptor, the client resource definitions, and the IBM bindings.

```
AppJAC.jar
+---META-INF
|   +---application-client.xml
|   +---client-resource.xmi
|   +---ibm-application-client-bnd.xmi
|   +---MANIFEST.MF
+---com
    +---loofa
        +---AppJAC.class
```

Figure 13.51: J2EE Application Client Java Archive (Application Client JAR) structure.

Figure 13.52 shows a J2EE Web Archive (WAR). It contains the J2EE Web component code, the Web resources, the Web deployment descriptor, the IBM bindings, and the IBM extensions.

```
AppWEB.war
+---META-INF
|   +---MANIFEST.MF
+---WEB-INF
    +---web.xml
    +---ibm-web-bnd.xmi
    +---ibm-web-ext.xmi
    +---classes
        +---com
            +---loofa
                +---AppServlet.class
```

Figure 13.52: J2EE Web Archive (WAR) structure.

Figure 13.53 shows a J2EE EJB Java Archive (EJB JAR). It contains the J2EE Enterprise component code, the EJB deployment descriptor, the IBM bindings, the IBM extensions, and other related meta data.

```
AppEJB.jar
+---META-INF
|    +---ejb-jar.xml
|    +---MANIFEST.MF
|    +---ibm-ejb-jar-bnd.xmi
|    +---ibm-ejb-jar-ext.xmi
|    +---ibm-ejb-access-bean.xmi
|    +---Table.ddl
|    +---backends
|    +---DB2UDBNT_V72_1
|    +---...
+---com
|    +---ibm
|    | +---...
|    |
|    +---loofa
|    +---Beer.class
|    +---...
|    +---websphere_deploy
|      +---...
|    +---DB2UDBNT_V72_1
|    +---...
+---org
     +---omg
         +---stub
             +---...
```

Figure 13.53: J2EE EJB Java Archive (EJB JAR) structure.

Figure 13.54 shows a J2EE Resource Adapter Archive (RAR). It contains the J2EE Resource Adapter component code and the resource adapter deployment descriptor.

```
AppCON.rar
+---META-INF
|    +---MANIFEST.MF
|    +---ra.xml
+---_connectorModule.jar
```

Figure 13.54: J2EE Resource Adapter Archive (RAR) structure.

IBM provides several tools to help package J2EE applications for WebSphere Application Server. These include WebSphere Studio Application Developer, Application Assembly Tool, and Assembly Toolkit for WebSphere Application Server. The Assembly

Toolkit for WebSphere Application Server replaces the Application Assembly Tool. Because of the date of its publication, this chapter covers only WebSphere Studio Application Developer. Figure 13.55 shows two views of a J2EE application in WebSphere Studio Application Developer.

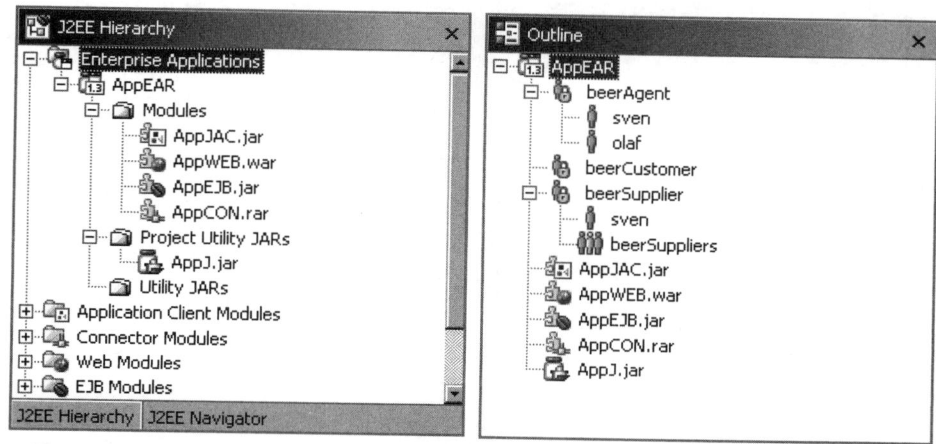

Figure 13.55: J2EE application views in WebSphere Studio Application Developer.

Figure 13.56 shows the Overview tab of WebSphere Studio Application Developer's Application Deployment Descriptor dialog. Note that it provides a summary of the modules contained within the application and the security roles defined for the application.

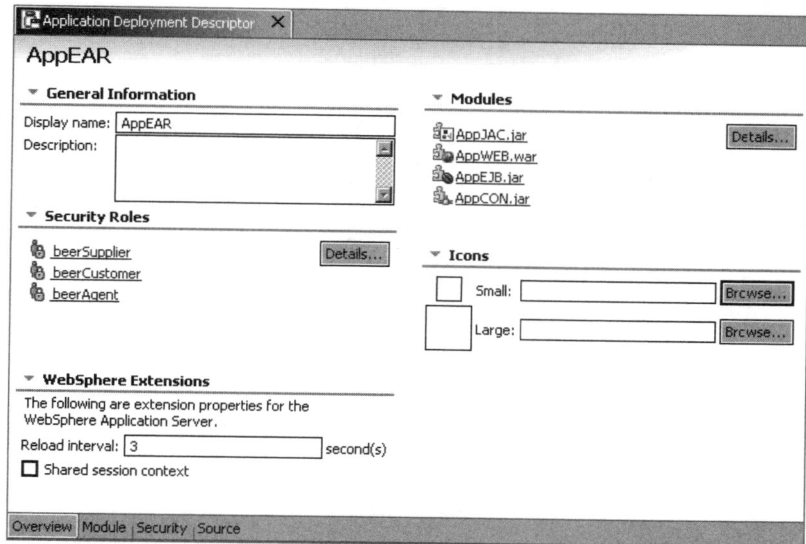

Figure 13.56: J2EE Application Deployment Descriptor Overview tab in WebSphere Studio Application Developer.

Figure 13.57 shows the Module tab of the Application Deployment Descriptor dialog. This tab provides a simple interface for packaging the different J2EE modules and regular Java archives in a J2EE application.

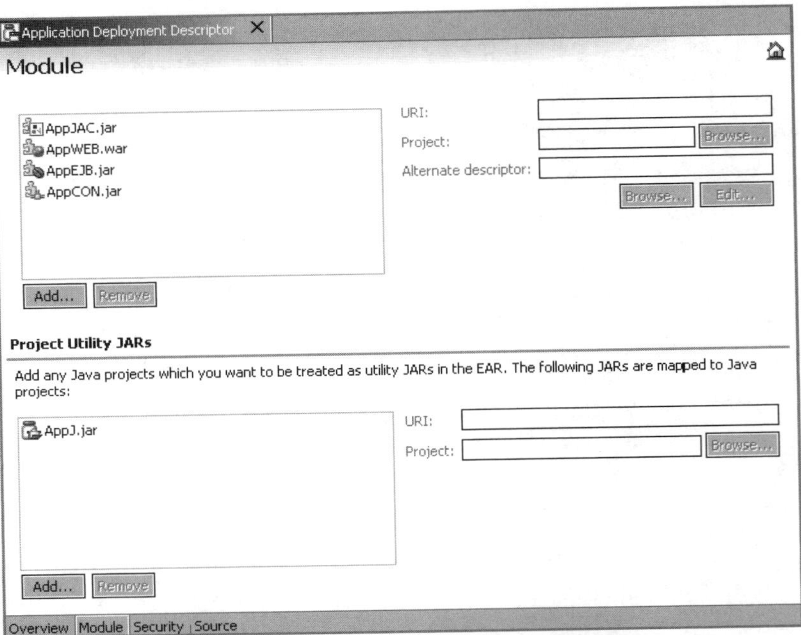

Figure 13.57: J2EE Application Deployment Descriptor Module tab in WebSphere Studio Application Developer.

Installing

Whereas the Administrator role typically configures the operational environment and installs applications, the Deployer role typically configures the application and installs it in operational environments. J2EE provides this overlap in responsibilities by design as shown in Figure 13.1. In fact, the Deployer role may wish to effect changes in the operational environment, and the Administrator may wish to configure the application. IBM provides tools for both development and operational environments.

WebSphere Studio Application Developer offers the Deployer role complete control of a J2EE application's configuration, but the tool also allows them to configure an operational environment and install J2EE applications in it. WebSphere Application Server offers the Administrator role complete control of an operational environment, but also allows them to configure and install J2EE applications. Although the tools have some overlap, they offer only a limited amount of each other's function.

For WebSphere Studio Application Developer, the Deployer role has access to many views in a workbench. Figure 13.58 shows the Server Configuration view in WebSphere Studio Application Developer. This view, among others, allows the Deployer role to install J2EE applications in a WebSphere Test Environment using a context menu.

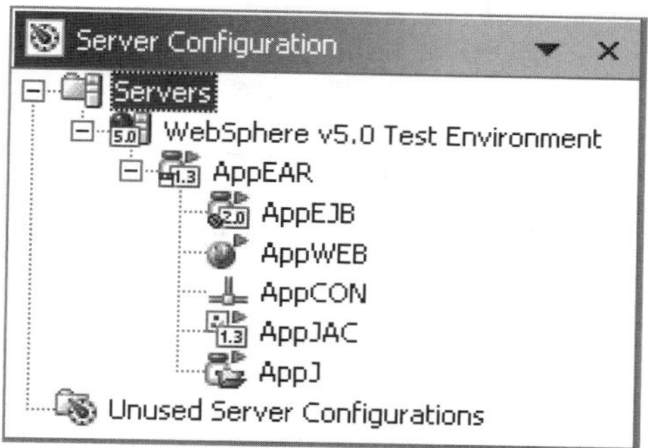

Figure 13.58: Server Configuration view in WebSphere Studio Application Developer.

Figure 13.59 shows the Server Configuration dialog in WebSphere Studio Application Developer. It allows the Deployer role to configure the WebSphere Test Environment.

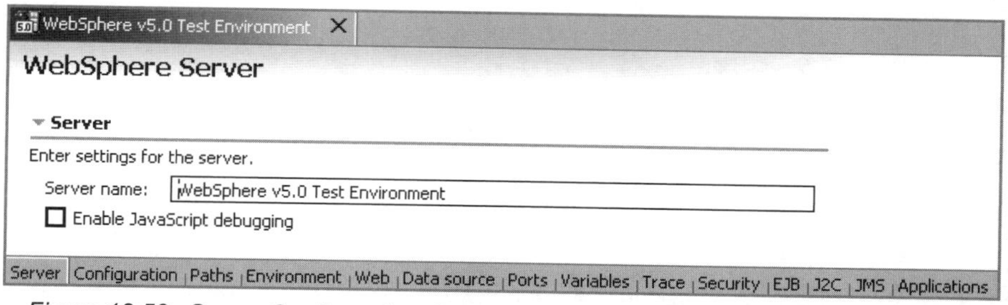

Figure 13.59: Server Configuration dialog in WebSphere Studio Application Developer.

For WebSphere Application Server, administrators and other roles have access to the admin console, the wsadmin shell, Java Control Language (JACL) scripts in the wsadmin shell, and Java Management Extension (JMX) MBeans to write administrative client programs. Figure 13.60 through Figure 13.64 show the typical process of installing an application in WebSphere Application Server using the WebSphere admin console. Note the contents of the many dialogs provided to configure the application.

Preparing for the application installation
Specify the EAR/WAR/JAR module to upload and install.
Path:
Browse the local machine or a remote server:
Local path:
C:\ears\AppEAR.ear
Browse...
Server path:
Choose the local path if the ear resides on the same machine as the browser. Choose the server path if the ear resides on any of the nodes in your cell context.
Context Root:
Used only for standalone Web modules (*.war)
You must specify a context root if the module being installed is a WAR module.
Next
Cancel

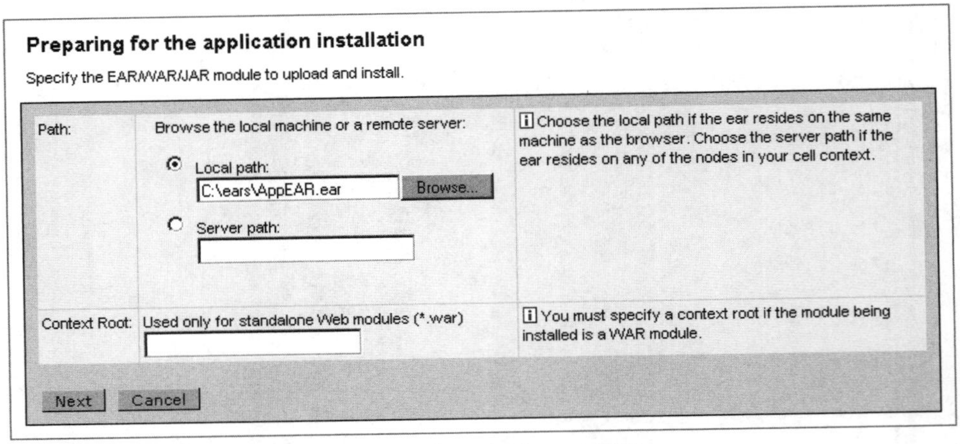

Figure 13.60: WebSphere admin console: selecting an EAR.

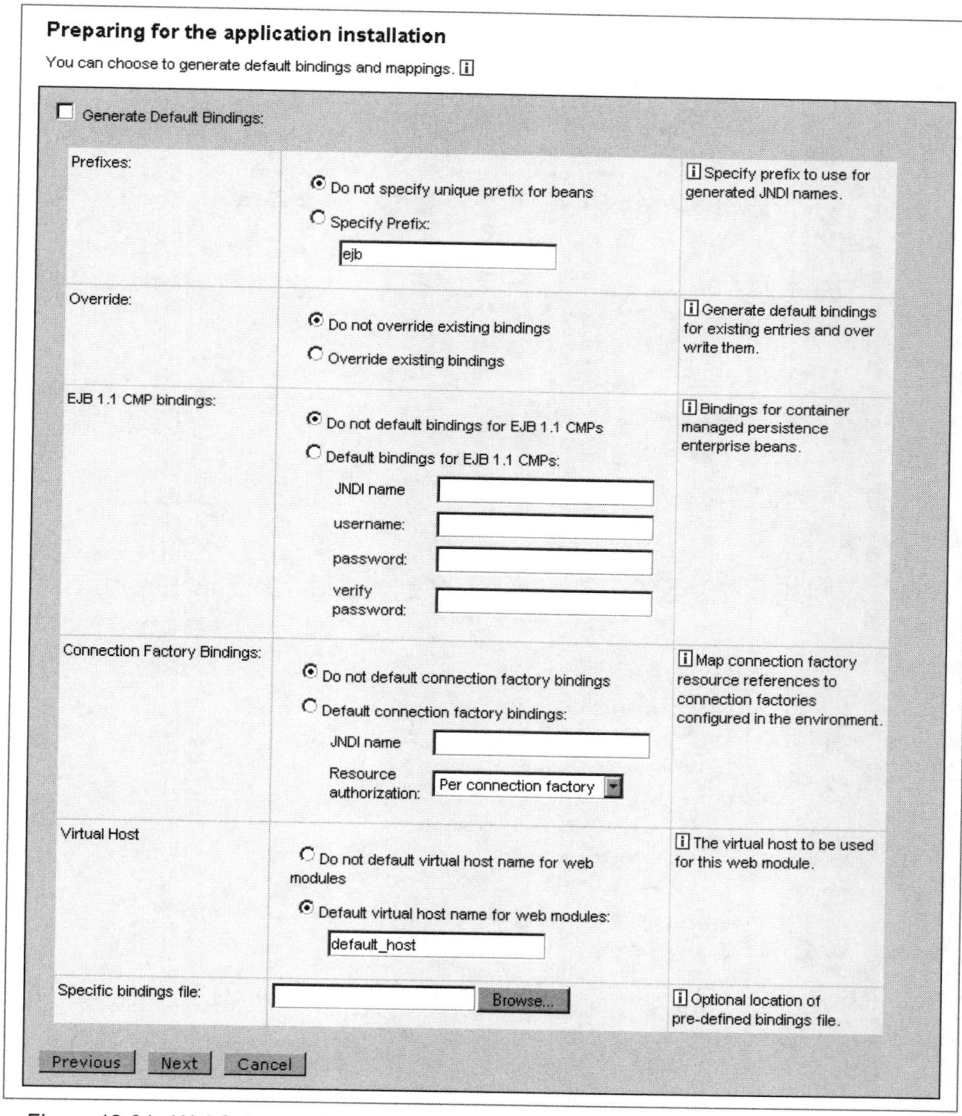

Preparing for the application installation

You can choose to generate default bindings and mappings.

☐ Generate Default Bindings:

Prefixes:	⦿ Do not specify unique prefix for beans ○ Specify Prefix: ejb	Specify prefix to use for generated JNDI names.
Override:	⦿ Do not override existing bindings ○ Override existing bindings	Generate default bindings for existing entries and over write them.
EJB 1.1 CMP bindings:	⦿ Do not default bindings for EJB 1.1 CMPs ○ Default bindings for EJB 1.1 CMPs: JNDI name username: password: verify password:	Bindings for container managed persistence enterprise beans.
Connection Factory Bindings:	⦿ Do not default connection factory bindings ○ Default connection factory bindings: JNDI name Resource authorization: Per connection factory	Map connection factory resource references to connection factories configured in the environment.
Virtual Host	○ Do not default virtual host name for web modules ⦿ Default virtual host name for web modules: default_host	The virtual host to be used for this web module.
Specific bindings file:	Browse...	Optional location of pre-defined bindings file.

Previous Next Cancel

Figure 13.61: WebSphere admin console: configuring bindings and mappings.

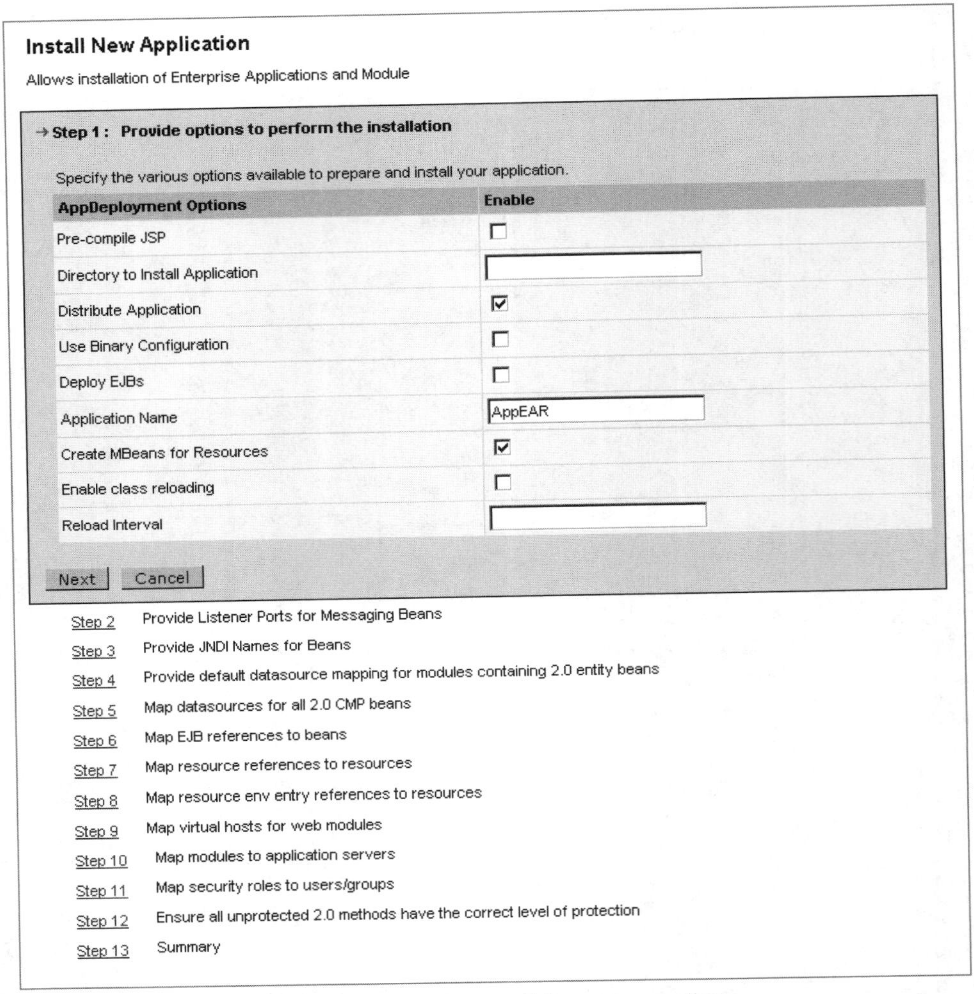

Install New Application

Allows installation of Enterprise Applications and Module

→ **Step 1 : Provide options to perform the installation**

Specify the various options available to prepare and install your application.

AppDeployment Options	Enable
Pre-compile JSP	☐
Directory to Install Application	
Distribute Application	☑
Use Binary Configuration	☐
Deploy EJBs	☐
Application Name	AppEAR
Create MBeans for Resources	☑
Enable class reloading	☐
Reload Interval	

Next Cancel

Step 2 Provide Listener Ports for Messaging Beans
Step 3 Provide JNDI Names for Beans
Step 4 Provide default datasource mapping for modules containing 2.0 entity beans
Step 5 Map datasources for all 2.0 CMP beans
Step 6 Map EJB references to beans
Step 7 Map resource references to resources
Step 8 Map resource env entry references to resources
Step 9 Map virtual hosts for web modules
Step 10 Map modules to application servers
Step 11 Map security roles to users/groups
Step 12 Ensure all unprotected 2.0 methods have the correct level of protection
Step 13 Summary

Figure 13.62: WebSphere admin console: specifying various options.

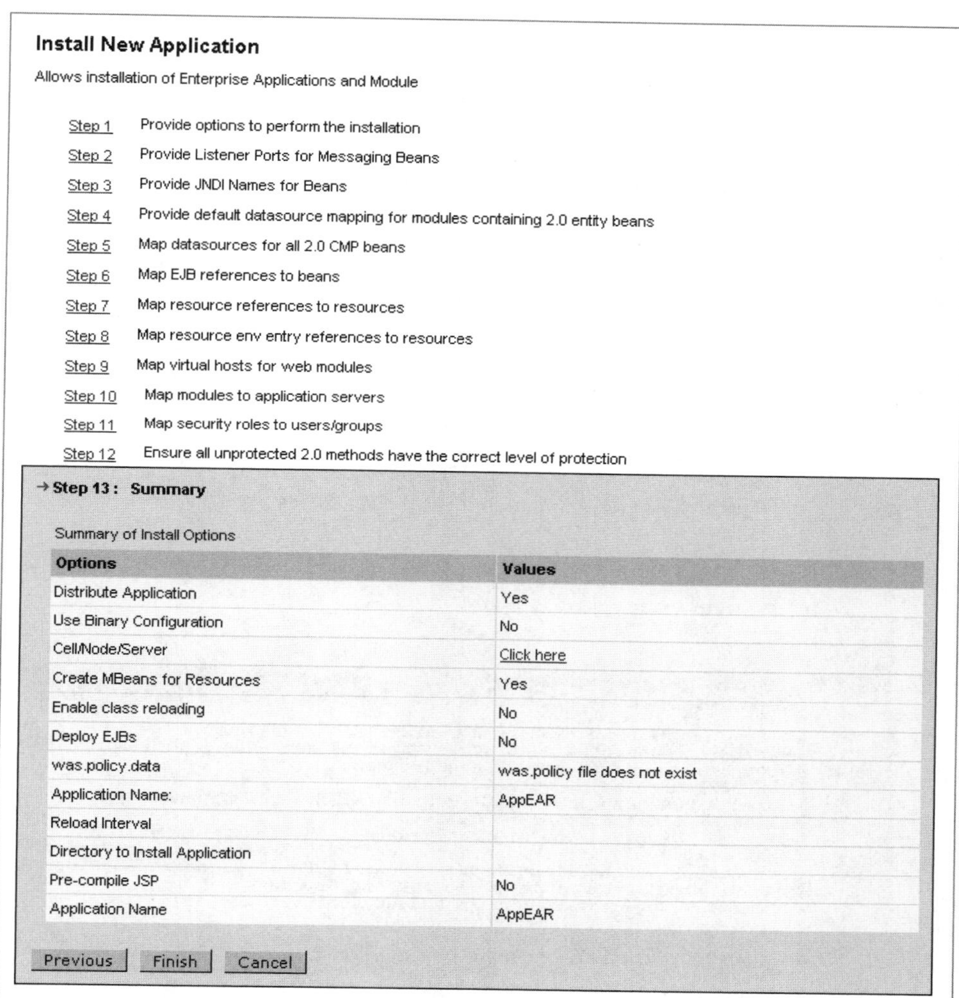

Figure 13.63: WebSphere admin console: summary of install options.

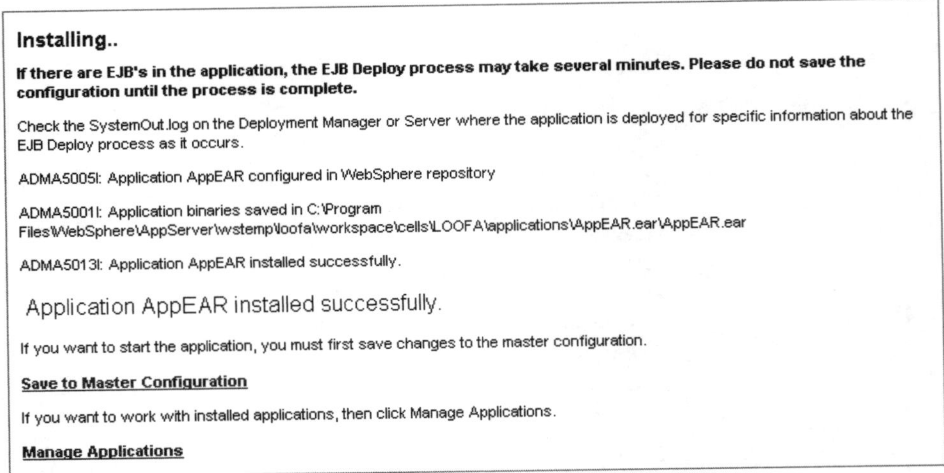

Figure 13.64: WebSphere admin console: simple install.

Figure 13.65 shows how to install and uninstall an application using wsadmin interactively.

```
Command Prompt - wsadmin

C:\Program Files\WebSphere\AppServer\bin>wsadmin
WASX7209I: Connected to process "server1" on node LOOFA using SOAP connector;  T
he type of process is: UnManagedProcess
WASX7029I: For help, enter: "$Help help"
wsadmin>$AdminApp install C://ears/AppEAR.ear {-appname App}
ADMA5016I: Installation of App started.
ADMA5005I: Application App configured in WebSphere repository
ADMA5001I: Application binaries saved in C:\Program Files\WebSphere\AppServer\ws
temp\Scriptf582dac561\workspace\cells\LOOFA\applications\App.ear\App.ear
ADMA5011I: Cleanup of temp dir for app App done.
ADMA5013I: Application App installed successfully.

wsadmin>$AdminApp uninstall App
ADMA5017I: Uninstallation of App started.
ADMA5104I: Server index entry for LOOFA was updated successfully.
ADMA5102I: Deletion of config data for App from config repository completed succ
essfully.
ADMA5011I: Cleanup of temp dir for app App done.
ADMA5106I: Application App uninstalled successfully.

wsadmin>
```

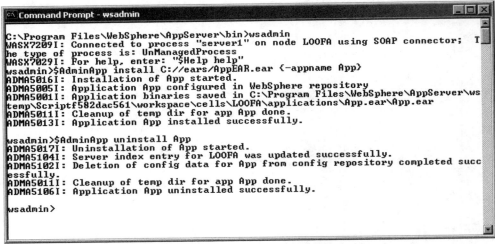

Figure 13.65: Installing and uninstalling a J2EE application using wsadmin.

Finally, Figure 13.66 shows how to install an application and save the WebSphere Application Server configuration using JACL.

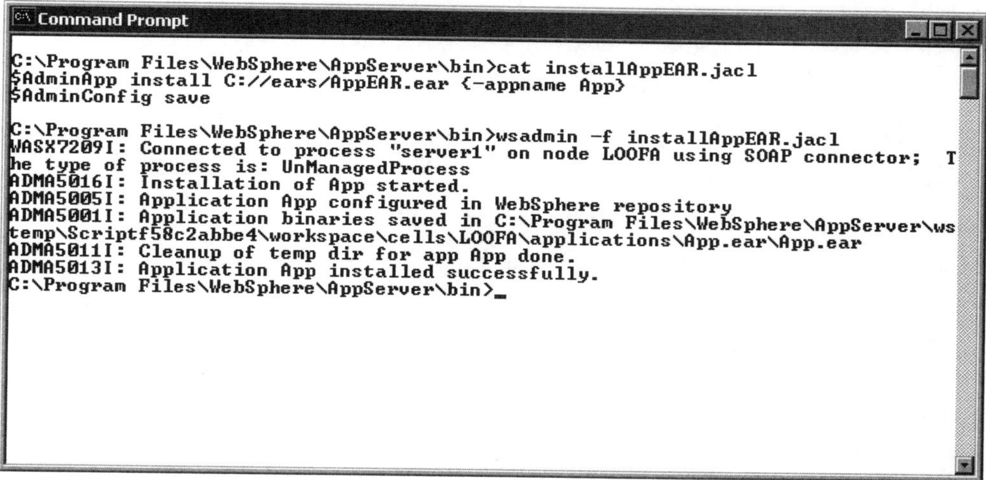

Figure 13.66: Installing a J2EE application using JACL.

Summary

Traditionally, developers use tooling appropriate for writing code. Likewise, administrators traditionally use tooling appropriate for operating code. J2EE bridges this clear separation with the roles discussed in this chapter. These additional roles muddy the waters of traditional software tooling. Whereas the evolution of traditional software tools remains governed by isolated software lifecycle roles, the survival of a new breed of tools depends on how well it thrives in the muddy environment that integrates these roles. WebSphere Studio Application Developer and the associated Eclipse project come from a concerted effort at IBM to create tooling that rapidly evolves to meet the needs of integrated software lifecycle roles.

Test yourself

Key terms

packaging

deployment

naming

deployment descriptors

environment entry references

resource manager connection factory references

resource environment references

EJB references

security role references

Review questions

1. List the roles defined by J2EE.
2. Compare the coarse security constraints provided by J2EE Web components against the fine-grained authorization in EJB components.
3. List the four types of J2EE deployment modules.
4. What types of archives can J2EE applications contain?
5. Describe the overlap in J2EE roles between the Administrator role and the Deployer role.

CHAPTER 14

WebSphere administration

Kameron Cole

Chapter topics

- *Performance-tuning tools*
- *Assessing the health of the Java Virtual Machine*
- *Assessing the health of the WebSphere Network*
- *Connection pooling (for Developers)*
- *Connection pooling (for Administrators)*
- *Miscellaneous parameter settings for performance enhancement*
- *Session Management*
- *The importance of classloaders*
- *Tracing*

Certification objectives

- *Manage end-user state and understand performance tradeoffs of using HTTP sessions*
- *Create, configure, and tune connection pools*
- *Interact with connection pools to obtain and release connections*
- *Use tracing and profiling tools to analyze and tune applications*
- *Explain implications of resource management on application design and implementation*
- *Identify misbehaving application components*
- *Describe the effects of a server failure on the application*
- *Validate operational parameters of application server to support the enterprise application*

This chapter is not intended to be an overview of the administration of WebSphere Application Server Version 5. Insofar as the certification test for which this book was intended is geared toward developers, so too is this chapter. Consequently, this chapter will deal with the issues on which enterprise developers and administrators will interact—basically, the types of tuning that a developer can do on an application; the types of application server tuning that will affect the performance of the application; production errors that pertain to and/or are caused by development; and, finally, the implications on the run time of application architecture and packaging.

Performance-tuning tools

The tuning of an application is a shared responsibility between the developer and the administrator. The kinds of things that each is responsible for tuning, however, are different. In general, the developer needs to look for the age-old memory leak and the unnecessary retention of unused resources. Also, the developer can make some relative judgments as to the length of method execution and whether those relative lengths are appropriate. (We say "relative" here because there is really no way that a developer can get absolute readings in terms of production performance.) A working definition, then, of the types of things that are left to the developer to tune would include those aspects of application performance that are limited to the boundaries of an application server—a Java Virtual Machine (JVM) or, specifically, those parts of the JVM that concern components but not the containers that manage those components.

The administrator is responsible for tuning those elements of the running of an application that begin at the boundary of the Application Server and extend beyond it. In later sections of this document, the reader will find a lengthy discussion of connection pooling parameters associated with DataSources. Since DataSources are configured by administrators and can be accessed by any application in a given WebSphere domain, DataSource tuning is clearly within the purview of the administrator. Also included would be the tuning of the various containers that process components within the application server: the client container, the web container, and the EJB container. Once the internal components of the application server and their containers have been tuned, the administrator must consider other servers that support the application server, namely the Web server and the database server. Finally, after each of the aforementioned elements is functioning at its "best" (according to criteria for acceptable performance established by administrative directives—not in terms of some "absolute best"), the administrator can improve performance by such measures as adding an IP sprayer, such as IBM WebSphere Edge Server, or cloning an application server.

The "Producers"

All of this tuning must begin with the collection of performance-related data; thus, that is where the discussion will begin.

The Performance Monitoring Infrastructure (PMI)

The Performance Monitoring Infrastructure is a set of WebSphere packages and libraries designed to cover four areas of performance monitoring: gathering, delivering, processing, and displaying. This infrastructure is compatible with and extends the JSR-077 specification (also known as J2EE™ Management); cf. *jcp.org/en/jsr/detail?id=077.*
Figure 14.1 will facilitate a short discussion of how these aspects are handled:

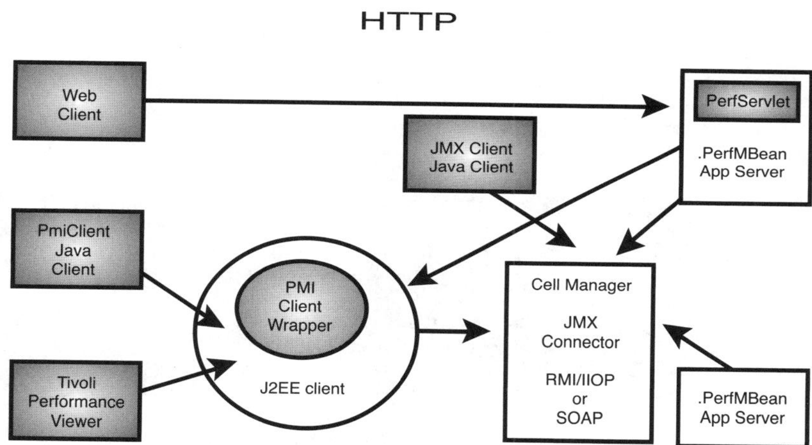

Figure 14.1: Client/server architecture of PMI. (Source: IBM WebSphere Application Server InfoCenter.)

Figure 14.1 shows that the PMI Session EJB (PerfMBean), running in the WebSphere cell manager, retrieves performance data from application servers (the "servers" in the client/server model), which is collected and made available for display to "clients," e.g., Tivoli Performance Viewer, the PerfServlet (not shown in the figure), and the Java Management Extensions (JMX) client, via the PmiClient interface (PMI client wrapper in Figure 14.1).

Another measurement subset of the PMI is the PMI request metrics, which measure the time a request spends in each of the WebSphere components (e.g., web container) and can report these times to Application Response Measurement (ARM) Time agents (see the section called "The Collectors" later in this chapter).

Enabling the PMI

To get started with the PMI, follow these steps (Figure 14.2):

1. Open the administrative console.
2. Click **Servers → Application Server** and then, in the right-hand pane, **YourServer**.

3. Scroll down the **Configuration** tab.
4. Click **Performance Monitoring Service**.
5. Make sure the **Startup** check box is checked.
6. Select the PMI modules and levels to set the initial specification level field (setting to Standard sets all levels to high).
7. Click **Apply** or **OK**.
8. Click **Save**.
9. Restart the server.

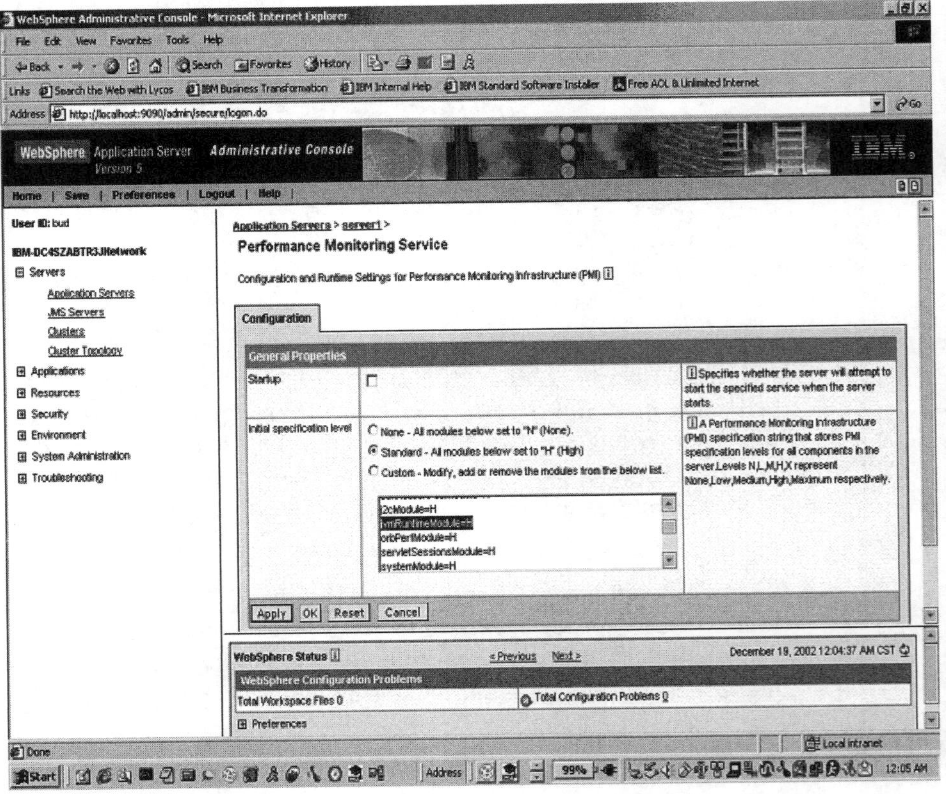

Figure 14.2: Turning on the PMI.

Java Virtual Machine Profiler Interface (JVMPI)

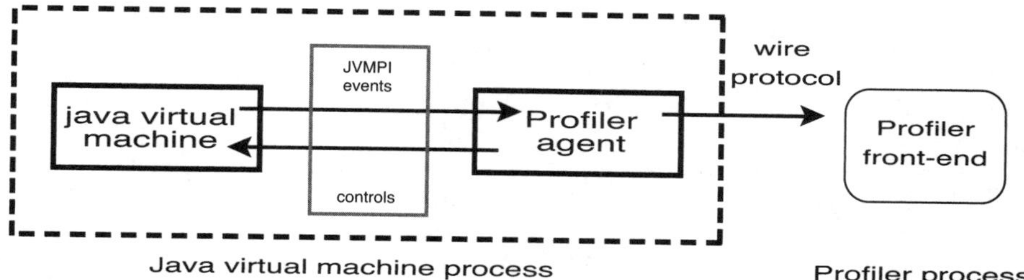

Figure 14.3: JVMPI client/server architecture.

As Figure 14.3 shows, the JVMPI is an interface that is conceptually very similar to the client and event listener interfaces in IBM WebSphere's PMI: "a two-way function call interface between the Java virtual machine and an in-process profiler agent" (*java.sun.com/products/jdk/1.2/docs/guide/jvmpi/jvmpi.html*). More focused on JVM memory usage, the JVMPI cannot provide performance data over the wide range of "servers" that PMI can. However, it offers greater detail in this data set (JVM memory) than PMI can. Thus, both profiling interfaces are made available to WebSphere Application Server's profiling tools, Tivoli Performance Viewer and PerfServlet, and WebSphere Studio Application Developer's Profiling perspective.

Enabling the JVMPI

With the PMI enabled, both the Performance Monitoring Infrastructure Servlet and the Tivoli Performance Viewer will be able to retrieve data using the PMI. At this point, we might enable the JVMPI as well, making our query of performance metrics as complete as possible. The steps in enabling the JVMPI are as follows (see Figure 14.4):

1. Open the administrative console.
2. Click **Servers → Application Servers** in the console navigation tree.
3. Click the application server for which JVMPI needs to be enabled.
4. Click **Process Definition.**
5. Click the Java Virtual Machine.
6. Type **-XrunpmiJvmpiProfiler** in the **Generic JVM arguments** field. Click **Apply**.
7. Now, return to the **Application Servers → YourServer → PMI Service** window (where you initially enabled the PMI). Switch your Initial Specification Level to **Custom**. Then set the jvmRuntimeModule level equal to **X** (Figure 14.5); note that M is for medium and X is for maximum.

8. Click **Apply** or **OK**.
9. Click **Save**.
10. Start the application server, or restart the application server if it is currently running.

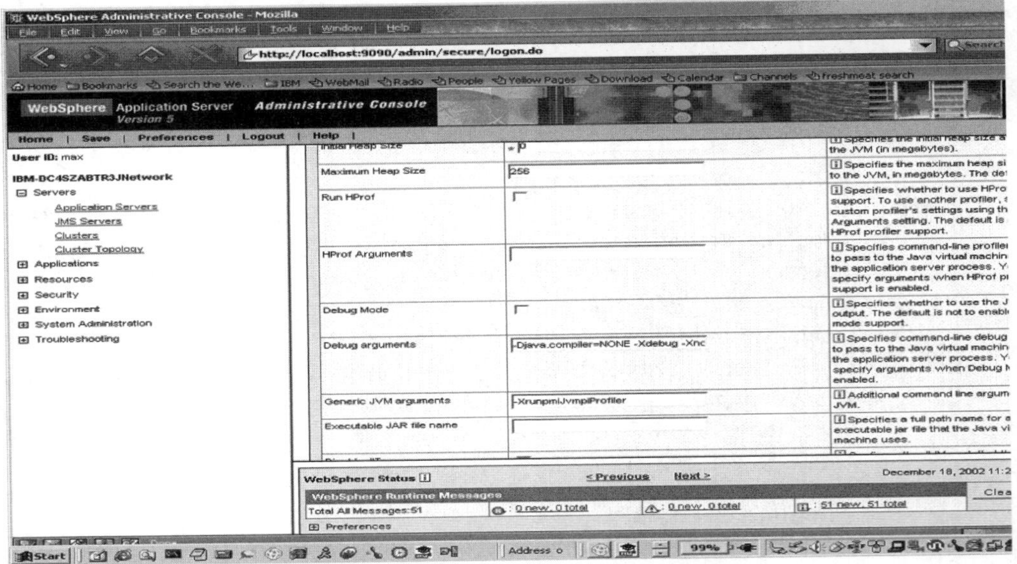

Figure 14.4: JVMPI enabled.

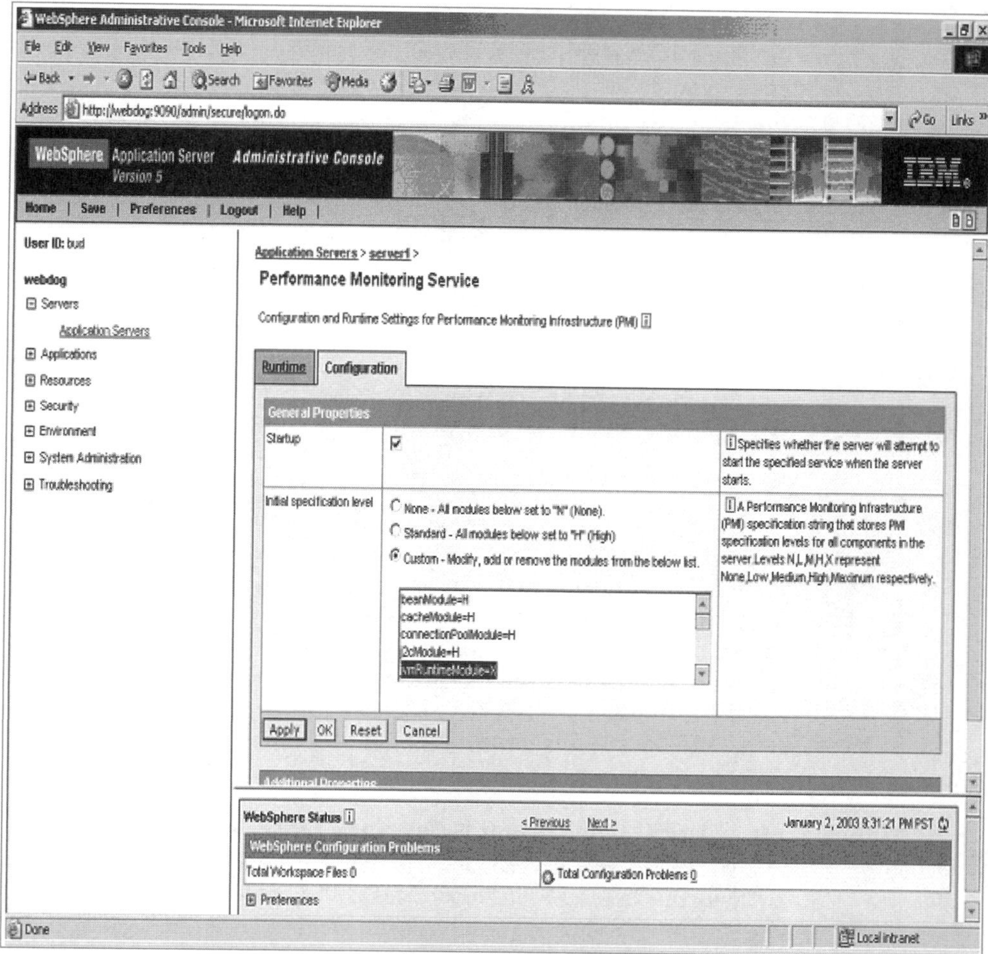

Figure 14.5: jvmRuntimeModule set equal to X for Maximum.

At this point, we have set up the "server side" of the PMI architecture. The discussion that follows covers the various "clients"—tools for collecting and viewing performance data produced by the PMI and JVMPI.

The "Collectors"

As mentioned earlier, the PMI is a client/server architecture. In the previous section, we focused on what would be referred to as the "servers"—the reporters of performance data. In this section, we will deal with "client" applications, which are developed for the collecting and presentation of the raw data.

WebSphere Studio Application Developer: Profiling perspective

WebSphere Studio Application Developer comes with a special perspective, uniquely designed to guide the developer in his/her particular tuning. This will be discussed in detail in Chapter 15.

WebSphere Application Server: Tivoli Performance Viewer (formerly called Resource Analyzer)

As seen in Figure 14.1, Tivoli Performance Viewer, formerly called Resource Analyzer, is a client to the PMI in a WebSphere Application Server. Its function is to organize collected data into objects in a hierarchical tree, the top of which is the Node. The node represents, as it has throughout the history of WebSphere, the physical machine. The immediate child of the node is the Server, which provides services but collects no data. The server contains Modules, which are channels for reporting component data (these can also contain Submodules). These modules would be, for example, the various connection pools, including J2C and JDBC connection pools, or the Object Request Broker (ORB) and the Web Container, which would have their respective thread pools as submodules (later we will discuss several of the modules in detail). The recorded data is controlled by an XML config file, which maintains a *uid* (unique identifier) for each datum reported in the module. The final division in the hierarchy is the Counter, which holds the results of a variety of calculations for the modules, with varying costs in terms of performance degradation. Each resource category (module) has an associated set of counters. Examples of counters include the number of active enterprise beans, the time spent responding to a servlet request, or the number of kilobytes of available memory. The data points within a module are queried and distinguished by the Mbean ObjectNames or PerfDescriptors.

The New Java Management Extensions (JMX) API

The JVMs in WebSphere Version 5 can be controlled programmatically with JMX, part of the javax.management package of J2EE. A concrete coding example using the JMX packages to programmatically set instrumentation levels and collect data can be found in the WebSphere Application Server Version 5 InfoCenter.

WebSphere Application Server: Performance Monitoring Infrastructure Servlet

As seen in Figure 14.1, the Performance Monitoring Infrastructure Servlet retrieves performance data through an HTTP request via the PMI. It can also be a client to the JVMPI. In this regard, it is very similar to the Tivoli Performance Viewer.

The Performance Monitoring Infrastructure Servlet comes with WebSphere Application Server as one of the Enterprise Applications in the <AS_ROOT>/installableApps directory. Installation is straightforward:

1. First, you will need to start the WebSphere Administrative Server if it has not already been started.

2. In the Admin Console, under the node you wish to monitor, drill down one level under Applications and select **Install New Application**.

3. In the "Preparing for the application installation" window, under "Specify the EAR/WAR/JAR module to upload and install," click **Browse**.

4. Navigate to the <WAS INSTALL>/installableApps folder, select **PerfServletApp.ear**, and click **Open**.

5. Back on the "Specify the EAR/WAR/JAR module to upload and install" panel, click **Next**.

6. You can accept the defaults for Generate Default Bindings. That is, do not generate any bindings; leave the existing bindings as they are. Click **Next**. You will be presented with five steps.
   - In "Step 1: Provide options to perform the installation," you must check the **Enable Class Reloading** checkbox; otherwise, you might leave the defaults, although we are not necessarily distributing this application.
   - In "Step 2: Map virtual hosts for Web modules," check **PerfServlet.**
   - In "Step 3: Map modules to application servers" check that the application server designated is the one you intend to test. Check **PerfServlet.** Click **Next**.
   - In "Step 4: Map security roles to users/groups," you can choose either Everyone, or All Authenticated.
   - In Step 5, click **Finish**. Depending on the amount of memory your machine has, the installation of the application may take a while.

7. When the installation completes, you will need to start the application. However, a warning at the top of the AdminConsole reminds you that you will need to save the configuration prior to starting the newly installed application. Click this warning, and then click the **Save** button.

8. To start the perfServletApp, go back to Enterprise Applications, find perfServlet App, and check the box next to it. Then, click **Start** in the menu bar at the top of this window. Because you checked Enable Class Reloading during the installation, you will not need to restart the server for changes to take effect. Open your Web your browser using the URL http://*yourHost:yourPort/wasPerfTool/servlet/perfservlet*. If you haven't enabled the PMI services yet, you will get something like the screen shown in Figure 14.6.

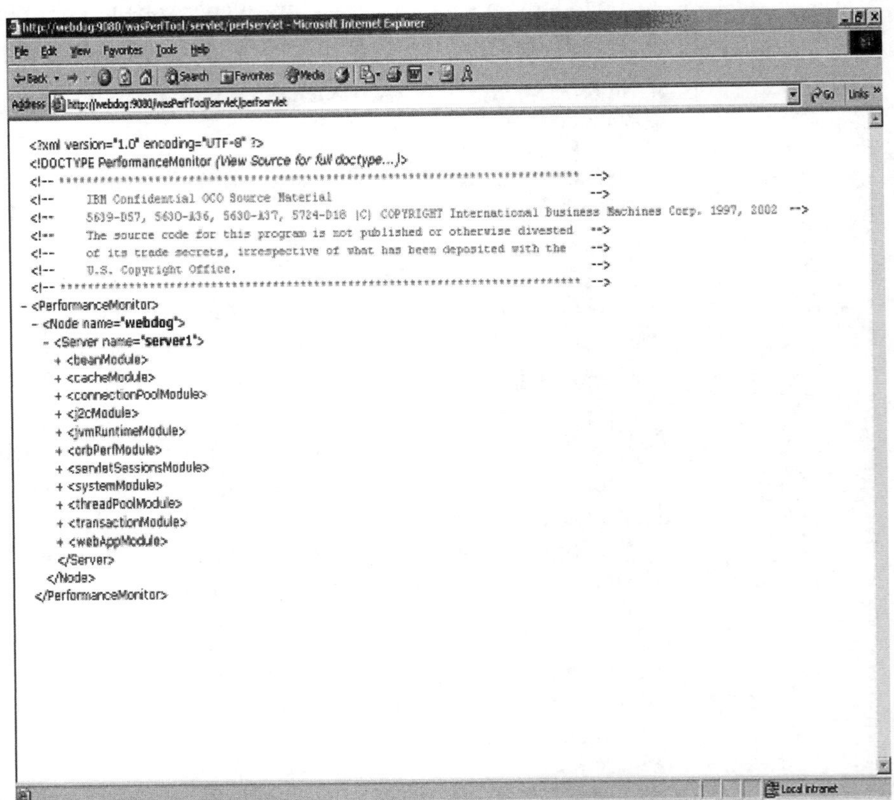

Figure 14.6: Performance Monitoring Infrastructure Servlet installed.

At this point, we would have one remaining step before we could collect our performance data—namely, to set the performance monitoring settings for those Application Server elements we wish to monitor. But which elements do we want to monitor? We need some framework to guide our performance data collection.

The discussion will now turn to two performance concepts that will guide us in selecting and analyzing performance data: the WebSphere Queuing Network and the "health" of the Java Virtual Machine.

Assessing the health of the Java Virtual Machine

The simplest and yet most fundamental notion to grasp in WebSphere is that "WebSphere" is a Java Virtual Machine. If the JVM is not tuned, then really nothing is tuned.

Healthy garbage collection patterns

One of Java's signature features is that it is a "managed" language; that is, the language doesn't stop after the byte code is generated. The use of memory is closely and continuously monitored and controlled. This was a design reaction to the programmatic management of memory in languages like C, and it supports a Java maxim that low-level maintenance tasks should be removed from the developer's list of burdens.

The process is very simple: At the point where memory has the potential to degrade performance, the "garbage collector" is executed. This utility applies a simple algorithm to traverse the "heap" in search of dereferenced objects, which can then safely be removed.

Although this process is ultimately meant to improve performance, it is in fact a heavy consumer of resources itself: The collection process is expensive in both time and CPU utilization. Thus, on a very simple level, the garage collector should run infrequently. However, with a decrease in frequency comes an increase in the amount of garbage to be collected, hence, an increase in the duration of the running of the algorithm. While the algorithm is running, the CPU is significantly compromised. Thus, long garbage collections are also not desirable.

As a happy medium, garbage collection should use between 5 and 20 percent of total application execution time; that is, if the duration of a single collection is, on the average, one fifth of the average time-span between collections, the overall collection load is around 20 percent of total application execution time. A proportion greater than this would indicate less than optimal garbage collection performance. Consider the screen shown in Figure 14.7:

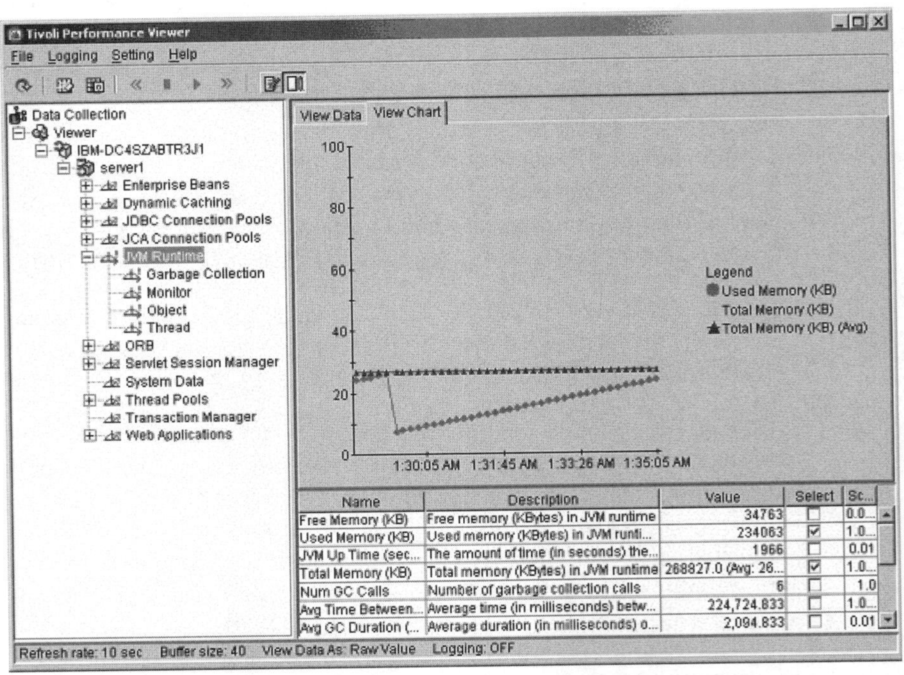

Figure 14.7: Optimizing JVM garbage collection.(Note that the JVMPI has been enabled for this JVM.)

Here we can see that if we divide the average GC duration (2094.833 milliseconds) by the average time between garbage collections (224,724.833 milliseconds), ratio is roughly 1 percent. This is, of course, a trivial example. The efficiency could be further optimized by increasing the numerator (average GC duration) tenfold, which would give us 10 percent, or twentyfold (roughly 44,000 milliseconds), which would give us 20 percent. Since the GC duration is a function of the number of objects on the heap, increasing the heap size would accomplish this.

If, in contrast to this example, the ratio is greater than 20 percent, it could indicate over-utilization of objects. To correct this in the most efficient way we would first discover which objects are causing the bottleneck using the JVMPI profiling in Tivoli Performance Viewer or the Profiling Perspective in WebSphere Studio Application Developer (see Chapter 15); then, we would use WebSphere optimization features such as object caches and pools. A less efficient solution would be the use of cloning.

Yet another, more elusive, cause of poor memory utilization is the infamous "memory leak." Java professionals are sometimes "deceived" by the notion of Java garbage collection: The assumption is that memory leaks have been eradicated by the management of garbage collection by the JVM. Since objects can be garbage-collected only if they are dereferenced, it is clear that, unless unused objects are set to null, unused objects can be retained, sometimes, recursively. This can be detected most easily using the Tivoli Performance Viewer. Consider Figure 14.8.

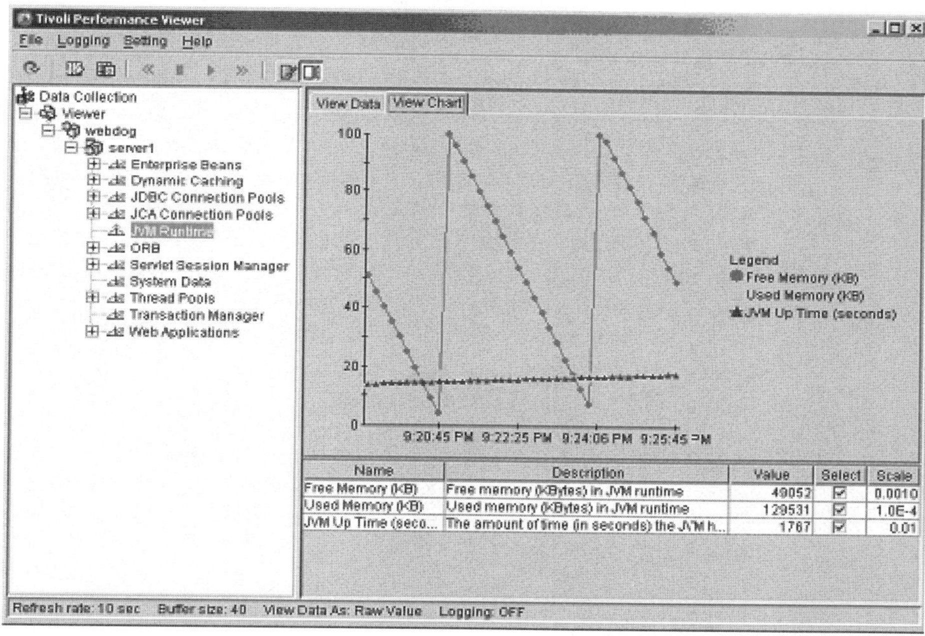

Figure 14.8: "Sawtooth" pattern.

The figure shows what is termed the healthy "sawtooth" pattern: First, the memory utilization constantly achieves 100 percent, which is ideal, since it means that the available memory is being completely utilized but not overutilized (i.e., causing "paging" into main memory); second, the garbage collection is completely emptying memory (i.e., consistently returning to 0).

In contrast, the "staircase" pattern indicates retained objects, which accumulate over time. If this is the case, the developers would need to do a thorough analysis of their object de-referencing, ideally using the Profiling perspective in WebSphere Studio Application Developer.

If the irregularity is noted only at peak utilization and returns to near-normal under light loads, then the cause could be heap fragmentation, which occurs when the garbage collector is able to free sufficient objects to satisfy memory allocation requests but does not have the time to compact available free space. This can also be caused by small objects (under 512 bytes). The objects are garbage-collected, but, due to the nature of the "heap" data structure, memory is not recovered.

Knowing this, the JVM developers have provided an "automatic compaction" flag, -Xcompactgc, which can be added to the JVM arguments. Since this is an additional process, it will lengthen the average GC duration, as mentioned earlier in this chapter. Thus, the ratio of duration to interval would need to be re-evaluated.

Gauging heap size

Adjusting the heap size is one of the first adjustments that can affect this proportion of collection duration to collection interval. A common misconception is that increasing the heap size will simply increase performance. Increasing the heap size allows more objects to be created and stay on the heap for a longer time before being collected as garbage. In contrast, small heap size forces the garbage collector to execute more frequently but collect a smaller number of objects. The perception in the large-heap scenario is that the application is running more efficiently, because the application runs for a longer time without having to "shut down" for garbage collection. However, when collection does eventually happen, performance falls off drastically for a significant amount of time. This reduction in performance, of course, would also be adjusted, referring to the duration-to-interval ratio discussed earlier.

When you begin to adjust the heap size, the initial and maximum heap sizes should be set to equal values. To illustrate the misconception that simply increasing the heap parameters will "automatically" improve performance, consider the set of measurements shown in Figure 14.9.

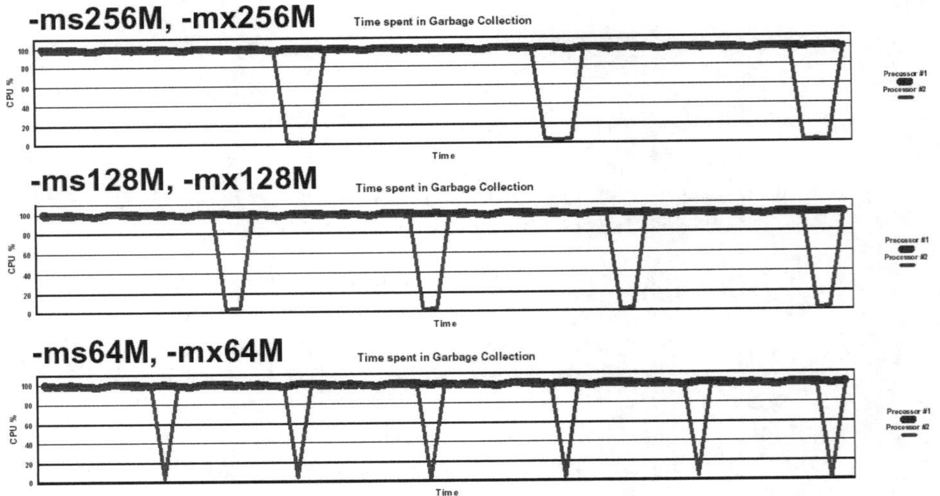

Figure 14.9: Varied JVM heap settings and their effects on garbage collection.

Note that all three sets of data result in an *equal* duration-to-interval ratio—roughly 15 percent for each, despite the fact that the heap size is increased from 64 megabytes to 256 megabytes. Although the number of GC's is decreased, the duration of the garbage collection is increased as a consequence.

When tuning a production system where the working set size of the Java application is not understood, a good starting value is to let the initial heap size be 25 percent of the maximum heap size. The JVM will then try to adapt the size of the heap to the working set size of the application.

Assessing the health of the WebSphere network

One of the most fundamental and accessible architectural aspects of WebSphere to tune is the system of "queues"—thread pools at junctures in the topology. It is with these queues we will begin our discussion of system tuning.

The WebSphere queuing network

Viewed from the application level, WebSphere Application Server is only one component in a series of components that, together, constitute the "path" between the client and the back end (see Figure 14.10). In this light, the WebSphere domain can be considered as a series of load-dependent queues; that is, the response time for the client is a function of the number of the service requests in the queues and the efficiency of this queuing network to process those requests.

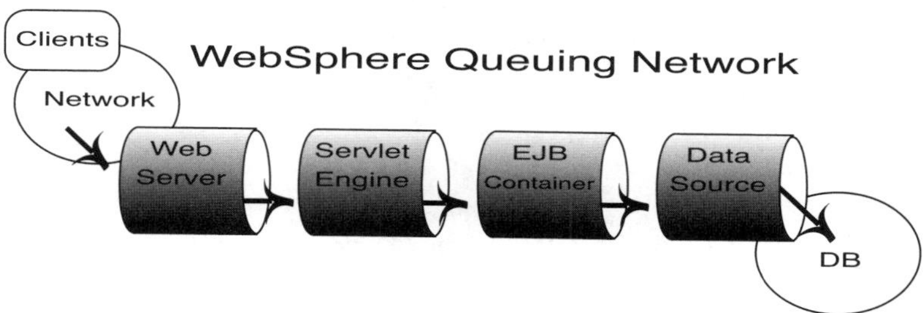

Figure 14.10: Queues: the network, the web server, Web Container (servlet engine), the EJB Container, the DataSource, and the database. (Source: IBM WebSphere Application Server InfoCenter)

The efficiency of these queues can be affected by "throttling" or "limiting" the capacity of the queue. Queues that have such a set limit are referred to as *closed*. When this limit is reached, requests are held in the queue, where they remain in the *waiting* state. Requests that are processing work or waiting for a response from the next element in the queue are considered *active*.

Two general principles govern the tuning of the WebSphere network:

- Always have work available for each element in the queue; that is, no element in the queue should ever be idle.
- Make sure that the "work" is ready for processing; that is, a request that has passed through the Web server is ready for processing by an Application Server.

Together, these two concepts form a principle called "upstream queuing." Upstream queuing implies that most of the requests should remain outside of the WebSphere queues, i.e., on the other side of the Web server (the "network" in Figure 14.11). Also, each queue should allow fewer requests than the queue in front of it.

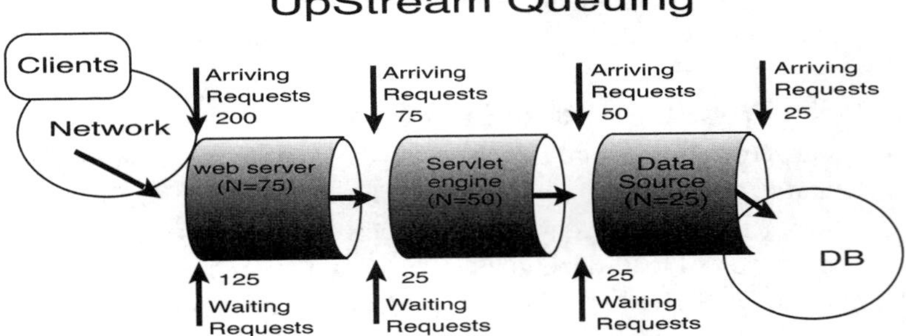

Figure 14.11: "Squeeze" requests toward the network side of the Web server. (Source: IBM WebSphere Application Server Info Center)

Of course, the numbers in Figure 14.11 are purely arbitrary. The WebSphere administrator's task is to discover the correct numbers. Here's where the PMI and its clients come into play.

Producing the throughput curve

The goal is to use the PMI tools to draw an accurate throughput curve to serve as a baseline for later adjustments. Several things are important to note when developing the baseline throughput curve:

- Use the production application. This means a tuned application should be used to tune the WebSphere network; that is, all bottlenecks at the application level must have been removed.

- Don't run the tuning on the production machine. All performance tuning is to be done *before* the application moves to production. A duplicate set of "test" servers is an absolute necessity.

- The goal of this level of testing is to discover the *saturation point*—where the utilization of all CPUs approaches 100 percent—of the WebSphere network, not to measure production performance. Th reason for this is that the measurement of performance affects performance; hence, the measurements will always be accurate. As in the automotive industry, performance testing is done to discover the limitations of a given system so that adjustments can be made to reduce those limitations to acceptable performance criteria. This does not imply, however, that the tests can be done without any knowledge of typical usage. On the contrary, the creation of a throughput curve requires at least one number—the maximum number of users expected at any given time.

There are three steps in producing the throughput curve: setting initial queue sizes, building up the load, and measuring the response times.

Setting the initial queue sizes for the throughput curve

To begin the baseline plotting, we will set all of the queues to an equal value, say 100.

The Web server

For this segment, the IBM HTTP Server will be used as example. All Web servers supported by WebSphere are thoroughly discussed in the WebSphere InfoCenter. In the IBM HTTP Server there is the parent httpd process, apache.sh or apache.exe, which spawns threads to be prepared to handle incoming requests. (These threads also appear as Apache processes, even though they are "lightweight" processes.) The setting for the Web server queue is slightly different for Linux and for other UNIX platforms than for Windows NT. For both platforms, the setting is found in the httpd.conf file (SERVER_ROOT/conf/httpd.conf). For Linux, the parameter is MaxRequestsPerChild, which applies to the number of *requests* each httpd child process will accept. When this number is reached, the child process dies. Under Windows NT, the directive is ThreadsPerChild, but it refers to the number of concurrent threads running at any given time in the Web server. The defaults for both platforms are very low—30 for Linux and 50 for Windows NT. For a start, try setting it to 100. (On either platform you must restart the Web server for the changes to be applied.)

The Web container

The next queue in the WebSphere network is the Web container. This queue is represented by the Maximum Size parameter. To set the parameter, start the Administrative Console and select the Application Server you intend to tune; select **Web Container**, then select **Thread Pool**. The screen shown in Figure 14.12 appears. Set the parameter, click **Apply**, and then save the configuration. You will need to restart the server for changes to take effect, but, since this is true for several other parameters we have to set, you should not restart at this point. Set the value to 100 as a starting point.

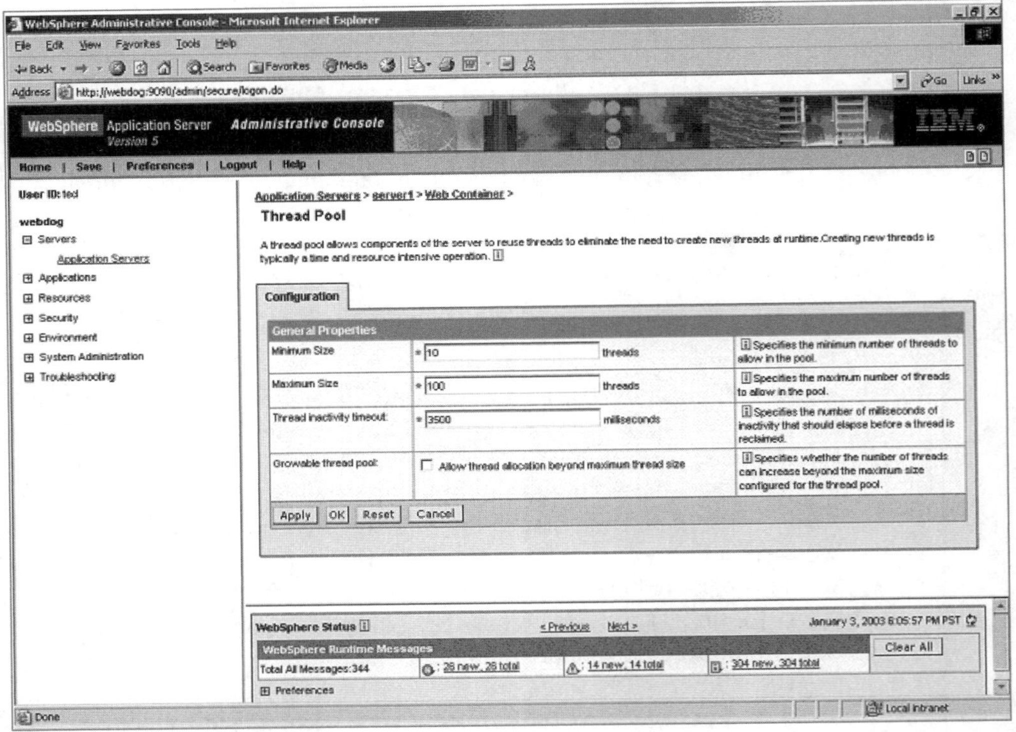

Figure 14.12: Setting the Web Container Queue.

EJB container

The queue for the EJB container is represented by the ORB thread pool size, which is set by selecting **ORB Service → Thread Pools** for the Application Server you intend to tune and entering the size on the screen shown in Figure 14.13.

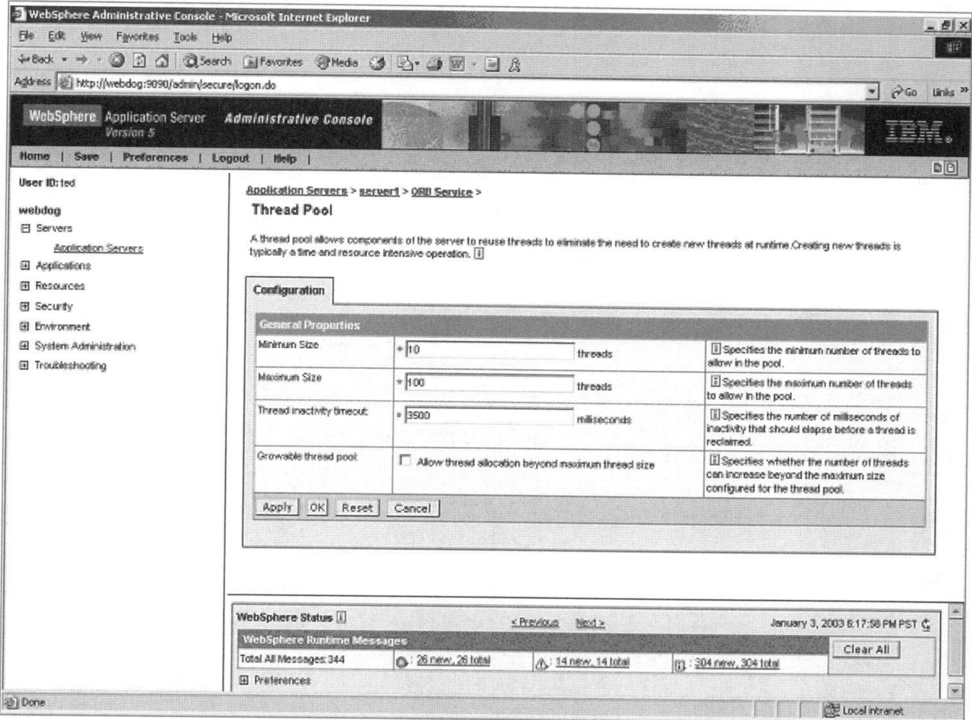

Figure 14.13: Initial setting for ORB thread pool, for defining throughput baseline.

DataSource

The final queue in the WebSphere network is the Connection Pool for a given DataSource. To close this queue, find the driver for the application you are tuning (in the WebSphere Administrative Console, select **Resources → JDBC Providers → MyProvider → MyDataSource → Connection Pools**). The window shown in Figure 14.14 appears. Set the Maximum pool size to **100**. (Remember, closing a queue implies setting the upper limit.)

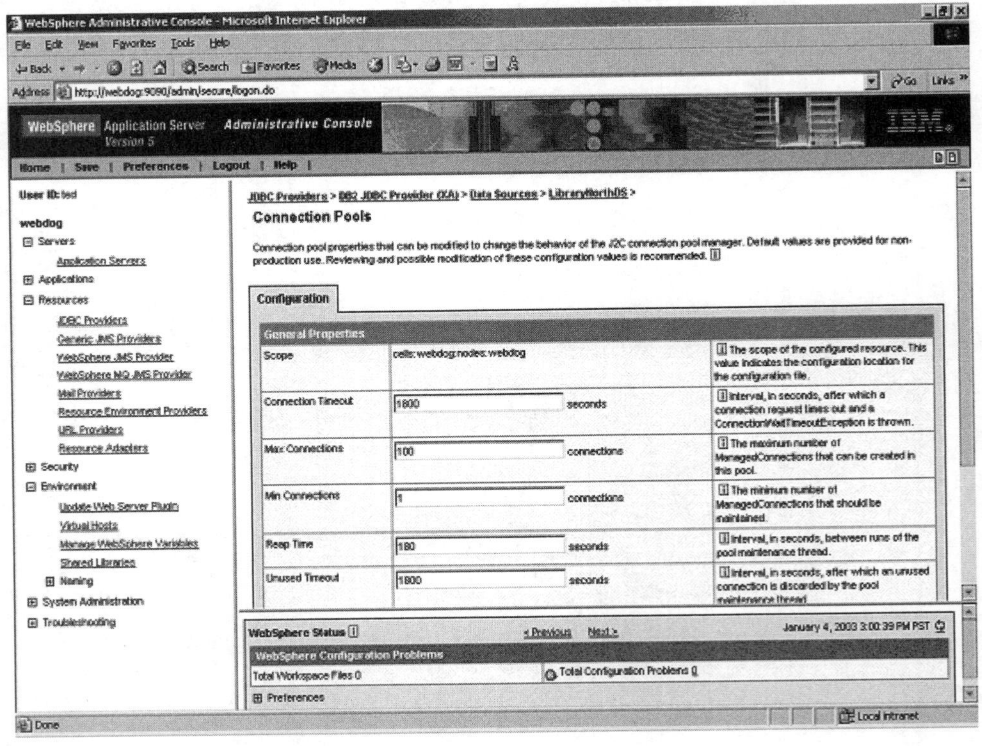

Figure 14.14: Setting the DataSource queue.

Building up the load

At this point, all the queues in the network have been set at equal values to each other. To build up the load, you will lead a load-generating tool, e.g., AKTools or Mercury Load Runner. The goal is to build up the load: Begin with one user and record the throughput (**requests per second**) and your response times (**seconds per request**). Load with two users and do the same. Continue to increase the number of users until your curve begins to "buckle" as shown in Figure 14.15.

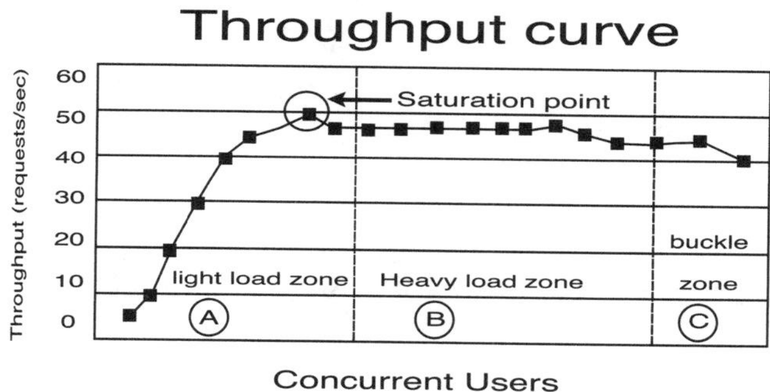

Figure 14.15: Establishing a throughput curve. (Source: IBM WebSphere Application Server InfoCenter)

The next section will discuss how to use the PMI tools to get the data for the throughput graph. At this point, however, it would be a good idea to give an analysis of the graph. Remember, the key in the analysis is the saturation point. More important is the cause of the saturation. The ideal cause of saturation is reaching the maximum utilization of the CPU used by the Application Server. This can be remedied by adding CPUs and placing Application Server Clones on those CPUs. Of course, first we should adjust our queues, as discussed in the following section, to achieve upstream queuing, recalling that the throughput curve is just the initial diagnostic. It gives us an important metric for future tuning adjustments. The saturation point observed earlier is referred to as Max Application Concurrency.

If the saturation point is reached without "maxing out" the CPUs, then the cause of saturation lies most likely in the application. In this case, the tuning analysis must turn to the JVM to discover application bottlenecks, as discussed in the section earliertitled "Assessing the Health of the Java Virtual Machine."

Obtaining the measurements

First, we need to obtain the data to draw our throughput curve. To do this, we will implement the PMI collection tools, Performance Monitoring Servlet, and Tivoli Performance

Viewer. In addition, Web server monitoring will be mentioned, using IBM HTTP Server as an example.

Enabling cross-platform monitoring of IBM HTTP server

Any implementation of the Apache Web server provides a module for accessing its status (for full documentation, see *www.apache.org/docs/mod/*), which we can enable in order to monitor the thread utilization. (Recall the MaxThreadsPerChild parameter we set earlier.) This is a cross-platform approach, since the module is available for Apache servers on all platforms. (There is an NT Performance Monitor, which could also be used to monitor Web server performance.) The enablement steps, all in the httpd.conf file, are as follows:

- Uncomment the following module directive, found at the top of httpd.conf (after a server restart, the module directive moves "up" in the httpd.conf, under ClearModuleList).

```
LoadModule status_module modules/ApacheModuleStatus.dll
```

- Uncomment the Location directive for server-status as follows:

```
<Location /server-status>
SetHandler server-status

#order deny,allow
#deny from all
#allow from .your_domain.com
</Location>
```

- Stop and start your IBM HTTP Server.
- In a Web browser, go to the URL **http://**<*your-host-name*>**/server-status** and click **Reload** to update status. Alternatively, if the browser supports refresh, go to **http://**<*your-host-name*>**/server-status?refresh=5** to refresh every 5 seconds.

From this page, you will be able to get the number of *waiting* requests; these are requests in the queue. The active threads are figured by subtracting the waiting threads from the MaxThreadsPerChild directive.

Enabling monitoring

We can use either the Performance Monitoring Infrastructure servlet or the Tivoli Performance Viewer to view the performance data of our queues. Before we use these tools, however, we will need to enable the PMI Service.

If you followed the steps under "Producing the Throughput Curve," then you might have already done this. If not, the steps (slightly different from those for the Tivoli Performance Monitoring Viewer, to be explained later in this section) are as follows:

1. Open the administrative console.
2. Select **Servers → Application Server → YourServer** in the console navigation tree.
3. Scroll down the Configuration tab.
4. Click **Performance Monitoring Service**.
5. Select the PMI modules and levels to set the initial specification level field. (Setting to Standard sets all levels to high.)

   By setting the Monitoring Level to High (or Maximum; in this case, the counters are the same for both), you will get the counters needed for the throughput curve: Average Response Time and Concurrent Requests (throughput). Click **OK** and then **Apply**. The server will need to be restarted for the settings to take effect.

Note: The term "concurrent users" in the throughput graph should not be confused here with Concurrent Requests, the counter we enable in the PMI. The number of "concurrent users" is the number of users that you feed into the system, using the load generation tool. The Concurrent Requests are the requests (fewer than the concurrent users) that are actually being processed; in fact, the number of requests processed per second, or, *throughput*

Now, start a browser, and enter the address **http://***<your-host-name>***:9080/wasPerfTool/servlet/perfservlet**. Scroll down the page until you find the name of the servlet you are monitoring, and then look for the two pertinent directives:

```
- <concurrentRequests>
     <PerfLoadInfo currentValue="0.0" integral="0.0" mean="0.0"
   time="1038284446112" timeSinceCreate="379906.0" uid="pmi12" />
  </concurrentRequests>
- <responseTime>
     <PerfStatInfo mean="0.0" num="0" sum_of_squares="0.0"
   time="1038284446112" total="0.0" uid="pmi13" />
  </responseTime>
```

Alternatively, you can set the monitoring levels from the Tivoli Performance Viewer:

First, start the Tivoli Performance Viewer from the command line. Navigate to *<SERVER INSTALLATION>*/**bin**. The syntax is

```
tperfviewer <NODE NAME> <PORT> <TRANSPORT PROTOCOL>
```

In the example shown in Figure 14.16, the Tivoli Performance Viewer is initialized to port 2809. Each subsequent installation of an Application Server will increment this port by 1.

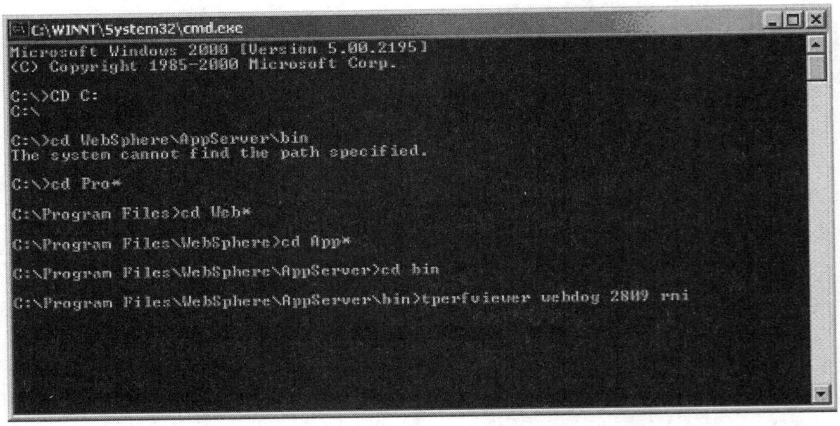

```
C:\WINNT\System32\cmd.exe
Microsoft Windows 2000 [Version 5.00.2195]
(C) Copyright 1985-2000 Microsoft Corp.

C:\>CD C:
C:\

C:\>cd WebSphere\AppServer\bin
The system cannot find the path specified.

C:\>cd Pro*

C:\Program Files>cd Web*

C:\Program Files\WebSphere>cd App*

C:\Program Files\WebSphere\AppServer>cd bin

C:\Program Files\WebSphere\AppServer\bin>tperfviewer webdog 2809 rmi
```

Figure 14.16: Starting the Tivoli Performance Viewer.

When the Tivoli Performance Viewer starts up, you will be presented with the screen shown in Figure 14.17.

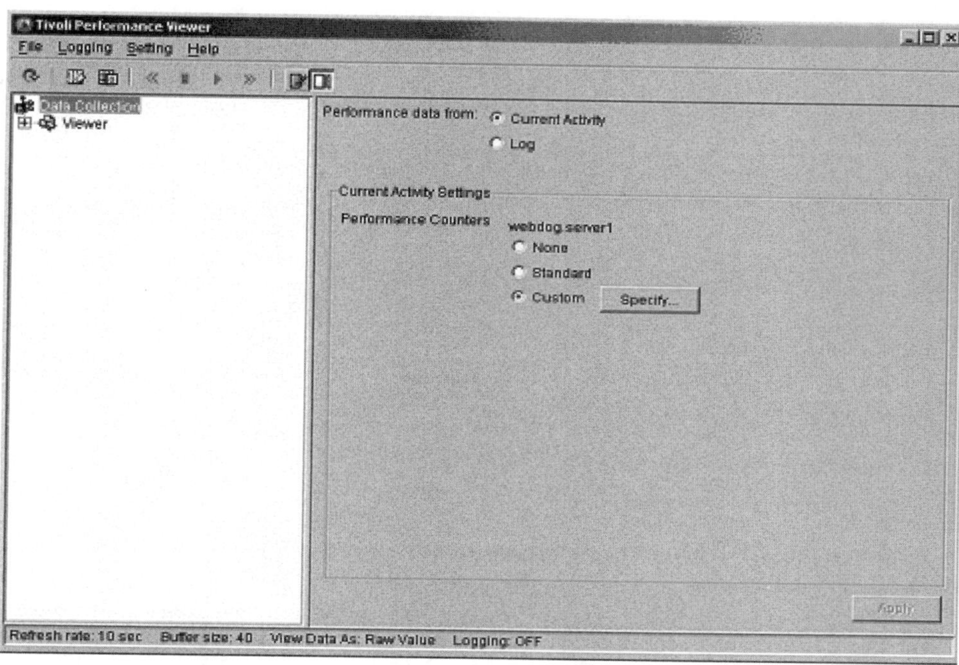

Figure 14.17: Throughput metrics in Tivoli Performance Viewer.

As mentioned earlier, if you choose Standard, all levels will be automatically set to High. This is sufficient for our purposes. However, for demonstration's sake, choose Custom, and then drill down until you find the Web Application and Servlet(s) that you intend to monitor. The assumption here is that you have already set the instrumentation levels for these resources, as for the Performance Servlet, as shown in the screenshot shown in Figure 14.18.

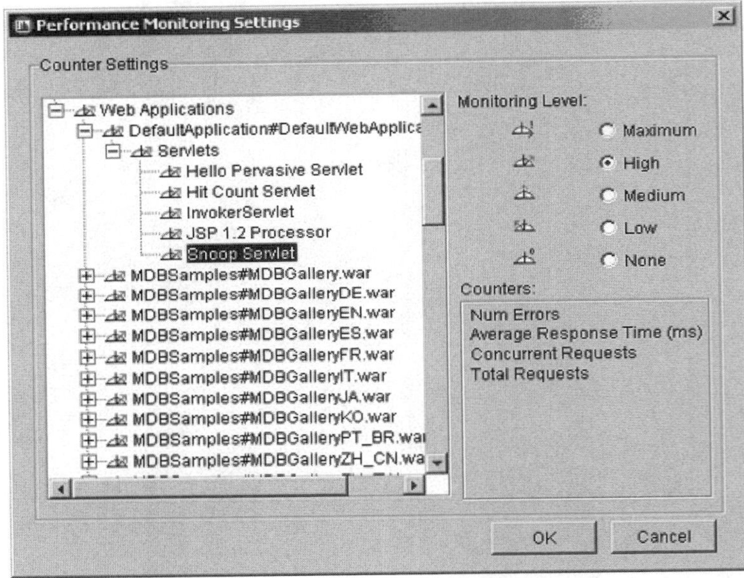

Figure 14.18: Setting the monitoring level for servlets.

Now the Tivoli Performance Viewer will display all the counters we have selected, as shown in Figure 14.19. The user interface can be set to numerical display or graphic, and the counters can be filtered at any time.

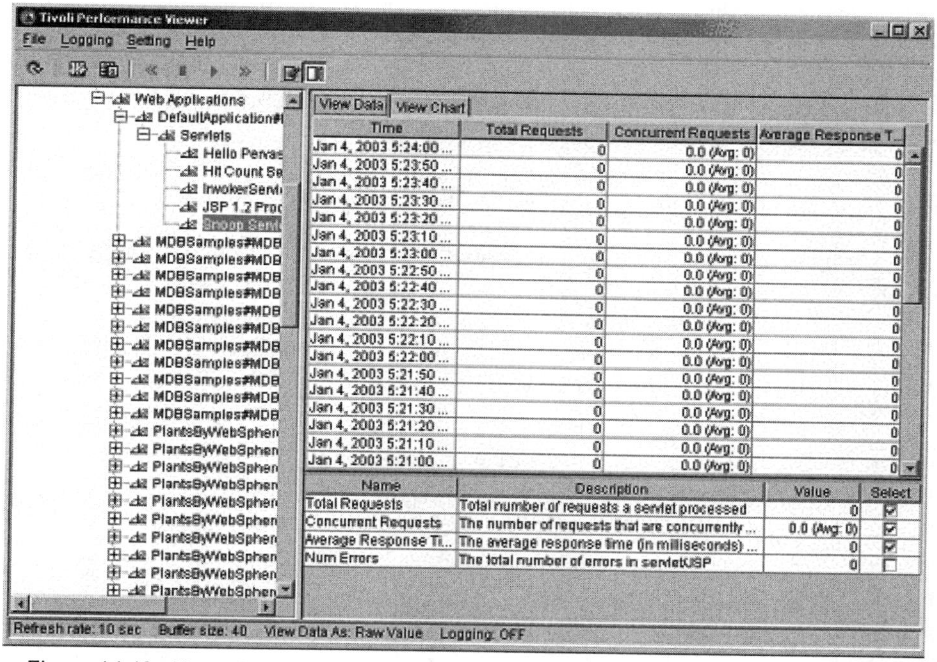

Figure 14.19: Numerical representations of throughput metrics in Tivoli Performance Viewer.

Note that we have focused solely on the throughput of a single servlet. Obviously, this was only for the purposes of demonstration, as the administrator would, in fact, need to produce throughput curve for all of the major and minor paths in the application. However, the steps will be identical to those in our examples.

Setting queue sizes for performance

So far, the goal has been merely to plot a rough throughput curve, which is why we set all the queue sizes to an arbitrary number, 100. Now the WebSphere administrator would need to return to each queue and give it a "realistic" setting.

The word "realistic" in this context is quite elusive. This comes as a surprise to some administrators, but a brief discussion should make this clear. The ambiguity of "realistic" stems from the ambiguity in another frequently misused phrase: "good performance." There is no reason to ask the administrator of another company, another Application Server, even another J2EE Application, what "good performance" is, since this a prescriptive metric, not descriptive. In other words, it is the development team, in conjunction with the administrators, in congress with the business people, who must all describe a "performance continuum" very early in the application development cycle, according to the expectations of the business and the realistic limitations of the programming model and hardware. We have seen that at one end of the continuum is the *saturation point*—the point at which, due to the limitations of the current equipment and workload distribution, the application's performance simply cannot improve. This can possibly be extended by the addition of more Application Server Clones, the addition of more processors—but only *possibly*, not *necessarily*. In any case, the continuum will have an upper bound. This upper bound does not necessarily represent "optimal" performance for this application. Further tuning will reveal *optimal* performance.

Somewhere in the middle of the continuum is the more practical, "realistic" *acceptable* performance range, with its lower extreme at the "bottom" of the continuum, the *minimum acceptable* performance. Once this metric is decided upon, it becomes a tacit guarantee that the end user will never experience performance lower than this boundary, and it is the constant work of the application team at least to maintain, but preferably to increase, this metric.

First, however, the application team must discover this "optimal" and "minimum" performance and possibly refine the saturation point derived from the initial throughput curve by setting queue values. This is also a question to which many request a "simple" answer. Unfortunately, the answer has many contingencies, the most significant of which is the usage pattern unique to each particular application. (This uniqueness of usage patterns in individual applications is the reason why only one application per application server is recommended for tuning.)

For example, in a robust "controller" design, every user action may be processed by a single servlet, the command servlet. Here, the command servlet would serve as a very convenient throughput measurement point, but clearly not a point of reference for tuning the queues subsequent to the Web container that contains the command servlet; that is, the usage pattern and path for one command can be radically different from those for another. One command could, for example, be a write-only command to a log that utilizes a singleton EJB, while another command, in contrast, could do millions of read-write operations using direct JDBC calls. Clearly, the demand on the DataSource Connection Pools would be at the far ends of the usage spectrum for these two paths. In many Web-based applications the bulk of requests may be handled at the Web server and never even reach any subsequent queue.

With these serious considerations in mind, the next section offer simple guidelines for each of the queues discussed.

EJB queuing

The most fundamental piece of usage-pattern information necessary for tuning the EJB queue is whether the EJB client is collocated in the same JVM as the EJB being called. This is significant because *WebSphere queuing in the ORB does not take place if the calling client is local.* In this case, the EJB method runs on the thread of the calling client, making any adjustment of the ORB thread pool (i.e., the "EJB queue") superfluous.

Once it has been established that the client-EJB relationship will always be remote, it is still not so much an issue of "queuing" as it is one of resource management. This is because the EJB queue cannot be *closed*. EJB requests are handled by the Object Request Broker, and thus the "EJB queue" corresponds to the ORB Thread Pool. As with most pooling mechanisms, threads in the pool are shared among requests. If requests are typically very short in duration, the pool size can be very small. Although we emphasize that there is no "magic" relationship implied here, the ORB Thread Pool could be set to half the number of Web container threads, for example.

On the other hand, the requests from servlets may utilize the ORB for the duration of a very complex and long method call, as is typical in the Session Façade pattern. In this case, the ORB threads and the Web container threads share a one-to-one relationship, and downstream queuing would be inappropriate: The ORB Thread Pool should be set equal to the Web container threads.

Note, however, that, as mentioned earlier, the ORB Thread Pool is open—that is, if no thread is available to process the request, a new thread is simply created and then discarded after the call completes. In other words, no actual queuing of requests ever occurs in the ORB. The setting of the ORB Thread Pool size has the effect, rather, of improving performance of the JVM by reducing the unnecessary, costly creation and destruction of threads.

To investigate the efficiency of ORB Thread Pool management, we can monitor a metric called Percent Maxed, using the Tivoli Performance Viewer, as shown in Figure 14.20:

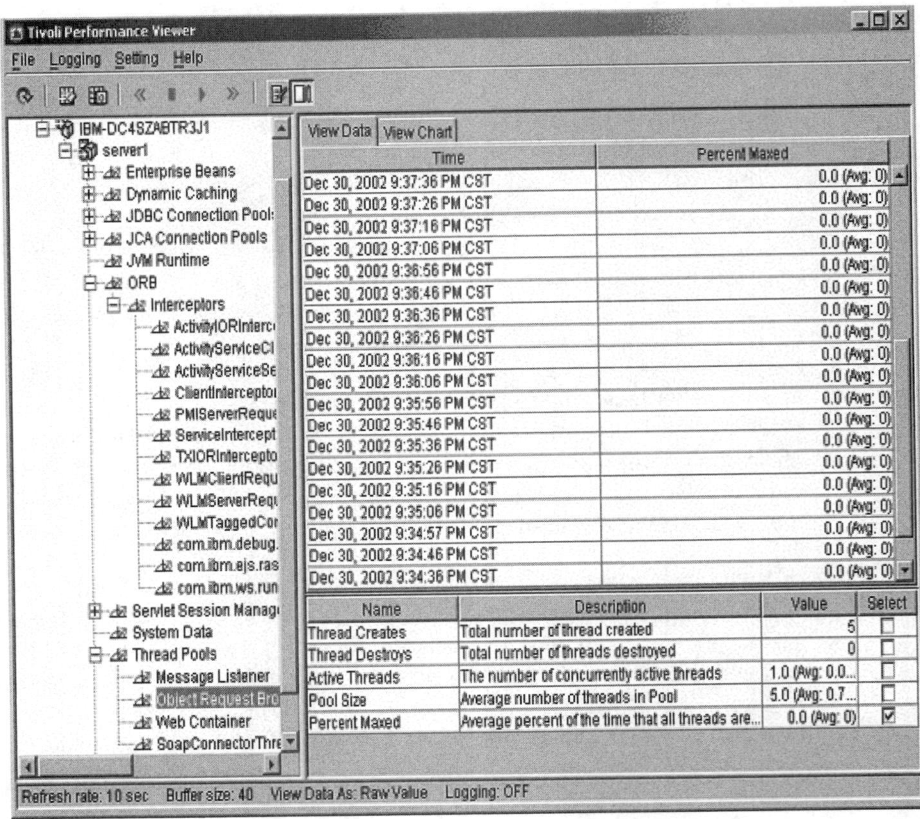

Figure 14.20: The Percent Maxed metric for the Orb Thread Pool.

Basically, if the value of Percent Maxed falls consistently in the double digits, the ORB may represent a bottleneck, which can be remedied by increasing the ORB Thread Pool size.

One final consideration is the effect of clustering (cloning) on EJB queuing. If, for example, an application uses an EJB server (i.e., an Application Server with only an EJB container), and this server is cloned, the location of that clone and the Workload Manager (WLM) Selection Policy for the ORB that routes requests to the EJB servers will be important factors. Consider, for example, that one clone of the EJB server is collocated with the calling Web container, and the other clone is located remotely from the Web container. If the WLM Policy were set to *random* or *round-robin*, there would be two distinct queuing patterns used by the same application. If, on the other hand, the WLM Policy included *local-preferred*, there would be no queuing.

Web container queuing

There is no simple formula for setting the size of the Web container queue. Considerations include the saturation point we have already discussed at length, the general notion, also already discussed, of upstream queuing or keeping the bulk of the work outside the Application Server, and some general rules for JVM management, which were discussed in the JVM Tuning section earlier in this chapter. The queue is closed by setting the Maximum Thread Size parameter. (Recall that closed implies that once the Maximum Thread Size is reached, the remaining request will remain queued, i.e., in the Web server.) Keep in mind that this queuing is at the heart of memory management. If, for example, each Servlet request requires *n* MB of memory, then the Maximum Thread Size guarantees that the memory utilization will never exceed

```
n X Maximum Thread Size
```

There are, however, WebSphere-exclusive features that may be set to improve the performance of the Web container significantly. These will be the topic of a later section.

Connection pooling (for developers)

This and the following sections on connection pooling are based largely on the article "WebSphere Connection Pooling" by Deb Erickson, Shawn Lauzon, and Melissa Modjeski (*www-3.ibm.com/software/webservers/appserv/whitepapers/connection_pool.pdf*).

The term "connection pooling" is used to refer to a mechanism in which a certain number of database connections are maintained by an application server and made available to applications. Connection pooling is in contrast with the practice of getting (building) a single connection per SQL query and then destroying it immediately after the SQL query has completed.

Parameters

In practice, DataSources are configured by WebSphere administrators. The JDBC 2.0 Optional API provides the developer with the ability to configure DataSources programmatically, but this is not a "best practice," because the developer should not be required to understand the parameter settings and their ramifications, as they pertain to performance. Performance tuning of DataSources is strictly the purview of the WebSphere administrator.

On the other hand, it is crucial that the developer understand how these parameters interact with her code. This will be the focus of the following section. The parameters of particular interest to the developer include the "timeout" parameters—CONN_TIMEOUT, UNUSED_TIMEOUT, and AGED_TIMEOUT—and are discussed in detail later. DISABLE_AUTO_CONN_CLEANUP is also relevant to developers and will also be discussed later in this chapter. Two simple observations about all of the parameters discussed are that, if set to 0, the feature is disabled (except in the case of MIN_CONNECTIONS); also, all values are in seconds.

Other parameters that affect performance but are not discussed here include MAX_POOL_SIZE, MIN_POOL_SIZE, and STATEMENT_CACHE_SIZE. UNUSED_TIMEOUT controls WebSphere's connection pool management, and thus performance. DATASOURCE_CLASS_NAME is set by the WebSphere administrator and is not present in the code. ERROR_MAP is used to map SQLExceptions to WebSphere exceptions, but its use should be sparse and preceded by a call to IBM support.

CONN_TIMEOUT

CONN_TIMEOUT is quite straightforward. It is the number of seconds an application will wait for a connection from the pool before throwing a com.ibm.ejs.cm.pool.ConnectionWaitTimeoutException. While the method call setLoginTimeout() is available to set this timeout programmatically, it is not a best practice, since one application would set the parameter for all applications, which simply duplicates the WebSphere administrator's setting the parameter.

You may find it useful to establish in your mind that there are really only two kinds of connections a developer deals with: allocated and unallocated (still in the pool). Since the application (and thus, the application developer) does not interact with the pooling mechanism directly, unallocated connections are beyond the scope of this discussion.

AGED_TIMEOUT

AGED_TIMEOUT affects an allocated connection (a connection that is being used by the application) after the set time limit by returning the connection back to the pool and marking that connection "stale" for that application. If the application tries to use this connection again, after it has been returned to the pool ("orphaning"), the WebSphere Application Server will throw the com.ibm.websphere.ce.cm.StaleConnectionException. (In fact, the connection is not yet "stale," but only "marked" for orphaning, the first time the timeout is reached. The second time the timeout is reached, the connection is returned to the pool.) You can see that this would require special coding, insofar as the developer cannot know the amount of time an end user will require to use the connection. Thus, the code needs to catch the StaleConnectionException specifically everywhere a connection is used. Then the catch block needs to get a "fresh" connection, perhaps in a do/while block.

```
Boolean retry;
do {
   try{
      conn = ds.getConnection();
      stmt = conn.createStatement();
      stmt.execute("SELECT * FROM EMPLOYEES");
    }
   catch(com.ibm.websphere.ce.cm.StaleConnectionException sce)
   {
      if (limit < //some time/number limit of retries)
      {
         retry = true;
         limit++;
      }
      else {// give up; throw an error}
      }
   finally
   {
        if (conn != null){conn.close();
               if(stmt != null) stmt.close();
   }
} while (retry)
```

Figure 14.21: Explicitly catch StaleConnectionException, close, and retry.

Figure 14.21 is a rough illustration of a coding pattern for handling really any connection problem.

- Catch the exception explicitly.
- Close the current (i.e., "stale") connection.
- Retry by getting a new connection.

The reason for a "limit" on the number of retries is that the cause of the StaleConnection Exception may not be transient. Often, a simple limit of 2 is set because a "true" StaleConnectionException is most likely thrown the very first time a connection is used. This would be the result of interaction with the AGED_TIMEOUT setting, discussed earlier. However, a database shutdown will make *all* connections in use by an application "stale." In this case, the developer might set a reasonable time-limit, based on required response time, giving the loop time to cycle through those connections previously obtained by the application (and thus now stale).

The behavior of StaleConnectionExceptions and their relationship to the AGED_TIMEOUT setting are also significantly influenced by transactions, as discussed in the following section.

DISABLE_AUTO_CONN_CLEANUP

This parameter specifies whether all database resources, including connections, are automatically closed (i.e., returned to the pool) at the end of a transaction. Since this is a "disable" parameter, setting it to false actually "enables" the behavior; thus, the default setting of false ensures that all resources are closed and connections returned to the pool at the end of transaction processing. The implications of this setting, in light of what we have discussed so far, are as follows:

- Any attempt to use a connection obtained within a transaction, after the transaction has completed, will result in a StaleConnectionException.
- Connections created within a transaction *cannot* be orphaned.

If set to "true," the code must explicitly call close(); otherwise, the connection will not be returned to the pool, *and* the application will soon run out of connections.

Connection pooling (for administrators)

This section need not be exclusive to administrators. The parameters discussed are likely to be under the control of the administrator, but the developer's awareness of them is crucial to communication.

Setting up a DataSource

With the advent of WebSphere Application Server Version 4, it became possible to configure a DataSource completely administratively, and that is the recommended method. In 3.5.x versions the developers still needed to hard-code database user ids and passwords; this necessity (although the possibility still exists) was removed in Version 4. Connections to the database were handled by a (single) connection manager (CM) in WebSphere Version 4 that is responsible for the connection pooling features of JDBC 2.0.

With the advent of WebSphere Version 5 and J2EE 1.3, a second type of connection manager architecture has been made available to support new features in the J2EE 1.3 specification. I emphasize the word *added*, so that there is no doubt that J2EE 1.2 connections are still supported in WebSphere Version 5. The new connection manager is implemented as a JCA style *connector*. The administrator must choose between the two different types of DataSource.

This choice is relatively simple: If you have a J2EE 1.2 application, you *must* choose the 4.0 DataSource.

If you are running a J2EE 1.3 application, your servlets (2.3) and JDBC calls *must* use the 5.0 DataSource.

Your EJB modules may be of different types in a J2EE 1.3 application, and this will determine your choice of DataSource. If your EJB module complies with EJB 1.1, you *must* choose the 4.0 DataSource. This applies to all types of 1.1 EJBs, e.g., CMP or BMP. For EJB 2.0 modules, all CMP beans (including 1.x CMPs) *must* use the 5.0 DataSource. The BMPs, of course, will be controlled by whether they use JDBC to call a relational database. If so, then the rule concerning all JDBC calls in a J2EE 1.3 application applies, and such BMP beans would have to use the 5.0 DataSource.

There are only a few parameter needed to configure a DataSource administratively. We will discuss these first, and then move on to "tuning" parameters. The reader may refer to Figure 14.22 for this discussion.

NAME

The NAME attribute, the reader will notice, is required, whereas the JNDI name is not. This is actually misleading, since the reality of the situation is completely the opposite: The JNDI name is absolutely crucial. In fact, if no JNDI name is supplied, the NAME attribute value is used for the JNDI name. (In single-server AEs (edition), both Name and JNDI Name are required.)

DATA_SOURCE_CLASS_NAME

This is the location of the "driver" class, which must implement either javax.sql. ConnectionPoolDataSource or javax.sql.XADataSource. It is provided by the database vendor, usually in a .zip or .jar archive. In Figure 14.22, this parameter is not shown: It was entered when the JDBC driver (in this case, SAMPLE DB DRIVER) was configured. The administrator must configure and install the driver on each node where it will run before configuring a DataSource that uses it.

From a WebSphere perspective, this is all that is required to create a DataSource; however, each database vendor will have other requirements. For example, if we use the *DB2ConnectionPoolDataSource* class as our driver, then we must also fill in DATABASE_NAME.

To do this, we must go to the Administrative Console and drill down: **Resources →** **JDBC Providers →**. Here you can select **New**, which will take you to the configuration dialog. For the purposes of this example, we have created a DB2 JDBC Provider (XA). Simply click **Apply** and save the configuration.

To create the DataSource, go back to the JDBC Providers menu, select the Provider you have just created, scroll down, and then select **DataSources,** followed by **New**.

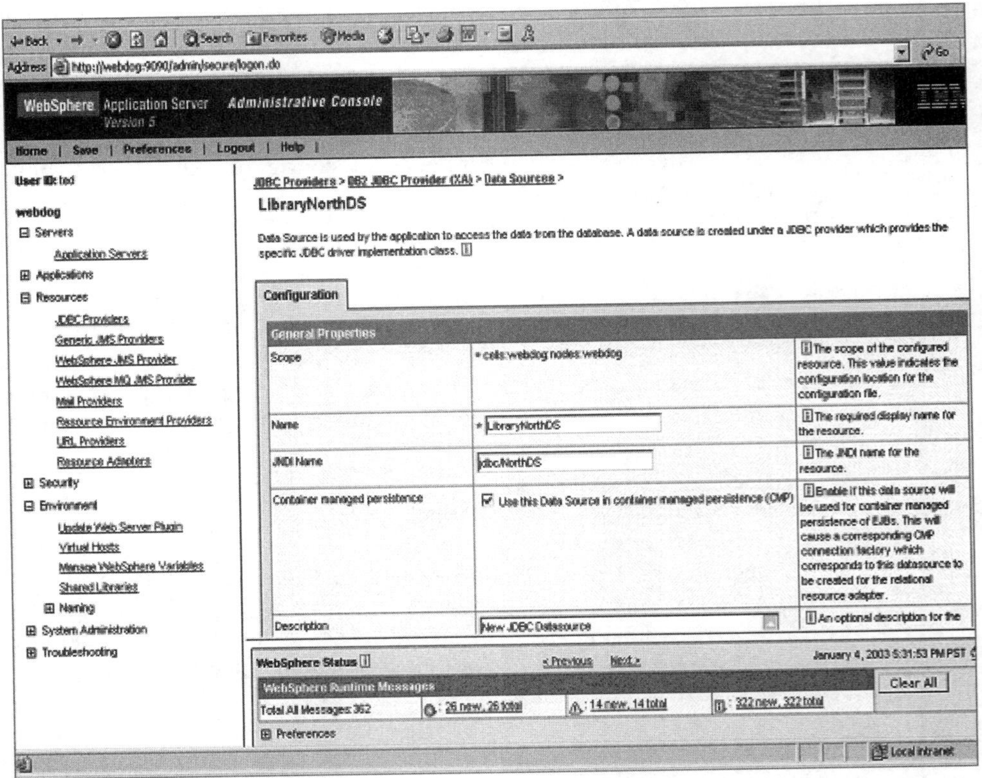

Figure 14.22: Creating a DataSource (WebSphere Application Server Version 5.0).

Once you've entered the two mandatory parameters, the DataSource is available for use by any program in the WebSphere domain. If the administrator chooses to configure the same DataSource on additional nodes, he/she need only be sure that the JDBC Provider (driver) has been installed on that node.

To configure the databaseName per our choice of property, you need to scroll down on the screen shown in Figure 14.23 and select **Custom Properties**:

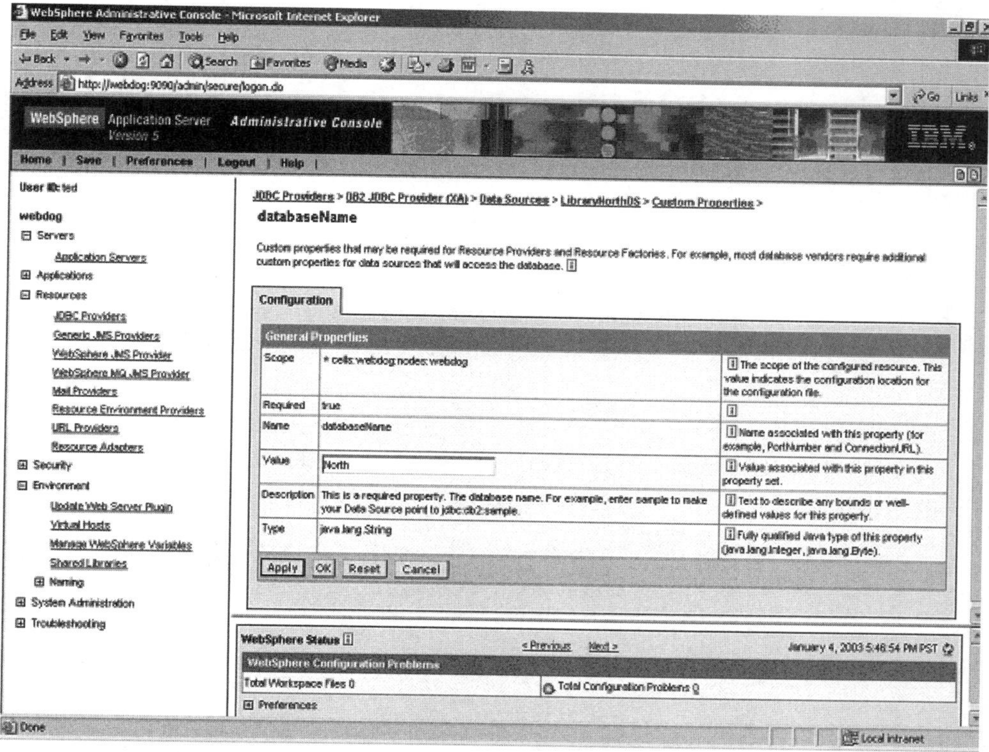

Figure 14.23: Setting the databaseName for a DataSource.

"Available for use" is, of course, not the same as "ready for use" in the minds of most administrators. What the administrator has at this point is an "untuned" DataSource, which uses the "factory presets." There are several key parameters that need to be customized for the unique environment the DataSource will be serving.

Settings for your Version 5.0 DataSource

Setting the userid and password parameters administratively is certainly more secure—not to mention more portable—than putting them all throughout your application code. However, these parameters are visible in clear text in the Version 5 *resources.xml* file, which, if not secured at the file-system level, could still be read by anyone. The J2C Authentication model offers you the alternative of defining these properties as an alias.

To define a new alias from the J2C Authentication Data Entries choice (see Figure 14.24), follow these steps:

1. If you are creating a new DataSource, you will not see the J2C Authentication Entries choice on the New DataSource page—just click **Apply**, and you will see it. It does appear on an existing data source's page.
2. Click **J2C Authentication Data Entries** in the Related Items section.
3. Click **New** on the J2C Authentication Data Entries page.
4. Fill in the fields on the resulting page. Click **Apply**.
5. Return to the data source page.
6. If by chance the new alias does not appear in the picklists (drop-down lists) for Component- or Container-managed Authentication Alias, close the page and reopen it.

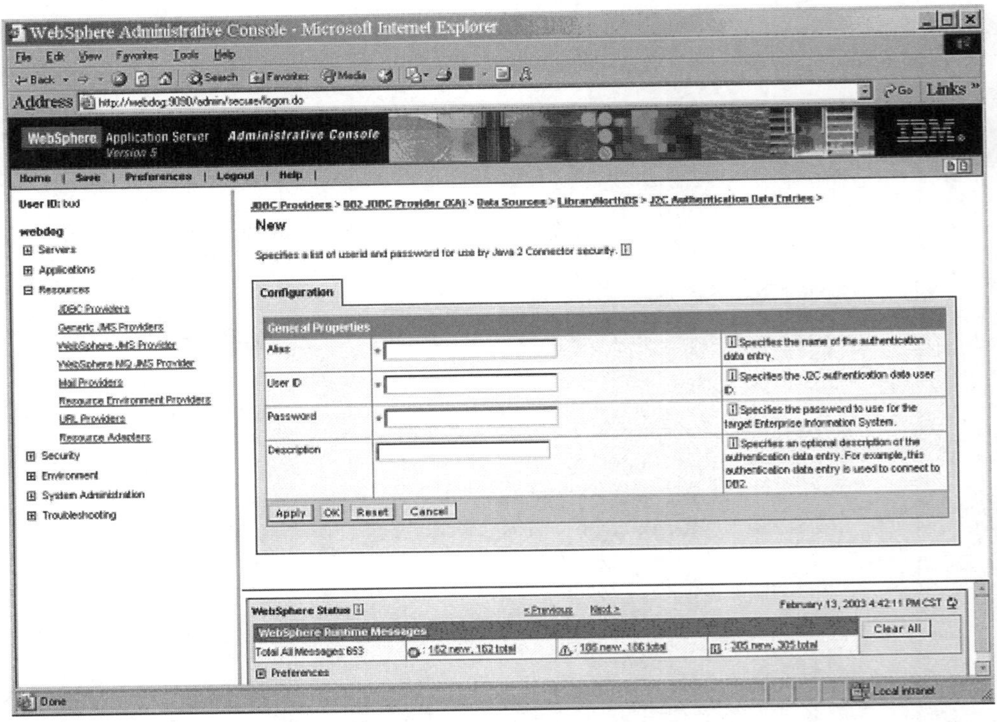

Figure 14.24: The New J2C Authentication Data Entries page.

These aliases are used to authenticate at runtime, either by the container or by the application, based on the res-auth tag in the deployment descriptor. This will dictate which of the drop-downs mentioned in Step 6 you will use to set your alias.

If you do not set one of these fields and your database requires the user ID and password to get a connection, then you receive an exception during run time. If your database does not require authentication (e.g., Cloudscape), then you needn't set up such an alias.

Shareable versus non-shareable DataSources (J2EE1.3)

In Version 5 of WebSphere, with the new requirements of J2EE 1.3, connection pooling has taken an interesting turn: It is possible for the developer/administrator to decide *not to use connection pooling*. Clearly connection pooling offers a great performance enhancement. It also provides greater scalability. However, these advantages also imply a certain degree of non-specificity of connections, which may not be acceptable in all applications.

A more readily graspable analogy here might be the familiar one of the HTTP session: Each user receives exclusive use of a session object for the duration of her session. Another important analogy would be the "handle" object in a Stateful Session EJB: When a user gets a stub for a particular Stateful Session EJB, and then does some other processing within the HttpSession, the user needs to wrap that stub in a Handle and place the Handle in the HttpSession. When that particular stub is required again some time later in the session the user retrieves the specific Handle and from it extracts that particular stub.

When applied to DataSources, the shareable connection would be similar to the connection pooling that developers became accustomed to in WebSphere Version 4: If a connection is marked as shareable, then all components within a sharing boundary (i.e., Transaction) may share or get the same connection. This means that, like Stateless Session EJB, the component requesting the connection may be given any viable connection in the pool.

On the other hand, if a connection is marked as unshareable, each call from a component to getConnection() will return the same connection, via a Connection handle object. This would be analogous to the Stateful Session EJB handle.

The key phrase with shareable connections is the word *may*. Despite the intention of the Developer (or whoever configures the connection), it is ultimately the J2EE Server that determines whether the connection will be shared. Following is an outline of the factors that determine sharing of a connection.

1. First, in the deployment descriptor, the DataSource must called using the same JNDI name, even though JNDI name is not, technically, a connection property.
2. Second, the resource-ref must be the same for calling components that expect to reuse the connection.
3. Third, the Resource Authentication must be the same.

The connection must be called by components within the same sharing scope. There are two such viable scopes: Transactions and LocationTransactionContainment (LTC). Within these boundaries, if the connection properties are the same, then the second call to get returns the same connection as on the first call. In this sense, the term *reuse* is more appropriate than *sharing*. In addition to get calls, reuse occurs with the following calls: use, commit/rollback, and close.

Changing the connection properties on the various calls by passing the ConnectionSpec attribute (an interface used by an application component to pass connection request-specific properties to the ConnectionFactory.getConnection method) on the get method, will force the connection to be unshareable (since, by definition, shareable connections are those that do not change the properties of a connection), *unless the properties in the ConnectionSpec Object are the same*. (It is recommended that the ConnectionSpec interface be implemented as a JavaBean to support tools; the properties on the ConnectionSpec implementation class must be defined through the getter and setter methods pattern. The interface is javax.resource.cci.ConnectionSpec.) In particular, the isolation level on a shareable connection can never be changed. This is outlined in the J2EE Specification. If you need various isolation level settings, then it is best to create multiple resource-refs and point them to the same DataSource.

Let's look at a concrete example involving EJB. First, to choose between shareable and unshareable, we open the ejb-jar.xml (the EJB deployment descriptor); see Chapters 5 and 6 in this book. Since the Shareable/Unshareable feature applies only when the resource-ref is the same for two or more components, we need to create a resource-ref in the deployment descriptor. In Application Developer, this is done on the References page of the deployment descriptor. Select **Add/EJB Resource Reference**. This yields the dialog box shown in Figure 14.25.

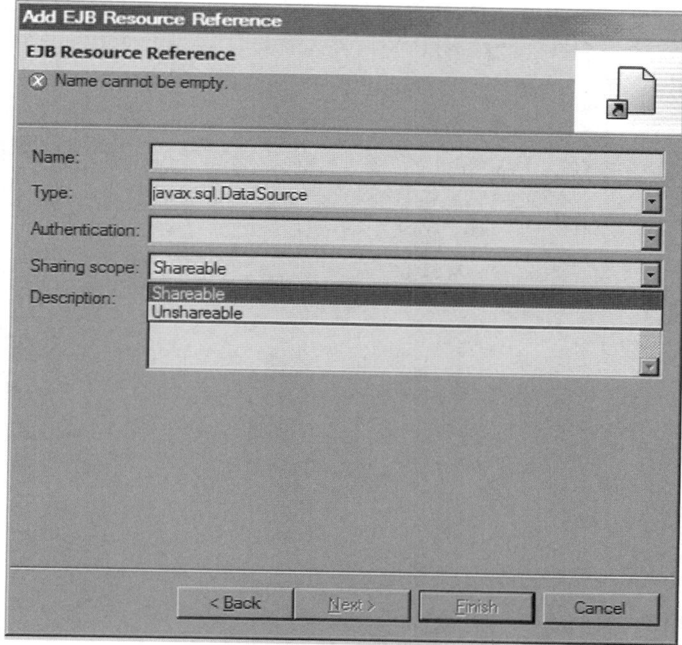

Figure 14.25: Setting up a shareable/unshareable connection.

In Figure 14.25, we have selected the javax.sql.DataSource as the Type.

If we select Unshareable as the Sharing Scope, we will be able to set the connection properties in get calls and be guaranteed that subsequent get calls by the same component will return the same Handle with the properties we set on the initial call. If we select Shareable, other components within the same sharing boundary will be able to reuse the Connection object, but we will generally not be allowed to set properties, since other components reusing this connection will not—indeed, should not—be aware of differences in connection properties. Connection properties can also be set by using Resource Adapters, but subsequent users are not guaranteed that the properties will be the same. In fact, if the subsequent call to the connection occurs outside of the sharing scope, even though the handle returned is the same, the connection will have to be "cleaned" before it is returned to the free pool.

Also, all other properties (e.g., Name and Authentication) must be configured the same for other components wishing to reuse this connection.

Earlier, we mentioned the use of sharing scope. If we choose to employ LTC, we will set this in the ejb-jar.xml, as well. On the Beans page of the deployment descriptor, scroll down until you find Local Transaction 2.0. Here, you can set the sharing boundary to either Bean Method or Activity Session. Next, you would set the Resolver to

ContainerAtBoundary (the only available setting). Finally, you could set the Unresolver to either Commit or Rollback, thus indicating the action the connection will take if the connection is interrupted. Figure 14.26 shows the configured deployment descriptor.

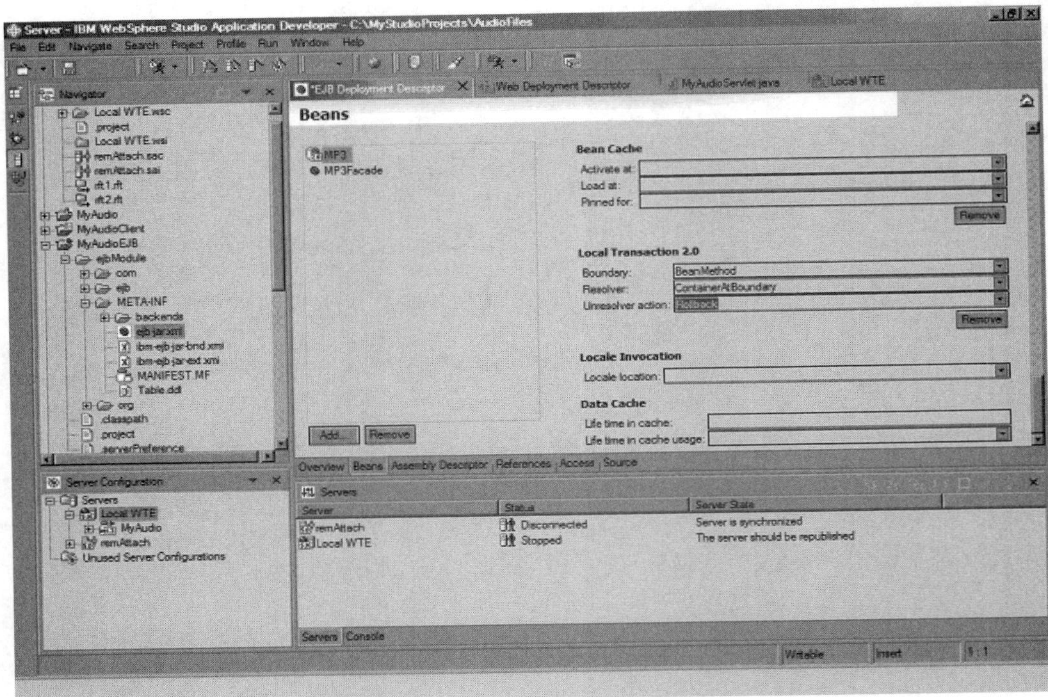

Figure 14.26: Configuring the sharing scope using LTC.

Finally, if you have decided on unshareable connections, you could set the isolation level. Still in the EJB deployment descriptor, go to the Access page. After scrolling down to the very bottom of the page, you will see the IsolationLevel settings. Since the isolation level is discussed at great length in Chapter 8 of this book, we will not discuss it here. Its only relevance to this topic is that the isolation level cannot be set for a Shareable DataSource.

DataSource tuning parameters

In much of tuning literature, these parameters receive the most significant treatment. Connection pooling, while clearly a powerful addition to the JDBC API, can also produce unwanted effects, if not properly understood.

Several of these parameters are set in the Administrative Console, under *<your DataSource>*/Connection Pools, as shown in Figure 14.27.

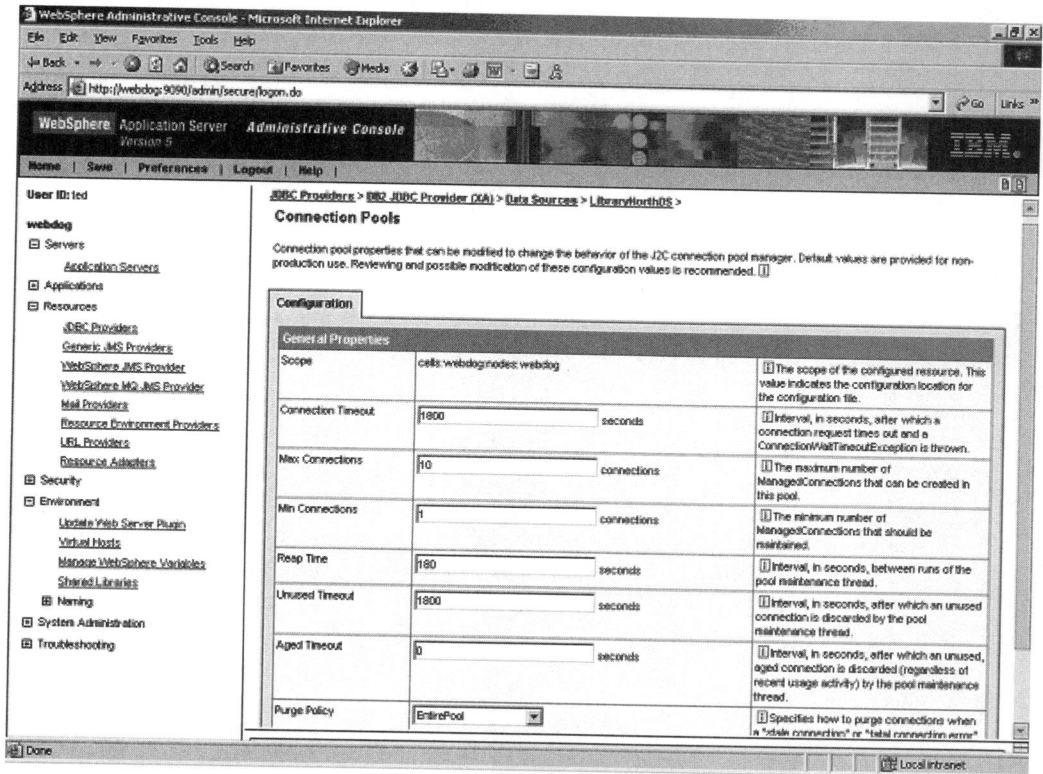

Figure 14.27: Setting Connection Timeout, Max Connections, Min Connections, Unused Timeout, and Aged Timeout.

CONN_TIMEOUT

As discussed earlier, CONN_TIMEOUT (Connection Timeout in Figure 14.27) is quite straightforward: the number of seconds an application will wait for a connection from the pool before throwing com.ibm.ejs.cm.pool.ConnectionWaitTimeoutException.

If this exception is being thrown frequently, it can mean that the application requires a longer value. (This would involve a discussion with the developer as to why the application requires this.) Of course, a higher setting in this case would fix the problem. However, another reason for frequent timeouts is that the MAX_CONNECTIONS is set too low, and there simply aren't enough connections available.

UNUSED_TIMEOUT

As mentioned earlier, it might be instructive to simplify connection into two groups:

- Allocated, i.e., out of the pool (not removed—just in use by the application)
- Unallocated, i.e., in the pool, not in use

The UNUSED_TIMEOUT (Unused Timeout in Figure 14.27) concerns unallocated connections. Allocated connections are governed by the AGED_TIMEOUT (below).

When a connection is either added or returned to the connection pool, the application server monitors the duration of its time in the pool. When the UNUSED_TIMEOUT is reached, the application server will remove the connection from the pool (i.e., destroy the connection), unless the destruction of this connection would result in the number of connections in the pool dropping below the MIN_CONNECTIONS (further discussed later in this chapter).

This is one of the main features of JDBC 2.0, Optional API: connection management. While having a pool of open connections is an incredible benefit to the performance of the application, it can also be very hard on the memory of the database (and, of course, the memory of the entire system). For this reason, the adjustment of this parameter can impact database stability, system stability, and, if the parameter setting is inconsistent with the performance requirements of the application that uses the DataSource, application performance can be degraded. In a later discussion, we will explore ways to collect data necessary to set this parameter correctly.

AGED_TIMEOUT

The allocated group, as indicated earlier, can be further subcategorized into "active allocated" and "inactive allocated." An allocated connection that has been active beyond the time set in the AGED_TIMEOUT parameter (Aged Timeout in Figure 14.27) will initially be marked for orphaning and, upon reaching the timeout a second time, truly orphaned, which means it will be returned to the pool, but marked as "stale" for the application that originally requested it.

Since this has been discussed in detail earlier in this chapter, the only additional comment here would be that the administrator should decide on the expected user time for connections and use that as a benchmark. If stale connections become a prominent pattern, then it is best to collect data on connection usage—perhaps users typically take longer than expected or there are other application-internal issues that are causing frequent orphaning of connections—and change the parameter. That is, although the developers will have robust code for handling stale connections, this should be viewed only as "triage" and not the solution to a significant problem.

MIN_POOL_SIZE

As the name implies, MIN_POOL_SIZE (Min Connections in Figure 14.27) is be the minimum number of connections required in the pool. The pool does not start at this size, but builds to it as applications request connections; thus, there is a "ramp-up" period in which users can experience lag while waiting for connections to be created. (The default for this parameter is 1, in which case the "ramp-up" consideration is moot.) Once achieved, the minimum number is always maintained in the pool. Through idling, the number of connections can return to this number (but not go below it, as discussed earlier). However, this number can be set to 0, which might be desirable for applications that reach a truly idle state, for example, at night.

To find the best number for this parameter, the administrator simply needs to use a monitoring tool (we will discuss several later) to determine the lowest number of connections required at any given time.

MAX_POOL_SIZE

This refers to the maximum number of connections possible in the pool (Max Connections in Figure 14.27). This can clearly have performance implications. A very large number of connections at peak time will involve significant overhead for both maintaining and managing the open connections. On the other hand, setting it too low will force applications to wait for a connection, which can result in the various timeouts discussed so far.

An easy misconception might be that setting the MAX_POOL_SIZE to a high number is the solution to application performance problems, since the application will never have to wait for a connection. It is actually not that simple: Clearly, the maintenance of a large number of potentially idle connections will severely affect the system, depending on how frequently the pool size needs to be re-adjusted (based on the UNUSED_TIMEOUT).

The "rule of thumb" for tuning this parameter is one connection per thread. Thus, the administrator would set the maximum DataSource connections equal to, for example, the MaxThreads parameter in the Web Container.

If, however, the application requires more than one connection per thread, the formula is

```
T * (C - 1)  + 1
```

where T is the maximum number of threads and C is the number of concurrent database connections necessary per thread.

STATEMENT_CACHE_SIZE

This parameter is relevant only for applications that use PreparedStatement java objects. (This is distinctive from the java.sql.Statement, which is not precompiled.) PreparedStatements are cached by WebSphere Application Server, per connection. Thus, if

PreparedStatement X is called on connection 1, the next user to receive connection 1 from the pool will have enhanced performance if he calls PreparedStatement X, as well.

The STATEMENT_CACHE_SIZE is set in the main window for your DataSource, as shown in Figure 14.28.

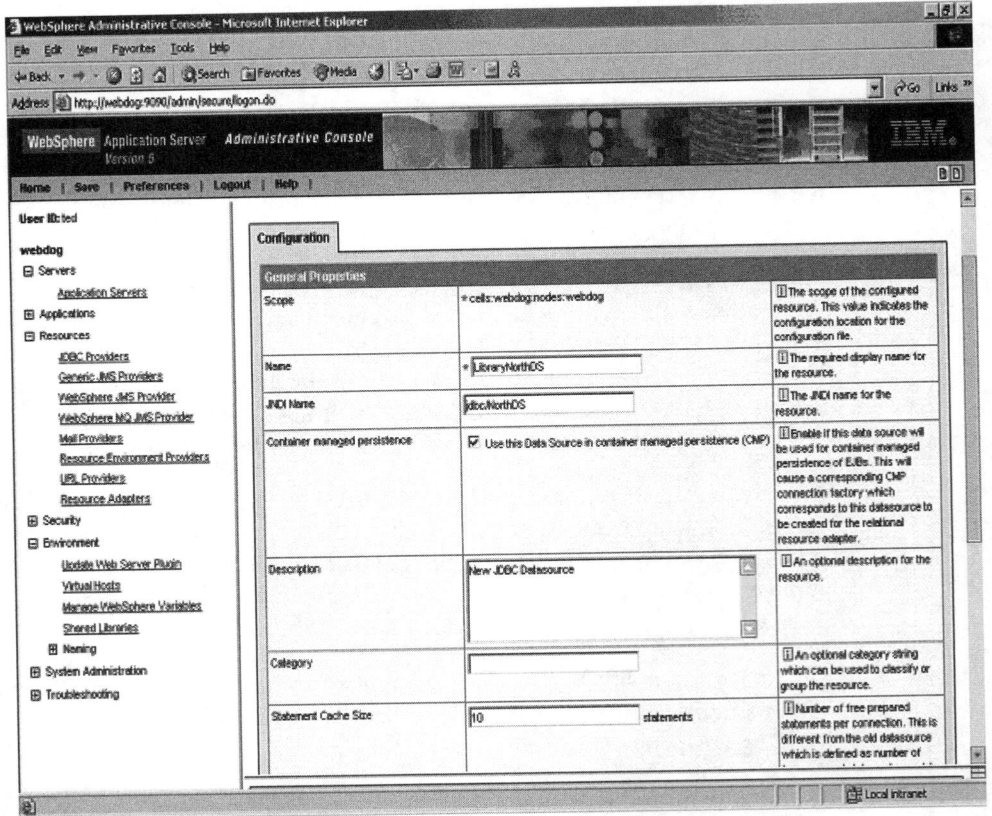

Figure 14.28: Setting the STATEMENT_CACHE_SIZE for a DataSource.

Miscellaneous parameter settings/architectural decisions for performance enhancement

Following is a collection of individual tuning parameters that can't necessarily be grouped in any one taxonomy, but are crucial to the complete tuning of a WebSphere environment.

For EJB

Pass-by-reference (NoLocalCopies) is an IBM optimization for EJB parameter passing that was introduced in WebSphere Application Server Version 4 and fully adopted as a standard in Version 5 (EJB 2.0) for local interfaces.

The EJB 1.1 Specification states that all methods calls are to be pass-by-value; The parameters passed are copied onto the stack prior to the call. This has a performance cost, which can be prevented by using WebSphere's pass-by-reference setting. This causes a reference to the object being passed as a parameter, not a copy of the object, to be passed. This setting can increase performance by 50 percent under the following conditions:

- The EJB client and EJB server are installed in the same WebSphere Application Server instance, and the client and server use remote interfaces.

For EJB 2.0 beans, interfaces can be local or remote (see Chapter 6). For local interfaces, method calls are pass-by-reference by default.

- Non-primitive object types are being passed as parameters—e.g., int and floats are always copied, regardless of the call model.

> **Warning:** Pass-by-reference can be dangerous and can lead to unexpected results. If an object reference is modified by the remote method, the change might be seen by the caller.

To set this property,

1. Click **Servers → Application Servers**. Then, click ORB Service.
2. Select **Pass by Reference** (see Figure 14.29).
3. Click **OK**.
4. Click **Apply** to save the changes.
5. Stop and restart the application server.

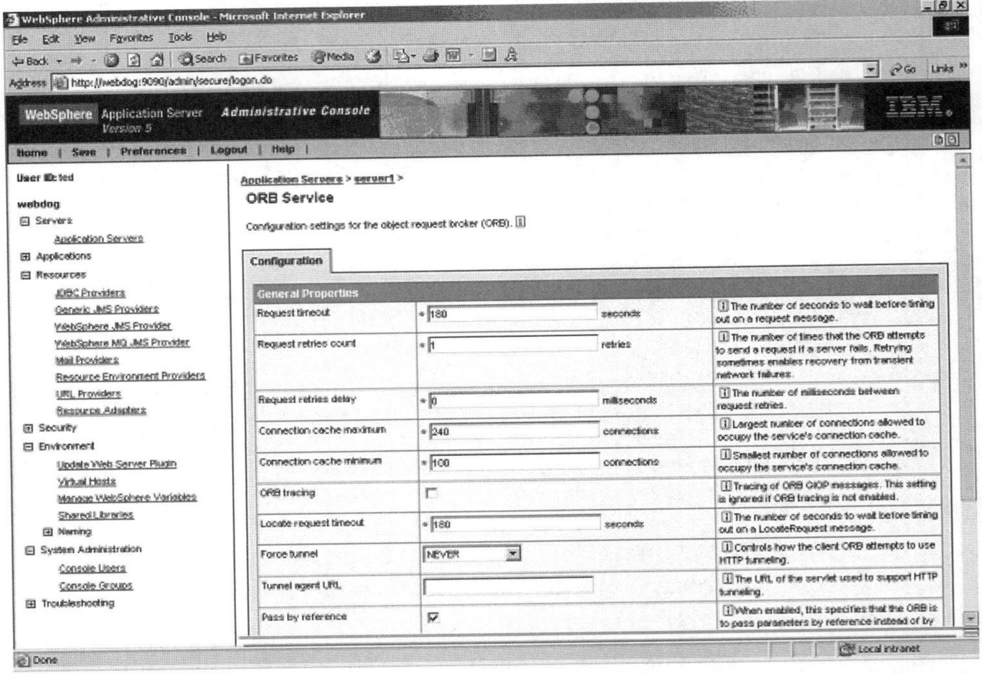

Figure 14.29: Setting "pass-by-reference."

For Web container

Several significant parameter settings and their effects are discussed in this section, with reference to the web container.

URL Invocation Cache

The Invocation Cache is an available option to the JVM. The goal is to speed mapping from URIs to servlets and JSPs. The Invocation Cache interacts directly with the Maximum Thread Size parameter (the web container queue), in that an Invocation Cache is created for each thread in the web container (see Figure 14.30).

The input value to the JVM is the desired size of the Invocation Cache. To set the parameter, use the following steps.

Note: that the instructions for setting this property in the Version 5 InfoCenter are not entirely correct: In the Version 5 Admin Console, the property is added under Custom Properties but is treated, in fact, as a System Property. The InfoCenter refers to the property as "System."

---

1. In the administrative console, click the application server you are tuning.
2. Click **Process Definition**.
3. Click **Java Virtual Machine**.
4. Add **-DinvocationCacheSize=xx** as a Generic JVM Argument *or* click **Custom Properties** (make sure you are on the Java Virtual Machine page); click**New** and add the property **invocationCacheSize** and the desired value (which should be something other than the default, which is 50).
5. Click **Apply** to ensure that the changes are saved.
6. Stop and restart the application server.

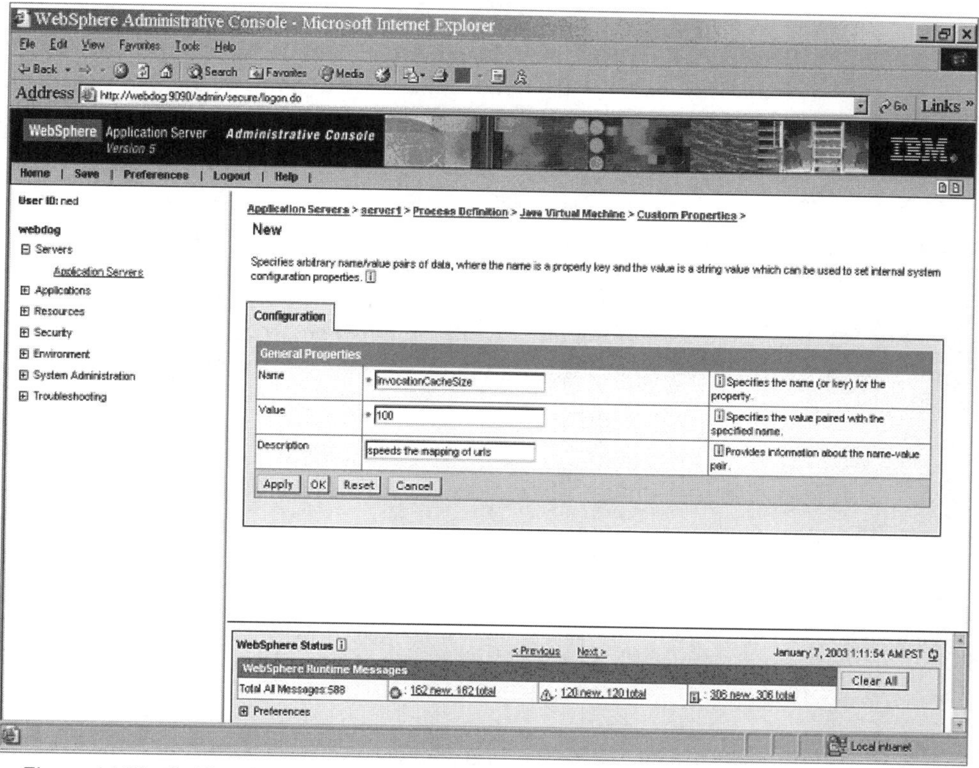

Figure 14.30: Setting the Invocation Cache size in the JVM.

This will, of course, have an impact on the Java heap; that is, in this example, assuming that each cache entry is around 2 KB, the Maximum Thread Size is 100 (from the throughput curve test), and the Invocation Cache is set to 100, as in Figure 14.30, then the Invocation Cache will require 20 MB of JVM memory.

The rule of thumb here is a one-to-one relationship between the unique URI/URL and the Cache entry. Thus, 50 unique servlet URIs would require an Invocation Cache size of 50 (since this is the default, no change need be made). With fewer URLs the size could actually be decreased. Note that each JSP constitutes a unique URL.

Servlet reload interval and reloading enabled

One of the important value-adds of WebSphere 4.x was the ability to modify virtually any aspect of a Web Module, be it servlet code or deployment descriptor information (web.xml), without reinstalling the J2EE Application or, more importantly, restarting the Application Server. This is a feature beyond the J2EE 1.2 Specification and pertains to WebSphere only. The feature has been extended and improved in Version 5 of the Application Server.

While this feature must be enabled for any type of dynamic update to be possible (recall that we had to enable this feature during the installation of the Performance Monitoring Infrastructure Servlet), the reload interval is initially set very low—every 3 seconds. While this is ideal for development, it is clearly unwarranted in a production application. There is, of course, no magic number here: It is entirely dependent on IT policies that govern code updates.

The enablement and the interval are both found in the ibm-web-ext.xmi file in each Web Module and can thus be changed only at application installation using either WebSphere Studio Application Developer or the Application Assembly Tool (AAT; see Figure 14.31). (A little thought will reveal that the dynamic reloading parameter itself is not affected by dynamic reloading; in other words, if one were to disable dynamic reloading directly in the file ibm-web-ext.xmi, would this change ever be read?)

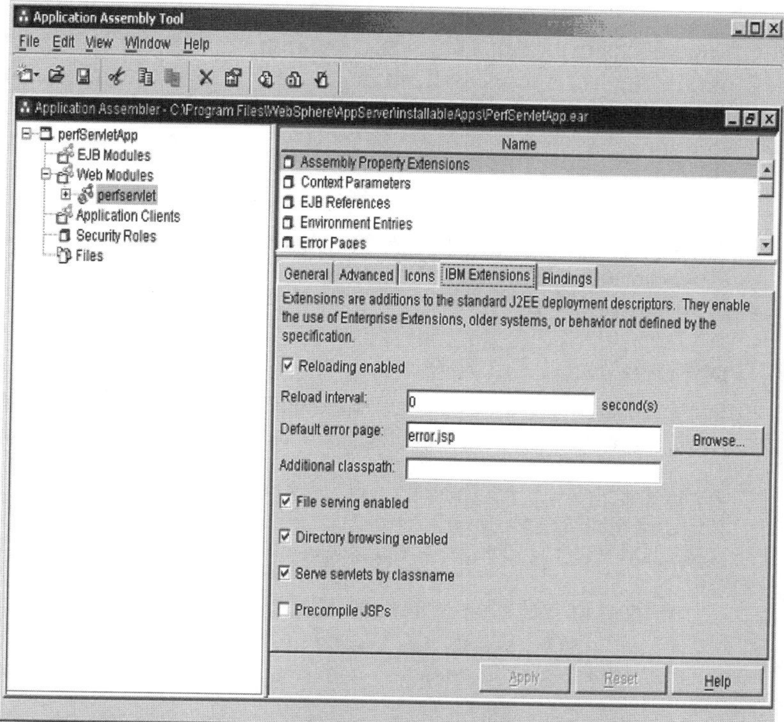

Figure 14.31: Enabling the auto-reload feature in AAT, and setting the interval.

Session management

There are basically four places where session data can be stored: cookies, the Servlet HttpSession object (i.e., in memory), the HttpSession persisted to a middle-tier persistence database, or the EJB layer (also involves persistence to a database, but no HttpSession object). Of these, the undisputed best in terms of performance is the HttpSession when the session stays within memory; that is, if the session grows very large, the JVM will begin to swap with hard-disk memory, which would have a seriously negative effect on performance.

Storing the session data in the EJB layer alleviates the memory limitations of the HttpSession but incurs latency penalties for the persistence aspect. The middle-tier database solution provided by WebSphere allows for software/hardware failover in a clustered/cloned environment. The decision as to which solution to use is, first, a question of the requirements of the application. If any cloning is involved or the session data is mission-critical (i.e., it must survive a JVM crash in a consistent state), or if the data footprint is larger than 2 KB, then the session data must be persisted with one of the persistence solutions and performance adjustments made to best compensate for the attendant persistence calls. The cookie solution is problematic at many levels; namely, it is unreliable for Internet applications, since users have the power to suppress cookies. Also, all the session data must be transported back and forth across the wire. The two solutions that can be influenced by WebSphere-specific tuning features are the HttpSession in memory and the HttpSession with middle-tier database persistence. These are the parameters that will be discussed in this section. Some of the parameters will influence either the database persistence solution or the session in memory solution; others would influence both. This scope of influence will be indicated next to the parameter name.

Persistence

For persistent Sessions, the performance hit will come in the updates to the persistent store. Careful decisions must be made when controlling these updates.

Write frequency (database persistence)

Performance can be improved by controlling the times the session is persisted to the database. WebSphere offers these options:

- End of service method (the default): Write session data at the end of the servlet's service() method call. There will always be an update for the timestamp, and the write would include any and all changes to the session data.
- Manual update: Write session data only when the servlet calls the IBMSession.sync() method. That is, the default end-of-service behavior can be turned off by extending IBM's implementation of the HttpSession API (com.ibm.websphere.servlet.session.IBMSession) so that session updates are called only explicitly from the code. At the end of the very first service() call when a session is first created, however, the session information is always written to the database.
- Time-based write: Write session data every so many seconds (called the *write interval*).

Write Contents (database persistence)

In addition to controlling when session data is written to the persistence database, WebSphere allows you to control exactly what is written, using the feature called Write Contents. The options for Write Contents are as follows:

- Write changed (the default): Write only session data that has been updated through setAttribute() and removeAttribute() method calls.
- Write all: Write all session data.

Write all is typically used when Java objects are maintained in the session: Instead of an explicit call to setAttribute() for each attribute that needs persisting in the session, *Write all* requires only the initial setAttribute() to bind the object to the session. This is clearly not a performance advantage; it has been discussed here only for completeness.

All of the above properties are set in the Session Manager, WebSphere Administrative Console (**Application Servers → server1 → Web Container → Session Management → Distributed Environment Settings**)(See Figure 14.32).

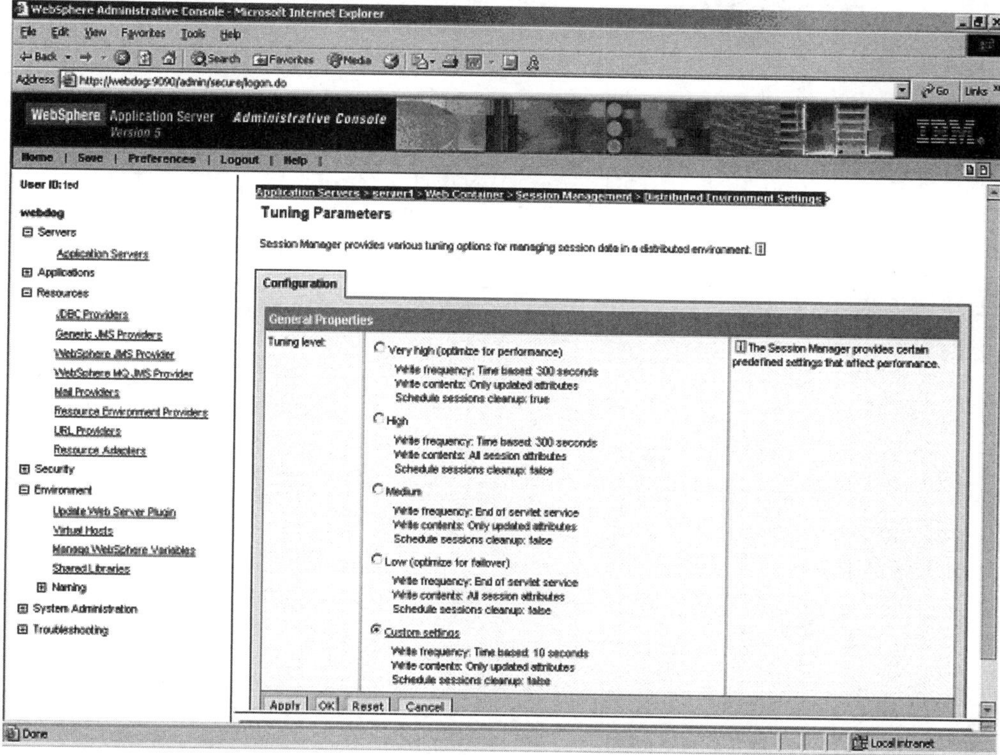

Figure 14.32: Session Persistence "preset" options.

For convenience, some common combinations of Write Frequency and Write Contents have been "preset," as seen in Figure 14.32. The administrator can also configure settings manually. To do so, select the **Custom Settings** radio button to bring up the screen shown in Figure 14.33.

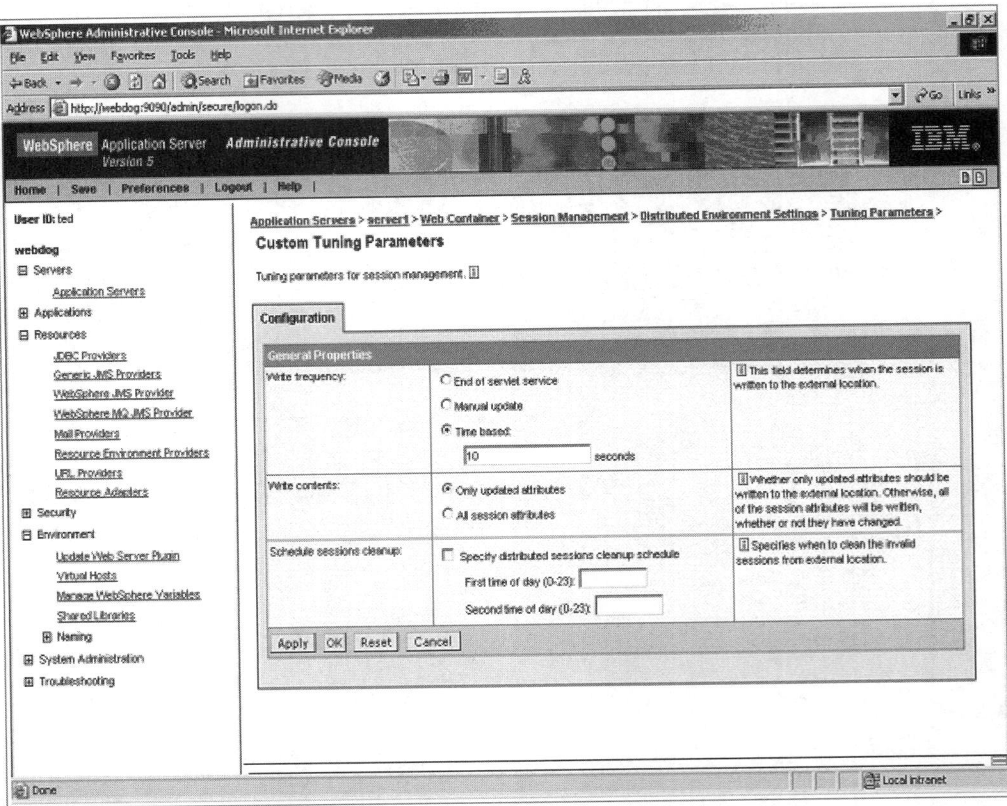

Figure 14.33: Configuring session persistence options manually.

Session affinity

The Servlet 2.3 Specification requires that a session be active in only one JVM at a time. This is sometimes misconstrued to mean that a session begun in one JVM must complete in that same JVM, but a careful re-reading of the requirement would clarify this point. In WebSphere 4.x the session affinity mechanism causes requests to be routed (through the WebSphere WebServer Plugin) through a particular Server Cluster Collection to the same JVM in which the session was begun. This is a clear performance benefit, since the session is cached in memory.

If, however, the original JVM crashes in a clustered environment, the original session can be re-created on any other functional Application Server, thus allowing the user to continue with the session. This is made possible only when WebSphere's session affinity mechanism is used in conjunction with WebSphere's session persistence mechanism, discussed earlier.

The process is straightforward. When a session is begun, the WebSphere Session manager creates a session cookie that contains the session id and an appended server id. (The default name of the session cookie is JSESSIONID, but the name can—and probably should, for security reasons—be changed in the Administrative Console, Session Manager Service, General tab.) The transience and domain of this cookie can be tightly configured as shown in Figure 14.34.

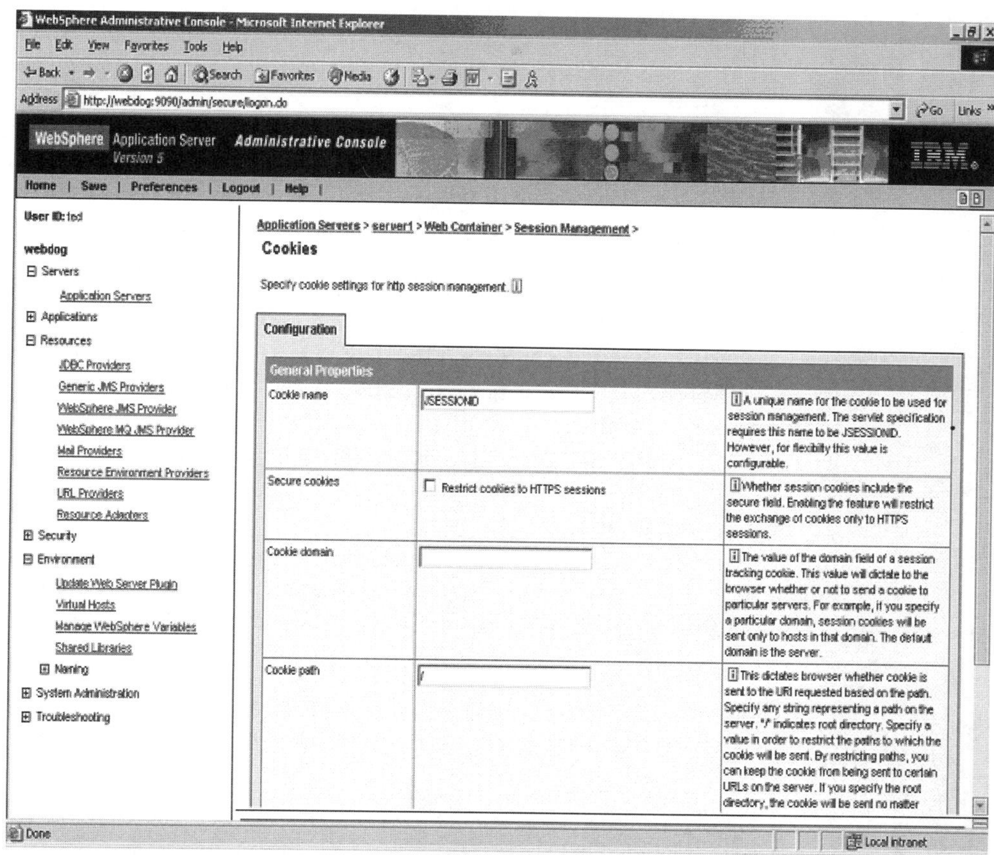

Figure 14.34: Configuring the session cookie.

Once this configuration is complete, an entry is added to the WebSphere WebServer Plugin for each URI in the URI Group (Figure 14.35).

```
<UriGroup Name="IBM-ZNQDCMTHX36_sampleApp/default_app_URIs">
        <Uri AffinityCookie="JSESSIONID" Name="/servlet/snoop/*"/>
        <Uri AffinityCookie="JSESSIONID" Name="/servlet/snoop2/*"/>
        <Uri AffinityCookie="JSESSIONID" Name="/servlet/hello"/>
        <Uri AffinityCookie="JSESSIONID" Name="/ErrorReporter"/>
        <Uri AffinityCookie="JSESSIONID" Name="*.jsp"/>
        <Uri AffinityCookie="JSESSIONID" Name="*.jsv"/>
        <Uri AffinityCookie="JSESSIONID" Name="*.jsw"/>
        <Uri AffinityCookie="JSESSIONID" Name="/j_security_check"/>
        <Uri AffinityCookie="JSESSIONID" Name="/servlet/*"/>
    </UriGroup>
```

Figure 14.35: Affinity entries in the Plugin.

Queuing and clustering

New with WebSphere Application Server Version 5 is the multi-server architecture. The Administration Server of previous versions, used to federate servers into a centrally administered domain, is gone. It has been replaced by the Deployment Manager in the Network Deployment packaging: Individual "base" servers can be federated by the Deployment Manager into a "Cell" (previously, "Domain"); or, similar or identical base servers can be linked together by a Node Manager into a "Cluster." While at first this seems the same as Server Groups/Models and Clones of previous releases, the differences are significant and require a good deal of reorientation on the part of the administrator. This book, however, is not intended to cover Clustering; rather, this section is intended to cover two specific problems that a developer, testing applications in a clustered environment, may encounter and how to diagnose and fix those problems.

Tuning a clustered set

If a managed server environment is functioning properly, it is advisable not to attempt to tune it. If, however, certain problems are encountered, there are parameters available to correct these. These specific situations will be discussed in this section.

Warning: This is not part of routine tuning. If the following are applied to a properly functioning managed server environment, the results will be detrimental.

---

1. Symptom: You are experiencing problems with requests sent to an ORB timing out. If you have a large network that is prone to a high degree of network latency, these timeouts could be due to a problem with clustering. When an application server receives a client request, a timeout period is initiated for sending back a

response to the request. Thus, high-latency, combined with clustering, might cause the server to time out waiting for the return of a request.

The solution, then, is to set the ibm.CORBA.RequestTimeout parameter to a large value. This interval is set by passing a -D option command line argument to the JVM and is expressed in seconds. Thus, the argument would be

```
-Dcom.ibm.CORBA.RequestTimeout=<timeout interval in seconds>
```

Note: There is no recommended value for this interval. It should be set only in response to a timeout problem.

2. Symptom: An application server in your clustered environment has gone down, but the selection policy continues to try to access it. Conversely, an application server has been "bounced", i.e., it is now running and should be available but is considered unavailable.

   The parameter that controls this behavior is ibm.websphere.wlm.unusable.interval**,** which indicates the interval in which the WLM client run time will not try to access a server that it has marked "unavailable." Thus, it is a type of refresh interval and should be changed only according to a particular situation that exists in the clustered environment; that is, there is no recommended interval (there couldn't be). There is a default value of 300 (seconds). The default scenario is, therefore, that the WLM attempts to access a managed server, but the server does not respond; thus, the server is marked as unavailable. If the WLM policy selects this server again before 300 seconds have elapsed, no attempt will be made by the runtime to access that server, regardless of the actual state of the server.

   The parameter is set by passing the following -D command line argument to the JVM:

   ```
   -Dcom.ibm.websphere.wlm.unusable.interval=<interval in seconds>
   ```

The importance of classloaders

One of the most basic concepts in the Java Virtual Machine specification is that of the classloader—actually, a Java class itself, implemented primarily by a Hashtable. The job of the classloader is to provide classes at runtime as they are requested by the application code. The goal of this section is to understand basic class loading behavior and WebSphere Version 5-specific class loading behavior.

Basic JVM class loading

These are the basic rules of JVM classloaders. These "rules" are enhanced, and even broken, by the WebSphere J2EE Servers. Understanding these fundamental rules thoroughly is essential to understanding how they affect the behavior of application code; it will also help in the understanding of their variants in WebSphere.

- **Every classloader is the child of the classloader before it**. This implies that classloaders are instantiated by the JVM in a specific and particular order that is either universal to all JVMs or specified by policy, as is the case with WebSphere classloaders. (Often the word "above" is used in the statement of this rule instead of "before." That metaphor may be helpful in some cases where we talk of a parent/child relationship, but, in fact, the ordering is essentially chronological.) The significance of this rule is found in the following item.
- **The default policy is to delegate class loading to the parent.** Upon request of a class, the parent Hashtable is searched; if the requested class is not found in the parent, then the original recipient classloader must fill the request. The stress here is on the word "must": If the original classloader cannot find the class, the search stops, and the ClassNotFoundException is thrown. If we use the "vertical" metaphor, we can say that classloaders can look "up", but not "down."
- **Once a class has been loaded, it cannot be loaded again by another classloader.** Any subsequent classes called by the loaded class will attempt to use the same classloader or look to the parent classloader tree.

Now that the basic rules have been established, we can examine the order and typology of the standard JVM classloaders and the WebSphere classloaders. The classloaders in the following discussion are numbered in the order in which they are created by the WebSphere runtime.

Standard JVM classloaders

There are three classloaders created by every JVM at startup: the bootstrap classloader, the extensions classloader, and the classpath classloader. Each has its own specific search path, as follows:

1. The *bootstrap classloader* searches the "bootstrap" path, typically jre/lib.
2. The *extensions classloader* searches the System Property java.ext.dirs, typically jre/lib/ext.
3. The *classpath classloader* searches the CLASSPATH Environment Variable. This variable can be set to anything, but, for a J2EE Server, it will surely contain j2ee.jar, which enables any libraries that depend on the J2EE APIs to be added to this classpath if we consider the foregoing rules. (However, the preferred method is to add a "shared" library.)

WebSphere classloaders

1. The *WebSphere extensions classloader* searches the WebSphere system property ws.ext.dirs and adds every J2EE and WebSphere JAR or ZIP file in this directory to the classpath of this classloader.

Very important: This classloader also loads all resource provider classes indicated by resource-refs in any application module if the resource provider is associated with the resource and if the provider indicates the directory of the provider classes (drivers).

---

2. A *shared library classloader* is created only if the shared library definition is associated with an application server. In this case, it is the parent of an application classloader and the child of the WebSphere extensions classloader, as indicated by its placement in this numerical list._If, on the other hand, the shared library definition is associated with an application, then a separate classloader is not created, and the shared library classes are loaded by the application module classloader (see the following rule).

3. *Application module classloaders* (numbered from 1 up) search classes contained in the corresponding application modules based on isolation policy and mode, described in the following discussions.

Classloader isolation policies

- The *application classloader policy* loads classes in EJB modules, resource adapters, dependency JARs, and, depending on the WAR classloader policy, potentially Web module classes. The policies are SINGLE and MULTIPLE. Simply put, if the policy is set to SINGLE, there will be only one classloader for the entire system; i.e., all classes in all application modules in all applications on the system will be loaded by this one alassloader.

Note: This may or may not include Web module classes; see the subsequent discussion.) In contrast, if the policy is set to MULTIPLE, each application will have its own classloader. Given the initial rules above, this means that applications using MULTIPLE will not be able to use or refer to classes in other applications, hence the term *isolation*; any attempt to do so will result in a ClassNotFoundException.

- The *WAR classloader policy* searches (according to the default policy, MODULE) WEB-INF/classes and WEB-INF/lib directories; that is, when this policy is set to MODULE, each Web module receives its own classloader, each of which is a child of the application classloader. (This policy is identical to the "Power Classloaders" in WebSphere Version 4.) If, however, the WAR policy is set to APPLICATION, then no new classloaders are created; instead, all classes in all WARs are loaded by the parent application classloader, which, given the application classloader policy, may be only one or one per application.

Classloader modes

There are two modes, and they are dependent upon the classloader isolation policy settings just outlined.

- PARENT_FIRST. This mode is identical to the default class loading rules outlined at the beginning of this section; that is, when a class is requested, the request is first passed to the parent classloader to fill and then returned to the child if the class cannot be found.
- PARENT_LAST. This mode is the exact opposite of PARENT_FIRST. It enables a child's version of a class to "override" the same class contained in a parent.

These modes are governed either by one of the isolation policies above or by the mode, as contained in the application determined implicitly by the choice of isolation policy, as follows:

- *The application classloader policy* determines the mode if the application classloader policy is set to SINGLE.
- The *mode,* set in the application, determines the mode of the application classloader if the application classloader's isolation policy is set to MULTIPLE.
- *The WAR classloader isolation policy* determines the mode (overrides the mode of the application classloader or the application) if the WAR's isolation policy is set to MODULE.

Examples of class loading

The following are two illustrative examples taken from the WebSphere Application Server Version 5 InfoCenter (Figures 14.36–14.39):

Example 1

```
Application Classloader policy: SINGLE
Application 1
       Module:   EJB1.jar
       Module:   WAR1.war
                 MANIFEST Class-Path: Dependency1.jar
                 WAR Classloader Policy = MODULE
Application 2
       Module:   EJB2.jar
                 MANIFEST Class-Path: Dependency2.jar
       Module:   WAR2.war
                 WAR Classloader Policy = APPLICATION
```

Figure 14.36: Classloader specifications for Example 1.

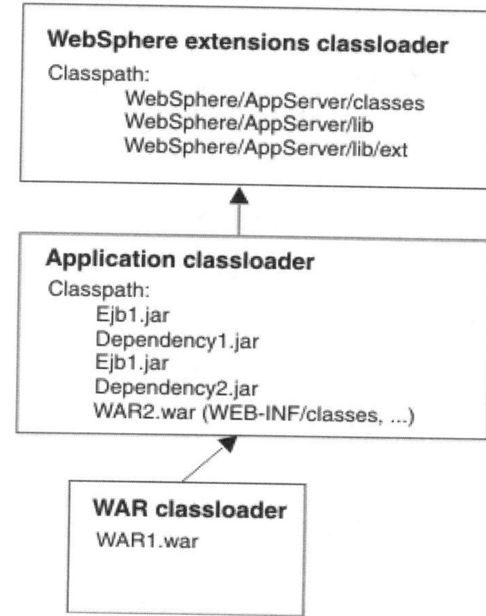

Figure 14.37: Classloader dependencies for Example 1.

The mode for application 1 would be set in the application classloader policy but overridden by its Web module's mode for the WAR classloader. All classes in application 2 would use only the application classloader, and thus use its mode setting.

Example 2

```
Application Classloader policy: MULTIPLE
Application 1
       Module:      EJB1.jar
       Module:WAR1.war
          MANIFEST Class-Path: Dependency1.jar
          WAR Classloader Policy = MODULE
Application 2
       Module:   EJB2.jar
          MANIFEST Class-Path: Dependency2.jar
       Module:   WAR2.war
          WAR Classloader Policy = APPLICATION
```

Figure 14.38: Classloader specifications for Example 2.

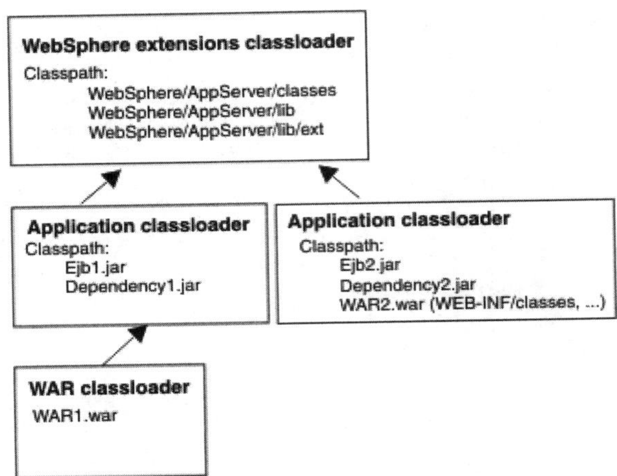

Figure 14.39: Classloader dependencies for Example 2.

The mode for application 1 would be set in the application and overridden by the WAR classloader policy mode setting. All classes in application 2 would use the same mode as set in the application.

Tracing

Tracing, when used in the context of WebSphere, does not mean tracing your running application. For that, you would use the OLT and Distributed Debugger.

The tracing referred to in WebSphere is the tracing of a managed (server) process, i.e., all of the Java objects that make up the runtime of the J2EE server. As such, tracing would be used for tuning only servers, not applications. In this light, it is not typically something that developers would do; that is, developers could only be effective when tuning (or observing) application-related resources. We will describe briefly how to enable tracing in both WebSphere Application Server Version 5 and the Version 5 WebSphere Test Environment (WTE).

For WebSphere Application Server, with the server running, trace enablement begins in the administrative console. As Figure 14.40 indicates, the "breadcrumb trail" to get to the trace settings is **Troubleshooting → Logs and Trace → Server1 → Diagnostic Trace**.

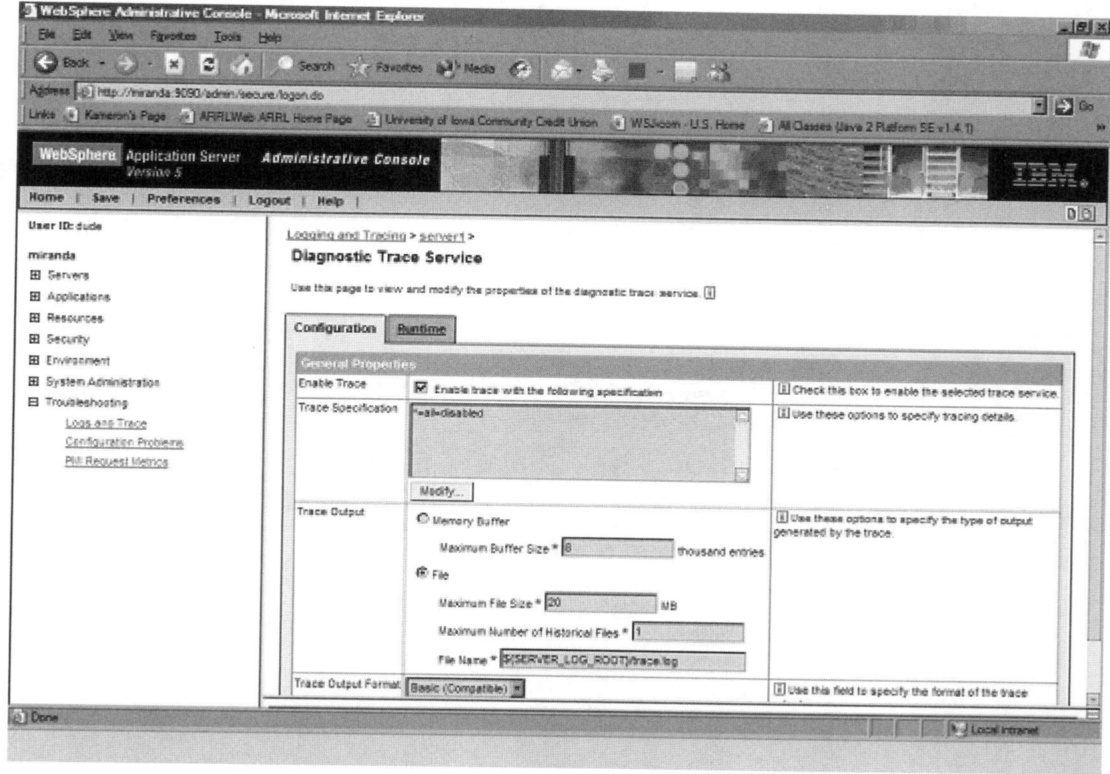

Figure 14.40: Trace settings in WebSphere Application Server Administrative Console.

If you compare this with Figure 14.41 (the "same" screen in Application Developer), you will note that you cannot set the buffer size for the trace output, nor anything about the output file, save its location. Also, you cannot configure the output format.

If you click **Modify . . .** , the administrative console will allow you to view/set all available objects using a GUI, as seen in Figure 14.41. Note, however, that the Modify button is available on both the Configuration and Runtime tabs: Any changes for tracing made in the Configuration tab would apply only at a start or restart of the server process; those entered in the Runtime tab would apply as soon as the changes were saved to the running server.

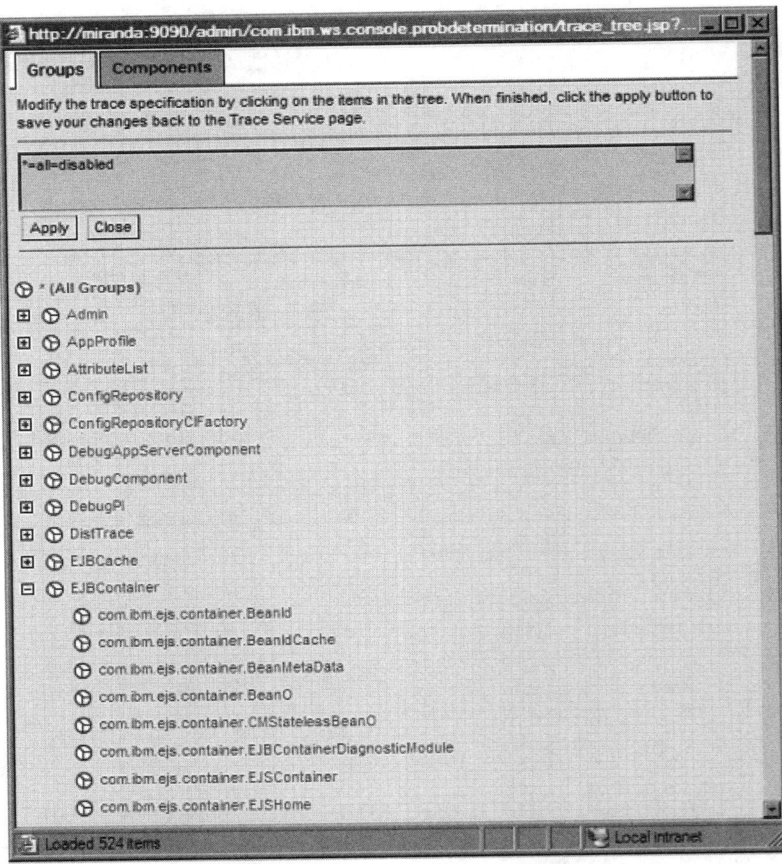

Figure 14.41: Setting tracing for objects using the GUI.

In Application Developer, you would open the server-cfg.xml and go to the Trace page. There, you simply check the **Enable** trace box and enter the trace string. Optionally, you could change the trace output file. Figure 14.42 shows the relevant server-cfg.xml page. Note that WebSphere Studio Application Developer does not provide the GUI that the WebSphere Application Server does; thus, the developer must find in the documentation the exact object names of the components.

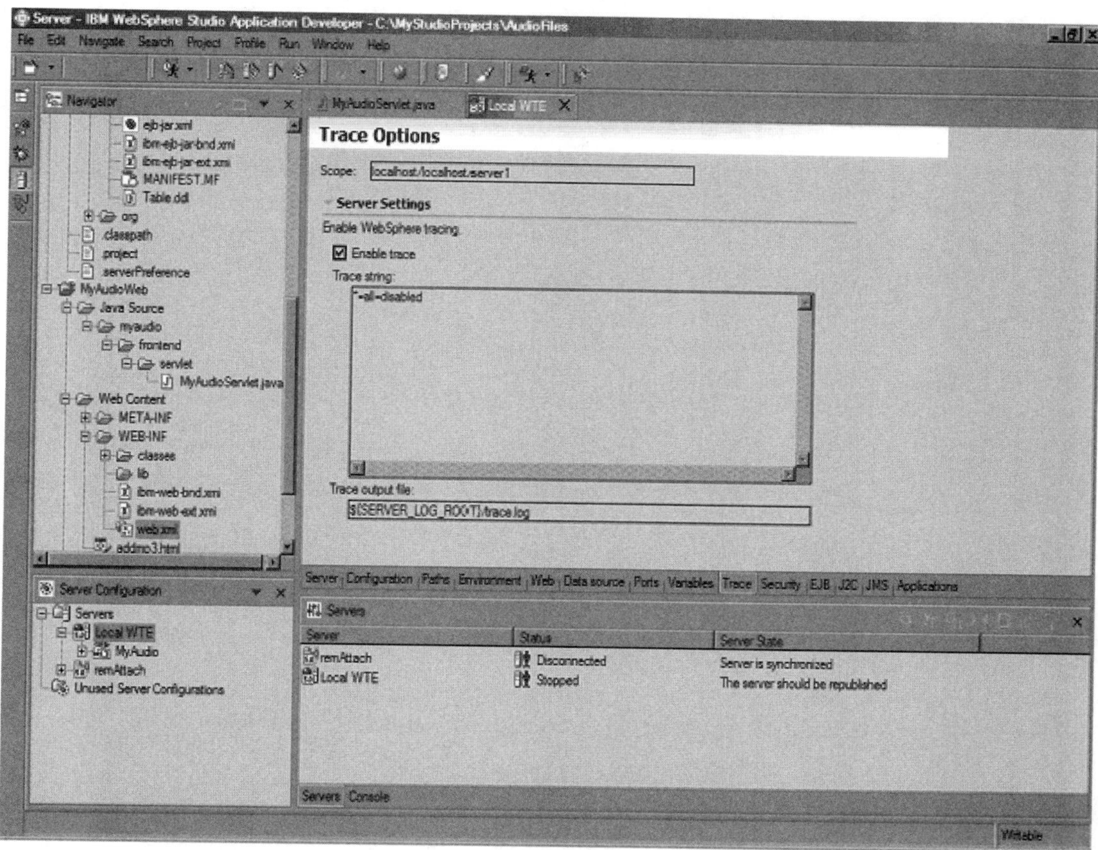

Figure 14.42: Enabling tracing in Application Developer.

Trace strings

Some discussion of trace strings is appropriate for the Enterprise Developer role, although it is a large topic and would need further study, either in the WebSphere Application Server InfoCenter or through the Application Developer's Help perspective.

The syntax for trace strings is listed in Figure 14.43.

```
TRACESTRING=COMPONENT_TRACE_STRING[:COMPONENT_TRACE_STRING]*

COMPONENT_TRACE_STRING=COMPONENT_NAME=LEVEL=STATE[,LEVEL=STATE]*

LEVEL = all | entryExit | debug | event

STATE = enabled | disabled

COMPONENT_NAME = COMPONENT | GROUP
```

Figure 14.43: Syntax of trace strings.

The following rules should be remembered

- No spaces are allowed in trace strings.
- Trace strings are parsed from left to right; thus, it is possible to use rules of exclusion when adding additional trace strings. For example, the string *abc.*=all=enabled,event=disabled* means that component *abc* will have all but event-level tracing enabled. Since there are only three levels of tracing (event, debug, and entryexit), this string could be equivalently rendered as *abc.*=debug=enabled,entryexit=enabled.*

Trace logs

You will note that in both trace GUIs, you are allowed to set the output file for the trace. In both cases, the default is: ${SERVER_LOG_ROOT}/trace.log. While this is fairly simple to find in WebSphere Application Server (you can check the value of the variable SERVER_LOG_ROOT in the Administrative Console, **Environment → Manage WebSphere Variables**), you have no such GUI in Application Developer.

A typical location for the Application Server trace log would be, on Windows, for example, C:\Program Files\WebSphere\AppServer\logs\server1\trace.log. In Application Developer, the SERVER_LOG_ROOT would be in your workspace directory, in a somewhat surprising location: The general path to the SERVER_LOG_ROOT would be <WORKSPACE_DIR>/.metadata/.plugins/com.ibm.etools.server.core/tmp#/logs/server1. So, in the case where I have a workspace located in C:\MyStudioApps\AudioFiles, I would find the trace.log at C:\MyStudioProjects\AudioFiles\.metadata\.plugins\com.ibm.etools.server.core\tmp3\logs\server1 (the number following "tmp" will change).

Summary

The purpose of this chapter was not to be an in-depth exploration of WebSphere Version 5 administration. As this book is intended principally for developers of J2EE applications, the focus of this chapter was on those aspects of the WebSphere Version 5 J2EE Server that influence the design of a J2EE application and its performance after it has been implemented, limited to those aspects that are under the control of the developer.

This chapter has focused almost solely (with the exception of the brief section on clustering) on the single-server WebSphere J2EE Server (informally known as the "Base" edition), as this is the edition most readily accessible to developers. Also, this is the server upon which the WebSphere Test Environment, part of WebSphere Studio Application Developer, is based.

In a very important sense, this chapter is limited in its scope by the J2EE 1.3 specification itself, insofar as the roles of Component Provider and System Administrator are clearly delimited. Stated another way, enterprise developers are not intended to be administrators, although they should be encouraged to understand many aspects of the administration of a J2EE Server, because this is the environment that hosts the applications they develop.

Test yourself

Key terms

Performance Monitoring Infrastructure (PMI)
Java Virtual Machine Profiling Interface (JVMPI)
Tivoli Performance Viewer
counter
Java Management Extensions (JMX)
WebSphere Queuing Network
throughput curve
closed queues
connection pooling
Classloader
tracing

Review questions

1. Tuning is done by both developers and administrators. Who does what?
2. Simply increasing heap size would seem to be an effective way to help the garbage collection process. Is it?
3. Is a sawtooth pattern in the plot of memory utilization over time a good thing?
4. Describe upstream queuing.

5. What happens when a queue is closed? Are there any queues that cannot be closed?
6. Compare vertical to horizontal clustering.
7. A developer can wrap all requests for a connection from the pool inside a try/catch block that catches a StaleConnectionException and retries to grab a new one. Normally the developer should limit the number of retries. Why?
8. A system is throwing a ConnectionWaitTimeoutException frequently. How should this be fixed?
9. Can session data be moved between servers in a cluster?

CHAPTER 15

Remote Debugger and Java Component Test Tools in WebSphere Studio

Doug Weatherbee

Chapter topics

- *Remote Debug background*
- *WebSphere application server debug procedures*
- *Component Test background and concepts*
- *The Component Test perspective*
- *Java Component Test procedures*

Certification objectives

- *Test and Debug enterprise components*
- *Identify misbehaving application components*

This chapter will describe two very useful tools in WebSphere Studio Application Developer: Remote Debugging and the Component Testing Framework. The chapter begins by providing background on Application Developer's Remote Debugger and then outlines the steps required for remotely debugging applications already deployed on a stand-alone WebSphere Application Server. The second half of the chapter describes Application Developer's Component Testing Framework and Perspective and concludes by outlining the procedures for creating, executing, and reviewing the results of Java Testcases.

Remote Debug background

This section of the chapter will outline the steps required to configure Application Developer to debug remotely applications already deployed on a stand-alone WebSphere Application Server. The chapter does not describe the fundamentals of how to use Application Developer's debugging tools. For a comprehensive discussion of Application Developer's debugging tools see *An Introduction to Web Application Development with IBM WebSphere Studio* by Gary Craig and Peter Jakab (IBM Press).

You can start a debug session in Application Developer for an application server that is running locally or remotely. Using Application Developer to debug code installed on a stand-alone WebSphere Application Server is very useful when your applications run differently outside of Application Developer's internal WebSphere Test Environment (WTE). Application Developer functions as a debug client to a WebSphere Application Server JVM running in debug mode. The Debug perspective and views function as normal. You will be able to set breakpoints in and step through your code as you normally would during a debug session with an Application Developer WTE debug session. The differences you may see are network delays when debugging an application server running on a remote host.

WebSphere Application Server debug procedures

In order to debug remotely an application deployed to WebSphere Application Server, you must, first, configure and start the Server to run in debug mode and, second, attach the Application Developer Debugger to your configured WebSphere Server.

Setting up WebSphere Application Server to run in debug mode

The WebSphere Application Server JVM has implemented Sun Microsystem's Java Platform Debugger Architecture (JPDA). The JPDA defines "three interfaces designed for use by debuggers in development environments for desktop systems" (Java Platform Debugger Architecture, Sun Microsystems, *java.sun.com/j2se/1.3/docs/guide/jpda/,* 1999). In order to activate the JPDA interfaces, the WebSphere Application Server Debugging Service must be configured to start in debug mode. In the WebSphere Administration Console go to **Servers → Application Servers → <YourServer> → Debugging Service**. Figure 15.1 displays the console window you should see.

You must select the **Startup** check box and then the **Apply** button. You will then be asked to save your configuration changes. The Debugging Service window contains three properties used to start the application server in debug mode: JVM debug port, JVM debug arguments, and Debug class filters. The JVM debug port is the port that the application server will open for the Application Developer debug client. The default port is **7777**. If you change this port, you must remember to make the corresponding changes in Application Developer. The JVM debug arguments are preset for you and include arguments to disable the Just In Time compiler and enable the required JPDA interfaces for your server to start in debug mode. After successfully saving your WebSphere configuration changes, you must start the application server.

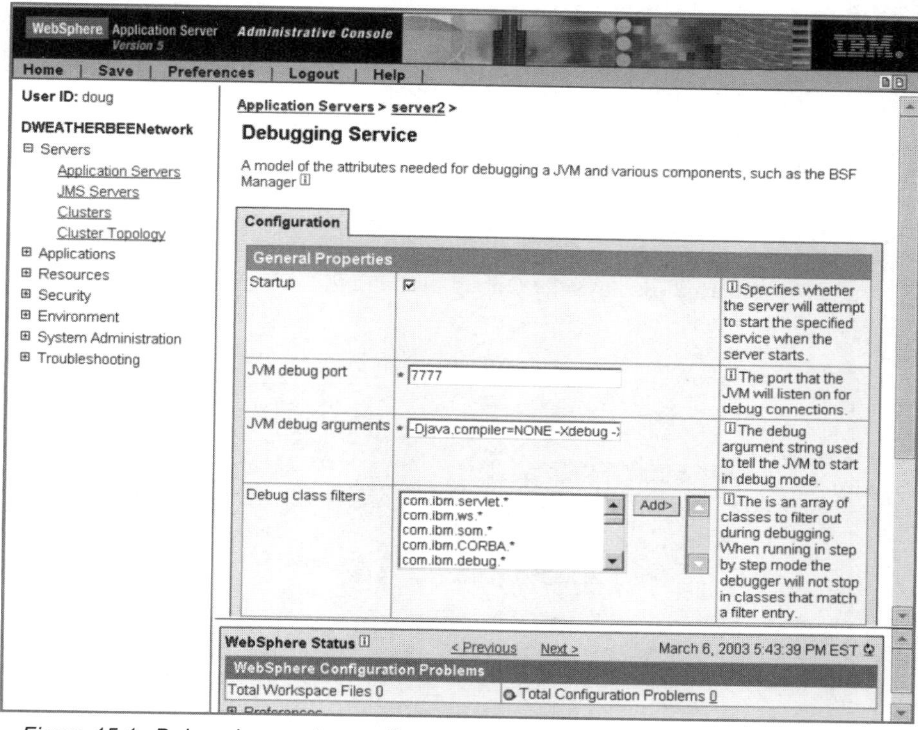

Figure 15.1: Debugging service configuration attributes.

Attaching the Application Developer debugger to the remote WebSphere application server

First, you should ensure that the enterprise application you have deployed to WebSphere Application Server is imported into Application Developer. Next, using the Launch Configurations dialog, you need to create a new WebSphere Application Server debug configuration. There are two ways to do this. By default, the Debug, Java, Java Browsing, Java Type Hierarchy, and J2EE perspectives contain a Debug button located on the workbench toolbar. Use the Debug button's drop-down menu and select **Debug. . . .** Figure 15.2 displays the Debug button and the Debug. . . menu item.

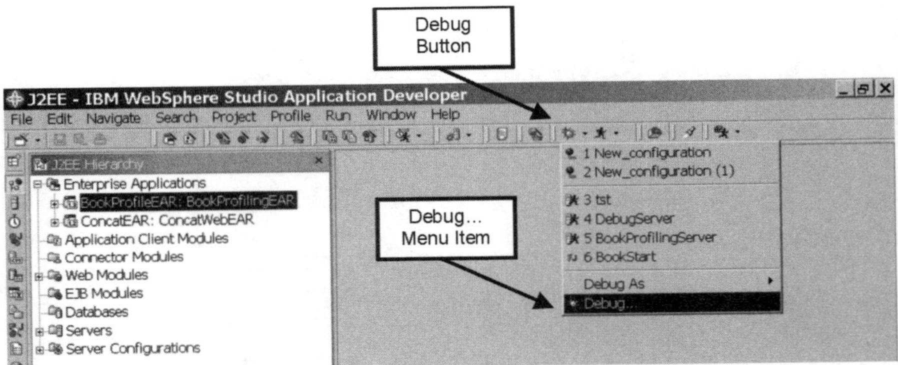

Figure 15.2: Debug button and Debug. . . menu item.

The second way to access the Launch Configuration dialog is to use the Debug perspective workbench Run menu. The Run menu contains a Debug. . . menu item that also invokes the Launch Configuration dialog. Figure 15.3 displays the Debug perspective's Run menu.

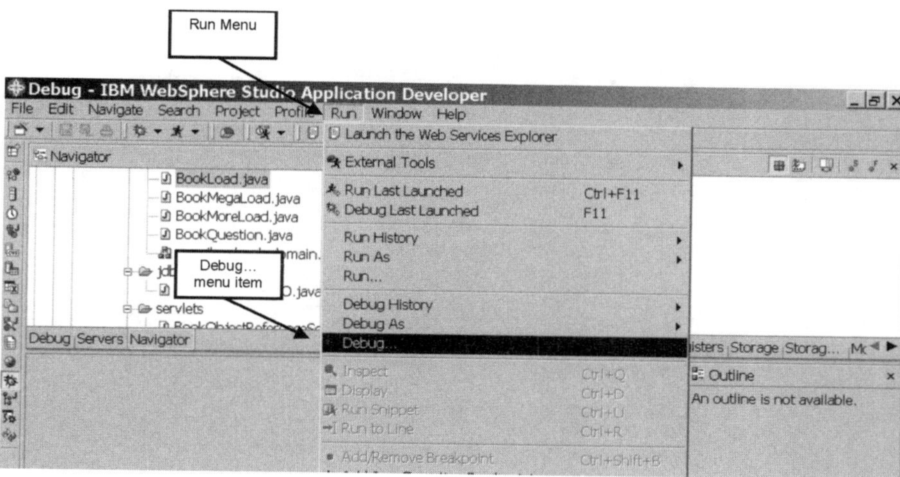

Figure 15.3: Debug perspective's Run menu.

Selecting the Debug. . . menu item from either the Debug button menu or the Run menu starts the Launch Configurations dialog. **Select WebSphere Application Server Debug** from the Launch Configurations list and click the **New** button. Figure 15.4 displays the Launch Configurations dialog.

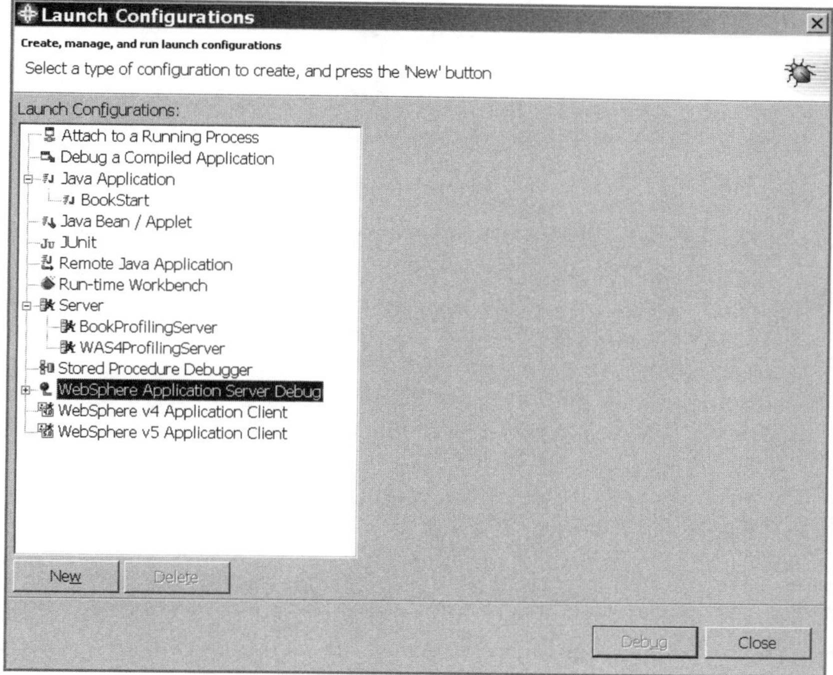

Figure 15.4: Launch Configurations dialog.

When you create a new WebSphere Application Server Debug configuration, there are three tabs of associated information: Connect, Source and Common. Figure 15.5 displays the Connect tab of the Launch Configurations dialog.

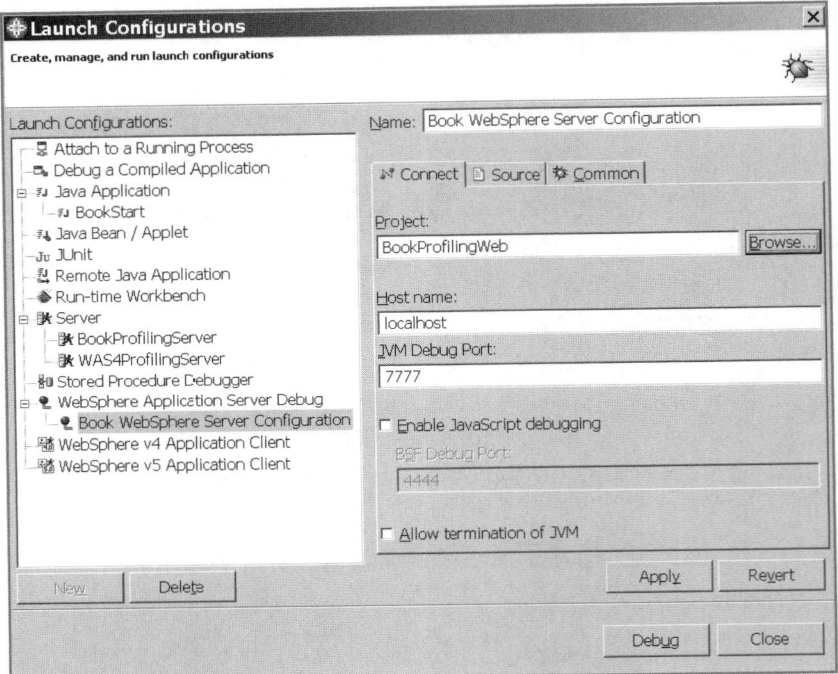

Figure 15.5: The Connect tab of the Launch Configurations dialog.

In the Connect tab, you must name your WebSphere Application Server Debug configuration. You must also provide a Project, usually a Web or EJB Project in the Enterprise Application, that you wish to debug. As stated earlier, you should have imported the enterprise application (if it was not already in your workspace) into Application Developer. You can use the Project Browse button to select either a Web or an EJB Project from that enterprise application. By default, **localhost** is entered as host name and **7777** as the JVM debug port. Depending on whether you are running WebSphere Application Server on the same machine as Application Developer or remotely, you may have to enter a new host name. As mentioned earlier, the default debug port of WebSphere Application Server is 7777; If you changed the port using the WebSphere Administrative Console, you would have to enter that port here.

The Source tab contains references to projects and JARs that contain your source code. The Debugger must have access to the source code of an application in order to display the text of the code. If the enterprise application modules (Web and EJB) and utility Java

Projects in your workspace contain source code, you do not need to deal with the Source tab. The Source tab's Source Lookup Path will be automatically created based on the paths of the selected Project in the Connect tab. If some or all of your source code resides elsewhere, you can add those references manually.

The Common tab allows you to specify that the configuration is used by you or can be saved in a project folder and shared, via a source control system, with other members of your development team. By default, when you launch WebSphere Application Server Debug configurations, the Debug perspective is opened. You can change this setting on the Common tab by using the Debug Mode drop-down list. The Common tab also has a Debug check box under Display in the favorites menu. If you would like the launch configuration to appear as a favorite debug configuration in the Debug button favorities menu or the Run menu Debug History menu item, select the **Debug** check box.

You should click the dialog's **Apply** button in order to save your configuration information. If you have already started WebSphere Application Server in debug mode, you can click the Launch Configuration dialog's **Debug** button. This will start a debug session between Application Developer and WebSphere Application Server. You will then need to run your enterprise application on the WebSphere Server by invoking a URL in a browser. Depending on whether you have set a breakpoint or enabled step-by-step debugging (see *An Introduction to Web Application Development with IBM WebSphere Studio* by Gary Craig and Peter Jakab [IBM Press] for information on debugger basics), Application Developer's Debugger will function as normal. The only difference may be increased response times. due to network traffic, as you step through.

Component Test background and concepts

The Component Test perspective provides various tools for creating and executing three types of Testcases: Java, HTTP, and manual. All Testcases are composed of blocks of testing tasks. Manual Testcases can be used to prompt and guide an actual person conducting application test tasks. A Manual Testcase can require the tester to record that a test task has passed or failed before moving on to the next task. In contrast, the HTTP and Java Testcases are automated tests written in Java. The HTTP Testcase is used to execute HTTP requests against a Web-based application component such as a servlet or JSP page. The Java Testcase is used to perform JUnit framework tests against model application code such as JavaBeans and other logic classes. The remaining sections of the chapter will focus on Application Developer's Java Testcase functionality.

The Component Test perspective

This section of the chapter will describe the range of Views and Editors available in the Application Developer Component Test perspective.

The Definition view

You define Java (and Manual and HTTP) Testcases in the Definition view of the Component Test perspective. You also define hosts on which your Testcases will run. Application Developer's Component Testing framework requires the use of the IBM Agent Controller to run your Testcases; therefore, in order for any Testcase to run, Agent Controller must be installed and running on the host machine where you intend to run your Testcases. After defining one or more Java Testcases and hosts in the Definition view, you can prepare the Testcase for execution by having Application Developer generate a Testcase Instance. A Java Testcase Instance includes generated classes implementing the JUnit Testcase framework. Like other JUnit code generators, you will need to edit the generated code in specific skeleton methods to include your actual application tests. The Application Developer Component Test tools provide generated testing framework code and an automated report-generating mechanism. You must provide the business logic tests. Figure 15.6 displays the Definition view with three hosts and two Testcases defined.

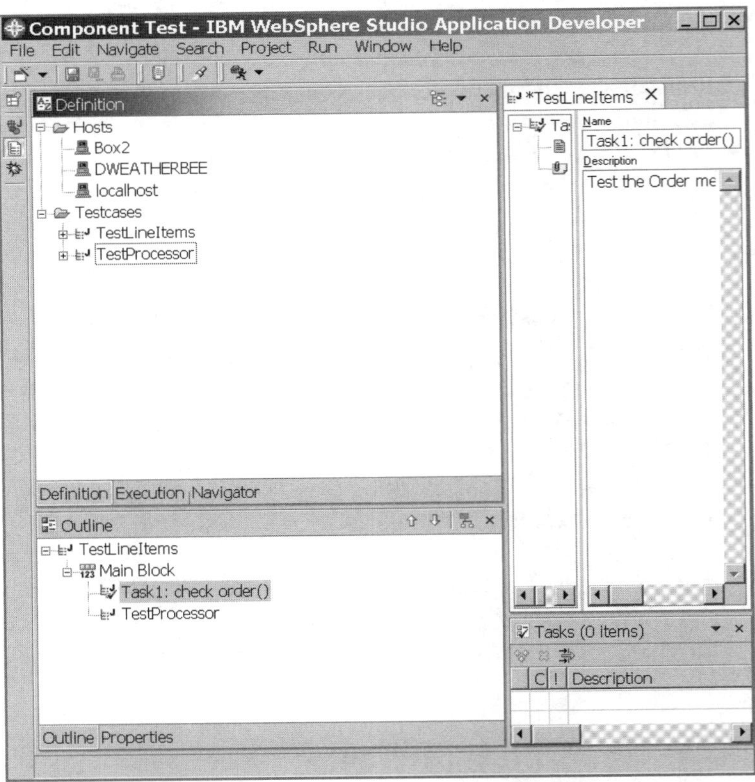

Figure 15.6: Definition view with three hosts and two Testcases.

The Execution view

The Execution view enables you to access and edit easily any of the JUnit Java Testcase Instance classes you generated while working in the Definition view. Once you have edited the generated classes by adding your specific application testing code, as you would in a JUnit Testcase, the Execution view also allows you to run the Testcases.

The Host editor

The Host editor allows you to define the IP address of the host machine you plan to run your Testcase on. Remember that you must have the IBM Agent Controller installed and running on the target host machine. To open the Host editor, double-click a host in the Definition view.

The Testcase editor

Java Testcases include several types of parts: Blocks, Tasks, Verification Points, and Delays. The Testcase editor is used in conjunction with the Outline view to define the names, descriptions, and other configuration information related to the Java Testcase parts. The Testcases Editor works with an XML file that stores the Testcase definitions. Once the Testcase XML file has been built using this editor, Application Developer will generate the concrete Testcase Instance JUnit classes. To open the Testcase editor, double-click a Testcase in the Definition view.

Note: The Testcase editor works with Testcases during the definition stage, prior to the generation of the Testcase Instance code. In contrast, the Testcase Instance editor is used to work with Testcase Instances and the generated code.

The Testcase Instance editor

The Testcase Instance editor is used in conjunction with the Outline view to access the concrete generated classes representing Testcase Blocks and Tasks as defined in the Testcase XML file (described above). The Testcase Instance editor can also be used to set configuration such as runtime classpaths. To open the Testcase Instance editor, double-click a Testcase Instance in the Execution view.

The Outline view

The Outline view in the Component Testing perspective is synchronized with the Definition and Execution views and the Testcase editors. When you are working with the Testcase editor, the Outline view provides context menus for creating and editing Testcase Blocks, Tasks, Verification Points, and Delays. When you are working with the Testcase Instance editor, the Outline view selections highlight the different editor pages associated with these Testcase parts. These editor pages include references to the generated JUnit classes that implement the parts.

The Prepare to Run wizard

The Prepare to Run wizard is used to generate the concrete generated classes representing Testcase Blocks and Tasks as defined in the Testcase XML file. The wizard is accessed through the Definition view by either selecting a Testcase context menu **Prepare** or the workbench **Run → Prepare Testcase** menu item.

Java Component Test procedures

Having discussed the major tools of Application Developer's Component Test perspective, we will outline how you create and run a Java Testcase.

Defining and adding hosts to projects

Before a Java Testcase can be created, a new host definition must be defined. The host definition contains a host name and an IP address. In the Definition view, select the context menu of **Hosts** and then choose **New → Hosts. . . .** The New Host wizard is opened. Using the wizard you define a host name and choose a Project folder in which to store the host configuration property file. Figure 15.7 displays the New Host wizard.

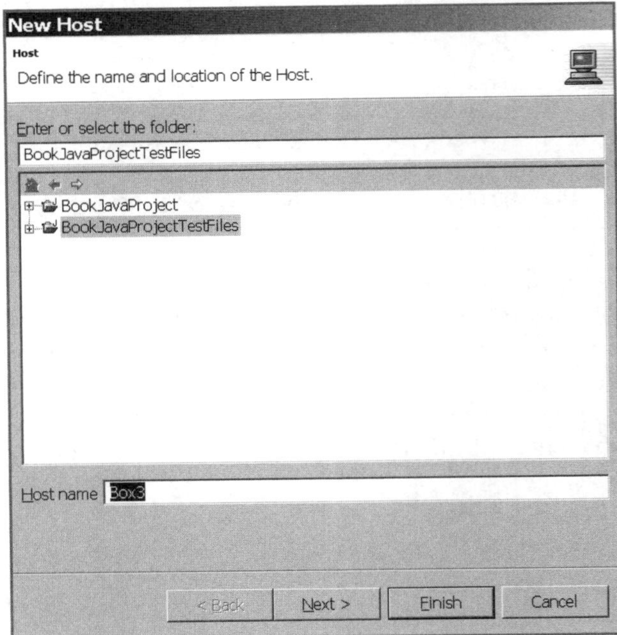

Figure 15.7: The New Host wizard.

Hosts define the machine on which the Testcase will be run. Using the IBM Agent Controller you can run Testcases on remote host machines.

Creating Java Testcases

In the Definition view, select the context menu of **Testcases** and then choose **New → Testcase. . .** The New Testcase wizard is opened. Using the Testcase page of the wizard you define a Testcase name and choose a Project folder in which to store the Testcase configuration property file. Figure 15.8 displays the first page of the New Testcase wizard.

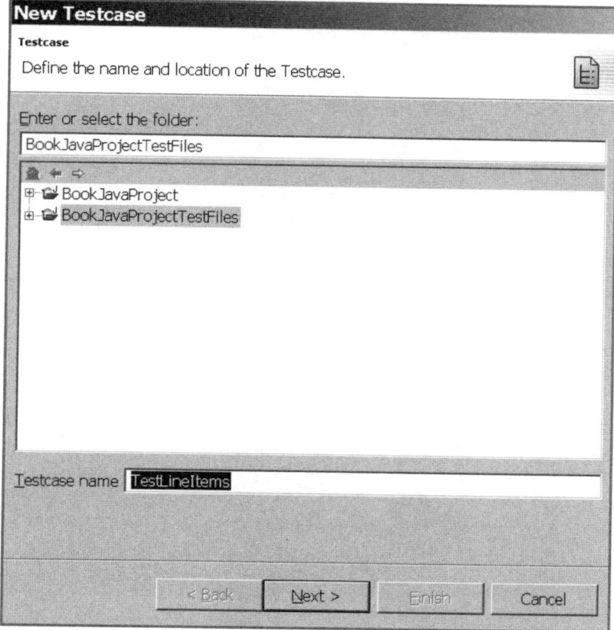

Figure 15.8: The first page of the New Testcase wizard.

The second page of the New Testcase wizard includes a list of the three types of Testcases. Figure 15.9 displays the second page of the New Testcase wizard.

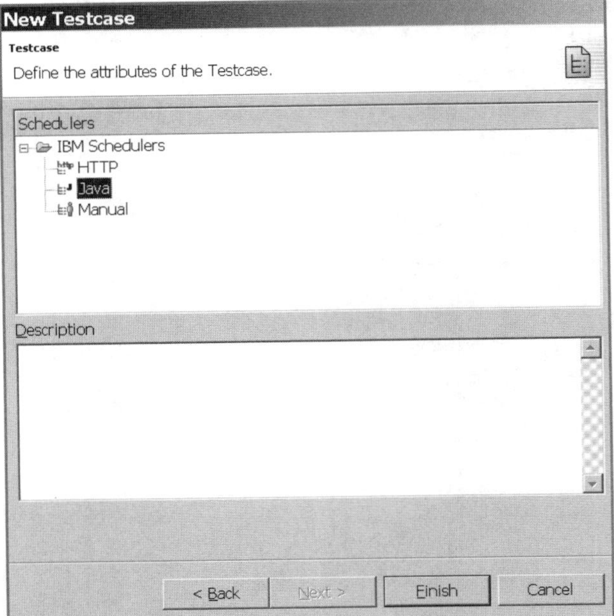

Figure 15.9: The second page of the New Testcase wizard.

Choose **Java Testcase** to define this as a Java Testcase. Then click the **Finish** button. The New Testcase wizard creates the Java Testcase and opens the new Testcase in the Testcase editor. Figure 15.10 displays the newly created Testcase opened in the Testcase editor.

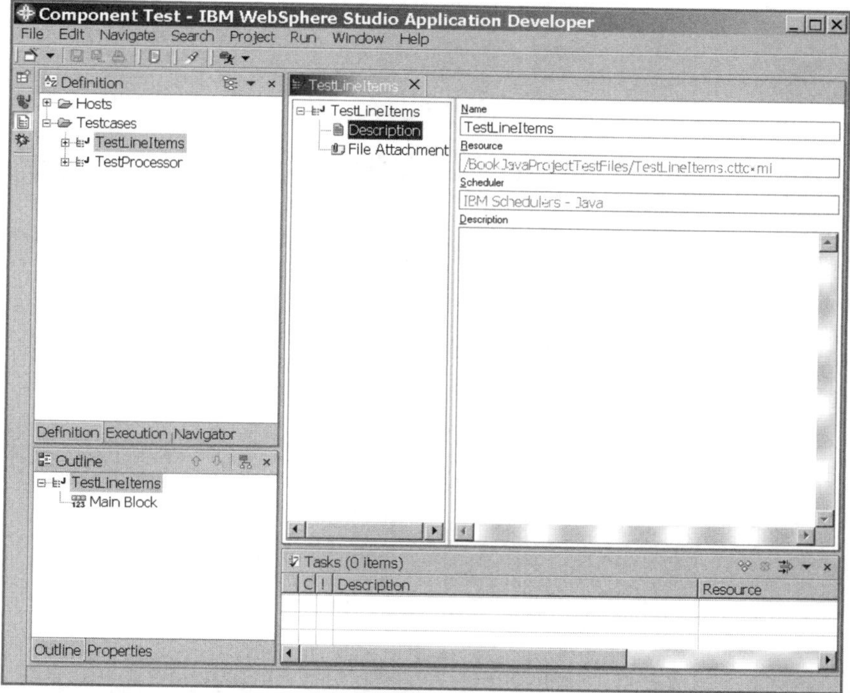

Figure 15.10: The newly created Testcase opened in the Testcase Editor.

After the Java Testcase is created, Blocks, Java Tasks, Verification Points, and Delays can be added.

Adding Blocks

Blocks organize a Testcase's Tasks, Delays, and Verification Points into logical groups. If required for proper test execution, the sequence and number of iterations of the Block contents can be customized using this editor. Every new Java Testcase has a Main Block. You can define Java Tasks, Delays, and Verification Points directly under the Main Block or create custom Blocks under the Main Block. When the Java Testcase JUnit classes are prepared, a new class for each Block, including the Main Block, will be generated.

Adding Java Tasks

Java Tasks define what will become method skeletons that will contain your test code. Java Tasks are contained in Blocks. When the Java Testcase JUnit classes are prepared, a new method skeleton, javaTaskInstance(), for each Java Task in the corresponding Block class will be generated. You will edit the generated Java Task method skeleton to include the necessary testing code for your application. To create a new Java Task, make sure the

Testcase is opened with the Testcase editor and select the containing Block in the Outline view. From the Block context menu select **New → Task → Java**. Figure 15.11 displays the Block context menu in the Outline view.

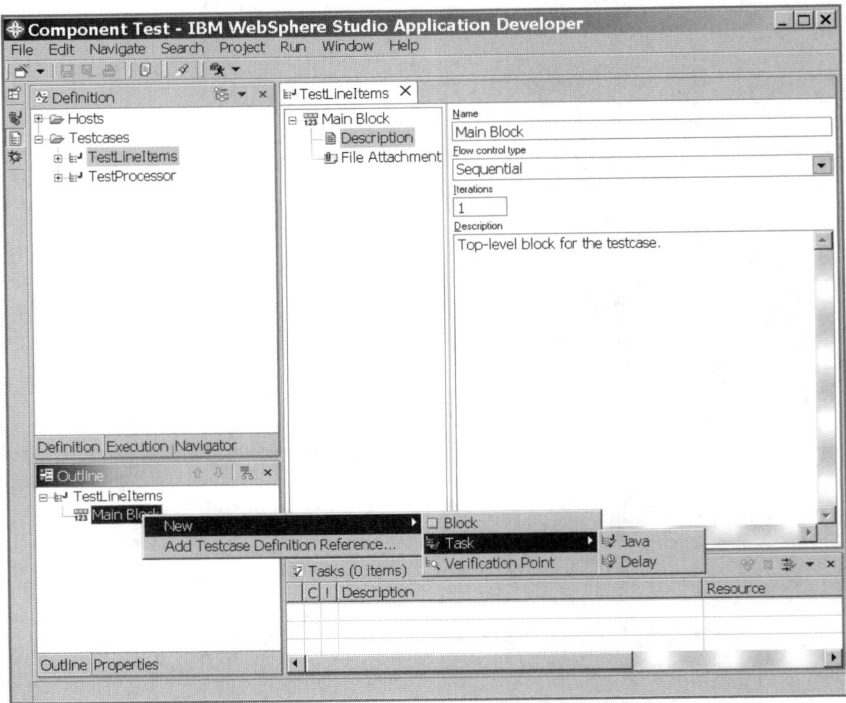

Figure 15.11: The Block context menu in the Outline view.

The Java Task will be created and added to the Outline view. The Testcase editor will also switch to the corresponding Java Task page, allowing you to change the Java Task name. Figure 15.12 displays the Java Task page of the Testcase editor.

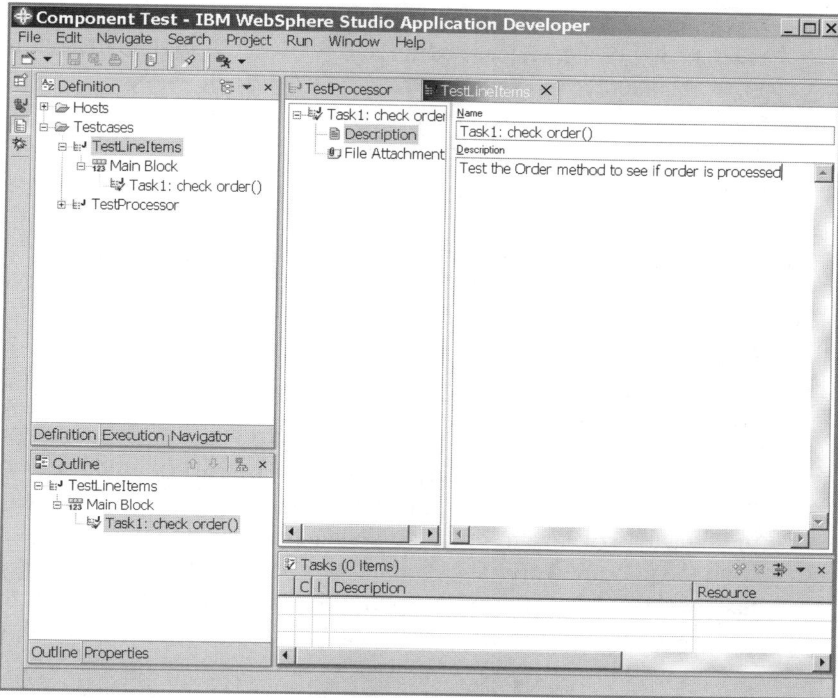

Figure 15.12: The Java Task page of the Testcase editor.

Adding Java Verification Points

Verification Points define what will become method skeletons that will contain code to check the progress of your test methods. Each Verification Point will become a method skeleton during code generation. Verification Points are optional definitions and generated methods. If your Java tests require periodic status checks during tests, then you can define a Verification Point and determine its placement in the Block's sequenced order. Similar to the Java Tasks, you will edit the generated Verification Point method skeleton, verifyPoint(), to include the necessary status-checking code for your application tests. To create a new Verification Point, make sure the Testcase is opened with the Testcase editor and select the containing Block in the Outline view. From the Block context menu select **New → Verification Point**.

Adding Delays

Delays define what will become generated methods that contain fully implemented code forcing the current thread to suspend. The duration of the thread delay is defined in the Delay page of the Testcase editor. Each Delay and its delay time will become a fully implemented method during code generation. You do not need to add code to the generated Delay methods. Delays are optional definitions and generated methods. If your Java tests require periodic delays during tests, then you can define a Delay and determine its placement in the Block's sequenced order. To create a new Delay, make sure the Testcase is opened with the Testcase editor and select the containing Block in the Outline view. From the Block context menu select **New → Task → Delay**.

Adding Testcase References

One Java Testcase can have a kind of pointer to another Java Testcase so that multiple associated Testcases can be run as groups. This is called a Testcase Reference. You can only reference testcases of the same type; for example, Java Testcase to Java Testcase. From the Block context menu, select **Add Testcase Definition Reference**.

Preparing and Running Java Testcases

After defining a Java Testcase, you will need to generate the skeleton classes, implement your test code, and finally run the tests.

Prepare to Run: Generating a Testcase Instance

Preparing to Run is the stage in which the generated code is created. In order to create the skeleton code, right-click the Testcase in the Definition view and select **Prepare** from the pop-up menu. The Prepare wizard is displayed, requiring you to define an Instance name and an Application Developer Project in which to store the Instance property file and the generated code. Figure 15.13 displays the Prepare wizard.

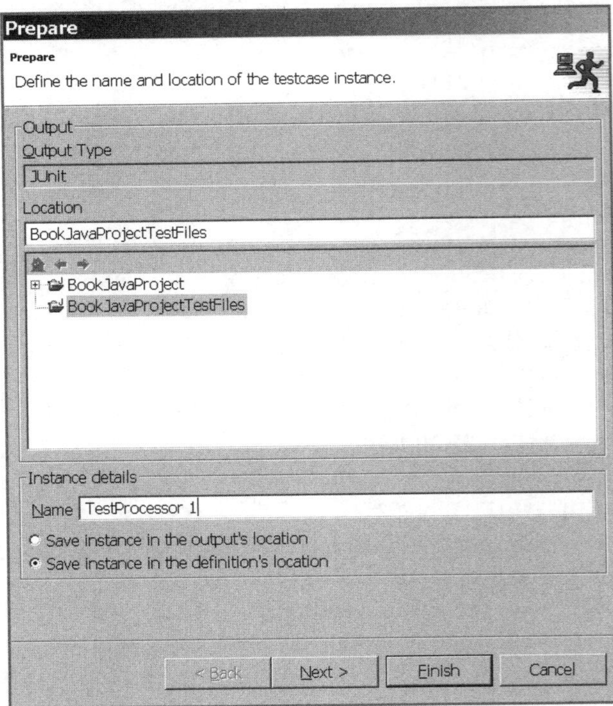

Figure 15.13: The Prepare wizard.

The second page of the Prepare wizard allows you to determine which host you will eventually run the Testcase Instance on. Figure 15.14 displays the Hosts page of the Prepare wizard.

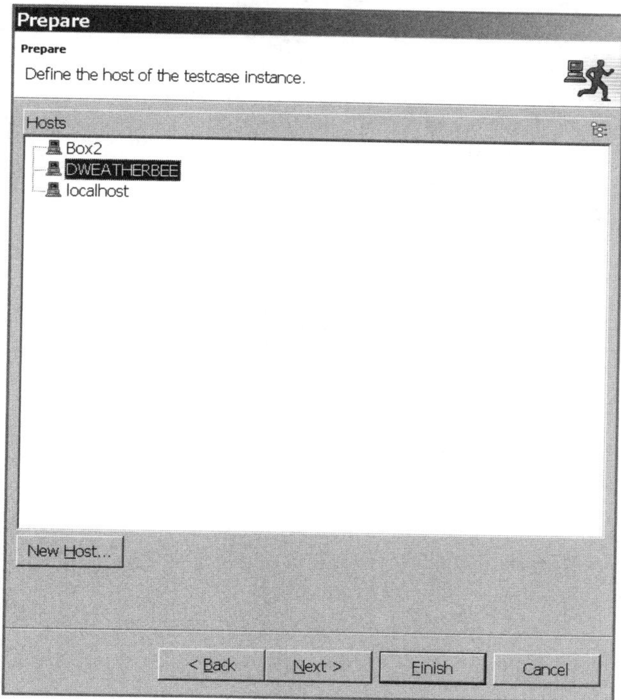

Figure 15.14: The Hosts page of the Prepare wizard.

Finally, click the **Finish** button. The Prepare wizard will generate at least three classes. One class is called JUnitScheduler and includes a main() method for executing the Testcase. You do not need to edit this class. The second class is assigned the name of the Testcase Instance from the Prepare wizard. It includes the instantiation of a JUnit TestSuite. The generated code includes the building of the TestSuite through the standard JUnit addTest(). The addTest() method actually adds classes that represent the Blocks in your testcase. You do not need to edit this code in the Testcase Instance generated class. The third class represents the main Block of the Testcase. If you created additional Blocks, there will one class per Block. The Block classes extend the standard JUnit Testcase class. The generated Block classes include the skeleton Java Task, Delay, and Verification Point methods. You will need to edit these Block classes and, in particular, the generated Java Task methods. You will implement your test code in these methods utilizing the standard JUnit assert and fail methods.

To edit the code associated with a particular Testcase Block, Task, Delay, or Verification Point, open the Testcase Instance editor by double-clicking your Testcase Instance in the Execution view. Select the Testcase element (Block, Task, Delay, or Verification Point) in the Outline view. This will switch the Testcase Instance editor to that specific element's page. Select **File Attachment** in the editor to view the class file associated with the Task, Delay, or Verification Point. Double-click the URL of the generated file to open a Java editor. Edit the appropriate skeleton method, adding your standard JUnit test code.

Running a Java Testcase

Once you have prepared your Java Testcase and edited the generated classes to include your test code, you can run the Testcase. In the Execution pane, right-click the testcase instance and select **Run**. The Run Testcase wizard will appear, asking you to enter an execution name. Figure 15.15 displays the Run Testcase wizard.

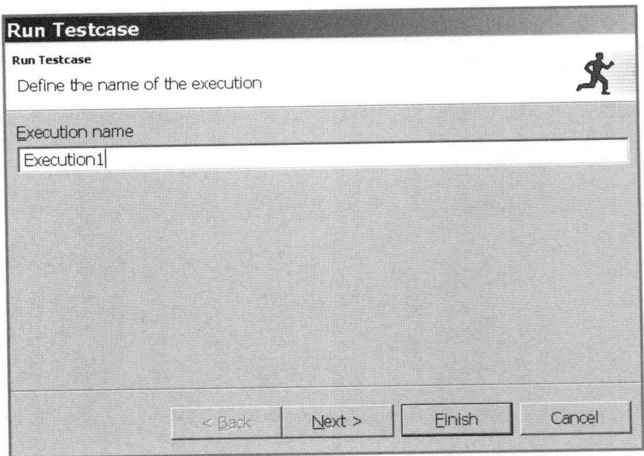

Figure 15.15: The Run Testcase wizard.

Testcases can be run multiple times, with each run being assigned an execution name. The second page of the wizard requires you to choose a host on which to run your Testcase.

Note: If you run the Testcase on a remote host. you must create a JAR file with the Testcase Instance and Business object code and install it on the remote box. Then, on the Environment page of the Testcase Instance editor, you must add the location of that remotely installed JAR to the classpath entry.

After the test has run, an Execution Results editor is automatically opened. You can review the detailed recorded test results by selecting the Testcase Instance in the Outline view and then selecting Event Log in the Execution Results editor. The Event Log will indicate whether different parts of your Testcase have passed or failed.

Summary

This chapter has described two very useful tools in WebSphere Studio Application Developer: Remote Debugging and the Component Testing Framework. The chapter began by providing background on Application Developer's Remote Debugger and then outlined the steps required for remotely debugging applications already deployed on a stand-alone WebSphere Application Server. The second half of the chapter described Application Developer's Component Testing Framework and Component Test perspective and concluded by outlining the procedures for creating, executing, and reviewing the results of Java Testcases.

Test yourself

Key terms

Java Platform Debugger Architecture (JPDA)	*JUnit*
WebSphere Application Server Debugging Service	*Block*
Testcase	*Task*
hosts	*Delay*

Review questions

1. JUnit is already built into Application Developer as a plug-in, usable from the Java perspective. What, then, is the purpose of the Component Test perspective? Why not simply use the Java perspective's JUnit Testcase and test suite wizards for everything?
2. What is the difference between the Definition view and the Execution view?
3. What is the purpose of the Agent Controller in the test context?
4. What three types of schedulers are available for Testcases?
5. To run a set of Testcases on a remote server, what additional step needs to be performed?

Appendix A—CD instructions

This book comes with two CDs containing trial versions of WebSphere Application Server, Version 5, and WebSphere Studio Application Developer, Version 5. This appendix provides a high-level overview of the WebSphere product installations. Detailed instructions are available on the CDs themselves.

Note: The trial versions will stop working after December 31, 2005.

Installation instructions

Prior to installing WebSphere Studio, you should install WebSphere Application Server. Otherwise you may experience problems later with the Agent Controller. Installing WebSphere Application Server will enable you to gain experience working with J2EE enterprise applications outside the WebSphere test environment of WebSphere Studio Application Developer.

After installing WebSphere Application Server, you can proceed to install IBM WebSphere Studio Application Developer, IBM Agent Controller, and the embedded messaging client and server. This establishes the development environment needed for building J2EE enterprise applications.

Note: The trial edition of WebSphere Studio Application Developer is good for only 60 days! We strongly suggest that you wait to install this software until you are actually ready to use it.

When the first CD is loaded into the drive, the WebSphere Studio Application Launcher shown in Figure A.1 should start up automatically. If the launcher starts, then click **Exit** as shown in Figure A.1, since we suggest that you defer installation of WebSphere Studio Application Developer until after you have installed WebSphere Application Server.

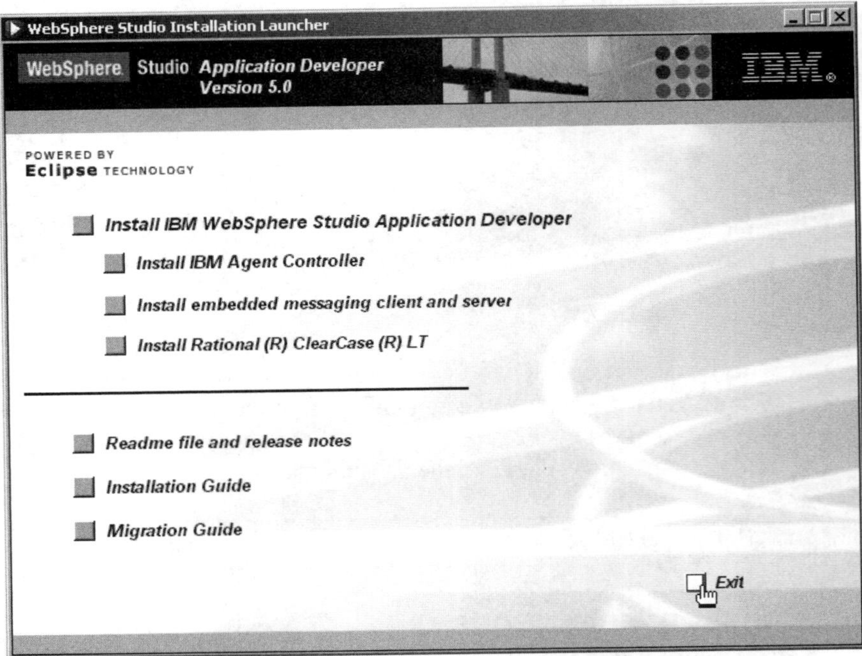

Figure A.1: WebSphere Studio Application Launcher with Exit button.

WebSphere Application Server

To install WebSphere Application Server, run the Install.exe program located in the **\wasv5inst\WAS50** directory on the first CD. The Installation wizard, shown in Figure A.2, is displayed. Select a language and click **OK**.

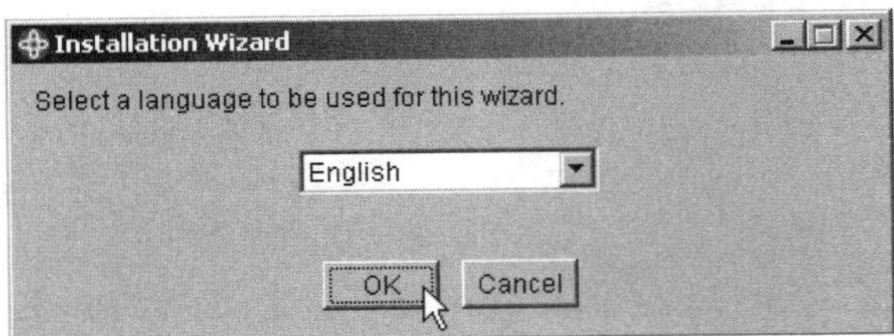

Figure A.2: Installing WebSphere Application Server.

We recommend accepting all the defaults during installation. We also recommend selecting the **Full** installation.

We recommend running both the WebSphere Application Server and the IBM HTTP Server as Windows Services. You will need to enter an ID and password with sufficient authority to perform these administrative tasks. Any user belonging to the Administrators group should have sufficient privileges.

Once the installation is complete, the First Steps program will be launched in a new window. You might want to take some time now to access the WebSphere InfoCenter from the IBM Web site, as shown in Figure A.3.

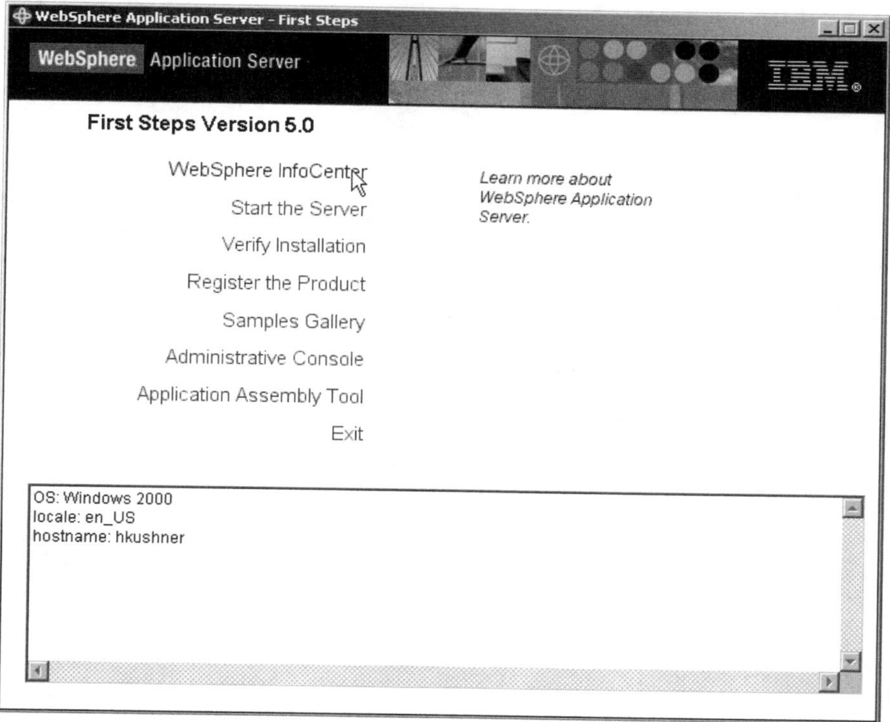

Figure A.3: The First Steps program.

You may also want to start the server and verify the installation using the menu option provided. If you do start the server, you should stop it before exiting the First Steps program.

WebSphere Studio Application Developer

As stated previously, when the first CD is loaded into the drive, the launcher should start up automatically. If this does not happen, then run the **setup.exe** program located in the root directory of the first CD. Click the button as shown in Figure A.4, and take a few minutes to review the Readme file and release notes (shown in Figure A.5) before proceeding.

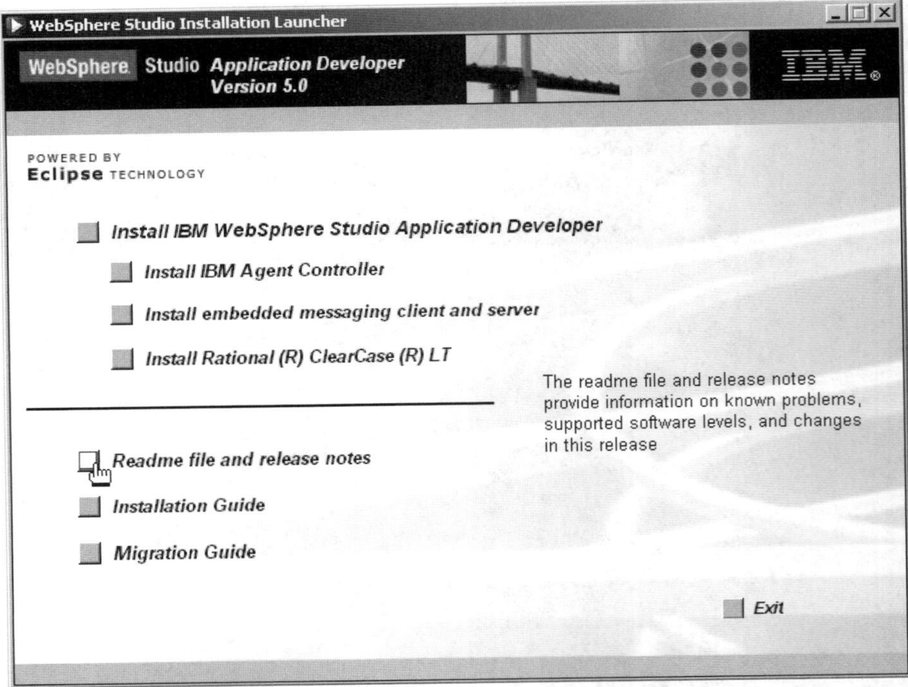

Figure A.4: The WebSphere Studio Installation Launcher: Opening the Readme file.

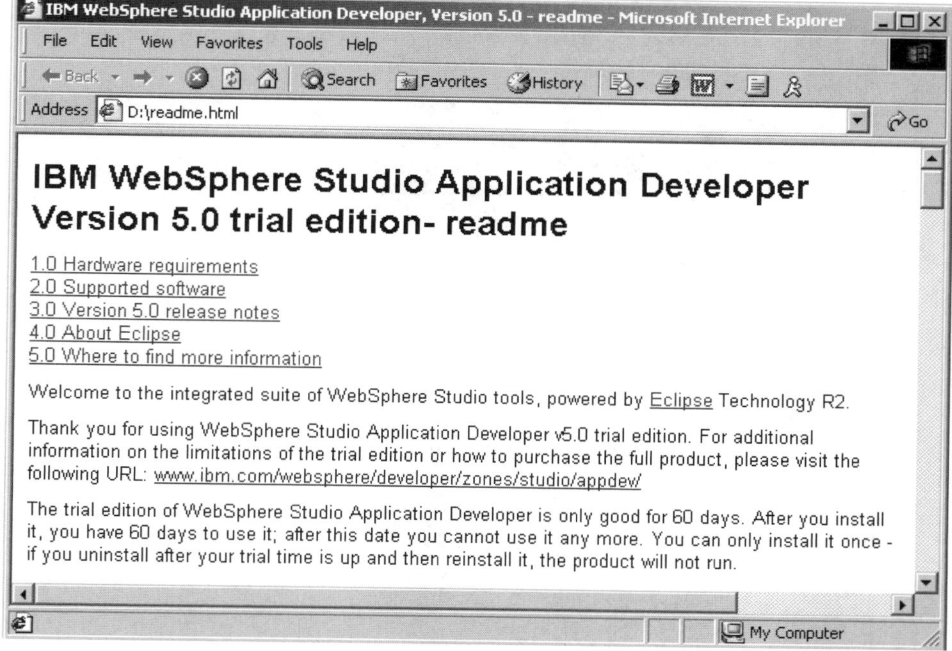

Figure A.5: The trial version Readme file.

Next, you should click the **Installation Guide** button as shown in Figure A.6. The Installation Guide opens, as shown in Figure A.7.

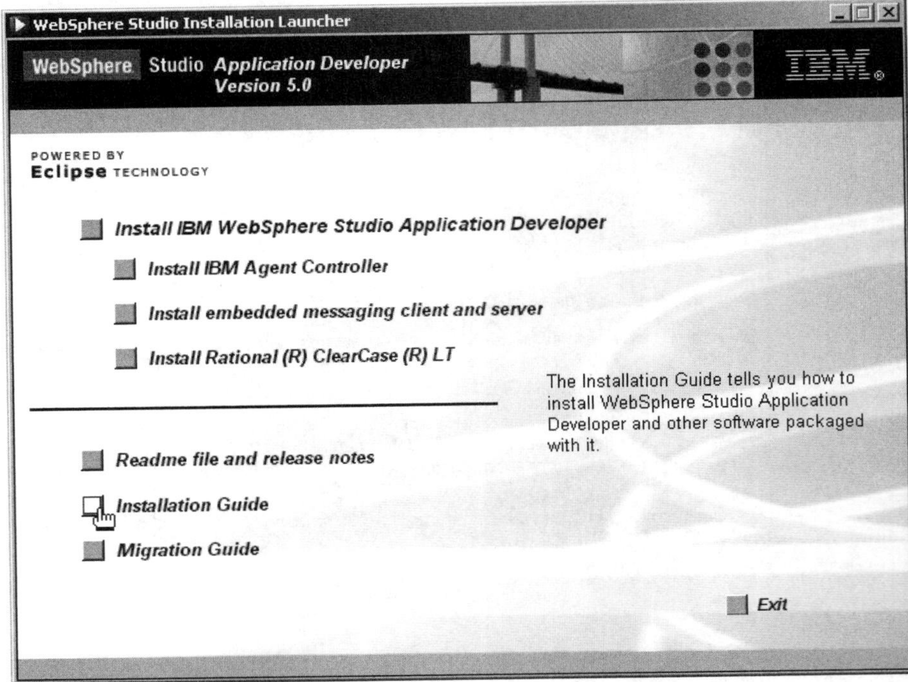

Figure A.6: Opening the Installation Guide.

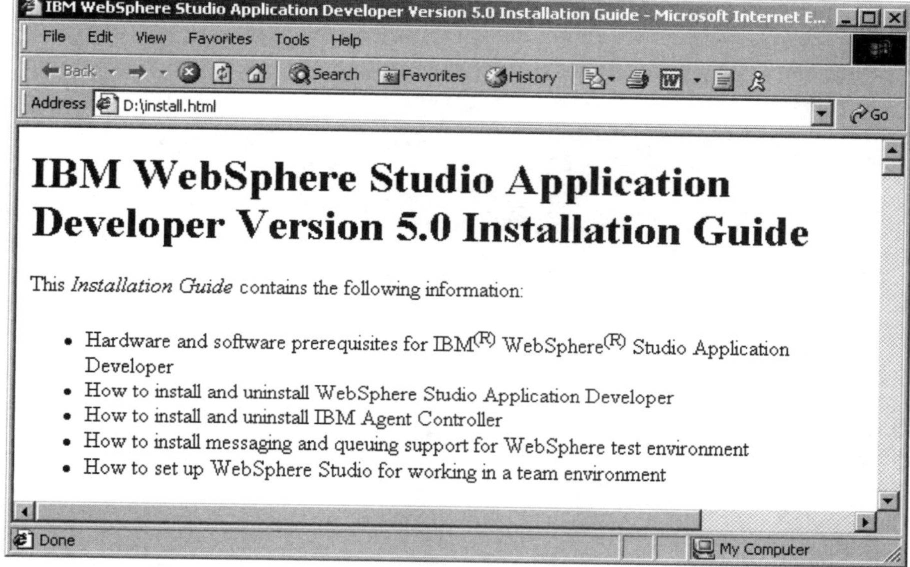

Figure A.7: The Installation Guide.

After reviewing the installation instructions, click the **Install IBM WebSphere Studio Application Developer** button, as shown in Figure A.8, to start the installation of WebSphere Studio Application Developer. We suggest that you accept all defaults.

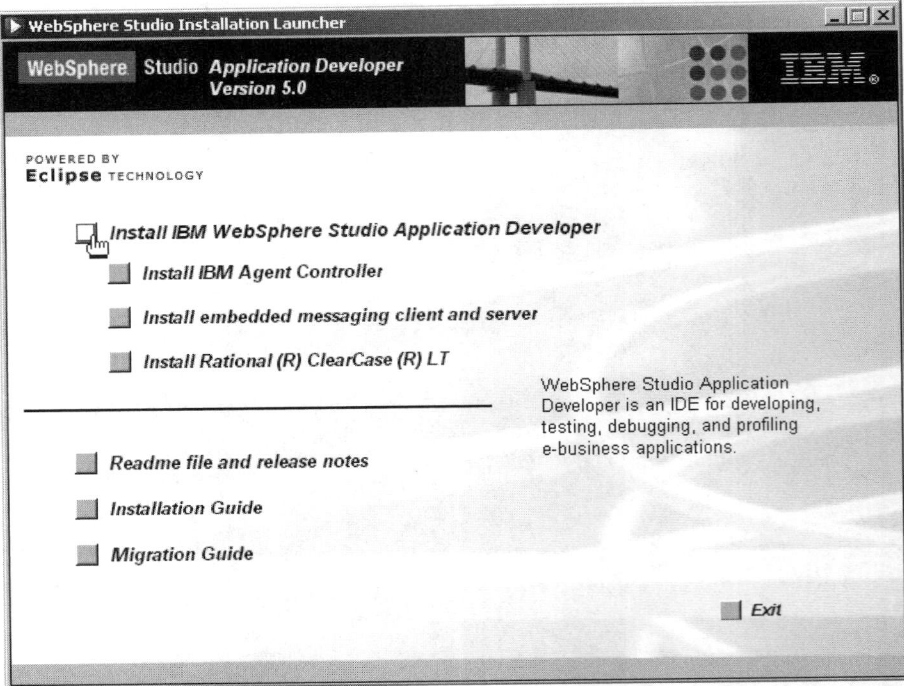

Figure A.8: Starting the IBM WebSphere Studio Application Developer installation.

Once the installation of WebSphere Studio Application Developer is complete, you can proceed to install the IBM Agent Controller and the embedded messaging client and server, as shown in Figures A.9 and A.10.

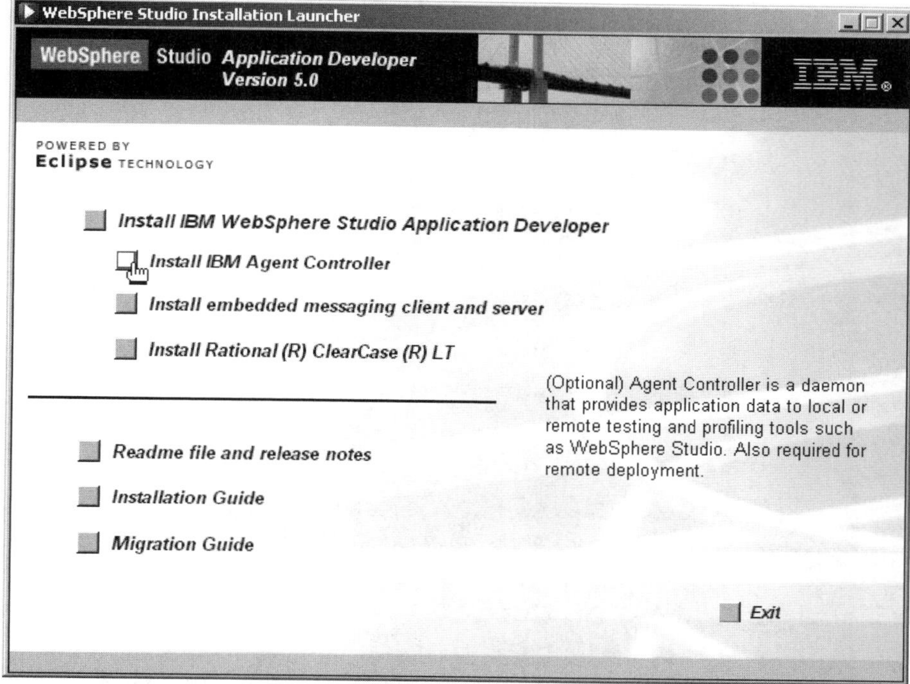

Figure A.9: Installing the IBM Agent Controller.

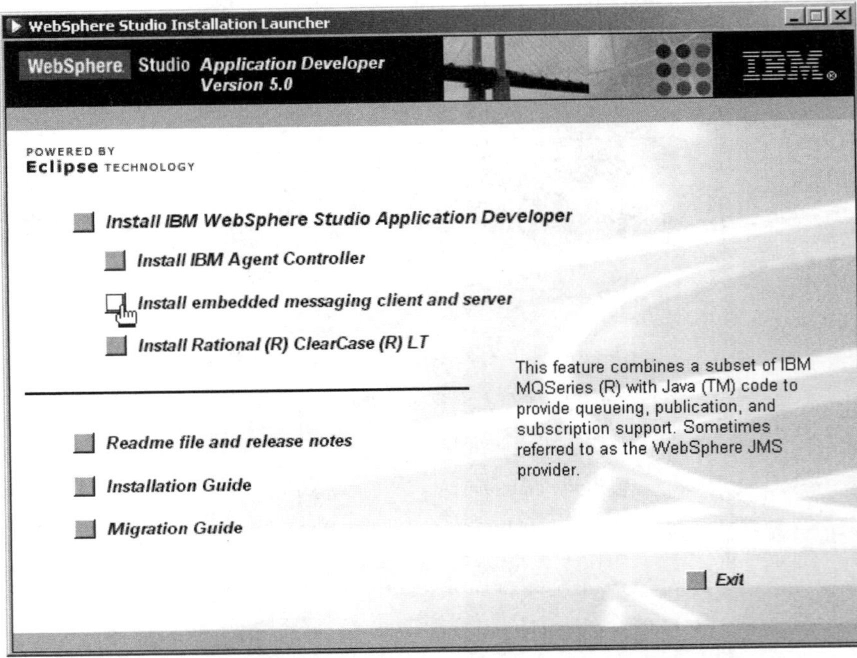

Figure A.10: Installing the embedded messaging client and server.

Additional files on the CDs

Both Disk 1 and Disk 2 have, in the root directory, a file named install.pdf, containing detailed instructions regarding installation of WebSphere Studio Application Developer, IBM Agent Controller, and messaging and queuing support for the WebSphere test environment.

Disk 2 has, in its root directory, the MyAudio.ear file, which is referenced in Chapter 2.

Database: DB2 or Cloudscape

Due to space limitations on the two CDs, we are unable to include a trial version of IBM DB2 Universal Database (UDB). However, you may wish to download and install it yourself. At the time of this writing, the following URL will take you to the IBM Web site from which to download this software.

```
http://www14.software.ibm.com/webapp/download/search.jsp?rs=db2udbdl
```

Rather than use DB2, you can also use the Cloudscape database that is shipped with WebSphere Application Server. Applications developed using Cloudscape can be migrated to DB2 UDB when they need to grow.

Appendix B—End of chapter questions with answers

Chapter 1: Introduction to IBM WebSphere

Key terms

Java	A platform-independent, object-oriented language from Sun Microsystems.
servlet	A server-side Java program that runs inside a Web container, most commonly used to respond to HTTP requests. Servlets are generally used as the "controller" in the Model-View-Controller pattern.
J2EE	Java 2 Enterprise Edition; an enabling technology that simplifies development of multi-tier enterprise applications, based on standard modular components, along with a standard set of services.
component	In J2EE, a pluggable module that runs within a container
container	In J2EE, a runtime process that provides runtime support for components. Each type of component (applet, application client, servlet, JSP page, or EJB) has its associated container. Containers were previously known as "engines."

Enterprise JavaBeans	(Abbreviated as "EJBs") Server-side components that simplify development of distributed, transactional, secure, and portable business components.
service	A support capability provided by an application server, such as transaction management, resource pooling, naming, or security.
framework	A collection of components, containers, and services that provides a means of building robust, scalable applications.
e-business	Electronic business, involving secure manipulation of data over the Web.
JavaServer Pages	(Abbreviated as "JSP") A set of tags and actions that can be placed inside a page otherwise written in HTML. A JSP page is automatically translated by the Web container into a servlet and is executed inside a Web container. JSP pages are generally used as the "view" in the Model-View-Controller architecture.
CORBA	Common Object Request Broker Architecture; a set of specifications, controlled by the Object Management Group, for services that enable secure, distributed, and transactional computing.
JavaBeans	Serializable Java classes that declare a public default (no-argument) constructor and expose feature that support introspection. JavaBeans are used effectively as the "model" in the Model-View-Controller pattern on the server.
applet	A client-side Java program that runs inside a Web browser. Applets have severe security restrictions (the so-called applet "sandbox"), which can be relaxed using digital signatures.
J2EE server	A program that manages the required J2EE containers, including the Web and EJB containers, and provides the required J2EE services. The J2EE server is also called an application server.

Review questions

1. List the services provided by a J2EE server.

   There are many ways to answer this. The services are transport and communications, directory and naming, resource processing and compilers, EIS interoperability enablement, security, email, asynchronous messaging, and transactions. A reasonable alternative (but equivalent) list would be distributed processing, location transparency, persistence, security, transactions, resource pooling, and lifecycle management.

2. What is the relationship between containers and components?

   Containers provide managed environments for component execution.

3. List the various roles defined by the J2EE architecture.

   The roles are Product Provider, Tool Provider, Application Component Provider, Application Assembler, Deployer, and System Administrator.

4. What is the difference between WebSphere Application Server and WebSphere Studio Application Developer?

   WebSphere Studio Application Developer is the development environment for J2EE components. WebSphere Application Server is the associated deployment environment. WAS is a J2EE server, providing all the required containers and services. WebSphere Studio Application Developer is an integrated development environment, providing compilers, verifiers, and deployment tools for J2EE components.

Chapter 2: Developing enterprise applications with WebSphere Studio

Key terms

perspective	A synchronized collection of views and editors in WebSphere Studio Application Developer. Perspectives are highly configurable. Several perspectives are already defined.
view	A window within a perspective in WebSphere Studio Application Developer that provides a particular representation of a resource. Views also provide a means of navigation.

IDE	Integrated Development Environment for developing, testing, and debugging.
workbench	The WebSphere Studio programming environment based on Eclipse.
workspace	The directory location of project files.
ear	Enterprise Archive; a compressed file containing all the components within an enterprise application.
war	Web Archive; a compressed file that contains all the components within a Web project.
deployment descriptor	An XML file used to configure components. Using deployment descriptors to change the behavior of programs is often called declarative programming.
modules	A set of packaged components in an enterprise application.
project	A collection of files on disk, used to represent conceptual components of an application.

Review questions

1. Looking at the MyAudio enterprise application, which parts of it (if any) are not portable?

   The JAR and WAR files should be transportable to another application server. The form of the web.xml and ejb-jar.xml deployment descriptors are part of the J2EE specification. Only those XML files that begin with "ibm" and have the extension .xmi are application server-specific. In general, they involve bindings and extensions specific to WebSphere.

   The files all live in the META-INF subdirectory of the various projects. The files are ibm-application-ext.xmi, ibm-application-client-bnd.xmi, ibm-ejb-access-bean.xmi, ibm-ejb-jar-bnd.xmi, ibm-ejb-jar-ext.xmi, ibm-web-bnd.xmi, and ibm-web-ext.xmi.

   Of course, all the CMP beans would have to be regenerated if a different database was used as well.

2. The so-called application client module also requires a container for execution. Why is this?

   The client-side application needs access to all the RMI stubs needed for remote access to the EJBs. It also needs the EJB classes themselves, in order

to use the proper types of references once the beans have been found via JNDI lookups. The client container also provides the ability to attach to the JNDI service.

3. What is the shortcut to bring up Code Assist?

   Use Ctrl+Space to bring up Code Assist.

4. How do you access a view that is not available in the current perspective?

   This can be done either by choosing Window → Show View to add it to the current perspective or by switching to a perspective where the view already exists.

Chapter 3: Servlets

Key terms

servlet	A standard Java class that runs on the server, generally invoked as a result of HTTP requests and coordinating HTTP responses. Servlets are generally used as the controllers in the MVC architecture.
request and response	HTTP protocol messages. Requests carry headers and any available form parameters. Responses carry the MIME type and send output to the browser.
cookies	Small text files (generally < 1K in size) containing name-value pairs, stored on the client and passed back and forth with each request and response. Cookies are used to help manage conversation state.
session	A series of URL requests from a common user. The HttpSession interface allows sessions to be configured, used to transmit information between resources, and timed out at assigned intervals. The session state is stored securely by the application server.
servlet listeners	Classes that implement the various servlet listener interfaces and are able to respond to events generated by the Web container.
servlet filters	Classes that process servlet requests and responses and deliver them to the servlet after this processing. Filters can “pipe” into each other as well, forming a filter chain.

Review questions

1. What are the types of requests that can be handled by servlets?

   HTTP requests; specifically, GET, POST, PUT, TRACE, OPTIONS, DELETE.

2. HttpServlet extends the abstract class GenericServlet, which contains the abstract method abstract void service(ServletRequest req, ServletResponse res). Whereas the HttpServlet class is also abstract, it contains no abstract methods. How is the service method implemented in HttpServlet? In other words, what happens when a GET request is received by an HttpServlet subclass?

   When a GET request is received, the container calls the service(ServletRequest, ServletResponse) method in your servlet. Since the version of this method in GenericServlet is overridden in HttpServlet, dynamic binding means that the one in HttpServlet is used (assuming you didn't override it yourself, which is almost always a bad idea).

   The implementation in HttpServlet casts each of the arguments to type HttpServletRequest and HttpServletResponse, respectively, and then calls service(HttpServetRequest, HttpServletResponse). This method decodes the request, determines its HTTP type, and dispatches it to the appropriate do*XXX* method. In this case, execution would pass to the doGet(HttpServletRequest, HttpServletResponse) method.

3. When a URL is typed into a browser, what kind of HTTP request is generated?

   The browser sends an HTTP GET request, so control ultimately is transmitted to the doGet() method in the servlet. Forms usually use the HTTP POST method.

4. How would you initialize attributes in a servlet? What method would you override? What method would you use to access values provided in the deployment descriptor?

   Override the init() method from GenericServlet in your servlet subclass. This method is executed only once, immediately after the servlet is instantiated but before it responds to any requests. Inside that method, use the getInitParameter(String) method from the ServletContext interface.

5. Describe the differences between the HttpSessionListener, HttpSessionBindingListener, and HttpSessionAttributeListener interfaces.

   The HttpSessionListener interface generates method calls when a session is created or destroyed. The HttpSessionBindingListener notifies an object when it is bound or unbound from a session. This is in contrast to the

HttpSessionAttributeListener, which notifies interested parties when any attribute is added, removed, or replaced in the session.

6. Google (*http://www.google.com*) search queries use an HTTP Get request. Why? Most forms use an HTTP Post request. Why is that?

   Get requests encode the form parameters in the URL. This makes them inappropriate for any form data that shouldn't be echoed (especially passwords). Google, on the other hand, wants to use Get requests so that the results of the query can be bookmarked for later use.

7. What's the difference between using the sendRedirect(String) method in the HttpServletResponse interface and calling forward(request, response) from a RequestDispatcher?

   The sendRedirect() call tells the browser to go to a new URL. A RequestDispatcher passes control to another resource (servlet or JSP page) but does so without notifying the browser. The RequestDispatcher therefore saves networking round trips and is useful when accessing resources not automatically available to the browser.

8. The HttpServletRequest class has both a getParameter(String) method and a getAttribute(String) method. What is the difference?

   Forms have parameters, while objects have attributes. Use the getParamter(String) method to access form parameters. Object references that should be passed to other locations are sent as attributes. Typically the session is used for this, but the request can be used as well. In the next chapter, the scope and usefulness of all the so-called implicit objects are discussed.

9. There is an addCookie(Cookie) method in the HttpServletResponse interface but no corresponding removeCookie(Cookie) method. How can you remove a cookie?

   Use the setMaxAge() method in the Cookie class. Using setMaxAge(0) causes the cookie to expire immediately ("go stale?") and be removed.

10. Application Developer provides a nice graphical front end on the XML-based Web deployment descriptor, which means a developer doesn't need to remember the various tags and rules for using them. The rules can be found, however, in a Document Type Definition (DTD) file. Its location appears at the top of the file, as part of the <!DOCTYPE> tag. What is the URL for the deployment descriptor DTD?

From the header of the web.xml file, using the Source tab, it is seen that the root element is <web-app>, the name of the DTD is "DTD Web Application 2.3," it is owned by "Sun Microsystems, Inc.", it is written in English, and it is located at the URL *http://java.sun.com/dtd/web-app_2_3.dtd*.

Chapter 4: JavaServer Pages (JSP)

Key terms

JavaServer Pages	(Abbreviated as "JSP") A system of tags that is combined with HTML to write dynamic J2EE Web components known as JSP pages. JSP pages are translated into servlets that generate output files rendered by browsers. JSP pages are normally used as the view in the MVC architecture.
comments	JSP tags of the form <!-- . . . --!> (HTML comments), and <%-- . . . --%> (JSP comments). HTML comments are seen by the client. JSP comments are ignored by the application server and are not seen by the client.
JSP directives	JSP tags of the form <%@ . . . %>. A JSP directive can be a page directive, an include directive, or a taglib directive.
JSP page directive	JSP tags of the form <%@ page . . . %>. Page directives represent translation-time instructions to the Web container regarding the generated servlet.
JSP include directive	JSP tags of the form <%@ include . . . %>. Include directives are used to include other resources prior to translation of the resulting page into a servlet.
JSP taglib directive	JSP tags of the form <%@ taglib . . . %>. Taglib directives are used to reference a custom tag library in the JSP page, making its associated tags available in the page.
JSP declarations	JSP tags of the form <%! . . . %>, used to declare fields and methods in the generated servlet.
JSP expressions	JSP tags of the form <%= . . . %>. The content of a JSP expression is written in the scripting language and evaluated at request time. The code resulting from the evaluation is inserted into output statements.

JSP scriptlets	JSP tags of the form <% . . . %>, used to embed scripting language statements within the page, enabling the generation of dynamic output.
implicit objects	Objects instantiated by the Web container and made available to the page. Commonly used implicit objects are *request*, *session*, and *application*. There is also an *exception* object, which is instantiated only if the isErrorPage attribute of the page directive is set to true.
JSP actions	Tags used for request processing by the Web container. The set of actions that begin with the prefix "jsp" are defined in the JSP specification and are automatically available on every page. Other actions are called custom actions and are backed by included tag libraries.
standard actions	Request-time tags defined in the specification. Among them are *jsp:include*, *jsp:forward*, *jsp:useBean*, *jsp:plugin*, and *jsp:getProperty* and *jsp:setProperty*.
tag library	A set of custom tags backed by Java classes that add functionality to JSP pages.
JSTL	The Java Standard Tag Library; a set of custom actions for common activities.
tag library descriptor	An XML file containing information about a tag library, such as its version, the required JSP version, the contained tags, whether they have attributes, whether attributes can be evaluated using request time expressions.
tag handler	A Java class that provides support for a custom JSP tag. The tag handler usually extends the class javax.servlet.jsp.tagext.TagSupport or javax.servlet.jsp.tagext.BodyTagSupport.
JavaBeans	Reusable "self-describing" Java components. Any Java class that supports introspection, implements Serializable, and provides a public default constructor can be used as a JavaBean. Typically a JavaBean has a set of properties and consistently named methods to get and set each property on a given instance of the bean.

Review questions

1. Describe the phases in the lifecycle of a JSP page.

   a. **Page translation:** **The page is parsed and a Java servlet is generated.**

   b. **Page compilation:** **The servlet resulting from page translation is compiled.**

   c. **Class loading:** **The compiled servlet class resulting from page compilation is loaded by the Web container.**

   d. **Instantiation:** **The loaded class is instantiated.**

   e. **Initialization:** **Before a request is handled, the jspInit() method is invoked.**

   f. **Request handling:** **The _jspService() method is called for each request.**

   g. **Destruction:** **The jspDestroy() method is called if and when the servlet is removed from service by the Web container.**

2. What method in the translated servlet is executed during every request?

   The complete signature is public void _jspService(HttpServletRequest req, HttpServletResponse resp) throws ServletException, IOException.

3. If a JSP page is altered, is it necessary to restart the server?

   According to the specification, if a JSP page is altered, the Web container is required to regenerate the servlet. Note that WebSphere provides this capability for servlets as well, though the specification does not require it. The only exception is that if a JSP page uses an include directive to incorporate another JSP page, and the included page is modified, the Web container is not required to notice it. In that case, the server would need to be restarted to pick up the change.

4. What is the difference between the include directive and the include action?

   The include directive affects behavior at translation time. The source code of the included file is added to the current file before translation begins. The include action occurs at request time, so the results of executing the included file are added to the current page.

5. Must variables appearing in a JSP page be declared in JSP declarations or JSP scriptlets before their first use?

   The entire page is translated into a servlet before the first request is handled, so the location of variable and method declarations in directives and scriptlets is arbitrary.

6. Does the order of scriptlets in a JSP page matter?

   Since scriptlet code is added to the _jspService() method, the order of scriptlets is significant.

7. Must scriptlet variables be initialized before their first use? What about variables in declarations?

   Since scriptlet variables are local variables inside the _jspService() method, they must be initialized before they are used. Variables in declarations become attributes of the translated servlet, and since attributes are automatically initialized by the Java compiler, they do not have to be initialized by the developer as well (as long as the default values are acceptable).

8. What packages are automatically included in every JSP page?

   The included packages are java.lang, javax.servlet, javax.servlet.http, and javax.servlet.jsp. All other packages must be imported using page directives, or the fully qualified class names must be used.

9. To which classes or interfaces do the implicit objects correspond?

a. application	**javax.servlet.ServletContext**
b. session	**javax.servlet.http.HttpSession**
c. request	**javax.servlet.http.HttpServletRequest**
d. response	**javax.servlet.http.HttpServletResponse**
e. out	**javax.servlet.jsp.JspWriter**
f. page	**java.lang.Object**
g. pageContext	**javax.servlet.jsp.PageContext**
h. config	**javax.servlet.ServletConfig**
i. exception	**java.lang.Throwable**

10. When are the implicit objects instantiated?

    The implicit objects are instantiated in the _jspService() method, so they cannot be used or accessed from declarations.

11. The <jsp:setProperty> tag has attributes called "name," "property," and "param." When are each used?

    The name attribute corresponds to the "id" attribute in the <jsp:useBean> tag, and represents the reference to the JavaBean instance. The <jsp:set-Property> tag is used to assign values to the bean's properties. If the names of the bean's properties exactly match the names of form variables in the

HTTP request, then simply writing <jsp:setProperty name= "..." property= "*" /> will set all the corresponding properties.

If any bean properties do not match the form variable names, then "property" is used for the bean property and "param" is the corresponding form parameter.

Chapter 5: Developing EJB—Session beans and the EJB architecture

Key terms

Enterprise JavaBeans	J2EE component and used to leverage J2EE services. EJBs, which are installed in an EJB container, can be either stateless Session beans, stateful Session beans, Entity beans using either bean-managed or container-managed persistence, or Message-Driven beans.
stateless Session beans	EJBs used for capturing business processes in which the values of properties are not preserved between method calls.
stateful Session beans	EJBs used for capturing business processes in which it is necessary to preserve the values of any properties, saving and restoring them from temporary storage as required.
home interface	The collection of creation methods (and, in the case of Entity beans, finder methods) for an EJB.
remote interface	The set of business methods implemented by the EJB.
local interface	The set of business methods implemented by the EJB but accessed from inside the same JVM that is managing the bean class.
object interface	The generic term for Local and Remote interfaces.
EJB container	An execution environment for EJBs that intercepts calls to the EJBs and provides any requested services, such as transactions or security. The EJB container also manages the lifecycle of the EJBs, instantiating, activating, and passivating them as necessary.
EJB component	The combination of home interface, remote interface, EJB class, and declarative services that compose an EJB.

CORBA	Common Object Request Broker Architecture; a set of specifications controlled by the Object Management Group. The CORBA specification predates the J2EE specification and forms the basis of much of it.
resource pooling	Instantiating a series of objects ahead of time that can be accessed and returned to the pool. Resource pooling is frequently used for stateless Session beans and database connections.
lifecycle management	For stateful Session beans, the process of activating and passivating beans as required in order to allow a small number of beans to serve a large number of clients efficiently.

Review questions

1. Can stateless Session EJBs have attributes?

   Stateless Session beans can (and often do) have attributes. The attributes are not guaranteed to retain their values between method invocations, however.

2. An application contains four EJB classes. Which one should be a stateless Session bean?
   a. TravelAgent
   b. CreditCardValidator
   c. Cruise
   d. Cabin

   The CreditCardValidator is a classic example of a stateless Session bean. It represents an encapsulated business method whose parameters represent the credit card information, which is specified each time the method is called. There is no state information to retain.

3. Which of these should be a stateful Session bean?
   a. TravelAgent
   b. CreditCardValidator
   c. Cruise
   d. Cabin

   TravelAgent is a classic stateful Session bean. Its methods represent business processes, and it represents a conversation between a single client and the server over multiple requests. Moreover, if the conversation is interrupted, the state can be temporarily preserved and resumed at a later time.

4. Why are stateless Session beans more efficient than stateful Session beans?

   Since stateless Session beans have no state to preserve, each instance is identical to every other. Consequently, they can be pooled by the application server. Each request can be assigned the next available bean, and after each request the bean can be simply returned to the pool.

5. What happens when Session beans are passivated and then activated?

   For stateful Session beans, the instance is serialized and placed in temporary storage, which can be on disk or in a temporary location in a database. Stateless Session beans cannot be passivated or activated. Each is assigned for a specific method call and returned to the pool immediately afterwards.

6. A Session bean requires a home interface, a remote interface, and a bean class. What interface must the bean class implement? What methods are in that interface?

   Session beans implement the javax.ejb.SessionBean interface, which has the following methods:

   - **void ejbActivate()**
   - **void ejbPassivate()**
   - **void ejbRemove()**
   - **void setSessionContext(SessionContext ctx)**

   The SessionBean interface extends javax.ejb.EnterpriseBean, which has no methods at all. The EnterpriseBean interface itself extends java.io.Serializable, which also has no methods to implement.

   Note that normally (as in the examples shown in the text), a getSessionContext() method is supplied by the developer, though it is not strictly necessary.

7. As a related question, if the Session bean class implements all the methods listed above, it will compile but not work. What additional method must be implemented, but does not appear in the interface?

   Session beans must also have an ejbCreate() method corresponding to each of the create() methods in the home interface. For stateless session beans, the home interface must have a create() method with no arguments, whose return type is the remote interface type. The bean class itself must then include the "public void ejbCreate()" method. Note that the return type on the ejbCreate() method is void.

   Stateful session beans may have additional create() methods that take arguments, which are used to set the values of the attributes. For each of these

additional methods, the bean class must have a corresponding ejbCreate() method with the same arguments, but also returning void.

As an additional difference, note that the create() method in the home interface must throw both javax.ejb.CreateException and java.rmi.RemoteException. The corresponding ejbCreate() methods, however, throw only the CreateException.

8. Most Session beans (even stateless ones) keep an attribute of type SessionContext. Why? What is the SessionContext used for?

   The SessionContext provides access to the container. SessionContext has the method EJBObject getEJBObject() and the corresponding one for local objects. SessionContext also extends EJBContext, which provides methods for accessing both security and transactional functionality as well as the environment itself.

   The SessionContext also allows a stateful session to access its specific reference, or handle, assigned to a particular client. This lets the client save the handle so that it can later access the same bean if desired.

9. Assume you already have a stateless Session bean implemented, and the bean class has attributes. You decide to change the type of bean from stateless to stateful. What changes need to be made?

   No changes at all need to be made to the code. The deployment descriptor, however, contains a tag called <session-type>, whose value is either Stateless or Stateful. Simply changing from one to the other is all that is necessary to switch the bean type.

   Of course, changing a stateful Session been to a stateless one might involve additional complications, because a stateful Session bean may have additional create() methods.

10. Notice that though the bean class has methods that correspond to those in the home and remote (or local) interfaces, the bean class does not actually implement those interfaces. Where are they implemented?

    The container itself generates classes that implement the home and object interfaces. These classes maintain a reference to the bean class supplied by the developer. Therefore, when methods are invoked on the interfaces, they call the method inside the implementation classes in the Web container, which then call back the various methods in the bean class. This "callback" process is the essence of EJB implementations; it allows the container to intercept calls and apply services as required.

Chapter 6: Developing entity EJBs with WebSphere Studio

Key terms

Entity bean	An object-oriented representation of data in a database. An Entity bean may represent a single record, or a join among tables.
Container-Managed Persistence (CMP)	Entity bean persistence in which the container generates the required SQL code necessary for maintaining the state of the bean. CMP beans are written using abstract bean classes. Details about which fields to persist and EJBQL statements to use are supplied in the deployment descriptor.
Bean-Managed Persistence (BMP)	"Do-it-yourself" Entity bean persistence in which the developer must supply all of the database code required to maintain the bean, using JDBC calls in the required ejbLoad(), ejbStore(), ejbCreate(), and ejbRemove() methods in the bean class.
finder methods	Methods that send SQL SELECT queries to the database to find a particular record or set of records to associate with an Entity bean. Finder methods return either object references or collections of object references.
primary key class	A class representing the primary key of a record in the database. Every Entity bean must have a class to contain the primary key. This class must be Serializable and must override both the equals() method and the hashCode() method appropriately.
home methods	Methods, added to the home interface of an Entity bean, that are used for logic that does not involve a specific instance of the bean but rather focuses on an entire set of the bean type.
EJBQL	Enterprise JavaBeans Query Language., a type of simplified, object-oriented, database-independent SQL for mapping Entity beans to data sources.
select methods	Private methods that allow a developer to query fields across all records of the bean type in the database.

CMP relationships	Also called, container-managed relationships (CMR), a feature that allows the user to specify one-to-one, one-to-many, and many-to-many relationships among Entity beans using the deployment descriptor.

Review questions

1. What type of method is found in the home interface of an Entity bean and not in the home interface of a Session bean?

   Entity beans have so-called "finder" methods, which are used to create a bean to represent data already existing in a database.

2. When would you use the ejbPostCreate() method in a bean class?

   Entity beans are not fully constructed until the ejbCreate() method returns. In order for a bean to refer to itself (for instance, to pass a reference to itself to other beans), it must use the ejbPostCreate() method. Note that this method returns void. This method is called by the container immediately after its associated ejbCreate() method returns.

   Note that an ejbPostCreate() method must be supplied for each ejbCreate() method and have the same parameter list, even if its implementation is empty. An associated create() method is also required in the home interface.

3. What is the difference between an Entity bean in the pooled state and one that is in the Ready state?

   Entity beans that have been pooled are associated with an entity context but have not yet been assigned data. They are, therefore, all identical. Clients can either assign them to a record (at which point they move to the Ready state) or use them to service requests that do not require state information.

4. If your primary key is only an int, what classes in the standard library can be used for primary key classes? When should you define your own?

   One natural choice would be to use the Integer class. Other classes could be used, such as Long or even String, as long as appropriate conversions are supplied. Note that all of these classes implement Serializable and have both equals() and hashCode() methods defined consistently.

   A developer can supply her own class in these cases, of course. A special primary key class must be defined if more than one field is used in the definition of a primary key. If you anticipate that other fields will be later added to a single-field primary key, it may be worth the trouble to define your own class at the beginning.

5. With Session beans, it was necessary to add an ejbCreate() method to the bean class and a create() method to the home interface, even though the SessionBean interface didn't require it. With Entity beans, there is an additional method that is required in the bean class. Which is it? What is required in the home interface as a result?

   Entity beans must have an ejbFindByPrimaryKey() method in the bean class. This method is used by the container for many operations. The analogous method in the home interface is findByPrimaryKey(). Interestingly enough, however, adding this method to the home interface is not required.

6. How does the behavior of the remove() method in Entity beans differ from the same method in Session beans?

   In stateless Session beans, the remove() method does nothing, since there is no state to deal with. For stateful Session beans, calling remove() on the home interface tells the container to dispose of the bean, thus freeing its state and returning it to the bean pool. In Entity beans, the remove() method actually deletes the associated data from the database before returning the bean to the pool.

7. In BMP, when should the developer call the ejbLoad() and ejbStore() methods?

   This is a trick question. Even though the developer supplies the needed SQL code to implement the ejbLoad() and ejbStore() methods, the container decides when to call the methods, even in bean-managed persistence.

8. Session beans implement Serializable partly so that they can be activated and passivated using secondary storage. Entity beans map to data in persistent storage. What is the purpose of activating and passivating them? Do they need to be Serializable?

   Entity beans naturally use the database when they are activated or passivated, rather than saving to disk or some other secondary storage mechanism. Still, activation and passivation are necessary so that the limited supply of Entity bean instances in the pool can service a much larger number of clients. The ejbActivate() and ejbPassivate() methods allow the container to notify the bean instance when it is being activated and passivated. This is done in case the bean instance needs access to some other transient resource and needs to manage that access.

   As to whether Entity beans need to implement Serializable or not, that's already done. The EntityBean interface in fact extends both EnterpriseBean and Serializable.

9. Consider an application that has an Entity bean representing an Order and an Entity bean representing an OrderItem. When an Order is deleted, all of its associated OrderItem instances should be deleted as well. How can this be implemented?

   Use CMP relationships to define a one-to-many association between the Order and its various OrderItem instances. In the wizard used to define this relationship, select the "Cascade delete" option.

10. Both Session beans and Entity beans have create() methods in their home interface, and corresponding ejbCreate() methods in the bean classes. How do the return types of these methods differ in the two types of beans?

    The ejbCreate() method in a Session bean returns void. In an Entity bean, it returns a reference of the primary key class.

11. In WebSphere Studio Application Developer, finder methods are not added using the normal wizard used to create the bean itself. How are finder methods added?

    The user needs to go to the deployment descriptor, scroll down to the Queries section, and click the Add button. This will trigger a wizard that can be used to add finder methods, complete with EJBQL statements as desired.

12. An application contains four EJB classes. Which should be Entity beans?
    a. TravelAgent
    b. CreditCardValidator
    c. Cruise
    d. Cabin

    The Cruise and Cabin classes map to data in a database. In addition, they represent data that will be shared among multiple clients. Both reasons suggest that these classes ought to be modeled as Entity beans.

Chapter 7: Message-Driven beans

Key terms

JMS	Java Message Service; a vendor-neutral set of interfaces for accessing message providers.
Message-Driven beans	(Abbreviated as "MDB") Stateless, transactional objects maintained by the EJB container, linked to a destination, from which they receive and consume JMS messages.

synchronous vs. asynchronous	Synchronous applications call methods and wait for their return before proceeding. Asynchronous communication involves calling a method or sending a message and then continuing normal processing without waiting for a return response.
producers and consumers	Producers generate messages and add them to message queues or topics. Consumers receive messages from the same sources.
destination	An abstract administered object that serves as the target for messages.
queue	A single, point-to-point connection between a producer and a consumer. The queue will continue to try to send the message until the consumer acknowledges that having received it.
topic	An implementation of the "publish-subscribe" paradigm. Consumers subscribe to a topic. When a producer generates a message and sends it to the topic, all subscribers are guaranteed to receive a copy.
message provider	A service that receives messages from producers and guarantees (in some sense) their delivery to consumers. It's like the container for the messaging system.
connection factory	An administered object used to create connections to JMS providers, similar to the way the DriverManager class allows easy access to JDBC drivers.
JMS message	The unit of communication in JMS, consisting of JMS headers, optional properties, and a body containing the content of the message.
listener port	A WebSphere-specific element that names a specific message destination. They abstract connection information, like JNDI information about the connection factory and the destination, in a manner similar to a data source.
message selectors	Filtering information used by the MDB to select only a portion of the available messages.

Review questions

1. List the defined types of JMS messages and their purposes.

   The types are:

   a. Object message, which encapsulates a single, serialized object

   b. Map message, which allows the creating of name-value pairs, where the names are String objects and the values are Java primitives; entries can be accessed sequentially or randomly by name.

   c. Text message, a message with a single string as its content

   d. Stream message, a message containing a stream of primitive values in the Java language, filled and read sequentially

   e. Bytes message, a message containing a stream of uninterpreted bytes

2. Normal EJBs require two interfaces (home and object) and a bean class. What do MDBs require?

   MDBs are not accessible to clients, so they do not require home or object interfaces. All an MDB requires is a bean class that implements both the javax.jms.MessageListener and javax.ejb.MessageDrivenBean interfaces.

3. MDBs are required to have an ejbCreate() method with no arguments, similar to stateless Session beans. In what other ways are MDBs like stateless Session beans?

   MDBs do not have attributes, and therefore do not maintain state. They are thus identical to each other, so they can be pooled the same way stateless Session beans are. MDBs likewise are not activated or passivated. Finally, though they must have an ejbRemove() method, removing an MDB simply returns it to the pool. The ejbRemove() method is simply for closing transient resources no longer needed by the bean.

4. A point-to-point application refers to a producer and a consumer. Is it possible to have more than one of either?

   A queue can have multiple producers, each of which can add messages to the queue. Only one consumer can be used, however, because when one consumer consumes a message, it no longer exists to be sent to the other consumer.

5. A developer needs to implement remote connectivity in an environment where networking faults are common. Are MDBs useful in this case?

   Since JMS providers guarantee delivery, an MDB is quite useful in a fault-filled environment. The provider will cache the messages and continue to try to deliver them until told not to, either via confirmation of receipt or user-configured conditions such as a time-out period.

6. Java classes can be written to act as message consumers without being MDBs. Why go to the trouble to create an MDB?

   As with other EJB types, the biggest benefit to EJBs is the container, which provides all the container-managed services. In the case of MDBs, the container provides location transparency, security, and scalability, among others. Message-driven beans can also participate in distributed transactions, either declaratively or through the Java Transaction API.

Chapter 8: Transactions

Key terms

JTA	Java Transaction API; a set of Java packages implemented on top of JTS for controlling transactions programmatically.
JTS	Java Transaction Service; a Java mapping of the CORBA OTS, implemented by service vendors.
ACID	Atomicity, consistency, isolation, and durability; the properties required of transactions.
atomicity	The requirement that all steps of a transaction must succeed or fail as a unit.
consistency	The requirement that transactions always leave the system in a consistent state.
isolation	The requirement that transactions can all be assumed to operate independently of each other.
durability	The requirement that committed transactions survive system failures.
commit	To make a transaction durable by executing all of its steps.
rollback	To undo the steps of a transaction so that the system is back in the consistent state from which the transaction began.
two-phase commit (2PC)	A protocol that allows multiple resources to update within a single transaction. First, all resources are told to prepare for a transaction. If all acknowledge readiness, they are all told to commit the transaction. If any fail, or are unable to acknowledge preparedness, the entire transaction rolls back.

bean-managed (programmatic) transaction demarcation	Controlling transactional behavior using the JTA.
container-managed (declarative) transaction demarcation	Allowing the container to control transaction behavior through configuration terms in the deployment descriptor.
OTS	Object Transaction Service; an API from the Object Management Group as an optional CORBA service for transactional behavior.
XA	A specification for distributed transactions.
TM	Transaction Manager; a program that ensures the ACID properties of transactions.
RM	Resource Manager; programs similar to a database management system that administer their associated resources.
transaction attributes	Specifications for the requirements for enterprise beans using container-managed transaction demarcation. The values are set in the deployment descriptor and must be one of the following: *RequiresNew*, *Required*, *NotSupported*, *Supports*, *Mandatory*, and *Never*.
transaction isolation	The guarantee that separate transactions do not directly affect one another, even when using the same database data. The following levels are normally supported: ReadUncommitted, ReadCommitted, RepeatableRead, and Serializable.
access intent policies	An IBM extension for EJB 2.0. Access intent policies are designed to replace the use of isolation levels and access intent modifiers in the deployment descriptor.

Review questions

1. Since the container can manage all transactions and can be configured easily using deployment descriptors, why should a developer ever use bean-managed transactions? What's the benefit of having the JTA at all?

   Through the JTA, transactions can be created that cover multiple systems, including different databases, message queues, and other legacy systems. A single unit of work can encompass them all and either commit or rollback as a unit. In addition, the transaction context can be propagated from one component to another without additional coding.

2. How can servlets and JavaServer Pages participate in transactions? Can they be configured to do so in the deployment descriptor?

   Web elements can use only bean-managed transactions. They acquire a UserTransaction reference via JNDI lookups. Only the EJB deployment descriptors allow the configuration of transaction attributes.

3. What types of Enterprise JavaBeans may use bean-managed transactions?

   Only Session beans can use bean-managed transaction demarcation. Entity beans must use container-managed transaction demarcation.

4. The transaction monitor is provided by the application server, even if the transactions are demarcated programmatically. How does an enterprise bean get access to the container—for example to acquire a UserTransaction reference?

   As with other services provided by the container, enterprise beans get access to the container from the EJBContext object. This is, in fact, one of the reasons that enterprise beans normally save their associate EJBContext (entity context or session context as the case may be) in an attribute of the bean implementation class.

5. According to the EJB 2.0 specification, CMP Entity beans that are persisted to a transaction data store should use only three of the possible six transaction attributes. Which are they?

   Entity beans using CMP should use only the transaction attributes Required, RequiresNew, and Mandatory. This is because Entity beans are normally assumed to be working with databases in a transactional manner.

6. What's the difference between the transaction attributes Required and Mandatory? Why would you use one over the other?

   The Required attribute means that a method will participate in a client's transaction if it has already started but will create a transaction itself if not. A

method declared Mandatory can be called only if a transaction is already occurring and will throw an exception otherwise. Mandatory ensures that the client controls the overall transaction, and other resources may be involved.

7. How can applets and application clients participate in transactions?

   According to the J2EE specification, applets and application clients do not require transaction support. In principle, they can do JNDI lookups to acquire a UserTransaction reference, but support for this is not uniform. In general, the best idea is to delegate transactional responsibilities to an enterprise bean.

8. When accessing a method, the container throws a TransactionRequiredException. With which transaction attribute was the method configured?

   The method must be using the Mandatory transaction attribute. Required will start a new transaction if one isn't already available.

9. A *system exception* occurs when one of the services supporting an application fails. Examples include a bad JNDI lookup or the inability to get a database connection. Normally the container wraps such an exception inside javax.ejb.EJBException, which is a subclass of java.lang.RuntimeException and therefore does not need to be declared. Such an exception causes the container to automatically roll back any open transactions. Say your application accesses a database, and if a particular value is incorrect, it throws a custom-made IncorrectValueException. How do you ensure that any existing transaction is rolled back, assuming you are using container-managed transaction demarcation?

   Here's one approach. In the method, create a try block that attempts the database operation. If the value is incorrect, then call the setRollbackOnly() method on the context before throwing the custom exception.

   In the matching catch block, catch the relevant exception (SQLException in this case) and rethrow an EJBException. For example:

```
public void updateData() {
    try {
        String s = getDataFromDB();
        if (isNotValid(s)) {
            ctx.setRollbackOnly();
            throw new InvalidDataException();
        }
        writeData();
    }
    catch (SQLException e) {
        throw new EJBException("Transaction failed due to SQLException: " +
e.getMessage());
    }
}
```

10. Transactions are also available in the JDBC package, where the Connection interface provides the methods setAutoCommit(boolean), commit(), and rollback(). This is in contrast to the JTA methods described in this chapter. What advantages do JTA transactions provide?

    A JTA transaction is controlled by the container. JTA transactions allow transaction boundaries to span multiple databases as well as other resources, which is not necessarily true of JDBC transactions.

    The major limitation of JTA transactions, however, is that they do not support nested transactions, which may be part of the available database functionality.

Chapter 9: Security

Key terms

authentication	The process of establishing that clients are who they say they are and that a particular client is valid within a given context.
authorization	The process of determining whether a given user is permitted access to requested resources.
access control list	A list of users and their permitted actions associated with a given resource.
capability list	A list of resources and corresponding permissions associated with a particular role.
secret key (symmetric) cryptography	Encryption that uses the same key to encrypt and decrypt the message. Secret key cryptography is generally faster, if less secure, than asymmetric methods.
public key (asymmetric) cryptography	Encryption that uses different keys to encrypt and decrypt a message. One key is exposed to the public, and the other is kept private. Asymmetric cryptography is more secure than symmetric but slower. Because of the relative cost in speed, asymmetric cryptography is often used to deliver a session (symmetric) key to the user.
SSL	Secure Socket Layer; a framework for negotiating a mutually acceptable set of encryption and key exchange protocols.

digital certificate	A signed message, issued by a certificate authority (CA), assuring the recipient that a particular key belongs to a particular user.
digital signature	A message appended to a document and encoded with the sender's private key. The public key can then be used to decode the message, implying that the message was encrypted with the corresponding private key and thus validating the message's source.
message digest	A short message representing the overall message content, used to validate the source of the message.
certificate authority (CA)	A company charged with validating identities and keys.
role-based security	Establishing categories of users and assigning permissions based on those categories.
HTTPS	The combination of HTTP used over SSL.
security constraints	Collections of Web resource collections, authorization constraints, and user data constraints used to secure a portion of an application.
Web resource collection	A set of URL patterns and servlet methods that is being secured.
authorization constraints	Defines the roles authorized to access a particular Web resource collection.
user data constraints	Requirements imposed on the transfer of data in order to satisfy the security constraints. Allowable values are None, Integral, and Confidential.
security role references	Mappings from an externally defined set of roles to roles defined within the application.
delegation	Allowing one EJB to invoke a method on another using a particular role.
user registry	Stores user and group names for authentication and authorization purposes. Examples are the local operating system's user registry, LDAP, or a custom user registry.
Simple WebSphere Authentication Mechanism (SWAM)	An authentication mechanism supplied by WebSphere that does not forward credentials. SWAM is best for environments that do not require distributed security.

Lightweight Third Party Authentication (LTPA)	A authentication mechanism, stronger than SWAM, that supports forwarding credentials and therefore single sign-on (SSO).
Java Authentication and Authorization Services (JAAS)	The J2EE security specification, part of J2SE v 1.4, which uses almost any underlying security systems to authenticate and authorize users.
global security	Security mechanisms defined on the server for managed domains.
Java Secure Sockets Extension (JSSE)	A set of Java packages that enable secure communication between clients and servers.

Review questions

1. How secure is a simple username/password combination?

   The simple answer is, not very. All a username/password combination does is verify that both parties to the current connection have been there before. Neither side is even guaranteeing that it has the same identity as before; just that they both know the username and password. Since these quantities can even be sent unencrypted, there really is very little assurance that either party is who it claims to be.

   If the initial setup of the username and password was done over SSL, then at least the values will be encrypted. Also, the party running the server often will register a public key with a certificate authority, which helps establish that it is who it says it is. Rarely will clients do the same, however. In addition, keys are not perfectly secure either.

   Securing systems is thus a trade-off between cost and efficiency. A simple username and password are fast and easy, but not very secure. Requiring both parties to purchase a certificate from a CA (and validating that the certificates themselves have not expired, or been revoked for any number of reasons) and then having all interactions occur over SSL is much safer, but also more expensive and slower. Most applications fall in between these two extremes.

2. A Web application uses basic authentication to validate users and wishes to switch to Form-based authentication. What changes are required?

   The developer needs to supply a login form that has as its action attribute *j_security_check* and must contain two fields: *j_username* and *j_password*. Also necessary is a file to capture unsuccessful logins.

In principle, this is all that is required. Like basic authentication, however, Form-based authentication sends information using clear text, however, so it is best to set up SSL communications for the forms.

3. A servlet using programmatic security checks to see whether a user is in a particular role by writing "if (req.isUserInRole('manager')) …." Unfortunately, this hard-codes the role name "manager" into the servlet. Worse, at the actual deployment location, the equivalent role is instead called "supervisor." What can be done to fix this situation?

   One easy way would be to edit the Web deployment descriptor. Inside the <servlet> tag for this particular servlet, add:

   ```
   <security-role-ref>
           <role-name>manager</role-name>
           <role-link>supervisor</role-link>
   </security-role-ref>
   ```

   One of the advantages to using Application Developer is that the GUI associated with the Web deployment descriptor will handle all the required tags and place them in the necessary locations and in the necessary order.

4. What's the difference between getUserPrincipal() in the HttpServletRequest class and getCallerPrincipal() in EJBContext?

   The method req.getUserPrincipal() returns a java.security.Principal reference (note that this is an interface in J2SE, not J2EE), which encapsulates the name of a currently authenticated user. If the user has not been authenticated, the method returns null.

   The method ejbContext.getCallerPrincipal() also returns a java.security.Principal reference that identifies the caller. The difference is that this method never returns null, so you don't have to worry about the subsequent call to getName() throwing a NullPointerException.

   Note also that the former method is useful in servlets or JSP pages, where the request object is available. The latter is used by EJBs, which may not have access to the request or response information.

5. A bank account manager is responsible for all accounts with balances less than \$1000. Can declarative security techniques be used to allow this manager to modify only those accounts?

   Unfortunately, no, or at least not easily. Declarative security is generally preferable to programmatic security, but the security privileges are configured by class, or at most by method. In order to use declarative security,

different methods would need to be created for each security role, which can get complicated quickly. In this case, programmatic security is probably easier to implement.

6. Several files are used in the process of setting up security for a J2EE application in WebSphere. Which are they?

   The Web deployment descriptor, web.xml, contains security resource collections and other associated information. The EJB deployment descriptor, ejb-jar.xml, has entries for security identification, security roles, and security role references. The EAR deployment descriptor, application.xml, defines security roles for the application itself. Additional, WebSphere-specific information is kept in the ibm-ejb-jar-ext.xmi and ibm-application-bnd.xmi files.

   Additional files are modified during deployment to an application server as well.

Chapter 10: JCA tools and supports

Key terms

J2EE Connector Architecture (JCA)	A specification describing how to enable J2EE components to interact in a standard way with heterogeneous EIS systems, including a set of system contracts, and associated APIs.
enterprise information systems (EIS)	The information infrastructure of an enterprise, which supplies services to its clients. Examples include legacy mainframe, database, and ERP systems.
resource adapter	A J2EE component, provided by EIS vendors, that allows access to the resource via JCA API calls. It provides connectivity between the EIS system and the application server by implementing the EIS side of the system contracts.
Resource Manager (RM)	A part of an EIS that supports transactional access to the EIS as part of the transaction management contract between the EIS and the transaction manager. The RM associates a global transaction with work performed on its individual data.

transaction manager (TM)	A part of an EIS that coordinates transactions across multiple resource managers, in accordance with the transaction management contract. The TM informs RMs to prepare, commit, or rollback as appropriate.
managed environment	In a managed environment, the application server is responsible for managing connections using a connection factory. In a non-managed environment, a client directly uses the low-level APIs exposed by the resource adapter to manage connection pooling.
Connection	An interface representing an application-level connection to the underlying EIS. The actual physical connection associated with a Connection instance is represented by a ManagedConnection instance.
system contracts	Services that are provided by the resource adapter, such as connection management, transaction management, and security.
Common Client Interface (CCI)	A standard client API for application components that provides interactions across heterogeneous EISs.
Resource Adapter Archive (RAR)	A file containing the JAR files and libraries necessary to deploy the resource adapter in a J2EE server.

Review questions

1. What types of systems are good candidates for being accessed by the JCA?

   Many different types of systems can be accessed, but the JCA is particularly suited for enterprise resource planning (ERP), mainframe transaction processing, and non-relational database systems, among others. Though often used as an example, relational databases are not good candidates for JCA, since they can be accessed more efficiently using data sources or directly via JDBC.

2. Can a call to an EIS system through JCA be enclosed in an XA transaction?

   Because the resource adapter supports the transaction management contract, calls can be made to multiple EIS systems, databases, and EJBs, all within a global, distributed transaction, if the source adapter implements the XAResource interface. (*Note:* Not all the resource adapters support XA Transaction; some of them support only Local Transaction.)

3. What services are provided by the security management contract?

   The security contract provides authentication of users, authorization of user access to specific resources, and secure communications between the J2EE server and the EIS system.

4. What services are provided by the connection contract?

   The most important service is resource pooling. Just as with JDBC, creating connections to external systems tends to be a relatively expensive operation involving limited resources. A resource providing a JCA adapter allows the application server to extend its normal resource pooling service to encompass the EIS as well.

5. Describe a typical process for using resources provided through the Common Client Interface of the JCA.

   Access to JCA resources starts by acquiring a reference to an instance of a class that implements the javax.resource.cci.ConnectionFactory interface, normally by using a JNDI lookup. This interface provides a method called getConnection(), which returns a reference to an instance of a class that implements the Connection interface. There is an overloaded getConnection() method, by the way, that takes a ConnectionSpec reference that can be used to configure the connection, for example, username and password.

   Once the Connection object has been acquired, methods such as createInteraction() are available to begin an interaction with the resource. This returns a reference of type Interaction, which has two overloaded execute() methods available. One takes an InteractionSpec reference to configure the interaction, as well as a Record reference to hold input data, and returns a Record reference that holds output data. The other uses a third input argument of type Record to hold the output results, and returns a boolean as the return type. Each executes the requested interaction. Note that Record is the superinterface of IndexRecord, MappedRecord, and ResultSet, and the user can select whichever is appropriate by using a RecordFactory, which itself is acquired from the ConnectionFactory.

   The interaction with the resource may return a Record with the output data, or it may come from the arguments. Either way, once the data has been extracted and used, the interaction and connection should be closed.

Chapter 11: Profiling analysis tools in WebSphere Studio

Key terms

Java Virtual Machine Profiler Interface (JVMPI)	An experimental interface provided by Sun, intended for tool vendors, allowing access by a profiling agent to Java Virtual Machine information at runtime.
profile	To measure, organize, and display visually the behavior of a program that is running in a Java Virtual Machine.
IBM Agent Controller (AC)	A daemon process that provides a bridge between a profiling agent and a profiling client.
memory leak	An allocated region of memory that can no longer be accessed from outside. In Java, the garbage collector significantly limits the impact of memory leaks by automatically reclaiming unused objects. Particularly long-lived objects (such as those stored in HttpSession objects) can become performance issues.
Java Profiling Agent	An in-process application that returns execution information to the profiling client in the form of XML fragments.
profiling client	A tool that provides a front-end for a profiling agent, displaying its results and enabling its configuration. In this case, WebSphere Studio Application Developer is the profiling client.
J2EE Request Profiler	A WebSphere profiling agent that focuses on tracking requests made from one WebSphere server to another.
monitor	A logical container for the profiling information collected from nodes in a distributed application server cluster.
Process object	A representation of a process being profiled; it appears in the Profiling Monitor view of the Profiling perspective.
process	A running Java Virtual Machine. Each process is shown with a process id number (PID) in the Profiling Monitor view.
agent	A visual representation of the mechanism running inside the JVM process, by which application data can be forwarded to attached clients. Examples are the Java Profiling Agent and the J2EE Request Profiler.

host	A physical machine or machine execution partition.
Base Time	The time taken by a method to execute, excluding methods it invokes.
Cumulative Time	The execution time of a method, including all methods it calls. The Cumulative Time also includes recursive executions.
filters	String patterns used to include and exclude classes and packages during a profiling session. Filters can be collected into Filter Sets.
Sequence Diagram	A Unified Modeling Language (UML) diagram that shows the flow of execution of a program. Object instances are arranged along the top. Messages between objects are shown as arrows between their lifelines. Time increases downward on a Sequence diagram.

Review questions

1. What flag is sent to the JRE to tell it to collect profiling data and return it to the Agent Controller?

   The java command is used with the -XrunpiAgent flag, which itself takes various arguments that allow properties to be turned on or off. This is a special case of the generic way to access a profiler, which is to use the java –Xrun command with information about the specific profiler following.

   It is also notable that starting a server in profiling mode sends the JVM flag -DPD_DT_Enabled=true to the process running the server. This is a special case of the -D*variable=argument* flag, which can be used to set system variables in any Java program.

2. How can basic profiling be done without a mechanism like the JVMPI?

   The static method System.getCurrentTimeMillis() returns a long value representing the current time, so simply calling that method before and after individual method calls can be used as a primitive profiling technique. Unfortunately, its measurements can be affected by many things, including other processes in the system or time spent waiting on I/O. The results say nothing, of course, about the state of the heap, thread starts, and so forth.

3. What is the purpose of the Object Reference view?

   The Object Reference view shows the current state of the object graph for an application. No objects that currently contain references can be garbage col-

lected. If an object is still referenced beyond its usefulness, it acts as a kind of memory leak for the application. An accumulation of too many objects will exhaust the available memory. Garbage collection is supposed to eliminate this, but if objects still have references (other than so-called "weak" references), they can't be garbage collected.

4. Profiling information is not automatically updated by Application Developer. Instead, the user needs to refresh the data by clicking a button. Why not update automatically?

   One of the difficulties with profiling processes is that the profiler itself can consume significant resources, which would throw off the measurement. By collecting data only when absolutely required, this interference can be minimized.

   Note that to minimize the impact of profiling displays, profiling trace data can be streamed to a file with the file extension .trcxmi and examined later.

5. Describe the hierarchy among monitors, hosts, processes, and agents.

   A profiling project contains a series of monitors. Each monitor can contain data that spans several hosts. Hosts have processes associated with them, each with its own process ID. A single process can be monitored by several agents.

6. When the Sequence Diagram view is generated during profiling, what is the source of the profiling data?

   The data comes from either the Java Profiling Agent or the J2EE Request Profiler. The Java profiling agent sends data from a particular JVM running a Java application. The J2EE request profiler supplies selective data from the request interception points in a J2EE application.

Chapter 12: Implementing clients

Key terms

Access beans	WebSphere-generated JavaBeans that simplify access to EJBs.
Data Class Access bean (DCAB)	A thin data class that maintains copies of subsets of an Entity EJB's data and keeps track of data changes.
Copy Helper Access bean (CHAB)	A mechanism for clients to access remote interfaces of Entity EJBs via generated proxies that cache the Entity EJB data locally.

JavaBean Wrapper Access bean (JWAB)	A mechanism for clients to access remote interfaces of both Session and Entity EJBs via a generated proxy.
bootstrap control of services	Configuration that occurs at application server process startup, through vendor configuration files or command-line arguments.
declarative control of services	Configuration that occurs at application, module, or component startup declaratively, through deployment descriptors.
dynamic control of services	Configuration that occurs at runtime, programmatically through API calls and dynamic properties.
Object Request Broker (ORB)	A term from Common Object Request Broker Architecture (CORBA) indicating a service that enables interactions between distributed components.
Java Naming and Directory Interface (JNDI)	An extension API that provides naming and directory services to applications written in Java, independent of any specific directory service implementation.
Web Services	Self-contained, self-describing, modular applications that can be published, located, and invoked via Web protocols.
Universal Description, Discovery, and Integration (UDDI)	An API for publishing and locating Web Services.
Simple Object Access Protocol (SOAP)	A protocol that uses XML over other protocols such as HTTP and SMTP. In SOAP RPC, the message involves an operation and its arguments. In SOAP Document Exchange, the message carries a document that the recipient must interpret.
Web Services Description Language (WSDL)	A document describing the location, data types, bindings, and operations associated with a Web Service.

Review questions

1. What types of Access beans does WebSphere Studio Application Developer provide? What type supports the best practices?

   Three types of Access beans exist: JavaBean Wrappers, Copy Helpers, and Data Classes. New applications create only Data Class Access beans as a best practice. In addition, the generated factory classes reduce the amount of coding required by EJB clients.

2. How does an EJB client typically access an EJB?

   The process involves first obtaining an initial context from the JNDI service. The client then uses the initial context to look up the home interface of the EJB. Once the client acquires the home interface, the client uses it to create an EJB proxy object that implements the EJB's local or remote interface. Finally, the client invokes methods on this proxy object to access the EJB.

3. Differentiate between a resource manager connection factory reference and a resource environment reference. Why would a client use each?

   A client declares a resource manager connection factory reference when it wants to configure a connection declaratively, i.e., through a deployment descriptor. It uses the resulting factory reference to get actual connections.

   A client declares a resource environment reference to access a resource that external services already manage.

4. What does the client obtain from an InitialContext?

   Clients use the InitialContext to obtain a proxy to a resource. The proxy handles communications with the resource, allowing external services to maintain control of the resource.

5. When acquiring a home interface to an EJB, the client does a JNDI lookup and then invokes static method PortableRemoteObject.narrow(Object, Class) to cast to the home interface type. Why go through the narrow() method instead of simply casting the reference directly?

   IIOP (Internet Inter-ORB Protocol) allows objects only to implement a single interface. Since the Context.lookup() method returns a reference of type Object, the resulting stub only implements Object methods. The narrow() method provides a protocol-independent mechanism for casting the Object reference to the desired type.

6. Can J2EE application clients also service requests from other J2EE components? How?

   Yes. Like any other Java client, J2EE application clients can implement the MessageListener interface and attach themselves to a JMS queue or topic. Alternatively, they can access ORB services directly to listen to other components in a manner similar to EJBs.

Chapter 13: Packaging and deployment

Key terms

packaging	The process of assembling modules from components and applications from modules.
deployment	Customizing and installing applications into an operational environment.
naming	A service allowing J2EE components to look up other components, external resources, or configuration information by name. Applications access the naming service through JNDI.
deployment descriptors	Configuration files used for declarative control of services. J2EE uses XML files for this purpose, along with associated document type definitions (DTDs).
environment entry references	References that allow the configuration of J2EE components for a particular application by using declarative values to customize their behavior.
resource manager connection factory references	References that allow J2EE components to access external resources with standard declarative controls appropriate for resource managers.
resource environment references	References that allow J2EE components to access external resources with minimal declarative control, such as components that external services already manage.
EJB references	References that allow J2EE components to resolve access to EJBs declaratively.
security role references	References to security roles required by a J2EE component to define authorization.

Review questions

1. List the roles defined by J2EE.

   - **The Application Component Provider role, which produces J2EE components**
   - **The Application Assembler role, which combines J2EE components into J2EE modules and J2EE applications**
   - **The Deployer role, which configures and installs J2EE applications into specific operational environments**

- **The Administrator role, which administers operational environments and installs J2EE applications in them**

J2EE also defines these additional roles.

- **The Tool Provider role, which provides the tooling for the different roles**
- **J2EE Product Provider role, which provides the server implementation**

In general, a single party may perform several roles.

2. Compare the coarse security constraints provided by J2EE Web components against the fine-grained authorization in EJB components.

   J2EE Web components define security constraints in the Web deployment descriptor, web.xml. A <security-constraint> element determines which security roles can access a set of resources by defining a <web-resource-collection> and associating with it an <auth-constraint> tag that lists the allowed <role-name> elements. An optional <user-data-constraint> defines access integrity and confidentiality.

   An EJB, however, can define permissions on a method-by-method basis, using a <method-permission> tag, which contains a series of <method> elements. J2EE components can also deny access to EJB methods regardless of permissions by using an <exclude-list> element.

3. List the four types of J2EE deployment modules.

   J2EE applications contain application client modules, Web modules, EJB modules, and resource adapter modules. Each runs inside its own type of container, which plugs into the overall system using connectors, services, and communications. Each also has its own deployment descriptor. The J2EE enterprise application also has a deployment descriptor.

4. What types of archives can J2EE applications contain?

   The application gets packaged in an enterprise archive, or EAR. The EAR can contain application client Java archives (client JARs), Web archives (WARs), EJB JARs, and resource adapter archives (RARs) as well as utility JARs.

   Each of the archives has its own internal file structure as well, which includes Java code, deployment descriptors, and manifests for the archive. Assembly of all these archives is greatly simplified by WebSphere Studio Application Developer.

5. Describe the overlap in J2EE roles between the Administrator role and the Deployer role.

Administrators configure operational environments (notably WebSphere Application Server) and install applications in them. Deployers configure applications (using WebSphere Studio Application Developer) and install them in operational environments.

The J2EE specification defines many roles in addition to these, but these two tend to map to distinct groups in actual organizations. Since the roles overlap by definition, organizations must provide good means for communication and interaction between the deployers and the administrators.

The Application Component Provider role and the Application Assembler role create an EAR, and the Deployer role deploys it to WebSphere Application Server and may install it. The Administrator role installs the application in WebSphere Application Server and configures the operational environment.

Chapter 14: WebSphere administration

Key terms

Performance Monitoring Infrastructure (PMI)	A set of WebSphere packages and libraries for gathering, delivering, processing, and displaying performance data.
Java Virtual Machine Profiling Interface (JVMPI)	A two-way function call interface between the JVM and an in-process profiling agent.
Tivoli Performance Viewer	Previously called the Resource Analyzer, a client to the PMI in WebSphere Application Server whose function is to organize the collected data into objects in a hierarchical tree.
counter	A holder for the results of various calculations. Examples include the number of active enterprise beans, the time spent responding to servlet requests, or the number of kilobytes of available memory.
Java Management Extensions (JMX)	A standard API for management and monitoring of J2EE applications.
WebSphere Queuing Network	A series of load-dependent queues constituting a path between the client and the back end
throughput curve	A plot of requests processed per second against the number of concurrent users. The point were the curve becomes flat is called the saturation point. Increasing users beyond this eventually reaches a buckle zone, where performance significantly degrades.

closed queues	Queues that have been "throttled" such that their available pools of threads have been limited. When the maximum thread size has been reached, further requests will remaining in the queue, waiting.
connection pooling	Instantiating a certain number of database connections ahead of time and serving them out on demand.
Classloader	A Java class that provides classes to an application at runtime as they are requested.
tracing	Tracing a managed process on the server through all the Java objects that make up the runtime environment of the server.

Review questions

1. Tuning is done by both developers and administrators. Who does what?

   Developers tune components, and administrators tune containers. Administrators also configure the services associated with the deployment environment, such as connection pools.

2. Simply increasing heap size would seem to be an effective way to help the garbage collection process. Is it?

   Garbage collection itself consumes resources, so it shouldn't be done too often. Running it infrequently, however, increases the amount of garbage to be collected during each run, increasing the individual running times.

   Increasing the heap size may cause the garbage collector to run less often, but each individual run can have a more significant impact on performance because there is so much to do.

3. Is a sawtooth pattern in the plot of memory utilization over time a good thing?

   The sawtooth pattern is ideal. It implies that memory usage increases toward 100%, at which time the garbage collector runns and empties memory completely. This implies that the garbage collector has sufficient resources not only to free the memory but to compact it as well, avoiding later fragmentation.

   The sawtooth is in contrast to a staircase pattern, which implies that there is a steady accumulation of retained objects over time.

4. Describe upstream queuing.

   Each queue should allow fewer requests than the one preceding it. This ensures that work is always available for each element in the queue and that work is always ready for processing.

5. What happens when a queue is closed? Are there any queues that cannot be closed?

   The EJB queue cannot be closed. The Web container queue can be. Closing a queue implies that future requests will remain in the queue, waiting until a resource is available. The fact that the EJB queue cannot be closed implies that when the application server runs out of threads for the EJB container, it will simply instantiate new ones.

6. Compare vertical to horizontal clustering

   Vertical clustering means adding additional JVMs to a single machine. This increases the load on that machine, which can be good if there are unused CPU cycles available. Multiple servers on a single machine also communicate very efficiently.

   Horizontal clustering adds servers on remote machines. While this incurs networking overhead, it has the advantage of surviving server failures.

7. A developer can wrap all requests for a connection from the pool inside a try/catch block that catches a StaleConnectionException and retries to grab a new one. Normally the developer should limit the number of retries. Why?

   StaleConnectionExceptions can result from a number of circumstances other than simply exceeding the time required for a particular connection to be made available. The cause may not be transient, as in the case of a database shutdown.

8. A system is throwing a ConnectionWaitTimeoutException frequently. How should this be fixed?

   The ConnectionWaitTimeoutException implies that the application waited for a connection from the pool longer than the defined CONN_TIMEOUT value. This could result from the timeout value being set too low. Alternatively, it may be that there aren't enough connections available in the pool, so increasing the pool size would seem to be in order. Increasing the number of connections uses extra memory, however, so their usage needs to be monitored as well.

The "rule of thumb" given in the text is that the maximum number of Data-Source connections should be equal to the maximum number of threads in the Web container.

9. Can session data be moved between servers in a cluster?

   Session data can propagate between servers if the <distributable /> tag is used in the Web deployment descriptor and if every element stored in the session is from a class that implements the Serializable interface.

   This process will incur performance penalties as well, so it should be used only if needed.

Chapter 15: Remote Debugger and Java Component Test Tools in WebSphere Studio

Key terms

Java Platform Debugger Architecture (JPDA)	A collection of three API interfaces to enable communication between debugging clients and the applications currently being debugged.
WebSphere Application Server Debugging Service	A service provided by the application server to send debugging information to clients. This service must be enabled on the application server for remote debugging to work.
Testcase	A set of Tasks organized into Blocks, used to test an application. Testcases are defined and then prepared to create an instance that can be executed.
hosts	Machines on which the tests are run.
JUnit	An open source, regression-testing framework, from *www.junit.org*, that provides an API for building Testcases for the unit testing of Java classes.
Block	An organized group of Tasks, Delays, and Verification Points within a particular Testcase.
Task	A method skeleton in a JUnit Testcase.
Delay	Part of a Testcase that contains code that suspends the test thread for a given period of time.

Review questions

1. JUnit is already built into Application Developer as a plug-in, usable from the Java perspective. What, then, is the purpose of the Component Test perspective? Why not simply use the Java perspective's JUnit testcase and test suite wizards for everything?

   It is true that Application Developer supplies wizards for generating JUnit testcases and test suites, and these capabilities are quite useful in their own right. What the Component Test perspective supplies is a complete framework for running multiple test cases, even across servers. In addition, HTTP testing is supplied and automated, which is beyond the basic JUnit capabilities.

2. What is the difference between the Definition view and the Execution view?

   The Definition view is used to define a Testcase. The Execution view is used after the Testcases have been prepared and instantiated. The relationship is analogous to that between classes and object instances.

3. What is the purpose of the Agent Controller in the test context?

   The Agent Controller is used to run Testcases on remote host machines.

4. What three types of schedulers are available for Testcases?

   Application Developer comes prepared to with a Java scheduler for Testcases that execute Java methods, an HTTP scheduler for Testcases that test HTTP interactions, and a manual scheduler for Testcases that will be executed by hand using an interactive dialog.

5. To run a set of Testcases on a remote server, what additional step needs to be performed?

   Testcases that are going to be run on a remote server need to be added to a JAR file, which is then installed on the remote host.

Index

Note: Boldface numbers indicate illustrations.

D

Note: Boldface numbers indicate illustrations.

Note: Boldface numbers indicate illustrations.

Note: Boldface numbers indicate illustrations.

Note: Boldface numbers indicate illustrations.

Q

R

S

Note: Boldface numbers indicate illustrations.

U

Note: Boldface numbers indicate illustrations.

X

Z

Note: Boldface numbers indicate illustrations.